CRITICAL MANAGEMEN

CRITICAL MANAGEMENT STUDIES

A Reader

Edited by

**Christopher Grey and
Hugh Willmott**

OXFORD
UNIVERSITY PRESS

OXFORD
UNIVERSITY PRESS

Great Clarendon Street, Oxford OX2 6DP

Oxford University Press is a department of the University of Oxford.
It furthers the University's objective of excellence in research, scholarship,
and education by publishing worldwide in

Oxford New York

Auckland Cape Town Dar es Salaam Hong Kong Karachi
Kuala Lumpur Madrid Melbourne Mexico City Nairobi
New Delhi Shanghai Taipei Toronto

With offices in

Argentina Austria Brazil Chile Czech Republic France Greece
Guatemala Hungary Italy Japan Poland Portugal Singapore
South Korea Switzerland Thailand Turkey Ukraine Vietnam

Oxford is a registered trade mark of Oxford University Press
in the UK and in certain other countries

Published in the United States
by Oxford University Press Inc., New York

© Introduction and Compilation Christopher Grey and Hugh Willmott 2005

The moral rights of the authors have been asserted
Database right Oxford University Press (maker)

First published 2005

British Library Cataloguing in Publication Data

Data available

Library of Congress Cataloging in Publication Data

Data available

Typeset by SPI Publisher Services, Pondicherry, India
Printed in Great Britain on acid-free paper by Biddles Ltd., King's Lynn, Norfolk

ISBN 0-19-928608-6 978-0-19-928608-9 (pbk.)
ISBN 0-19-928607-8 978-0-19-928607-2
1 3 5 7 9 10 8 6 4 2

Contents

Contents

List of Contributors

Paul S. Adler, Marshall School of Business, University of Southern California, USA

Mats Alvesson, University of Lund, Sweden

P. D. Anthony, formerly of the University of Cardiff

James R. Barker, Department of Management, United States Air Force Academy, USA

Loren Baritz, Department of History, University of Massachusetts, Amherst, USA

Stewart Clegg, School of Management, University of Technology, Sydney, Australia

Bill Cooke, Manchester Business School, The University of Manchester, UK

Stanley Deetz, University of Colorado, Boulder, USA

David Dunkerley, School of Humanities and Social Sciences, University of Glamorgan, UK

Christopher Grey, Judge Institute of Management, University of Cambridge, UK

Heather Hopfl, Department of Accounting, Finance, and Management, University of Essex, UK

David Knights, School of Business and Economics, University of Exeter, UK

Richard Marsden, Centre for Integrated Study, Athabasca University, Canada

C. Wright Mills (1916–62), formerly Professor of Sociology at Columbia University, USA

Martin Parker, The Management Centre, University of Leicester, UK

Rosemary Pringle, School of Social Sciences, University of Southampton, UK

Paul Thompson, Department of Human Resource Management, University of Strathclyde, UK

Barbara Townley, Management School, University of Edinburgh, UK

Hugh Willmott, Judge Institute of Management, University of Cambridge, UK

Edward Wray-Bliss, Nottingham University Business School, University of Nottingham, UK

Acknowledgements

P. D. Anthony, 'Management Ideology'. Extract reprinted from *The Ideology of Work* by P. D. Anthony (Routledge, 1977).

L. Baritz, 'The Servants of Power'. Extract reprinted from *The Servants of Power* by L. Baritz (1960). Copyright © 1960 L. Baritz. Reprinted by permission of the author.

S. Clegg and D. Dunkerly, 'Introduction: Critical Issues in Organizations'. Reprinted from *Critical Issues in Organizations*, edited by S. Clegg and D. Dunkerly (Routledge, 1977)

C. Wright Mills, 'The Higher Circles'. From *The Power Elite, New Edition* by C. Wright Mills, copyright © 1956, 2000 by Oxford University Press Inc. Used by permission of Oxford University Press, Inc.

M. Alvesson and S. Deetz, 'Critical Theory and Postmodern Approaches in Organization Studies'. Reprinted from *The Handbook of Organization Studies*, edited by S. Clegg, C. Hardy, and W. Nord (Routledge 1996).

D. Knights, 'Changing Spaces: The Disruptive Impact of a New Epistemological Location for the Study of Management'. Reprinted from the *Academy of Management Review* (Copyright © 1992 The Academy of Management).

Richard Marsden, 'The Politics of Organizational Analysis'. Reprinted from *Organization Studies* (© EGOS, 2002), by permission of SAGE Publications Ltd.

Paul Adler, 'Market, Hierarchy and Trust: The Knowledge Economy and the Future of Capitalism'. Reprinted from *Organization Science* (Copyright © 2001 INFORMS).

James R. Barker, 'Tightening the Iron Cage: Concertive Control in Self-Managing Terms'. Reprinted from *Administrative Science Quarterly* (© 1993 Cornell University, Johnson Graduate School of Management), by permission of *Administrative Science Quarterly*.

Bill Cooke, 'The Managing of the (Third) World'. Reprinted from *Organization* (© SAGE Publications, 2004), by permission of SAGE Publications Ltd.

Heather Hopfl, 'The Making of the Corporate Acolyte: Some Thoughts on Charismatic Leadership and the Reality of Organizational Commitment'. Reprinted from the *Journal of Management Studies* (© Blackwell Publishing, 1992) by permission of Blackwell Publishing Ltd.

R. Pringle, 'Sexuality at Work'. Reprinted from *Secretaries Talk* by R. Pringle (London, Verso, 1989).

Barbara Townley, 'Performance Appraisal and the Emergence of Management'. Reprinted from the *Journal of Management Studies* (© Blackwell Publishing, 1993) by permission of Blackwell Publishing Ltd.

Hugh Willmott, 'Studying Management Critically'. Reprinted from the *Journal of Management Studies* (© Blackwell Publishing, 1987) by permission of Blackwell Publishing Ltd.

Martin Parker, 'Managerialism and its Discontents'. Extract reprinted from *Against Management* by Martin Parker (Policy 2002). Reprinted by permission of Polity.

Paul Thompson, 'Brands, Boundaries and Bandwagons: A Critical Reflection on Critical Management Studies'. Reprinted from *Critical Realist Applications in Organisation and Management Studies* edited by Steve Fleetwood and Stephen Ackroyd (Routledge, 2004).

Edward Wray-Bliss, 'Abstract Ethic, Embodied Ethics: The Strange Marriage of Foucault and Positivism in Labour Process Theory'. Reprinted from *Organization* (© SAGE Publications, 2002), by permission of SAGE Publications Ltd.

1 Introduction

Christopher Grey and Hugh Willmott

A Critical Management Studies Reader?

There seems something perverse in producing a Reader of critical work. For the very notion of a Reader entails assumptions that, from a critical perspective, appear questionable. The selection of contributions implies the existence of an underlying field with a clear and settled identity and set of boundaries which are then mapped by the Reader. In these terms, Critical Management Studies (CMS) looks like an unpromising candidate for a Reader. As a newly emergent area or genre that has yet to 'settle' in this way, so there is considerable room for debating its scope as well as its distinctive or most illustrious works. However, the difficulties of editing a CMS Reader go deeper. For a core proposition of the 'criticality' which is a defining feature of CMS is a broadly constructivist ontology[1] which asserts that the world—in this case, the world that passes for CMS—is not 'out there', ready to be mapped by skilful cartographers but, rather, that in the very process of drawing any such map, this world is itself shaped. In short, albeit in a small way, publishing a Reader creates, rather than simply distils or reflects, what it ostensibly maps: identifiable landmarks and distinctive boundaries of 'The Field'.

Moreover, from a critical standpoint, the process of producing a Reader involves ascriptions of hierarchy: this text merits inclusion, that one does not; this text exemplifies the field, that one is marginal. Critical studies (in many variants) are inclined to problematise the activity that generates such pairings. Instead of assuming their authority, critical thinking worries about how the pairings have been produced and legitimised, and the effects that such exercises of power have for what is counted as knowledge. As a consequence, the operation of pairings is viewed as disciplinary, contestable, possibly elitist and certainly suspicious. All of which might lead one to conclude that editing a CMS Reader is not just a hazardous task but an impossible and indefensible one. One of our aims in this introductory chapter is to explain why we do not believe this to be so.

Another common, and related, proposition of critical studies is the value of reflexivity. By this, we do not mean only a recognition that the author (or in this case editor) actively participates in the creation of text. More broadly, reflexivity points to the importance of accounting for the very possibility of CMS as 'something' about which an account (e.g. in the form of a Reader) can be given. That it is possible to conceive of a 'CMS Reader' bespeaks of an already accomplished construction. CMS has become the term in use (or, in a usually pejorative meaning, brand) for the activities and outputs of a growing community of academics. Shortly, we will explore how and why that has come about; and, in doing so, our concern is less with the development of a broadly shared 'orientation'—which we have already suggested includes, for example, a minimally constructivist epistemology and a degree of reflexivity—than with the development of an 'institution'. By institution, we mean to imply the way that CMS is articulated through a series of formally organized activities and expressions such as the CMS conference, the CMS division of the American Academy of Management and its associated 'manifesto'; and, more generally, the growing sense amongst both those who identify strongly with it and those who are hostile to it, that CMS has somehow become, in some difficult-to-pin-down sense, a distinctive approach, a school or, even, a movement, albeit one that comprises very diverse voices.[2] And, of course, the production of a Reader in CMS may, in this light, be interpreted as another—encouraging or unwelcome moment—in the process of its institutionalization.

It would be naïve to think that such institutionalization can be thought of exclusively in terms of the formation and development of what passes for CMS. Rather, CMS grows out of, and is nested within, a wider institutional context— namely, that of business and management schools, and beyond that the sphere of higher education principally, but not exclusively, in developed capitalist societies. We will return later to the implications of this, but for now we simply assert that it is unsatisfactory to think of the current popularity of CMS, and its potential influence, as being somehow a function of whatever identity or qualities are ascribed to it. To put it another way, if the same kinds of ideas had been developed within, say, the fields of sociology or economics, then they would have a different, and we would argue lesser, potential for influence. To take the present instance, the existence of this Reader is at least partially attributable to the existence of a large population of academics, schools, programmes and students whom it has the opportunity to enrol and to convince of its relevance. In the remainder of this introductory chapter we will suggest that this 'double institutionalization' (i.e. the institutionalization of

CMS within the institutional context of university business schools) places a particular inflection upon what CMS can be and what it may achieve, and that an understanding of this explains why it is not, after all, so perverse to produce a critical Reader.

The Appeal of CMS

The first use of the capitalised phrase *Critical Management Studies* was in the title of the edited collection of the same name that appeared in1992 (Alvesson & Willmott, 1992). Its appearance seems to have acted as a catalyst for work positioning itself under this label. It was an unintended and unexpected outcome, except in the general sense that all authors hope that their work will have some influence and be taken up by others. That the identity, badge or brand CMS was subsequently embraced indicates something more than whatever merits the contributions to that collection may have had. It chimed with a series of developments within the business and management research community in particular, those since the late 1970s in, predominantly but by no means exclusively, Europe.

In a reflection upon CMS, Fournier & Grey (2000) identified a number of factors that, they suggest, have increased the resonance and appeal of CMS, including:

- The rise of managerialism associated with the hegemony of the New Right;
- The crisis of western (and especially North American) management in the face of globalised capitalism;
- The crisis of positivism in management research and the development of epistemological and methodological alternatives.

Moreover, it was suggested that these coincided with some specific factors in the UK, where CMS has probably been most prominent, including:

- The existence of an influential Marxist tradition within social science;
- The rapid growth of business schools in the 1980s, a growth which was contemporary with, or post-dated, the factors listed above;
- The way that this rapid growth drew in faculty members trained in social science from outside the business schools;
- The tendency of such faculty to be predisposed to publish academic articles and thereby to be valued within intensified systems of monitoring and valuing research output.

Needless to say, several of these factors existed in countries other than the UK, most notably in Scandinavia and the Antipodes.

These factors contributed to a receptive climate in which the development of CMS might be possible. What the deployment of the CMS term seems to signify, then, is the unfolding of a conceptual umbrella that has been found to be useful in enabling those engaged in seemingly unrelated projects to recognise some family resemblances. It has provided a kind of common cause and legitimation: if others were doing similar work, if it was an approach with its own traditions, adherents and institutions, then it could be perhaps be worthwhile to espouse membership of a group that was filling this expanding tent. Why? Because of what we said earlier about CMS being linked to business schools. Since these were—and are—by and large 'uncritical' in orientation, those going in different directions face a degree of scepticism, isolation, indifference and perhaps even downright hostility. CMS offers a 'badge' of relative respectability in the face of this hostility.

In a few schools, pockets of critically-oriented faculty had been recruited in the 1980s by those of a like mind. They were able to be supportive of each other intellectually in various internal political fights (e.g. over appointments and curricula), as well as in presenting a distinctive approach to external audiences. It is also worth noting that these groups emerged in a number of the longest established, largest and most prestigious of UK departments based primarily around undergraduate and postgraduate, and not simply MBA, programmes. Elsewhere, academics who felt some affinity with an emergent CMS movement were more isolated; and, in virtually all cases, critics are by definition in the minority. In this context, the take-up of the CMS label should be seen as a deft, or at least expedient, move that confers a degree of protection and legitimation of marginal orientations, especially those departments that lacked a 'critical mass' of critically-oriented faculty. This move was not necessarily made self-consciously but that does not detract from the point. In a context where central figures doing critical work were publishing in respected journals, were winning research council grants, and were being promoted to senior positions, identifying with CMS became a progressively less risky and more attractive option for academics who were disillusioned, or were never entranced, by the mainstream. So the adoption of CMS as a term is an embryonic form of institutionalization and it arises primarily because CMS developed within, and out of, the institution of the business school within higher education.

As an embryonic institution CMS incorporates a number of features, and indeed ambiguities, that facilitate its appeal and expansion. First, it is not directed at any particular management specialism. It can therefore include accounting, marketing, etc. rather than be confined to more overarching, generalist areas, such as organizational behaviour or strategy. Second, it is concerned with *studies*, not study—which suggests that there is room for considerable diversity and fluidity. Even if the theoretical centre of gravity shifts—perhaps from Marxist or Frankfurt conceptions of criticality to more post-structuralist approaches, the catch-all label can still be used.[3] Third, the 'critical' in management studies may be directed at current manifestations of 'management' or it may be directed at its 'study'. But, of course, the two targets are linked, for if the critique of the (mainstream) study of management is successful, then a new, critical form of studying management develops—one which engages in the critique of management. Indeed, for it to be a critique—for CMS to mean something different to 'management studies'—it must necessarily seek to challenge and replace a dominant orthodoxy or, more probably, to supplement the diverse currents that comprise the orthodoxy within what Whitley (1984) has aptly described as the 'fragmented adhocracy' of management studies.

Common Threads in CMS

The issue of the point and distinctiveness of CMS can be approached in another way by attempting to elucidate common threads or themes that run through work that is widely regarded as most central to or exemplary of CMS. For example, it has been suggested that CMS organises itself around three inter-related core propositions: de-naturalization, anti-performativity and reflexivity (Fournier & Grey 2000). De-naturalization refers to what is crucial to any oppositional politics. Whatever the existing order may be, it becomes taken for granted or naturalized and often is legitimised by reference to nature and necessity. It's just how things are, the way of the world: *of course* men dominate women, whites dominate blacks, capital dominates labour. Whether based on evolution or social function, the answer is the same: There Is No Alternative. In management, naturalization is affirmed in the proposition that someone has to be in charge, that of course they know more, or else they would not be in charge, so of course they deserve more money. Hierarchy is taken as natural; the idea that coordination implies superiority is taken as natural; the idea that hierarchical coordination licenses higher rewards than production is taken as natural; markets are natural; greed and competitiveness are natural and so on. CMS questions these kinds of assertions and thereby de-naturalizes them.

Anti-performativity, which is perhaps a special case of de-naturalization, denies that social relations should (naturally) be thought of as exclusively instrumentally: in terms of maximizing output from a given input. This feature is important because most knowledge of management presupposes the over-riding importance of performativity. It is taken to be the acid test of whether knowledge has any value. So, knowledge of management has value only if it can be shown how it can, at least in principle, be applied to enhance the means

5

of achieving established (naturalized) ends. The term 'anti-performative' emphatically does not imply an antagonistic attitude towards *any* kind of 'performing'. Rather, 'performative' is used in a somewhat technical sense to identify forms of action in which there is a means-ends calculus that pays little or no attention to the question of ends. In effect, ethical and political questions and issues are unacknowledged or assumed to be resolved. It follows that issues of a fundamentally ethical and political character—such as the distribution of life chances within and by corporations or the absence of any meaningful democracy from working life—are ignored or if not ignored then only marginally adjusted through, for example, 'involvement' and 'consultation'. Efforts are then directed at the matter of how limitations and 'dysfunctions' within the established system can be ameliorated without significantly changing or disrupting the prevailing order of privilege and disadvantage. CMS challenges the monocular focus on performativity.

Finally, 'reflexivity' refers to the capacity to recognise that accounts of organization and management are mediated by those, typically researchers, who produce these accounts, and who themselves are embedded in particular conditions and traditions of research. In this way, CMS presents a methodological and epistemological challenge to the objectivism and scientism of mainstream research where there is an assumption and/or masquerade of neutrality and universality. Under the guise of the production of value-free facts, such research is inattentive to (i.e. unreflexive about) the assumptions which guide both its choice of what to research and the manner in which that research is conducted. Little encouragement is given to students or other research users (e.g. managers, policy-makers) to interrogate the assumptions and routines upon which conventional knowledge production is founded or to question the commonsense thinking (e.g. about what counts as 'scientific') and disciplinary paraphernalia (e.g. tenure, control of journals, etc.) that safeguard their authority. CMS sees such questioning as mandatory.

Business Schools: The Institutional Context of CMS

Taken together the three features identified by Fournier and Grey (2000) stake out a terrain for CMS that is compatible with diverse theoretical assumptions, and yet suggests some boundaries that operate to differentiate CMS from orthodox and managerialist positions. Yet there is another and much more straightforward way of defining CMS which brings us back to an appreciation of its marginality within business schools. One does not have to spend very much time in business schools to appreciate that the content of their textbooks, lectures and publications is predominantly 'right wing' in the sense of being implicitly or explicitly supportive of the institutions and values of corporate capitalism. Equally, when reading what have become key texts in CMS, or attending CMS conferences, it soon becomes apparent that these are broadly 'left wing'. It might seem odd that an ostensibly oppositional grouping has formed within a distinctly capitalist institution. To make sense of this, we must take some account of the history of business school education that to date has developed primarily within the broader context of higher education.

As departments in universities, which most of them are, business schools are required to conform to the values and norms of the wider institution by exhibiting at least a degree of 'academic respectability'. Gaining and retaining their place within institutions of higher education requires business schools to subscribe, at least minimally, to the liberal virtues of diversity, and to contribute to knowledge through peer review. Put bluntly, business schools located in established universities which jealously guard their hard-won reputation and independence cannot simply appoint consultants or gurus as professors, even though it might be the wish of some corporate patrons and students to do precisely that. Instead, tenured staff are required to have a modicum of academic respectability—as demonstrated through publication in esteemed journals and supportive references from established academics in prestigious institutions.

The publication in the 1950s of the influential Ford and Carnegie reports established the model of the (US) business school that was subsequently copied across the world (Whitley et al. 1981). Their common demand was for business education to be set upon an analytical, scientific foundation with a heavy emphasis upon positivist philosophies and methods. That meant hiring and promoting a core faculty who could at least minimally comply with these requirements. As a consequence, the recruits to business schools were drawn primarily from existing university departments, attracted by new opportunities as well as a more applied approach to academic disciplines and the increased scope for teaching and pursuing research within less rigidly defined disciplinary boundaries.

During the 1950s and for the following decades, a positivist model of science was in the ascendant, nurtured by the oppressive climate of the Cold War and anxieties about the credentials and respectability of *social* science. A degree of relaxation accompanied the broader liberalization of the late 1960s and 1970s, together with the increasing esteem enjoyed by the now expanded business schools and the growth of their corporate clients. Across the social sciences, the positivist hegemony began to be pluralized by varieties of hermeneutic and pragmatist research. In business schools, there emerged a grudging (and repressive) tolerance for post-positivist research, a development propelled by a growing disillusionment with the practical applicability of the knowledge produced by positivist science as much as by the theoretical critique of positivism.

The dominance of the positivist model of science had acted to exclude critical thinkers from business schools who, in any event, were unlikely to view them as a preferred place of employment. With the faltering of the positivist hegemony, 'top' management journals began to publish some broader-based research (even if this sometimes meant no more than accepting qualitative papers). In turn, this enabled a broader base of faculty to develop, some of whom were sympathetic to the hiring and promotion of even more broadly based faculty. In their ranks could be found those who were critically orientated not just methodologically but also politically.

By the 1980s and 1990s, it began to matter less whether authors complied with positivist norms than that they published in the most prestigious journals whose editors and referees were now more likely to be sympathetic to critical work. Business schools continue to appoint and promote faculty on the basis of what they publish. To be sure it is still the case that the 'top' journals publish primarily mainstream work. But by institutionalising the academic status of business schools through the requirement to publish in academic journals, an unintended consequence has been to legitimate critical work to the extent that it is published in these journals. Moreover, to the extent that faculty employed for their (critical) research publication are also engaged in teaching it follows that this too has become susceptible to critical influence.

But why, it might be asked, should business or management education take place in universities? Of course, much business education does occur elsewhere, either within corporations or through other providers. What distinguishes universities is their state-ratified advantage in awarding, and regulating the supply, of the scarcest and most prized of business qualifications. In principle, the same forms of 'quality control' are applied to the award of business degrees—undergraduate as well as postgraduate—as are applied to, say, astronomy or zoology. Moreover, and this is no less important, degrees confer a particular status and authority upon their holders. There is a strong association between possessing a degree and the mastery of a body of knowledge to which only the initiated are deemed to have access. All things being equal, then, potential and practicing managers have preferred to acquire a qualification with the prestigious stamp of a higher education institution impressed upon it than any other kind of certificate, no matter how relevant its attainment may or may not be for the practical, day-to-day conduct of their work. And up until now, at least, there has been no shortage of customers willing to pay high fees for the business school imprimatur, calculating that it is worth the investment in terms of projected future income which is derived from the differentiating benefit of the qualification.

From the demand-side of students, then, there is a clear interest in having business education provided by universities. This has been so ever since—indeed it was a principal reason for—the foundation of business schools. Engwall (1997:

90) noted that for the many philanthropists who funded early business schools 'their intention was primarily to raise the status of business men' rather than having any particular concern with what was taught in the new institutions. For example, writing of Gustav Mevissen, creator of the business school at Cologne at the turn of the century, Locke (1989: 71, cited in Engwall ibid: 91) concludes that 'concerned to raise the low status of businessmen, he thought . . . to raise the businessman's social status by conferring college degrees on members of the business estate'. Business schools continue to be key institutions in the social mobility project that transforms ordinary businessmen (and increasingly women) into the high flyers of global capitalism.

On the supply side, many universities were hesitant in accommodating business education as it apparently departed from other, potentially comparable, forms of vocational study (e.g. medicine, architecture). The latter seemed to be based upon well-established, academically respectable *disciplines* whereas management and business were more comparable to *trades*, like plumbing. The condition of their entry was a willingness to comply, at least minimally, with the established disciplines and trappings of higher education. As we have emphasized, that meant recruiting staff with academically respectable backgrounds—for example, degrees in economics to teach marketing; degrees in mathematics to teach operational research; degrees in social science to teach organizational behaviour—who ostensibly could provide business education with some analytical, scientific foundations. And for universities to recruit and retain academically qualified staff for their business schools, it was necessary to ensure that they enjoyed conditions of service (e.g. salary), promotion procedures based upon publication in refereed journals, and academic freedom that paralleled those applied across the institutions in which business schools were to be established.

Of course any reservations that universities may have had about establishing business schools were assuaged not just by insisting on a degree of conformity to standard understandings of academic work, but by the prospect of the income streams produced by large populations of students and alumni with deep pockets. In many countries, and with a growing insistence in recent years, universities have also been required to demonstrate their utility through an engagement with the corporate world. Castigated as 'ivory towers', they have been encouraged to become more entrepreneurial and to justify themselves in terms of their economic benefit to society rather than in purely 'academic' terms. In tandem with this, the eroding willingness to fund universities through taxation meant that the search was on to find new ways of raising income through profit-generating courses. It is easy to see how business schools could satisfy both of these demands whilst, if they were designed in the way suggested above, allowing many of the traditional features of the university to remain relatively intact.

The Institutionalization of CMS within Business Schools

So how is this relevant to CMS? Our proposition is that a condition of development of CMS is its positioning in university business schools. Of course, we are not suggesting that this was part of the planning of business schools but, rather, that it is unintended consequence. The nesting of business schools within universities, primarily for reasons of status on the part of students and necessity on the part of universities, opened up a space within which CMS has been able to emerge and even flourish. Both universities and students have an interest in the business schools conforming in some degree to the norms of academia. Certainly any attempt to overtly proscribe the politics of management research would be incompatible with this interest. Moreover, if critical work could be published in established peer-review journals then this would offer not just a certain amount of cultural capital necessary to justify, defend and expand its presence but would also serve to legitimate CMS as contributing to the academic standing required of business schools.

This does not mean that CMS was an inevitable development: the positioning of business schools was a condition of possibility for CMS that has been fulfilled as an effect of other circumstances. These circumstances crucially include a widespread disillusionment with the (positivist) model of science that was assumed to provide the appropriate foundation for business education. Despite vigorous attempts (e.g. Pfeffer 2000), it has proved impossible to establish and police a single, agreed set of criteria or a 'paradigm' for determining what is 'scientific'—a difficulty that has been compounded by wider debates in the social sciences about the difficulties of developing value-free, objective knowledge, and to which proponents of CMS have very actively contributed (e.g. Willmott 1997). Over the past two decades, there has been a gradual but steady process of fragmentation and disintegration as diverse theories, perspectives and schools have emerged to disrupt the hope of a unified approach. It is surely no coincidence that CMS has been most in evidence in countries, such as the UK, where the widespread development of business schools post-dates the onset of this fragmentation.

Disillusionment with the project of establishing a single set of criteria for assessing knowledge has been accompanied and reinforced by the gap between what practitioners find relevant and what the unified programme has been able to deliver. Irrespective of the intellectual credibility of its claims to provide objective knowledge of business, practitioners have not found its outputs particularly pertinent or illuminating. This is not just because the findings presented in top journals are presented in a language that is impenetrable to practitioners but because their aim is to provide generalizable knowledge when practitioners are wrestling with particular, contextually bounded issues. As practitioners perceive it, 'scientific' journal articles are generally written for other academics, not for them. To put this another way, the form as well as the content of journal-based knowledge makes it very difficult for practitioners to incorporate insights into their existing ways of thinking about management and business. Since CMS departs from the mainstream's scientistic conception of knowledge, it can offer a different approach to students of management. In principle, it explores the possibility of developing a different kind of knowledge that is less alien, albeit that it may be ideologically less appealing, and thus presents a different kind of barrier to its absorption by practitioners. This is much less the challenge of showing practitioners how the fruits of (positivist) knowledge have practical application than it is one of encouraging and enabling them to examine critically their established beliefs and practices.

Beyond the business school and the institutions of higher education, the wider world is changing in ways that may also make CMS more relevant and attractive. Post 9/11 and post Enron there is an emergent awareness of the relativity and contingent viability of dominant, Western values and forms of knowledge. Associated with this, there is greater scepticism about many types of authority as well as, paradoxically, a retreat into apparent givens and certainties (e.g. fundamentalism, evidence-based policy making, etc). And there is a growing awareness of issues—business ethics, diversity, environmentalism, neo-imperialism—that have direct relevance for the everyday conduct of management, yet have been largely excluded from, or trivialised by, orthodox research and also from textbook accounts of business. CMS appeals to faculty and students with an interest in these issues and who are frustrated by their exclusion from, or managerialist handling within, teaching and research undertaken within business schools. For those who sense that management involves issues that extend beyond the standard fare of orthodox textbooks and leading journals, CMS commends an approach that is politically as well as epistemologically differentiated from the mainstream.

This changing and fragmented landscape, whilst opening up possibilities for CMS, presents certain difficulties. The contradictions are manifold. CMS relies for its existence upon the business schools which it critiques. A large part of the reason for its growth has been its contribution to legitimizing business schools as academically respectable and pluralistic. These contradictions cannot be resolved, but one thing is certain. It is no good to see CMS as a route for escaping from the context of business schools; they are necessarily, and for the foreseeable future, the place where it is implanted. They are also the place from which CMS is most likely to exert whatever influence it may be capable of having.

So then the question becomes: how is that influence to be achieved? Within a multiple and polyphonic situation, CMS may be no more than another voice in the Babel of voices. From this point of view, it is necessary to weld together those with more-or-less shared perspectives if its contribution is to be heard and to become influential. This is where attempts to institutionalise CMS become important. The label 'CMS' is itself an important part of such a process as are the conferences, workshops, journals and so on that have been established in recent years. And so we come back to the issue of producing this Reader. It does indeed stake out a territory, draw attention to antecedents, identify 'landmark' contributions and do all of those things which many adherents of CMS find, in other contexts, problematic. But it is our contention that this, and other, acts of institutionalization are necessary moves if critical studies of management are to be sustained and, indeed, thrive, and thereby have an effect upon the theory and practice of management. For whilst it is possible to draw attention, as we have done, to the growth of CMS it nevertheless remains a marginal and vulnerable phenomenon. Just as a peculiar set of circumstance have been conducive to its growth, so too is it easy to envisage circumstances which would render it liable to decline. It is only by institutionalizing CMS, not just inside business schools but within journals, funding bodies and other forums that its shallow roots can go deeper, with an improved prospect of changing the theory and practice of management. A Reader is a small contribution to that endeavour.

....

A Critical Management Studies Reader

Having devoted so much attention to the rationale for a CMS Reader, it remains the case that the task of selecting material for inclusion is a difficult one. We are acutely aware of the many outstanding pieces of work which we have not been able to include. In particular, we are aware that we have produced a collection which is heavily skewed towards contributions from the fields of organization studies, human resource management and general management. This fails to do justice to critical work on, in particular, accounting, information systems, strategy and marketing. To a large extent this is simply because of space requirements. It also reflects the fact that it is in the former areas that the influence of CMS has to date been felt most strongly. And it may, not entirely unreasonably, be claimed that it is work in these areas that has informed the development of critical studies in more specialised fields of management. What we have also entirely ignored is work on the implications of CMS for management education. But some selection is inevitable, and in the additional readings at the end of this chapter we indicate the availability of collections which provide useful surveys of some of the areas we have neglected.

Even with these restrictions, we were still faced with an enormous array of potential contributions. In the introduction to each section we will discuss what we have included but, briefly, we wanted to illustrate four themes. First we wanted to at least gesture towards the very large number of works which undertook the critical study of management before that term was in use. Mainstream management research is typically ignorant of its own history and it is important that CMS should not be similarly myopic. Hence we begin with a section on **Anticipating CMS**. Second, we wanted to draw some distinction between **Studying Management Critically** and **Critical Studies of Management** which form sections two and three of this volume. The distinction is by no means clear cut but denotes something like, on the one hand, principles which might inform any critical study of management and, on the other hand, instances of such studies. The former sets out something of what makes CMS distinctive from management studies in general, whilst the latter illustrates the range of insights that CMS can generate. That is not, we hope, to draw too much of a line between theoretical and empirical work: indeed, one of the great strengths of CMS is surely to imbricate theory and empirics in contrast to the abstract modelling and atheoretic descriptivism of much of the mainstream. Finally, we wanted to demonstrate the capacity of CMS to engage reflexively with itself so as to indicate that it is not a cut-and-dried body of knowledge. **Assessing CMS**, the fourth section, contains a selection of works offering internal or external critical discussions of CMS itself.

In the end, like a fantasy football team, our selection can be argued about. Everyone will have their favourite texts and their preferred authors. In the main we have chosen, within the confines of the space available, works which we have found influential, valuable and provocative, but we have also aimed at a collection which we hope will appeal to a broad cross-section of the CMS 'community'. We hope it will provide a useful resource for academics and students with an established or emergent interest in CMS.

Notes

1. A proposition that is shared by 'critical realists' who are otherwise hostile to constructionism.
2. This understanding resonates with Lynch's (1998: 14) account of the 'construction-ist movement' in social science which he describes as 'a fragile coalition of marginal, nomadic, academic bands. The knowledge produced by these bands is stitched together less by adherence to a body of dogma, technical protocols, master narratives or clear-cut ideologies than by a tolerance of diverse "voices"'.

3. Some critics of CMS, such as Thompson (this volume), assert that it excludes those, such as critical realists and neo-marxists, who do not subscribe to post-structuralism. We can only re-state that this is not our understanding of CMS and indeed that CMS must be a broad church if it is to advance any meaningful political project. See Grey (2005).

References

Alvesson, M. & Willmott, H. (eds) (1992). *Critical Management Studies*. London: Sage.

Engwall, L. (1997). 'Mercury and Minerva: A Modern Multinational Academic Business Studies on a Global Scale', in Alvarez J. L. (ed.), *The Diffusion and Consumption of Business Knowledge*. London: Macmillan, pp. 81–109.

Fournier, V. & Grey, C. (2000). 'At the Critical Moment: Conditions and Prospects for Critical Management Studies', *Human Relations* 53, 1: 7–32.

Grey, C. (2005). 'Critical Management Studies: Towards a More Mature Politics', in Howcroft D. & Trauth E. (eds), *Handbook of Critical Information Systems Research*. London: Edward Elgar (in press).

Lynch, M. (1998), 'Towards a Constructivist Genealogy of Social Constructivism' in I. Velody and R. Williams, eds., *The Politics of Constructionism*, London : Sage, pp 13–32

Pfeffer, J. (2000), 'Barriers to the Advance of Organizational Science,' in Frost P., Lewin A. & Daft R. (eds), *Talking About Organization Science*. Thousand Oaks: Sage, pp 39–61.

Whitley, R., Thomas, A. & Marceau, J. (1981), *Masters of Business: The Making of a New Elite?* London: Tavistock.

Whitley, R. (1984). 'The Fragmented State of Management Studies: Reasons and Consequences', *Journal of Management Studies* 21, 3: 331–348.

Willmott, H. C. (1997), 'Management and Organization Studies as Science? Methodologies of OR in Critical Perspective', *Organization* 4, 3: 309–344.

Additional Reading

The works listed below are a small selection of other Readers and edited collections which include many works relevant to CMS. Another useful source of such material is the proceedings of Critical Management Studies Conferences which can be found at: www.mngt.waikato.ac.nz/research/ejrot/

Alvesson, M. and Willmott, H. C. (2004). *Studying Management Critically*, London: Sage.

Brownlie, D., Saren, M., Wensley, R. and Whittington, R. (eds) (1999). *Rethinking Marketing*, London: Sage.

Collinson, D. (ed.) (2000). *Organisational Studies: Critical Perspectives on Business and Management*. London: Routledge (4 vols).

Cooper, D. and Hopper, T. (eds) (1990). *Critical Accounts*. London: Macmillan.

Grey, C. and Antonacopoulou, E. (eds) (2004), *Essential Readings in Management Learning*. London: Sage.

Howcroft, D. and Trauth, E. (eds) (2005). *Handbook of Critical Information Systems Research*. London: Edward Elgar.

Jackson, M. and Keys, P. (eds) (1990). *OR and the Social Sciences*, London : Plenum.

Mills, A. and Tancred, P. (eds) (1992). *Gendering Organizational Analysis*. London: Sage
Prasad.

1. ANTICIPATING CRITICAL MANAGEMENT STUDIES

Although CMS has gained force as a *label* over the last decade, the *substance* of its analysis has long existed, prompted by a variety of religious and political critiques of the role of management in the identification and subjugation of 'labour' as an abstract, instrumental factor of production. Without going back that far, from the 1950s onwards it is possible to find a growing chorus of concern about both the dominance of large organizations (e.g. Whyte 1956) and of management and managerialism within society. Much of this concern was articulated in terms of the formation of a technocratic elite linking business, politics and the armed forces—the so-called 'military-industrial complex'. Such an analysis is exemplified by the work of **C. Wright Mills** from whose book *The Power Elite* (1959) we take an extract. The significance of the analysis is its focus upon the systemic nature of managerial dominance. Within Marxism this had long been recognised. Yet, traditionally, it was in ways which treated managers either as bearers of the interests of capital or as a particularly privileged segment of labour (Dumenil & Levy 1993). It was not until later that more sustained attempts to theorise managerial dominance were made by Marxists (e.g. Marglin 1980).

The proposition that management needs to be thought of both in terms of managerial dominance and in terms of its systemic nature—regardless of the details of how these are apprehended—seems to us to be central to CMS. Without such an understanding, CMS would be no more than a series of 'complaints' about this or that aspect of management. To become a critique of any significance it is necessary to locate such complaints within an overall conception of how they fit together and why they are significant. Wright Mills' work is illustrative of one such conception. Whilst eschewing notions of a knowing, conspiratorial elite, he nevertheless insists upon a sceptical stance towards those who would deny domination, particularly when such denials are made by those who hold power, or who speak on behalf of the power elites. Mills shows that it is possible to trace formal and informal connections within elites which perpetuate their domination, and that these elites sustain and are sustained by key institutions. Inevitably many parts of his analysis now seem dated—and in this and some other readings in this section the gendered use of language is jarring—but what remains for CMS is both the example of a sceptical intellect and the sense that the critique of management matters because of its imbrication with wider social and political concerns.

Management studies is very much bound up with managerial power. **Loren Baritz's** book *The Servants of Power* (1960) is an early and prescient analysis of this. Baritz suggests that industrial sociologists and psychologists have 'put themselves on auction' to the power elites. He points in particular to the promise of such social scientists to offer managers ever more effective means of control of employees, especially through the various techniques associated with 'human relations theory'. This represents the alignment of social science with a particular and partial set of interests and the incorporation of managerial assumptions into the practice of research. Of course, as Baritz points out, the capacity of social science to actually deliver on its managerial promises may be more limited than it claims, but nevertheless it contributes, in particular, to the development of ever more sophisticated techniques of ideological manipulation in the workplace.

The enrolment of social science in the service of managerial power is very much the hallmark of the mainstream of management studies, which has grown hugely since Baritz's time, and it is this which provides the impetus for CMS. **Clegg & Dunkerley's** (1977) work, the introduction to which is reproduced here, is an explicit and early call to embrace a far broader set of issues than the mainstream allows. These issues include 'sexism, power [and] capitalist development' whose exclusion is seen to reflect and reinforce the sectional interests of management. Clegg & Dunkerley's work articulates what still remains at the heart of CMS, even though some CMS writers, under the influence of post-structuralism, might now worry about the apparent ease of access to the organizational 'realities' that it invokes.

Nearly thirty years on, Clegg and Dunkerley's characterization of the mainstream is depressingly familiar. It is still the case that management studies is dominated by a North American orthodoxy which seeks to unify the field around a positivist and managerialist agenda; and it is still to some extent the case that the issues Clegg & Dunkerley raise are marginalised, but no longer invariably ignored, in the standard textbooks. On the other hand, the very flourishing of CMS which we discussed in the introduction to this volume is indicative of the way that the kinds of concerns they articulate have been taken up and developed, not just in organization theory but across the management field. Indeed it is relevant and ironic to note that CMS has become sufficiently established to now be a target of criticism—from none other than Stewart Clegg (2005)!

Perhaps there is a pattern here. Also published in 1977 was **P. D. Anthony's** *The Ideology of Work* from which we reproduce an extract. There are some significant continuities with Clegg & Dunkerley and Baritz. In particular, there is a sense that (mainstream) management studies (including organization theory) contributes to the ideological projects of management and managerialism. It is again a servant of power. This occurs precisely by a concealment of its own ideological positioning through the adoption of a supposedly, although in Anthony's view bogus, scientific language. This of course is precisely the language encouraged by the middle-range, managerial positivism attacked by Clegg & Dunkerley. For Anthony, the deployment on a massive scale of managerialist ideology has been steadily transforming—or 'modernizing', to use the preferred, seemingly progressive and neutral, managerialist terminology—not just business organizations but professions and government.

Although the analysis is different, this echoes the way that Mills' work points CMS towards a wide array of social institutions. Even more noticeably, Anthony's work prefigures the now commonplace observation of what has become an even more extensive managerialization of diverse institutions (e.g. Clarke & Newman 1997). But Anthony's account of managerial ideology explains that it is also a way in which the behaviour and belief of managers and others is shaped. This pre-figures the substantial attention CMS has devoted to subjectivity and it also opens up the great significance of management education—derided by Anthony as 'theocratic'—as a bearer of managerial ideology, a significance which has also noticeably increased in the intervening years.

Again it is difficult to know how to evaluate the continuing purchase of Anthony's work. So much of *The Ideology of Work* still resonates. Yet, just as some current CMS writers are suspicious of the notion of organizational 'realities', they may be uneasy with the identification of certain forms of knowledge as 'ideology', if this implies a form of bogus knowledge to be contrasted with 'science'. Nonetheless, it is probably fair to say that some version of Anthony's stance is widely held amongst adherents of CMS, and indeed may be conceived as a central element of its 'conventional wisdom'. And this is where we see a pattern. For it is again ironic that CMS has been the target of withering attack from P. D. Anthony (1998) himself.

References

Anthony, P. (1998). 'Management Education: Ethics versus Morality', in Parker M. (ed.), *Ethics and Organizations*. London: Sage, pp. 269–281.

Clarke, J. & Newman, J. (1997). *The Managerial State*. London: Sage.

Clegg, S. (2005). 'For Management', *Management Learning* (forthcoming).

Dumenil, G. & Levy, D. (1993). 'The Emergence and Functions of Managerial and Clerical Personnel in Marx's *Capital*', in Garston N. (ed), *Bureaucracy: Three Paradigms*. Boston MA: Kluwer, pp. 61–81.

Marglin, S. (1974). 'What do Bosses Do? The Origins and Functions of Hierarchy in Capitalist Production', *Review of Radical Political Economics* 6: 60–102.

Whyte, W. (1956). *The Organization Man*. New York: Simon & Schuster.

2 Management Ideology

P. D. Anthony

What we have called the recruitment of social science in the service of management concerned first the utilization of the psychologist's techniques and expertise. The application of psychology extended from an initial concern to improve methods of selection and training to a much more general concern with the individual's motivation in which, finally, the business organization and the tasks which it requires to be performed are both changed in order to make work become the satisfier of fundamental human needs. Work becomes a much more valued and valuable activity, we are the more likely to regard it as a central life interest, to take its performance requirements seriously, and to become deeply involved in its distribution of rewards when these rewards include our own psychological health.

But, powerful though this new appeal of work is meant to be, it is not yet omnipotent. The individual worker is not the sole determinant of his own behaviour, even when his environment has been controlled in order to encourage his individual decisions to be those of which the organization which controls his environment would approve, there still remains the uncontrolled influence of groups and the informal social structure of the work place. The next extension of control is therefore to exert some influence over the social system. The end result is to be able to propose to the worker that the social system is his in that it, like his work, has been constructed in order to take account of his wishes and his needs so that its objectives become his own. The end result is achieved when the application of authority and power is no longer necessary to assist in the achievement of the organization's goals because the goals have been internalized by those who are to pursue them. While the goals are left untouched (indeed there are instances in management literature when the goals, in terms of production, have been increased) the apparatus of bureaucratic authority is concealed or dismantled. As McGregor

(1960 : 31) put it: 'There is nothing inherently wrong or bad about giving an order or making a unilateral decision. There are many circumstances however, when the exercise of authority fails to achieve the desired results. Under such circumstances, the solution does not lie in exerting more authority or less authority; *it lies in using other means of influence*' (McGregor's emphasis).

The apparatus can be dismantled because its use is unnecessary or a nuisance, because 'other means' are a more effective substitute for authority in achieving goals about which there is often no real debate. The manager has come to rely more and more heavily on the psychologist and the sociologist for the determination of other means which are appropriate to his own particular situation. The manager's life has become much more complicated as the result of this dependence because he is constantly being told about the unreliability of the old saws, clichés, and principles by which he used to direct his affairs. This new complexity does not necessarily challenge the legitimacy of managerial authority, rather it seeks to point out its limits 'and even to improve its effectiveness by analysing the barriers to managerial control' (Child 1969 : 205).

However, it is not our business to discuss the theory and practice of management except in so far as it influences an ideology of work. In this respect we see a strange departure from the ideological evolution which we have been observing. While, at every previous stage, we have seen improvements in the appeal to work associated with attempts to make the appeal more legitimate, now that legitimacy appears to be more firmly established than ever, the appeals to work seem to diminish in frequency and force. Such appeals as are now directed by managers at workers are much more likely to require their continued presence at work rather than the expenditure of greater effort and enthusiasm while there. Appeals are now normally concerned with the avoidance of disputes or absence.

Is this the end of ideology? In a limited sense, it is. The whole approach which we have been outlining under the heading of the recruitment of the social scientist is essentially to make any managerial exhortation for effort unnecessary and redundant. To continue to appeal *to* the workers *by* managers would indeed be a contradiction of the new understanding that management is now seeking to bring about; the continuation of a process of exhortation would be a confession that the process of social and psychological integration had failed.

The major necessity now is not that workers should be appealed to for greater effort but that their managers should be appealed to to bring about the conditions which will encourage it—to some extent, from workers but, more so, from managers themselves. The ideological onslaught is now almost entirely directed at managers and it is no longer composed of a naive, Smilesian appeal for hard work.

The ideology of work is now essentially a managerial syndrome. It contains several strands, the first of which, concerned with the construction of an environment which the worker will find, in every sense, rewarding, we have examined at some length. A second strand consists of a more direct appeal for managerial effort and hard work. This strand is supported by a whole mass of techniques designed to measure, monitor, control, and reward managers' performance. Despite its apparent technical complexity, this is the element in the managerial appeal which is the most simple and most directly related to the evolution emerging from the protestant ethic to Smiles and beyond; it concerns the motivation of the manager. A third strand consists of the continued search for a legitimate foundation upon which appeals and authority can be based.

This third element takes us very close to a discussion of the whole controversy concerning managerialism. In the sense that this involves a debate about whether or not managers are established as an elite, a group or a class, which has ultra-national similarities, is concerned to advance its own power and influence and to control access to membership and the behaviour of its personnel, in this, macro sense, we can avoid it. But in the more limited sense that we have concluded that it is now managers and managers alone who are concerned with the direction of appeals concerning the commitment to work and are therefore involved in legitimating their own authority in work, in this sense, we are concerned with an aspect of managerialism.

This particular aspect of managerialism has two important characteristics which distinguish it from previous attempts at establishing the legitimacy of authority in industry. The first is the sheer scale of the ideological effort. Previous ideological appeals were often implicit in entrepreneurs' speeches and writings, occasionally they were given explicit and coherent form in the writings of specialist apoligists or propagandists like Robert Owen, Andrew Ure, or Samuel Smiles. Currently, ideology plays a very considerable part in the curricula of management courses at universities, polytechnics, technical colleges and industrial staff colleges.

The ideological element is not always instantly recognizable for what it is. We would not identify it as ideology as readily, for example, as we would that part of Chinese educational curricula which are devoted to Marxist-Leninist theory and the contributions of Chairman Mao. One reason for our difficulty is that much of the ideological element in management education appears to be concerned with objective, scientific, research-based conceptualization of practical managerial problem-solving. Thus Child (1969 : 250), referring to a survey of management teachers which he carried out in 1964, concluded that 'at the time considerable emphasis was given in courses to discussions about increasing the discretionary content of work and employees participation within organizational affairs. This strongly supports the view that neo-human relations has become the new "orthodoxy" in management education.' The continued popularity of courses with titles such as 'A day with Herzberg' suggests that little has happened subsequently to require an amendment of this judgement. The content of these courses has, of course, become more sophisticated in that they are now likely to take account of 'plural frames of reference' and the recognition of the 'reality of conflict' but we have suggested, if not established, that the intention behind these more complex contributions remains the same.

The intention, quite apart from the disguise of scientific language, is two-fold: to provide a basis for the control of subordinates by facilitating their integration in work, and to reinforce the integration of managers. A great deal of management education, that part of it concerned with behavioural science, is in fact theocratic, it is designed to establish a sense of unity of purpose and of values largely by providing managers with a common language and a system of concepts. Management education is truly ideological in this sense, that it aims to influence behaviour by inculcating beliefs and expectations. Dissemination of an ideology by way of management training has these two latent functions: it helps to promote the internal solidarity of management and it helps to justify its authority over subordinates. The manufacture and spread of an ideology also gives a more spiritual or cultural appearance—particularly when it emanates from universities—to what would otherwise be a purely money-grubbing and materialist pursuit. This confers a welcome dignity and it helps, as we have noted, to shift the basis of control over managers from a remunerative to a normative base.

An ideological explanation of this element in managerial education also explains the astonishing absence of controversy. Perhaps we have quoted at sufficient length from some of the influential sources in this area to illustrate that much of them are based on uncertain theory applied by questionable logic to unrelated circumstances. Much of the behavioural sciences do not fulfil the most elementary tests of the validity of scientific method. This is not an idle accusation. It has been argued by a number of authoritative analysts of scientific method that scientific propositions are advanced as the result of a hypothetical-deductive method in which the resultant theories, although they can never be proved, continue to stand while the scientist rigorously looks for evidence to *overthrow* them. The scientist's theories stand for as long as he fails to upset them. This is the opposite of the way in which most behavioural scientists go about their work; they advance theories which they have 'proved' as the result of a singularly hasty search for evidence that will *support* them.

If there are methodological problems concerning the validity of behavioural science theory these problems are multiplied by the time unrealiable theories have been vulgarized by consultants and then simplified by teachers in order to transmit them to managers, whose knowledge of basic behavioural science theory may be nil. Perhaps we can understand why there is no controversy. It would be hard to find another field of educational activity in which intelligent, and sometimes educated minds, were so harmoniously disposed. There may be occasional disagreement about educational methods, never about doctrine.

On the very rare occasions when a manager, or come to that one of his teachers, meets someone carrying another set of doctrines based uon different values, he reacts with bewilderment.

Let me illustrate with two examples, perhaps in this context we should really call them 'case studies'.

The first example comes from a staff college where industrial relations specialists had prepared a project report on productivity bargaining. In the general atmosphere of complete consensus with which the report was presented, I ventured, as visiting adjudicator, to say that there was a very different view concerning productivity bargaining, that Cliff (1970 : 11) had described productivity bargaining as 'part of a determined offensive by the employing class' which is 'aimed at finding a *permanent* solution to employers' problems' and that this view was not without support from workers. The result was laughter. It seemed that these specialists in labour relations were so insulated from a view that would be either familiar or acceptable to their trade union opposite numbers that they thought it was a joke.

The second example goes some way to explain the sense of cloistered privacy in which those discussions are often conducted. Fox (1971 : 172), in discussing 'New Modes of Joint Regulation' explains that 'only by fully recognizing and accepting the constraints imposed by the aspirations of its subordinates, and working through these constraints towards a new synthesis, can management now enjoy any creative role in its handling of the social organization' and that this recognition was embodied in the growing number of managements who had engaged in productivity bargaining. This new form of bargaining enabled both management and 'employee collectivities' 'to achieve a major reconstruction of the normative system which leaves all the parties conscious of having improved their position' (Fox 1971 : 174). Productivity bargaining offers 'something to the aspirations of all the parties involved. It represents a joint struggle to accommodate conflicting demands to the survival or growth needs of the coalition.' And how does this particular sociologist respond to a counter-view of productivity bargaining, from a party who is *not* conscious of having improved his position? He refuses to discuss any attack upon productivity bargaining (the underlying assumptions of which he so obviously approves) by simply identifying the ideological source of the opposition. Thus: 'Finally, one would predict that the new modes of regulation involving as they do a closer collaborative pattern of relationships would be condemned by those whose anti-management stance is ideological and total.

25

The perspectives and behaviours required for integrative bargaining are incompatible with the class war' (Fox 1971 : 175).

Fox's response suggests an approach that is itself basically ideological. This is illustrated first because, having gone further than most in acknowledging a counter-view, he cannot apparently discuss it but can only discount it by reference to its own ideological commitment—'one would predict...'. Second, the identification of the enemy is loose, ambiguous, and general, as it often is in ideological accounts. 'Those whose anti-management stance is ideological'—but who are they? 'Those committed to the class struggle'. Ah, then, the communist party? But communists are demonstrably not anti-management. Indeed Cliff, (1970) making an equally 'predictable' attack on productivity bargaining gives and criticizes many instances of communists who have supported it. Finally, Fox's account illustrates a basic refusal to enter into a discourse. This is a rare departure in the development of European thought, even the most arid schoolmen were prepared to debate the potential density of angels upon pins. The sociologists' pronouncements are, we are intended to believe, value free, so that their defence cannot be contaminated by conducting it in terms of the concealed values on which it rests. But if any attack must always be ideological, does this not prove, at least, that a conflicting ideology will find values underlying the sociologists' case to disagree with?

The ideological content of managerialism is illustrated by one other characteristic, its ambition. We have observed, ever since Tawney (1925) commented on the 'revolution which was to set a naturalistic political arithmetic in the place of theology, substitute the categories of mechanism for those of theology...', the gradual domination of economic interests and work-related values. This domination has reached the point where the values of management culture can be described as having these three components:

The first is the value system of economic rationality analysed by Weber, prominent in which are such principles as the measured weighing of utilities and costs; the use of money as the universal measure of value, and the importance of maximising-behaviour and of capital accounting. The second major component is the value-system of economic growth: the philosophy which measures national success by performance in the international league-table of Gross National Product. This philosophy is now virtually world-wide and completely transcends fundamental differences in political and social systems. The third component is the closely associated notion of technological progress; the philosophy that finds terminal as well as instrumental value in extending human control over material resources. These three components constitute the dominant culture of industrial societies .... (Fox 1971 : 68)

In this sense, the political, economic, and social lives of industrialized communities are suffused with managerial values. But managerial ideology is ambitious in another sense. There are signs that the transcendence of its values is not enough, that the demand is emerging for its supremacy to be explicitly acknowledged.

While claims to managerial legitimacy once rested upon analogies with government and with political democracy, so that management drew credibility and authority by comparisons with established political systems the argument and the analogy is now beginning to run in the opposite direction. Governments and political systems are now being recommended to model themselves on management. The expertise, authority, and objectivity of managers is offered to governments and the British government begins to emulate that of the USA in its willingness to give senior ministerial posts to managers who next have to be found Parliamentary seats. Sometimes the offers of assistance are more wholehearted, as when Lord Robens and Sir Paul Chambers advocated government by businessmen as more efficient. There is even support for more managerialism from the politicians; Roszak (1970 : 11) quotes the late President Kennedy:

What is at stake in our economic decisions today is not some grand warfare of rival ideologies which will sweep the country with passion, but the practical management of a modern economy. What we need are not labels and clichés but more basic discussion of the sophisticated and technical questions involved in keeping a great economic machinery moving ahead.

Management, meanwhile, makes more modest claims to achieve new influence. It has now become common-place to talk of the management of areas of activities which were previously regarded as the province of professionals. In medicine the nurses have been gradually forced to abandon a close professional attachment to patient care in favour of a typically hierarchical structure in which the superordinate levels are concerned with administration or management of the ward or the hospital and in which the subordinate levels have been subjected to specialism and the recruitment of auxiliary labour. Massive courses of management education are now directed at the nurses, the main ingredients of which are a grounding in the behavioural sciences and the constant attempt to make the nurses see themselves as essentially engaged in managerial activities. Nurses are often accompanied by hospital administrators who are very ready to admit the newcomers to the highly regarded ranks of management in which the administrators, of course, are already well established. This process has the additional advantage that, apart from 'converting' the nurses, it solves the serious status problems of the administrators in an erstwhile professional structure by changing the structure so that administrators can see themselves at its centre, while the old professionals become the newcomers. The process would be even more satisfactory if the doctors could also be persuaded to become claimants for managerial status; the hospital administrators would be delighted to assist them with instruction and advise. The further development of status inversion has, however, not met with the entire approval of the doctors who stubbornly continue to regard themselves as professionals and who, as yet show no great enthusiasm for managerial treatment.

In other professions (apart from the law) there are similar signs of conversion. Headmasters conscientiously attend behavioural science courses on motivation and the management of scarce resources. Architects show signs of having been so thoroughly committed to a process of employment and management by institutions and organizations that there are even signs of a revolt.

All these developments suggest a rampant managerialism that is no longer content to camouflage its values and disguise itself in a society in which other institutions (like the professions) and other activities (like politics) are paid the greatest respect. And apart from overt claims to influence, there is the 'broad power' in:

the position that corporate management occupies as task setter or style leader for the society as a whole. Business influence on taste ranges from the direct effects through the design of material goods to the indirect and more subtle effects of the style of language and thought purveyed through the mass media—the school of style at which all of us are in attendance every day. Further, these same business leaders are dominant social models in our society: their achievements and their values are to a large extent the type of the excellent, especially for those strata of society from which leaders in most endeavours are drawn. (Kaysen in Bendix and Lipset 1967 : 234)

In such a society, the crudities of a straightforward ideology of work are no longer necessary and no longer effective. Economic enterprise, and those who are responsible for its control and whose own value is measured by its results, have virtually succeeded in transforming society so that politics, as well as theology, have been transformed from 'the master interest of mankind into one department of life with boundaries which it is extravagant to overstep'.

....

References

Child, J. (1969). *British Management Thought*. London: Allen and Unwin.

Cliff, T. (1970). *The Employers Offensive*. London: Pluto Press.

Fox, A. (1971). *A Sociology of Work in Industry*. London: Collier-Macmillan.

Kaysen, C. (1967). 'The Corporation: How Much Power?', in Bendix and Lipsett (eds), *Class, Status and Power*. London: Routledge and Kegan Paul.

McGregor, D. (1960). *The Human Side of Enterprise*. New York: McGraw Hill.

Roszak, T. (1970). *the Making of a Counter Culture*. London: Faber and Faber.

Tawney, R. H. (1925). *Thomas Wilson, A discourse upon usury*. London: Bell.

3 The Servants of Power

Loren Baritz

Henry Ford II, 1946: 'If we can solve the problem of human relations in industrial production, we can make as much progress toward lower costs in the next 10 years as we made during the past quarter century through the development of the machinery of mass production.'[1] By the middle of the twentieth century, industrial social science had become one of the most pregnant of the many devices available to America's managers in their struggle with costs and labor, government and the consuming public. But, even then, industrial social science remained richer in its promise than in its accomplishments, impressive as these had been. It was often what social science *could* do in the next five, ten, or twenty years that justified to managers their current support of its practitioners. Thus far, social scientists had contributed to management a useful array of techniques, including testing, counseling, attitude research, and sociometry. All to the good, certainly; but much was left to do. And most of what was left, as Henry Ford correctly pointed out, was centered in the area of human relations. The reason that an understanding of human relations assumed such monumental proportions was that, in an age of governmental regulations and more powerful unions, costs continued to rise. American management came to believe in the importance of understanding human behavior because it became convinced that this was one sure way of improving its main weapon in the struggle for power, the profit margin.

The promise of industrial social science has not been a subject about which America's managers have had to guess. The industrial social scientists themselves have, throughout their professional history, made explicit their aspirations, their hopes for the future, and their unbounded faith in the centrality of their discipline to the problems of modern life. The history of this explication of faith began, appropriately enough, with Walter Dill Scott, who argued in 1911 that a knowledge of the laws of psychology would make it possible for the businessman to control and therefore raise the efficiency of every man in his employ, including his own. At about the same time, a lecturer at the University of Wisconsin's School of Commerce assured his students that a knowledge of psychology would increase their 'commercial proficiency by fifty per cent.' Workers, according to Hugo Münsterberg's 1913 statement, would have their wages raised, their working hours reduced, mental depression and dissatisfaction with work eliminated, all through the application of psychology to industry. He assured Americans that a 'cultural gain ... will come to the total economic life of the nation.' A knowledge of psychology, reported another psychologist, would provide the business executive with the skills needed to influence the behavior of his workers. Psychologist G. Stanley Hall went all out: 'Our task', he said, 'is nothing less than to rehumanize industry.'[2]

During the 1920's and 1930's psychologists reported that 'the fate ... of mankind' depended on the help they could give to managers. Indeed, according to James McKeen Cattell, the founder of the Psychological Corporation, 'The development of psychology as a science and its application to the control of human conduct ... may in the course of the coming century be as significant for civilization as has been the industrial revolution.' Specific tasks were also outlined for the psychology of the future. For example, General Motors' sit-down strikes of 1937 could have been avoided through the use of psychology, said a psychologist. If psychologists were as effective in industry as they had been in education, said another, 'something akin to an industrial Utopia would arise.' Over and over again these men assured anyone who cared to listen that many of the world's problems would disappear if only executives would be more receptive to the advances of psychology.[3]

Even problems of general moment were thought to be solvable through the work of industrial psychologists; the factory, said M.I.T. psychologist Douglas McGregor, 'is a microcosm in which we may well be able to find answers to some of the fundamental problems of modern society.' Industrial conflict would disappear, reported other psychologists, if their conclusions were implemented in industry. In fact, said still another, if psychology were more widely accepted by management, 'the advancement of our emotional, social, and economic life' would be more certain. *'Potentially the most important of sciences for the improvement of man and of his world-order'* is the way Robert M. Yerkes, a psychologist at Yale, described his discipline in 1946.[4]

Sociologists, too, tried to make clear what they could do if they were given the chance, though they were usually more restrained than the psychologists. They recognized that managers determined the kinds of opportunities the sociologists had, and hence, if the claims of sociology were frustrated, the managers themselves would be at fault. If all was in order, however, if managers cooperated, sociologists could 'provide useful analytical tools and profitable guides for activity.' Other sociologists believed that they could help managers 'think more effectively about their human problems.' Perhaps this was why one sociologist accepted employment with a petroleum company in 1943 to explain why the CIO was able to organize its men. Margaret Mead thought her colleagues could help make the anonymous industrial worker feel important. Focusing on the top echelon of the business hierarchy, some sociologists were dissatisfied with what they saw. A different type of social control was needed, and they believed that they were the men to point the way to the future. The powers of the sociological elite would be concentrated on the subelite of managers who needed to be led and 'clarified.' All that was needed was some cooperation from those who wielded managerial power.[5]

It was precisely this need for managerial cooperation that made the social scientists' conception of what they could do in the future seem at best a trifle grandiose and at worst silly. As part of the bureaucratization of virtually every aspect of American life, most industrial social scientists labored in industry as technicians, not as scientists. Not professionally concerned with problems outside the delimited sphere which management had assigned to them, not daring to cross channels of communication and authority, they were hemmed in by the very organization charts which they had helped to contrive. And the usual industrial social scientist, because he accepted the norms of the elite dominant in his society, was prevented from functioning critically, was compelled by his own ideology and the power of America's managers to supply the techniques helpful to managerial goals. In what should have been a healthful tension between mind and society, the industrial social scientist in serving the industrial elite had to abandon the wider obligations of the intellectual who is a servant of his own mind.

Casting his characteristically wide net, sociologist C. Wright Mills pointed out that 'the intellectual is becoming a technician, an idea-man, rather than one who resists the environment, preserves the individual type, and defends himself from death-by-adaption.' Unless psychologists raised their sights and became concerned with broader social problems, said another observer, they would not 'rise to the level of professional persons but will degenerate into mere technicians.'[6]

The technician's role was literally forced upon industrial social scientists by the nature of their industrial positions. Hired by management to solve specific problems, they had to produce. The problem was best stated by two of the most astute psychologists of the 1920's: 'Research, to be successful, has to be carried out under the most favorable conditions, and only the business man himself can say whether these conditions shall be provided.'[7]

A few industrial social scientists learned that they could not even rely on the much touted practicality of business executives. One psychologist employed by an advertising agency said in 1955 that he 'had expected that the businessman would be hard headed and practical.... To my surprise and frustration,' he went on, 'they have accepted an awful lot of research mish mush.... Hard headed businessmen hell!'[8] Managers, however, have usually been sufficiently practical, from their own point of view, to realize that controls over research programs were necessary. Demanding that the social scientists in their employ concentrate exclusively on the narrow problems of productivity and industrial loyalty, managers made of industrial social science a tool of industrial domination. Some social scientists warned that this procedure would result in a 'distorted view of industry,' but failed to see that this was precisely what sophisticated managers wanted.[9]

Even Elton Mayo, of Hawthorne fame, feared that the forced status of technician would seriously limit the effectiveness of industrial social scientists, whose science would thereby be strangled. Because of the control of management over the nature and scope of their work, Mayo said, 'the interesting *aperçu*, the long chance, may not be followed: both alike must be denied in order that the [research] group may "land another job."' The long-range effects would be even worse, because the 'confusion of research with commercial huckstering can never prosper: the only effect is to disgust the intelligent youngster who is thus forced to abandon his quest for human enlightenment.'[10]

Management, in short, controlled the industrial social scientists in its employ. Managers did not make use of social science out of a sense of social responsibility, but out of a recognized need to attack age-old problems of costs and worker loyalty with new weapons designed to fit the needs and problems of the twentieth century. Thus, the recent arguments that American industry has entered a new era of social obligations and responsibilities[11] have missed the main point in the motivation of managers. When fulfilling putative social obligations became smart business, smart managers became socially conscious. Walter Reuther is characteristic of the small group that has refused to be seduced by the sophisticated rhetoric of managers, their spokesmen, and the articulate academicians who insist that the American business civilization is the best of all possible worlds. Trying to educate a congressional committee, Reuther said that his extensive experience with employers had taught him that 'the one sure way of making them [employers] socially responsible is to make them financially responsible for the social results of what they do or fail to do.'[12] Because of the general climate of opinion today, it is perhaps necessary to repeat what in previous years would have been a cliché unworthy of serious argument: managers, as managers, are in business to make money. Only to the extent that industrial social scientists can help in the realization of this goal will management make use of them.

Managers are forced by the necessities of the business world to measure their personal success or failure by the yardstick of the balance sheet; they have occasionally made considerable effort to clarify the thinking of industrial social scientists who just might be of help in improving the financial condition of the firm and therefore improving the position of the manager. It will be recalled that one of the main obstacles to easy interchange between managers and social scientists had long been the managers' conviction that social scientists were ignorant about the nature and purposes of industry. To employ an expert who did not recognize either the values or necessities of business might prove dangerous. Articulating what many managers felt, an executive of a large utility company, for example, in 1951 laid down the law to social scientists specifying the attitudes business expected of them:

First—a willingness to accept the notion that businessmen perform a useful function in society, and that their methods may be necessary to accomplish this function. . . .

Second—a willingness to accept the culture and conventions of business as necessary and desirable. . . .

Third—a willingness to obtain personal satisfaction from being a member of a winning team, perhaps an anonymous member.

Fourth—a willingness and ability to practice the good human relations principles that he knows.[13]

How unnecessary was this managerial fear of the industrial social scientist. The popular image of the impractical and absent-minded professor who was either a political liberal or perhaps even worse blurred the perception of the hard-headed managers of the business life of the nation. For, throughout their professional history, industrial social scientists, without prodding from anyone, have accepted the norms of America's managers. If this attitude had not tended to influence their work, it would deserve merely passing mention. But this commitment to management's goals, as opposed to the goals of other groups and classes in American society, did color their research and recommendations. These men have been committed to aims other than those of their professional but nonindustrial colleagues. Though the generalization has weaknesses, it seems that making a contribution to knowledge has been the essential purpose of only a few industrial social scientists. Reducing the pressures of unionism while increasing the productivity of the labor force and thereby lowering costs have been among their most cherished goals, because these have been the goals which management has set for them.

Managers, of course, had the power to hire and fire social scientists. If a social scientist was to be kept on the payroll, he had to produce. The judge of whether he was producing was his boss. His boss was interested in the specific problems of the business including those that threatened managerial control. Thus industrial social scientists have usually been salaried men, doing what they were told to do and doing it well—and therefore endangering those other personal, group, class, and institutional interests which were opposed to the further domination by the modern corporation of the mood and direction of American life. Endangered most have been the millions of workers who have been forced or seduced into submission to the ministrations of industrial social scientists. For these men and women there has been little defense, because organized labor generally has been apathetic to the movement, and because, even had labor been more active, management has played the game from a dominant position. Recently, however, there have been a few hints indicating that organized labor is beginning to make use of social-science techniques itself.[14] In any case, to date nothing seems to stand in the way of increased industrial exploitation of social science, and the industrial social scientists themselves have been especially willing.

The position these social scientists have taken regarding the ethics and politics of power obtrudes as a red thread in the otherwise pallid canvas on which they have labored. From the pioneers in industrial psychology to the sophisticated human-relations experts of the 1950's, almost all industrial social scientists have either backed away from the political and ethical implications of their work or have faced these considerations from the point of view of management. Aptly, it was Hugo Münsterberg who first formulated the comfortable and self-castrating position that industrial psychologists should concern themselves with means only, not with goals, aims, or ends, which could and should be determined only by the industrial managers themselves. Scientific method was clearly on Münsterberg's side, for science cannot solve political problems, and psychology, he argued, was a science which must be impartial. Thus, he insisted that his colleagues should not pander 'to selfish fancies of either side'—that is, capital or labor—but should remain detached and scientific observers of the industrial situation. Other early leaders in the development of industrial psychology quickly picked up Münsterberg's cue and explicated his position: 'Psychology will always be limited by the fact that while it can determine the means to the end, it can have nothing to do with the determination of the end itself.'[15]

During the 1920's the political stance desirable for social scientists was made even more clear. Moving from the justification by objectivity to a recognition of the industrial facts of life, psychologists were told that 'business results are the main object.' Objectivity was lifeblood to a true science, but the industrial manager would instruct his hired specialists about those problems or subjects that required analysis. 'The pursuit and enlargement of psychological knowledge is merely a by-product of business efforts,' psychologists were further cautioned. Confusion was compounded when, late in the decade, another industrial psychologist explained his position: workers who were justifiably dissatisfied were not fit subjects for psychological analysis because such a situation was an 'economic or ethical problem.' The obverse held: where workers were treated fairly and still were dissatisfied, there was the spot for psychological inquiry.[16] The controlling question of who determined the justification of employee dissatisfaction was unanswered, as of course it had to be. Moving from the academic to the industrial world, it seemed relatively clear that managers would at least suggest where psychological analysis should occur, which is to say that the decision about the justification of employee satisfaction or dissatisfaction was one that management made. The social scientist applied his tools where he was told to apply them.

Of major importance in this subordination of industrial social science to the pleasure of management were the assumptions made by the Hawthorne researchers. Perhaps this was the area in which the work of Elton Mayo was the most significant. For Mayo, more than any other single individual, directed the course of industrial research—obliquely, to be sure, through the statement of his attitudes and assumptions, which proved so comfortable that many disciples made them their own.

Mayo's unshakable conviction was that the managers of the United States comprised an elite which had the ability and therefore the right to rule the rest of the nation. He pointed out, for instance, that many of America's managers were remarkable men without prejudice.[17] According to one of his critics, Mayo believed that 'management is capable, trained, and objective. Management uses scientific knowledge, particularly engineering knowledge, for making decisions. Political issues are illusions created by evil men. Society's true problems are engineering problems.'[18] With this frame of reference, Mayo throughout his inquiring and productive life ignored labor, power, and politics. Indeed, he ignored the dignity that is possible in the age of the machine, despite his contrary arguments idealizing what for him was the soothing past, the pre-industrial America. And in his myopia his colleagues and the larger movement of industrial human relations shared.[19]

But the commitment of social science to management derived not alone from Mayo's assumptions about the nature of the industrial world and of American civilization. Quite as important were the implications of the substantive research done at the Hawthorne Works of the Western Electric Company. The counseling program developed there, for example, led most industrial social scientists to conclude that, because workers felt better after talking to a counselor, even to the point of commenting about improved pay rates which the company had not changed, most workers did not have compelling objective problems. Much of industrial unrest was simply a function of faulty perception and conceptualization on the part of labor. One counselor, also an industrial consultant, put it this way:

At least half of the grievances of the average employee can be relieved merely by giving him an opportunity to 'talk them out.' It may not even be necessary to take any action on them. All that they require is a patient and courteous hearing, supplemented, when necessary, by an explanation of *why* nothing can be done. . . . It is not always necessary to yield to the worker's requests in order to satisfy them.[20]

More and more industrial psychologists heeded the injunction of one of their colleagues who, in 1952, said that 'the psychologist must reorient his thinking from what is good management of the individual to what is good personnel management and, ultimately, good business.'[21]

The industrial social scientists' view of labor and unionism adds further depth to our understanding of their sweeping commitment to management. What kind of man is he who labors and why does he join a union? He is the kind of man, the early industrial psychologists agreed, who is stupid, overly emotional, class conscious, without recreational or aesthetic interests, insecure, and afraid of responsibility. He is a man who, when banded together in a union with others of like sort, is to be distrusted and feared. This blue-collar man joins a union, psychologists and sociologists eventually postulated, because of a personality maladjustment, one that probably occurred early in life.[22] The need for an equalization of power between labor and management, the need for economic sanctions, were not seen as the real reasons why men join unions. Rather, said psychologist Robert N. McMurry:

The union also serves the worker in another way. Being somewhat authoritarian, *it may tell him what to do. He no longer has to think for himself.* . . . Once he has been relieved of personal responsibility for his actions, *he is free to commit aggressions which his conscience would ordinarily hold in check.* When this is the case, his conscience will trouble him little, no matter how brutal and anti-social his behavior may be.

Granting such premises, solely for the sake of discussion, one is forced to conclude with McMurry, whose position was rather typical, that 'where management is fair and is alert to discover and remove sources of employee dissatisfaction, a union is not necessary.'[23]

The social scientists' view of industrial conflict further illuminates their commitment to management. Throughout their professional history, the majority of industrial social scientists insisted that as soon as management took the trouble to study or to authorize studies of its workers, to learn their wants, instincts, desires, aspirations, and motivations, management would be able to do something about the demands of labor before such demands tied up the lifeline of industry and resulted in a strike. Understanding human relations, in short, was the only certain way to avoid conflict. Thus the demand of labor for wages was merely camouflage, argued the social scientists, masking more real and human needs of appreciation, understanding, and friendliness.[24]

Because of his impact, Elton Mayo's formulations have always been important, and his statement of the problem of conflict was no exception. His early approach to conflict, and one that was to become rather representative of a large segment of industrial social science, was based on the postulate of the primacy of the individual in all social processes, including labor-management conflict. Before the Hawthorne researches broadened his vision, Mayo believed that '"industrial unrest" has its source in obsessive preoccupation.' And again: 'There is a real identity between labor unrest and nervous breakdown.'[25] Conflict to Mayo was neither inevitable nor economic. It was a result of the maladjustment of a few men on the labor side of the picture. Even after Hawthorne forced Mayo to grow, he remained firm in his conviction that conflict was an evil, a symptom of the lack of social skills. Cooperation, for him, was symptomatic of health; and, since there was no alternative in the modern world, cooperation must mean obedience to managerial authority. Thus collective bargaining was not really cooperation, but merely a flimsy substitute for the real thing.[26]

The nature of the social sciences in the twentieth century was, and is, such as to encourage the type of thinking of which Mayo is a good representative. His illusions of objectivity, lack of integrative theory, concern with what many have called the 'wrong problems', and, at least by implication, authoritarianism, virtually determined the types of errors he committed. Such errors are built into modern social science.

The problem of objectivity has proved to be especially troublesome to modern social scientists. During the depression of the 1930's, for instance, some social scientists warned that a rigid insistence on objectivity would place power in the hands of partisans who would not trouble themselves with such matters. In other words, social scientists, by providing, without interpretation or advocacy, techniques and concepts useful to men engaged in struggles for power, became by default accessories to the power politics of American government and industry, while insisting that they were innocent of anything of the sort. The insistence on objectivity made an impartial *use* of their research findings virtually impossible.[27]

Only after World War II did many social scientists, including Mayo, blame their difficulties on a lack of theory.[28] But the more general belief that 'the chief impetus to the field of industrial sociology has come from observational studies in industry rather than inference from theoretical principles'[29] discouraged a concentrated effort to tie together the many dissociated studies with some kind of underlying theory. Data were piled on data; statistical analyses were pursued with increasing vigor.

Only rarely was any attempt made to explain, in a broader framework, the significance and relationships of psychological and sociological research. 'Lacking an objective scale of values', said one industrial psychologist, 'we have accumulated a vast body of data on what some of us suspect are either the wrong problems, or false or misstated questions, or altogether minor ones.'[30] In 1947 the criticism was fully developed:

The human problems of industry and economic relationships lie at the very heart of the revolutionary upheavals of our century. One might expect industrial psychologists to be fired by the challenge of these issues. But most of us go on constructing aptitude tests instead—and determining which of two advertising slogans 'will sell more of our company's beauty cream.'[31]

This concentration on wrong or trivial problems was a result of the fact that social scientists, especially those who applied their science to the desires or needs of power groups, were not in command of their activities. They have not been, and are not, free agents. Clearly, however, industrial social scientists have not been forced to accept the assumptions, biases, and frames of reference of America's industrial elite. These specialists, like virtually every other group in American society, freely shared the assumptions of this elite. Most managers have had no trouble in getting social scientists to grant managerial premises because such premises have also been assumed by the social scientists. According to some analysts, this acceptance and sanction of America's power status by social scientists can most easily be explained by reference to the social scientists themselves. Said a sociologist, 'American social scientists have seldom, if ever, been politically engaged; the trend towards the technician's role has, by strengthening their a-political professional ideology, reduced, if that is possible, their political involvement, and often, by atrophy, their ability even to grasp political problems.' Hence industrial social scientists have had no qualms about serving 'the needs of the business side of the corporation as judged by the business manager.' This, another sociologist believed, made 'something less than a scientist' of any social scientist directly involved in the power relationships of the modern bureaucracies.[32]

The classic statement of the position of the industrial psychologist in relation to the powers for which he worked was made, in 1951, by the eminent industrial psychologist W. V. Bingham, who said that industrial psychology 'might be defined as psychology directed toward aims other than its own.'[33] Who, then, should set the aims for industrial psychologists? Obviously, managers would have no scruples against telling the social-science specialists on their payrolls how they should earn their money. With Bingham's definition in mind, most industrial social scientists did not hesitate to do what they were told. 'The result', reported one of *Fortune's* editors, 'is not a science at all; it is a machine for the engineering of mediocrity.... Furthermore,' he continued, 'it is profoundly authoritarian in its implications, for it subordinates the individual to the group. And the philosophy,' he concluded, 'unfortunately, is contagious.'[34]

A handful of industrial social scientists bitterly complained of this willing acceptance by almost all of their colleagues of the control of their science and their research by the managers and spokesmen of that ubiquitous concentration of power: the modern corporation. The psychologist Arthur Kornhauser was one of the first, when in 1947 he called industrial psychology a management technique rather than a social science, and complained that 'psychological activities for industry... are characterized by the fact that business management constitutes a special interest group which manifests its special viewpoint in respect to research as in other matters.... Certain areas of research are tabu', he went on. 'Certain crucial variables must not be dealt with. We must avoid,' he concluded, 'explicit analysis of the broad and basic problems of *power and authority* in economic life.' On rare occasions an industrial sociologist expressed similar attitudes. In the same year, for instance, Wilbert E. Moore, then of Princeton, warned his audience of sociologists that the persistent managerial assumptions underlying so much of their work would reduce their profession to a refined type of scientific management dedicated to the exploitation of labor.[35] But such expressions were unusual and not representative of the opinions of most industrial social scientists. Most of these specialists remained content to develop and refine further the techniques in which management expressed an interest, and either did not bother about or approved of the implications of their research.

Despite the avowed or implicit hostility of virtually all industrial social scientists to organized labor, union leaders traditionally have been either unaware of or indifferent to the work of these specialists. With time, however, at least since the Second World War, a few labor leaders have spoken against the entire social-science movement as it was then implemented in industry. No major union has, however, taken action on the national level to counteract this movement.[36]

One labor leader has been especially troubled about the industrial use of social science; his formulation of the problem serves to highlight the basic difficulties of labor in a social-science world that is built on the assumptions of management. First of all, he wrote, social scientists so complicate the bargaining relationship that control is taken out of the hands of the inadequately informed workers and their representatives; experts are required to get through the maze of confusion, and democracy becomes impossible. 'The essence of unionism,' he continued, 'is not higher wages, shorter hours or strikes—but self-government. If, as some unions apparently believe, higher benefits are the essential objective, then unionism becomes another, and more subtle, form of paternalism.... As for me,' he concluded, 'I would prefer to receive lower benefits than to lose control of my bargaining relationship. Unfortunately, and this is the nub of the problem, many workers prefer higher benefits to democracy.'[37] The issues at stake in this man's dilemma are profound, and the impotence of all unions, including his own, to resist, as well as the general apathy of other labor leaders, causes rot at the heart of American unionism. But the industrialist's keen awareness of the problems pushes him forward in his use of social scientists to complicate and confuse bargaining, to reduce grievances, and to squelch militant unionism.

A final question remains. What difference does it make if social scientists have found a place in industry and generally have shared the points of view of management? Are not social scientists an esoteric group of academicians with little or no contact with reality? What if they have been hostile to interests other than those that pay them?

The difference is great. Many managers have not hesitated to make explicit the point that their use of social scientists and their skills is for the purpose of human control. Through group conferences, management hopes to pressure the recalcitrant individual into conforming with his more right-thinking colleagues. Cessna Aircraft and Atlantic Refining have furnished good examples of this approach. American Telephone & Telegraph has been convinced that it is possible through an understanding of motivation to 'influence' a given employee. The Life Insurance Sales Research Bureau said that 'in learning to shape people's feelings and control their morale, we shall be doing nothing more difficult than we have already done in learning how to fly.... We need not "change human nature," we need only to learn to control and to use it.' General Foods took the position that 'leadership' and persuasion would prove most effective in directing the thinking and conduct of its workers. Other businessmen and social scientists have agreed that the main business of business is the control of human conduct.[38]

A few social scientists were concerned, however, about the implications of their growing effectiveness with a science of behavior. Would this not lead to the most insidious and relentless form of exploitation ever dreamed of? One industrial social scientists argued that control in a complex and interdependent society is inevitable:

Society has always outlawed certain techniques for getting people to do what one wants them to do. As our understanding of behavior becomes more and more refined, we will have to refine equally the moral judgment on the kinds of coercion—however subtle—that are approved and disapproved.[39]

Control, in other and more simple words, is a given; what needs to be changed is the system of morals that disapproves of control. Slim hope for the future, this. But *Business Week* has assured us that there is nothing to worry about. 'There's no sign,' reported this organ of business interests, 'that the science of behavior is getting ready to spawn some monster of human engineering, manipulating a population of puppets from behind the scenes.'[40]

Business Week is wrong. Social scientists by now have evolved a series of specific techniques whose results have delighted management. Especially through the use of group pressures has management shoved its people into line. Majority opinions, even when directly contrary to visual fact, sway the attitudes of others who would rather not trust their own eyes than suffer the stigma of being unusual. This social scientists have proved.[41] 'If a manager's superior,' said the personnel director of Continental Oil, 'has had difficulty in developing a cooperative attitude within that manager, the group technique can frequently help in developing the appropriate attitude.' Even *Business Week* was forced to admit that the pressures of the group on the individual members were so relentless that this was 'one good way to change what they [managers] want.' The Harwood Manufacturing Company and American Cyanamid both learned to lean heavily on group techniques to assure the continuation of management control.[42]

Through motivation studies, through counseling, through selection devices calculated to hire only certain types of people, through attitude surveys, communication, role-playing, and all the rest in their bag of schemes, social scientists slowly moved toward a science of behavior. Thus management was given a slick new approach to its problems of control. Authority gave way to manipulation, and workers could no longer be sure they were being exploited. Said C. Wright Mills:

Many whips are inside men, who do not know how they got there, or indeed that they are there. In the movement from authority to manipulation, power shifts from the visible to the invisible, from the known to the anonymous. And with rising material standards, exploitation becomes less material and more psychological.[43]

Many industrial social scientists have put themselves on auction. The power elites of America, especially the industrial elite, have bought their services—which, when applied to areas of relative power, have restricted the freedom of millions of workers. Time was when a man knew that his freedoms were being curtailed. Social scientists, however, are too sophisticated for that. The fires of pressure and control on a man are now kindled in his own thinking. Control need no longer be imposed. It can be encouraged to come from within. Thus the faith that if 'people develop propaganditis', the effectiveness of control would be weakened[44] seems to miss the point. A major characteristic of twentieth-century manipulation has been that it blinds the victim to the fact of manipulation. Because so many industrial social scientists have been willing to serve power instead of mind, they have been themselves a case study in manipulation by consent.

Over the years, through hundreds and hundreds of experiments, social scientists have come close to a true science of behavior. They are now beginning to learn how to control conduct. Put this power—genuine, stark, irrevocable power—into the hands of America's managers, and the work that social scientists have done, and will do, assumes implications vaster and more fearful than anything previously hinted.

41

....

Notes

1. Henry Ford II, 'Human Engineering Necessary for Further Mass Production Progress,' *Automotive and Aviation Industries*, XCIV, 2 (Jan. 15, 1946), 39.
2. George R. Eastman, *Psychology for Business Efficiency* (Dayton, 1916), 9, 12; G. Stanley Hall, address to Vocational Educational Association of the Middle West, Jan. 17, 1919, in Lionel D. Edie (ed.), *Practical Psychology for Business Executives* (New York, 1922), 36; T. Sharper Knowlson, *Business Psychology* (Libertyville, Ill., 1912), 11, 12; Hugo Münsterberg, *Psychology and Industrial Efficiency* (New York, 1913), 244, 306–309; W. D. Scott, *Increasing Human Efficiency in Business* (New York, 1911). 6–7.
3. Floyd H. Allport *et al.*, 'Psychology in Relation to Social and Political Problems,' in Paul S. Achilles (ed.), *Psychology at Work* (New York, 1932), 252; Walter V. Bingham, 'The Future of Industrial Psychology,' *JCP*, I, 1 (Jan.–Feb., 1937), 9–11; George C. Brandenburg, 'Personality and Vocational Achievement,' *JAP*, IX, 3 (1925), 282; Harold E. Burtt, *Principles of Employment Psychology* (Boston, 1926), 508; J. McKeen Cattell, 'Retrospect: Psychology as a Profession,' *JCP*, I, 1 (Jan.–Feb., 1937), 1; Edgar A. Doll, 'Preparation for Clinical Psychology,' *ibid.*, III, 5 (Sept.–Oct., 1939), 139–140; Eliott Frost, 'What Industry Wants and Does Not Want from the Psychologist,' *JAP*, IV, 1 (March, 1920), 23–24; George W. Hartmann, 'Summary for Psychologists,' in Hartmann and Theodore Newcomb (eds.), *Industrial Conflict* (New York, 1939), 544; Edward N. Hay, 'Sizing Up Job Applicants,' *Personnel Journal*, XVIII, 7 (Jan., 1940), 261; Harry W. Hepner, *Psychology in Modern Business* (New York, 1931), 436; Forrest A. Kingsbury, 'Applying Psychology to Business,' *Annals*, CX (Nov., 1923), 11; Morris Viteles, 'The Clinical Viewpoint in Vocational Selection,' *JAP*, IX, 2 (1925), 135; Viteles, *Industrial Psychology* (New York, 1932), 4; Robert M. Yerkes, 'What is Personnel Research?' *Monthly Labor Review*, XIV, 1 (Jan., 1922), 11.
4. W. V. Bingham, 'Industrial Psychology and Government,' *JAP*, XXIV, 1 (Feb., 1940), 3; Milton L. Blum, *Industrial Psychology and its Social Foundations* (New York, 1949), 1; Orlo L. Crissey, 'Personnel Selection,' in *Current Trends in Industrial Psychology* (Pittsburgh, 1949), 81; George Katona, *Psychological Analysis of Economic Behavior* (New York, 1951), 282–283; C. H. Lawshe *et al.*, *Psychology of Industrial Relations* (New York, 1953), v; Douglas McGregor, 'Foreword,' *Journal of Social Issues*, IV, 3 (Summer, 1948), 4; Willard E. Parker and Robert W. Kleemeier, *Human Relations in Supervision* (New York, 1951), v, 11–12; May Smith, *An Introduction to Industrial Psychology* (London, 1943), 5–6; Harold C. Taylor, 'Industrial Psychology and the Community,' in *Current Trends*, 197; Robert M. Yerkes, 'Psychology in World Reconstruction,' *JCP*, X, 1 (Jan.-Feb., 1946), 2.
5. William F. Whyte to Elton Mayo, April 27, 1943, Mayo MSS; John S. Ellsworth, Jr., *Factory Folkways* (New Haven, 1952), 1; Delbert C. Miller and William H. Form, *Industrial Sociology* (New York, 1951), 100; Eugene Staley *et al.* (eds.), *Creating an Industrial Civilization* (New York, 1952), 180; W. F. Whyte, 'Social Science and Industrial Relations,' *Personnel*, XXVII, 4 (Jan., 1951), 266; William H. Whyte, Jr., *Is Anybody Listening?* (New York, 1952), 219–220.

6. Warren W. Coxe, 'Professional Problems of Applied Psychology,' *JCP*, IV, *3* (May-June, 1940), 103; V. E. Fisher and Joseph V. Hanna, *The Dissatisfied Worker* (New York, 1931), 246; C. Wright Mills, *White Collar* (New York, 1953), 157.

7. Arthur W. Kornhauser and Forrest A. Kingsbury, *Psychological Tests in Business* (Chicago, 1924), 174–175.

8. Quoted from a personal letter whose author prefers to remain unidentified.

9. Frank W. Braden to L. Baritz, Sept. 13, 1955; John G. Darley, 'An Overview of the Conference and its Controversies,' in Harold Guetzkow (ed.), *Groups, Leadership and Men* (Pittsburgh, 1951), 263–264; Arthur Kornhauser, 'The Contribution of Psychology to Industrial Relations Research,' *Proceedings of the First Annual Meeting, Industrial Relations Research Association, Cleveland, Dec. 29–30, 1948* (N.P., 1949), 174; Fred Massarik and Paula Brown, 'Social Research Faces Industry,' *Personnel*, XXX, *6* (May, 1954), 455; C. Wright Mills, 'The Contribution of Sociology to Studies of Industrial Relations,' *Proceedings of IRRA*, 204.

10. Elton Mayo in F. J. Roethlisberger and William J. Dickson, *Management and the Worker* (Cambridge, 1939), xiii–xiv.

11. See, e.g., Howard Bowen, *Social Responsibilities of the Businessman* (New York, 1953), *passim*.

12. Quoted in U.S. Congress, *Automation and Technological Change*, Hearings before Subcommittee on Economic Stabilization of the Joint Committee on the Economic Report, 84th Cong., 1st Sess., Oct. 14–28, 1955 (Washington, 1955), 105.

13. 'Industry Appraises the Psychologist,' *Personnel Psychology*, IV, *1* (Spring, 1951), 63–92.

14. See, e.g., Murray Kempton, 'Pre-Tested Miracles,' *New York Post*, Jan. 3, 1957, 26.

15. H. L. Hollingworth and A. T. Poffenberger, *Applied Psychology* (New York, 1917), 20; Hugo Münsterberg, *Business Psychology* (Chicago, 1915), 181–182.

16. Harold E. Burtt, *Psychology and Industrial Efficiency* (New York, 1929), 273; C. F. Hansen, 'Psychology in the Service of the Life Insurance Business,' *Annals*, CX (Nov., 1923), 190.

17. Elton Mayo, 'The Fifth Columnists of Business,' *Harvard Business School Alumni Bulletin*, XVIII, *1* (Autumn, 1941), 33.

18. William H. Knowles, *Personnel Management* (New York, 1955), 156.

19. See, e.g., Lewis Corey, 'Human Relations Minus Unionism,' *Labor and Nation*, VI, *2* (Spring, 1950), 48; W. A. Koivisto, 'Value, Theory, and Fact in Industrial Sociology,' *AJS*, LVIII, *6* (May, 1953), 564–567; Mills, 'Contribution of Sociology,' *Proceedings of IRRA*, 209n.

20. Robert N. McMurry, *Handling Personality Adjustment in Industry* (New York, 1944), 13–14.

21. John H. Gorsuch, 'Industrial Psychology's Growing Pains,' *Personnel*, XXIX, *2* (Sept., 1952), 154.

22. See, e.g., Hepner, *Psychology in Modern Business*, 578–583; Morris S. Viteles, 'The Role of Industrial Psychology in Defending the Future of America,' *Annals*, CCXVI (July, 1941), 157; C. R. Walker and R. H. Guest, *The Man on the Assembly Line* (Cambridge, 1952), 134; William F. Whyte, 'Who Goes Union and Why,' *Personnel Journal*, XXIII, *6* (Dec., 1944), 216–217.

23. McMurry, *Handling Personality Adjustment*, 15, 17.

24. E.g., Arthur W. Ayers, 'Personality Considerations in Collective Bargaining,' *JCP*, VIII, *3* (May–June, 1944), 144; George C. Homans, 'Industrial Harmony as a Goal,' in Arthur Kornhauser *et al.* (eds.), *Industrial Conflict* (New York, 1954), 49; Elton Mayo, 'The Great Stupidity,' *Harper's*, CLI (July, 1925), 231; Ross Stagner, 'Psychological Aspects of Industrial Conflict: II—Motivation,' *Personnel Psychology*, III, *1* (Spring, 1950), 1; U.S. Bureau of Labor Statistics, *Strikes in 1941 and Strikes Affecting Defense Production* (B.L.S., Bull. No. 711; Washington, 1942), 17; B.L.S., *Strikes in 1942* (B.L.S. Bull. No. 741; Washington, 1943), 14; B.L.S., *Strikes in 1943* (B.L.S. Bull. No. 782; Washington, 1944), 18; B.L.S., *Strikes and Lockouts in 1944* (B.L.S. Bull. No. 833; Washington, 1945), 1; T. N. Whitehead, 'Human Relations within Industrial Groups,' *HBR*, XIV, *1* (Autumn, 1935), 2.

25. Elton Mayo, 'The Irrational Factor in Human Behavior,' *Annals*, CX (Nov., 1923), 122; Mayo, 'Mental Hygiene in Industry,' in Henry C. Metcalf (ed.), *The Psychological Foundations of Management* (New York, 1927), 276; Mayo, 'Orientation and Attention,' *ibid.*, 270–271.

26. Reinhard Bendix, 'Bureaucracy,' *ASR*, XII, *5* (Oct., 1947), 502; Bendix and Lloyd H. Fisher, 'The Perspectives of Elton Mayo,' *Review of Economics and Statistics*, XXXI, *4* (Nov., 1949), 314; Elton Mayo, 'Research in Human Relations,' *Personnel*, XVII, *4* (May, 1941), 265; Miller and Form, *Industrial Sociology*, 79.

27. Hadley Cantril and Daniel Katz, 'Objectivity in the Social Sciences,' in Hartmann and Newcomb, *Industrial Conflict*, 12; Robert S. Lynd, *Knowledge for What?* (Princeton, 1939), 116, 119–120, 128, 185–186.

28. E.g., Herbert Blumer, 'Sociological Theory in Industrial Relations,' *ASR*, XII, *3* (June, 1947), 272; Douglas McGregor, 'Industrial Relations,' *Advanced Management*, XIV, *4* (Dec., 1949), 2–6.

29. Wilbert E. Moore, 'Current Issues in Industrial Sociology,' *ASR*, XII, 6 (Dec., 1947), 651.

30. George W. Hartmann, 'Summary for Psychologists,' in Hartmann and Newcomb, *Industrial Conflict*, 541–542.

31. Arthur Kornhauser, 'Industrial Psychology as Management Technique and as Social Science,' *American Psychologist*, II, *7* (July, 1947), 224.

32. Mills, 'Contribution of Sociology,' *Proceedings of IRRA*, 206; Mills, *White Collar*, 82; Lynd, *Knowledge for What?* 178.

33. Walter V. Bingham, 'Psychology as a Science, as a Technology, and as a Profession,' in John Elmgren and Sigvard Rubenowitz (eds.), *Applied Psychology in Industrial and Social Life* (Göteborg, 1952), 24.

34. Whyte, *Is Anybody Listening?* 209.

35. Kornhauser, 'Industrial Psychology,' *American Psychologist* (1947), 225; Moore, 'Current Issues,' *ASR* (1947), 654.

36. Solomon Barkin to L. Baritz, Dec. 6, 1955; Otis Brubacker to L. B., Dec. 15, 1955; Sylvia B. Gottlieb to L. B., Dec. 2, 1955; Carl Huhndorff to L. B., Nov. 29, 1955; Solomon Barkin, 'A Pattern for the Study of Human Relations in Industry,' *Industrial and Labor Relations Review*, IX, *1* (Oct., 1955), 95–99; Barkin, 'Technology and Labor,' *Personnel Journal*, XVIII, *7* (Jan., 1940), 239.

37. Quoted from a personal letter whose author prefers to remain unidentified.

38. F. H. Allport, *Social Psychology* (Boston, 1924), 408; American Telephone & Telegraph Co., Personnel Relations Dept., 'Motivation and the Job,' *Human Relations in Management* (New York, 1949), 2; Atlantic Refining Co., *A Manual on Conference Leadership* (N.P., N.D.), 3–4, 6; Willard Beecher, 'Industrial Relations in the Light of Individual Psychology,' *American Journal of Individual Psychology*, XI, 2 (1955), 124; Cessna Aircraft Co., Personnel Dept., *How to Win Workers (Or—Hosswhippin' Won't Work)* (Wichita, [1942 (?)]), 4; General Foods Corp., Dept. for Personnel Administration, *Solving Problems by Practicing Consultative Supervision* (N.P. [1949]), 4; Knowles, *Personnel Management*, 59; Life Insurance Sales Research Bureau, *Morale and Agency Management*, Vol. I: *Morale: The Mainspring of Management* (Hartford, 1940), 22; U.S. Congress, Senate, *Violations of Free Speech and Rights of Labor*, Hearings before a Subcommittee of the Committee on Education and Labor, U.S. Senate, 75 Cong., 1st Sess., on S. Res. 266, Part 6, 'Labor Espionage, General Motors Corp.,' Feb. 15–19, 1937 (Washington, 1937), 2037.

39. Mason Haire, 'Group Dynamics,' in Kornhauser, *Industrial Conflict*, 384–385.

40. 'People: What's Behind Their Choices—in Buying, in Working,' *Business Week*, Aug. 14, 1954, 50–60.

41. S. E. Asch, 'Effects of Group Pressure upon the Modification and Distortion of Judgments,' in Guetzkow, *Groups, Leadership and Men*, 189–190.

42. Richard Crow, 'Group Training in Higher Management Development,' *Personnel*, XXIX, 6 (May, 1953), 458; 'Group Meetings Pay Off,' *Business Week*, May 20, 1950, 82, 84; Alfred Marrow, 'Group Dynamics in Industry,' *Occupations*, XXVI, 8 (May, 1948), 476; 'People,' *Business Week*, Aug. 14, 1954, 50–60; 'Psychologists at Work,' *ibid.*, Sept. 19, 1953, 52–53.

43. Mills, *White Collar*, 110.

44. Harold L. Wilensky, 'Human Relations in the Workplace,' Industrial Relations Research Association, *Research in Industrial Human Relations* (New York, 1957), 40–41.

4 Critical Issues in Organizations

Stewart Clegg and David Dunkerley

In the social sciences one can find many volumes whose titles proclaim them to be in some sense 'critical'. Indeed, such is the apparent increased frequency with which such terms are used that one might be forgiven for supposing them to be of devalued currency. Yet, here is another volume sufficiently audacious as to claim to address Critical Issues in Organizations. Such a claim cannot be lodged lightly. It behoves anyone who proposes it to argue in what way their volume is 'critical' in such a way as to be distinct from other contributions.

Many other texts on organizations exist. You may well be familiar with some of them. If so, then you will be aware of the bewildering state of disarray that exists in these texts, and which passes as 'organization theory'. Given the antecedents of organization theory such diversity is hardly surprising. The study of organizations has developed in a number of specific ways, serving different ends which have ranged from improving organizational 'effectiveness' to providing theoretical direction for those claiming a purely academic interest. Regardless of the objectives, it is clear that to speak of a body of 'organization theory' is to refer to a body of knowledge that, for pragmatic reasons, has developed both unevenly and atheoretically.

Of course, we are not alone in recognizing the problems confronting the analysis of organizations. Such problems pre-occupy professional conventions and papers. But while similar conclusions may be reached, the prescriptions suggested are quite dissimilar to those which we imply. By way of displaying contrast consider the following example. At the 1974 American Sociological Association Convention, Jerald Hage pleaded strongly for 'a new wave of attempts to create general organizational theory' (Hage, 1974, p.19). His solution was cast in terms of formal middle-range sociological theory emphasizing theoretical and operational definitions and linkages. Such an analysis presumes a certain value to what has 'preceded it, which we, and our contributors, would question. To reason as Hage does is to remain secure within the convention of thesis, whilst neglecting the dialectic of antithesis. To credit as synthetic a conversation which is conducted entirely within one thesis concerning the nature of social reality, and the appropriate way of 'regarding' it, is seriously to devalue the dialectical metaphor. But the Hage plea is in many respects entirely consistent with some aspects of contemporary American theorizing in sociology. The suggested approach would, we suspect, draw heavily upon the work of methodologists such as Blalock for its 'theory', while its paramount organizational input would be that style of research whose hegemony is maintained by the pages of the 'Administrative Science Quarterly'.

Complementary to, and sometimes in opposition to, the developments and suggestions which emanate from the tradition of 'Administrative Science Quarterly', the study of organizations has progressed in Europe. A distinctively European tradition is emergent. Methodological, theoretical and critical issues which once seemed to be condemned to silence are being re-awakened, renewed and discussed. Much of this discussion has centred on the on-going critique currently being developed by members of the 'groupe théoretique' of the European Group for Organizational Studies (EGOS). The group has a short history to date, having emerged from the first meeting of EGOS in 1975 as a viable focus of interest among researchers. Nearly all the contributors to this volume are currently engaged in this on-going critique. The focus of the critique has been on the development of an 'institutional' approach to the study of organizations, a focus which is represented in all of the papers collected here. This speaks to our common commitment to re-awaken some critical issues for discussion.

Our 'issues'—sexism, power, capitalist development, organizational transactions and interactions, the historical interpenetration of state and capital—are not yet found in the indexes of most texts on organizations. We hope to remedy this state of affairs through posing this absence as problematic. Thus, it would seem to be no accident that the majority of texts on organization theory place greater emphasis upon concepts such as individual motivation, needs and satisfactions, than upon the structural features of power, exploitation and historical change. The eagerness with which management theorists have adopted many of the ideas from organization theory lends further support to the argument. However, considering the way in which organization theory has almost ignored Marx, or interpreted Weber in the narrowest possible way as a progenitor of modern theories of organization structure, then this is not surprising. The interests of management and the interests of organization theory have all too often been in harmony.

A critical theory cannot allow its interest to be so defined. The function of our papers is to enable one to grasp and understand the reality of that 'life' which organizations find themselves imposed in and on. As such we distinguish our analyses from those fictions preserved in the ideology of organization theory, where the freedom of 'exchanges', 'social constructions', and the 'satisfaction' of 'needs' reigns dominant. In contrast, our papers show contemporary sources of 'unfreedom' as occasioned through organizations. We attempt thus to begin conversation with others who have been both mastered and victimized by the formulations that we oppose here.

So it is not that our 'critical issues' are 'in organizations'. They are not. They are not 'in' organizations in terms of the wide-spread consciousness of their members, any more than they are yet 'in' the widespread consciousness of the members of organization theory. Nor can our issues be constrained 'within' the boundaries of organizations. Such closure to social issues and theory is part of the stance we oppose. Our issues are 'in organizations' only in so far as *organization* is the metaphor under which we collect our thoughts and reflections. Organization serves merely as the rubric and the locus of our analysis. Only in as much as we constitute them as such are our issues *in* organizations.

In an organization theory where life has been analysed, paralysed and reduced to a series of quantifiable variables, our issues would remain unspoken. This volume is an attempt to speak this silence. For all of us, in our various voices, this articulates itself through redressing the scant consideration given to issues which are historically located, politically potent, economically relevant, and socially significant.

We neither propose to 'synthesize' existing theory, nor to 'broaden' it by importing yet another fledgling sociological stance. Rather, we propose to overcome existing organization theory. In that organizations have been left too much to the ideologists of administration, their continued existence as an ontological realm of self-sufficient enquiry has survived critical scrutiny for too long. We wish to call into question the continued existence of such a state of affairs.

References

Hage, J. (1974). 'The State of Organizational, Theory', American Sociological Association.

5 The Power Elite

C. Wright Mills

The truth about the nature and the power of the elite is not some secret which men of affairs know but will not tell. Such men hold quite various theories about their own roles in the sequence of event and decision. Often they are uncertain about their roles, and even more often they allow their fears and their hopes to affect their assessment of their own power. No matter how great their actual power, they tend to be less acutely aware of it than of the resistances of others to its use. Moreover, most American men of affairs have learned well the rhetoric of public relations, in some cases even to the point of using it when they are alone, and thus coming to believe it. The personal awareness of the actors is only one of the several sources one must examine in order to understand the higher circles. Yet many who believe that there is no elite, or at any rate none of any consequence, rest their argument upon what men of affairs believe about themselves, or at least assert in public.

There is, however, another view: those who feel, even if vaguely, that a compact and powerful elite of great importance does now prevail in America often base that feeling upon the historical trend of our time. They have felt, for example, the domination of the military event, and from this they infer that generals and admirals, as well as other men of decision influenced by them, must be enormously powerful. They hear that the Congress has again abdicated to a handful of men decisions clearly related to the issue of war or peace. They know that the bomb was dropped over Japan in the name of the United States of America, although they were at no time consulted about the matter. They feel that they live in a time of big decisions; they know that they are not making any. Accordingly, as they consider the present as history, they infer that at its center, making decisions or failing to make them, there must be an elite of power.

On the one hand, those who share this feeling about big historical events assume that there is an elite and that its power is great. On the other hand, those who listen carefully to the reports of men apparently involved in the great decisions often do not believe that there is an elite whose powers are of decisive consequence.

Both views must be taken into account, but neither is adequate. The way to understand the power of the American elite lies neither solely in recognizing the historic scale of events nor in accepting the personal awareness reported by men of apparent decision. Behind such men and behind the events of history, linking the two, are the major institutions of modern society. These hierarchies of state and corporation and army constitute the means of power; as such they are now of a consequence not before equaled in human history—and at their summits, there are now those command posts of modern society which offer us the sociological key to an understanding of the role of the higher circles in America.

Within American society, major national power now resides in the economic, the political, and the military domains. Other institutions seem off to the side of modern history, and, on occasion, duly subordinated to these. No family is as directly powerful in national affairs as any major corporation; no church is as directly powerful in the external biographies of young men in America today as the military establishment; no college is as powerful in the shaping of momentous events as the National Security Council. Religious, educational, and family institutions are not autonomous centers of national power; on the contrary, these decentralized areas are increasingly shaped by the big three, in which developments of decisive and immediate consequence now occur.

Families and churches and schools adapt to modern life; governments and armies and corporations shape it; and, as they do so, they turn these lesser institutions into means for their ends. Religious institutions provide chaplains to the armed forces where they are used as a means of increasing the effectiveness of its morale to kill. Schools select and train men for their jobs in corporations and their specialized tasks in the armed forces. The extended family has, of course, long been broken up by the industrial revolution, and now the son and the father are removed from the family, by compulsion if need be, whenever the army of the state sends out the call. And the symbols of all these lesser institutions are used to legitimate the power and the decisions of the big three.

The life-fate of the modern individual depends not only upon the family into which he was born or which he enters by marriage, but increasingly upon the corporation in which he spends the most alert hours of his best years; not only upon the school where he is educated as a child and adolescent, but also upon the state which touches him throughout his life; not only upon the church in which on occasion he hears the word of God, but also upon the army in which he is disciplined.

If the centralized state could not rely upon the inculcation of nationalist loyalties in public and private schools, its leaders would promptly seek to modify the decentralized educational system. If the bankruptcy rate among the top five hundred corporations were as high as the general divorce rate among the thirty-seven million married couples, there would be economic catastrophe on an international scale. If members of armies gave to them no more of their lives than do believers to the churches to which they belong, there would be a military crisis.

Within each of the big three, the typical institutional unit has become enlarged, has become administrative, and, in the power of its decisions, has become centralized. Behind these developments there is a fabulous technology, for as institutions, they have incorporated this technology and guide it, even as it shapes and paces their developments.

The economy—once a great scatter of small productive units in autonomous balance—has become dominated by two or three hundred giant corporations, administratively and politically interrelated, which together hold the keys to economic decisions.

The political order, once a decentralized set of several dozen states with a weak spinal cord, has become a centralized, executive establishment which has taken up into itself many powers previously scattered, and now enters into each and every cranny of the social structure.

The military order, once a slim establishment in a context of distrust fed by state militia, has become the largest and most expensive feature of government, and, although well versed in smiling public relations, now has all the grim and clumsy efficiency of a sprawling bureaucratic domain.

In each of these institutional areas, the means of power at the disposal of decision makers have increased enormously; their central executive powers have been enhanced; within each of them modern administrative routines have been elaborated and tightened up.

As each of these domains becomes enlarged and centralized, the consequences of its activities become greater, and its traffic with the others increases. The decisions of a handful of corporations bear upon military and political as well as upon economic developments around the world. The decisions of the military establishment rest upon and grievously affect political life as well as the very level of economic activity. The decisions made within the political domain determine economic activities and military programs. There is no longer, on the one hand, an economy, and, on the other hand, a political order containing a military establishment unimportant to politics and to money-making. There is a political economy linked, in a thousand ways, with military institutions and decisions. On each side of the world-split running through central Europe and around the Asiatic rimlands, there is an ever-increasing interlocking of economic, military, and political structures. If there is government intervention in the corporate economy, so is there corporate intervention in the governmental process. In the structural sense, this triangle of power is the source of the interlocking directorate that is most important for the historical structure of the present.

The fact of the interlocking is clearly revealed at each of the points of crisis of modern capitalist society—slump, war, and boom. In each, men of decision are led to an awareness of the interdependence of the major institutional orders. In the nineteenth century, when the scale ᶠ all institutions was smaller, their liberal integration was achieved in the automatic economy, by an autonomous play of market forces, and in the automatic political domain, by the bargain and the vote. It was then assumed that out of the imbalance and friction that followed the limited decisions then possible a new equilibrium would in due course emerge. That can no longer be assumed, and it is not assumed by the men at the top of each of the three dominant hierarchies.

For given the scope of their consequences, decisions—and indecisions—in any one of these ramify into the others, and hence top decisions tend either to become coordinated or to lead to a commanding indecision. It has not always been like this. When numerous small entrepreneurs made up the economy, for example, many of them could fail and the consequences still remain local; political and military authorities did not intervene. But now, given political expectations and military commitments, can they afford to allow key units of the private corporate economy to break down in slump? Increasingly, they do intervene in economic affairs, and as they do so, the controlling decisions in each order are inspected by agents of the other two, and economic, military, and political structures are interlocked.

At the pinnacle of each of the three enlarged and centralized domains, there have arisen those higher circles which make up the economic, the political, and the military elites. At the top of the economy, among the corporate rich, there are the chief executives; at the top of the political order, the members of the political directorate; at the top of the military establishment, the elite of soldier-statesmen clustered in and around the Joint Chiefs of Staff and the upper echelon. As each of these domains has coincided with the others, as decisions tend to become total in their consequence, the leading men in each of the three domains of power—the warlords, the corporation chieftains, the political directorate—tend to come together, to form the power elite of America.

. . .

There is, of course, no one type of corporate hierarchy, but one general feature of the corporate world does seem to prevail quite widely. It involves a Number One stratum at the top whose members as individuals—and increasingly as committees—advise and counsel and receive reports from a Number Two stratum of operating managers.

It is of the Number One stratum that the very rich and the chief executives are a part. The Number Two men are individually responsible for given units, plants, departments. They stand between the active working hierarchies and the directing top to which they are responsible. And in their monthly and yearly reports to the top executives, one simple set of questions is foremost: Did we make money: If so, how much? If not, why not?

Decision-making by individual executives at the top is slowly being replaced by the worried-over efforts of committees, who judge ideas tossed before them, usually from below the top levels. The technical men, for example, may negotiate for months with the salesmen over a tubeless tire before the chief executives descend to operation-level conferences. Theirs is not the idea nor even the decision, but The Judgment. On the top levels this judgment usually has to do with the spending of money to make more money and the getting of others to do the work involved. The 'running' of a large business consists essentially of getting somebody to make something which somebody else will sell to somebody else for more than it costs. John L. McCaffrey, the chief executive of International Harvester, recently said, '... he [a business president] seldom lies awake very long thinking about finances or law suits or sales or production or engineering or accounting problems... When he approaches such problems the president can bring to bear on them all the energy and the trained judgment and past experience of his whole organization.' And he goes on to say what top executives do think about at night: 'the biggest trouble with industry is that it is full of human beings.'

The human beings on the middle levels are mainly specialists. 'We sit at our desks all day,' this chief executive continues, 'while around us whiz and gyrate a vast number of special activities, some of which we only dimly understand. And for each of these activities, there is a specialist... All of them, no doubt, are good to have. All seem to be necessary. All are useful on frequent occasions. But it has reached the point where the greatest task of the president is to understand enough of all these specialties so that when a problem comes up he can assign the right team of experts to work on it... How can he maintain the interest of and get full advantage from the specialists who are too specialized to promote? On the one hand, the company absolutely requires the skills of the specialists in order to carry on its complicated operations. On the other hand, he has to get future top management from somewhere. And that somewhere has to be largely within the existing company, if he is to have any management morale at all... we live in a complicated world—a world that has spiritual and moral problems even greater than its economic and technical problems. If the kind of business system we now have is to survive, it must be staffed by men who can deal with problems of both kinds.'

It is below the top levels, it is where the management hierarchies are specialized and varied by industrial line and administrative contour, that the more 'bureaucratic' types of executives and technicians live their corporate lives. And it is below the top levels, in the domain of the Number Two men, that responsibility is lodged. The Number One stratum is often too high to be blamed and has too many others below it to take the blame. Besides, if it is the top, who is in a position to fix the blame upon its members? It is something like the 'line' and 'staff' division invented by the army. The top is staff; the Number Two is line, and thus operational. Every bright army officer knows that to make decisions without responsibility, you get on the staff.

On the middle levels, specialization is required. But the operating specialist will not rise; only the 'broadened' man will rise. What does that mean? It means, for one thing, that the specialist is below the level on which men are wholly alerted to profit. The 'broadened' man is the man who, no matter what he may be doing, is able clearly to see the way to maximize the profit for the corporation as a whole, in the long as well as in the short run. The man who rises to the top is the broadened man whose 'specialty' coincides with the aims of the corporation, which is the maximizing of profit. As he is judged to have realized this aim, he rises within the corporate world. Financial expediency is the chief element of corporate decision, and generally, the higher the executive, the more he devotes his attention to the financial aspect of the going concern.

Moreover, the closer to the corporate top the executive gets, the more important are the big-propertied cliques and political influence in the making of his corporate career. This fact, as well as the considerations for co-optation that prevail, is nicely revealed in a letter that Mr. Lammot du Pont wrote in 1945 in response to a suggestion from a General Motors executive that General George C. Marshall be appointed to the board of directors. Mr. du Pont discussed the proposal: 'My reasons for not favoring his membership on the board are: First his age [The General was then 65]; second, his lack of stockholdings, and third, his lack of experience in industrial business affairs.' Mr. Alfred P. Sloan, chairman of General Motors, in considering the matter, generally concurred, but added: 'I thought General Marshall might do us some good, when he retires, following his present assignment—assuming he continues to live in Washington; recognizing the position he holds in the community and among the government people and the acquaintances he has—and he became familiar with our thinking and what we are trying to do, it might offset the general negative attitude toward big business, of which we are a symbol and a profitable business, as well. It seems to me that might be some reason, and in that event the matter of age would not be particularly consequential.'

In considering other appointments, Mr. Sloan wrote to W. S. Carpenter, a large owner of du Pont and General Motors: 'George Whitney [G. M. director and chairman of J. P. Morgan & Co.] belongs to the board of directors of quite a number of industrial organizations. He gets around a lot because he lives in New York where many contacts are easily and continuously made. Mr. Douglas

[Lewis W. Douglas, a G. M. board member, chairman of the Mutual Life Insurance Company, former Ambassador to Great Britain] is, in a way, quite a public character. He seems to spend a great deal of time in other things. It seems to me that such people do bring into our councils a broader atmosphere than is contributed by the "du Pont directors" and the General Motors directors.'

Or examine a late case of corporate machination that involved the several types of economic men prevailing in higher corporate circles. Robert R. Young—financial promoter and speculator—recently decided to displace William White, chief executive of the New York Central Railroad and a lifetime career executive in railroad operation. Young won—but did it really matter? Success in the corporate world does not follow the pattern it follows in the novel, *Executive Suite*, in which the technologically inclined young man, just like William Holden, wins by making a sincere speech about corporate responsibility. Besides the favors of two friends, each a leading member of the very rich, Mr. Young's income, over the past seventeen years—most of it from capital gains—is reported to be well in excess of $10 million. His yearly income is well over a million, his wife's, half a million—and they manage to keep, after taxes, some 75 per cent of it. But then, no fiction known to us begins to grasp the realities of the corporate world today.

II. STUDYING MANAGEMENT CRITICALLY

Critical studies of management share the view that much of what passes for scientific or objective knowledge of management is little more than a recycled version of the thinking of elite groups institutionalized as received wisdom. Such thinking is collusive in reproducing a status quo that is systematically but unnecessarily exploitative, subjugating and/or restrictive by dint of its divisions of class, gender, ethnicity and so on. Studying management critically involves challenging and disrupting this knowledge in a way that opens up the possibility of alternative ways of managing which are less socially divisive and ecologically destructive.

Each reading in this section makes a contribution to an on-going debate about how critique should be advanced. A central axis of this debate is signalled in the title of **Mats Alvesson and Stanley Deetz's** 'Critical Theory and Postmodernism'—labels that are widely used to indicate a basic divergence within critical studies Alvesson and Deetz associate critical theory primarily with the Frankfurt School (e.g. Horkheimer, Marcuse, Habermas; see Alvesson and Willmott 1992) but it also includes critical realist thinking, which has been influential for the study of management (e.g. Fleetwood and Ackroyd 2004) and is illustrated by Marsden's contribution. Advocates of forms of critical theory continue to believe that an objective knowledge of reality can, albeit tentatively, be established. But this, they contend, requires a (more critical) version of science that can challenge, and will replace, methodologies compromised by a reliance upon the institutionalized predilections of privileged groups and, more specifically, the commonsense realist preference to conceive of the empirical world as a reified given that has an equivalence to the externality of the natural world. In principle, the benefit of such an approach resides in its (critical) scientific capacity to demonstrate and dissolve the bias and partiality of what is presented, in the mainstream, as a neutral and objective knowledge of management. In this way, it is anticipated, management will become founded upon a more enlightened body of knowledge.

The 'postmodernist' approach, in contrast, is more doubtful about the project of 'out-trumping' received wisdom by playing a *critical* science card. It questions whether the establishment of neutral, objective knowledge is ever possible; and it anticipates that claims to be neutral and authoritative risk its imposition, as a mono-culture, in the name of objectivity. Postmodern scepticism is informed by the understanding that all knowledge is inescapably partial; and that grand narratives, such as Science, masquerade as absolute and conclusive, albeit falsifiable, bodies of knowledge when they are inherently limited and contingent. For postmodernists, it is not a matter of rejecting science, or even reforming it to make it more critical but, rather, of re-evaluating the sense of the universalising pre-eminence and authority that is ascribed to it. Alvesson and Deetz illustrate these concerns when they discuss 'the philosophy of presence', 'hyperreality' and 'resistance'.

These two strands of CMS are illustrated by the remaining pieces reproduced in this section. In 'The Politics of Organizational Analysis', **Richard Marsden** commends a critical realist stance that offers an alternative to mainstream, positivist interpretations of the theory and practice of science. This presupposes the existence of 'real, yet non-empirical entities . . . which generate observable events', such as magnetic fields and, in the social world, social structures. The theory of science favoured by empiricists and positivists, it is argued, enables them only to produce knowledge of events and their correlation. In contrast, critical realists claim to disclose real, causal entities, of which events are simply their manifest form. That is to say, critical realism moves 'retroductively' from empirical events to the structural mechanisms that are understood to be a condition of their appearance. These mechanisms are conceived to be real, albeit that they are not tangible or measurable, because they have causal powers—powers that are retroduced from their effects, in the form of events. For example, events, including power struggles between individuals and groups within organizations, it is argued, can be explained by reference to wider structures (and power relations) in society: 'the real underlying relations which structure behavioural interaction'. Critical realist analysis aspires to be revelatory and emancipatory by laying bear the underlying mechanisms—for example, of class privilege or gender domination—that are otherwise ignored, or obscured and effectively denied, in mainstream analyses of management.

Marsden argues for a reading of Foucault as a critical realist, something that, as he acknowledges, goes rather against the grain of most interpretations of his work, including that of David Knights, as having a stronger affinity with postmodern forms of analysis. This is done primarily by suggesting that Foucault and critical realists share a depth metaphor in which attention is given to the conditions of possibility (considered to be comparable to causal mechanisms) that give rise to specific events or ideas, or which are constitutive of surface phenomena of investigation—such as 'management'or 'madness'. **David Knights**, in contrast, contends that Foucault rejects a presumption of 'the existence of essential relations that appearances conceal'—a presumption that Knights associates with modernist, 19th century ontologies. He is critical of the way positive science, including much economics, examines the value chain of production and exchange independently of the social relations that constitute its elements. But he does not conceive of these relations as causal mechanisms which generate the empirical entities that comprise that production and exchange. Indeed, he might well argue that, for Foucault, critical realism offers itself as a prime target in the 'struggle against the *coercion* of a theoretical, unitary, formal and *scientific* discourse'.

There are of course many ways of studying management critically which are not captured by this small selection of readings. Nevertheless, these represent perhaps the principle cleavage within CMS. They also show that this cleavage need not be an unbridgeable gulf. There are points of commonality as well as difference within the traditions of critical theory and post-structuralism and postmodernism, and both differ less sharply from each other than they do from mainstream, managerialist and positivist approaches to the study of management.

References

Alvesson, M. and Willmott, H. C. (eds) (1992). *Critical Management Studies*, London: Sage

Fleetwood, S. and Ackroyd, S. (eds) (2004). *Critical Realist Applications in Organization and Management Studies*, London: Routledge.

6 Critical Theory and Postmodernism: Approaches to Organizational Studies

Mats Alvesson and Stanley Deetz

Anyone who has followed the writings in critical theory and postmodernism during the last decade or so understands the difficulties we face in trying to provide a short, understandable and useful overview of this work. The two labels refer to massive bodies of literature, most of which are difficult to read. Compared to most other research perspectives treated in this *Handbook*, most of the various critical theory and postmodernist positions are still relatively new to management studies. Texts in the field cross many traditional disciplinary divisions. Many researchers draw on both traditions; others argue for irreconcilable differences between them. The differences and conflicts both within and between these two general headings have filled many pages both within and outside of organization studies. It might well be argued that nothing at once fair, coherent and brief can be written on this topic. But striving to understand these literatures is important.

The general projects of critical theory and postmodernism do not represent fad or simple fascination. Certainly some popular accounts on postmodernism invite such a critique, and we do not believe that this label is necessarily the best or will last. We believe that postmodernism—and critical theory for that matter—should be studied not because they are new and different, but because they provide unique and important ways to understand organizations and their management. Initially we will consider the social and historical context giving rise to these approaches and why the themes they address are becoming increasingly important to organization studies. We will then demonstrate ways postmodern and critical theories of organizations are different from other approaches to organization studies as well as different from (and within) each other. As the chapter develops, we will consider different ways of doing postmodern and critical work. In addition to reviewing and discussing existing work, we will sketch some fruitful lines of development between and within these two approaches. Despite their importance, in the treatment of neither critical theory nor postmodernism will we cover gender issues in any specific or detailed way since this volume has a chapter devoted to feminist approaches.

Researchers in organization and management studies came to critical theory and postmodern writings relatively late, with critical theory emerging in the late 1970s and early 1980s (for example, Benson 1977; Burrell and Morgan 1979; Frost 1980; Deetz and Kersten 1983; Fischer and Sirianni 1984) and the postmodernism writings in the late 1980s (for example, Smircich and Calás 1987; Cooper and Burrell 1988). This is no surprise given the 'modernist' assumptions embedded in organizations and the rather dogmatic and exclusionary character of dominant research traditions of either a positivist or a Marxist bent. Part of the reason both critical theory and postmodern writings have now found fertile ground in management studies is the decline and disillusionment of what is broadly referred to as modernist assumptions by both organizational theorists and practitioners. As will be developed, the attack on the modernist tradition is central to both critical and postmodern studies.

The increased size of organizations, rapid implementation of communication/information technologies, globalization, changing nature of work, reduction of the working class, less salient class conflicts, professionalization of the work force, stagnant economies, widespread ecological problems and turbulent markets are all part of the contemporary context demanding a research response. Some of these lines of development have weakened the soil for Marxism and other critiques of domination but improved it for the alternative orientations discussed here. Many of these developments provided a growing crisis in the heart of the modernist discourse with its instrumental rationality and connection to state democracies. Management in a modernist discourse works on the basis of control, the progressive rationalization and colonization of nature and people, whether workers, potential consumers, or society as a whole. But there are structural limits to control. The costs of integration and control systems often exceed the value added by management within the corporation. The shift from manufacturing to service industries as the most typical economic form in the Western world also has implications for control forms (Alvesson 1987). As the cost of control grows and the means/end chains grow longer, strategy and instrumental reasoning are strained. Themes like corporate culture, identity, quality management, service management and the renewed call for leadership, soul, and charisma during the late 1980s and early 1990s, illustrate this. Objects for management control are decreasingly labour power and behavior and increasingly the mind-power and subjectivities of employees. These new social conditions provide a new urgency and new areas of application for postmodern and critical theory work in organization studies—consider the amount of critical theory work on organizational culture (see Alvesson 1993a and Willmott 1993 for overviews)—but have little to do with their formation. These rather indicate the new social conditions to which critical theory and postmodern writing have provided innovative and instructive analyses.

While these new conditions have provided opportunity for organizational changes, we think little is gained by proclaiming a new postmodern period, or talking about postmodern organizations (Alvesson 1995). Empirical indications are highly selective and weak (Thompson 1993). The portrayal of one's own time as unique and a time of great transition is an unfortunate tendency of many periods in Western thought (Foucault 1983). Theoretically, this enterprise is equally unconvincing. The talk about postmodern organizations often means a relabeling of what is also called organic, adhocratic or post-Fordist organizations, with little or no conceptual gains and quite a lot of confusion (Parker 1993, Thompson 1993). For example, Peters (1987) or even Clegg (1990) talk about significant changes in organizations that we think can be usefully explored using postmodern and critical theory discourses, but they do not. We are only interested in these theoretical approaches and what they offer to organization studies, not in claims of organizations as postmodern.

What is then included under the umbrella concepts of critical theory and postmodernism? Sometimes critical theory is given a broad meaning and includes all works taking a basically critical or radical stance on contemporary society with an orientation towards investigating exploitation, repression, unfairness, asymmetrical power relations (generated from class, gender, or position), distorted communication, and false consciousness. We, however, use the term here with a more restricted meaning, referring to organization studies drawing concepts primarily, though not exclusively, from the Frankfurt School (Adorno, Horkheimer, Marcuse and Habermas). Much of the foundation for this work is summarized, though not without some conceptual confusions, in Burrell and Morgan's (1979) radical humanism paradigm and in Morgan's (1986) images of domination and neuroses.

Postmodernism is in many ways much harder to delimit. In the social sciences, the term has been used to describe a social mood, a historical period filled with major social and organizational changes, and a set of philosophical approaches to organizational and other studies (Featherstone 1988; Kellner 1988; Parker 1992; Hassard and Parker 1993). We will focus on this last designation, emphasizing the more socially and politically relevant writings and the use of conceptions of fragmentation, textuality, and resistance in organization studies. These philosophically based approaches to organization studies have emerged out of works of Derrida and Foucault in particular, and to a lesser degree Baudrillard, Deleuze and Guattari, and Laclau and Mouffe. Much more so than with critical theory this is a wide group of writers and positions with quite different research agendas. Still their work shares features and moves that can be highlighted in treating them together.[1]

Their themes include focusing on the constructed nature of people and reality, emphasizing language as a system of distinctions which are central to the construction process, arguing against grand narratives and large-scale theoretical systems such as Marxism or functionalism, emphasizing the power/knowledge connection and the role of claims of expertise in systems of domination, emphasizing the fluid and hyperreal nature of the contemporary world and role of mass media and information technologies, and stressing narrative/fiction/rhetoric as central to the research process.

We emphasize the critical edge of postmodernism. We see it as part of a broader critical tradition which challenges the status quo and supports silenced or marginalized voices. This is a common emphasis, but by no means the only one. Many postmodernist ideas have been utilized for different political purposes. The critique of foundations and utopian ideals has been understood by some as leaving a distinctly apolitical, socially irrelevant, or even neo-conservative stance (Habermas 1983; Margolis 1989; Sarup 1988). The absence of a political stance grounded in a systematic philosophy has been a source of complaint, but this does not mean that a different, more 'local' and 'responsive', political stance is absent (see Walzer 1986). Sometimes people distinguish between 'reactionary postmodernism' and a 'postmodernism of resistance' (Foster 1983; Smircich and Calás 1987). Like the majority of authors in social science and organization theory, we choose the latter route in our account. Most applications in social science have taken postmodern conceptions in a radical/critical direction—although an unconventional one.

The Development of Critical Theory and Postmodernism

Every historical period has probably had its particular equivalences of traditionalists, modernists, critical theorists, and postmodernists—those who lament the passing of a purer time, those instrumentally building a future, those concerned with disadvantaged segments and the direction of the future, and those seeing fragmentation and decay mixed with radical potential. In faster transitional periods as compared to relatively stable periods the mix of these figures is probably different. Remembering this more situates the historical account of critical theory and postmodernism than denies it as being interesting. Here we wish first to situate them in the history of ideas. Let us be clear at the start: all such social histories are types of fiction. They often serve present social purposes more than record the past. They are reconstructions which give us a particular way to think about the present. The history is interesting because of its productive capacities. The developmental accounts of critical theory and postmodernism are no exceptions.[2] These accounts emphasizing unity and distinction, while purposive fictions, highlight central features of these bodies of work.

Theoretical Sources of Inspiration and Distinction

Both critical theory and postmodern writers position their work in regards to four specific developments in Western thought. The way they respond to and partly use mixes of these developments accounts for many of the differences between and within postmodernism and critical theory. These are (1) the power/knowledge relation arising with Nietzsche's perspectivalism, (2) a non-dualistic constructionist account of experience and language arising with phenomenological hermeneutics and structural linguistics, (3) a historically based social conflict theory arising from Marx, and (4) a complex human subject arising from Freud. The first posed a challenge to any possible foundations for knowledge: all knowledge claims primarily reference social communities filled with specific power relations rather than an essential world or knowing subjects. The second situated all perspectives within specific social/historical/linguistic contexts: the intersubjectivity preceding any subjectivity or objectivity is structured in specifiable ways. The third removed the innocence of social/historical/linguistic perspectives by positioning them within materially produced social divisions and denied any smooth unitary historical development. And the fourth provided for a complex, conflict ridden, and often mistaken *subject* in place of a knowing, unitary, autonomous *person*, thereby challenging any claim to simple rationality and a clear and fixed identity. Together people, realities, and social relations become nonessential constructions, constructed under specific conditions of power and contestation, and filled with opacities, contradictions, and conflict suppression. These different concepts provide the historically specific tools for encountering the dominant discourses of the time.

These shared intellectual heritages should not prevent us from emphasizing the differences in how critical theory and postmodernism draw upon them. Postmodernism typically, for example, uses Freud much more unconventionally than critical theory, and merges psychoanalytic ideas with language philosophy in efforts to deconstruct and show the fragmentation of the subject.

Important sources of inspiration that are clearly different from critical theory and postmodernism include structuralist language theory (Saussure), which postmodernism draws heavily upon, and Weberian notions of the rationalization process of modern society, which is central for critical theory. In addition, critical theory is inspired by German moral philosophy and its faith in autonomy and reason (Hegel, Kant). Embedded in these choices are long term oppositions between French and German cultural contexts. If it were not for this historical context some of the differences would not be as clear. For example, Horkheimer and Adorno's (1979) cultural criticism of administratively induced control contingent upon the conception of progress in the Enlightenment can be read as sounding as close to Foucault as to Habermas's recent writings. But few would think of them in that way. It is interesting to note that Foucault, when towards the end of his life became acquainted with the Frankfurt School, expressed himself very positively, almost over generously, about it:

if I had been familiar with the Frankfurt School . . . I would not have said a number of stupid things that I did say and I would have avoided many of the detours which I made while trying to pursue my own humble path—when, meanwhile, avenues had been opened up by the Frankfurt School. (1983 : 200)

Critical Theory and Postmodernism Responses to Modernism

Since both postmodernism and critical theory writings are filled with attempts to distinguish themselves in comparison to the modernist project, a brief rendition of the latter may be helpful—though since it is familiar we will not be long. Kant described the Enlightenment as the escape from self-inflicted tutelage. In pre-Enlightenment communities, personal identities, knowledge, social order, and dominant historical narratives were carried and legitimized by tradition, though individuals actively 'inflicted' the tradition upon themselves. The Enlightenment promised an autonomous subject progressively emancipated by knowledge acquired through scientific methods. It noted the rise of reason over authority and traditional values. Its science developed and in time proclaimed a transparent language (freed from the baggage of traditional ideology) and representational truth, a positivity and optimism in acquisition of cumulative understanding which would lead to the progressive enhancement of the quality of life. The Enlightenment enemy was darkness, tradition, ideology, irrationality, ignorance, and positional authority. Each of these themes of the Enlightenment are deeply embedded in modernist management theory.

In the organizational context, we use the term 'modernist' to draw attention to the instrumentalization of people and nature through the use of scientific-technical knowledge (modeled after positivism and other 'rational' ways of developing safe, robust knowledge) to accomplish predictable results measured by productivity and technical problem-solving leading to the 'good' economic and social life, primarily defined by accumulation of wealth by production investors and consumption by consumers. Modernism initially represented emancipation over myth, authority, and traditional values through knowledge, reason, and opportunities based on heightened capacity. Early twentieth century organization studies were organized around development of modernist over traditional discourses. Taylor's and Weber's treatment of rationalization and bureaucratization showed from the start the corporation as a site of the development of modernist logic and instrumental reasoning. The traditional was marginalized and placed off in the private realm. While writings in human relations, quality of work life, and later cultural studies would continue to claim a place for traditional values and norms with their particular logics, each would be 'strategized' and brought to aid further rationalization of work for the sake of convenience, efficiency, and direction of the work effort. 'Performativity' would come to be valued over any earlier Enlightenment narrative of emancipation or human values (Lyotard 1984). In fact in the new age embellishment one could even be emancipated from the body's emotions and bring the body's spirit and faith under rational control. Foucault's (1977; 1980; 1988) demonstrations, and critical treatment, of the rise of self-surveillance and bio-power as control systems described the furthest development of self-rationalization in modernity. Critical theory and postmodernism open new discussions. In particular critical theory showed how modernism itself was based on myths, had acquired an arbitrary authority, subordinated social life to technological rationality and protected a new dominant group's interests (Horkheimer and Adorno 1979). The old conflict between a modern and a traditional discourse where the modern laid claim to all the positive terms is suddenly displaced by a new set of conflicts, those arising from the problems of modernity itself.

Both critical theory and postmodernism see their work as responses to specific social conditions. Contemporary society as a result of science, industrialization, and communication/information technologies has developed positive capacities but also dangerous forms of domination. Both critical theory and postmodernism describe Western development as one where a progressive, instrumental modernism gradually eclipsed traditional society with fairly clear payoffs but also great costs. They agree that something fundamental has gone awry and that more technical, instrumental 'solutions' will not fix it. While their diagnoses are similar (to use a less than totally adequate medical metaphor), they differ in their pronouncement and response. Critical theorists see the modernists' project as sick and see hope for reconstruction in recovery of good parts and redirecting the future. Postmodernists pronounce its death and proclaim the absence of a thinkable future.[3]

The critical theorists, especially Habermas (1984; 1987), focus on the incompletion of the positive potentialities of enlightenment. Different forces have utilized their power and advantages to force new forms of tutelage, often *consentful* in character. As we will discuss in regards to organizational studies, critical theorists have focused on the skewing and closure of the historical discourse through reification, universalization of sectional interests, domination of instrumental reasoning, and hegemony. In different ways they hope to recover a rational process through understanding social/historical/political constructionism, a broader conception of rationality, inclusion of more groups in social determination, and overcoming systematically distorted communication. Central to this is the critique of domination and the ways those subjugated actively participate in their own subjugation. The politically astute intellectual is given an active role in the production of an enlightened understanding. The hope is to provide forums so that different segments of the society and different human interests can be part of a better, more moral, historical dialogue, so that each may equally contribute to the choices in producing a future for all.

The postmodernists also focus on the dark side of the Enlightenment, its destruction of the environment and native peoples, its exclusions, and the concealed effects of reason and progress, but postmodernists see the entire project as wrong. The problem is not who or what participates in it. The project is inherently problematic. They seek to find the 'nonenlightened' voices, the human possibilities that the Enlightenment itself suppresses. This discourse is filled with the pronouncement of the end of the historical discourse of progress and emancipation and its endless deferral of social promise, that more technology, more knowledge and increased rationality will somehow accomplish the promise. Man (the humanist subject as a coherent entity with natural rights and potential autonomy) is pronounced dead and in *his* place appears the decentred, fragmented, gendered, classed subject; the grand narratives of theory and history are replaced by disjoined and fragmented local narratives potentially articulated and sutured; and metaphysics with its philosophies of presence and essence has lost terrain to the celebration of multiple perspectives and a carnival of positions and structurings. The future is endlessly deferred and without positive direction, but life can be made more interesting through deconstruction and the recovery of suppressed conflicts and marginalized groups. The intellectual has no privileged position or special knowledge, but can only act in situational, local ways like all others. Since there can be no theory of history or projection into the future, resistance and alternative readings rather than reform or revolution become the primary political posture.

Opening the Tensions and Providing Temporary Unities

In this section we will show a way of thinking about research positions that makes critical theory and postmodernism similar in contrast to other approaches to organizations and different from each other. To do this we will use a grid similar to the popular one by Burrell and Morgan (1979) but with changes that highlight similarities and differences more usefully (see Deetz 1994a; 1996 for development).[4] See Figure 1.

The consensus–dissensus dimension focuses on the relation of research practices to the dominant social discourses. Research perspectives can be contrasted based on the extent to which they work within a dominant set of structurings of knowledge, social relations, and identities, called here a 'consensus' discourse, and the extent to which they work to disrupt these structurings, called here 'dissensus' discourse. This dimension is used to show a significant way that we can think about what makes postmodernism and critical theory different from other current research programs. The second dimension focuses on the origin of concepts and problem statements as part of the constitutive process in research. Differences among research perspectives can be shown by contrasting 'local/emergent' conceptions with 'elite/*a priori*' ones. This dimension will be used to show one way to interestingly think about the difference between the postmodernism and critical theory discourses.

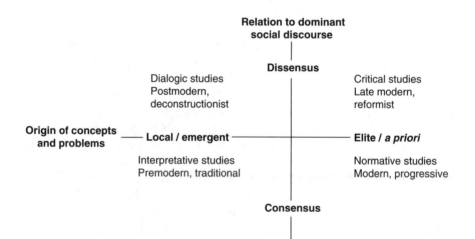

Fig. 1. *Contrasting dimensions from the metatheory of representational practices* (adapted from Deetz 1994c)

The two dimensions together attempt to show what is negotiable and not in research practice, how research reports are organized, and the anticipated political outcome of the research activity (the direction in which it points, whether or not it has a practical effect). Unlike Burrell and Morgan we do not wish to suggest that the grid identifies paradigms but rather we propose that it shows particular discourses which develop mobile but specifiable relations to each other and position particular types of conflicts and contradictions internal to them. Each of these issues will be taken up briefly below. We recognize that in naming these positions and the bodies of work exemplifying them, some things are pulled together that are still different in many now hidden ways and bipolar contrasts are created that change a continuous world to a discontinuous one. We hope the reader will work with us to see the various conceptualizations as interesting ways to call attention to similarities and differences that matter rather than as devices for division and classification. The differences between critical theory and postmodernism are often contested and many researchers draw on both traditions. Still it is useful to give some account of what makes these *different* traditions that do not easily collapse into each other.

The Consensus—Dissensus Dimension

Consensus or dissensus should be understood not primarily as agreement and disagreement but rather as presentation of unity or of difference, the continuation or disruption of a coherent dominant discourse, trust or doubt as basic anticipation. Key to this dimension is the argument from the dissensus end that people, orders, and objects are constructed in work, social interaction, and the process of research, and hence the perceived world is based on political processes of determination which often demonstrate domination and could/ should be contestable; while the consensus discourse provides the identities of people, social orders, and objects as natural, or if constructed, legitimate and given awaiting discovery by the researcher. When a construction view is advocated by certain consensus researchers, it tends to emphasize the natural, organic and spontaneous nature of the constructions, rather than, as in the version of dissensus seekers, its arbitrary and political character. To save space, see Table 1 for conceptualization of this dimension.

Local/Emergent—Elite/A Priori Dimension

The local/emergent—elite/*a priori* dimension will be used here primarily to call attention to a central difference between postmodern and critical theory positions but it also contrasts normative and interpretative studies. Table 2

Mats Alvesson and Stanley Deetz

Table 1. Characterizations of the consensus–dissensus dimension

Consensus	Dissensus
Trust	Suspicion
Hegemonic order as natural state	Conflicts over order as natural state
Naturalization of present	Present order is historicized and politicized
Integration and harmony are possible	Order indicates domination and suppressed conflicts
Research focuses on representation	Research focused on challenge and reconsideration (re-presentation)
Mirror (reflecting) dominant metaphor	Lens (seeing/reading as) dominant metaphor
Validity central concern	Insight and praxis central concern
Theory as abstraction	Theory as opening
Unified science and triangulation	Positional complementarity
Science is neutral	Science is political
Life is discovery	Life is struggle and creation
Researcher anonymous and out of time and space	Researcher named and positioned
Autonomous/free agent	Historically/socially situated agent

Source: adapted from Deetz (1996)

Table 2. Characterizations of the local/emergent-elite/*a priori* dimension

Local/emergent	Elite/*a priori*
Comparative communities	Privileged community
Multiple language games	Fixed language game
Particularistic	Universalistic
Systematic philosophy as ethnocentric	Grounded in hoped-for systematic philosophy
Atheoretical	Theory driven
Situational or structural determinism	Methodological determinism
Nonfoundational	Foundational
Local narratives	Grand narrative of progress and emancipation
Sensuality and meaning as central concerns	Rationality and truth as central concerns
Situated, practical knowledge	Generalizable, theoretical knowledge
Tends to be feminine in attitude	Tends to be masculine in attitude
Sees the strange	Sees the familiar
Proceeds from the other	Proceeds from the self
Ontology of 'otherness' over method	Epistemological and procedural issues rule over substantive assumptions

Source: adapted from Deetz (1996)

presents an array of these contrasts. On the elite side, the discourse produces the researcher as a stronger agent with privileged insights—at least having the ability to produce reliable knowledge—and makes clear the commitment to political agendas.

The *a priori* set of conceptions demonstrates implicit or explicit alliances with different groups in society. For example, to the extent that normative researchers' concepts align with managerial conceptions and problem statements and are applied *a priori* in studies, the knowledge claims are intrinsically biased toward certain interests as they are applied within the site community. The knowledge claims become part of the same processes that are being studied, reproducing world views and personal identities, and fostering particular interests within the organization (see Knights 1992). Feminists and those primarily concerned with class analysis, while usually in sympathy with most aspects of postmodernism, often turn to critical theory (or a similar position) to acquire a political agenda based on preconceptions of social divisions and forms of domination that are considered general (see Fraser and Nicholson 1988; Flax 1990). While such conceptions from critical theory are critical of elite groups in the move to create a more equitable society, they tend to privilege the conceptions of disadvantaged groups or intellectual ideals, and hence produce their own, usually temporary, elitism. The local/emergent conceptions see social groupings themselves as constructions, power and domination as dispersed, and the research agenda as itself dominating. Words like 'women', 'worker', 'poor', 'owners', and so forth are accepted not as representations of 'reality', but as power-laden distinctions. An ordinary conception of political action as end-directed is thus difficult to sustain in either interpretative or postmodern (dialogic) work.

A Sketch of Alternative Research Approaches

The relation of postmodern and critical theory to each other and to normative and interpretative work can be shown by comparing the discourse they generate in regard to issues in organization studies. See Table 3. Since we will use these characterizations to build our discussion of studies in critical theory and postmodernism, we will not discuss them here.

Critical Theory and Organizational Research

The central goal of critical theory in organizational studies has been to create societies and workplaces which are free from domination, where all members

Table 3. Prototypical discursive features

Issue	Normative	Discourse Interpretative	Critical	Dialogic
Basic goal	Law-like relations among objects	Display unified culture	Unmask domination	Reclaim conflict
Method	Nomothetic science	Hermeneutics, ethnography	Cultural criticism, ideology critique	Deconstruction, geneology
Hope	Progressive emancipation	Recovery of integrative values	Reformation of social order	Claim a space for lost voices
Metaphor of social relations	Economic	Social	Political	Mass
Organization metaphor	Marketplace	Community	Polity	Carnival
Problems addressed	Inefficiency, disorder	Meaningless-ness, illegitimacy	Domination, consent	Marginaliza-tion, conflict suppression
Concern with communication	Fidelity, influence, information needs	Social acculturation, group affirmation	Misrecognition, systematic distortion	Discursive closure
Narrative style	Scientific/technical, strategic	Romantic, embracing	Therapeutic, directive	Ironic, ambiva-lent
Time identity	Modern	Premodern	Late modern	Postmodern
Organizational benefits	Control, exper-tise	Commitment, quality of work life	Participation, expanded knowledge	Diversity, creativity
Mood	Optimistic	Friendly	Suspicious	Playful
Social fear	Disorder	Depersonaliza-tion	Authority	Totalization, normalization

Source: adapted from Deetz 1996

have an equal opportunity to contribute to the production of systems which meet human needs and lead to the progressive development of all. Studies have focused externally on the relation of organizations to the wider society by emphasizing the possible social effects of colonization of other institutions and the domination or destruction of the public sphere, and internally on the domination by instrumental reasoning, discursive closures, and consent processes within the workplace. As indicated, critical researchers tend to enter their studies with a full set of theoretical commitments which aid them analytically to ferret out situations of domination and distortion. Organizations are largely seen as political sites, and thus general social theories and especially theories of decision-making in the public sphere are seen as appropriate (see Deetz 1992; 1995).

Critical theorists sometimes have a clear political agenda focused on the interests of specific identifiable groups such as women, workers, or people of color, but usually address general issues of goals, values, forms of consciousness and communicative distortions within corporations. Increasingly important to critical studies is the enrichment of the knowledge base, improvement of decision process, and increases in 'learning' and adaptation. Their interest in ideologies considers the difficulties of disadvantaged groups in understanding their own political interest, but is more often addressed to limitations on people in general, challenging technocracy, consumerism, careerism, and exclusive concern with economic growth. Most of the work has focused on ideology critique which shows how specific interests fail to be realized owing partly to the inability of people to understand or act on these interests. In the context of management and organization studies, it should be emphasized that critical theory, compared to Marxism, is not anti-management *per se*, even though one tends to treat management as institutionalized and ideologies and practices of management as expressions of contemporary forms of domination. Critical theory can offer much to management and managers. Contributions include input to reflection on career choices, intellectual resources for counteracting totalitarian tendencies in managerially controlled corporate socialization, and stimulation for incorporating a broader set of criteria and consideration in decision-making— especially in cases where profit and growth do not clearly compete with other ends or where uncertainty exists regarding the profit outcomes of various alternative means and strategies (Alvesson and Willmott 1996; Chapter 8; Deetz 1995: ch. 4). Two principal types of critical studies can be identified in organization studies: ideological critique and communicative action.

Ideology Critique

The earliest ideological critiques of the workplace were offered by Marx. In his analysis of work processes he focused primarily on practices of economic exploitation through direct coercion and structural differences in work relations between the owners of capital and the owners of their own labor. However, Marx also describes the manner in which the exploitative relation is disguised and made to appear legitimate. This is the origin of ideology critique. Economic conditions and class structure still were central to the analysis whether this misrecognition of interests was a result of the domination of the ruling class's ideas (Marx 1844) or of the dull compulsions of economic relations (Marx 1867).

The themes of domination and exploitation by owners and later by managers have been central to ideology critique of the workplace in this century by Marxist inspired organization theorists (for example, Braverman 1974; Clegg and Dunkerley 1980; Edwards 1979; Salaman 1981). Attention by analysts from the left focused on ideology since workers often seemed to fail to recognize this exploitation and their class-based revolutionary potential in the industrial countries. Gradually these later analyses became less concerned with coercion and class and economic explanations as their focus changed to why coercion was so rarely necessary and to systemic processes that produced active consent. Issues of 'workers' self-understanding of experience' become more central (for example, Gramsci 1929–35; Burawoy 1979; Willmott 1990). To an increasing degree, ideology critiques do not only or even strongly address class issues, but broaden the picture and study how cultural-ideological control operates in relationship to all employees, including levels of management (Hodge et al. 1979; Czarniawska-Joerges 1988; Deetz and Mumby 1990; Kunda 1992). Ideology produced in the workplace would stand alongside that present in the media and the growth of the consumer culture and welfare state as accounting for workers' failure to act on their own interests. Ideology would also account for professionals' and managers' failure to achieve autonomy in relationship to needs and wants and the conformist pressure to standardize paths for satisfying these (conspicuous consumption, careerism, and self-commodification: see Heckscher 1995). This would fill out the tradition of ideology critique.

A considerable amount of critical work has addressed management and organization theory as expressions, as well as producers, of ideologies which legitimize and strengthen specific societal and organizational social relations and objectives (Burrell and Morgan 1979; Alvesson 1987; Alvesson and Willmott 1996; Steffy and Grimes 1992). Academics, particularly those in management studies, are often viewed as ideologists. They serve dominant groups through socialization in business schools, support managers with ideas and vocabularies for cultural-ideological control at the workplace level, and provide the aura of science to support the introduction and use of managerial domination techniques.

Four themes recur in the numerous and varied writings about organizations working from the perspective of ideology critique: (1) the naturalization of social order, or the way a socially/historically constructed world would be treated as necessary, natural, rational and self-evident; (2) the universalization of managerial interests and suppression of conflicting interests; (3) the domination by instrumental, and eclipse of competitive, reasoning processes; and (4) hegemony, the way consent becomes orchestrated.

Naturalization

In naturalization a social formation is abstracted from the historical conflictual site of its origin and treated as a concrete, relatively fixed, entity. As such the reification becomes the reality rather than life processes. Through obscuring the construction process, institutional arrangements are no longer seen as choices but as natural and self-evident. The illusion that organizations and their processes are 'natural' objects and functional responses to 'needs' protects them from examination as produced under specific historical conditions (which are potentially passing) and out of specific power relations. In organization studies, organismic and mechanistic metaphors dominate, thereby leading research away from considering the legitimacy of control and political relations in organizations (Morgan 1986). Examining the naturalization of the present and the reifications of social processes helps display the structural interrelation of institutional forces, the processes by which they are sustained and changed, and the processes by which their arbitrary nature is concealed and hence closed to discussion. Ideology critique reclaims organizations as social-historical constructions and investigates how they are formed, sustained, and transformed by processes both internal and external to them (see Lukács 1971; Benson 1977; Giddens 1979; Frost 1980; 1987; Thompson 1984; Deetz 1985; 1994d). The self-evident nature of an organizational society, the basic distinctions and division of labor between management and workers, men and women, and so forth are called into question by ideology critique which demonstrates the arbitrary nature of these phenomena and the power relations that result and sustain these forms for the sake of discovering the remaining places of possible choice.

Universalization of Managerial Interests

Lukács (1971) among many others (see Giddens 1979) has shown that particular sectional interests are often universalized and treated as if they were everyone's interests. In contemporary corporate practices, managerial groups are privileged in decision-making and research. Management is ascribed a superior position in terms of defining the interests and interest realizations of the corporation and thereby of wide segments of the population. The interests of the corporation are frequently equated with specific managerial self-interests. For example, worker, supplier, or host community interests can be interpreted in terms of their effect on corporate—i.e. universalized managerial—interests. As such they are exercised only occasionally and usually reactively and are often represented as simply economic commodities or 'costs'—for example, the price the 'corporation' must pay for labor, supplies, or environmental clean-up (Deetz 1995). Central to the universalization of managerial interest is the reduction of the multiple claims of ownership to financial ownership. The investments made by other stakeholders are minimized while capital investment is made central. Management by virtue of its fiduciary responsibility (limited to monetary investors) speaks for (and is often conceptually equated with) the corporation (Storey 1983). In such a move, since the *general* well-being of each group is conceptually and materially tied to the *financial* well-being of the corporation as understood by management, self-interest by nonmanagerial stakeholders is often ironically reinterpreted as accomplished by minimizing the accomplishment of their own self-interests. In ideological critique managerial advantages can be seen as produced historically and actively reproduced through ideological practices in society and in corporations themselves (see Tompkins and Cheney 1985; Knights and Willmott 1985; Lazega 1992; Deetz 1992). Critical studies explore how interest articulation is distorted through the dominating role of money as a simple and powerful medium (Offe and Wiesenthal 1980) and confront productivity and consumption with suppressed values such as autonomy, creativity and pleasure as objectives for the organization of work (Burrell and Morgan 1979; Willmott and Knights 1982; Alvesson 1987).

The Primacy of Instrumental Reasoning
Habermas (1971; 1975; 1984; 1987) has traced the social/historical emergence of technical rationality over competing forms of reason. Habermas described *technical reasoning* as instrumental, tending to be governed by the theoretical and hypothetical, and focusing on control through the development of means—ends chains. The natural opposite to this Habermas conceptualizes as a *practical interest*. Practical reasoning focuses on the process of understanding and mutual determination of the ends to be sought rather than control and development of means of goal accomplishment (Apel 1979). As Habermas described the practical interest: 'a constitutive interest in the preservation and expansion of the intersubjectivity of possible action-oriented mutual understandings. The understanding of meaning is directed in its very structure toward the attainment of possible consensus among actors in the framework of a self-understanding derived from tradition' (1971 : 310). In a balanced system these two forms of reasoning become natural complements. But, in the contemporary social situation, the form and content of modern social science and the social constitution of expertise align with organizational structures to produce the domination of technical reasoning (see Stablein and Nord 1985; Alvesson 1987; Alvesson and Willmott 1992; 1996; Mumby 1988; Fischer 1990). To the extent that technical reasoning dominates, it lays claim to the entire concept of rationality and alternative forms of reason appear irrational. To a large extent studies of the 'human' side of organizations (climate, job enrichment, quality of work life, worker participation programs, and culture) have each been transformed from alternative ends into new means to be brought under technical control for extending the dominant group interests of the

corporation (Alvesson 1987). Sievers, for example, suggests that 'motivation only became an issue—for management and organization theorists as well as for the organization of work itself—when meaning either disappeared or was lost from work; that the loss of meaning is immediately connected with the way work has been, and still is organized in the majority of our Western enterprises' (1986 : 338). The productive tension between technical control and humanistic aspects becomes submerged to the efficient accomplishment of often unknown but surely 'rational' and 'legitimate' corporate goals.

Hegemony

Although Gramsci's (1929–35) analysis and development of the concept of 'hegemony' aimed at a general theory of society and social change with the workplace as one component, his conceptions have been widely used as a foundation for an examination of the workplace itself (for example, Burawoy 1979; Clegg 1989). Gramsci conceives of hegemony as a complex web of conceptual and material arrangements producing the very fabric of everyday life. Hegemony in the workplace is supported by economic arrangements enforced by contracts and reward systems, cultural arrangements enforced by advocacy of specific values and visions, and command arrangements enforced by rules and policies. These are situated within the larger society with its supporting economic arrangements, civil society (including education/intellectuals/media), and governmental laws.

The conception of hegemony suggests the presence of multiple dominant groups with different interests and the presence of power and activity even in dominated groups. The integration of these arrangements, however, favors dominant groups and the activity of both dominant and dominated groups is best characterized as a type of produced 'consent'. The hegemonic system works through pervading common sense and becoming part of the ordinary way of seeing the world, understanding one's self, and experiencing needs (see Angus 1992). Such a situation always makes possible a gap between that inscribed by the dominant order and that which a dominated group would have preferred. As Lukes argued, 'Man's wants themselves may be a product of a system which works against their interests, and in such cases, relates the latter to what they would want and prefer, were they able to make the choice' (1974 : 34). A number of studies have investigated a variety of 'consent' processes (for example, Burawoy 1979; Kunda 1992; Vallas 1993). Several studies have shown how employees 'strategize their own subordination', achieving marginal gains for themselves through subordination but also perpetuating dominant systems which preclude their autonomy and ability to act on their own wider interests (see Burawoy 1985; Deetz 1995; 1998; Willmott 1993).

Organization studies in the 1980s and 1990s have exhibited a rather wide body of critical theory addressing corporate culture or proceeding from

Mats Alvesson and Stanley Deetz

cultural perspectives on organizations, where culture and cultural engineering are defined as pointing towards hegemony (for example, Alvesson 1993a; Alvesson and Willmott 1996; Deetz 1985; Jermier 1985; Knights and Willmott 1987; Mumby 1988; Rosen 1985). Willmott, for example, has explored how 'corporate culture programmes are designed to deny or frustrate the development of conditions in which critical reflection is fostered. They commend the homogenization of norms and values within organizations . . . Cultural diversity is dissolved in the acid bath of the core corporate values' (1993 : 534). In practice, as Willmott and other critical theorists point out, management control strategies are seldom fully successful. Resistance and some level of cultural diversity normally prevail. The role of critical theory, but even more so postmodernism, can be seen as trying to preserve and reinforce this diversity.

A Critique of Ideology Critique
Each of these four concerns raised in various ideological critiques has value. Yet, limitations of ideology critique have been demonstrated by many. Three criticisms appear most common. First, ideology critique often appears *ad hoc* and reactive. Most studies explain after the fact why something didn't happen rather than making predictive and testable statements about the future. Second, it appears elitist. Concepts like false needs and false consciousness which were central to early studies presume a basic weakness in insight and reasoning processes in the very same people it hopes to empower. The irony of an advocate of greater equality pronouncing what others should want or how they should perceive the world 'better' is not lost on either dominant or dominated groups. And, third, the accounts from early studies of ideology critique appear far too simplistic. According to the Abercrombie et al. (1980) critique of the 'dominant ideology thesis', the conception of the dominant group remains singular and intentional, as if an identifiable group worked out a system whereby domination through control of ideas could occur and its interest could be secured.

A more sophisticated critique, coming from postmodernism, points out that the idea of the centred agent-subject is as central to ideology critique as it is to dominant groups and the systems that advantage them. The hope for a rational and reflective agent who is capable of acting autonomously and coherently may in itself be a worthy target of ideology critique. The modern corporation's legitimacy is based on both the assumption of the existence of such an individual and its ability to foster that individual's development. Ideology critique does not, on the whole, question this basic notion of the individual, even though authors are quick to point to the discrepancy between actual production of people and a potential development.

Clearly, the power of ideology critique can be maintained without falling to these criticisms and many critical theorists have accomplished this as they have pulled the concept of ideology away from traditional Marxism. They have responded to the critics by (a) advocating research that empirically investigates expressions of dominating systems of thought in particular communicative situations rather than explains outcomes (for example, Alvesson 1996; Knights and Willmott 1987; Rosen 1985); (b) refraining from directive statements regarding what people should do (revolt, liberate) but emphasizing the problematization of dominating beliefs and values (Deetz 1992); (c) recognizing pluralistic qualities, but still insisting that there are strong asymmetries between various interests and perspectives; and (d) treating ideologies as dominating without seeing them as a simple instrument or in the interest of an elite group, thus showing that elites may have internalized and may suffer from the effects of dominating sets of ideas (such as pollution or through work processes: Heckscher 1995).

Another response to the problems of ideology critique is the development of a communicative perspective within critical theory. It represents a development from a focus on socially repressive ideas and institutions to the explorations of the communicative processes through which ideas are produced, reproduced and critically examined, especially in decision-making contexts.

Communicative Action

Unlike earlier advocates of critical theory, Habermas's work since the late 1970s has reduced the significance of traditional ideology critique and has concentrated instead on building a systematic philosophy in which theory and communicative action are of pivotal importance (Habermas 1984; 1987). This project retains many of the features of ideology critique, including the ideal of sorting out constraining social ideas from those grounded in reason, but it envisages procedural ideas rather than substantive critique and thus becomes quite different from traditional ideology critique. It also introduces an affirmative agenda, not based on a utopia, but still a hope of how we might reform institutions along the lines of morally driven discourse in situations approximating an ideal speech situation.

Habermas separates two historical learning processes and forms of rationality, the technological-scientific-strategic, associated with the system world, and the communicative-political-ethical, associated with the lifeworld, and tries to contribute to the latter. He argues for the systematic improvement of the lifeworld through an expanded conception of rationality focusing on the creation and re-creation of patterns of meaning. The lifeworld can be regarded as fully rational—rather than instrumentalized or strategized—to the extent that it permits interactions that are guided by communicatively achieved understanding rather than by imperatives from the system world—such as those contingent upon the money code or formal power—or by the unreflective reproduction of traditional cultural values (Habermas 1984).

Communicatively achieved understanding is dependent on undistorted communication, the presence of free discussion based on goodwill, argumentation and dialogue. On the basis of undistorted, rational discussion he assumes that consensus can be reached regarding both present and desirable states. He maintains that in language itself and the way it is used there are certain conditions for achieving this ideal: the expectation and the wish to be understood and believed, and the hope that others will accept our arguments and other statements (see Thompson 1984; Deetz 1992: chs. 6 and 7). Without such expectations and ambitions there is little point in either statements or discussions. Undistorted communication provides the basis for the 'highest' (or perhaps the widest, most reflective) form of rationality, namely communicative rationality. Here it is not power, status, prestige, ideology, manipulation, the rule of experts, fear, insecurity, misunderstanding or any other form of mischief that furnishes a base for the evolving ideas. Decision-making becomes based on the strength of the good, well-grounded argument provided in an open forum rather than authority, tradition, ideology, or exclusion of participants.

This concept of communicative rationality carries with it connotations based ultimately on the central experience of the unconstrained, unifying, consensus-bringing force of argumentative speech, in which different participants overcome their merely subjective views and, owing to the mutuality of rationally motivated conviction, assure themselves of both the unity of the objective world and the intersubjectivity of their lifeworld. (Habermas 1984 : 10)

Communicative rationality thus denotes a way of responding to (questioning, testing and, possibly, accepting) the validity of different claims. Communicative action thus allows for the exploration of every statement on a basis of the following (universal) validity criteria: comprehensibility, sincerity, truthfulness and legitimacy. Communicative action is therefore an important aspect of social interaction in society, in social institutions and in daily life. The ideal speech situation, which enables communicative rationality and is in turn pervaded by it, exists under the following conditions: 'the structure of communication itself produces no constraints if and only if, for all possible participants, there is a symmetrical distribution of chances to choose and to apply speech-acts' (Habermas, cited by Thompson and Held 1982 : 123). Of course, the ideal speech situation is not a quality of ordinary communication, but a counterfactual anticipation we make when we seek mutual understanding, trying to accomplish the form of argumentation we presuppose we are able to step into when we seek to step aside from the flow of everyday action and check a problematic claim. As we will suggest in looking at critical theory's contribution, such an ideal when used as an analytic frame in organization studies can provide much guidance to restructuring discussions and decision-making in organizations (for example, Lyytinen and Hirschheim 1988; Power and Laughlin 1992).

We will not here repeat the critique of Habermas's theory (see Thompson and Held 1982; Fraser 1987; Burrell 1994), but just mention that it over stresses the possibility of rationality as well as value of consensus (Deetz 1992) and puts too much weight on the clarity and rationality potential of language and human interaction. To some extent, it relies on a model of the individual as potentially autonomous and clarified, but this assumption plays a less central role compared to earlier critical theory, as the focus is not on consciousness, but on the structure of communicative interaction as the carrier of rationality. But still Habermas can be criticized for his 'benign and benevolent view of human kind' (Vattimo 1992), which counts on knowledge and argumentation to change thought and action, a position about which postmodernists are highly skeptical.

The Contribution of Critical Organization Studies

Critical studies in organization theory have utilized the ideas sketched above, developed these and illustrated their relevance for the understanding of modern organizations, in particular corporations. Alvesson and Willmott (1996) have pointed at some metaphors for organizations and management from critical theory: organization as technocracy, mystification, cultural doping and colonizing power. These draw attention to how management expertise leads to passivity on the part of other organizational participants, how ambiguity and contradictions are masked, how the engineering of values and definitions of reality tend to weaken low-level and other marginal groups in the negotiation of workplace reality and, respectively, how the codes of money and formal power exercise a close to hegemonic position over workplace experiences and articulated values and priorities. As indicated above, two basic foci can here be pointed at: one content oriented, emphasizing sources of constraints; one process oriented, emphasizing variation in communicative action in organizations.

Critical theory draws attention, for example, to the narrow thinking associated with the domination of instrumental reason and the money code. Potentially, when wisely applied, instrumental reason is a productive form of thinking and acting. However, in the absence of practical reason (aiming at politically and ethically informed judgment), its highly specialized, means-fixated and unreflective character makes it strongly inclined to also contribute to the objectification of people and nature and thus to various forms of destruction. Most salient are (1) constrained work conditions where intrinsic work qualities (creativity, variation, development, meaningfulness) are ignored or subordinated to instrumental values (Alvesson 1987; Sievers 1986); (2) the development and reinforcement of asymmetrical social relations between experts (including management elites) and non-experts (Alvesson and Willmott 1996; Fischer 1990; Hollway 1984); (3) gender bias in terms of styles of reasoning, asymmetrical social relations and political priorities (Calás and Smircich 1992a; 1992b; Mumby and Putnam 1992; Ferguson 1984; Hearn and Parkin 1987); (4) extensive control of employees' mindsets and a freezing of their social reality (Deetz and Kersten 1983; Frost 1987; Mumby 1987); (5) far-reaching control of employees, consumers and the general political-ethical agenda in society, though mass media and lobbying advocating consumerism and the priority of the money code as a yardstick for values and individual and collective political decision-making (Alvesson and Willmott 1996; Deetz 1992); and (6) destruction of the natural environment through waste and pollution (Shrivastava 1995; Stead and Stead 1992).

In the guise of technocracy, instrumental rationality has pretenses to neutrality and freedom from the value-laden realms of self-interest and politics. It celebrates and 'hides' behind techniques and the false appearance of objectivity and impartiality of institutionalized sets of knowledge, bureaucracy and formal mandates. Not surprisingly, technocracy is promoted by each of the management 'specialisms' as they claim a monopoly of expertise in their respective domains. Human resource specialists, for example, advance and defend their position by elaborating a battery of 'objective' techniques for managing the selection and promotion of employees (Hollway 1984; Steffy and Grimes 1992). Strategic management institutionalizes a particular way of exercising domination through legitimizing and privileging the 'management' of the organization—environment interface, producing some actors as 'strategists' and reducing others to troops whose role is to subordinate themselves and to implement corporate strategies (Shrivastava 1986; Alvesson and Willmott 1995). The concept of technocracy draws attention to some of the darker and more disturbing aspects of so-called 'professional management'. It points to a restricted understanding of human and organizational goals: those that are identified and validated by experts. By associating management with technocracy and its instrumentalization of reason, the domination of a narrow conception of reason is at once exposed and questioned.

The domination of groups, ideas and institutions producing and drawing upon the idea of technocracy leads to a technocratic consciousness (Habermas 1970; Alvesson 1987). Here basic conflicts between different ideals and principles are seen as dissolving as a consequence of the development of more and more rational methods. In work organizations, conflicts between practical reason (emphasizing the removal of repression) and instrumental reason (focused on the maximization of output) are portrayed as avoidable through the use of optimal management methods such as job enrichment, QWL, TQM, corporate culture and so forth, which simultaneously produce human well-being and development as well as high quality and productivity. Basic political issues are then transformed into technical problemsolving.

Habermas's ideas may also be used in a pragmatic way, more suitable for social science and organization studies than the original philosophical-theoretical version. With the communicative turn in Habermas's work, there follow possibilities for a more applied and empirical development in the use of critical theory. This means, as Forester argued, 'putting *ideal* speech aside' and expanding the exploration of 'the *actual* social and political conditions of "checking", of political voice, and thus too of possible autonomy' (1993 : 3, italics added). Forester (1985; 1989; 1992; 1993) has developed a 'critical pragmatism' based on an independent and creative reading of Habermas. Forester's work is particularly interesting as it combines theoretical sophistication with an empirical and applied orientation and can serve as an example here of what critical can look like in practice. To Forester, an empirically oriented critical theory should be '(1) empirically sound and descriptively meaningful; (2) interpretatively plausible and phenomenologically meaningful; and yet (3) critically pitched, ethically insightful, as well' (1993 : 2).

In following this through, Forester (1989) distinguishes between unavoidable and socially unnecessary disturbances, between socially *ad hoc* problems and more socially systematic, structure-related sources of distortions. Organizations may be understood as structures of systematically (nonaccidentally and possibly avoidable) distorted communications or as social/communicative infrastructures mediating between structural relations and social actions in economic and working life contexts. Irrespective of the extent to which distortions can be avoided in practice, knowledge and insight of these distorted communications are certainly of value. From a communication perspective, organizations can be assessed and evaluated according to whether they approximate dogma (closed communication) or dialogue (open communication) (see Deetz 1992: ch. 7). As Forester argued:

When organizations or polities are structured so that their members have no protected recourse to checking the truth, legitimacy, sincerity, or clarity claims made on them by established structures of authority and production, we may find conditions of dogmatism rather than of social learning, tyranny rather than authority, manipulation rather than cooperation, and distraction rather than sensitivity. In this way critical theory points to the importance of understanding practically and normatively how access to, and participation in, discourses, both theoretical and practical, are systematically structured. (1983 : 239–40)

Forester views the organizing of attention as a crucial feature of administrative and organizational processes of social reproduction. He draws upon

Habermas's (1984) model of reproduction, which includes (1) cultural reproduction of world views (ideas, knowledge, beliefs), (2) social integration, in
which norms, obligations and patterns of social membership are reproduced,
and (3) socialization, in which social identities, motives and expressions of the
self are altered and developed. At stake in specific communicative / organizational acts (and struggles) are thus the reproduction / challenging / reformula-
tion of beliefs, consent and identity; Crucial research as well as practical
questions include 'what makes possible or impedes a worker's finding out
information at the workplace, challenging rules or norms, or expressing
needs, feelings, his or her identity, way of being?' (1993 : 131). The problem
here, Forester notes, is to link control structures to daily experience, voice and
action. Such an account becomes a structural phenomenology: it is structural
because it maps 'the systematic staging and framing of social action; it is
phenomenology because it explores the concrete social interactions (promises,
threats, agreements, deals, conflicts) that are so staged' (1993 : 140). Forester
(1992) illustrates his approach through a sensitive reading of a mundane,
seemingly trivial empirical situation, a city staff planning meeting. He explores
his data—twelve lines of transcript from the meeting—and shows how Habermas's pragmatic validity claims are productive in exploring how social and
political relations are established, reordered, and reproduced as the staff talk
and listen.

Postmodernism and Organizational Research

Much has been made of the multiple uses of the term 'postmodern' and the
different versions of it (Alvesson 1995; Thompson 1993). We will not here deny
the variation within the stream. Nevertheless, in contexts such as the present
one it can be helpful to produce common themes in which variations in key
authors' agendas are downplayed and commonalities highlighted. In postmodernism as a philosophically based research perspective, which is our major
concern in this chapter, the following, on the whole interrelated, set of ideas is
often emphasized: (a) the centrality of discourse—textuality—where the constitutive powers of language are emphasized and 'natural' objects are viewed as
discursively produced; (b) fragmented identities, emphasizing subjectivity as a
process and the death of the individual, autonomous, meaning-creating subject
where the discursive production of the individual replaces the conventional
'essentialistic' understanding of people; (c) the critique of the philosophy of
presence and representation where the indecidabilities of language take precedence over language as a mirror of reality and a means for the transport of
meaning; (d) the loss of foundations and the power of grand narratives where

an emphasis on multiple voices and local politics is favored over theoretical frameworks and large-scale political projects; (e) the power/knowledge connection where the impossibilities in separating power from knowledge are assumed and knowledge loses a sense of innocence and neutrality; (f) hyperreality—simulacra—replace the 'real world' where simulations take precedence in contemporary social order; and (g) research aims at resistance and indeterminacy where irony and play are preferred to rationality, predictability and order. Let us consider each briefly.

The Centrality of Discourse

Postmodernism grew out of French structuralism by taking seriously the linguistic turn in philosophy. In this sense postmodernists in the French tradition made a move on structuralist thought similar to the one Habermas made on ideological critique in the German tradition. As systematically distorted communication replaces false consciousness in critical theory, textual/discursive fields replaced the structure of the unconscious in postmodern thought. Both used these to fight a two front war, the objectivists on the one hand with their science aimed at predicting/controlling nature and people, and humanists on the other privileging the individual's reported experience and unique human rights, and advancing a naive version of human freedom. Focusing on language allowed a constructionism which denied the objectivist claim of certainty and objective truth and the humanists' reliance on essential claims which lead them to miss the social/linguistic politics of experience. As discussed later, the linguistic turn enabled a postmodern rejection of humanism through a critique of autonomy and unitary identities and a rejection of objectivism through a critique of the philosophy of presence and representation.

To note the primacy of discourse is to suggest that each person is born into ongoing discourses that have a material and continuing presence. The experience of the world is structured through the ways discourses lead one to attend to the world and provide particular unities and divisions. As a person learns to speak these discourses, they more properly speak to him or her in that available discourses position the person in the world in a particular way prior to the individual having any sense of choice. As discourses structure the world they at the same time structure the person's subjectivity, providing him/her with a particular social identity and way of being in the world. The person, *contra* humanism, is always social first and only mistakenly claims the personal self as the origin of experience.

There are two major versions of this theme. One emphasizes discourses in a special linguistic sense, where language in use is intrinsically related to meaning and perception. All perception and meaning entails a 'seeing as' and this 'seeing as' is described as a fundamental 'signifying' or 'language' relation. The distinctions historically carried in language enable a reproduction of specific 'seeing as' relations. Different discourses are always possible—although they may be more or less powerful or marginal. As a linguistic phenomenon, discourse is weakly coupled to material practices in this version (Weedon 1987). Another, Foucauldian version views discourses as systems of thought which are contingent upon as well as inform material practices which not only linguistically, but also practically through particular power techniques (clearly visible in prisons, psychiatric hospitals, schools, factories, and so forth), produce particular forms of subjectivity (Foucault 1977; 1980). In both versions, human subjectivity can be relatively open or closed. Discursive closure according to the first version is temporary, though often continually reproduced, while Foucault tends to emphasize a more systematic fixation of subjectivity as a result of the network of power relations in operation.

Many organizational researchers have used this insight productively. Most, but not all, have followed Foucault in their development. For example, Knights and Morgan used Foucault's discursive practices to show the construction of person and world in the discourse of corporate strategy. They argue that 'strategic discourse engages individuals in practices through which they discover the very "truth" of what they are—viz. "a strategic actor" ' (1991 : 260). They point at a number of power effects of corporate strategy discourse, including the sustaining and enhancement of the prerogatives of management, the generation of a sense of personal security for managers, the expression of a gendered masculinity for (male) management, and the facilitation and legitimization of the exercise of power.

Fragmented Identities

The position on the 'person' follows directly from the conception of discourse. Postmodernism rejects the notion of the autonomous, self-determining individual with a secure unitary identity as the centre of the social universe. Even though many other traditions have done so also (for example, behaviourists, structuralists), postmodernists have pushed this point strongly and in a sophisticated manner.

There are two versions of this critique of a secure unitary identity. The first suggests that the Western conception of *man* has always been a myth. It represents a rather ethnocentric idea. Freud's work on tensions and conflicts as central for the human psyche is used to show the growing awareness in Western thought of the fundamental inner fragmentation and inconsistency, but postmodernists go further in their deconstruction of the Western self-image. The conception of a unitary self is considered a fiction used to suppress those conflicts and privilege masculinity, rationality, vision, and control. To the extent that dominant discourses spoke the person (and produced the person as the origin of thought), the person gained a secure identity but participated in the reproduction of domination, thus marginalizing the other parts of the self and other groups. The sense of autonomy served to cover this subservience and give conflict a negative connotation.

The other version suggests that the view of the individual as coherent, integrated and (potentially) autonomous has become false in the contemporary historical and cultural situation. If identity is a social production, identity will be relatively stable in homogeneous and stable societies with few dominant discourses. In contemporary, heterogeneous, global, teleconnected societies the available discourses expand greatly. They also change rapidly. The individual comes to be spoken by so many discourses that fragmentation is virtually inevitable (Gergen 1991). As society becomes more fragmented and hyperreal or virtual (discourse is disconnected from any world reference, images reference images) the identity-stabilizing forces are lost.[5] Such a position suggests the possibility of tremendous freedom and opportunity for marginalized groups and aspects of each person to enter the discourse, but also insecurities which lead to normalization strategies in which people 'voluntarily' cling themselves to consumer identities offered by commercial forces or organizational selves through the orchestration of corporate cultures (Deetz 1995; Willmott 1994). This loose self is also very susceptible to manipulation and can be jerked about in the system, leading to ecstasy but domination without any dominant group as in Baudrillard's (1983; 1988) conception of simulation. These two versions—emphasizing human nature *per se* or only the contemporary, Western variant as discursively produced and fragmentary—are often a matter of emphasis (see Gergen 1991; 1992).

This view of the human subject however creates difficulties in developing political action. Flax (1990) for example shows the awkward position it leaves women in. If gender is treated as a social construction and dominant discourses have produced marginality and a sense of women being 'others'—taking all the negative terms in the linguistic system and discourse—then ridding society of strong gender ascriptions, making gender irrelevant in many situations, is a good idea. One should simply stop talking about 'men' and 'women', and stop reproducing this pervasive and powerful distinction (except in specific situations where it makes practical sense, i.e. in relationship to childbirth and a few diseases). But to accomplish such a move in the contemporary situation requires women to organize and show that gender is an issue across nearly all social situations. And similarly with the issue of experience: if women's experience arises out of an essential difference (bodily and/or socially produced), it cannot be denied as important and needing to be taken into account, but to make the essentialist argument denies social constructionism and can easily be used in a society where men have resources to further stigmatize women. Theoretical tensions are not easily escaped (see Fraser and Nicholson 1988). Ironically, however, this type of deep tension and inability to develop a single coherent position appears at the same time to weaken postmodern work and give it its reason for being. Such tensions have led some researchers to borrow from critical theory conceptions to add a clearer political program (see Martin 1990) and others to focus on more local forms of resistance (see Smircich and Calás 1987).

Important implications for organizational analyses follow from the destabilization of human actors and their organizing processes. Linstead suggests that 'organization then is continuously emergent, constituted and constituting, produced and consumed by subjects' and argues for investigations that move 'towards those processes which *shape* subjectivity rather than the process by which individual subjects act upon the word' (1993 : 60). Knights and Willmott (1989) have provided such work, demonstrating the way being subjected leads to particular forms of subjugation. Pringle (1988) has shown how the identity of a 'secretary' becomes constructed and reproduced. Deetz (1994c; 1998; 1997) has shown how the nature of 'knowledge-intensive' work situates the production of specific work identities. In a similar way, Townley (1993) applied Foucault's analysis to the discourse of human resource management. In this work, Townley argued that the basic unit of analysis in understanding human resources management was 'the nature of exchange embodied in the employment relation'. Since this relation in itself is indeterminant, the exchange relation is organized through imposing order on the inherently undecidable. The construction of knowledge in human resource management 'operates through rules of classification, ordering, and distribution; definition of activities; fixing of scales; and rules of procedure, which lead to the emergence of a distinct HRM discourse' (1993 : 541). This body of knowledge operates to objectify (determine) the person, thus both constraining and subordinating the person's fuller social and personal character.

The Critique of the Philosophy of Presence

Normative social science as well as most of us in everyday life treat the presence of objects as unproblematic and believe that the primary function of language is to re-present them. When asked what something is we try to define it and list its essential attributes. Postmodernists find such a position to be illusionary in the same way as the conception of identity. The *stuff* of the world only becomes an *object* in a specific relation to a being for whom it can be such an object. Linguistic and nonlinguistic practices thus are central to object production.

Such a position has been familiar for some time in works as varied as Mead, Wittgenstein, and Heidegger, but continues to lead to misunderstandings, the most common being the claim of relativism. The position is not, however, relativistic in any loose or subjective way. Those making the charge misunderstand the conception of objects or the strength of the conception of discourse. Most postmodernists are not concerned with the chance of being called relativistic, they are more concerned with the apparent stability of objects and the difficulty of unpacking the full range of activities that produce particular objects and sustain them.

As mentioned in the section of fragmented identities, postmodernists differ in the extent to which they describe discourse in textual versus a more extended form. On the whole, however, they start with Saussure's demonstration that the point of view creates the object. He meant this to attend to the importance of the value-laden nature of the system of distinctions in language, but the linguistic and nonlinguistic practices quickly interrelate. Let us use a brief example. A 'worker' is an object (as well as a subject) in the world, but neither God nor nature made a 'worker'. Two things are required for a 'worker' to exist: a language and set of practices which makes possible unities and divisions among people, and something to which such unities and divisions can be applied. The questions 'What is a worker really?', 'What is the essence of a worker?', 'What makes one a worker?' are not answerable by looking at the something that can be described as a worker, but are products of the linguistic and nonlinguistic practices that make this something into an object. In this sense, a worker is not an isolated thing. To have a worker already implies a division of labor, the presence of management ('nonworkers'). The 'essence' of worker is not the properties the 'object' contains but sets of relational systems including the division of labor. The focus on the object and object properties is the mistake; the attention should be to the relational systems which are not simply in the world but are a human understanding of the world, are discursive or textual. The meaning of 'worker' is not evident and present (contained there) but deferred to the sets of oppositions and junctures, the relations that make it like and unlike other things.

Since any something in the world may be constructed/expressed as many different objects, limited only by human creativity and readers of traces of past understandings, meaning can never be final but is always incomplete and indeterminate. The appearance of completeness and closure leads us to overlook both the politics in and of construction and the possibilities for understanding that are hidden behind the obvious. Language is thus central to the production of objects in that it provides the social/historical distinctions that provide unity and difference. Language cannot mirror the reality 'out there', or people's mental states (Shotter and Gergen 1989; 1994). Language is figural, metaphorical, full of contradictions and inconsistencies (Brown 1990; Cooper

89

and Burrell 1988). Meaning is not universal and fixed, but precarious, fragmented and local (Linstead and Grafton-Small 1992). Organizational researchers have used these conceptions to deconstruct objects of organizational life including the bounded concept of an organization itself. Perhaps among the most productive have been those studying accounting practices. The bottom line, profit and loss, expenses, and so forth have no reality without specific practices creating them (Hopwood 1987; Power and Laughlin 1992; Montagna 1986). Others have looked at knowledge and information (Boland 1987). And yet others have examined reporting practices (Sless 1988) and categories of people (Epstein 1988). Each of these shows the conditions necessary for objects to exist in organizational life. Any attempt at representation is thus always partial (one-sided and favoring a side). The making of distinction through language use is both a necessary condition of life with others, and yet inevitably limiting in that it hides important alternative distinctions (see Bourdieu 1984; 1991).

The Loss of Foundations and Master Narratives

The power of any position has been traditionally gathered from its grounding. This grounding could be to either a metaphysical foundation—such as an external world in empiricism, mental structures in rationalism or human nature in humanism—or a narrative, a story of history, such as Marxism's class struggle, social Darwinism's survival of the fittest, or market economy's invisible hand. With such groundings, positions are made to seem secure and inevitable and not opportunistic or driven by advantage. Certainly much organizational theory has been based on such appeals as has critical theory in its morally guided communicative action.

Again, as in the case of identity, postmodernists take two different but not incompatible stances, one categorical (valid throughout history and social context) and one interested in recent historical trends (thus overlapping the philosophy/periodization distinctions). Following the first position, foundations and legitimating narratives have always been a hoax. They have been used (usually unknowingly) to support a dominant view of the world and its order. Feminists, for example, have argued that the historical narrative has always been *history*. Empiricists' appeal to the nature of the external world covered the force of their own concepts (and those borrowed from elite groups), methods, instruments, activities, and reports in constructing that world.

Following the second position, other postmodernists note the growing social incredulity toward narratives and foundational moves. Lyotard (1984) showed the decline of grand narratives of 'spirit' and 'emancipation'. The proliferation of options and the growing political cynicism (or astuteness) of the public lead to a suspicion of legitimating moves. This conception is not far from Habermas's idea of legitimation crises in late capitalistic society (Habermas 1975). In Lyotard's sense perhaps all that is left is local narratives. Such a position has led to sensitive treatments of how stories in organizations connect to grand narratives and how different ones have a more local, situational character (see Martin 1990; Deetz 1997). Others have used this opening to display the false certainty in the master narratives in management (Jehenson 1984; Ingersoll and Adams 1986; Carter and Jackson 1987; Calás and Smircich 1991).

Not all postmodernists see this as necessarily positive. Certainly the decline of foundations and grand narratives takes away a primary prop of dominant groups' offer of security and certainty as a trade for subordination. But the replacement is not necessarily freedom and political possibility on the part of marginalized groups. Lyotard demonstrated the rise of 'performativity' where measures of means toward social ends become ends in themselves (see also Power 1994). Access to computers and information—contingent less upon knowledge integrated in the person ('scholarship') than upon financial resources—has become a significant source of knowledge and power. Along with this comes new forms of control directed not by a vision of society and social good but simply by more production and consumption.

Certainly the loss of grand integrative narratives has not been missed by management groups. One could perhaps say that corporate 'visions' and 'cultures' are strategic local narrative constructions to provide the integration and motivation in a pluralistic society formerly provided by wider social narratives. On the other hand one could say that these forms of management control represent large-scale systematic efforts which resemble grand narratives, though at a corporate level. Perhaps the development of management control can be seen as corporate grand narratives taking over some of the functions of political programs. The decline of vision, hope and community in politics has paved the way for management ideologies and practices that may fill parts of the vacuum (Deetz 1992). Postmodernists point to the precarious nature of this kind of project. Corporate cultures, for example, are seen as text and corporate members then become readers who 'bring awareness of other texts, other cultural forms, other evocations and explosions of meaning to their reading of any text, and enter into the text, changing its nature and reproducing it as they consume it' (Linstead and Grafton-Small 1992 : 344).

The difficulty in postmodernism with this, as in the concept of fragmented identities, is how to generate a political stance in regard to these developments. If one rejects an essentialist foundation and believes that more than local resistance is needed, some kind of combination between postmodernism and critical theory may well provide the best remaining option. We will come back to this.

Mats Alvesson and Stanley Deetz

The Knowledge/Power Connection

Within postmodern writings power is treated far different from most writings on organizations. Foucault has been the most explicit (Foucault 1977; 1980; see Clegg 1994). The power that is of interest is not that one possesses or acquires. Such appearances of power are the outcome of more fundamental power relations. Power resides in the discursive formation itself—the combination of a set of linguistic distinctions, ways of reasoning and material practices that together organize social institutions and produce particular forms of subjects. As mentioned before, language is here less strictly focused than in many other variants of postmodernism. Following the earlier example, the discourse that produces a 'manager' both empowers and disempowers the group of individuals formed as that object. It simultaneously provides a solidarity and interests and sets into play conflicts, material and symbolic resources, self-understandings, and the same for others such as professionals and workers. Power thus resides in the demarcations and the systems of discourse that sustain them, including material arrangements, for example, recruitment and selection procedures, office arrangements, reward and control structures, inclusion/exclusion in significant meetings, and so forth. One of the most useful terms entering into organizational studies from this has been Foucault's (1977) concept of discipline. The demarcations provide forms of normative behavior supported by claims of knowledge. Training, work routines, self-surveillance, and experts comprise discipline in that they provide resources for normalization. Normative experts in particular and the knowledge they create provide a cover for the arbitrary and advantaging discursive practices and facilitate normalization (Hollway 1984; 1991). Townley's (1993) work, already discussed, carefully showed how the development of the human resource expert and human resource knowledge was used as a way to 'determine' and subordinate employees. Such knowledge can also be utilized by employees to engage in self-surveillance and self-correction of attitudes and behaviors toward norms and expectations established by others (Deetz 1995: ch. 10; 1998).

Hyperreality

Postmodern writings vary in terms of how they handle the relation of language to the nonlinguistic realm of people and world. A strict linguistic focus and a strict critique of the philosophy of presence leave little interest in references to a pre-formed and relatively constant extra-textual reality. Most postmodernists treat the external as a kind of excess or 'otherness' which serves as a resource for formations and also prevents language systems from becoming closed and purely imaginary. While the referent has no specific character it always exceeds the objects made of it, and thus reminds one of the limited nature of all systems of representation and their fundamental indeterminacy (Cooper 1989). The presence of 'otherness' in the indeterminacy provides a moment to show the domination present in any system, to open it up, and to break the sealed self-referentiality of some textual systems.

Many existing linguistic or representational systems are shown to be self-referential by postmodernists. Such systems are not anchored in a socially produced as objective world, nor do they respect the excess of an outside. They produce the very same world that they appear to accurately represent. For example, contemporary media and information systems have the capacity to rapidly construct images which replace, more than represent, an outside world. Such systems can dominate the scene with an array of reproduced imaginary worlds. The referent disappears as anything more than another sign; thus signs only reference other signs; images are images of images. Such systems can become purely self-referential, or what Baudrillard calls *simulations* (see Deetz 1994b). In such a world, in Baudrillard's analysis, signs are disconnected from opening a relation to the world and the 'model' response to a 'model' world replaces responsive action in an actual changing one. Signs reach the structural limit of representation by referencing only themselves with little relation to any exterior or interior. Baudrillard expresses this relation as follows:

The form-sign [present in a monopolistic code] describes an entirely different organization: the signified and the referent are now abolished to the sole profit of the play of signifiers, of a generalized formalization in which the code no longer refers back to any subjective or objective 'reality', but to its own logic ... The sign no longer designates anything at all. It approaches its true structural limit which is to refer back only to other signs. All reality then becomes the place of semi-urgical manipulation, of a structural simulation. (1975 : 127–8)

The world as understood is not really a fiction in this situation since there is no 'real' outside which it portrays falsely or which can be used to correct it. It is properly imaginary; it has no opposite, no outside. Baudrillard used the example of the difference between feigning and simulating an illness to show the character of this postmodern representation: 'feigning or dissimulation leaves the reality principle intact; the difference is always clear, it is only masked; whereas simulation threatens the difference between "true" and "false", between "real" and "imaginary". Since the simulator produces "true" symptoms, is he ill or not? He cannot be treated objectively either as ill, or not ill' (1983 : 5). These ideas have inspired some organization studies emphasizing the imaginary character of modern organizations (Berg 1989; Alvesson 1990; Deetz 1994c; 1995). As is common with postmodern ideas in organization theory, these studies do not follow the source of inspiration to its full (extreme) consequences.

Mats Alvesson and Stanley Deetz

Research as Resistance and Indeterminacy

The role of postmodern research is very different from more traditional roles assigned to social science. It primarily serves to attempt to open up the indeterminacy that modern social science, everyday conceptions, routines, and practices have closed off. The result is a kind of anti-positive knowledge (Knights 1992). The primary methods are deconstruction and resistance readings and genealogy. These terms have been used in many different ways and in the short space here we can do little beyond a sketch. Deconstruction works primarily to critique the philosophy of presence by recalling the suppressed terms (the deferred term) which provides the system and thus which allows the positive terms to appear to stand for an existing object. When the suppressed term is given value both the dependency of the positive term on the negative is shown and a third term is recovered which shows a way of world making that is not dependent on the opposition of the first two (see Cooper 1989; Martin 1990; Calás and Smircich 1991; Mumby and Putnam 1992). The resistance reading is less narrowly focused on terms. It both demonstrates the construction activity and provides indeterminacy based in the excess of the outside. The positive and the polar construction are both displayed as acts of domination, subjectivity doing violence to the world and limiting itself in the process. In this move, conflicts that were suppressed by the positive are brought back to redecision and the conflictual field out of which objects are formed is recovered for creative redetermination—constant dedifferentiation and redifferentiation. Given the power of closure and the way it enters common sense and routines, especially in simulations, such rereadings require a particular form of rigor and imagination. The rereadings are formed out of a keen sense of irony, a serious playfulness, and often guided by the pleasure one has in being freed from the dull compulsions of a world made too easy and too violent. A good example of such readings is Calás and Smircich's (1988) account of a mainstream positivist journal article—where they start with the question 'Why should we believe in this author?' and then point at the rhetorical tricks involved in order to persuade the reader. Another interesting example is Sangren's (1992) critical review of Clifford and Marcus's *Writing Culture* (1986). Sangren, drawing upon Bourdieu (1979), uses their points about the politics of representation—intended to indicate the problems of ethnographies in mirroring cultures and exemplified through important anthropological works—against themselves, showing how representations of Clifford, Marcus and co-authors of earlier work can be seen in terms of politics. Particular kinds of representations are used that create the impression that earlier works are flawed and that there is a large and open space for novel contributions (and the career options) of the new heterodoxy (Clifford, Marcus et al.) and their more informed view on the politics of representation.

The point of social science is not to get it right but to challenge guiding assumptions, fixed meanings and relations, and to reopen the formative capacity of human beings in relation to others and the world, qualities that Gergen (1978) and Astley (1985) displayed as essential to any important theory. As Sangren (1992) illustrates, the challenge of dogma, fixed ideas and reopenings easily implies new dogmas, fixations and closures. Postmodernism is in no way immune to such implications (Alvesson and Sköldberg 1996).

One outcome of the themes reviewed above—in particular the critique of the philosophy of presence and the loss of master narratives, but also hyperreality and the focus on resistance—is a strong current interest in experimenting with different styles. This is prominent in anthropology (Clifford and Marcus 1986; Geertz 1988; Marcus and Fisher 1986; Rose 1990) but also in organization theory (for example, Calás and Smircich 1991; Jeffcutt 1993; Linstead and Grafton-Small 1990). Typically, 'realist' ways of writing are superseded or complemented by other styles, for example, ironic, self-ironic or impressionistic ones. In an investigation of texts in organizational culture and symbolism, Jeffcutt shows how it is 'distinguished by heroic quests for closure; being dominated by authors adopting representational styles that privilege epic and romantic narratives over tragic and ironic forms. These representational strategies expose an overriding search for unity and harmony that suppresses division and conflict' (1993 : 32). Perhaps the inspiration to develop new ways of writing will turn out to be one of the most powerful and interesting contributions of postmodernism.

Relating Critical Theory and Postmodernism

Critical theory and postmodernism, as has been shown, are both alike and different. Each has much to contribute to organizational studies, and we believe that they have a contribution to make together. Without considering postmodern themes, critical theory easily becomes unreflective in regard to cultural elitism and modern conditions of power; and without incorporating some measure of critical theory thought—or something similar that provides direction and social relevance—postmodernism simply becomes esoteric. Both draw attention to the social/historical/political construction of knowledge, people, and social relations, including how each of these appears in contemporary organizations. And they share a view that domination is aided, and both people and organizations lose much, if we overlook these construction activities by treating the existing world as natural, rational and neutral. In critical theory's language, the concern is reification; in postmodernism, the philosophy of presence. Based on this naturalization and freezing of contemporary social reality, important conflicts—options for reconsiderations and questioning—are lost and different groups of people as well as vital values are marginalized and disadvantaged. Both see organizations and the social sciences that support them as relying increasingly on a form of instrumental reasoning privileging the means over ends and aiding dominant groups' ability to invisibly accomplish their ends. Habermas describes this in terms of 'instrumental technical reasoning', Lyotard in terms of 'performativity'.

The differences are also important. Critical theory sees the response in terms of an expanded form of morally guided communicative reasoning leading to individual autonomy and better social choices. Through reflections on the ways ideology—taken for granted cultural ideas as well as specific messages engineered by powerful agencies—enters into person/world/knowledge construction and by providing more open forums of expression and a type of discourse aimed at mutual understanding, there is hope for the production of social consensus and social agreements that better fulfill human needs. The grand narrative of enlightenment might, according to critical theory, yet be advanced. But postmodernism rejects such reflection and consensus, suspecting the replacement of old illusions with new ones, and the creation of new elites and new forms of marginalizations. Critical theory replies: without reflection, consensus and rationality, there is no politics, no agenda for a constructive alternative. Postmodernism counters: politics are by necessity local and situational; responsiveness is more important than systematic planning. Critical theory responds: local politics is too weak to confront system-wide gender and class dominations as well as global poverty and environmental problems. Postmodernism maintains: organizing against domination both props up and solidifies dominant groups; it creates its own forms of domination. The difference is in a sense the same as between a push and pull theory. Critical theory wants us to act and provides direction and orchestration; postmodernism believes that such a move will be limited by the force of our own subjective domination and encourages us to get out of the way and allow the world to pull us to feelings and thought heretofore unknown; but critical theory does not have enough faith to let go. And so on.

But there are ways to think them both at once, though not necessarily through some new synthesis. We have a need for both conflict and consensus, for resistance and plans. The issue is not which but the balance, choosing the right moments (Deetz 1992). To say that consensus implies domination means not that we should not make the best decisions we can together, but that we need to continue to look for domination and be ready to move on. To say that resistance lacks a clear politics does not mean that it is not doing something important and ultimately may be the only way we can see through dominations that we like or that benefit *and* limit us.

One option is thus to work with unresolved tensions within a text where one follows different themes of postmodernism and critical theory without attempting synthesis, working with the tensions and contrastive images. Examples of this include work by Martin (1990; 1995), Knights and Willmott (1989) and Deetz (1994c; 1998). Another version is to allow space for various discrete voices in texts through organizing these around conversations between various theoretical perspectives or interest groups (Alvesson and Willmott 1996; Chapter 7) or to conduct multiple interpretations of the same phenomenon (Alvesson 1996; Morgan 1986), such as interpreting a phenomenon from both critical theory and postmodernist (and perhaps other) positions. Another way of combining insights from critical theory and postmodernism is to see both as metatheories useful as inspiration for reflexivity rather than as theories directly relevant for guiding and interpreting studies of substantive matters (Alvesson and Sköldberg 1996). Still another option is to restrict the approach to the careful study of language use and communicative practices in 'real' social settings, which is done by discourse and conversation analysis (I. Parker 1992; Potter and Wetherell 1987) and constructivists (Shotter and Gergen 1994; Steier 1991). Such studies can be used to sensitize us to the power effects of language and ground Habermasian and postmodernist ideas in portions of organizational reality (Forester 1992). Such a language focus avoids the philosophy of presence but maintains an empirical context.

Perhaps the greatest criticism of critical theory and even more so postmodernism is the lack of clear empirical studies. Part of the criticism arises from a narrow view of the notion of 'empirical', but researchers can still be faulted for doing many conceptual essays without extended field experience and reports. Critical theory's and postmodernism's strong critique of empiric*ism*, and their emphasis on data as constructions open to a multitude of interpretations, do not mean that reflective empirical work is not worth doing. Many texts have limited feelings for organizational contexts and the lives of real people. Much can be gained by allowing organizational participants to 'say something' that is not immediately domesticated by theories locating the material in an all too predictable 'bureaucracy', 'patriarchy', 'capitalism', 'managerialism' pejorative discourse, an all-embracing Foucauldian power concept, or a pacification and fragmentation of subjects as mere appendices of discourses. An empirical turn may also reduce the tendency of negativity in much of critical theory and some postmodernism. Having said this, we must acknowledge that recently more empirical work has been done, particularly with a critical theory orientation (for example, Rosen 1985; 1988; Knights and Willmott 1987; 1992; Alvesson 1996) but also using postmodern themes (Martin 1990; 1995; Deetz 1998; 1997). What is lacking, in particular, is serious efforts to ground ideas of local resistance in specific empirical contexts. There is a lot of talk of resistance in the postmodernist industry, but it is highly theoretical and generalized and remains quite esoteric. We need to go further than repeat programmatic slogans and use and refine the idea in close contact with the lives of subjects in organizational settings.

We will for space reasons not indulge in further treatment of these responses to various critiques of traditional ways of doing research brought forward by postmodern authors in particular, but in many cases also by authors not waving the postmodern flag. Suffice to say that there are various paths that address the middle ground between more traditional realist and hermeneutic epistemologies—where there is space for empirical studies of organizational phenomena—on the one hand and a postmodern philosophy threatening to turn all social science into a quite esoteric literary criticism on the other hand.

....

Notes

1. Quite often when people talk about postmodernism and its shadow modernism, the former position is a kind of synthesis and social science adaptation of what has been expressed by the gurus referred to. This means that there is not necessarily a one-to-one relationship between what one can find clear support for in key texts of Derrida, Foucault, etc. and what is summarized as a postmodernist position. We will here follow this practice and hold back doubts regarding the reasons for summarizing partly quite different authors and intellectual themes (cf. Alvesson 1995)—a move for which these people would probably have little sympathy.
2. We should note before going on that one of the functions of histories is to produce a number of scholars/texts (a) as a school of thought, and (b) as new or different both for the professional advantages of its practitioners and as a way of demarking a community. It is interesting to note that this history production is important not for forerunners or gurus—who often resist labels such as postmodernism—but for followers and supporters. The political and identity-confirming advantages are clearest for these people.
3. As on many issues, there are variations here amongst postmodernists. Derrida does not directly address the issue. Foucault comes closest in supporting a critical theory view against social engineering as a solution, although he is not without ambiguity on this point. Lyotard appears to have mixed feelings about this matter. The majority of social science authors advocating postmodernism share the skepticism of critical theory on this point.
4. The discussion in this section is adapted from Deetz's (1996) discussion of the problems of Burrell and Morgan's (1979) paradigm divisions. Several revisions of Burrell and Morgan are crucial. The term 'normative' is used to describe most of the same research positions that Burrell and Morgan called 'functionalist'. This frees the description from a particular school of sociological thought and draws attention to both their search for the normal, the regularity, and the value-laden nature of

their use in 'normalizing' people, and the existing social conditions. 'Dialogic' draws attention to the relational aspect of 'postmodernism' and avoids the periodicity issue. Note too that critical work is shown with more affinity to 'normative' work (rather than the total opposition in Burrell and Morgan's 'functionalist/radical-humanist' configuration) because of their directive qualities in contrast to the strong 'otherness' guidance in interpretative and dialogic work. The *a priori/* elite—local/emergent dimension replaces the subjective–objective dimension in Burrell and Morgan. The subject/object dualism on which their dimension was based is severely flawed. First it tends to reproduce the subject–object dualism that is present in the philosophies underlying 'normative' research but not the other positions. Second, it misplaces normative research, overlooking its subjectivity in domination of nature and in defining people's experience for them. And third, it fails to highlight the constructionist quality of all research programs.

5. This is then basically a sociological or periodization type of postmodern psychology, and is also to some extent used by authors who do not see themselves as postmodernist or talk about postmodernism, for example, Berger et al. (1973) or Lasch (1978; 1984).

References

Abercrombie, N., Hill, S. and Turner, B. S. (1980). *The Dominant Ideology Thesis*. London: Allen and Unwin.

Alvesson, M. (1987). *Organization Theory and Technocratic Consciousness: Rationality, Ideology, and Quality of Work*. Berlin, New York: de Gruyter.

—— (1990). 'Organization: from substance to image?', *Organization Studies*, 11: 373–94.

—— (1993a). *Cultural Perspectives on Organizations*. Cambridge: Cambridge University Press.

—— (1993b). 'The play of metaphors', in J. Hassard and M. Parker (eds), *Postmodernism and Organizations*. London: Sage.

—— (1995). 'The meaning and meaninglessness of postmodernism: some ironic remarks', *Organization Studies*, 15.

—— (1996). *Communication, Power and Organization*. Berlin/New York: de Gruyter.

Alvesson, M. and Sköldberg, K. (1996). *Towards a Reflexive Methodology*. London: Sage.

Alvesson, M. and Willmott, H. (eds) (1992). *Critical Management Studies*. London: Sage.

—— —— (1995). 'Strategic management as domination and emancipation: from planning and process to communication and praxis', in C. Stubbart and P. Shrivastava (eds), *Advances in Strategic Management*, vol. 11. Greenwich, CT: JAI Press.

—— —— (1996). *Making Sense of Management: a Critical Analysis*. London: Sage.

Angus, I. (1992). 'The politics of common sense: articulation theory and critical communication studies', in S. Deetz (ed.)., *Communication Yearbook 15*. Newbury Park, CA: Sage, pp. 535–70.

Apel, K.-O. (1979). *Toward a Transformation of Philosophy*, translated by G. Adey and D. Frisby. London: Routledge & Kegan Paul.

Astley, G. (1985). 'Administrative science as socially constructed truth', *Administrative Science Quarterly*, 30: 497–513.

Baudrillard, J. (1975). *The Mirror of Production*, translated by M. Poster. St Louis: Telos Press.

—— (1983). *Simulations*. New York: Semiotext(e).

—— (1988). 'Simulacra and simulations', in M. Poster (ed.)., *Jean Baudrillard: Selected Writings*. Stanford: Stanford University Press, pp. 166–84.

Benson, J. K. (1977). 'Organizations: a dialectical view', *Administrative Science Quarterly*, 22: 1–21.

Berg, P. O. (1989). 'Postmodern management? From facts to fiction in theory and practice', *Scandinavian Journal of Management*, 5: 201–17.

Berger, P., Berger, B. and Kellner, H. (1973). *The Homeless Mind: Modernization and Consciousness*. New York: Random House.

Boland, R. (1987). 'The in-formation of information systems', in R. Boland and R. Hirschheim (eds), *Critical Issues in Information Systems Research*. New York: Wiley, pp. 363–79.

Bourdieu, P. (1979). *Outline of a Theory of Practice*. Cambridge: Cambridge University Press.

Bourdieu, P. (1984). *Distinctions: a Social Critique of the Judgement of Taste*. Cambridge: Cambridge University Press.

Bourdieu, P. (1991). *Language and Symbolic Power*. Cambridge, MA: Harvard University Press.

Braverman, H. (1974). *Labor and Monopoly Capital*. New York: Monthly Review Press.

Brown, R. H. (1990). 'Rhetoric, textuality, and the postmodern turn in sociological theory', *Sociological Theory*, 8: 188–97.

Burawoy, M. (1979). *Manufacturing Consent*. Chicago: University of Chicago Press.

Burawoy, M. (1985). *The Politics of Production: Factory Regimes under Capitalism and Socialism*. London: Verso.

Burrell, G. (1994). 'Modernism, postmodernism and organizational analysis 4: the contribution of Jürgen Habermas', *Organization Studies*, 15: 1–19.

Burrell, G. and Morgan, G. (1979). *Sociological Paradigms and Organizational Analysis*. Aldershot: Gower.

Calás, M. and Smircich, L. (1988). 'Reading leadership as a form of cultural analysis', in J. G. Hunt et al. (eds), *Emerging Leadership Vistas*. Lexington, MA: Lexington Books.

—— —— (1991). 'Voicing seduction to silence leadership', *Organization Studies*, 12: 567–602.

—— —— (1992a). 'Feminist theories and the social consequences of organizational research', in A. Mills and P. Tancred (eds), *Gendering Organizational Analysis*. London: Sage.

—— —— (1992b). 'Rewriting gender into organizational theorizing: directions from feminist Perspectives', in M. Reed and M. Hughes (eds), *Rethinking Organization: New Directions in Organizational Theory and Analysis*. London: Sage.

Carter, P. and Jackson, N. (1987). 'Management, myth, and metatheory—from scarcity to postscarcity', *International Studies of Management and Organization*, 17(3).: 64–89.

Clegg, S. (1989). *Frameworks of Power*. London: Sage.

—— (1990). *Modern Organization: Organization Studies in the Postmodern World*. London: Sage.

Clegg, S. (1994). 'Weber and Foucault: social theory for the study of organizations', *Organization*, 1: 149–78.

Clegg, S. and Dunkerley, D. (1980). *Organization, Class and Control*. London: Routledge & Kegan Paul.

Clifford, J. and Marcus, G. E. (eds) (1986). *Writing Culture*. Berkeley, CA: University of California Press.

Cooper, R. (1989). 'Modernism, postmodernism and organizational analysis 3: the contribution of Jacques Derrida', *Organization Studies*, 10: 479–502.

Cooper, R. and Burrell, G. (1988). 'Modernism, postmodernism and organizational analysis: an introduction', *Organization Studies*, 9: 91–112.

Czarniawska-Joerges, B. (1988). *Ideological Control in Nonideological Organizations*. New York: Praeger.

Deetz, S. (1985). 'Critical-cultural research: new sensibilities and old realities', *Journal of Management*, 11(2).: 121–36.

—— (1992). *Democracy in the Age of Corporate Colonization: Developments in Communication and the Politics of Everyday Life*. Albany, NY: State University of New York Press.

—— (1994a). 'The future of the discipline: the challenges, the research, and the social contribution', in S. Deetz (ed.)., *Communication Yearbook 17*. Newbury Park, CA: Sage. pp. 565–600.

—— (1994b). 'Representative practices and the political analysis of corporations', in B. Kovacic (ed.)., *Organizational Communication: New Perspectives*. Albany, NY: State University of New York Press, pp. 209–42.

—— (1994c). 'The micro-politics of identity formation in the workplace: the case of a knowledge intensive firm', *Human Studies*, 17: 23–44.

—— (1994d). 'The new politics of the workplace: ideology and other unobtrusive controls', in H. Simons and M. Billig (eds), *After Postmodernism: Reconstructing Ideology Critique*. Newbury Park, CA: Sage, pp. 172–99.

—— (1995). *Transforming Communication, Transforming Business: Building Responsible and Responsive Workplaces*. Cresskill, NJ: Hampton Press.

—— (1996). 'Describing differences in approaches to organizational science: rethinking Burrell and Morgan and their legacy', *Organization Science*.

—— (1997). 'The business concept, discursive power, and managerial control in a knowledge-intensive company: a case study', in B. Sypher (ed.)., *Case Studies in Organizational Communication*, 2nd edn. New York: Guilford Press.

—— (1998). 'Discursive formations, strategized subordination, and self-surveillance: an empirical case', in A. McKinlay and K. Starkey (eds), *Managing Foucault: a Reader*. London: Sage.

Deetz, S. and Kersten, A. (1983). 'Critical models of interpretative research', in L. Putnam and M. Pacanowsky (eds), *Communication and Organizations*. Beverly Hills, CA: Sage.

Deetz, S. and Mumby, D. (1990). 'Power, discourse, and the workplace: reclaiming the critical tradition in communication studies in organizations', in J. Anderson (ed.)., *Communication Yearbook 13*. Newbury Park, CA: Sage, pp. 18–47.

Edwards, R. (1979). *Contested Terrain: the Transformation of the Workplace in the Twentieth Century.* New York: Basic Books.

Epstein, C. (1988). *Deceptive Distinctions.* New Haven: Yale University Press.

Featherstone, M. (ed.). (1988). *Postmodernism.* Newbury Park, CA: Sage.

Ferguson, K. (1984). *The Feminist Case against Bureaucracy.* Philadelphia: Temple University Press.

Fischer, F. (1990). *Technocracy and the Politics of Expertise.* Newbury Park, CA: Sage.

Fischer, F. and Sirianni, C. (eds) (1984). *Critical Studies in Organization and Bureaucracy.* Philadelphia: Temple University Press.

Flax, J. (1990). *Thinking Fragments: Psychoanalysis, Feminism and Postmodernism in the Contemporary West.* Berkeley, CA: University of California Press.

—— (1983). 'Critical theory and organizational analysis', in G. Morgan (ed.)., *Beyond Method.* Beverly Hills, CA: Sage.

—— (ed.). (1985). *Critical Theory and Public Life.* Cambridge, MA: MIT Press.

—— (1989). *Planning in the Face of Power.* Berkeley, CA: University of California Press.

—— (1992). Critical ethnography: on fieldwork in a Habermasian way', in M. Alvesson and H. Willmott (eds), *Critical Management Studies.* London: Sage.

—— (1993). *Critical Theory, Public Policy, and Planning Practice.* Albany: State University of New York Press.

Foster, H. (1983). *Postmodern Culture.* London: Pluto Press.

Foucault, M. (1977). *Discipline and Punish: the Birth of the Prison*, translated by A. S. Smith. New York: Random House.

—— (1980). *Power/Knowledge.* New York: Pantheon.

—— (1983). 'Structuralism and post-structuralism: an interview with Michel Foucault, by G. Raulet', *Telos*, 55: 195–211.

—— (1988). 'Technologies of the self', in L. Martin, H. Gutman and P. Hutton (eds), *Technologies of the Self.* Amherst, MA: University of Massachusetts Press, pp. 16–49.

Fraser, N. (1987). 'What's critical about critical theory? The case of Habermas and gender', in S. Benhabib and D. Cornell (eds), *Feminism as Critique.* Cambridge: Polity Press.

Fraser, N. and Nicholson, L. (1988). 'Social criticism without philosophy: an encounter between feminism and postmodernism', *Theory, Culture & Society*, 5: 373–94.

Frost, P. J. (1980). 'Toward a radical framework for practicing organizational science', *Academy of Management Review*, 5: 501–7.

—— (1987). 'Power, politics, and influence', in F. Jablin, L. Putnam, K. Roberts and L. Porter (eds), *Handbook of Organizational Communication.* Newbury Park, CA: Sage.

Geertz, C. (1988). *Work and Lives: the Anthropologist as Author.* Cambridge: Polity Press.

Gergen, K. (1978). 'Toward generative theory', *Journal of Personality and Social Psychology*, 31: 1344–60.

—— (1991). *The Saturated Self: Dilemmas of Identity in Contemporary Life.* New York: Basic Books.

—— (1992). 'Organization theory in the postmodern era', in M. Reed and M. Hughes (eds), *Rethinking Organizations*. London: Sage.

Giddens, A. (1979). *Central Problems in Social Theory*. London: Macmillan.

Gramsci, A. (1929–35). *Selections from the Prison Notebooks*, translated by Q. Hoare and G.N. Smith. New York: International, 1971.

Habermas, J. (1970). *Toward a Rational Society*. London: Heinemann.

—— (1971). *Knowledge and Human Interests*, translated by J. Shapiro. London: Heinemann.

—— (1975). *Legitimation Crisis*, translated by T. McCarthy. Boston: Beacon Press.

—— (1983). 'Modernity—an incomplete project', in H. Foster (ed.)., *Postmodern Culture*. London: Pluto Press.

—— (1984). *The Theory of Communicative Action. Vol. 1: Reason and the Rationalization of Society*, translated by T. McCarthy. Boston: Beacon.

—— (1987). *The Theory of Communicative Action. Vol. 2: Lifeworld and System*, translated by T. McCarthy. Boston: Beacon Press.

Hassard, J. and Parker, M. (eds) (1993). *Postmodernism and Organizations*. London: Sage.

Hearn, J. and Parkin, W. (1987). *'Sex' at 'Work': the Power and Paradox of Organisation Sexuality*. Brighton: Wheatsheaf.

Heckscher, C. (1995). *White-collar Blues: Management Loyalties in an Age of Corporate Restructuring*. New York: Basic Books.

Hodge, H., Kress, G. and Jones, G. (1979). 'The ideology of middle management', in R. Fowler, H. Hodge, G. Kress and T. Trew (eds), *Language and Control*. London: Routledge & Kegan Paul.

Hollway, W. (1984). 'Fitting work: psychological assessment in organizations', in J. Henriques, W. Hollway, C. Urwin, C. Venn and V. Walkerdine (eds), *Changing the Subject*. New York: Methuen, pp. 26–59.

—— (1991). *Work Psychology and Organizational Behavior*. London: Sage.

Hopwood, A. (1987). 'The archaeology of accounting systems', *Accounting, Organizations and Society*, 12: 207–34.

Horkheimer, M. and Adorno, T. (1979). *The Dialectics of Enlightenment* (1947).. London: Verso.

Ingersoll, V. and Adams, G. (1986). 'Beyond organizational boundaries: exploring the managerial myth', *Administration and Society*, 18: 360–81.

Jeffcutt, P. (1993). 'From interpretation to representation', in J. Hassard and M. Parker (eds), *Postmodernism and Organizations*. London: Sage.

Jehenson, R. (1984). 'Effectiveness, expertise and excellence as ideological fictions: a contribution to a critical phenomenology of the formal organization', *Human Studies*, 7: 3–21.

Jermier, J. (1985). '"When the sleeper wakes": a short story extending themes in radical organization theory', *Journal of Management*, 11(2).: 67–80.

Kellner, D. (1988). 'Postmodernism as social theory: some challenges and problems', *Theory, Culture and Society*, 5(2–3).: 239–69.

Knights, D. (1992). 'Changing spaces: the disruptive impact of a new epistemological location for the study of management', *Academy of Management Review*, 17: 514–36.

Knights, D. and Morgan, G. (1991). 'Corporate strategy, organizations, and subjectivity: a critique', *Organization Studies*, 12: 251–73.

Knights, D. and Willmott, H. (1985). 'Power and identity in theory and practice', *Sociological Review*, 33: 22–46.

—— (1987). 'Organizational culture as management strategy', *International Studies of Management and Organization*, 17(3).: 40–63.

—— (1989). 'Power and subjectivity at work: from degradation to subjugation in social relations', *Sociology*, 23: 535–58.

—— (1992). 'Conceptualizing leadership processes: a study of senior managers in a financial services company', *Journal of Management Studies*, 29: 761–82.

Kunda, G. (1992). *Engineering Culture: Control and Commitment in a High-Tech Corporation*. Philadelphia: Temple University Press.

Lasch, C. (1978). *The Culture of Narcissism*. New York: Norton.

—— (1984). *The Minimal Self*. London: Picador.

Lazega, E. (1992). *Micropolitics of Knowledge: Communication and Indirect Control in Workgroups*. New York: Aldine de Gruyter.

Linstead, S. (1993). 'Deconstruction in the study of organizations', in J. Hassard and M. Parker (eds), *Postmodernism and Organizations*. London: Sage.

Linstead, S. and Grafton-Small, R. (1990). 'Theory as artefact: artefact as theory', in P. Gagliardi (ed.)., *Symbols and Artefacts: Views of the Corporate Landscape*. Berlin/New York: de Gruyter.

—— —— (1992). 'On reading organizational culture', *Organization Studies*, 13: 331–55.

Lukes, S. (1974). *Power: a Radical View*. London: Macmillan.

Lukács, G. (1971). *History and Class Consciousness*, translated by R. Livingstone. Cambridge, MA: MIT Press.

Lyotard, J.-F. (1984). *The Postmodern Condition: a Report on Knowledge*, translated by G. Bennington and B. Massumi. Minneapolis: University of Minnesota Press.

Lyytinen, K. and Hirschheim, R. (1988). 'Information systems as rational discourse: an application of Habermas's theory of communicative action', *Scandinavian Journal of Management*, 4: 19–30.

Marcus, G. and Fischer, M. (1986). *Anthropology as Cultural Critique*. Chicago: University of Chicago Press.

Margolis, S. (1989). 'Postscript on modernism and postmodernism: both', *Theory, Culture & Society*, 6: 5–30.

Martin, J. (1990). 'Deconstructing organizational taboos: the suppression of gender conflict in organizations', *Organization Science*, 11: 339–59.

Martin, J. (1995). 'The organization of exclusion: the institutionalization of sex inequality, gendered faculty jobs, and gendered knowledge in organizational theory and research', *Organization*, 1: 401–31.

Marx, K. (1844). *Economic and Political Manuscripts of 1844*, translated by M. Miligan. New York: International, 1964.

—— (1867). *Das Kapital*, Bd 1. Berlin: Dietz, 1967.

Montagna, P. (1986). 'Accounting rationality and financial legitimation', *Theory and Society*, 15: 103–38.

Morgan, G. (1986). *Images of Organization*. Newbury Park, CA: Sage.

Mumby, D. K. (1987). 'The political function of narrative in organizations', *Communication Monographs*, 54: 113–27.

—— (1988). *Communication and Power in Organizations: Discourse, Ideology, and Domination*. Norwood, NJ: Ablex.

Mumby, D. K. and Putnam, L. (1992). 'The politics of emotion: a feminist reading of bounded rationality', *Academy of Management Review*, 17: 465–86.

Offe, C. and Wiesenthal, H. (1980). 'Two logics of collective action: theoretical notes on social class and organizational form', in M. Zeitlin (ed.)., *Political Power and Social Theory*, vol. 1. Greenwich, CT: JAI Press.

Parker, I. (1992). *Discourse Dynamics*. London: Routledge.

Parker, M. (1992). 'Post-modern organizations or postmodern organization theory?', *Organization Studies*, 13: 1–17.

—— (1993). 'Life after Jean-François', in J. Hassard and M. Parker (eds), *Postmodernism and Organizations*. London: Sage.

Peters, T. (1987). *Thriving on Chaos*. New York: Alfred A. Knopf.

Potter, J. and Wetherell, M. (1987). *Discourse and Social Psychology: Beyond Attitudes and Behaviour*. London: Sage.

Power, M. (1994). 'The audit society', in A. Hopwood and P. Miller (eds), *Accounting as Social and Institutional Practice*. Cambridge: Cambridge University Press, pp. 299–316.

Power, M. and Laughlin, R. (1992). 'Critical theory and accounting', in M. Alvesson and H. Willmott (eds), *Critical Management Studies*. London: Sage, pp. 113–35.

Pringle, R. (1988). *Secretaries Talk: Sexuality, Power and Work*. London: Verso.

Rose, D. (1990). *Living the Ethnographic Life*. Newbury Park, CA: Sage.

Rosen, M. (1985). 'Breakfast at Spiro's: dramaturgy and dominance', *Journal of Management*, 11(2).: 31–48.

—— (1988). 'You asked for it: Christmas at the Bosses' expense', *Journal of Management Studies*, 25(5).: 463–80.

Salaman, G. (1981). *Class and the Corporation*. Glasgow: Fontana.

Sangren, S. (1992). 'Rhetoric and the authority of ethnography', *Current Anthropology*, 33(Supplement).: 277–96.

Sarup, M. (1988). *An Introductory Guide to Post-Structuralism and Post-Modernism*. Hemel Hempstead: Harvester Wheatsheaf.

Shotter, J. and Gergen, K. (eds) (1989). *Texts of Identity*. London: Sage.

Shotter, J. and Gergen, K. (1994). 'Social construction: knowledge, self, others, and continuing the conversation', in S. Deetz (ed.)., *Communication Yearbook 17*. Newbury Park, CA: Sage.

Shrivastava, P. (1986). 'Is strategic management ideological?', *Journal of Management*, 12.

—— (1995). 'Ecocentric management for a risk society', *Academy of Management Review*, 20: 118–37.

Sievers, B. (1986). 'Beyond the surrogate of motivation', *Organization Studies*, 7:335–52.

Sless, D. (1988). 'Forms of control', *Australian Journal of Communication*, 14: 57–69.

Smircich, L. and Calás, M. (1987). 'Organizational culture: a critical assessment', in F. Jablin, L. Putnam, K. Roberts and L. Porter (eds), *Handbook of Organizational Communication*. Newbury Park, CA: Sage, pp. 228–63.

Stablein, R. and Nord, W. (1985). 'Practical and emancipatory interests in organizational symbolism', *Journal of Management*, 11(2).: 13–28.

Stead, W. E. and Stead, J. G. (1992). *Management for a Small Planet*. Newbury Park, CA: Sage.

Steffy, B. and Grimes, A. (1992). 'Personnel/organizational psychology: a critique of the discipline', in M. Alvesson and H. Willmott (eds), *Critical Management Studies*. London: Sage.

Steier, F. (1991). 'Reflexivity and methodology: an ecological constructionism', in F. Steier (ed.), *Research and Reflexivity*. London: Sage.

Storey, J. (1983). *Managerial Prerogative and the Question of Control*. London: Routledge & Kegan Paul.

Thompson, J. (1984). *Studies in the Theory of Ideology*. Berkeley, CA: University of California Press.

Thompson, J. B. and Held, D. (eds) (1982). *Habermas: Critical Debates*. London: Macmillan.

Thompson, P. (1993). 'Post-modernism: fatal distraction', in J. Hassard and M. Parker (eds), *Postmodernism and Organizations*. London: Sage.

Tompkins, P. and Cheney, G. (1985). 'Communication and unobtrusive control in contemporary organizations', in R. McPhee and P. Tompkins (eds), *Organizational Communication: Traditional Themes and New Directions*. Newbury Park, CA: Sage, pp. 179–210.

Townley, B. (1993). 'Foucault, power/knowledge, and its relevance for human resource management', *Academy of Management Review*, 18: 518–45.

Vallas, S. (1993). *Power in the Workplace: the Politics of Production at AT&T*. Albany, NY: State University of New York Press.

Vattimo, G. (1992). *The Transparent Society*. Baltimore: John Hopkins University Press.

Walzer, M. (1986). 'The politics of Foucault', in D. Hoy (ed.)., *Foucault: a Reader*. Oxford: Basil Blackwell. pp. 151–68.

Weedon, C. (1987). *Feminist Practice and Poststructuralist Theory*. Oxford: Basil Blackwell.

Willmott, H. (1990). 'Subjectivity and the dialectic of praxis: opening up the core of labour process analysis', in D. Knights and H. Willmott (eds), *Labour Process Theory*. London: Macmillan.

—— (1993). 'Strength is ignorance; slavery is freedom: managing culture in modern organizations', *Journal of Management Studies*, 30(4).: 515–52.

—— (1994). 'Bringing agency (back). into organizational analysis: responding to the crises of (post).modernity', in J. Hassard and M. Parker (eds), *Towards a New Theory of Organizations*. London: Routledge.

Willmott, H. and Knights, D. (1982). 'The problem of freedom: Fromm's contribution to a critical theory of work organization', *Praxis International*, 2: 204–25.

7 Changing Spaces: The Disruptive Impact of a New Epistemological Location for the Study of Management

David Knights

Positive knowledge and positivism (the set of methods that deny the distinctive nature of the social in contrast to natural phenomena) are almost indistinguishable. The desire to represent a closure on reality frequently involves an unreflexive use of methods (e.g., experiments, hypothesis testing, quantifications) assumed to be successful in the natural sciences and readily transferrable to the domain of the social sciences. Clearly, one of the conditions that makes it possible to treat knowledge as a correspondence between representations and the reality to which they supposedly refer is a positivist belief in the ontological continuity of the natural and the social world (Douglas 1970). The collapse into positivism, then, is not all that surprising.

But insofar as they fail to acknowledge their own participation in the constitution of social reality, qualitative researchers, who claim a distance from positivist beliefs, also have a tendency to be unreflexive about the representations they produce. Whether quantitative or qualitative methods are used, representational approaches to knowledge production rest on a privileging of the consciousness of the researcher who is deemed capable of discovering the 'truth' about the world of management and organizations through a series of representations. In the process of reflecting and reproducing a dualism between the subject or agent (e.g., researcher) and the object or subject matter of knowledge, the search for representations of reality denies or obscures the process through which an academic discipline constitutes the object of its discourse in its own image (Game 1991).

Numerous critiques, both of a general and a specific organizational focus, have been targeted on positivism (see Bernstein 1976; Burrell & Morgan 1979; Cicourel 1964; Douglas 1970; Feyerabend 1972; Habermas 1972; Silverman 1970; Winch 1958), and there is no intention here of repeating them yet again, not least because there is a danger of merely replacing one set of positivities with another. The concern here, by contrast, is not to displace those positive forms of knowledge, which are the object of criticism by a superior representation of reality, but to show how they rely for their production on that which they cannot know (e.g. subjectivity or the way in which human beings are categorized or categorize themselves) or choose to ignore (e.g. power). More specifically, this article draws from the way in which Michel Foucault's archaeological and genealogical analysis disrupts knowledges that are built on representations deeming to reflect reality. Primarily, it focuses upon what may be seen as the 'trouble-making' implications of Foucault's work for the epistemological foundations of management and organizational studies as an empirical and positive form of knowledge. Indeed, far from dismissing the object of its criticism, Foucault's archaeological and genealogical analyses acknowledge a parasitical dependence on the production of positive knowledge because this is precisely the condition that makes it possible to generate their particular mode of critique.

Although not attempting to offer universal guidelines or blueprints, this article suggests that Foucault's insights allow us to make a virtue out of necessity. Rather than collaborate in the myth of progress that underlies the demand for stable and positive management knowledge, we can celebrate the conditions of subjectivity that make this mythology impossible to sustain. The article is structured as follows: The first section presents some of the central features of Foucault's work. This provides the foundation for the second section, where an attempt is made to subject Michael Porter's (1980; 1985) thesis on strategy to a genealogical analysis as an example of how the study of management and organizations might be deconstructed. The implications of an archaeological and a genealogical analysis for methodology are discussed in the third section before some final conclusions are drawn.

AN OVERVIEW OF FOUCAULT'S WORK

The work of Michel Foucault is both extensive and complex mainly because throughout his career he continuously sought to advance radical redirections and to focus on a different set of analytical objects. A conventional way of breaking down the complexity of Foucault's work is to separate it into three historically chronological phases: the archaeological period, the genealogical period, and the ethical period (Burrell, 1988; Dreyfus & Rabinow, 1982; Smart, 1985), which are outlined next.

The archaeological period relates to Foucault's earlier work, when he was concerned with identifying or uncovering common features underlying a wide range of diverse and discontinuous sets of discourses. In his most famous archaeological text, *The Order of Things: An Archaeology of the Human Sciences*, Foucault (1973) focused on the historical, social, and philosophical rules and regularities (or the 'unconscious of knowledge') that underlie the formation of the human sciences, but which would ordinarily elude the conscious awareness of the scientist. In particular, he was concerned with showing how a set of classical disciplines, apparently as distinct and discrete as grammar, political economy, and natural history, shared a set of rules and procedures for rendering statements true. Of most interest to this article's focus on the management sciences is Foucault's emphasis on the transition to modernism, or 'when man [sic] constituted himself in Western culture as that which must be conceived of and that which is to be known' and, thereby, became the 'object of science' (Foucault 1973: 345). At this point, the classical disciplines closest to human life were transformed as theorists began to generate representations of a linguistic, economic, and biological nature drawn from objectified observations of speaking, producing, and living subjects, respectively. This transformation whereby human beings become the objects as well as the subjects or agents of knowledge is, according to Foucault, 'an event in the order of knowledge' (1973 : 345). It is an event that underlies the 'perpetual controversy between the sciences of man and the sciences proper—the first laying an invincible claim to be the foundation of the second' (Foucault 1973 : 345), while having some difficulty with regard to their own foundation and justification (ibid : 346).

This difficulty is even greater for the management and organizational sciences, which emulate the rules and procedures of positive knowledge (e.g. biology, economics, and linguistics). Although biology, for example, may have been subjected to political manipulation (e.g. the Lysenko affair), management knowledge is never independent of the power that managers and their corporations exercise. But as Rabinow (1986 : 10) made clear, 'Foucault, never intended to isolate discourse from the social practices that surround it'; those who examine these newer disciplines, therefore, must also draw on insights deriving from a genealogical analysis.

In his archaeological period, Foucault investigated the rules and procedures that made it possible for writers within a number of discrete and disparate disciplines to make statements that claimed the status of truth. In his genealogical investigations, by contrast, analogous discourses and institutions were shown to engage a multiplicity of unconnected strategies and tactics in exercising their power over subjects. Foucault explored the various conditions that rendered it possible for these 'technologies of power' to emerge historically.

David Knights

Genealogy contrasts sharply with conventional history, which in emulating the methods of the positive sciences focuses on the historical event as developing sequentially through time and space and subject to a 'discoverable' set of causal determinants which preceded it. Frequently, the assumption underlying such an analysis is the enlightenment idea that history unfolds in a unilinear and 'progressive' manner and that its course is strongly influenced by particular individuals (the 'great man' thesis). Foucault countered these views first by suggesting that institutions and the discourses surrounding them often emerge out of a series of accidents and arbitrary or superficial localized events. So, for example, Foucault (1979b : 191) traced the 'birth of the sciences of man' not to major philosophical breakthroughs in the great academies but to such 'lowly' events as the development of files and records constituting 'the individual as a describable, analysable object' (Foucault, 1979a : 190) within institutions of correction, mental asylums, hospitals, and schools. Foucault's second counter to conventional history was to remove all trace of the human subject from the center of his analysis; he argued that social practices and their discursive formations are independent of those who speak for them (Foucault 1973, 1979a). By this, Foucault did not mean to imply that the intentions of subjects are nonexistent but merely that their outcomes in aggregated sets of social practices are wholly independent of what was intended (see Dreyfus & Rabinow 1982).

The discourses of psychiatry, medicine, and the human sciences and the institutional practices (e.g. internment, hospitalization, imprisonment) in which they are embedded may be seen as methods for dividing up populations between 'the mad and the sane, the sick and the healthy, the criminals and the "good boys"' (Foucault 1982: 208). In short, these disciplines and institutions exercise power through the 'normalizing' procedures of exclusion and surveillance whereby 'deviants' (e.g., the sick, paupers, criminals) are physically segregated and the 'incompetent' are marginalized through hierarchical distinction.

In reflecting on his genealogical period, Foucault (1980) declared that he had been concerned with power all along but, in his third period, a disruption for those who would seek to categorize him, he argued that 'it is not power, but the subject, which is the general theme of my research' (Foucault 1982: 209). According to this refocusing of his work, there are 'three domains of genealogy' (Foucault quoted in Rabinow 1984 : 351): those in which the study of the history of subjects of knowledge is sought, those that concern the subjects of power acting on others, and those that focus on the way people constitute themselves as ethical subjects or moral agents. From this point of view, his work has dealt with three different modes of objectifying human practice, each of 'which transform human beings into subjects' (Foucault 1982 : 208) in distinct yet overlapping ways.

First, through archaeology Foucault examined those discourses claiming the status of science which, for example, generate representations of a linguistic, economic, and biological nature, and thus, objectify speaking, producing, and living subjects, respectively. Second, through genealogy he studied the diverse ways in which objectifying or stereotyping individuals or groups has the effect of dividing them internally from themselves and externally from others. The stigma attached to the mad, the sick, the criminal, the black, the poor, the unemployed, and so on, provides an objectification that not only classifies and contains the deviant but also 'normalizes' the rest of the population. Through discipline and punishment (see Foucault 1979), an example is made of the deviant whose visibility is a constant reminder to others to conform. Finally, in the ethical period, Foucault was concerned with *subjectification*, or those ways in which individuals objectify themselves so as to recognize, and become committed to, a particular sense of their own subjectivity. This latter mode focuses on the active self-formation of subjects (see Davidson 1986) and examines particular discourses and practices, within the domain of sexuality, for example. This mode reveals how individuals are transformed into subjects who secure this meaning and reality through identifying with a particular sense of their own sexuality.

The implications that this third period has for organizational analysis are not so clear. This is mainly because Foucault (1987, 1988) found it necessary to delve further back into history to periods (e.g., ancient Greece and classical Rome) when the formation of subjects was not 'contaminated' by the object-ifications of the human sciences. Despite this problem, Foucault's discussion of the continuities and breaks in the history of how individuals have come to 'recognize themselves as subjects of sexuality' (1987 : 4), for example, is of particular importance to understanding the subjective self-formation process in contemporary society. Though not extending as far back into the historical past to illustrate specific genealogies, the analysis of sexuality (e.g. Burrell 1984; Calás & Smircich 1992; Hearn, Sheppard, Tancred-Sheriff & Burrell 1991) and subjectivity more generally (e.g. Knights 1990; Knights & Morgan 1991; Miller & O'Leary 1987; Robson & Cooper 1989; Rose 1989) have become increasingly important to the study of organizations, as will be indicated in the following illustration of strategy.

At this point it may be helpful to present the principal contrasts between the forms of positive knowledge and what is recommended here as an approach informed by Foucault's insights. The left-hand side of Table 1 summarizes the approach of the positive forms of knowledge, which concentrate exclusively on representations of human life. The right-hand side presents ideas that counter such knowledge and that are consistent with the epistemological space which, it may be argued, the studies of management and organization occupy (that is, the place between the representations of the positive forms of knowledge and

David Knights

Table 1. Contrasting Positive and Antipositive Knowledge

Features Associated With Positive Forms of Knowledge	Ideas That Counter the Positive Approaches to Knowledge
1. Treats their subject matter as a "given," exactly like the natural sciences.	1. Refuses either to focus only on the representations of human existence or to reduce subjectivity to an objectification of apparent subjective 'characteristics'; instead, the power matrix, which is the background to the production of such representations and objectifications and 'characteristics,' is examined.
2. Develops laws, rules, or statistical probabilities concerning their respective objects.	2. Recognizes the goals of a science of management and organizations as a claim to status, respectability, and legitimacy, but one that is open to ridicule because it is incapable of standing up to the rigor of the methods it has set. That is, its emulation of the positive sciences locates it in the trap of having to provide causal explanations, invariable laws, and predictions, the possibility of which would demand that knowledge of management could be independent of, or truly ignore, the conditions (e.g. an elusive subjectivity) of its own production.
3. Acquires the status of sciences.	3. Suggests an analysis that does *not* use evidence exhaustively to establish a set of causal relations but selectively to render a problem intelligible. This is the genealogical approach, which in displaying the conditions that made it possible for management knowledge to develop, points to the precarious and unreliable character of that knowledge.
4. Becomes an integral part of power relations through their impact on standards of public health (biology), correct grammar (linguistics), and the management of the economy (economics).	4. Encourages management and organization theorists to confront the way in which power and knowledge influence one another and to refrain from engaging in the practice of power while projecting the pretense

Table 1. Contrasting Positive and Antipositive Knowledge—continued

Features Associated With Positive Forms of Knowledge	Ideas That Counter the Positive Approaches to Knowledge
	of value neutrality. It recognizes how management knowledge results from, and contributes to, a particular disciplinary regime.
5. Produces truths (i.e. the norms of what it is to be a healthy, speaking, and productive subject) through their power effects.	5. Perceives truth as an effect of power–knowledge relations rather than the outcome of correct scientific procedure or method. Students of management and organization, therefore, must avoid presuming that when the practical recommendations of a research project 'work,' this is so simply because the theory underlying them is true. The 'truth' of our knowledge is much more a result of it being seen as true and, as a consequence, drawn upon in the exercise of power. At the same time it has to be recognized that 'the achievement of 'true' discourses (which are incessantly changing, however) is one of the fundamental problems of the West' (Foucault 1988: 112).

the social, political, economic, and philosophical conditions that make these studies possible).

The alternatives suggested on the right-hand side demand a different way of understanding knowledge. They should be thought of as unconventional objects or commodities. Clearly, according to conventional thinking, knowledge is represented by such items as certificates of accreditation or qualification and through what Friere (1972) calls the 'banking' concept where knowledge is seen as something to accumulate in the 'dusty' vaults of the brain or more likely the 'paper mountains' of unread, if not indigestible, notes stored in teachers' and students' files. But knowledge can never be so concrete or certain: The conditions that make it possible—namely, human subjectivity—are precisely those that render it precarious. Far from representing knowledge, certificates are merely the outcome of a set of disciplinary practices that involve classifying students along the dimensions of hierarchical gradings and individualizing them through invoking competitive tension. Because these conditions involve philosophical, political, economic, and social dimensions, which are always in some degree of flux, the knowledge they render possible is continually subjected to disruption and dislocation. Epistemologically then, we are 'condemned' to a critical or reflective position with respect to the output of positive accounts of management and organization. At the cost of its own potential demise, archaeological and genealogical analysis must continue to unsettle, to disturb, and, ultimately, to undermine the stability and reputability of positive forms of knowledge.

In raising irresolvable questions about the conditions that make positive knowledge possible, the central impetus of Foucault's enterprise is deeply disturbing to the mainstream membership within management and organization studies. As Silverman and Gubrium (198: 5) put it, Foucault's work is 'profoundly discomfiting to all versions of Enlightenment thought' for it deconstructs 'their polarities of theory/practice, fact/value, reason/emotion, science/ideology, and society/individual' . . . 'by revealing the very practices and technologies which deploy such representations.'

Critical studies of organizations and management (e.g. Burrell & Morgan 1979; Clegg 1979, 1990; Clegg & Dunkerley 1977, 1980; Morgan 1983, 1986; Perrow 1979, 1981; Zey-Ferrell & Aiken 1981) do not escape the discomfort because Foucault's project is a 'radical activism' that rejects any firm foundations; it subscribes neither to an objective truth (which contemporary power glosses over) nor to the existence of essential relations that appearances conceal. He refuses to let 'comfortable' assumptions and practices alone, whether these support a conservative or critical account of organizational and social life. Instead, he is forever questioning ideas and turning upside down the institutions that support these ideas. Because critical theorists of management tend to cling precisely to these 19th-century ontologies and to the humanist faith in liberation that grounds them, they too are profoundly threatened by a project that continually undermines knowledge, including the knowledge that it has produced.

Foucault's radical activism does not sanction or facilitate a solid and stable program to which individuals can readily attach themselves and secure some sense of identity (Knights & Willmott 1985, 1989). Although not by direct design, it usually involves a revolutionary upheaval of the discourses and practices. In order to illustrate some of these ideas, this article briefly outlines how a study of a discourse on strategy can be informed by a reading of Foucault.

A Foucauldian Approach to the Study of Strategy

The field of discourse that produces prescriptions on strategy and/or describes how management seeks to design and implement corporate and business strategies combines elements of each of the three modes of objectification wherein individuals are transformed into subjects. It therefore can be examined from the point of view of an archaeological, a genealogical, and an ethical account of social practices. However, experts in corporate and business strategy remain comparatively unreflective with respect to the objectifying effects of strategic discourse and practice. They tend simply to promote strategy as a management tool for rendering organizational activities more calculable (Hoskin 1990) or the market more controllable (Ansoff 1965; Hofer & Schendel 1978), but without acknowledging how certain features of strategic discourse may be self-fulfilling in their effects, if only because they are drawn upon in the exercise of power (Foucault, 1980). Consultants might be excused because of their concern with understanding the social processes through which their recommendations are effective, but students of management and organization cannot afford to be self-satisfied since their raison d'être is to provide an analysis of events and not merely a descriptive or prescriptive record.

Although the genesis of strategy as a modern concept may be traced back to the mid-19th century and the development of the Pennsylvania railroad in the United States (Hoskin 1990), the proliferation of strategic discourses and practices on a large scale seems to have occurred only after the second world war (Bracker 1980) and, more recently, primarily in relation to the problem of securing competitive advantage in external markets (Porter 1980, 1985, 1990). This proliferation of the discourse was both a condition and consequence of large numbers of corporations seeking to transform their practices to coincide with the standards of strategic planning in relation to 'the long-term goals and objectives' (Chandler 1962 : 13) of the organization and the means to their achievement. Within the conventional literature, strategy was seen and celebrated as an essential component of 'rational' organization and control. This was a rationality that enabled management in organizations to assess the prevailing, and forecast the future, environmental conditions with respect to their impact primarily on the market potential or competitive advantage of the business.

Strategy discourse can be seen as transcending a number of the artificial boundaries surrounding the academic disciplines that make up the social and management sciences, but the representations it produces align most comfortably with the comparatively new discipline of marketing. Although a genealogy of the discourse of marketing so far has not been produced, it would not diverge sharply from a similar analysis of strategy (Knights & Morgan 1991)

despite the views of business history academics (e.g. Chandler 1962), organization theorists (e.g. Miles & Snow 1978; Mintzberg 1978), and accounting
historians (e.g. Hoskin 1990). Undoubtedly it is the case that strategy is related
in complex ways to changes in organizational structure (Chandler 1962). So, for
example, as the multidivisional or multinational corporation developed, new
strategies of management control were necessary whereby geographically
dispersed and/or product-distinct operating business units had to go 'to
market' as if they had no parent corporation backing. Equally, corporate
strategy would be a means of rendering an organization's activities calculable
and recordable and thereby accountable (Hoskin 1990). Furthermore, the
strategy that is realized in an organization is frequently divergent from what
was intended (Mintzberg 1978). It may be argued, however, that a major
condition making it possible for a discourse on strategy to arise and to
proliferate was the growing importance of markets and their control as the
capitalist organization mastered production difficulties only to find itself beset
with problems of distribution and consumption. As early as the late 19th
century, Marx had anticipated this in his argument about the excess productive
capacity of capitalist organization (Baran & Sweezy 1966). Clearly marketing,
both as an academic discourse and a management practice, was a response to
problems regarding the market and consumption with which 20th-century
business practitioners have been confronted.

The relationships between the discourses and practices of marketing and
those of strategy are important not only to the genealogical analysis of their
genesis and development but also to an understanding of their archaeology and
the ethics which they embrace. The underlying rules of formation of what
Foucault termed the positive sciences of life, language and production, were
the conditions that made it possible for the proliferation or transition of a range
of discourses distinct from, but focusing on phenomena (i.e., human representations) that are analogous to those studied in biology, linguistics, and economics. Among these were a variety of disciplines in which the activities of
business and the various functions of management were examined, and these
became known as the management sciences.

Through their association with one or another of these new management
disciplines, proponents of strategy discourse have been able to make statements
claiming the status of truth about organizations, decision making, and the
relationship of strategies to specific environments and markets. Their claim to
truth derives mainly from emulating the procedures concerning the production
and operation of representations within the positive sciences but without
questioning whether it is appropriate to objectify human behavior in this
way. Instead, the procedures for representing the outcome of human activity
in the form of second-order constructs of, for example, markets, demand
and supply schedules, company accounts, selection techniques, or collective

bargaining are simply taken for granted. Claiming merely to report or represent the 'reality' observed, those who conduct positive studies seem oblivious to how their representations actually constitute the subjectivity of management, as practitioners draw upon these studies in their exercise of power. Subjectivity can, however, never be finally 'fixed' in knowledge if only because of the power of subjects to alter their behavior on the basis of such knowledge, thus transforming or undermining the conditions that made its production possible. Knowledge in the human sciences, therefore, changes immediately when it enters the public domain and begins to inform the behavior of those to whom it is meant to refer. Despite this, practitioners are in a position to define their strategic practices as successful and, thus, render the knowledge used in the exercise of power to be self-fulfilling in its truth effects.

Therefore, the systems of truth surrounding marketing concepts such as strategy were a product of power exercised by large corporations, government, and business schools within which there was a positive incitement to generate 'knowledge' of markets and how to manage them. Strategy was a discourse that entered management practice as an element of corporate government rationality, or what Foucault (1979; see also Burchell, Gordon & Miller 1991) described as *governmentality*. It was part of that whole edifice described by Foucault (1979 : 16) as the art or science of government wherein 'the notion of economy came to be able to focus onto a different plane of reality, which we characterise today as "economic", ... [and] ... it became possible to indentify problems specific to the population.' This constitutes a transformation from the classical legal framework of sovereign rule to a modern system of government, 'which has as its primary target the population and as its essential mechanism apparatuses of security' (Foucault 1979 : 19).

It may be suggested that the security of populations can best, or only, be achieved through state welfare agencies and, of course, these represent one important mechanism, but the art of government is to promote levels of economic wealth and prosperity sufficient not only to fund public welfare, but also to render it unnecessary. Clearly, liberal government has followed a diversity of approaches in managing the problem of security; socialists have sought to ensure a greater equitability of wealth distribution, whereas conservatives have emphasized the importance of the free market in stimulating economic growth. Every facet of liberal government, however, has sought to intervene for purposes of improving the productive performance of industry as an important means to establishing economic prosperity and social security.

Strategy can be seen as an important discourse in this whole enterprise of governmentality. It may be located archaeologically in that set of rules which allowed representations of human activity to become objects of knowledge, and its genealogy can be linked to the problem of markets and how they were to be managed by corporate government, on the one hand, and to the increasing importance of the economy as modern governments assume responsibility for the prosperity and security of populations, on the other.

Foucault's mode of analysis offers insights into the discourse and practice of strategy in intimating how its rules of formation are analogous to those of the positive sciences and its genesis and development are closely linked with the problems of governmentality. In order to illustrate these ideas more concretely, this article now focuses on Michael Porter's (1980, 1985) work on strategy and competitive advantage. This focus compensates slightly for the slippage into a 'grand narrative' that an examination of strategic discourse in general invokes. It also addresses a discourse that has been highly successful in 'spreading the word of strategy' among both academics and practitioners and, thereby, is not only familiar to theorists and practitioners but also has figured prominently in the exercise of power both within academia and corporations. In subjecting Porter's work to this kind of analysis, however, there is no suggestion that what is produced is superior; this article merely offers a different way of rendering more inteligible the discourse and practice of strategy, as constituted by a particular author.

The Porter Model of Strategy

Porter's discourse can be aligned directly with Foucault's three modes of objectification: representation, the dividing practices, and subjectification. The objectification that Focault described as representation appears quite explicitly in Porter's (1980, 1985) treatment of the modern business as 'a collection of activities that are performed to design, produce, market, deliver, and support its product. All these activities can be represented using a value chain' (1985 : 36).

The value chain consists of a set of primary and support activities associated with product-to-market processes, and it is the principal analytical framework that a business must construct in order to develop a competitive advantage (Porter 1985 : 36). The value chain 'is a basic tool for diagnosing competitive advantage' (Porter 1985: 59). This competitive advantage, according to Porter (1980, 1985), can be secured either by the company's becoming a *cost leader* or by its adapting a system of *market differentiation*. Each of these representations, whether normative or descriptive, is presumably derived from a mixture of academic work, consulting, and common sense, but none is treated as problematical. Instead, Porter followed the rules and procedures of the positive sciences in constructing, classifying, and ordering representations, adding the appropriate causal connections between them and, thus, claiming the status of scientific truth for his statements.

Yet research in progress (Kerfoot, Knight & Morgan 1992) conducted in a major financial services group in England, which involves 'tracking' the annual business strategy cycle presented at meetings and found in documents, suggests that Porter's model is difficult to follow. Although his work on strategy has been guiding the bank's group strategy for some time, senior managers have found that neither differentiation nor cost leadership is a feasible strategy in the pursuit of competitive advantage. Differentiation does not work because financial service products are easily limitated and there are a limited range of service possibilities; cost leadership seems impossible to operationalize because the costs of even their own operations, let alone those of competitors, are not calculable.

Despite these debilitating obstacles to applying the model, senior management appears reluctant to abandon the model of competitive strategy developed by Porter in their deliberations over strategic planning. This, it may be argued, is because a certain amount of investment has already gone into existing planning programs and, in the absence of a better positive model, management clings to its previous strategies. However, one (unintended) effect of managing an organization in terms of specific strategies is to transform individuals into subjects who secure their sense of reality through such positive commitments. But the positive nature of the model comes at the expense of giving any attention to subjectivity which, in the example here, is its major virtue. This is because the assumption underlying such positive models is that the behavior of organizational members can be ignored as it is expected to conform to the 'rational' imperatives for controlling uncertainty implicit in the theory of competitive strategy.

Porter objectifies business, then, through developing a series of representations that are not dissimilar from those produced in the positive sciences. In the same way that linguistics represents language as independent of the speaking subject, economics treats production and exchange as if they were independent of laboring subjects, and biology objectifies the body as if it were separate from living beings, so the business corporation is represented as a set of activities and value chains that are detached from those managers, workers, and consumers who constitute them. Analogous to the positive knowledge he emulates, Porter's success as both a 'management scientist' and a guru for practitioners is partly an effect of forgetting, neglecting, or denying the subjectivity that is the condition rendering his representations possible. In other words, having erased 'the traces of its own construction, the representation becomes the "reality"' (Bloomfield & Vurdubakis 1991 : 7).

By contrast, when this subjectivity in the form of culture, politics, and career is admitted and the rationality informing strategic decision making is thereby questioned (e.g. Child & Smith 1987; Johnson 1987; Pettigrew 1985, 1988; Smircich & Stubbart 1985), the ensuing muddied waters weaken the impact of strategy discourse on practitioners. Indeed, it could be argued that there is an inverse relation between academic and practitioner credbility in the field of strategy.

The second mode of objectification deployed by Porter is that of the dividing practices where he elevates those businesses whose operations most clearly resemble his model and support the view that competitive advantage is to be secured either by becoming a cost leader, through differentiation or by focusing on a narrow segment of the market. Those companies trapped or 'stuck in the middle' (Porter 1980 : 41–44) because they are neither cost leaders nor differentiators are denigrated as failures—condemned with almost the same vehemence and stigma as has been attached to insanity, criminality, and poverty in earlier representations of this behavior.

Now suppose it could be assumed that Porter's analyses were scientific and, therefore, a perfect guide to business practice, in the way that he professes. This assumption, of course, is to ignore his critics (e.g. Knights & Morgan 1991; Pettigrew 1985; 1988) but, more important, it demands that both the conditions that make it possible to generate such models and the process of their construction are unproblematical. And as has already been suggested, the conditions rendering it possible to produce models of strategy are far from unproblematical. First, they involve all those features of the positive sciences illustrated on the left side and challenged on the right side of Table 1; second, they are constructed as if independent of the kind of power that makes them self-fulfilling as true discourses.

Yet even if these reservations are put aside, it is quite clear that if every business adopted the strategies advocated by Porter they could not all secure a competitive advantage because if the thesis is 'true,' the competitive advantage of each would be canceled out in direct proportion to their success in achieving the strategy. The 'truth' of his thesis is then dependent on it being adopted selectively or differentially rather than universally within an industry. So not only is its very condition of existence made possible by the subjectivity that allows for alternative strategies, but it is also the probability that subjects (i.e. managers) will be unable to follow its guidelines perfectly or will fail to follow them at all that provides the conditions of possibility with respect to its truth and plausibility. Clearly, Porter's theory of strategy is a form of knowledge that is only advantageous in competitive terms when combined with the exercise of unequal or differential power, which is precisely the kind of power that comes from a privileged access to this knowledge deriving from exclusive contract consultancy arrangements. Because of the inevitable distortions in translation from text to management practice, Porter's books can appear to offer rational solutions to business without these solutions being undermined by their application. But what makes these distortions possible are the self-same conditions of subjectivity that are necessary yet blithely ignored or erased in the constitution of Porter's theory of competitive strategy in the first place. In short, the universality of Porter's analysis of strategy only remains plausible if it is inadequate, either in its construction or application.

If the effect of Porter's work was an objectification of business only at the level of representation and the dividing practices, it may not have been so popular among practitioners. Yet when applied to business, Porter's framework can have certain positive and 'productive' consequences for subjects that are neither anticipated nor understood by theorists or practitioners. These consequences for behavior can be understood in terms of the third mode of objectification—the transformation of individuals into subjects. For example, members of an organization whose hierarchical position gives them privileged access to certain knowledge or representations relating to strategy are transformed into subjects who exercise power through, and gain a sense of meaning and reality from, practices that are informed by strategic discourse. But it is a power that is equally as subjugating for those lower in the hierarchy who are subjected to it as to those through whom it is exercised. It:

applies itself to everyday life which categorizes the individual, marks him [sic] by his own individuality, attaches him to his own identity, imposes a law of truth on him which he must recognize and which others have to recognize in him. (Foucault 1982 : 212)

When Porter's theory of competitive advantage is taken up by management, it begins to have these consequences whereby individual managers and employees are transformed into subjects who secure meaning, purpose, and identity through engaging in practices that reflect and support the strategies perceived to improve competitive advantage. In short, the strategy discourse provides a kind of 'rallying cry' for the organizational troops but one that appears to be grounded in systematic analysis of a 'scientific' nature. This use of competitive advantage does not mean that, like sheep, everyone subscribes to the strategies as constituted by senior practitioners' interpretations of Porter's model. Indeed, the gist of the critique of the 'processual' approach (Mintzberg & Waters 1982; Pettigrew 1985) to strategy is precisely to question the assumption that behavior automatically follows a prescribed strategy. Internal politics within an organization may result in members relating in diverse ways to the formal strategies that a company adopts, although regardless of their content, these practices often will be legitimized by, or performed in the name of, official strategies or policies (Burns & Stalker 1961). Even though it has been established that neither cost leadership nor cost differentiation are feasible strategies for a company to use in the pursuit of competitive advantage, the bank reported on previously still continues to justify various practices precisely in terms of the presumed competitive advantage deriving from such strategies.

No less than other theorists, Porter constitutes the problems (e.g. cost leadership, cost differentiation, the value chain) that his theory is designed to resolve. But his work is attractive to management also because it contributes to the transformation of management practice into an expertise that is supported by knowledge. As a rational basis for managerial prerogative, this expertise provides some illusion of control, legitimacy, and security in the face of uncertainty. It feeds on the representations of reason and rationality, fact and truth that reflect and reproduce particular 'masculine' conceptions of reality that are embedded in a disembodied propensity to 'speak for others' (Seidler, 1989 : 17) through applying a series of 'rational' and 'technical' solutions to organizational problems. That management is a male-dominated occupation is not in dispute (Cockburn 1983, 1990; Collinson, Knights & Collinson 1990; Kanter 1977), but strategic planning quite clearly develops out of that regime of rationality within which 'the successful manager was the "man" who could control his emotions, and [where] women were perceived as "temperamentally unfit" for management because they were too emotional' (Kanter, quoted in Pringle 1989 : 88). In contrast to Kanter, who sees job segregation as reflecting the power of men to exclude women from management, it may be argued that the discourse on rationality itself, of which strategy is one of its latest manifestations, sustains a 'particular kind of masculinity based on the exclusion of the personal, the sexual and the feminine from any definition of "rationality"' (Pringle 1989 : 88). It is a form of rationality in which the masculine preoccupations with conquest and domination are exalted (Kerfoot & Knights 1991). Strategy establishes that cause through which 'a masculine ethic of independence and commitment assumes a power over the environment and a sense of control' (Bologh 1990 : 229). As Weber and many existentialists have insisted, it is necessary to serve 'some cause outside the self' (Pringle 1989 : 232) if life is to remain meaningful. Those who use strategy deploy depersonalized knowledge and expertise to secure an instrumental control over large numbers of people and objects both inside and outside of the organization, they aim to improve and extend 'systems of purposive rational action' (Habermas 1971 : 81). Although these 'externalities' can never be controlled and are for this reason a threat to managerial masculinity, the existence of a strategy provides an occasion whereby such externalities can be continually (re)constituted as objects of conquest and where reason and calculability (Hoskin 1990) can be brought to bear upon the problem of uncertainty.

Strategic control and expertise are drawn from an entire range of knowledge that emanates from the bureaucratic and academic application of rational, technical, and scientific principles to the sphere of human affairs. Although not distinctive in this respect, the discourse of strategy does offer a more 'productive' means of involving individuals in their own subjective and organizational self-discipline. Such involvement is not necessarily an intended consequence, for in being identified predominantly as a means of managing the environment (e.g. markets), strategy appears to have little to do with conventional conceptions of the internal control of labor. Insofar as a successful implementation of strategy is expected to generate competitive advantage, it promises 'security' both for the organization and its members. This is so if only because competitive advantage is a condition of the possibility of growth in a market economy that ordinarily results in an expansion of resources (e.g. incomes, career promotions). Accordingly, employees readily accept delegated responsibilities for the business strategy when they are 'cascaded' down the hierarchy and, in so doing, collaborate in the constitution, or self-formation, of their own identity as subjects of strategy.

Scientific strategic discourse provides existential comfort to practitioners and academics alike because it generates a rationale for specific interventions directed at security and control; it also makes strategic actors feel like subjects who can 'make a difference' in managing uncertainty as part of what it means to pursue success (Knights & Morgan 1991 : 264). Furthermore, it is a demonstration to outsiders (i.e. bankers, investors, the state) that the organization is in rational control of its destiny (Knights & Morgan 1991 : 264).

As has been suggested, strategic discourse and practice represent a set of power–knowledge relations that constitutes the subjectivity of managers and employees. This is not meant to imply that individuals are merely passive and reactive to strategic discourses and practices; indeed, the very effectiveness of strategy is how it engages individuals actively in the meanings and interpretations that it invokes. Resistance to strategy may occur because it violates a particular organizational culture (e.g. paternalism) or treats its own historical self-formation and development as natural and inevitable. Thus, the exercise of strategic power is not a monolith, and the relations in which it is exercised are not necessarily coordinated and coherent, one with another. There are gaps, contradictions, and discontinuities, and these can be exploited by members of an organization seeking to resist the impact of strategic planning. Likewise, subjectivity is not a unified and an integrated whole; individuals are very often as divided within themselves as they are from one another. Their subjectivity is composed of a complex web of complementary and conflicting as well as coherent and inconsistent meanings, purposes and identities, all of which generate as much tension as stability. These discrepancies and discontinuities provide space for resistance to strategy, but the latter (the subjectivity of individuals and their resistance) is not to be seen as somehow outside of power relations.

It is clear, then, that although the constitution of subjects is an effect of the exercise of power, their historical formation is not a one-way process in which individuals are passive victims; their transformation into subjects through power does not guarantee subjugation for they frequently resist the forms of subjectivity that are its 'normalized' effects. For example, not all practitioners and organizations 'buy into' the Porter model on strategy and competitive advantage, and quite clearly other discourses will threaten its hegemony. They may question the rigidity of the model and, thereby, its restrictive impact on the speed with which organizations may respond to change (Mintzberg & Quinn 1990). Individuals also may criticize the model because it does not take account of sociopolitical relations both inside and outside of any particular organization (Knights & Morgan 1991; Knights & Murray 1992; Pettigrew 1985, 1988).

Methodological Implications

It may already be apparent that the epistemological location of management studies in the space between representations of management and their conditions of possibility involves a method where the aim is *not* to establish precise accounts of a phenomenon in terms of a set of causally related, abstract variables. Rather the objective is to render a problem more intelligible paradoxically through a process which, as in the case of Porter's thesis on competitive strategy, actually problematizes both the conditions of a theory's formation and its consequences. With respect to Porter's thesis, one important condition of its existence and plausibility was a certain inadequacy either at the level of its construction or the level of its application. For if the content were true and its application perfect across a broad range of companies, competitive advantage would remain elusive rather than be the logical outcome of following the theory.

An archaeological investigation of management and organization discourse would seek to uncover the philosophical, political, social, and economic rules of formation that underlie the development of specific management theories. In Porter's analysis of strategy, these rules of formation are analogous to those that secure knowledge in the positive sciences; his view of an organization is as a set of representations that are directed toward an objectified pursuit of competitive advantage. Porter offers strategy solutions to the problem of competitive advantage that he has constructed behind what appear as mere representations (see Butler 1990 : 2). What he fails to consider are the social relations of production that are the conditions of possibility for any organizational accomplishment. Instead, organization or management as a subject is discursively constituted by a mode of power and representation that, it is claimed, will save it from its own competitive failures. This preoccupation with pragmatic intervention on the basis of objectifications of organizations and managerial subjects derived from common sense observations is unreflective of how this theory constitutes what it claims merely to represent—namely, strategy and its managerial agents. For what is constituted out of this mixture of conceptual prescriptions and descriptions is a new discourse on strategy claiming the status of scientific knowledge. Thus, this discourse has a considerable impact on the subjectivity of practitioners, and strategy becomes a guiding principle of organizational life.

By contrast, a genealogical analysis would be used to examine the conditions of possibility for such knowledge to be drawn upon in the exercise of power. Researchers using it would also explore the effects of this power in sustaining and modernizing particular management regimes by the mechanisms of discipline and surveillance, and through the procedures of normalizing and individualing subjects. Porter's objectifications of competitive advantage and its relationship to three distinct strategies were rendered possible and plausible as a mode of discourse because of a number of conditions. Among these were the changes in ownership from owner-manager to public corporation, the necessity to provide accounts and rationalizations for creditors and shareholders, the development of multidivisional and multinational companies, the growth of management education generating new disciplines, the increasing importance of the market and consumption in Western economies (Knights & Morgan 1991) and perhaps, of most importance, the growing crisis of confidence in American businesses to meet the demands and challenges of global competition (Dent 1990). Porter's discourse on strategy is designed precisely to discipline modern management regimes into emulating the model he presents.

Following Foucault, the genesis and proliferation of a discourse like strategy cannot be traced to some essential origin, but has to be seen as emerging out of a set of accidental and unpredictable conditions that happen to coincide at a particular point in history. The intelligibility of strategy, then, is best captured by examining specific 'localized' events, some of which may be tied to the institutional context of its formation as a particular discourse, and not through the application of universal abstract laws. In the case of Porter's work, this examination may involve explorations of events and discourses beyond the broader conditions of the American business economy and of the specific content of his completed texts. Focusing on localized discourses and practices at Harvard, for example, would enable the analyst to establish not only some of the conditions that rendered the development of Porter's particular approach to strategy possible but, more important, to reveal the arbitrary and accidental events in its formation to show how its history was neither necessary, continuous, nor inevitable. This kind of analysis would apply equally to all rival views on strategy, including the one developed in this article.

Indeed, in the study of management and organization we should, as Foucault (1980 : 85, emphasis added) suggests with respect to genealogy, 'struggle against the *coercion* of a theoretical, unitary, formal and scientific discourse.' In the previous discussion of Porter's theory, the pretensions of its claim to universal truth were exposed as self-contradictory but not as a basis for imposing some alternative totalizing narrative. Rather, Foucault's approach is in direct opposition to advancing grand, global, and totalizing narratives of universal truth. Its users refrain from producing imperialistic knowledge that denies the validity of all other points of view. As Foucault (1984 : 385, emphasis added) pointed out in an interview just before his death: 'My attitude isn't a result of the form of critique that claims to be a methodical examination in order to reject all possible solutions except for the valid one.' At the same time, it is not another version of 'that easy post-modernism of the "anything goes" variety' (Huyssen 1990 : 271), for the users of genealogical analysis are continually engaged in a kind of 'trouble making' that fosters resistance to new conventional wisdom and expertise. They are simply concerned with avoiding what has been described as the desire for community, which 'denies difference in the concrete sense of making it difficult for people to respect those with whom they do not identify' (Young 1990 : 311).

Summary and Conclusion

This article has focused attention on the diverse and, complex contribution that Foucault's writings have made, to intellectual inquiry, and it has sought to show how this contribution might be relevant to the study of management and organizations. It began with a brief synopsis of Foucault's work as conventionally divided into the archaeological, the genealogical, and the ethical periods, which could be characterized respectively as distinct modes of objectification whereby individuals or organizations, for example, are represented and classified through knowledge, divided both internally and from one another through power, and transformed into self-disciplinary subjects through ethics. These modes of objectification were then deployed as a way of illustrating the kind of analysis that could be produced within the management and organizational sciences with particular reference to the work of Michael Porter on business strategy. Finally, the article enumerated some of the methodological implications of following an archaeological and a genealogical approach, again illustrating where appropriate through reference to Porter's analysis of strategy.

A major implication of the archaeological approach is that it points to a change in the epistemological space that management studies occupies, recognizing this form of study to lie between positive knowledge (i.e., biology, economics, and linguistics) and the conditions of subjectivity that make these positive studies possible. Recognizing this new epistemological position would lead students of management studies in the direction of a genealogical mode of analysis, which seeks to show how power may intervene in organizations either to sustain or to undermine positive knowledge. Power may sustain positive knowledge when management exercises the taken-for-granted notions of rank and hierarchy as it generates norms and judgments of competence regarding subjects within the organization. In this case, the use of positive knowledge is often self-fulfilling in the sense that it transforms individuals who are subjected to its power effects in the direction of identifying with, and thereby becoming committed to, those practices which are an outcome of its application (Foucault 1982). In contrast, critical knowledge is continually being developed which is disruptive and undermining of this positive knowledge in demonstrating the flimsy and accidental conditions of its production. It raises serious questions and creates considerable tension regarding the status of prevailing knowledge and practices.

This critical examination of positive forms of knowledge in the management / organizational field has considerable implications not just for the epistemological and methodological approaches to research but also for the lives of those who are its producers. For if nothing else, the impact of Foucault's work is to disturb and disrupt what is readily taken for granted, and this extends well beyond the realms of 'professional' activities and their objects. Notwithstanding the 'illusions of grandeur' aspired to by those who claim the respectable status of 'science' for their endeavors through emulating its methods and vocabulary, some students of management and organizations are troubled by the 'creeping' instability and uncertainty surrounding the knowledge they seek to produce. I would argue that this instability and uncertainty is what animates the defense of positivism against its critics (see Donaldson 1985; Marsden. In press; Review Symposium 1988). It is also reflected in the clamour with which the various subdisciplines (e.g., accounting, marketing, personnel management, and organization studies) borrow copiously from economics, statistics, psychology, and sociology in an attempt to gain a positive theoretical advantage on the 'world' that they study.

In conclusion then, the distinctive nature of this approach is its capacity to disturb and threaten the stability of positive forms of management science and to disrupt both totalizing and erudite knowledge, which offer political technologies in the name of technical expertise. The conditions of subjectivity that render a piece of positive knowledge possible are necessarily precarious. This is so if only by virtue of the transformation of subjectivity that occurs as a result of the exercise of power deploying that knowledge. In short, management knowledge generates precisely the kinds of changes that will result in a disruption of the conditions that made such knowledge possible in the first place. Only the resistance of power to new knowledge would limit its disruptive and destabilizing potential, but that course would demand a reactionary conservatism that even managers, much less management theorists, would find hard to force.

David Knights

Acknowledgement

Thanks go to colleagues and students in the Manchester School of Management who have suffered through my preoccupations with these ideas and (often unintentionally) have helped me to formulate them. Particular thanks goes to Chris Grey, Anne Loft, and Hugh Willmott, who offered criticisms of an earlier draft, and to Theo Vurdubakis, whose intellect is a constant inspiration.

References

Ansoff, H. I. (1965). *Corporate strategy.* New York: McGraw-Hill.

Baran, P. A., and Sweezy, P. M. (1966). *Monopoly Capital: An Essay on the American Economic and Social Order.* Harmondsworth, England: Penguin.

Bernstein, R. (1976). *The Restructuring of Social and Political Theory.* Oxford: Basil Blackwell.

Bloomfield, B., and Vurdubakis, T. (1991). *Inscribing Organisations and Technology: The Textual Construction of Reality.* Unpublished manuscript, Manchester School of Management, University of Manchester Institute of Science and Technology.

Bologh, R. W. (1990). *Love or Greatness: Max Weber and Masculine Thinking—A Feminist inquiry.* Boston: Unwin Hyman.

Bracker, J. (1980). 'The Historical Development of the Strategic Management Concept', *Academy of Management Review.* 5: 219–224.

Burchell, G., Gordon, C., and Miller, P. (1991). *The Foucault Effect: Studies in Governmentality.* London: Harvester Wheatsheaf.

Burns, T., and Stalker, G. M. (1961). *The Management of Innovation.* London: Tavistock.

Burrell, G. (1984). 'Sex and Organizational Analysis', *Organisation Studies.* 5: 97–118.

—— (1988). Modernism, Postmodernism and Organizational Analysis 2: The Contribution of Michel Foucault. *Organization Studies,* 9: 221–235.

Burrell, G., and Morgan, G. (1979). *Sociological Paradigms and Organisational Analysis.* London: Heinemann.

Butler, J. (1990). *Gender Trouble: Feminism and the Subversion of Identity.* New York: Routledge.

Calás, M. B., and Smircich, L. (1992). 'Voicing seduction to silence leadership,' *Organisation Studies,* 12: 567–602.

Chandler, A. D., Jr. (1962). *Strategy and Structure.* Garden City, NY: Doubleday.

Child, J., and Smith, C. (1987). 'The context and process of organizational transformation—Cadbury Limited in its sector'. *Journal of Management Studies,* 24: 565–593.

Clcourel, A. V. (1964). *Method and Measurement in Sociology.* Glencoe, IL: Free Press.

Clegg, S. R. (1979). *The Theory of Power and Organisation.* London: Routledge & Kegan Paul.

—— (1990). *Modern Organizations.* London: Sage.

Clegg, S. R., and Dunkerley, D. (eds) (1977). *Critical Issues in Organizations*. London: Routledge & Kegan Paul.

—— —— (1980). *Organisation, Class and Control*. London: Routledge & Kegan Paul.

Cockburn, C. K. (1983). *Brothers: Male Dominance and Technological Change*. London: Pluto.

—— (1990). 'Men's power in organizations', in J. Hearn and D. Morgan (eds), *Men, Masculinities and Social Theory*. Boston: Unwin Hyman, pp. 72–89.

Collinson, D., Knights, D., and Collinson, M. (1990). *Managing to Discriminate*. London: Routledge.

Davidson, A. I. (1986). 'Archaeology, genealogy and ethics', in D. C. Hoy (ed.), *Foucault: A Critical Reader*. Oxford: Basil Blackwell, pp. 221–223.

Dent, J. F. (1990). 'Strategy, organization and control: Some possibilities for accounting research', *Accounting, Organizations and Society*, 15(1–2): 3–25.

Donaldson, L. (1985). *In Defence of Organization Theory: A Reply to the Critics*. Cambridge: Cambridge University Press.

Douglas, J. D. (1970). *Understanding Everyday Life*. London: Routledge & Kegan Paul.

Dreyfus, H. F., and Rabinow, P. (1982). *Michel Foucault: Beyond Structuralism and Hermeneutics*. Brighton: Harvester Press.

Feyerabend, P. (1972). *Against Method*. London: New Left Books.

Foucault, M. (1973). *The Order of Things: The Archeology of the Human Sciences*. New York: Vintage Books.

—— (1979). 'Governmentality', *Ideology and Consciousness*, 6: 5–22.

—— (1979a). *Discipline and punish*. Harmondsworth: Penguin.

—— (1980. *Power/Knowledge*, in C. Gordon, (ed.). Brighton: Harvester Press.

—— (1982). 'Afterword: The subject and power', in H. F. Dreyfus and P. Rainbow (eds), *Michel Foucault: Beyond Structuralism and Hermeneutics*. Brighton: Harvester Press, pp. 208–26.

—— (1984). 'Polemics, politics, and problematizations: An interview with Michel Foucault', in P. Rabinow (ed.), *The Foucault Reader*. Harmondsworth: Penguin, pp. 381–90.

—— (1987). *The Use of Pleasure: The History of Sexuality* (vol. 2). London: Penguin.

—— (1988). *The Care of the Self: The History of Sexuality* (vol 3). New York: Vintage Books.

Friere, P. (1972). *Pedagogy of the Oppressed*. Harmondsworth: Penguin.

Game, A. (1991). *Undoing the Social: Towards a Deconstructive Sociology*. Milton Keynes: Open University Press.

Habermas, J. (1971). *Toward a Rational Society*. London: Heinemann.

—— (1972). *Knowledge and Human Interests*. London: Heinemann.

Hearn, J., Sheppard, D. L., Tancred-Sheriff, P., and Burrell, G. (eds) (1989). *The Sexuality of Organization*. London: Sage.

Hofer, C. W., and Schendel, D. (1978). *Strategy Formulation: Analytical Concepts*. St. Paul, MN: West.

Hoskin, K. W. (1990). *Using History to Understand Theory: A Reconsideration of the Historical Genesis of "Strategy."* Paper presented at the European Institute for

Advanced Studies in Management Workshop on Strategy. Accounting, and Control, Venice, Italy.

Huyssen, A. (1990). 'Mapping the postmodern', in L. J. Nicholson (ed.), *Feminism/ Postmodernism*. New York: Routledge, pp. 234–77.

Johnson, G. (1987). *Strategic Change in the Management Process*. Oxford: Blackwell.

Kanter, R. M. (1977). *Men and Women of the Corporation*. New York: Basic Books.

Kerfoot, D. J., and Knights, D. (1991). *Management, Manipulation and Masculinity: From Paternalism to Corporate Strategy in Financial Services*. Paper presented at the 10th European Group for Organizational Studies, Vienna, Austria.

Kerfoot, D. J., Knights, D., and Morgan, G. (1992). *Corporate Strategy in Action*. Paper to be presented to the Knowledge Workers in Contemporary Organizations Conference. Lancaster University, England.

Knights, D. (1990). 'Subjectivity, power and the labour process', in D. Knights and H. Willmott (eds), *Labour Process Theory*. London: Macmillan, pp. 297–335.

Knights, D., and Morgan, G. (1991). 'Strategic Discourse and Subjectivity: Towards a Critical Analysis of Corporate Strategy in Organizations', *Organisation Studies*, 12: 251–273.

Knights, D., and Murray, F. (1992). 'Politics and pain in managing information technology', *Organization Studies*, 13: 211–228.

Knights, D., and Willmott, H. (1985). 'Power and identity in theory and practice', *Sociological Review*, 33: 22–46.

—— —— (1989). 'From Degradation to Subjugation in Social Relations: An Analysis of Power and Subjectivity at Work'. *Sociology*, 23: 535–558.

Marsden, R. (In press). Donaldson: A critical note. *Organization Studies*.

Miles, R. E., and Snow, C. C. (1978). *Organization Strategy, Structure and Process*. Tokyo: McGraw-Hill.

Miller, P., and O'Leary, T. (1987). 'Accounting and the construction of the governable person', *Accounting, Organizations and Society*, 12: 235–265.

Mintzberg, H. (1978). 'Patterns in strategy formation', *Management Science*, 24: 934–948.

Mintzberg, H., and Waters, J. (1982). 'Tracking strategy in an entrepreneurial firm', *Academy of Management Journal*, 25: 465–499.

Mintzberg, H., and Quinn, J. B. (1990). *The Strategy Process: Concepts, Contents and Cases*. Englewood Cliffs, NJ: Prentice-Hall.

Morgan, G. (ed.) (1983). *Beyond Method*. Beverley Hills, CA: Sage.

—— (1986). *Images of Organizations*. London: Sage.

Pettigrew, A. (1985). 'Culture and Politics in Strategic Decision Making and Change', in J. M. Pennings (ed.), *Strategic Decision Making in Complex Organizations*. New York: Jossey Bass.

—— (ed.) (1988). *The Management of Strategic Change*. Oxford: Basil Black well.

Porter, M. E. (1980). *Competitive Strategy*. New York: Free Press.

—— (1985). *Competitive Advantage*. New York: Free Press.

—— (1990). *The Competitive Advantage of Nations*. New York: Free Press.

Pringle, R. (1989). *Secretaries Talk*, New York: Verso.

Rabinow, P. (ed.), (1984). *The Foucault Reader*. Harmondsworth: Penguin.

Review Symposium, (1988). 'Offence and defence: A symposium with Hinings, Clegg, Aldrich, Karpik, and Donaldson', *Organization Studies*, 9: 1–32.

Robson, K., and Cooper, D. (1989). 'Power and management control', in W. F. Chua, E. A. Lowe, and A. G. Puxty (eds), *Critical Perspectives in Management Control*. London: Macmillan, pp. 79–114.

Rose, N. (1989). *Governing the Soul: The Shaping of the Private Self*. London: Routledge.

Senidler, V. J. (1989). *Rediscovering Masculinity*. London: Routledge.

Silverman, D. (1970). *The Theory of Organisations*. London: Heinemann.

Silverman, D., and Gubrium, J. F. (1989). Introduction, in J. F. Gubrium and D. Silverman (eds). *The Politics of Field Research*. London: Sage, pp. 1–12.

Smart, B. (1985). *Michel Foucault*. London: Horwood & Tavistock.

Smircich, L., and Stubbart, C. (1985). 'Strategic management in an enacted world,' *Academy of Management Review*, 10: 724–736.

Winch, P. (1958). *The Idea of Social Science*. London: Routledge & Kegan Paul.

Young, I. M. (1990). 'The ideal of community and the politics of difference,' in L. J. Nicholson (ed.), *Feminism/Postmodernism*. New York: Routledge, pp. 300–230.

Zey Ferrell, M., and Aiken, M. (eds). (1981) *Complex Organizations : Critical Perspectives*. Glenview, Il: Scott, Foresman.

8

The Politics of Organizational Analysis

Richard Marsden

Introduction

In this paper I want to pursue some issues raised in Donaldson's *In Defence of Organization Theory: A Reply to the Critics* (1985), but left unexplored in 'Offence and Defence in Organization Studies: A Symposium' (*Organization Studies*, Special Issue, 1988).

Donaldson notes that 'much of the discussion around conventional organization studies' raises the fundamental question, can there be a science of organizations? (Donaldson 1985 : 75; also Hinings 1988 : 4). This question raises two issues: the ontological status of organizations and the epistemological status of organization theory (Burrell and Morgan 1979 : 298–299). It was the application to organizations of the techniques of the natural sciences, and the consequent belief that organizations are hard, concrete things, that the critics Donaldson claims to have 'routed' (Donaldson 1988 : 28) took issue with (Burrell and Morgan 1979 : 398; Clegg and Dunkerley 1980 : 257–262). Their criticisms of positivist organization theory, according to Donaldson, 'turn out to be a misappreciation of the philosophy of science' or reflect a 'misunderstanding of sociological theory' (Donaldson 1985 : 173 and 51). In assessing this remark, it is important to note that their critique was not simply anti-positivist—as Donaldson assumes (Donaldson 1988 : 28)—but contained the seeds of the then emerging realist concept of science (Bhaskar 1978; Keat and Urry 1975; Burrell and Morgan 1979; Clegg 1983). Realism repudiates positivism's account of the practice of the natural sciences and provides a comprehensive alternative to this usurper of the title of science (Bhaskar 1978 : 8). Introducing realism into the debate about organization theory changes its terms entirely. Criticisms of positivist organization theory can be substantiated by drawing on this rival concept of science; they do not 'misappreciate' philosophy of science or 'misunderstand' sociological theory. Donaldson's defence of positivist organization theory is doubly wrong: not only is he mistaken in defending the application of natural science techniques to social phenomena (Donaldson 1985 : 75), positivism is not even an accurate account of what natural scientists actually do (Bhaskar 1978; Holton 1968).

I have four broad aims in this paper:

First, to introduce realism as a means of resolving the impasse within organization theory, characterized by Donaldson in terms of pro-and anti-positivism.

Second, to critique Donaldson's defence of positivist organization theory by drawing on developments in the philosophy of realism subsequent to the criticisms he attempts to rebut, particularly the work of Roy Bhaskar (1978, 1986, 1989a, 1989b).

Third, to argue that the limitations of critical organization theory, and its susceptibility to Donaldson's positivist counter-attack, are attributable to a failure to develop this realist alternative and to the consequent persistence of an empiricist ontology (a refusal to acknowledge the reality of non-empirical things) which is presupposed by positivism's theory of knowledge and left unscathed by its critique.

Finally, to reconcile the critics' earlier problematization of epistemology and ontology (Burrell and Morgan 1979; Clegg and Dunkerley 1980) with their recent interest in postmodernism (Burrell 1988; Cooper and Burrell 1988; Clegg 1989a, 1989b; Clegg 1990) by developing a realist reading of Foucault and by explaining its significance for organizational analysis.

··

What is Realism?

Any theory of knowledge entails a theory of the objects of knowledge. Disinterest in such philosophical matters is not legitimate option. The question is not whether ontology, but which? The ontology of realism is distinguished by its acceptance of the possible existence of real, yet non-empirical entities—e.g. quarks, magnetic fields, social structures—which generate observable events. It takes issue with empiricism for collapsing within the category of experience three ontologically distinct levels of reality: real, non-empirical networks of organically connected structures ('the real'), which take the form of events ('the actual'), some of which are conceptually mediated in experience ('the empirical'). Thus 'the empirical is only a subset of the actual, which is itself a subset of the real' (Bhaskar 1989a : 190). These three levels of reality are inter-related, but distinct and irreducible: structures can exist but counteract and so produce no actual events, and events can occur without being experienced (Bhaskar 1989a : 16).

This ontology turns on its head the conventional primacy of the empirical. Since observation is conceptually mediated, the empirical is tenuous, subject to reinterpretation and expands with our knowledge. The primary object of science is not empirical patterns of events but the real entities of which they are the phenomenal form. As Bhaskar (1986 : 106) puts it, 'the world consists of things, not events'.

This ontology has significant epistemological and methodological implications.

Realism rejects empiricism's constant conjunction model of causation, in which cause and effect are seen as temporally and spatially distinct events, for appearances may mislead and causally related things may not be constantly conjoined. Causation, rather, is an object's capacity to act and is intrinsic to its internal structures and mechanisms. This capacity, or causal power, exists independently of its exercise and of experience of constant conjunctions among its phenomenal forms. Causal powers can be possessed unexercised, exercised unrealized and realized unperceived (Bhaskar 1989a : 16). Typically, events are conjunctions of multiple causes which may not be apparent to experience. On this basis, science is primarily interested in the causal powers of the mechanisms that cause things to happen, rather than the flux of empirical events.

Realism's refutation of the constant conjunction model of causality entails rejection of the deductive—nomological model of explanation, and the related belief that prediction and explanation are symmetrical; for if appearances may mislead and empirical regularities are a poor guide to causal mechanisms, then events cannot be deduced from covering laws. Science reasons 'retroductively' from empirical appearances to underlying essences or structures: what mechanisms would have to exist for the empirical world to appear in the form it does? (Sayer 1979). Realism's concern is with the intrinsic nature of objects, their properties, dispositions and capacities to act. The task is to develop models and explanatory theories that describe the powers and tendencies of the mechanisms of real objects, such that were they 'to represent correctly these structures and mechanisms, the phenomena would then be causally explained' (Keat and Urry 1975 : 35).

The realist stance toward theory is expressed in the notion of object constitution: 'to conceptualise in opposition to the empirical *melange*, a non-empirical but real (stratified) subject of enquiry, designating the proper focus of scientific thought' (Bhaskar 1986 : 105, n. 4). This is done by making 'real' (as opposed to nominal) definitions, i.e., statements with ontological commitments which describe the basic nature of the entity or structure. For example, 'a real definition of water would be that its molecules are composed of two atoms of hydrogen and one of oxygen' (Outhwaite 1987 : 45). The abstractions of object constitution are not generalizations from the empirical, nor concepts under which similar categories of events are grouped, but attempts to designate the necessary connections between internally or organically related objects that generate the empirical. 'The "abstract", though non-empirical, may nevertheless designate what is real' (Bhaskar 1986 : 108). 'Correspondence rules', refer not to the relationship between observational and theoretical terms, as in positivism, but to the causal relations between these real entities and their forms of appearance (Keat and Urry 1975 : 38).

Real definition and object constitution is critical, for only when we have defined what a thing is can we hypothesize on its causal mechanisms, i.e. what it has done, can do, and may do. This ontology, within which theory maps real relations rather than simply providing a framework for ordering facts, emphasizes conceptual precision. Theory is expressed in language, confirmed in dialogue. Language in science is analogous to geometry in physics: precision in meaning rather than accuracy of measurement is the arbiter of theory (Bhaskar 1989b : 46).

Although realism stresses the importance of concept formation, it warrants no theoreticism or idealist structuralism: it is a concept of applied science. Though imagined for theory construction, the reality of hypothetical entities or structures can be demonstrated through empirical testing (Bhaskar 1989a : 20), according to criteria of exhaustiveness, independence and consistency (Hanson 1958; Sayer 1979). Theoretical work is the 'retroduction' from manifest phenomena to generative structures ('the real'). It gains a knowledge of what structures are like and what they can do. Applied work is the 'retrodiction' (Bhaskar 1986 : 108) from resolved components to their antecedent causes. It gains a knowledge of structures' 'contingent modes of articulation in time' (Bhaskar 1986 : 108), i.e. what they actually do (the actual'). Scientific activity is, therefore, a movement in thought from conceptions of manifest phenomena (the 'empirical') to the description and explanation of the generative mechanisms of their essential relations. On this basis, knowledge of surface phenomena is then revised and explained. As Bhaskar (1986 : 68) puts it, knowledge 'does not lie exposed on the face of the world, prone to the gaze of the casual observer. Rather it is, for the most part, hidden encrusted in things, needing to be excavated in the theoretical and practical labours of the most arduous kind'. Continuing the metaphor of depth, as we dig deeper, through successive levels of reality, the boundary of the empirical world expands.

Realism takes issue with empiricism's conception of society as a mass of separable events and sequences comprised of atomistic individuals, and conceives the social relationally. The combined actions of individuals (or social practice) are objectified in social structures: a *sui generis* reality, both the medium within which social practice occurs, constraining and enabling, and the outcome of that practice. These structures are just as real as their natural counterparts, but differ in being concept- and activity-dependent. While social practices are conceptualized in experience their interconnections seldom are (Bhaskar 1986 : 159), for they are not spontaneously apparent in the observable pattern of social events and are typically obscured by ordinary sense experience. Social structures are non-empirical entities—real, not because we can see or touch them, but because they have causal powers—and are identifiable only through the theoretical and practical work of the social sciences (Marsden 1982 : 245). By this relational conception of the social, it is the ensemble of social structures, their tendencies and powers, that comprises 'society' (Bhaskar 1989a : 79): 'Society, as an object of enquiry, is necessarily "theoretical" in the sense that, like a magnetic field, it is necessarily unperceivable; so that it cannot be empirically identified independently of its effects. It can only be known, not shown to exist' (Bhaskar 1989a : 82).

Contrary to positivism's theory/practice dichotomy, realism recognises that ordinary people theorize and, in this sense, categories are internally related to and constitutive of social relations, rather than externally descriptive of them. For this reason, categories are both an inseparable part of the object, and therefore something to be explained rather than taken for granted, and their critique is an epistemic entrée to the 'real', i.e. social structures. The realist conception of experience thus contains both an ontological dimension, the generative mechanisms between social relations and categories, and an epistemological dimension, the conceptualization of social relations through a critique of their corresponding categories. Hence, the internal relationship between social relations and concepts is both epistemic and causal (Bhaskar 1986).

Bhaskar's 'transformational model of social activity' (Bhaskar 1986 : 122–129; also Giddens 1976 : 121) is a framework within which many of the troublesome methodological dualisms of social science, such as agency/structure, subjective/objective, idealism/materialism can be resolved in a manner which avoids voluntarism or reification (Reed 1988). However, realism's a priori concept of science provides no blue-print for empirical enquiry; it is for practicing social scientists to put realism to work. They are increasingly doing so. Realist approaches are particularly evident in geography and the sociology of space (Massey and Meegan 1975; Gregory and Urry 1985). We might also note Whittington's (1989) use of realism to reconcile agency and structure in his approach to strategic choice, which he advances as a corrective to the environmental determinism of traditional organization studies, such as Donaldson (1987). The exemplar of a relational conception of the social and a transformational model of social activities remains Marx's conception of social relations of production, which he developed through a critique of the categories of political economy. To make this association is not to deny the possibility of a non-Marxist realist social science or to claim that Marxism is necessarily a *valid* science: it is the mode of analysis that is significant. It is sufficient to note that realism is active within a remarkable re-construction of traditional Marxism— Sayer's *The Violence of Abstraction*—from which those interested in the organization of production might profit.

To reiterate: the significance of the ontology of realism lies in its unorthodox conceptions of reality, causality and explanation, the relational nature of the social and the internality of social relations and their concepts. It doesn't necessarily reject quantitative techniques, but asks what they are measures of and questions their explanatory value (see Clegg 1988 : 8; Donaldson 1988 : 29; Sayer 1984, especially Chapter 6). It is not a panacea for every problem within organization theory, nor does it underwrite any particular substantive analysis, but it can, I think, act as an under-labourer, 'in clearing the ground a little, and removing some of the rubbish that lies in the way to knowledge' (Locke, cited in Bhaskar 1989a : vii).

In the light of this précis of realism, in the next section, I would like to examine Donaldson's defence of positivist organization theory and to present a realist conception of 'organization'.

Donaldson: A Realist Critique and Alternative

Let us start with Donaldson's position on what he takes to be the cornerstone of the critique of positivist organization theory: the incommensurability of paradigms (Donaldson 1988 : 31). Donaldson opposes this because he thinks it inevitably entails intellectual apartheid and relativism (Donaldson 1985 : 37; Donaldson 1988 : 31).

I want to clarify, at the outset, some misunderstandings regarding paradigms and incommensurability which stem from Burrell and Morgan's (1979) *Sociological Paradigms and Organizational Analysis* (henceforth SPOA) by drawing on a little known reflexive interview with one of its authors, Gareth Morgan (Mills 1987/88). There are two issues: is Burrell and Morgan's use of 'paradigm' consistent with Kuhn, and does incommensurability mean that rival paradigms cannot be rationally evaluated? The answer to both questions is no.

SPOA's aim is to explore the philosophical and sociological assumptions shaping organizational analysis. When the book was written, in the mid 1970s, these assumptions were rarely reflected upon, questioned or challenged (Mills 1987/88 : 43). The reputation of Burrell and Morgan as 'critics' (Aldrich 1988;

Donaldson 1985, 1988) belies the remarkably nonpartisan nature of SPOA. Each of the four paradigms is critically, but sympathetically presented: 'When we were writing the book, we weren't committed so much to one paradigm over the other. . . . In fact, the whole book is based upon the ability to put oneself in different paradigms, to see from within these paradigms. That was the strategy that was used in trying to write the book: you locate yourself in the paradigm, you explore, you try to present in its terms, although a little bit of a critical edge comes in here and there' (Morgan, cited in Mills 1987/88 : 43). The entire purpose of this exercise was to open up to discussion the implicit assumptions of these paradigms at a time when the dominance of organization studies by functionalism militated against this. Herein lies the book's critical nature.

The term 'paradigm' is certainly derived from Kuhn, but Burrell and Morgan's usage is broader, in two senses (Burrell and Morgan 1979 : 36). First, they use the term as a classificatory device to structure their thesis that 'all theories of organization are based on a philosophy of science and a theory of society' (Burrell and Morgan 1979 : 1). 'What we did, not necessarily consciously at the time, was to take the metaphor of a map as a way of trying to lay out social theory and organization theory. As you know, a map is a classificatory device, and, for a lot of people, one of the major strengths of *Sociological Paradigms* is that it is a road map of social theory and organization studies' (Morgan, cited in Mills 1987/88 : 44). Second, Burrell and Morgan's 'paradigms' are ideal types of opposing metatheoretical assumptions and not, as they are for Kuhn, actual opposing substantive explanations. It is for these two reasons, I think, Morgan says, 'in retrospect, we probably shouldn't have selected that term (paradigm) at all. We should have talked about sociological world views and organizational analysis, or reality assumptions and organizational analysis' (Morgan, cited in Mills 1987/88 : 43).

Burrell and Morgan's call for 'paradigm closure' and 'isolationism' (Burrell and Morgan 1979 : 397)—used by Donaldson to damn the critique of positivism—must be understood in its historical context. It is far from being a philosophical axiom and incitement to relativism. Their prescription is, in fact, a strategy for achieving plurality and diversity in organizational analysis, a guard against 'dominant orthodoxies swamping promising heterodoxies and stunting the growth of innovative theoretical development' (Reed 1985 : 184). Their statements on 'isolationism' are always qualified by reference to the dominance of functionalism.

Donaldson's position on the incommensurability of paradigms is mistaken on two counts. Not only does he mistake Burrell and Morgan's strategy for plurality and diversity in organizational analysis for a principle of relativism, but he also misunderstands Kuhn by confusing and conflating 'incompatibility', 'incommensurability', and 'incomparability'. Bernstein clarifies their distinction:

138

'Kuhn did not introduce the incommensurability thesis in order to call into question the possibility of *comparing* theories and rationally evaluating them, but to clarify what we are *doing* when we compare theories. . . . for Kuhn rival paradigm theories are logically *incompatible* (and, therefore, really in conflict with each other); *incommensurable* (and, therefore, they cannot always be measured against each other point-by-point); and *comparable* (capable of being compared with each other in multiple ways without requiring the assumption that there is or must always be a common, fixed grid by which we measure progress)'. (Bernstein 1983 : 86)

Donaldson, however, convinced that rival paradigm groups are prevented 'from understanding and communicating' with each other (Donaldson 1985 : 38) and having demonstrated, to his own satisfaction, that this is not the case in organization theory (Donaldson 1985 : 40–46), reprimands Aldrich for his temerity in persisting in the belief that 'organization theory is composed of distinct paradigms' (Donaldson 1988 : 31). On the contrary, for Donaldson, 'various "paradigms" are not incommensurable concepts, theories, metatheories or epistemologies' but 'references to a variety of dependent variables and a variety of, and debate between, independent variables' (Donaldson 1988 : 31). Missing entirely Burrell and Morgan's point about the emasculation and incorporation of rival paradigms by the positivist techniques of functionalism (Burrell and Morgan 1979 : 398–399), Donaldson inadvertently proves it.

There is certainly a way of choosing between theories, even incommensurate ones: 'we can allow quite simply that a theory T_A is preferable to a theory T_B, even if they are incommensurable, provided that T_A can explain *under its descriptions* almost all the phenomena that T_B can explain under its descriptions *plus* some significant phenomena that T_B cannot explain' (Bhaskar 1989 : 19). This is, in fact, what Donaldson proposes for functionalist organization theory—widening organization theory by assimilating its rivals so as to incorporate their criticisms. 'Moves to widen conventional frameworks are to be applauded, moves to eradicate traditional concepts and objects of study are to be resisted' (Donaldson 1985 : 122). It is important to note that Donaldson does not achieve this widening of conventional frameworks: he simply says it can be done. A skeptic might want to reserve judgement until it is accomplished. Given this promise of a broadening of organization theory, it is interesting to note that Donaldson's defence mechanisms entail its *narrowing*.

The first defence mechanism I want to examine is Donaldson's vigilant distinction between organization and society. This social relationship is expressed in the physical metaphor internal/external and by micro/macro levels of analysis. Organization, a relatively micro-phenomenon (Donaldson 1985 : 123), is a sub-system of society; organization theory is a sub-discipline of sociology (Donaldson 1985 : 117–18). Organization theory deals with those parts of the social structure located inside the organization (Donaldson 1985 : 119, 102–3); sociology is concerned with the wider society. By means of this distinction, organization theory is protected from the criticisms of those who argue for a sociology of organization: wrong level, different object of study. In this way, the possibility of a Marxian theory of organizations, for example, is dismissed as a contradiction in terms: 'Marxism is a theory of society therefore it cannot be a theory of organizations' (Donaldson 1985 : 127). This distinction, however, raises the problem of the relationship between organization and society, for Child (1988a : 13) the lacuna in Donaldson, and poses the interesting question of how society can exist in anything but organizational form.

A second defence is the scope of organization theory. Its focus is goal-oriented behaviour coordinated towards an objective (Donaldson 1985 : 7–9, 120–1). Organization theory, according to Donaldson, does not attempt to explain everything that happens within the 'legal envelope' of organizations (Donaldson 1985 : 8). To be precise, organization theory studies a narrow sub-set of a sub-system of society. Donaldson protests therefore that 'the gambit of delineating phenomena which organization theory cannot handle, and then using this to "prove" the "inadequacy" of the "approach" is both widespread and invalid' (Donaldson 1985 : 120). However, this argument can be turned around. A common defence of normal science is to restrict the range of theory to only those phenomena it can explain (Kuhn 1970 : 100). For Donaldson, that which organization theory cannot explain is not the business of organization theory; it is either without organization (i.e. society, the wrong level) or within organization, but beyond its subset. While he allows for the possibility of expanding organization theory, by definitional fiat, he seeks to delegitimate expansion of the explanatory power of its critics.

The remaining defence against the critics is the teleological account of positivist organization theory by Donaldson (1985 and 1988) and Hinings (1988). Organization theory is presented as a new discipline struggling to define and legitimate itself apart from its origins in Weberian sociology. Critics are construed as attempting to 'reclaim' organization theory for sociology (Hinings 1988 : 2), imposing upon it criteria drawn from classical sociological theory (Donaldson 1985 : 8). For Donaldson, sociology is problematic in two major respects: it is concerned with the wrong level (the 'wider society') and it is outmoded—sociology is always 'classical', never contemporary. The image is of a child (organization theory) struggling to achieve independence from over-possessive parents (sociology). This account neatly reverses the popular impression: critics become conservative custodians of an old orthodoxy, and Donaldson's defence of what has been practiced in North American business schools for the best part of fifty years becomes the 'brilliant' midwife of a new discipline (Hinings 1988 : 3). In fact, the institutional segregation of organization theory from sociology (organization from society) is an accomplished fact in North America, and the issues raised by the critique have been largely ignored (Hinings 1988 : 5).

I want to relate the institutionalization of organization theory to the meta-phors of battle—'paradigm warriors', 'possession of the field', 'routing'—used by participants to the debate over Donaldson's defence (Aldrich 1988; *Australian Journal of Management* 1989; Donaldson 1988). Kuhn's observations on profes-sional socialization into normal science offer insights into the *realpolitik* of academia which are apposite here. Paradigmatic change is not a purely cerebral affair, but depends on the outcome of political conflicts between custodians and opponents of a paradigm. Resistance to change is the norm; breakthroughs typically occur when the hegemony of the 'invisible college' is broken. The simple, if unspoken, truth is that universities are organizations of power—as every graduate student and untenured faculty knows only too well—and positivism has functioned as a hegemonic method within them. This dominant concept of science, deference to which is a rite of passage in North America, has established control over the production of knowledge. It specifies what is knowable (ontology) and how it is to be known (epistemology): together they have shaped the scope and content of organization studies and the nature of rules (of research practice, criteria for success) governing the academic profession. It is because of this that Donaldson is able to defend organization theory in the name of science. The comments of Hinings (1988) and Aldrich (1988) are observations on this political reality. By virtue of its institutional power, positivist organization theory largely ignores criticism: it cannot invali-date or disarm it. Aldrich's citation count (Aldrich 1988), which he uses to question the critics' impact on 'established ways of thinking about organiza-tions' (Aldrich 1988 : 20), is no assessment of the validity of a critique: it is as much a measure of insularity.

Donaldson's defence misses the central point of the 'moves to eradicate traditional concepts and objects of study' (Donaldson 1985 : 122). Yet it is implicit in his very formulation of the problem of incommensurability: 'to say of two theories that they conflict, clash or are in competition presupposes that there is something—a domain of real object or relations existing and acting independently of their (conflicting) descriptions—*over* which they clash. Hence incommensurable theories must share a part world in common. If they do not, then no sense can be given to the concept of scientific change, and *a fortiori* to the notion of a clash between the theories for they are now no longer alternatives' (Bhaskar 1989a : 19). The problem of incommensurability, then, points to the existence of an ontological dimension, to the real object or relations over which theories clash: in this case, 'organization'. For this reason, the entire debate between positivist organization theory and its critics hinges on the ontological status of 'organization' and its relationship to 'society' (Clegg and Dunkerley 1980; Burrell and Morgan 1979). *This* is what critics of positivist organization theory were getting at, but, because their critique was confined to epistemology, they failed to develop the realist alternative to the empiricist ontology of positivism which would have enabled them to sustain an alternative conception of 'organization'. Bhaskar's assessment, that there can be no going back from the critique of positivist epistemology, but yet without an adequate social ontology there can be no going forward, is particularly apposite in the case of organization theory (Bhaskar 1989a : 11).

I should like to pursue this issue by utilizing the previous discussion of realism to sketch a very different account of the conceptual development of positivist organization theory to that of Donaldson and, in the process, to account for its conceptual fault lines—organization/society, internal/external, and formal/informal structure—which are active in Donaldson's defence. Convention looks to the origins of organization theory in Weber, but I want to argue that the theoretical imperative to an organization theory came from neo-classical or marginalist economics, not sociology, and that organization theory has developed within, and been constrained by, the implicit social ontology of economics.

Economics, Power and Private Property

The ontology of economics is empiricist (Marsden 1982). It conceives the social as a series of empirical regularities among a mass of atomistic individuals, events and things. Blind to their non-empirical connections, economics abstracts individuals from their social context to form 'homo economicus' and abstracts material things from the social relations that produced them to form the 'economy'. It then develops an a priori model of rational economic action between these abstractions. This double abstraction expels from economic analysis 'power' and 'social relations', the nature of the employment relationship and the organization of work. These problems are delegated by economics to complementary, but subordinate, disciplines—such as organization studies—which developed within the theoretical space of economists' implicit social ontology. Weber mediated the relationship between economics and organization theory by elucidating the implicit social theory of marginalism and theorizing the institutional conditions required by the market (Clarke 1982). He remains the chief analyst of organization theory's backcloth, the economy/society distinction.

The relationship between this lacuna within economics and the need for a theory of organizations is clear if we look not to Barnard, as is customary, but to Coase's, now classic, *The Nature of the Firm*, published the previous year, in 1937. The problem for economic theory is that it assumes the direction of resources within the firm directly depends on the price mechanism, yet, evidently, resources within the firm are directed by the power of command of one group of people over another. What needs explaining is the existence of 'islands of conscious power in this ocean of unconscious cooperation [the price mechanism] like lumps of butter coagulating in a pail of buttermilk' (Robertson, cited in Coase 1937 : 388). The problem in economic theory is, if the price mechanism coordinates the distribution of resources, 'why is such organization necessary?' (Coase 1937 : 388). The theoretical imperative to the development of organization theory was provided by the need to fill this 'gap' in economic analysis, i.e., the problem of theorizing 'power' and 'organization'.

This theoretical imperative combined with the influence of practical theorists, such as Barnard (1938), to define the object of knowledge of organization studies as control and coordination within the corporation. Broad definitions of organizations in terms of families arranging picnics (Donaldson 1985 : 8) should not deflect attention from the fact that organization theory is active in business and the predominant form in which business is organized is the corporation. That's why it is institutionalized in business schools, why businesses invest millions of dollars in these schools and why organization theory permeates the M.B.A. The corporation is remarkable as the only form of social organization to take the form of private property (Ellerman 1983 : 271). The conceptual fault lines of organization theory stem from a misconception of this peculiar form of social organization. Just as economics abstracts from the social relations of production to form 'the firm', so organization theory abstracts from them to form its analogue, 'the organization', which is precisely a 'legal envelope' (Donaldson 1985 : 8, 120). By abstracting 'organization' from 'society' in this way, the corporation's connections with the social relations which constitute this form of private property are conceptually severed and it is effectively de-juridified. The exclusive nature of private property is mirrored in the conceptual exclusion of society from organization. This is the basis for the internal/external metaphor usually applied to the organization/society relationship: a *physical* metaphor suggestive of walls and fences quite unsuited to social realities, but apt for the boundary of property. The social relationship between the propertied and the propertyless transcends its corporate organizational form. It is only the categorical dichotomies of organization theory that prevent recognition of the causal connections between the behaviour of people within organizations and this broader social relationship structuring their interactions.

The ontological status of this object—'organization'—is defined by the intersection of an empiricist concept of causation, by which cause and effect are taken to be spatially and temporarily distinct empirical events, and an empiricist ontology, which delimits possible objects of knowledge to the observable. This ontology is the basis for the—much criticized—positivist epistemological position that explanation is deduced from covering laws documenting empirical regularities, and a theory/practice dichotomy in which theory is seen as descriptive of an external reality, rather than constitutive of it.

Organizations are thus construed as empirical things consisting of behavioural regularities within a particular space and time—visible, habituated action, identified and known by ' "seeing" what sorts of people do what sorts of things in a regular way' (Manicas 1980 : 71)—which are measured by positivist techniques, objectified as 'structure' and construed as the focus of organization theory (Donaldson 1985 : 8; see also Pugh et al. 1963; Whitley 1977). In this way, organizations are restricted to what is observable and to what is measurable: 'power' and 'social relations' repeatedly slip through the conceptual net attached to this philosophical framework.

The abstraction of corporations from the relations of exclusion which constitute this form of private property retains within this legal envelope the structure of property rights underwriting managerial authority and bestowing management's right to direct production and appropriate its product. Management's ultimate right is the right to exclude, enforced through trespass law (Vincent-Jones 1987). This structure of rights is theorized in economics as capitalist rationality, embodied in accounting practices and propagated in an ideology which construes management as allocating resources on the basis of an impartial interpretation of market signals. This abstracted structure is 'formal' organization: it is what is supposed to happen—because economic theory tells us it will, and management ideology tells us it should. The underside of property rights and managerial authority, workers' indirect or negative control—basically their power to say 'no!'—i.e. behaviour inconsistent with this structure of rights and economic model—is what actually happens and what is labelled 'informal' (Clegg and Dunkerley 1980 : 226).

The major complaint against the implicit ontology of positivist organization theory is that it inhibits an understanding of power. Organization theory conflates the empirical with the non-empirical pattern of events with causal laws, and exercising power with its capacity. The capacity of power is beyond the remit of organization theory: it is dependent on resources in society, accepted as a given and located *outside* organizations. Hence, the aim of organization theory is not a 'sociological explanation of power, but an explanation of power distribution and how power works *within* organizations' (Hinings 1988 : 4, my emphasis). An understanding of power is inhibited by the divorce between exercising power and its capacity (Clegg 1977), a divorce institutionalized in the distinction—insisted upon by Donaldson and supported by Hinings—between organization theory and sociology, the 'organizational' and the 'societal'. A misconception of power is no philosophical nicety, but has an impact on the teaching of organizational political analysis and skills—which are, after all, the essence of management (Baddeley and James 1987). This point might be considered by positivists when assessing the regular complaints that management education is poor preparation for the real world.

Realism, Power and 'Organization'

It was, of course, the divorce between organization and society which stimulated sociologists of organizations to attempt to restore their connections by rethinking organizational power in terms of 'control' (Clegg and Dunkerley 1980; Salaman and Thompson 1980). However, much depends here on the ontological status of 'organization' and 'society', and on the nature of control. Control is the actuation of power. The concept of power operationalized by the control approach to organizations is the radical version developed by Lukes (1974 : 34): 'A exercises power over B when A effects B in a manner contrary to B's interests'. Lukes's innovation of real or objective interests widened the scope of enquiry beyond the actual or threatened use of observable sanctions to latent, unobservable conflict and to the shaping of perceptions and preferences contrary to people's real interests. Thus, perception of power was an epistemological problem: real interests could be obscured by false consciousness and ideological analysis, such as organization theory (Clegg and Dunkerely 1980 : 58). Marxian analysis located the origins or capacity of power outside the organization, at the interface of classes and in the instruments of the state, and from its economic analysis of the conflicting real interests of management and labour, deduced an imperative to control exercised within the organization, at the point of production. The injunction, then, to study organizations in the context of the wider society, expressed the radical concept of power, which itself grew out of the critique of epistemology.

The radical concept of power stimulated a wide-ranging critique which radicalized a cluster of disciplines and caused their convergence around the organon of control, an approach applied to a wide range of substantive issues, from accountancy, industrial relations, deviancy, labour process to organizations. Any assessment of the relative merits of positivist organization theory *vis-á-vis* the sociology of organizations must recognize the limitations of 'control'—now evident in the incipient deconstruction of labour process analysis (Burawoy 1985; Storey 1985; Cohen 1987; Cohen 1989; Knights and Willmott 1990) and the mounting interest in Foucault and postmodernism (Cooper and Burrell 188; Burrell 1988; Clegg 1989a, 1989b, 1990)—and their origins in 'the lack of a good, general theory of power' (Bray and Littler 1988 : 567).

For realism, the limitations of the radical concept of power are explicable in terms of its underlying empiricist social ontology which, despite their other differences, it shares with elitist and pluralist concepts of power (Isaac 1987). All agree that power is rooted in the regular conjunctions between temporally and spatially distinct events, A and B. In other words, their common focus is on the *lateral* relations between social behaviour: the more powerful is said to cause the behaviour of the less powerful because his/her behaviour regularly antecedes it (Isaac 1987 : 85). The essence of the injunction of the sociology of organizations is simply to examine the lateral connections between society and organizations (a relationship expressed in the hyphenation of 'political' and 'economy'). In short, like positivist organization theory, it fails to recognize the ontological depth of experience.

For realism, power is a concept referring to necessary properties or non-observable causal mechanisms of objects, rather than their contingent effects. For example, 'to assert that conductivity is a power of copper is to claim that copper possesses the enduring capacity to conduct electricity, by virtue of its intrinsic nature, in this case its atomic structure' (Isaac 1987 : 74). *Social* powers are 'those capacities to act possessed by social agents in virtue of the enduring relations in which they participate' (Isaac 1987 : 80). Thus power must be understood relationally, in terms of the real underlying relations which structure behavioural interaction. It is the relationship which bestows both parties with a capacity or power to act and causes the behaviour of both A and B, rather than the behaviour of one causing that of the other. In accordance with realism's stratified ontology, a power may be real without being exercised, and it can be exercised without producing an empirical effect, e.g., due to the presence of countervailing powers. The actual exercise of power, of course, depends on political skill and is contingent on the circumstances of its deployment. Thus contrary to the behavioural focus of empiricism, realism conceives power as a *vertical* relation between social structures and social action, the depth of which is expressed in its category of 'experience'. The essential point is that, for realism, capacities to act—'powers'—are a property of the nature of the social relations between people, and these relations are construed as non-empirical structures analogous to the atomic structures that account for conductivity (Isaac 1987 : 75). On this basis, theorizing 'power' is a matter of conceptualizing the causal mechanisms of social structures, or in formal realist terminology, constituting objects in thought. I might add, it was precisely this problem that Clegg and Dunkerley addressed, although they identified it by the Althusserian term, theoretical object (Clegg and Dunkerley 1980 : 1, 262, 502; Clegg 1988 : 9).

While realism can agree with positivist organization theory that 'organizations' are observable patterns of behaviours, discrete in time and space, its primary concern is not temporally ordered correlations between these behaviours, but the causal mechanisms of the social structures generating these phenomena. These structures comprise people who are causally connected but not necessarily physically co-present, therefore they transcend the traditional parameters of organization theory. It is this complex ensemblage of structures that comprises society (Bhaskar 1989a : 76 and 78). Conceived thus, the relationship between organization and society is that between the empirical and non-empirical, conceptually-mediated activity and structure, the subjective and the objective. It is ill-described by the physical metaphor of internal/ external, for this reflects a constant conjunction concept of causality within a flat or horizontal, empiricist ontology. The appropriate metaphor is depth. Organization and society are not external, contingently connected entities, but internally related objects: indivisible aspects of the same social reality. Contrary to Donaldson, in no way is society external to organization.

Foucault: A Realist Reading

The last critical work examined by Donaldson (1985) was published in 1981. The critics of positivist organization theory, who Donaldson claims to have 'routed' (Donaldson 1988 : 28; Child 1988b), have long since advanced their ideas in a development which can be construed as an auto-critique. The first of a series of articles by Cooper and Burrell (1988) which considered the implications of postmodern theory for organizational analysis appeared in the same issue as the 'Offence and Defence' Symposium. This was followed shortly afterwards by articles on Michel Foucault by Burrell and by Clegg (Burrell 1988; Clegg 1989a; see also Burrell 1984; Clegg 1989b, 1990). With the intention of building on these, I want to investigate further Foucault's potential contribution to organizational analysis in the light of my account of realism.

There is no point in repeating Burrell's (1988) introduction, but a brief précis of Foucault helps focus attention on my argument. The relevant text is Foucault's *Discipline and Punish: The Birth of the Prison*, an account of how the privatization of property triggered the privatization of power (Foucault 1977 : 85–7). This book is less a history of the prison, more an analysis of power and its modern form, 'disciplines'. Disciplines are meticulous methods of controlling the operation of the body that work through exploring, breaking down and rearranging this operation (Foucault 1977 : 137–8). The instruments of discipline—hierarchical observation, normalizing judgement, the examination—determine norms or rules of conduct and shape (or 'normalize') people to fit them. The Foucauldian thesis is that disciplines originated in monasteries, became diffused during the eighteenth and nineteenth centuries and are present today in the constitution of a variety of interconnected organizational forms—prisons, asylums, hospitals, armies, corporations—where their techniques are developed and refined. The privatization of power is graphically illustrated in the book's opening pages by the description of the gruesome details of that very public and violent form of punishment—hanging, drawing and quartering—and the private and silent punishment of the timetabled regimen of the prison, eighty years later. This illustration is a metaphor, the prison is a laboratory of power and microcosm of a disciplinary society. A close examination of the machinery of imprisonment can reveal the logic and operating principles of disciplinary mechanisms dispersed throughout society.

Juxtaposing realism with this emerging postmodern, Foucauldian genre in organizational analysis raises the question of their relationship and compatibility. Can my realist defence of the critics' earlier critique of positivist organization theory from Donaldson's counter-critique be reconciled with their recent interest in Foucault and the postmodern? To the best of my knowledge, the relationship between realism and Foucault has never been systematically examined. The typical postmodern reading of Foucault, as a relativist idealist hostile to meta-narrative, and the close association between realism and the materialism of its exemplar—Marx—has left a widespread impression that realism and Foucault are incompatible and has discouraged their cross-fertilization.

Is a realist reading of Foucault possible then? I believe it is. Foucault is an empirical, historical researcher into the nature of power. He denies being a theorist of power (Kritzman 1988 : 39); indeed, he seems averse to theorizing and declares himself an empiricist (Kritzman 1988 : 106). Yet, deeply embedded within his detailed analyses of concrete historical situations and events there is a rich and complex model of the mechanisms of power which is of direct relevance to organizational analysis (Burrell 1988; Clegg 1989a, 1989b). However, because Foucault prioritizes empirical detail over conceptual precision, there is little conceptual consistency and development within and between his texts. As a result, this implicit model of power is 'exploratory rather than coherent and well-finished' (Cousins and Hussain 1984 : 226). His empirical work can be similarly described. In Foucault's own, somewhat harsh, words, it is indecipherable, disorganized, inconclusive, repetitive and disconnected, a muddle that does little more than mark time: 'it advances nowhere' (Foucault 1980 : 78). They are 'just fragments', it's up 'to you or me to see what we can make of them' (Foucault 1980 : 79).

The conceptual and empirical incoherence of Foucault's work renders it susceptible to a variety of interpretations (Burrell 1988 : 222), each of which discern, or impose, some unity. There are two broad sets of responses to Foucault. Both are impediments, in my view, to understanding Foucault's significance for organizational analysis. Historiographers criticize Foucault for failing to meet the requisite standards of empirical evidence. They allege his evidence is insufficient and conflicting, he is careless over dates and places and his topics are not even 'discussed in a temporal order' (Giddens 1987 : 213). Postmodernists welcome his work as a celebration of heterogeneity and difference, fragmentation and indeterminacy, and as an alternative to the totalizing discourse or metanarrative of science (Cooper and Burrell 1988; Burrell 1988). Broadly speaking, the first group rejects his work for failing to meet modernist criteria, the second welcomes it for this very reason.

To correct these interpretations I want to present an alternative reading of Foucault based on critical realism and to argue that Foucault seeks 'to establish the ontological foundations of modern institutions' (Clegg 1989b : 153). This reading is based on several points of resemblance between Foucault and realism which are suggestive of a *prima facie* case for their compatibility. These can be stated simply, thus:

1. They share the metaphor and terminology of depth.
2. Each is concerned, in different ways, with what Bhaskar calls 'object constitution'.
3. Both are critical of and provide compatible alternatives to positivism and empiricism.
4. They share a non-empiricist concept of causation and a similar approach to time and space.
5. They provide compatible alternatives to the positivist dichotomy between practice and theory, or power and knowledge.
6. They provide compatible critiques of, and alternatives to, conventional approaches to 'power'.
7. Both are critical of 'traditional' Marxism.

Foucault contends that his work is best understood not as a solution, but as various ways of formulating a problem: explaining the relationship between experience, power and knowledge (Kritzman 1988 : 71). 'For my part', Foucault explains, 'it has struck me that I might have seemed a bit like a whale that leaps to the surface of the water disturbing it momentarily with a tiny jet of spray and lets it be believed, or pretends to believe, or wants to believe, or himself does in fact indeed believe, that down in the depths where no one sees him any more, where he is no longer witnessed nor controlled by anyone, he follows a more profound, coherent and reasoned trajectory' (Foucault 1980 : 79). This metaphor of the whale is redolent of the metaphor of ontological depth of realism. Foucault is undoubtedly a skilled analyst of surface events, but his work does not preclude other analyses, such as realism. The idea I want to develop is that the set of problems Foucault attempts to formulate can be better understood if we explore the ontological underside to his empirical studies of these events. 'Down in the depths', Foucault does indeed follow a 'coherent and reasoned trajectory'—a glimpse of which is revealed in his interviews— which realism can help explicate and develop.

Problematization

Like realism, Foucault's purpose is to de-mystify the category of the 'real' by showing how objects of knowledge are constituted. Foucault refers to this as 'problematization', the notion common to all his work since *Madness and Civilization* (Kritzman 1988 : 257). Paraphrasing Foucault: problematization is not the representation of a pre-existing object, nor the creation by discourse of an object that does not exist, but a concern with how objects are practically and conceptually constituted (Kritzman 1988 : 257). In considering the compatibility of Foucault and realism much depends, however, on the nature of 'objects'. I want, therefore, to deduce something of their nature from Foucault's comments on sexuality, madness and criminality.

An object, for Foucault (1981 : 127), 'is the set of effects produced in bodies, behaviors, and social relations' by the deployment of a series of conceptual and practical operations—in a word, 'disciplines'. For example, 'the convergence of internment and medicine' (Cousins and Hussain 1984 : 139), organized in the form of the asylum. An object is a network of social relations organized or synthesized into empirical form by this complex disciplinary technology. 'Objects' are simply regulated forms of social relationships, forms of politically organized subjection (Abrams 1988), and, as such, also forms of experience—such as madness, illness, sexuality, and criminality. They are real, historical constructs—like the objects of realism, concept- and activity-dependent—what Foucault calls the 'historical *a priori*' (Foucault 1980 : 236).

These objects have an outside or a surface (observable behaviour, events) and—I suggest—an inside or structure, referred to by Foucault as the mobile system of relationships and syntheses between an object's constitutive elements (Foucault 1980 : 236). The surface corresponds to practice, the interior corresponds to the product of practice—its structure of interconnections. The latter is largely a hidden domain, for while social practices are conceptualized, their interconnections seldom are. As Foucault puts it, 'people know what they do; they frequently know why they do what they do; but what they don't know is what they do does' (Foucault, cited in Krips 1990 : 173).

Foucault depicts the existence of these objects by detailed empirical descriptions of the practices constituting them (Foucault 1971; 1976; 1977), by examining concretely and in detail the way in which power is exercised—its 'great surface network' (Foucault 1981 : 105). For the most part, he is concerned with the 'how' of practice, only latterly (in Foucault 1977 and 1984) with the 'what' of the product of that process, its structure or 'anatomy'. Foucault describes the exterior of the necessary relations comprising these objects, i.e. he empirically isolates necessary from contingent relations. Realism can assist in developing an understanding of the interior of these objects, i.e. the nature of the causal connections between their heterogeneous, constitutive elements (Foucault 1980 : 194).

Causality, Time and Space

A misunderstanding of the nature of these objects is the source of the chief difficulties of understanding Foucault, particularly his methods of examining them. Convention distinguishes between Foucault's early archaeological and later genealogical work (Burrell 1988). This characterization poses the problem of the relationship between discourse and power: is Foucault an archaeologist of discourse or a genealogist of power? (Smart 1983). It is important to counter this interpretation, for it encourages an idealist interpretation of Foucault and mystifies Foucault's significance as an empirical researcher.

I want to examine Foucault's methodology by considering his work as the gradual formulation of a problem which is intelligible only if we use his later work as a retrospective vantage point. As Foucault says, 'one always finds what is essential after the event; the most general things are those that appear last' (Kritzman 1988 : 257). I propose that we consider Foucault's texts, as he examines those of others, not laterally or horizontally, in terms of chronological periods, but as the laying down of epistemic sediments. On this basis, I shall argue, archaeology and genealogy are complementary methods working in different dimensions, not discrete methods representing different periods of his work.

To make sense of archaeology and genealogy, I want to introduce the idea that Foucault employs a realist concept of causality, and that this informs his approach to time and space. For Foucault, causally connected things need not occur in the same time and space; the 'here-and-now' is not necessarily epistemologically significant (Urry 1985 : 23). This is evident in his conception of power and history. Power, for Foucault, is a quality of social relations which 'are perhaps among the best hidden things in the social body' (Kritzman 1988 : 118). These relations are hidden, I suggest, because they are among people who are spatiotemporally discrete. They are non-empirical, but real entities, transcending time, space and organizational forms. Similarly, the conventional view of history which restricts it to a chain of past events, and of historiography as the narrative description of the sequence of these events, is based on a particular, constant conjunction, view of causation to which Foucault does not subscribe. Foucault employs a two-dimensional view of time. Time exists in a horizontal dimension as a sequence of events, and in a vertical dimension as 'layers of epistemic organization' of ideas of those events (Giddens 1987 : 213). Epistemic structure is the 'deep memory' of an historical process, it constitutes a history of the development of an object (Bollas 1987). These horizontal and vertical dimensions of time correspond to genealogy and archaeology, respectively; both methods synthesize material that is spatiotemporally discrete.

Archaeology is a method of unearthing from beneath the surface of ideas and categories ('local discursivities') the object of which is the historical—materialist condition of their existence (Foucault 1980 : 233). We might recall Bhaskar's words as an apt justification for this method: knowledge 'does not lie exposed on the face of the world prone to the gaze of the casual observer. Rather it is, for the most part, hidden encrusted in things, needing to be excavated in the theoretical and practical labours of the most arduous kind' (Bhaskar 1986 : 68). Foucault chose the term archaeology to:

suggest that the kind of analysis I was using was out-of-phase, not in terms of time but by virtue of the *level* at which it was situated. Studying the history of ideas, as they evolve, is not my problem so much as trying to discern *beneath them* how one or another object could take shape as a possible object of knowledge. Why, for instance did madness become, at a given moment, an object of knowledge corresponding to a certain type of knowledge? By using the word "archaeology" rather than "history", I tried to designate this desynchronisation between ideas about madness and *the constitution of madness as an object*. (Kritzman 1988 : 31, *my emphasis*)

If we heed Foucault's remarks concerning 'level' and 'time' then archaeology should not be regarded as a digging back through chronological time, or the past, and the assemblage of its remnants in the 'museum of modern knowledge', as Harvey (1989 : 56) puts it. Rather, it is a digging beneath present categories to uncover the object they represent. Archaeology is a method of abstraction consistent with realism. Whereas positivism generalizes from the particular and deduces an understanding of the local from general, covering laws, Foucault's archaeology extracts knowledge of general causal mechanisms, diffuse throughout society, from their particular manifestations. As Burawoy (1985 : 18) puts it, 'every particularity contains a generality; each particular factory regime is the product of general forces operating at a societal or global level'. Archaeology is a method of extracting 'the general from the particular' (Burawoy 1985 : 18). Its aim is to produce a model or analytics to grasp the situational logic (Atkinson 1971 : 174–9; Van Velsen 1967 : 141–9; Kritzman 1988 : 105) of localities and contexts by explicating the rationale or micro-physics of the infinitesimal mechanisms of power operating there.

True, Foucault abandoned the term archaeology (1988 : 31), but the *concept* remains. 'Archaeology' was replaced—I suggest—not by 'genealogy', but 'analytics' (Foucault 1981 : 82): a model or 'grid of analysis' that describes the nature and constitution of an object and grasps its logic and rationale. The shift from 'archaeology' to 'analytic' coincides with a shift in Foucault's interest from the 'how' to the 'what' of power, from an uncritical acceptance of sovereign power to an attempt to define disciplinary power (Foucault 1980 : 92 and 183–4). Foucault makes clear that this analytics of power can be constituted only if it frees itself from the juridico—discursive representation of power (Foucault 1981 : 82); 'we must', he says, 'construct an analytic of power that no longer takes law as a model and a code' (Foucault 1981 : 90). Necessarily then, the excavation of the 'micro-physics' of power entails a critique of those systematizing theories and descending analyses which represent power in terms of law and 'the state' (Marsden 1992). An analytic, then, is a model depicting the constitution or structure of objects and is developed through a critique of their constitutive categories.

Genealogy, on the other hand, is a method of determining the constitution of objects (Foucault 1980 : 117) by means of a detailed empirical description of their practical, historical formation. Concrete events are conjunctures of a multiplicity of diverse practices, constituted by a 'mobile system of relationships and syntheses', which genealogy reveals through selecting material from the flux of empirical events. Like that Victorian realist, Marx, Foucault's empirical work is concrete, 'because it is the concentration of many determinations, hence unity of the diverse' (Marx 1973 : 101). The 'synthesis' noted above is significant, for the combination of these elements and processes 'qualitatively modifies each constitutive entity' (Urry 1985 : 26), and is one important reason why for both realism and Foucault there can be no 'general' theory.

This realist interpretation recasts conventional understanding of Foucault's methodology. Rather than representing discrete periods of his life's work, archaeology and genealogy are methods of analysis operating in different dimensions: ontological depth and chronological time, 'theory' and 'history', abstract and concrete. In Foucault's words: ' "archaeology" would be the appropriate methodology of this analysis of local discursivities, and "geneal-ogy" would be the tactics whereby, on the basis of the descriptions of these local discursivities, the subjected knowledges which were thus released would be brought into play' (Foucault 1980 : 85). Moreover, these methods are com-plementary: 'it is a question of forming a different grid of historical decipher-ment by starting from a different theory of power; and, at the same time, of advancing little by little toward a different conception of power through a closer examination of an entire historical material' (Foucault 1981 : 90–1). This interpretation of his methodology accounts for Foucault's retrospective de-scription of all his work as genealogy (Foucault 1980 : 85–6).

Realism and Foucault: A Convergence

To summarize, Foucault's synthesis of material discrete in time and space, his explanation of the practical and conceptual constitution of seemingly self-evident things, and his unearthing of an object's microphysics beneath the surface flux of empirical events—all this is consistent with realism's critique of and alternative to positivism's conception of causality, ontology and theory. Yes, genealogies are 'precisely antisciences' (Foucault 1980 : 83)—but anti-*positivist* sciences.

Recognition of realism's and Foucault's common purpose is hindered by the different terms used to describe it and the different methods they favour. Their common purpose is to capture the causal mechanisms of social forms of experience. Bhaskar calls this 'object constitution', Foucault 'anatomy'. Their respective methods are critique and genealogy. Critique 'retroduces' from categories to their constitutive social conditions, thereby creating concepts that map real, non-empirical social structures. Genealogy uncovers the layers of epistemic organization of objects of knowledge through a reconstruction of the history of their formation. Critique and genealogy are complementary moments of historical materialist analysis (Sayer 1987), for they approach a common task from different directions. Theorists grant logical priority to critique over empirical research. They direct attention to relevant historiographic terrain. We theorize a thing and then describe it by writing its history. Foucault—being no social theorist—reverses the order of priority. He presents a genealogy of the practical constitution of politically organized subjection— madness, criminality, sexuality—and leaves us with the problem of theorizing about what he has done. Hence the volume of secondary literature.

Finally—and crucially, for organizational analysis—realism and Foucault provide complementary critiques of positivism's theory–practice dichotomy and of empiricist concepts of power. Realism's notion of the internality of social relations and categories is compatible with Foucault's notion of power–knowledge. Foucault shows how the control of an object requires knowledge of its nature. The mechanisms of disciplinary power are simultaneously instruments for the formation and accumulation of knowledge. Disciplining is an act of both individualization and of categorization. Power and knowledge, conceived by positivism as independent, are internally related and combine to form 'power–knowledge', a concept analagous to 'space–time' (Hawking 1988 : 15–34). Foucault thus dissolves the traditional, positivist distinctions between power and knowledge, practice and theory. We should, says Foucault, 'abandon a whole tradition that allows us to imagine that knowledge can exist only where the power relations are suspended and that knowledge can develop only outside its injunctions, its demands and interests' (Foucault 1977 : 27).

Realism and Foucault provide complementary critiques of and alternatives to conventional concepts of power which typically conceive it in terms of negation and repression of the actions of the powerless by the powerful (i.e. 'control'). For Foucault, while power disciplines, it also enables and produces. For realism, 'Rather than A getting B to do something B would not otherwise do, social relations of power typically involve both A and B doing what they *ordinarily* do' (Isaac 1987 : 96). There can be no power without resistance because it is the relationship between A and B that causes the behaviour of both: 'it is not the behaviour of the slave that is caused by the behaviour of the master; rather, the master–slave relationship is the material cause of the behaviour of both the master *and* the slave' (Isaac 1987 : 85–6). Realism and Foucault can agree that power is relational, that the mechanisms of social relations are non-empirical, that while social practices are conceptualized their interconnections seldom are and therefore must be revealed through abstraction and reconstructed through empirical history. Realism is concerned with what power is; Foucault with the exercise and effects of power.

This realist reading of Foucault corrects postmodern and historiographic interpretations, which, I maintain, obscure what Foucault has to say, and inhibit the deployment of his ideas in organizational analysis. Postmodernist interpretations of Foucault, distrustful of 'any narrative that aspires to coherence' (Harvey 1989 : 350), are fuelled by his criticisms of 'theory' and science and by his preoccupation with the micro-physics of power. Because power is local and fragmentary it cannot be connected or represented by a meta-theory: 'incredulity towards meta-narratives' is Lyotard's definition of the post-modern (cited in Harvey 1989 : 45). We might note Foucault's lack of familiarity with this interpretation: 'What are we calling post-modernity?', he asks of an interviewer, 'I'm not up to date'. 'I've never clearly understood what was meant in France by the word "modernity"', he says, 'neither do I grasp the kind of problems intended by this term—or how they would be common to people thought of as being "post-modern"' (Kritzman 1988 : 33–4). Characterizing Foucault as a postmodernist is a mistake: he is no postmodernist. It is specifically *positivist* science, and its implicit empiricist ontology and conception of theory, that Foucault opposes. He rejects 'the generalization of relatively specific and localised empirical developments into large-scale general laws of development' (Urry 1985 : 37), and its corollary, the explanation of local events by appeal to some overarching, general theory. Foucault opposes this positivist method for two reasons. It is unable to explain the micro-physics of power and it disqualifies or discredits ('subjugates') local knowledges with the potential to do so. Foucault does not deny the existence of a general law of power—indeed he argues that the logic of power relations developed over time and across space—Foucault denies only that a knowledge of this logic can be deduced from covering laws based on empirical generalizations. Certainly, there are general laws, but they cannot be deduced from generalizations. The laws of power relations—their microphysics—are analogous to the laws of fluid dynamics: invariant in every river, but every river is different (Harvey 1989 : 343–4). How the logic of power unfolds in practice depends on its context; power is always negotiated and therefore contingent on political skill and the circumstances of its deployment (Isaac 1987).

This, then, is the basis of Foucault's opposition to 'general theory', which is used to sustain a postmodernist interpretation of his work.

Equally, the historiographers' criticisms of Foucault are rendered redundant by a realist interpretation. Reading Foucault is uncomfortable for those accustomed to orthodox modes of writing history, for he does not provide a narrative of a sequence of events, topics are not discussed in temporal order and there are breaks in the description when the reader expects continuity (Giddens 1987 : 213). Although true, these criticisms are based on a misunderstanding of Foucault's project. Foucault's aim is to delineate an object through a description of the practices, diverse in time and space, which constitute it; it is not to develop a narrative of the sequence of past events, ideas or institutions. An analogy with psychoanalysis is helpful. From the narrative of psycho-analysis the analyst 'retroduces' a model of the structure of the analysand's ego, an unconscious organizing process evolved from a dialectic between this inner core and the external environment (Bollas 1987 : 8). Ego structure is the internalization of a process; a form of 'deep memory' (Bollas 1987 : 50); it constitutes a 'history of the development of the person' (Bollas 1987 : 50). The aim of psychoanalysis is not to research the analysand's biography but to discern the structure of the ego from the 'private logic of sequential association. . . . implied in the patient's discourse' (Bollas 1987 : 1). This logic of association is unlikely to be confined to co-join events within the same space and time. The relationship between events is more important than the details of their chronological sequence and location. The object of psychoanalysis does not exist within conventional understandings of time and space: nor does Foucault's. He is an historian of the constitution of objects, not a narrator of the sequence of events. Sexuality, for example, is an object in the sense that the ego is an object. 'What I want to make apparent is precisely that the object "sexuality" is in reality an instrument formed a long while ago, and one which has constituted a centuries-long apparatus of subjection' (Foucault 1980 : 219). Just as the psychoanalyst uses knowledge of the analysand's ego to inform understanding of his or her present and past, so Foucault's work informs understanding of taken-for-granted objects by accounting for their historical formation. In this sense, Foucault is an historian of the present and a philosopher of the past.

Situational Logic and Organizational Ethnography

To reiterate, 'organization' is the name of an abstraction from the corporation which is reified and construed as a self-evident concrete object, constituted by behavioural regularities, and generalized in explanation of diverse social forms:

'first of all, an abstraction is made from a fact; then it is declared that the fact is based on the abstraction' (Marx 1976 : 481). It is just this positivist conception of organization—reality as a well-marked out closed space, an internal milieu inhabiting an external environment (Cousins and Hussain 1984 : 261)—that Foucault challenges.

Disciplines are precisely organizing principles. They are techniques that partition and organize time, space and movement; micro-political mechanisms that explore, break down and rearrange the operation of the body, materialized in the architecture of buildings. These organizing techniques are enforced through hierarchical observation, normalizing sanctions and the examination, which combine to determine norms or rules of conduct—activity, behaviour, speech, sexuality—and shape (or 'normalize') people to fit them. Foucault's significance for organizational analysis is that through research of a variety of eighteenth and nineteenth century institutions—penitentiaries, insane asylums, elementary schools, military institutions—he showed how these self-evident things are actually constituted.

A realist reading of Foucault is helpful to organizational analysis in two ways. First, it helps explicate and develop Foucault's model of discipline by creating the theoretical space within which to imagine (Bhaskar 1989 : 19) and explore the interior or underside of his empirical studies of power. This is necessary for, as Foucault acknowledges, his work refers to problems that could not be made explicit because of the way he posed them (Kritzman 1988 : 243). For example, the central theme of his work—'problematization', how objects are practically and conceptually constituted—was never sufficiently isolated (Foucault 1988 : 257). Foucault's problems were inadequately formulated, I suggest, because he lacked an alternative ontology to the positivism he so thoroughly undermined. Second, by insisting on the necessity of substantive analysis, realism disentangles Foucault's work from his epigones' 'overblown theory dressed up in unnecessary jargon' and reveals it as a perceptive guide to empirical research, not a new language of armchair theorizing (Silverman 1985 : 82).

The empirical method of Foucault's theory is organizational ethnography. Ethnography restores the connections between 'organization' and 'society', severed by positivist abstractions, by demonstrating the situational logic of those causal mechanisms of structures constraining and enabling social action, its medium and outcome. In Foucault's words, we must research at 'the point where power reaches into the very grain of individuals, touches their bodies and inserts itself into their actions and attitudes, their discourses, learning processes and everyday lives' (Foucault 1980 : 39). This is the final rebuke to positivist organization theory. Despite their professed affection for real, hard, empirical data, positivists seldom dirty their hands with ethnography. Indeed, they have seen to it that this 'method of enquiry combining social theoretical ideas with techniques for data collection' (Rosen 1991 : 4–5) is 'almost totally

Richard Marsden

absent from the administrative science literature' (Rosen 1991 : 22; *apropos* Burrell and Morgan 1979 : 399). The preoccupation with the ethnography of Silverman—that first organizational 'paradigm warrior' (Aldrich 1988 : 19)—is a lesson to us all (Silverman 1991).

Ethnographers practice a very different type of abstraction to positivists: not the extrapolation from sample to population, but the abstraction of the general—the micro-physics of power—from the particular (Burawoy 1985 : 18). Ethnography builds 'on other studies, not in the sense that they take up where the others leave off, but in the sense that, better informed and better conceptualized, they plunge more deeply into the same thing' (Geertz, in Rosen 1991 : 19). Each particular organizational form is shaped by social forces diffuse throughout society. These cellular forms of power contain the genetic code of the larger body politic. They are not simply microcosms of this body: they constitute it, just as actual cells do. That much sought-after but elusive 'wider society' or external 'environment' does not, in fact, exist (Donaldson 1985 : 121; Child 1988).

We cannot generalize or extrapolate from Foucault's analysis of French social history to explain contemporary modes of organizing in, say, Canada, Britain or the United States. The idea is absurd (we might recall why Foucault opposed 'general theory'). Foucault's model of power has far more productive applications. First, it can drive critiques of existing 'descending' analyses, reconceptualize what passes in the name of—here—organization studies, and thereby develop Foucault's model and re-orient empirical enquiry. Second, this model can be applied in substantive research, assessed according to criteria of exhaustiveness, independence and consistency (Hanson 1958; Sayer 1979 : 115; Isaac 1987 : 68–9; Clegg 1989b : 126) and revised or transformed accordingly. The Foucauldian thesis—that disciplines are present in the constitution of a variety of interconnected organizational forms, where these techniques are developed and refined—is immensely plausible, but manifestly testable: though in a realist, rather than a positivist, way (Sayer 1984). I would like to conclude by suggesting three substantive areas that lend themselves to the approach to organizational analysis advocated here:

1. While I reject the characterization of Foucault as a postmodernist, his model is a potent tool in the empirical analysis of the historical–geographical condition of postmodernity: the transformation in the experience of space and time now evident in the organization of production, architecture and urban design (Harvey 1989; Zukin 1991; Soja 1989; Jameson 1991). Foucault compels organizational analysts to venture beyond the *cordon sanitaire* of positivism (Clegg 1988 : 11) and take geography seriously.
2. A Foucauldian analysis reveals the rules and techniques of accountancy, human resource management and industrial relations as procedures for

transforming micro-political problems into technical problems which more detailed knowledge and better management techniques promise to resolve (Smart 1983). They are organizational 'technologies of the self' (Martin et al. 1988): means to observe, examine and normalize employees' performance and behaviour (Townley 1990, 1991, 1992, 1993; Marsden and Townley 1991).

3. Finally, a realist reading of Foucault, when combined with Sayer's (1987) realist reconstruction of 'traditional' Marxism, paves the way for a *rapprochement* between Marx and Foucault and for their combined analysis of the organization of those primary structures within capitalism: social relations of production (Marsden 1992). Is not Foucault's account of the breaking down and reconstitution of the body precisely an account of how production relations are organized into empirical forms, how labour is made a productive power or 'force' (Sayer 1987; Marsden 1992; Foucault 1977 : 26)?

Conclusion

The relationship between 'organization' and 'society' is that between the empirical and the non-empirical; they are sides (front and back) of the same social relations; vertically, not horizontally, connected. Foucault's model of disciplinary practices is an account of how non-empirical social relations are organized, across space and through time, into empirical forms. Power–knowledge is a property of social relations, materialized in the rules of disciplinary practices. Politicking over these rules constitutes the ontological foundations of organizations, structuring their architecture, constituting subjectivity, training the body, shaping the self. It is the task of the ethnographer to grasp the situational logic of these rules of organizational life. Like capital, an organization isn't a thing, it's a process: the site of these practices, resistance to and struggles against them. Better, 'organizing', 'ruling' or 'modes of regulation'. *This* is why 'the boundaries of the organization . . . cannot be specified *a priori*' (Clegg 1989a : 110). 'Organizations'—schools, hospitals, corporations, trade unions, armies, asylums, prisons—are apparently discrete, but actually part of an interlocked structure (Burrell 1988 : 232). Contrary to Donaldson, 'there is no outside' (Foucault 1977 : 301).

The inner connections between organization and society—between an apparent surface and a deep structure—can never be grasped by a positivist organization theory, for its flat ontology cannot recognize the depth of social objects. It disavows the possibility of non-empirical things and so is blind to the causal connections between society and its organizational forms, thus conceiving them as self-contained islands in a societal sea. It denies the theoretical space within which the relationship between organization and society may be conceptualized; makes impossible the real definitions of object constitution; reduces abstract concepts to heuristic devices and construes abstraction as the generalization from the empirical. These are the characteristics contained within positivist organization theory, institutionalized in business schools, protected by its hegemonic method and vigorously defended by Donaldson. It is important to stress, in considering his defence, that the critique of organization theory was not simply anti-positivist, but also contained the seeds of an emerging realist ontology. It is the argument of this paper that an understanding of realism obviates Donaldson's defence and provides the basis for an alternative—Foucauldian—conception of organizations.

Acknowledgements

The thesis of this paper stems from a paper on 'The Politics of Industrial Relations Theory' that Gibson Burrell and I presented at the Industrial Relations Research Unit, Warwick University, in June 1989, which made me think for the first time about the relationship between realism and Foucault. I would like to acknowledge the comments of Richard Hyman, Gibson Burrell, Paul Edwards, O. S. reviewers Mike Reed and David Knights and Co-Editor Hans Pennings, and participants at the 'Towards a New Theory of Organizations' Conference, Keele University, April 1991, where I presented an earlier version. Conversations with Stewart Clegg helped a lot too. Finally, Barbara Townley provided detailed comments throughout the paper's development. I thank them all: the usual disclaimers apply.

References

Abrams, P. (1988). 'Notes on the difficulty of studying the state', Journal of Historical Sociology, 1/1: 58–89.

Aldrich, H. (1988). 'Paradigm warriors: Donaldson Versus the Critics of Organization Theory'. Organization Studies, 9/1: 19–25.

Atkinson, D. (1971). Orthodox Consensus and Radical Alternative: a Study in Sociological Theory. London: Heinemann.

Australian Journal of Management (1989). Editor's preface to Donaldson (1989),' 14/2: 244.

Baddeley, S., and James, K. (1987). 'Owl, fox, donkey or sheep: political skills for managers', Management Education and Development, 18/1: 3–19.

Barnard, C. I. (1938). The Functions of the Executive. Cambridge, MA: Harvard University Press.

Bernstein, R. J. (1983). Beyond Objectivism and Relativism: Science, Hermeneutics, and Praxis. Philadelphia: University of Pennsylvania Press.

Bhaskar, R. (1978). *A Realist Theory of Science*. Hemel Hempstead: Harvester Wheatcheaf.

—— (1986). *Scientific Realism and Human Emancipation*. London: Verso.

—— (1989a). *Reclaiming Reality: A Critical Introduction to Contemporary Philosophy.* London: Verso.

—— (1989b). *The Possibility of Naturalism: a Philosophical Critique of the Contemporary Human Sciences*, 2nd edn. Hemel Hempstead: Harvester Wheatcheaf.

Bollas, C. (1987). *The Shadow of the Object: Psychoanalysis of the Unthought Known*. New York: Columbia University Press.

Bray, M., and Littler, C. R. (1988). 'The Labour Process and Industrial Relations: Review of the Literature', *Labour and Industry*, 1/3: 551–587.

Burawoy, M. (1985). *The Politics of Production: Factory Regimes under Capitalism and Socialism*. London: Verso.

Burrell, G. (1984). 'Sex and Organizational Analysis', *Organization Studies*, 5/2: 221–235.

Burrell, G. (1988). 'Modernism, Postmodernism and Organizational Analysis 2: the Contribution of Michel Foucault'. *Organization Studies*, 9/2: 221–235.

Burrell, G., and Morgan, G. (1979). *Sociological Paradigms and Organizational Analysis: Elements of the Sociology of Corporate Life*. London: Heinemann.

Child, J. (1988a). 'On Organizations in their Sectors'. *Organizations Studies*, 9/1: 13–19.

—— (1988b). 'Letter to the Editor', *Organization Studies*, 9/1: 143–144.

Clarke, S. (1982). *Marx, Marginalism and Modern Sociology: From Adam Smith to Max Weber*. London and Basingstoke: Macmillan.

Clegg, S. R. (1977). 'Power, Organization Theory, Marx and Critique', in *Critical Issues in Organizations*, S. R. Clegg and D. Dunkerley (eds). London: Routledge and Kegan Paul, pp. 21–40.

—— (1983). 'Phenomenology and Formal Organizations: a Realist Critique', in *Re-Search in the Sociology of Organizations*, Vol. 2, S. Bacharach (ed.). Greenwich, Conn.: JAI Press pp. 109–52.

—— (1988). 'The Good, the Bad and the Ugly'. *Organization Studies*, 9/1: 7–12.

—— (1989a). 'Radical revisions: power, discipline and organizations', *Organization Studies*, 10/1: 97–115.

—— (1989b). *Frameworks of Power*. London: Sage.

—— (1990). *Modern Organizations: Organization Studies in the Postmodern World*. London: Sage.

Clegg, S. R., and Dunkerley, D. (1980). *Organization, Class and Control*. London: Routledge & Kegan Paul.

Coase, R. (1937). 'The Nature of the Firm', *Economica* IV: 386–405.

Cohen, S. (1989). 'The Critical Discourse on "Social Control": Notes on the Concept as a Hammer', *International Journal of the Sociology of Law*, 17: 347–357.

Cohen, Sheila (1987). 'A Labour Process to Nowhere?' *New Left Review*, 165: 34–50.

Cooper, R., and Burrell, G. (1988) 'Modernism, Postmodernism and Organizational Analysis', *Organizational Studies*, 9/1: 91–112.

Cousins, M., and Hussain, A. (1984). *Michel Foucault*. New York: St. Martin's Press.

Donaldson, L. (1985). *In Defence of Organization Theory: A Reply to the Critics*. Cambridge: Cambridge University Press.

Donaldson, L. (1987). 'Strategy and Structural Adjustment to Regain Fit and Performance: in Defence of Contingency Theory', *Journal of Management Studies*, 24/1: 1–24.

—— (1988). 'In Successful Defence of Organization Theory: a Routing of the Critics', *Organization Studies*, 9/1: 28–32.

Ellerman, D. P. (1983). 'The Employment Relation, Property Rights and Organizational Democracy', in *Organizational democracy and political processes*, Vol. 1. C. Crouch and F. A. Heller (eds). Chichester: Wiley, pp. 265–78.

Foucault, M. (1971). *Madness and Civilization: a History of Insanity in the Age of Reason*. London and New York: Tavistock.

—— (1976). *The Birth of the Clinic: An Archaeology of Medical Perception*. London: Tavistock.

—— (1977). *Discipline and Punish: the Birth of the Prison*. London: Penguin.

—— (1980). *Power/Knowledge: Selected Interviews and Other Writings, 1972–1977*. New York: Pantheon.

—— (1981). *The History of Sexuality. Volume I: An Introduction*. Harmondsworth: Penguin.

Giddens, A. (1976). *New Rules of Sociological Method: a positive critique of interpretative sociologies*. London: Hutchinson.

—— (1987). 'Structuralism, Post-Structuralism and the Production of Culture' in *Social Theory Today*, A. Giddens and J. H. Turner (eds). Oxford: Polity Press/Blackwell, pp. 195–223.

Gregory, D., and Urry, J. (eds) (1985). *Social Relations and Spatial Structures*. New York: St Martin's Press.

Hanson, N. (1958). 'The Logic of Discovery', *The Journal of Philosophy*, 55/25: 1073–1089.

Harvey, D. (1989). *The Condition of Postmodernity: An Enquiry into the Origins of Cultural Change*. Oxford: Blackwell.

Hawking, S. (1988). *A Brief History of Time: From the Big Bang to Black Holes*. London: Transworld.

Hinings, C. R. (1988). 'Defending Organization Theory: a British View from North America', *Organization Studies*, 9/1: 2–7.

Holton, G. (1968). 'Mach, Einstein, and the Search for Reality', *Daedelus*, 67: 636–673.

Isaac, J. C. (1987). *Power and Marxist Theory: A Realist View*. Ithaca: Cornell University Press.

Jameson, F. (1991). *Postmodernism: The Cultural Logic of Late Capitalism*. Durham: Duke University Press.

Keat, R., and Urry, J. (1975). *Social Theory as Science*. London: Routledge & Kegan Paul.

Knights, D., and Willmott, H. (1990). *Labour Process Theory*. London: Macmillan.

Krips, H. (1990). 'Power and Resistance'. *Philosophy of the Social Sciences* 20/2: 170–182.

Kritzman, L. D., (ed.) (1988). *Michel Foucault: Politics, Philosophy, Culture: Interviews and Other Writings, 1977–1984*. London and New York: Routledge.

Kuhn, T. S. (1970). *The Structure of Scientific Revolutions*. London: University of Chicago Press.

Lukes, S. (1974). *Power: A Radical View*. London and Basingstoke: Macmillan.

Manicas, P. T. (1980). 'The Concept of Social Structure'. *Journal for the Theory of Social Behaviour* 10/2: 65–82.

Marsden, R. (1982). 'Industrial Relations: A Critique of Empiricism'. *Sociology*, 8/2: 232–250.

Marsden, R. (1992). ' "The State": A Comment on Abrams, Denis and Sayer'. *Journal of Historical Sociology* 5/3: 358–377.

Marsden, R., and Townley, B. (1991). 'Deconstructing Industrial Relations: Power, Rules and Foucault'. Paper presented at the Canadian Industrial Relations Association Conference, Kingston, Ontario, June.

Marx, K. (1973). *Grundrisse: Foundations of the Critique of Political Economy.* Harmondsworth: Penguin.

Marx, K., and F. Engels (1976). 'The German Ideology' in *Karl Marx and Frederick Engels: Collected Works.* Vol. 5, 23–539. New York: International Publishers.

Massey, D., and R. Meegan, (eds) (1975). *Politics and Method: Contrasting Studies in Industrial Geography.* London and New York: Methuen.

Mills, A. J. (1987/88). 'An Interview with Gareth Morgan: "Sociological paradigms and organizational analysis" ', *Aurora*, 11/2: 42–46.

Outhwaite, W. (1987). *New Philosophies of Social Science: Realism, Hermeneutics and Critical Ttheory.* London: Macmillan.

Pugh, D. S., Hickson, D. J., Hinings, C. R., Macdonald, K. M., Turner, C. and Lupton, T. (1963). 'A Conceptual Scheme for Organizational Analysis'. *Administrative Science Quarterly* 8: 289–315.

Reed, M. I. (1985). *Redirections in Organizational analysis.* London and New York: Tavistock.

—— (1988). 'The Problem of Human Agency in Organizational Analysis'. *Organization Studies* 9/1: 47–68.

Rosen, M. (1991). 'Coming to Terms with the Field: Understanding and Doing Organizational Ethnography'. *Journal of Management Studies*, 28/1: 1–24.

Salaman, G., and Thompson, K. (eds) (1980). *Control and Ideology in Organizations.* Cambridge, Mass.: MIT Press.

Sayer, A. (1984). *Method in Social Science: A Realist Approach.* London: Hutchinson.

Sayer, D. (1979). *Marx's Method: Ideology, Science and Critique in 'Capital'.* London: Harvester.

—— (1987). *The Violence of Abstraction: the Analytic Foundation of Historical Materialism.* Oxford: Blackwell.

Silverman, D. (1985). *Qualitative Methodology and Sociology: Describing the Social World.* Aldershot: Gower.

—— (1991). 'On Throwing away the Ladders: Rewriting the Theory of Organisations'. Paper presented at the 'Towards a New Theory of Organizations' Conference, Keele University, England, 3–5 April, 1991.

Smart, B. (1983). *Foucault, Marxism and Critique.* London: Routledge & Kegan Paul.

Soja, E. W. (1989). *Postmodern Geographies: The Assertion of Space in Critical Social Theory.* London: Verso.

Storey, J. (1985). 'The Means of Management Control', *Sociology*, 19/2: 192–211.

Townley, B. (1990). 'Foucault, Power/Knowledge and its relevance for HRM'. Paper presented at Employment Research Unit Annual Conference: 'Employment Relations and the Enterprise Culture', Cardiff Business School, September.

Richard Marsden

Townley, B. (1991). 'Managing by Numbers: Personnel Management and the Creation of a Mathesis'. Paper presented at the 3rd Annual Interdisciplinary Perspectives on Accounting Conference, Manchester, July.

—— (1992). 'In the Eye of the Gaze: The Constitutive role of Performance Appraisal' in *Managing Organizations in 1992: Strategic Responses*, P. Barrar and C. Cooper (eds), 155–202. London: Routledge.

—— (1993). 'Performance Appraisal and the Emergence of Mmanagement'. *Journal of Management Studies* 30/2: 27–44.

Urry, J. (1985). 'Social Relations, Space and Time' in *Social Relations and Spatial Structures*. D. Gregory, and J. Urry (eds), New York: St. Martin's Press. pp. 21–48.

Van Velsen, J. (1967). 'The Extended-Case Method and Situational Analysis', in *The craft of Social Anthropology*. A. L. Epstein (ed.), London: Tavistock. pp. 129–149

Vincent-Jones, P. (1987). 'Theory and Method Reconsidered: A Marxist Analysis of Trespass Law'. *Economy and Society* 16/1: 75–119.

Whittington, R. (1989). *Corporate Strategies in Recession and Recovery: Social Structure and Strategic Choice*. London: Unwin Hyman.

Whitley, R. D. (1977). 'Concepts of Organization and Power in the Study of Organizations'. *Personnel Review* 6/1: 54–59.

Zukin, S. (1991). *Landscapes of Power: From Detroit to Disney World*. Berkeley: University of California Press.

III. CRITICAL STUDIES OF MANAGEMENT

This section presents a diverse selection of studies that subject aspects of management to critical analysis. They range from the self-styled 'speculative' (e.g. Adler) through the analysis of texts (e.g. Townley) and critique (e.g. Cooke) to ethnography (e.g. Barker). They encompass attentiveness to issues of gender, postcolonialism, established and emergent forms of control, the knowledge economy, leadership and the position of management in society. They also engage elements of both critical theoretic (e.g. Adler) and postmodern (e.g. Pringle) thinking (see Section 2). In this respect, they are indicative of the diversity of critical studies of management, yet are unrepresentative as they cannot possibly do justice to the vast range of issues and approaches that are considered within the umbrella of CMS. What they share, in their different ways, is a concern to redress the criticism that studies of managerial work, and of management more generally, take inadequate account of its wider, institutional formation, and its increasingly influential role in the reproduction and remaking of established national and international institutions.

Paul Adler reflects upon the role and fate of trust in the organization and management of capitalist organizations and societies. Trust, Adler contends, is not readily reducible to 'market' (reliance upon the price mechanism) or 'hierarchical' (reliance upon authority) forms of economic coordination; and it becomes more central to, and mutates within, more knowledge-intensive forms of business organization. Trust is associated with 'community' where coordination relies upon goodwill and 'informality' that, it is suggested, become crucial in an era where reliance upon 'markets' and 'hierarchies' alone, or even in combination, is insufficiently effective in coping with the competitive pressures and complexities of knowledge intensity that combines a more educated workforce with the manufacture of products/services that embody advanced forms of science and technology. Such pressures operate to reward those who can find ways of facilitating collaboration between divisions within hierarchies, and between competitors within markets; and this lubricant, Adler argues, takes the form of 'trust' based less upon tradition and deference to authority, as illustrated in **Heather Hopfl's** commentary upon instilling organizational commitment though the charismatic delivery of corporate platitudes, than upon a reciprocated respect for integrity and competence. Yet, while a 'reflective' concept of 'trust' is identified by Adler as a necessity for competitive success in knowledge-intensive markets, he also views it as unattainable within capitalist firms. For its realization, he argues, requires the replacement of 'autocratic governance and owner control' by 'participative governance and multistakeholder control'.

An example that comes close to such control within a capitalist enterprise is provided by **James Barker's** study of teamwork within ISE, a small manufacturing company. The details and context of the case cannot be explored here but suffice it to say that this enterprise complies with Adler's concept of the high-tech knowledge intensive organization as it manufactured transmission circuit boards and its survival necessitate flexibility and responsiveness to rapidly changing market conditions. Indeed, it was the prospect of failing to meet this challenge that led to a reorganization of its manufacturing operations so that, in the words of the vice president, 'the resources of the whole organization' were 'marshalled' to be maximally responsive to 'customer needs'. At the centre of this change was the introduction of self-managing teams in which team members would recruit, co-direct, discipline and even fire their own members and would also be responsible for every aspect of the manufacturing process—from fabrication to packaging. The outcome, after a period of some confusion and fumbled efforts, was the emergence of what Barker terms 'concertive control' where employees at the plant became so identified with their role as self-managers that they place extreme normative pressures upon themselves and their team mates to act 'responsibly'. This, to be clear, was not simply to safeguard their jobs but because a strong emotional investment was made in their team as well as in their productive activity. In effect, the team became a 'gilded' cage in which each member desired, and felt compelled to obey, its norms, and faced scrutiny, ostracism and shame when these were transgressed. New recruits either 'either obeyed the rules and became integrated into this system, or they found the door'. There was zero tolerance of slackness or resistance. There was also a progressive clarification and tightening of the role of 'co-ordinator', a role which, as one of the coordinators confided 'feel(s) like a supervisor, I just don't get paid for it'. Barker observes that ISE employees actively formalized, codified and rigidified their work to provide a sense of stability that had been absent during the previous period of experimentation. This was not a typical, impersonal, hierarchical application of rule but,rather, a different, concertive, 'value-based' form of 'communal-rational' control in which team members were, seemingly, in control of their work : they were 'their own masters' as well as 'their own slaves'. This example suggests a possible, dystopic configuration of market, hierarchy and trust, in which market pressures prompt and facilitate a preparedness to flatten, but not democratise, hierarchy by trusting employees who willingly became self-managing.

The limits of the devolution of control from management to employees found at ISE could be interpreted as a confirmation of 'the contradiction between socialized production and private appropriation' identified by Marx and invoked by **Hugh Willmott** in his review of studies of managerial work. Willmott argues that even the least managerial accounts of managerial work are informed by a liberal-pluralist perspective that fail to situate what managers do within the wider structure of domination, and therefore fail to appreciate how the technical division of labour is fundamentally a class division that operates to secure the process of private appropriation through socialized production. But Willmott is also at pains to argue that the interests of capital, like those of labour, have to be organized and that for this they depend upon salaried experts, such as managers, who occupy an ambivalent position, and are capable of organizing their work and that of employees for their own material or symbolic improvement. From this standpoint, what managers do and what management is cannot plausibly regarded as a neutral technology or as serving the interests of the dominant, capitalist class. To do so simply ignores how such interests are interpreted, rather than pre-given, by managers who have a vested interest in their careers and in undertaking projects (e.g. of self-aggrandisement or career enhancement) that are not necessarily sought or even endorsed by shareholders, a situation that the latter have sought to rectify by emphasising the primacy of shareholder value and the issuing of stock options to senior executives. The comparative openness or contingency of capitalist relations of production is illustrated by Willmott by drawing upon Giddens' theory of structuration which is applied to a reinterpretation of Nichols and Beynon's classic study of worker-management relations at a chemicals plant.

Bill Cooke addresses the global significance of management by examining its extension into the ideology and operation of international public institutions. Here, 'management' an almost religious as an ethos is viewed less as a function within organizations than as 'a global, institutional (more than organizational) modernizing change agent'. Specifically, he explores how Development Administration and Management (DAM), including the World Bank's involvements in Third World development, relies upon ostensibly 'progressive' managerial thinking in which participation is placed in the service of technocratic intervention that is intended to produce neo-liberal political order. Cooke argues that the latter objective is cloaked in an ostensibly neutral managerialism which welcomes 'participation' and, for example, welcomes 'trust' just so long as it is consonant with achieving the desired political reforms—a refrain that echoes Barker's study of ISE. The familiar markets and hierarchies of a neo-liberal political order are assumed to provide the only viable and defensible model of organization whilst their attainment and minimal maintenance is understood to be facilitated by a managed form of participation in which radical ideas are appropriated for highly restrictive and conservative objectives. In Adler's terms, there is an attempt, by invoking the aura of management, to instil trust, but it is an endeavour driven by, and subordinated to, the goal of establishing institutions that are commensurate to neo-imperialist ambitions of the First World.

Whereas Cooke's invitation is to shift our analytical gaze from the world of organization(s) to explore the role of management in building institutions and nation-states, **Rosemary Pringle** emphasises the embodied qualities of mundane organizing practices where gender and sexuality are potent yet unspoken and arguably suppressed dimensions of everyday work relationships. The ethos of modern, bureaucratic organization is *impersonality*: people are expected to interact with each other as bundles of skills and competences, not as sexual, gendered beings. Pringle challenges this view to show how, for example, masculinist values and priorities—such as the emphasis upon rationality that is prized as a distinctively male attribute or at least deemed deficient in most women (and therefore makes them inherently ill-suited to managerial work)—are institutionalized within bureaucracies. Far from being eliminated by bureaucracy, patriarchy is seen to be sustained by it. What, then, if women contrive to desexualise their work relations and emulate masculine codes of behaviour in order to improve their position within the power hierarchy? They risk being complicit in reproducing a form of organization that systematically negates their femininity. In the terminology of Adler's contribution, hierarchy is then triumphant. Yet, focussing upon the boss-secretary relationship, Pringle argues that this routinely departs from impersonality, claiming that it is frequently 'based upon personal rapport, involves a degree of intimacy, day-to-day familiarity and shared secrets unusual for any but lovers...'. Why might this be? One possible answer returns us the importance of 'trust' in mediating and lubricating politically complex and sensitive areas of work (e.g. gate-keeping) or the security to be found in a sense of community. But another is that the intimacies of the boss-secretary relationship are less a functional necessity of effective organization than they are a valued, sexualized space of polymorphous pleasure actively (re)produced, though not unequivocally, by its occupants. More widely, organizational work is seen to be accomplished by gendered, sexual beings who engage, more or less knowingly, in well-rehearsed or novel 'strategies and counter-strategies of power' that include sundry, mild or ruth-less, forms of harassment and seduction. On occasion, harassment is mixed with seduction—as in Heather Hopfl's example of the missionary manager who delivers a messianic message to the assembled congregation of seemingly dutiful managers but does not hear their scathing, cynical observations after tongues have been loosened by the flow of drink in the hotel bar. It is then that that voice is given to 'the underlying anxieties, perplexities and conflicts' of managerial work. A modernist stance, in which Pringle includes feminism, inclines toward an outlawing or tabooing of such strategic practices by fully implementing the rationalist project of impersonality. A postmodernist position, including postfeminism, leans towards an acceptance of the pervasiveness of such strategies and, in the case of women, commends a reassertion of their 'rights to be subjects rather than objects of sexual discourses'.

The Foucauldian influence upon Pringle's study of sexuality at work is also apparent in Barbara Townley's discussion of performance management. She commends the deconstruction of management so that it is re-membered as a theoretical construct, rather than analysed as if it were a 'pre-given entity'. She also follows Foucault in conceiving of power as a relation rather than as a possession, which leads her to examine the mechanisms, rather than the agents to whom power is commonsensically attributed. In this formulation, power acts to constitute and to position individuals in relations of interdependence through an operation of technologies, such as performance appraisal systems. For Townley, the Foucauldian notion of power/knowledge is illustrated by how appraisal 'render(s) aspects of existence thinkable, calculable, and thus manageable' so that, over time, it operates to 'sediment' a form of organization that is 'hierarchical, centralized and disciplinary'. It is through the introduction of such mechanisms that the practices identified as 'management' become established and take on the appearance of pre-given entities. Moreover, appraisal does not simply act to monitor and control the appraisee but also to assess the diligence and competence of each appraiser who is required to appraise in a uniform manner. And the effect of such mechanisms, even when consistently applied, is unpredictable. Instead of offering reassurance that traces of nepotism are expelled by the introduction of an standardised, impartially administered procedure, formal appraisal may arouse anxieties and create divisions when it is seen to encourage certain kinds of behaviour valued by markets and hierarchies (e.g. research output, teaching ratings) whilst failing to recognise and positively value other, equally important qualities such as colleagueship, 'good citizenship' and trust. Then, instead of, or perhaps in addition to, securing managerial control, it may prompt forms of resistance when, for example, appraisal 'conflict(s) with long established patterns of relationships between colleagues or personal definitions of what "the job" entails'.

Critical Studies of Management

Taken together, these studies indicate at least something of the range of CMS. In so doing, they demonstrate that CMS involves not simply a reactive critique of mainstream management studies but can offer compelling, alternative accounts of management and organizations.

9

Market, Hierarchy, and Trust: The Knowledge Economy and the Future of Capitalism

Paul S. Adler

Introduction

Considerable attention has been focused recently on data suggesting that the secular trend toward larger firms and establishments has stalled and may be reversing (Brynjolfsson et al. 1994). Some observers argue that the underlying new trend is toward the disintegration of large hierarchical firms and their replacement by small entrepreneurial firms coordinated by markets (Birch 1987). This argument, however, understates the persistence of large firms, ignores transformations underway within these firms, and masks the growth of network relations among firms. How, then, should one interpret the current wave of changes in organizational forms?

Zenger and Hesterly (1997) propose that the underlying trend is a progressive swelling of the zone between hierarchy and market. They point to a proliferation of hybrid organizational forms that introduce high-powered marketlike incentives into firms and hierarchical controls into markets (Holland and Lockett 1997, make a similar argument). This proposition is more valid empirically than a one-sided characterization of current trends as a shift from hierarchy to market. The 'swelling-middle' thesis is also a step beyond Williamson's (1991) unjustified assertion that such hybrid forms are infeasible or inefficient. However, this paper argues that Zenger and Hesterlys' thesis, too, is fundamentally flawed in that it ignores a third increasingly significant coordination mechanism: trust.

In highlighting the importance of trust, this essay adds to a burgeoning literature (e.g. *Academy of Management Review* 1998; further references below); my goal is to pull together several strands of this literature to advance a line of reflection that positions trust as a central construct in a broader argument. In outline, the argument is, first, that alongside the *market* ideal-typical form of organization which relies on the price mechanism, and the *hierarchy* form which relies on authority, there is a third form, the *community* form which relies on trust. Empirically observed arrangements typically embody a mix of the three ideal-typical organization forms and rely on a corresponding mix of price, hierarchy, and trust mechanisms. Second, based on a well-established body of economic and sociological theory, I argue that trust has uniquely effective properties for the coordination of knowledge-intensive activities within and between organizations. Third, given a broad consensus that modern economies are becoming increasingly knowledge intensive, the first two premises imply that trust is likely to become increasingly important in the mechanism mix. I present indices of such a knowledge-driven trend to trust within and between firms, specifically in the employment relationship, in interdivisional relations, and in interfirm relations. Fourth, I discuss the difficulties encountered by the trust mechanism in a capitalist society and the resulting mutation of trust itself. Finally, the concluding section discusses the broader effects of this intra- and interfirm trend to trust, and argues that this trend progressively undermines the legitimacy of the capitalist form of society, and simultaneously lays the foundations for a new form.

Both the theory and the data underlying these conclusions are subject to debate: I will summarize the key points of contention, and it will become obvious that we are far from theoretical or empirical consensus. In the form of an essay rather than a scientific paper, my argument will be speculative and buttressed by only suggestive rather than compelling evidence. My goal, however, is to enrich organizational research by enhancing its engagement with debates in the broader field of social theory.

The Limits of Market and Hierarchy

Knowledge is a remarkable substance. Unlike other resources, most forms of knowledge grow rather than diminish with use. Knowledge tends, therefore, to play an increasingly central role in economic development over time. Increasing knowledge-intensity takes two forms: the rising education level of the workforce (living or subjective knowledge) and the growing scientific and technical knowledge materialized in new equipment and new products (embodied or objectified knowledge).

Recapitulating a long tradition of scholarship in economics and organization theory, this section argues that neither market nor hierarchy, nor any combination of the two, is particularly well suited to the challenges of the knowledge economy. To draw out the implications of this argument. I will assume that real institutions, notably empirically observed markets and firms, embody varying mixes of three ideal-typical organizational forms and their corresponding coordination mechanisms: (a) the hierarchy form relies on the authority mechanism, (b) the market form relies on price, and (c) the community form relies on trust. For brevity's sake, an organizational form and its corresponding mechanism will be referred to as an organizing 'mode.' Modes typically appear in varying proportions in different institutions. For example, interfirm relations in real markets embody and rely on varying degrees of trust and hierarchical authority, even if their primary mechanism is price. Similarly, real firms' internal operations typically rely to some extent on both trust and price signals, even if their primary coordination mechanism is authority.

Hierarchy uses authority (legitimate power) to create and coordinate a horizontal and vertical division of labor. Under hierarchy, knowledge is treated as a scarce resource and is therefore concentrated, along with the corresponding decision rights, in specialized functional units and at higher levels of the organization. A large body of organizational research has shown that an institution structured by this mechanism may be efficient in the performance of routine partitioned tasks but encounters enormous difficulty in the performance of innovation tasks requiring the generation of new knowledge (e.g. Burns and Stalker 1961, Bennis and Slater 1964, Mintzberg 1979, Scott 1992, Daft 1998). When specialized units are told to cooperate in tasks that typically encounter unanticipated problems requiring novel solutions, tasks such as the development of a new product, the hierarchical form gives higher-level managers few levers with which to ensure that the participating units will collaborate. By their nonroutine nature, such tasks cannot be preprogrammed, and the creative collaboration they require cannot be simply commanded. Similarly, the vertical differentiation of hierarchy is effective for routine tasks, facilitating downward communication of explicit knowledge and commands, but less effective when tasks are nonroutine, because lower levels lack both the knowledge needed to create new knowledge and the incentives to transmit new ideas upward. Firms thus invariably supplement their primary organizational mode, hierarchy/authority, with other modes that can mitigate the hierarchy/authority mode's weaknesses.

The market form, as distinct from the actual functioning of most real markets, relies on the price mechanism to coordinate competing suppliers and anonymous buyers. With standard goods and strong property rights, marginal pricing promises to optimize production and allocation jointly. The dynamics of competition, supply, and demand lead to a price at which social welfare is Pareto optimal (that is, no one's welfare can be increased without reducing someone else's). A substantial body of modern economic theory has shown, however, that the price mechanism fails to optimize the production and allocation of knowledge (Arrow 1962, Stiglitz 1994). Knowledge is a 'public good'; that is, like radio transmission, its availability to one consumer is not diminished by its use by another. With knowledge, as with other public goods, reliance on the market/ price mode forces a trade-off between production and allocation. On the one hand, production of new knowledge would be optimized by establishing strong intellectual property rights that create incentives to generate knowledge. On the other hand, not only are such rights difficult to enforce, but more fundamentally, they block socially optimal allocation. Allocation of knowledge would be optimized by allowing free access because the marginal cost of supplying another consumer with the same knowledge is close to zero.

Over several decades, discussion of this trade-off between production and allocation was framed as a debate at a macroeconomic level over the relative merits of market, hierarchy in the form of central planning, and intermediate forms such as regulated markets and market socialism (Arrow and Hurwicz 1977, Stiglitz 1994). This 'mechanism design' literature has more recently been applied to the analysis of individual firms (Miller 1992)—with the same results. On the one hand, hierarchy could simply mandate the free availability of knowledge and thus outperform market as far as allocation is concerned. On the other hand, hierarchy would have far greater difficulty than market in creating the incentives needed to optimize the production of new knowledge. Formal modeling has shown that neither market nor hierarchy nor any intermediate form can resolve the dilemma, leaving us stuck in a 'second-best' equilibrium (Miller 1992).

Recent research on knowledge and coordination mechanisms has highlighted the importance of tacit knowledge. The recognition of the importance of tacit knowledge does little, however, to restore confidence in the ability of the market form to assure optimal outcomes. First, tacit knowledge brings with it all the challenges of hidden knowledge in principal/agent relations. Second, notwithstanding the current scholarly interest in tacit knowledge, codified forms of knowledge continue to be an important factor in economic growth. The reasons are straightforward: The transfer of knowledge is much more costly when the knowledge is of a tacit kind, and the generation of new knowledge is usually much faster when it builds on a base of explicit rather than tacit knowledge.

As knowledge becomes increasingly important in the economic development of firms and nations, the question of whether we can improve on the second-best allowed by market and hierarchy is posed with increasing urgency. Much recent economic scholarship has, however, argued for resignation: The second-best achievable in pure or mixed markets and hierarchies is redefined as the best feasible and 'relatively efficient' (Alchian and Demsetz 1972, Williamson 1975). This resignation is not warranted. Hierarchy and market are not the only possible organizational forms. Community is an alternative (Ouchi 1980, Dore 1983, Bradach and Eccles 1989, Powell 1990).

The Power of Community and Trust

Community

Community is a term with many interpretations (Kirkpatrick 1986). However, the salience of some such notion is demonstrated by what we know of both intra- and interfirm relations.

Analysis of action within real firms reveals the ubiquity and importance of 'informal' organization—this is one of the founding insights of organization theory (see Scott 1992, ch. 3). Views differ as to how best to conceptualize the informal organization and its differentiation from the formal structures of hierarchy. Without preempting this ongoing debate, we can posit that the informal organization constitutes its members as a community.

DIMENSIONS	COMPONENTS
sources	• familianty through repeated interaction • calculation based on interests • norms that create predictability and trustworthiness
mechanisms	• direct interpersonal contact • reputation • institutional contest
objects	• individuals • systems • collectivities
bases	• consistency, contractual trust • competence • benevolence, loyalty, concern, goodwill, fiduciary trust • honesty, integrity • openness

Fig. 1. *Dimensions and Components of Trust*

Analysis of real market relations between firms reveals a similar dependence on informal ties (Macaulay 1963). Pure-spot market relations between anonymous buyers and sellers is in reality rather unusual. Firms transact primarily with long-standing partners, and in the continuity of their relations, shared norms and understandings emerge that have their own efficacy in shaping interactions.

Trust

Trust is the key coordinating mechanism in the community form. Following Gambetta (1988), one could define trust as the subjective probability with which an actor assesses that another actor or group of actors will perform a particular action, both before she or he can monitor such action (or independently of his or her capacity ever to be able to monitor it) and in a context in which it affects his or her own action. This broad definition captures many uses of the word, including the possibility of feared as well as welcomed actions. Another narrower and more benign definition is confidence in another's goodwill (Ring and Van de Ven 1992).

The difference between these definitions obliges us to make a short digression on the notion of trust. Both the generation of trust—i.e. its sources and mechanisms—and its targets—i.e. the objects and the features of those objects in which we invest our trust—are manifold.

First, we can distinguish three *sources* of trust. Familiarity through repeated interaction can lead to trust (or distrust). Interests can lead to a calculative form of trust via a sober assessment of the costs and benefits to the other party of exploiting my vulnerability. Values and norms can engender trustworthy behavior that leads to confidence (Liebeskind and Oliver 1998). (We should note that there is some confusion in the literature about precisely what it is about values and norms that creates trust. We might reasonably distinguish a spectrum running from weaker forms of trust based on the predictability imparted to other actors' behavior by their adherence to any stable norm, to stronger forms of trust based on the predicted benevolence of actors with whom we share norms that privilege trustworthiness; see Ring 1996.) Empirically, all three sources of trust are important in the real world of business (cf. Williamson 1993), and in practice, although excessive focus on the calculative form can undermine the normative form, all three tend to be intertwined complements.

Second, we can distinguish three *mechanisms* by which trust is generated. As Coleman (1990) points out, trust can be engendered by direct interpersonal contact, by reputation through a network of other trusted parties, or by our understanding of the way institutions shape the other actor's values and

behavior. Like the three sources, the three mechanisms are primarily complements rather than substitutes: They tend to build on each other.

Third, we can distinguish three generic *objects* of trust: Our trust can be in a
person, an impersonal system, or a collectivity. Social psychologists have
focused most of their efforts on the first (Bigley and Pearce 1998), and indeed
some social theorists would reserve the concept of trust for interpersonal
relations and use the term 'confidence' to refer to related assessments of
abstract systems (Luhmann 1979, Seligman 1997). Notwithstanding the ter-
minological issue, sociologists such as Barber (1983), Zucker (1986), Giddens
(1990), and Shapiro (1987) highlight the importance to the functioning of
contemporary society of confidence/trust in anonymous systems such as
money and law. The concept of procedural justice (e.g. Brockner and Siegel
1996) is one form of system trust familiar to organizational researchers. The
importance to comparative economic performance of trust in a collectivity—
that is, generalized trust in others who are part of that collectivity—is fore-
grounded by Fukuyama (1995).

Finally, we can distinguish the features of those objects in which we feel
trust, often referred to in the literature as the *bases* of trust. The list of bases
invoked by various authors is long and partially overlapping, and none of the
typologies has a strong theoretical foundation. They include the other party's
consistency (Sako 1992, 'contractual trust'), competence, benevolence (or
loyalty, concern, or Sako's 'goodwill trust'), honesty (or integrity), and openness. While much of the discussion of bases has taken interpersonal trust as its
context, it is clear that system and collectivity trust also have diverse bases (see
e.g. Barber 1983, on fiduciary trust—i.e. benevolence—and competence trust
in government). Like sources and mechanisms, both objects and bases are
primarily complements: Community, system, and interpersonal trust typically
buttress each other, as do the various bases (e.g. Kurland 1996).

Community/Trust as a Third Mode

While trust is a complex, multifaceted phenomenon, the complementarities
between the components of each of its four key dimensions enable trust to
function as a highly effective coordinating mechanism. Groups whose cohesion
is based primarily on mutual trust are capable of extraordinary feats. Trust is
therefore usefully seen as a third coordination mechanism that can be combined in varying degrees with price and authority.

The thesis that trust constitutes a third coordination mechanism contrasts
with three other views. Williamson (1991) suggests we see market and hierarchy as two discrete alternatives, and declares trust to be irrelevant to business
transactions. The 'swelling middle' thesis invites us to see a continuum

between these points, but implicitly assumes a trade-off between mechanisms, and still ignores trust. Ouchi's (1980) discussion includes trust but still implies a three-way trade-off.

It is more fruitful. I submit, to map institutions in three dimensions according to the salience of community/trust, market/price, and hieararchy/authority modes (Figure 2). This three-dimensional representation has the advantage of allowing us to think of the way the various modes combine in different settings. In the absence of trust, market coordination takes the form of spot markets. However, trust can be combined with the price mechanism in the form of 'relational contracts' (Macneil 1980), as found in long-term partnership-type supplier relations (Bradach and Eccles 1989, Sako 1992, Uzzi 1997). Hierarchy often appears in a low-trust form, as reflected in the colloquial, pejorative use

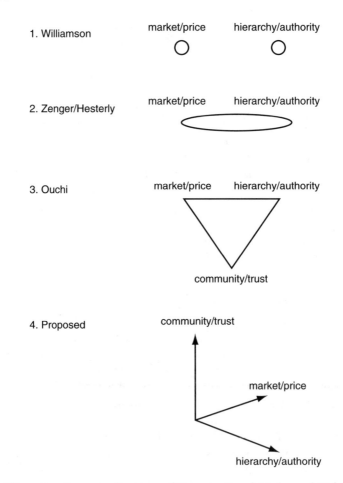

Fig. 2. *Alternative Conceptualizations of Organizational Modes and Hybrids*

of the term 'bureaucracy,' and in cases such as those presented by Crozier (1964). However, hierarchy can be combined with trust, as in the 'representative,' 'dynamic,' and 'enabling' types of bureaucracy described respectively by Gouldner (1954), Blau (1955), and Adler and Borys (1996).

Market and hierarchy too are often combined, as reflected in the mix of incentives and authority typically found in employment relations, in relations between divisions and headquarters within large multidivisional firms, and in relations between firms and their suppliers. Sometimes this market/hierarchy mix takes a low-trust form, but sometimes trust is an important third ingredient. Within firms, high-trust hybrids can be found in 'collaborative' multidivisional corporations characterized by high levels of interdivisional and interlevel trust (Eccles 1985). Between firms, high-trust hybrids can be found in keiretsu-type configurations characterized by high-trust, hierarchically structured, market relations (Gerlach 1992, Dyer 1996). Figure 3 summarizes these alternatives, building on the framework suggested by Figure 2.

I should note that under this view, the growing importance of 'network' forms of organization within and between firms does not so much answer the question motivating this essay as it poses a further question: Figure 2 suggests that we ask of these networks whether the content of their constituent ties is market exchange, hierarchical authority, or community trust. Korczynski (1996) and Carney (1998) contrast high-trust and low-trust network forms,

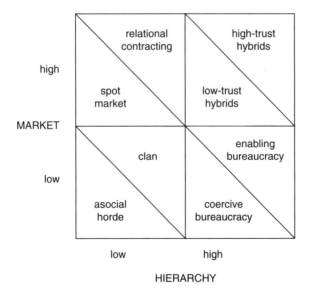

Fig. 3. *A Typology of Institutional Forms (low trust forms in lower left triangles, high trust forms in upper right triangles)*

and show that the low-trust form can help lower costs but performs relatively poorly in generating or sharing new knowledge.

A Hypothesis: The Trend to Trust

Using these three-dimensional schemas, we can map the vector of change in the mix of organization modes associated with the increasing knowledge-intensity of the economy. Compared to pure authority and price, trust makes possible an enlarged scope of knowledge generation and sharing. Trust can dramatically reduce both transaction costs—replacing contracts with handshakes—and agency risks—replacing the fear of shirking and misrepresentation with mutual confidence. Trust can thus greatly mitigate the coordination difficulties created by knowledge's public good character. Also, insofar as knowledge takes a tacit form, trust is an essential precondition for effective knowledge transfer. Therefore, as knowledge management becomes an increasingly important performance determinant, I hypothesize that trust becomes an increasingly attractive mechanism to economic agents.

In the following sections, I will adduce some evidence—suggestive, but certainly not compelling—that firms are indeed being drawn to increasing reliance on trust. A constellation of somewhat contradictory trends is developing as firms attempt to deal more effectively with the knowledge management challenge. First, firms are sharpening marketlike processes. Second, they are developing more effective hierarchical processes. And third, in apparently growing numbers, they are adopting approaches to knowledge management that rely on community and trust between employees and managers, between divisions within the corporation, and between firms and their suppliers. The evidence I present for a trend to trust is not compelling, but given the stakes, it is sufficient to warrant a preliminary assessment and an exploration of its implications.

Employment Relations

Viewed over the longer period, the economy's growing knowledge-intensity is pushing the employment relationship in several somewhat contradictory directions. A trend to trust may nevertheless be emerging.

First, one can identify a range of efforts to strengthen the authority mechanism in the employment relation. In response to competitive pressures, firms are fine-tuning their management structures and planning processes, demanding greater accountability at every level, and enforcing more discipline in the planning and execution of operations. The most common motivation for these efforts appears to be greater efficiency and control, but firms sometimes see this refinement of hierarchy as a path to more effective knowledge management too. It is under this latter rationale that many firms are introducing more formalized procedures such as TQM and highly structured product and software development processes. Many firms are also developing more elaborate project planning and human resource planning techniques to ensure that the right mix of skills is available to support the development and launch of innovative products. They are developing more complex metrics, the 'balanced scorecard' for example (Kaplan 1996), that go beyond market performance criteria for the assessment of these projects. Firms are attempting to identify their 'core competencies' and nurture development of these competencies over the longer term, even when purely market-based financial assessments do not support such risky investments.

Second, alongside these refinements of hierarchy, one sees efforts designed to strengthen the market form of the employment relation. Downsizing and contingent employment are sometimes seen as ways not only to reduce labor costs and increase 'numerical' (head-count) flexibility, but also as paths to greater flexibility in the mix of knowledge and skills available to the firm (head-content). Reliance on market-type mechanisms is also visible in the shift, albeit modest, toward contingent compensation at lower levels in the organizational hierarchy, creating higher-powered incentives for performance in general and for risky innovation and knowledge creation in particular (Lawler et al. 1998). These efforts are most often motivated by efficiency and flexibility concerns, but here again, improvements in knowledge management capability are sometimes seen as another benefit. Firms like Microsoft invoke both motives when they use market relations in the form of large pools of contingent contract employees and high-powered stock incentives for regular employees.

Third, firms are trying to improve their knowledge management capabilities by strengthening employee trust. The rationale is explicit. Effective *development* of knowledge—whether new concepts in the research lab, new products in the development department, or process refinement suggestions on the shop floor—depends on employee commitment and on collaborative teamwork for which mutual trust is a critical precondition (Bromiley and Cummings 1995). Effective *sharing* of knowledge depends equally critically on a sense of shared destiny, which in turn both depends on and engenders a sense of mutual trust (e.g. Nahapiet and Ghoshal 1998). Firms like 3M and Hewlett Packard thus attempt to create high levels of community and trust by providing material and nonmaterial expressions of commitment to their employees (Collins and Porras 1994).

Trust is a crucial ingredient both in high-commitment vertical relations between employees and management and in collaborative horizontal relations between specialist groups. Building on many decades of research on the critical role of informal organization in innovation, community—particularly in the form of 'communities of practice' (Wenger 1998)—is increasingly recognized as the organizational principle most effective in generating and sharing new knowledge.

In the language of transaction cost economics, we would say that when the firm needs high levels of firm-specific knowledge and when metering individual output is difficult—conditions that are arguably typical in knowledge-intensive firms—the most efficient form of the employment relation is that of a 'relational team' (Williamson 1981). Notwithstanding Williamson's own reservations regarding the use of the notion of trust in sociological research (1993), relational teams seem in practice to rely on high levels of trust. As illustration, consider a recent book on knowledge management by two particularly thoughtful observers of its practice, Thomas Davenport and Laurence Prusak (1998). They appear at first to advance a thesis contrary to mine, arguing for the need for improved 'knowledge markets' within and between firms. But this, it turns out, is merely a metaphor, since the 'currencies' of these markets are reciprocity, repute, and altruism, and 'mutual trust is at the heart of knowledge exchange' (Davenport & Prusak 1998 : 35).

Note the complex three-way tensions between market/price, hierarchy/authority, and community/trust. On the one hand, in some cases the three modes function as mutually exclusive substitutes. Efforts to sharpen market forms can undercut efforts to strengthen trust. Downsizing, for example, is rarely a propitious time for a shift toward teamwork. Efforts to improve hierarchical planning processes often require that market forms be moderated, and changes in the structure of hierarchy can be hampered by the long-term stability implied by strong trust. On the other hand, these three modes can be mutually supportive if they are designed and implemented appropriately. Employee participation, for example, is one way to link community and hierarchy so that the two are complements rather than substitutes (Adler et al. 1999). While Figure 2 represents the three mechanisms as three orthogonal dimensions, it is not intended to pre-empt questions of substantive interdependencies. Unfortunately, these interdependencies have so far eluded compelling theorization. See e.g. Hirschman (1970) on the variable relationship between exit (read: market) and voice (read: community). For now, all we can say is that hierarchy, market, and community are sometimes complements and sometimes substitutes.

Some Counterarguments

The hypothesis that as the knowledge-intensity of the economy increases, firms will be drawn in increasing numbers to higher-trust forms of the employment relation runs counter to a long tradition in sociology. This tradition draws on several theoretical perspectives: Here I review some that pertain directly to the employment relationship. In a subsequent section. I return to others of more general import.

A venerable line of sociological scholarship has argued that the capitalist employment relation is an essentially low-trust one. The hallmarks of the capitalist firm—scientific management and mass production—are engines of war against community: fragmenting workers' roles, separating conception and execution, and centralizing control. From this vantage point, writings in the human relations tradition and, more recently, on empowerment are seen as ideological inflation of a thin veneer of trust that managers try to overlay on the underlying reality of domination. Indeed, the concept of trust was rarely invoked in industrial sociology until Alan Fox's 1974 study—which argued that trust was systematically undermined in capitalist firms. His argument seemed so convincing that the topic essentially disappeared for another decade (Heisig and Littek 1995).

Some contributors to this sociological tradition work from the Marxist theoretical premise that the core or the employment relation is an inescapable struggle between workers and managers over work intensity (e.g. Braverman 1974, Burawoy 1979). Researchers working in this perspective highlight the deceptive nature of management efforts to inculcate a sense of trust in workers and the 'false consciousness' of workers who take the bait.

Other contributors are grounded in Weber rather than Marx, and for these the hypothesis of a trend to trust in the employment relationship arouses skepticism rather than radical hostility. Weberians, like Marxists, remind us that a trend to trust would be likely to encounter enormous impediments in the rivalry of competing social groups. These scholars can point to a substantial body of research accumulated over many decades that documents the frequency and potency of both management and worker opposition to 'progressive' management ideas. Enlightened self-interest does not diffuse easily in a society where so many personal, organizational, and contextual factors encourage managers, and sometimes workers, to choose hierarchy and market over community/trust.

As a result of these impediments to trust, scholars in these traditions expect to find a trendless pattern of fluctuation in the employment relation's mechanism mix. Consistent with this interpretation. Ramsay (1977) argues that trust in the employment relation has fluctuated over the century as a function of the balance of power between labor and management. Barley and Kunda (1992) and Abrahamson (1997) document cyclical swings between the rhetorics of rational control and normative commitment in management discourse over the last century.

Paul S. Adler

The Hypothesis Reaffirmed

These Marxist and Weberian objections are, however, not convincing. The radical skepticism of trust in the traditional Marxist view is justified only if one accepts that the interests of workers and managers are never even partly congruent. This assumption appears empirically implausible. Moreover, it is based on an unfortunately narrow reading of Marx (Adler 1990). It ignores Marx's insights into the role of community within the firm, expressed in his analysis of 'cooperation' and the 'collective worker'—a collective that includes managers in their 'productive,' as distinct from 'exploitative,' roles (Carchedi 1977).

Once this facet of Marx's analysis is retrieved, it is no longer difficult to conceive of a progressive expansion of trust under capitalist relations of production. Trust, under this view, becomes a feature of work organization, and as such it is at the intersection of the forces of production (society's accumulated productive resources) and the relations of production (the structure of ownership and control of these resources)—embodying both structures simultaneously and subject to the dynamics of both (Adler 1997). Insofar as its trajectory is shaped by fundamentally antagonistic capitalist relations of production, the growth of trust is necessarily limited; but insofar as it is shaped by the forces of production, trust grows cumulatively with the progressive expansion of those forces. In sum, this alternative reading of Marx suggests the possibility of a trend to trust, albeit a trend that is limited in its form and extent by the persistence of capitalist relations.

The version of Weber invoked by those skeptical of a trend to trust is a somewhat truncated one too. In its insistence on the enduring conflict between competing social groups, this reading downplays the importance Weber attached to rationalization in the development of modern society. As traditional bases of domination are displaced by rational–legal ones, the authority of managers within the firm is increasingly a function of the perceived legitimacy of their claim to expertise and to functional necessity. The brute assertion of positional prerogative loses legitimacy, and some kind of trust becomes increasingly critical to the exercise of authority. (Below, I take up the question of which kind of trust.)

Nor is an expansion of trust contradicted by evidence of fluctuations in the mix of mechanisms constituting employment relations. A closer look at the data cited by Barley et al. suggests that a secular trend line underlies these cycles. In both the sequence of rational control phases—from scientific management (whose dominance Abrahamson dates from 1894 to 1921) to systems rationalism (1944–1971) and to reengineering (1990–)—and the sequence of normative commitment phases—from welfare and personnel management (1921–1944) to culture-quality (1971–1990)—we observe the growing importance of themes of employee consent and trust. In the normative approaches, for example, there is a clear shift from the earlier emphasis on paternalism, to relatively impersonal bureaucratic norms of procedural justice, to the recent emphasis on empowerment and mutual commitment.

Perhaps more striking is the trend to trust found in the sequence of control rhetorics. Within two or three years of publishing a text popularizing a rather brutally coercive method of business process reengineering (Hammer and Champy 1993), both James Champy and Michael Hammer published new volumes (Champy 1995, Hammer 1996) stressing the importance of the human factor and the need for job redesigns that afford employees greater autonomy. The undeniably autocratic character of much early reengineering rhetoric and its rapid 'softening' compares favorably with unilateral and enduring forms of domination expressed in post-war systems rationalism. It compares even more favorably with the even more unilateral and rigid rhetoric in turn-of-the-century scientific management: scientific management only softened its relations with organized labor after nearly two decades of confrontation (Nyland 1998).

Clearly, there is a gap—often a huge one, as Marxist and Weberian commentators have pointed out—between these trends in rhetoric and the reality of the employment relation. However, this long-term evolution of rhetoric both reflects and reinforces a real trend to trust. It reflects the evolving expectations of an increasingly educated (read: knowledge-intensive) workforce and the evolving needs of an increasingly advanced (ditto) economy. And it reinforces that trend because the rhetoric of trust legitimizes the idea that management authority depends on employee consent.

Interdivisional Relations

Large multibusiness corporations are under increasing pressure to show real benefits for asserted synergies. A first result of this pressure is the trend to divest unrelated businesses in the interest of 'focus.' Therefore, the increasingly common configuration is that of related-diversified firms, that is, firms in which divisions are neither integrated vertically as suppliers and users nor totally independent of each other. However, in related-diversified firms, if divisions seek only to meet their own divisional objectives, they will behave in ways that are detrimental to the firm's global objectives. A second result of the performance pressure on large corporations is, therefore, a cluster of innovations that appear to be pushing beyond the limits of market and hierarchy and towards greater collaboration.

The multidivisional corporation is in effect a miniature economy in which business units function as miniature firms. Such a corporation must struggle with precisely the dilemma of knowledge management articulated in the market/plan debate. Headquarters' hierarchical control over divisions might help assure the dissemination across divisions of existing knowledge, but such control undermines incentives for the divisions to create new knowledge. The more common approach gives divisions profit and loss responsibility and engenders the corresponding problems of the market form. When divisions function as autonomous profit centers and charge a market-based price for sales of intellectual assets to sister divisions, the effectiveness of the corporation as a whole suffers because the optimal allocation of knowledge assets is blocked (Kaplan 1984; for an example at TRW, see *Business Week* 1982). Because one division's use of these knowledge assets does not preclude their use by another, the corporation would benefit from a regime of free sharing among divisions.

Eccles (1985) finds that in the microeconomy of the firm there is no mix of transfer prices and hierarchical procedures that simultaneously can optimize incentives to invest in the development of new knowledge and to share the results of those development efforts. Not surprisingly, this finding supports at a micro level the prediction of Arrow's and Hurwicz's (1997) analysis of whole economies. The multidivisional form of the corporation was constructed to counterbalance the merits and limits of hierarchy, as embodied in the functional form, with those of market, as embodied in the holding-company form. In this, the M-form resembles the intermediate cases of regulated market or market socialism mentioned above. However, even this hybrid model becomes increasingly inefficient when the corporation must encourage simultaneously the creation of new knowledge within divisions and the sharing of existing knowledge across divisions (Miller 1992).

In response to these problems and to their growing urgency in an increasingly knowledge-intensive economy, multidivisional firms are actively experimenting with new ways to stimulate collaboration between profit centers within the firm. The notion of core competencies, as articulated by Prahalad and Hamel (1990), is premised on the insight that corporate competitiveness depends on bodies of expertise that are typically distributed across divisions rather than contained within them. Collaboration across divisions, therefore, is a critical, not a secondary issue (see also Porter 1985, Pt. III on 'horizontal strategy'). Collins and Porras (1994) document a whole panoply of mechanisms designed to encourage a bond of common identity and a norm of sharing. Davenport and Prusak (1998) describe a range of methods used in large firms to enhance the trust and shared identity needed for the easy flow of ideas across divisional boundaries.

These shifts in interdivisional relations are reflected in changes in corporate control systems. Eccles' (1985) research shows that the most effective transfer pricing scheme in such cases is based neither on market prices nor on internal costs but on what he calls 'rational trust.' Under rational trust, division managers' confidence in top management's ability to evaluate and reward performance fairly is based on two measures: first, the judicious use of quantitative measures of subunit performance, and second, the enlightened use of subjective measures of the subunit managers' contributions to total company performance, even when these contributions hurt their subunits' own performance (Eccles 1985 : 279).

Consistent with Eccles' argument, empirical research finds that in firms with relatively high levels of knowledge-intensity, where collaboration between divisions is therefore at a premium, headquarters commonly use subjective judgments of how well division managers help their peers. These subjective judgments both assess and require trust, in contrast with the more traditional approaches that rely exclusively on quantitative, market performance-based formulae or hierarchical-bureaucratic criteria to determine division managers' bonuses (Gupta and Govindarajan 1986, Lorsch and Allen 1973, Salter 1973, Hill et al. 1992).

The shift to trust is not, however, unproblematic. The ethos of common destiny that underpins trust blurs the allocation of accountability and decision rights at the heart of both hierarchy and market forms. Powerful actors resist this blurring. Within hierarchies, superiors resist giving up the ease of control afforded by the principle of accountability (see e.g. Ashkenas et al. 1993 : 125). Unilateral control is a far simpler organizational process to manage than shared control. More fundamentally, as agents of owners, senior managers are themselves held accountable to brutally simple norms imposed by the product and financial markets. The implacable, anonymous irrationality of the market often makes a mockery of efforts to create and sustain trust. Senior executives, whose fortunes are tied to the firm's market performance, cannot, therefore, commit more than half-heartedly to trust (Hyman 1987).

Notwithstanding this resistance, increasing knowledge-intensity appears to encourage a trend to trust in interdivisional relations. This trend might help explain the proliferation of titles such as chief technology officer and chief knowledge officer. These positions have broad responsibility for building cross-division knowledge and sharing, but typically they have no formal authority—they rely on trust in their attempts to build more trust (Adler and Ferdows 1992, Earl and Scott 1999). As firms learn how to infuse trust into the immensely complex task of coordinating action in multidivisional firms, and in particular as they learn how to combine trust with the necessary elements of hierarchy and market, Eccles' 'rational trust' model appears to be gaining legitimacy.

Interfirm Relations

In parallel with these trends toward trust in employment and interdivisional relations, firms are increasingly infusing trust into their relations with other firms. Alliances and other forms of interfirm networks are proliferating, and the consensus in the field is that this proliferation is driven in large measure by the challenge of growing knowledge-intensity. Here, too, firms are juggling market/price, hierarchy/authority, and community/trust modes, and scholars are debating their relative importance (e.g. *Organization Science* 1998). While some argue that trust is increasingly important in interfirm relations, others argue that firms are unlikely to suspend self-interest in alliances and that trust may often be a result rather than a cause (Koza and Lewin 1998). Whether trust plays an independent causal role is an open question; in this section, I present the case for the affirmative.

First, we should note the countertendencies. On the one hand, we see some firms imposing ever sharper market discipline on their suppliers by aggressively demanding lower prices and moving rapidly to cut off suppliers who cannot deliver (e.g. Ashkenas et al. 1993 : 240). On the other hand, we see firms trying to force improvements in their supplier base by introducing more complex 'hierarchical contracts' (Stinchcombe 1985) into their market relations. Such hierarchical elements control not only product specifications but also the supplier's internal processes. Korczynski (1996), for example, documents a trend toward a low-trust combination of market and hierarchical relations between management contractors and building contractors in the U.K. engineering construction industry in the 1980s and 1990s. Hancké (1997) makes a similar diagnosis of the evolution of subcontracting relations in the French automobile industry.

We also see, however, a growing number of firms building long-term, trust-based partnerships with their suppliers. A burgeoning body of research shows that when firms need innovation and knowledge inputs from suppliers rather than just standardized commodities, no combination of strong hierarchical control and market discipline can assure as high a level of performance as trust-based community (Dyer 1996, Sako 1992, Helper 1991, Bensaou and Venkataraman 1995, Ring 1996, 1997). By contrast, Korczynski's (1996) study shows how low-trust relations in the UK construction industry enabled schedule and cost improvements but were unable to stimulate the creation of new knowledge.

The hierarchy/authority mode of interfirm relations clearly risks impeding innovation by stifling the upward flow of new ideas from subordinate suppliers. Their narrow specialization leaves them without the technological know-how needed for innovation, and their subordination leaves them few incentives to contribute innovative ideas to customers.

The market/price mode facilitates innovation by creating incentives to generate new ideas, but this mode, too, impedes innovation because suppliers and customers of innovations have difficulty agreeing on a price for these innovative ideas. The suppliers are not sure what price would cover their costs, for two reasons. First, the main source of a firm's innovative ideas is society's total stock of knowledge rather than assets held privately by the innovating firm. Given the public-good character of much of that knowledge stock, identifying or justifying a 'raw materials' cost for new ideas generated from this knowledge stock is difficult. Second, an innovative idea is just as likely to arise during free time as on the job, so identifying a 'transformation' cost is difficult. Whereas competition between suppliers of most other types of goods drives prices toward their marginal costs, no comparably grounded 'supply schedule' guides the price of knowledge.

The customer side is no easier. The potential customer for an innovation typically cannot judge the worth of the idea without having its secret revealed, and intellectual property protection is cumbersome and expensive. Moreover, intellectual property rights, compared to property rights in other kinds of assets, lack a legitimating material substratum. We have already pointed out the difficulty of determining the price of knowledge based on its production cost; the alternative basis would be rent, but rent is only a viable price-form when the asset in question is not reproducible and is rivalrous in use, whereas knowledge (at least in its codified forms) is reproducible at close to zero cost and nonrivalrous in use. Its price is therefore less grounded in any material considerations: it is purely a function of convention and relative power. Lacking a legitimating material basis, intellectual property is amongst the most contentious of forms of property. Perhaps that is why patent rights are so often bundled and bartered in dyadic trade rather than sold on open markets.

These implications of growing knowledge-intensity for the market form were identified by Marx more than a century ago (1973 : 700). The forces of production of modern industry are progressively socialized—increasingly, they take the form of society's total knowledge stock. As a result, labor inputs and production costs become increasingly irrelevant to the formation of prices, and the price mechanism becomes an increasingly unreliable basis for economic calculation. The difficulties encountered by efforts to create 'metrics' for knowledge management are perhaps more fundamental than commonly recognized.

Hierarchy and market are relatively more effective for the governance of low-knowledge—intensity transactions where efficiency, rather than innovation, is critical. Where knowledge management is the critical task, the more effective approaches rely on long-term partnership-style relationships based on 'goodwill' trust, as well as competence- and contract-trust (Sako 1992, Bensaou and Venkataraman 1995, Ring 1997). Thus, trust is at the heart of effective knowledge-intensive interfirm networks (Powell 1990).

As with the employment relation, the most effective approaches to knowledge management in interfirm relations deploy a complementary mix of price, authority, and trust mechanisms. Toyota, for example, rarely allows itself to become dependent on a single supplier, and tries to maintain two sources for any noncommodity inputs. Toyota always makes these suppliers aware of the ultimate power of the market test. However, the relationships between Toyota and these suppliers are hardly composed of anonymous, arms-length, spot-market transactions. First, these contracts embody a comprehensive set of documents specifying in detail product requirements and management processes. Second, these hierarchical documents are embedded within a long-term, high-trust, mutual-commitment relationship.

While some observers might argue that Japanese firms like Toyota put so much emphasis on trust because of the importance of this norm in the broader Japanese culture, the evidence appears strong that such a trust-heavy mix of mechanisms is productively superior in a broad range of cultures. Two indicators come from the US auto industry. First, Dyer and Chu (1998) find that, compared to their US counterparts, Japanese auto firms established recently in the United States were able rapidly to create higher-trust relations with their US-owned suppliers. Second, in response to this Japanese challenge, US auto manufacturers have shifted toward higher trust relations with their suppliers. The percentage of US auto parts producers who provide sensitive, detailed information about their production process to their customers grew from 38 percent to 80 percent during the 1980s (Helper and Sako 1995). However, in the case of supplier relations, unlike that of employment relations, research has not yet assessed whether such a shift is more than a swing of the pendulum back to what may been relatively high-trust relations in interfirm relations in earlier periods of capitalism (see, e.g. Sabel and Zeitlin 1997).

Evidence for a trend to interfirm trust is stronger in the proliferation of multilateral network forms of organization for the most knowledge-intensive tasks and industries (Nelson 1988, Powell 1990, Liebeskind et al. 1996). The multiplication of such tasks and industries over time warrants the hypothesis that the proliferation of high-trust multilateral interfirm networks is not just a pendulum swing. Patent pooling and cooperative R&D consortia have multiplied in recent decades. Formal professional and technical societies and informal community ties among scientists constitute other, less direct forms of interfirm networking whose importance appears to be growing.

One should not ignore the countervailing forces. These high-trust network forms may be more productive, but because the market principle is also present, they suffer the risk of opportunistic defection. Self-interested behavior can sometimes encourage trustworthiness, particularly when the 'shadow of the future' is long. However, self-interest does not reliably ensure the diffusion and persistence of trust-based networks, and whole regions can find themselves stuck at low-trust and poor-performing equilibria. However, when these regions are subject to competition from regions that have attained a higher-trust, higher-performing equilibrium, one sometimes observes serious, sustained, self-conscious efforts to create trust (Sabel 1992). Some of these efforts succeed. One might hypothesize that if efforts to create trust as a response to competition do not succeed, economic activity will tend to shift to higher-trust regions. In either case, the trend towards trust seems likely to emerge, if only at a more global level.

The Difficulties of Trust

The preceding overview of changes within and between firms suggests that all three coordination mechanisms—price, authority, and trust—have a role to play in the knowledge economy, but that trust is becoming increasingly important in this mix. Relative to their respective low-trust forms, the high-trust forms of intraorganizational, interdivisional, and interfirm relations encourage more effective knowledge generation and dissemination. The objective need for trust is, to be sure, counterbalanced by the resistance of those whose prerogatives would be threatened by it, but the defense of these prerogatives is increasingly inconsistent with the interests of economic performance. I leave empirical testing of this argument to another occasion, and focus here on the theoretical obstacles. The section above on employment relations discussed several such obstacles. We must now broaden that discussion.

A first obstacle is posed by some economists and sociologists who argue that trust can never, even in principle, become a stable and dominant mechanism. Theoretical economists such as Arrow do not deny that trust would greatly improve the effectiveness of markets; and organizational economists such as Williamson add that trust would also no doubt improve the effectiveness of hierarchy. However, economic theory argues that trust, like knowledge itself, is a public good, and that the spontaneous working of the price mechanism (assumed to be the dominant one) will generate too large a free-rider problem, and consequently will fail to produce the optimal quantity of trust. In repeated games, tit-for-tat co-operation—a minimal form of community—may emerge, but the emergence of cooperation is neither necessary nor predictable. Economists therefore doubt that trust can ever become a stable, dominant mechanism.

The flaw in such reasoning is in the assumption that individuals' preferences are essentially egotistical and exogenous. If people have a propensity for altruism that coexists and competes with the propensity for egoism, and if the relative importance of these two propensities varies with the circumstances, then there is no reason to believe that trust cannot become an important, even dominant, mechanism of coordination in the right circumstances (Ring and Van de Ven 1992).

Some sociologists, too, have expressed skepticism of trust, based on the intuition that trust is far easier to destroy than to create and that its most powerful forms are those that accumulate over long periods (e.g. Putnam 1993, Hardin 1992). Evans (1996) contrasts this 'endowment' view with a 'constructibility' view of trust and social capital. While future empirical research might perhaps east light on the relative merits of these views, common experience tells us that trust can be created, at least under some conditions. Sable (1992) describes the processes by which previously distrustful actors can overcome the temptation to free-ride and deliberately create the trust they recognize as being in their common interest (see also Ring 1997).

Assuming that trust can emerge, a second obstacle arises: Trust has its own dark side. Trust can fail us because it makes betrayal more profitable (Granovetter 1985). More fundamentally, it can fail us because its success can prove dysfunctional. Trust-based institutions are often exclusivistic and elitist, particularly when the source of trust is shared norms or familiarity. These institutions are poorly equipped to deal with the knowledge management challenge. Social psychologists have shown that trust within teams can lead to complacency and poor performance in innovative tasks (Kim 1997). When trust based on familiarity or norms becomes the dominant mechanism, firms can come to look like premodern 'clans' with the associated traditionalistic domination, and whether this domination takes an autocratic or a paternalistic form, such organizations are clearly handicapped in their knowledge management. When suppliers become trusted partners, the risk of discrimination against potential new suppliers grows correspondingly, reducing innovative potential (Uzzi 1997, Kern 1998). In the language of sociology, one would say that in settings governed by norm- or familiarity-based trust, ascribed status often replaces achieved status—which is surely not a promising move in a dynamic knowledge economy.

The most appropriate theoretical response to this challenge is to invoke the potential complementarities between price, authority, and trust. The downsides of trust and closed communities can be mitigated by the presence of market and hierarchy. Compared to traditional normative trust, the pure, low-trust market is a powerful lever for creating opportunities, especially opportunities for knowledge development. Uzzi's (1997) study of the New York women's apparel industry, for example, shows how firms combine arm's-length market relations with trust-based social relations in their supplier and customer networks. Uzzi argues that firms that balance trust and market can maintain trust's benefits while avoiding the rigidity associated with exclusive reliance on trust relations. Communitarians sensitive to the risks of closed communities make a parallel argument for the importance of hierarchy: at the level of specific organizations, the pure, low-trust bureaucratic hierarchy is a powerful lever for assuring equity and stability, and at a more macro-societal level, a healthy society needs a mutually supportive combination of community and hierarchy in the form of government and law (Walzer 1999).

A third and potentially greater obstacle is identified by several currents of social theory that argue that the overall dominance of the price mechanism in capitalist society tends over time to corrode the foundations of trust. Hirschman (1982) reviews these arguments in his discussion of 'self-destructive' views of market-based society. Scholars inspired by both Marxist and reactionary thought and by writers such as Weber, Simmel, and Durkheim have argued that the 'cash nexus' characteristic of the market-based capitalist form of society progressively undermines the social conditions of capitalism's effectiveness. First, the market undermines the familiarity source of trust by corroding the traditional bonds of community and extended family, leading to the anonymity of urban life. And second, the market undermines the normative source of trust by corroding traditional shared beliefs, leading to 'the dissolution of pre-capitalist bonds of loyalty and obedience' (Schumpeter 1976). Without the buttressing effect of familiarity and traditional shared norms, self-interested calculative trust alone provides only an unreliable foundation for capitalism: '[self-] interest is what is least constant in the world' (Durkheim 1984 [orig. 1893]; see also Ring 1996 on 'fragile trust', and Barney and Hansen 1994, on 'weak form' trust).

Hirschman (1982) points out, however, that this self-destructive view has competed with another, more benign view of the effect of the market of society. He labels this benign view the '*doux commerce*' (Fr: gentle commerce) thesis. Thomas Paine in *The Rights of Man* (1951 [1792]: 215) expressed it in the proposition: '[Commerce] is a pacific system, operating to cordialise mankind, by rendering Nations, as well as individuals, useful to each other.' Markets may undermine the strong ties of closed community, but they weave an ever-broader web of weaker ties that draws us into 'universal inter-dependence' (Marx and Engels 1959 : 11). A host of observers (but few social theorists) argue that capitalism encourages the emergence of 'modern' norms such as industriousness, frugality, punctuality, probity (Rosenberg 1964). Some of these modern virtues are arguably propitious for the propagation of at least some forms of trust.

In the contest of these two views, the self-destruction thesis has fared better than the *doux commerce* view. Durkheim's celebration of organic versus mechanical solidarity, for example, echoes Paine's view of the importance of functional interdependence in modern society, but Durkheim was notably pessimistic concerning the possibility of the spontaneous emergence of the requisite normative foundations. Marx's celebration of capitalism's civilizing effects were eclipsed by his denunciation of its inhumanity. Indeed, Hirschman shows that the *doux commerce* thesis all but disappeared after the eighteenth century.

Toward Reflective Trust

My summary of the corrosive effects of the market distinguished its effects on the three sources of trust: market society seems inimical to strong forms of familiarity trust; market society encourages calculative trust, but such trust alone is unreliable; and market society dissolves the traditional foundations of normative trust. Given the ineluctable quality of the first and second of these effects, the burden of a hypothesized trend to trust must fall on normative trust. Is there any reason to believe that normative trust can be sufficiently renewed to meet the challenge of the knowledge economy? Further research is needed to test the proposition, but the available evidence suggests that alongside the apparently irresistible decline of traditional trust, we might be observing the gradual emergence of a distinctively modern form of trust.

Leadership is one domain in which some of the tensions between the old and new forms of trust seem to manifest themselves. While some leaders at both the corporate and national levels still seek to legitimize their authority by reference to tradition, a growing number appear to have accepted that if leadership is going to support effective knowledge management, then leadership's legitimacy must be based on more rational norms. The trust that leaders build must be an inclusive, open, democratic kind, or knowledge creation and sharing will falter (Bennis and Slater 1964, Bennis and Nanus 1997). Charismatic bases of leadership, as Weber predicted, still wax and wane in popularity, continually finding new pertinence, but the balance between traditional and rational bases seems to be shifting progressively in favor of rationality. Within firms, leadership seems to have shifted toward a form of trust consonant with the ethos of 'fact-based management', independent inquiry, and collaborative problem-solving rather than traditionalist deference to established authority.

A modern form of normative trust can be distinguished from its premodern form. The modern form is less blind and tradition bound. It is more 'studied' (Sabel 1992), 'rational' (Eccles 1985), and 'tentative' (Barnes 1981). Its rationality is not of the purely calculative kind assumed by economics. Norms play a central role in modern trust, but these norms do not derive their legitimacy from affective sources such as tradition or charisma, nor from their own calculative, purposive-rational utility. Rather, the legitimacy of modern trust is derived from grounding in open dialogue among peers. Habermas (1990) has attempted to characterize this form of legitimization in terms of the 'ideal speech situation', and Apel (1987) in the 'ideal community of communication.'

The modern form of trust might be labeled 'reflective.' The values at work in modern trust are those of the scientific community: 'universalism, communism, disinterestedness, organized skepticism' (Merton 1973 : 270). Modern trust is inclusive and open. Referring to the discussion above of the bases of trust, one could hypothesize that whereas traditional trust elevates loyalty over the other bases (Schumpeter's 'precapitalist bonds of loyalty and obedience'), modern trust ranks integrity and competence more highly (Butler and Cantrell 1984, Schindler and Thomas 1993; see Gates 1998 for a case study of the shift from loyalty to competence in the basis of trust among President's staff in the White House).

From these considerations, I tentatively conclude that the efficacy of trust for knowledge management and the likelihood of its growth over time are maximized if: (a) trust is balanced by hierarchical rules to ensure stability and equity; (b) trust is balanced by market competition to ensure flexibility and opportunity; and (c) trust is modern and reflective rather than traditionalistic and blind. Space does not permit, but a parallel argument can be made concerning traditional and modern forms of community. Much of the debate around communitarianism has been diverted into an unproductive contrast between community and individual rights. As Lakoff (1996) argues, a more fruitful and urgent debate would be over alternative forms of community.

Trust and Universalism

Before exploring the broader implications of a trend toward reflective trust, one possible further objection should be addressed: As a norm, reflective trust appears to conflate two poles of the fundamental Weberian distinction between particularism and universalism. Is reflective trust therefore a self-contradictory notion?

Carol Heimer (1992) poses this problem nicely in her discussion of forms of organization based on interpersonal networks. Network forms of organization require a significant departure from the 'universalist' orientation articulated by Weber and highlighted by Talcott Parsons as one of the distinguishing features of modernity. To build trust, actors must adopt a more 'particularistic' orientation, acknowledging the obligation to reciprocity entailed by relations with specific others, rather than relying on universal norms to guide their conduct (1992).

To reinforce the point, Heimer quotes a quip about Parsons (an unfair one, I am told by others) to the effect that he was 'so universalistic that he wouldn't help a friend' (1992 : 143). Is the idea of a modern form of trust which avoids the limitations of particularism essentially wrong-headed? If trust is necessarily particularistic, does it necessarily suffer the limitations of its traditional form? These limitations would hobble trust's ability to coordinate knowledge-intensive activity.

These questions call for a more nuanced analysis than space permits. For the present purposes, however, it is sufficient to point out that particularism and universalism need not be polarities on a one-dimensional spectrum. They might better be conceived as conceptually independent dimensions, even if broadly speaking they tend to occur in inverse correlation. Traditionalistic trust is indeed high on particularism and low on universalism, and both pure markets and pure bureaucracies are high on universalism and low on particularism, but we can easily imagine a normative orientation and an associated form of trust that is high on both dimensions. This is precisely the modern condition: The ethical dilemmas characteristic of the modern era are those engendered by simultaneous commitments to particular others and to universal principles.

It should be mentioned that under some construals, 'modernity' would be characterized somewhat differently, as an epoch in which universalism prevailed and particularism was shunned—at least as the socially legitimate normative orientation, if not always in daily life. Under this view, the current epoch should be seen as 'post-modern' precisely because its ethos legitimates the simultaneous and paradoxical embrace of both universalism and particularism. Maxims such as 'Think globally, act locally' come to mind.

Trust and Capitalism

So far, the argument has focused on the implications of an economywide trend—growing knowledge-intensity—for intra- and interfirm relations. If, however, the trend to trust prevails, one must surely expect some reciprocal effect of firm-level changes at the aggregate, economywide level. Organizational research and social theory might both be enriched if these implications could be seen more clearly. The final set of speculations in this paper leads to the hypothesis that if capitalism undermines traditional trust and fosters modern trust, a new form of society will be likely to emerge.

Schumpeter provides the starting point. Paraphrasing and extending Marx, Schumpeter wrote:

Capitalism creates a critical frame of mind which, after having destroyed the moral authority of so many other institutions, in the end turns against its own: the bourgeois finds to his amazement that the rationalist attitude does not stop at the credentials of kings and popes but goes on to attack private property and the whole scheme of bourgeois values. [...] The capitalist process not only destroys its own institutional framework but it also creates the conditions for another. Destruction may not be the right word after all. Perhaps I should have spoken of transformation. The outcome of the process is not simply a void that could be filled by whatever might happen to turn up; things and souls are transformed in such a way as to become increasingly amenable to the socialist form of life. With every peg from under the capitalist structure vanishes an impossibility of the socialist plan. (1976 : 143, 162).

In Schumpeter's view, large corporations developed means of institutionalizing innovation and regulating competition. The firm typical of competitive capitalism—owned and led by an entrepreneur—was thus progressively displaced by the large, bureaucratic firm with dispersed ownership and professional managers. Market was progressively displaced by hierarchy. Property was, in the process, progressively socialized—but not socialized enough to eliminate capitalism's tendency to periodic crises or its other negative externalities. The earlier form of capitalism derived legitimacy from its support for the entrepreneurial function: Competitive capitalism's obvious flaws were the price to be paid for the productive energy of entrepreneurship. But capitalism's own development, and in particular the shift to large bureaucratically organized firms, makes capitalism's dysfunctions appear increasingly unnecessary and therefore intolerable: Witness, for example, the US government's bailout of Chrysler. The legitimacy of capitalism as a form of society based on private ownership of productive resources is progressively undermined. Moreover, by the same process, capitalist development 'creates the conditions for another' institutional framework that replaces private ownership by public ownership—socialism.

The logic of the present essay argues for both the continuing pertinence of Schumpeter's thesis and the need to revise it. Schumpeter's underlying contrast was between market (externally coordinating entrepreneurial firms) and hierarchy (internally coordinating oligopolistic firms, and eventually coordinating activity across entire economies). This contrast and Schumpeter's analysis of it have continuing pertinence: Both the persistent crisis tendencies of capitalism and the incapacity of markets to cope effectively enough with the growing knowledge-intensity of modern society reinforce Schumpeter's concerns about the efficacy of market coordination. Also, the long-term trend toward larger firms and bigger government confirms his prognosis of the growing importance of hierarchy.

A critic might argue that this prediction is at variance with the real trends observed in the United States and elsewhere in the advanced industrial economies over the last couple of decades, where an intensification of global and

domestic competition and a wave of deregulation have reasserted the dominance of the market. The Schumpeterian view, however, invites us to enlarge
our temporal horizon: If one considers the changes witnessed over the last 50
to 100 years, Schumpeter's prediction of the replacement of market by hierarchy becomes more plausible. The last couple of decades have made little
progress in 'turning back the clock.' Even if the average size of establishments
has stabilized, the weight of large firms relative to small in the economy has
grown, and the weight of (federal and state) government relative to private
industry has grown too.

Schumpeter's thesis, however, also needs revision. Both the continued
vitality of small entrepreneurial firms in the capitalist knowledge-creation
process and the demise of state socialism give us reasons to doubt the efficacy
of hierarchy alone as a form capable of effectively structuring firms and
societies. Schumpeter's implicit market-hierarchy model must be extended to
include trust: We must add a dialect of trust to Schumpeter's market-hierarchy
dialectic. On the one hand, over the longer run, the economy's increasing
knowledge-intensity undermines the efficacy and therefore legitimacy of (low-
trust) market and hierarchy. Market's costly fluctuations and manifest failures
and hierarchy's coercive domination and alienating specialization reveal the
inadequacies of these two forms relative to the knowledge-management challenge. Low-trust market thus loses legitimacy as a model of governance of
interfirm and interdivisional relations, and (low-trust) hierarchy loses legitimacy as a model of governance of employment relations. On the other hand, the
gradual infusion of trust into hierarchies and markets popularizes and legitimates a range of more participative and democratic notions of how firms
should be run (Levine 1995, Lawler et al. 1998) and of how society and the
economy as a whole should be governed (Lodge 1975, Unger 1975, Etzioni
1988).

Do these trends, however, spell the demise of capitalism? Hirschman (1982)
criticizes Schumpeter and other proponents of the self-destruction thesis for
ignoring capitalism's ability to adapt to pressures such as these. Hirschman
argues that through a series of innovations from factory legislation to social
security to countercyclical macroeconomic management, demands to socialize
the economy have been accommodated within a basically capitalist framework.
At a micro level of intra- and interfirm relations, one could follow Hirschman
and point to the evidence that trust can indeed infuse hierarchy and market
relations without provoking crisis: As argued above, the three forms are often
complementary.

These complementarities should, nevertheless, not obscure the fact that in a
capitalist society the varying combinations of market, hierarchy, and community operate under the overall predominance of the market. If, as I argued
above, the three basic coordination modes are sometimes substitutes and only

sometimes complements, then it follows that all three modes cannot peacefully co-exist in any proportions. There is little doubt which of the three dominates in advanced economies today. While the functioning of a market-based economy is greatly enhanced by modest doses of hierarchy and community, the dominance of the market form places limits on the growth of hierarchy and community. Whatever hierarchy and community are created within and between firms, market pressures that are beyond any actor's control—in the form of unpredictable market fluctuations and crises—can force management to renege on its commitments (laying off employees or breaking supply relationships) or can simply force the firm out of business. In an era of globalization, intensified competitive rivalry, and international financial crisis tendencies, the dominant role of the market has been brutally brought back into focus.

It is against this backdrop that Schumpeter's thesis acquires its force. The development of greater knowledge–management capability will necessitate the displacement of the market as the dominant form. However, whereas Schumpeter saw the progressive displacement of market by hierarchy, first in large corporations, then at the societal level in the form of socialism, this essay suggests a 'friendly amendment' to Schumpeter's thesis: The institutional framework likely to emerge from capitalism's development is not any form of socialism but a form characterized by high levels of trust. If socialism can be construed as a form of society in which hierarchy dominates market at both the firm level and the economywide level, then the form of socialism that can successfully confront the challenges of modern, knowledge-intensive industry will have to be one in which hierarchy is combined with high levels of trust.

Opinions are divided as to whether the most viable form of postcapitalist society will prove to be one based on comprehensive centralized but democratic planning or a form of market socialism in which markets supplement democratic planning (Nove 1982). What seems indubitable, however, is that the planning process must be one in which citizens feel a high degree of trust. Evidence for this assertion comes first from the demise of (decidedly low-trust) state socialism. While external pressures clearly played a role in this demise, low-trust central planning was also a key factor. Evidence also comes from research on the vitality of industrial districts in regions such as Northern Italy. Whereas Putnam (1993) argues that long-standing community ties in those regions created a fabric of horizontal trust, which in turn led to high levels of civic engagement and economic prosperity, critics have shown the economic vitality of these regions stems not only from horizontal trust but also from the vertical trust earned and enjoyed by active local governments (e.g. Tarrow 1996). This is also the lesson of Evans' (1995) analysis of the importance for economic development of governments with high levels of 'embedded autonomy.'

The various configurations of capitalist and postcapitalist socretal forms can be located in a typology that reflects at the macrosocietal level the typology presented earlier of institutional forms at the firm level (see Figure 4). Indeed, substitution of the three terms of Figure 3—market, hierarchy, and community—with corresponding dimensions already well established in sociological analysis—market, state, and civil society—is conceptually straightforward. (Concerns voiced by critics of this market/state/civil society trichotomy focus on the way much prior research fell prey to 'classificatory angst' (Edwards and Foley 1988 : 128), and degenerated into arguments over whether a given institution falls into this or that type. The approach suggested by this paper avoids that dead end by using these ideal-types to understand the hybrids in which they are typically presented.)

For trust to become the dominant mechanism for coordination *within* organizations, broadly participative governance and multistakeholder control would need to replace autocratic governance and owner control—even if hierarchy, in a high-trust form, continued to characterize large-scale enterprise. And, for trust to become the dominant mechanism for coordinating *between* organizations, comprehensive but democratic planning would need to replace market competition as the dominant form of resource allocation—even if market retained an important subsidiary role. If capitalism can be defined as a form of society characterized by (hierarchically controlled) wage labor and

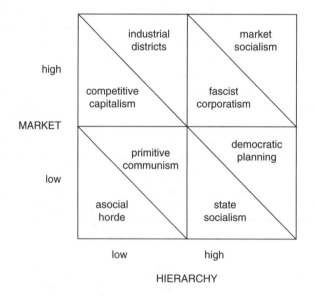

Fig. 4. *A Typology of Societal Forms (low trust forms in lower left triangles, high trust forms in upper right triangles)*

(market coordinated) competing firms, then such a trust-based form of society would surely qualify as postcapitalist. A host of institutional components of capitalism, notably property rights, corporate law, labor law, and even the form of government, would need to change accordingly. 'Vertical trust'—trust in government—would have to be radically increased.

This extension of Schumpeter's thesis must immediately acknowledge that we know little about what any postcapitalist form of society might look like. The demise of state socialism has highlighted the importance of combining hierarchy with high levels of trust and the possible value of market as a subordinate mode, but whether and how such combinations can be attained and sustained is still an open question. Indeed, the central thesis of this essay is that the trends at work today in the fabric of intra- and interfirm relations might give us valuable clues to the answer.

Acknowledgments

This article is based on a presentation at the University of California Berkeley Forum on 'Knowledge and the Firm', September 1997. Contributors were asked to err on the side of interesting provocation, thus the speculative nature of this article. It has benefited from the comments of several colleagues who bear no responsibility for the author's reluctance to accept their advice: Eileen Appelbaum, Nick Argyres, Reinhardt Bachmann, Rose Batt, Warren Bennis, David Finegold, Susan Helper, Peter Kim, Marek Korczynski, Nancy Kurland, David Levine, Arie Lewin, Julia Liebeskind, Larry Prusak, Peter Ring, and Carroll Stephens. *Organization Science* referees offered valuable suggestions and challenges.

References

Abrahamson, E. (1997). 'The Emergence and Prevalence of Employee Management rhetorics: The Effects of Long Waves, Labor Unions, and Turnover, 1875–1992', *Acad Management J*, 40(3) 491–533.

Academy of Management Review (1998). Special topic forum on trust in and between organizations, 23(3).

Adler, P. S. (1990). 'Marx, Machines and Skill', *Tech Culture*, 31(4) 780–812.

—— (1997). 'Work Organization: From Taylorism to Teamwork', *Perspectives on Work*, (June) 61–65.

—— B. Borys (1996). 'Two Types of Bureaucracy: Coercive Versus Enabling', *Admin Sci Quart*, 41(1) 61–89.

Paul S. Adler

Adler, P. S., K. Ferdows (1992). 'The Chief Technology Officer: A New Role for New Challenges', in L. R. Gomez-Mejia and M. W. Lawless (eds), *Advances in Global High-Technology Management: Top Management and Executive Leadership in High Technology*, Vol. 2. Greenwich CT: JAI Press, pp. 49–66.

—— B. Goldoftas, D. I. Levine (1999). 'Flexibility Versus Efficiency? A Case Study of Model Changeovers in the Toyota Production System', *Organ Sci*, 10(1) 43–68.

Alchian, A. A., Demsetz, H. (1972). 'Production, Information Costs, and Economic Organization', *Amer Econom Rev*, 62(5) 777–795.

Apel, K.-O. (1987). 'The Problem of Philosophical Foundations in Light of a Transcendental Pragmatics of Language', in K. Barnes, J. Bohnmann, and T. McCarthy (eds), *After Philosophy: End or Transformation?* Cambridge MA: MIT Press, pp. 250–90.

Arrow, K. (1962). 'Economic Welfare and the Allocation of Resources for Invention. Universities-National Bureau Committee for Economic Research', in *The Rate and Direction of Inventive Activity*. Princeton, NJ: Princeton University Press, pp. 609–625.

—— L. Hurwicz (eds) (1977). *Studies in Resource Allocation Processes*. Cambridge MA: Cambridge University Press.

Ashkenas, R., Ulrich, D., Jick, T., and Kerr, S. (1993). *The Boundaryless Organization*. San Francisco CA: Jossey-Bass.

Barber, B. (1983). *The Logic and Limits of Trust*. New Brunswick NJ: Rutgers University Press.

Barker, J. R. (1993). 'Tightening the Iron Cage: Concertive Control in Self-Managing Teams', *Admin Sci Quart*, 38 408–437.

Barley, S. R., Kunda, G. (1992). 'Design and Devotion: Surges of Rational and Normative Ideologies of Control in Managerial Discourse', *Admin Sci Quart*, 37 363–399.

Barnes, L. B. (1981). 'Managing the Paradox of Organizational Trust', *Harvard Bus Rev*, (March–April) 59(2) 107–116.

Barney, J. B., Hansen, M. H. (1994). 'Trustworthiness as a Source of Competitive Advantage', *Strategic Management J*, 15 (Special Issue) 175–216.

Bell, D. (1993). *Communitarianism and Its Critics*. Oxford: Clarendon Press.

Bennis, W. G., Nanus, B. (1997). *Leaders: Strategies for Taking Charge*, 2nd edn, New York: HarperBusiness.

—— Slater, P. E. (1964). 'Democracy is Inevitable', *Harvard Bus Rev*, (March–April).

Bensaou, M., Venkataraman, N. (1995). 'Configurations of Interorganizational Relationships: A Comparison between U.S. and Japanese Automakers', *Management Sci*, 41(9) 1471–1492.

Bigley, G. A., and Pearce, J. L. (1998). 'Straining for Shared Meaning in Organization Science: Problems of Trust and Distrust', *Acad Management Rev*, 23(3) 405–421.

Birch, D. L. (1987). *Job Creation in America*. New York: Free Press.

Blackburn, P., Coombs, R., and Green, K. (1985). *Technology, Economic Growth and the Labor Process*. New York: St Martin's Press.

Blau, Peter M. (1955). *The Dynamics of Bureaucracy*. Chicago IL: University of Chicago Press.

Bradach, J., Eccles, R. (1989). 'Markets Versus Hierarchies: From Ideal Types to Plural Forms', W. R. Scott (ed.), *Ann Rev Soc*, 15 97–118.

Braverman, H. (1974). *Labor and Monopoly Capital*. New York: Monthly Review Books.

Brockner, J., Siegel, P. (1996). 'Understanding the Interaction between Procedural and Distributive Justice: The Role of Trust', in Roderick M. Kramer, Tom R. Tyler (eds), *Trust in Organizations*. Thousand Oaks CA: Sage, pp. 390–413.

Bromiley, P., Cummings, L. L. (1995). 'Transaction Costs in Organizations with Trust', in Robert J. Bies, R. J. Lewicki, Blair L. Sheppard (eds), *Research on Negotiations in Organizations*. Greenwich CT: JAI.

Brynjolfsson, E., Malone, T. W., Gurbaxani, V., Kambil, A. (1994). 'Does information technology lead to smaller firms?', *Management Sci*, 40(12) 1628–1644.

Burawoy, M. (1979). *Manufacturing Consent*. Chicago IL: University of Chicago Press.

Burns, T., and Stalker, G. (1961). *The Management of Innovation*. London: Tavistock.

Business Week (1982). 'TRW leads a revolution in managing technology'. (November 15).

Butler, J. K., Cantrell, R. S. (1984). 'A Behavioral Decision Theory Approach to Modeling Dyadic Trust in Superiors and Subordinates', *Psych Reports*, 55 19–28.

Carchedi, G. (1977). *The Economic Identification of Social Classes*. London: Routledge & Kegan Paul.

Carney, M. (1998). 'The Competitiveness of Networked Production: The Role of Trust and Asset Specificity', *J Management Stud*, 35(4) 457–479.

Champy, J. (1995). *Reengineering Management*. New York: HarperBusiness.

Coleman, R. (1990). *Foundations of Social Theory*. Cambridge MA: Belknap Press.

Collins, J. C., and Porras, J. I. (1994). *Built to Last*. New York: HarperCollins.

Crozier, M. (1964). *The Bureaucratic Phenomenon*. Chicago, IL: University of Chicago Press.

Daft, R. L. (1998). *Essentials of Organization Theory and Design*. Cincinnati, OH: South-Western College Publishing.

Davenport, T. H., Prusak, L. (1998). *Working Knowledge*. Boston, MA: Harvard Business School Press.

Dore, R. (1983). 'Goodwill and the Spirit of Market Capitalism', *British J Soc*, 34 459–482.

Downs, A. (1967). *Inside Bureaucracy*. Boston, MA: Little, Brown.

Durkheim, E. (1984). *The Division of Labor in Society*. New York: Free Press, W. D. Halls, trans.

Dyer, J. H. (1996). 'Does Governance Matter? Keiretsu Alliances and Asset Specificity as Sources of Japanese Competitive Advantage', *Organ Sci*, 7(6) 649–666.

—— W. Chu. (1998). 'The Determinants of Interfirm Trust in Supplier–Automaker Relationships in the U.S., Japan and Korea. Unpublished, Wharton.

Earl, M. J., Scott, I. A. (1999). 'What is a chief knowledge officer?', *Sloan Management Rev*, (Winter) 40(2) 29–38.

Eccles, R. (1985). *The Transfer Pricing Problem*. Lexington MA: Lexington.

Edwards, B., and Foley, M. W. (1998). 'Civil Society and Social Capital Beyond Putnam', *Amer Behavioral Scientist*, 42(1) 124–139.

Etzioni, A. (1988). *The Moral Dimension*. New York: Free Press.

Evans, P. (1995). *Embedded Autonomy: States and Industrial Transformation*. Princeton NJ: Princeton University Press.

—— (1996). 'Government Action, Social Capital and Development: Reviewing the Evidence on Synergy', *World Development*, 24(6) 1119–1132.

Fox, A. (1974). 'Beyond Contract: Work, Power and Trust Relations', London: Faber and Faber.

Fukuyama, F. (1995). 'Trust: The Social Virtues and the Creation of Prosperity', New York: Free Press.

Gambetta, D. (ed.) (1988). *Trust: Making and Breaking Cooperative Relations*. Oxford: Basil Blackwell.

Gates, H. L., Jr. (1998). 'The end of loyalty', *The New Yorker*, (March 9) 34–44.

Gerlach, M. L. (1992). *Alliance Capitalism: The Social Organization of Japanese Capitalism*. Berkeley CA: University of California Press.

Giddens, A. (1990). *The Consequences of Modernity*. Stanford CA: Stanford University Press.

Gouldner, A. W. (1954). *Patterns of Industrial Bureaucracy*. New York: Free Press.

Granovetter, M. (1985). 'Economic Action and Social Structure: The Problem of Embeddedness', *Amer J Soc*, 91 481–510.

Gupta, A. K. V. G. (1986). 'Resource Sharing Among SBUs: Strategic Antecedents and Administrative Implications', *Acad Management Rev*, 29(4) 695–714.

Habermas, J. (1990). *Moral Consciousness and Communicative Action*. Cambridge MA: MIT Press.

—— (1993). *The Philosophical Discourse of Modernity*. Cambridge MA: MIT Press.

Hammer, M. (1996). *Beyond Reengineering*. New York: HarperBusiness.

—— and Champy, J. (1993). *Reengineering the Corporation*. New York: HarperBusiness.

Hanck, B. (1997). 'Trust or Hierarchy? Changing Relationships Between Large and Small Firms in France', *Small Bus Econom*, 11(3) 237–252.

Hardin, R. (1992). 'The Street-Level Epistemology of Trust.', *Politics and Society*, 21 505–529.

Harvey, D. (1990). *The Condition of Modernity*. Cambridge MA: Blackwell.

Heimer, C. (1992). 'Doing Your Job and Helping Your Friends: Universalistic Norms about Obligations to Help Particular Others in Networks', in N. Noria and R. G. Eccles, (eds), *Networks and Organizations: Structure, Form, and Action*. Boston MA: Harvard Business School Press. pp. 143–64.

Heisig, U., Littek, W. (1995). 'Trust as a Basis of Work Organization', in W. Littek and Tony Charles (eds), *The New Division of Labour: Emerging Forms of Work Organization in International Perspective*. Berlin/New York: de Gruyter, pp. 17–56.

Helper, S. (1991). 'Strategy and Irreversibility in Supplier Relations: The Case of the US Automobile Industry', *Bus History Rev*, 65(4) 781–824.

—— and Sako, M. (1995). 'Supplier Relations in the Auto Industry in Japan and the USA: Are they converging?', *Sloan Management Rev*, (Spring) 36(3) 77–84.

Hill, C., Hitt, M., and Hoskisson, R. (1992). 'Cooperative vs. Competitive Structures in Related and Unrelated Diversified Firms', *Organ Sci*, 3(4) 501–521.

Hirschman, A. O. (1970). *Exit, Voice, and Loyalty*. Cambridge MA: Harvard University Press.

—— (1982). 'Rival Interpretations of Market Society: Civilizing, Destructive or Feeble?', *J Econom Literature*, 20: 1463–1484.

Holland, C. P., and Lockett, A. G. (1997). 'Mixed Mode Network Structures: The Strategic Use of Electronic Communication by Organizations', *Organ Sci*, 8(5) 475–488.

Hyman, R. (1987). 'Strategy or Structure? Capital, Labour and Control', *Work, Employment and Society*, 1(1) 25–55.

Kaplan, R. S. (1984). 'The Evolution of Management Accounting', *The Accounting Rev*, (July).

—— (1996). *The Balanced Scorecard: Translating Strategy into Action*. Boston MA: Harvard Business School Press.

Kern, H. (1998). 'Lack of Trust, Surfeit of Trust: Some Causes of the Innovation Crisis in German Industry', Cristel Lane and Reinhard Bachmann (eds), *Trust Within and Between Organizations*. New York: Oxford University Press, pp. 203–213.

Kim, P. H. (1997). 'Working Under the Shadow of Suspicion: The Implications of Trust and Mistrust for Information Sharing in Groups', Unpublished. Los Angeles CA: University of Southern California.

Kirkpatrick, F. G. (1986). *Community: A Trinity of Models*. Washington, DC: Georgetown University Press.

Korczynski, M. (1996). 'The Low Trust Route to Economic Development: Interfirm Relations in the UK Engineering Construction Industry in the 1980s and 1990s', *J Management Stud*, 33(6) 787–808.

Koza, M., Arie, P., Lewin, Y. (1998). 'The Co-Evolution of Strategic Alliances', *Organ Sci*, 9(3) 255–264.

Kurland, N. B. (1996). 'Trust, Accountability, and Sales Agents' Dueling Loyalties', *Bus Ethics Quart*, 6(3) 289–310.

Lakoff, G. (1996). *Moral Politics: What Conservatives Know That Liberals Don't*. Chicago IL: University of Chicago Press.

Lawler, E. E., III, Mohrman, S. A., Ledford Jr., G. E. (1998). *Strategies for High Performance Organizations*. San Francisco CA: Jossey-Bass.

Levine, D. (1995). *Reinventing the Workplace: How Business and Employees Can Both Win*. Washington, DC: Brookings Institution.

Lewicki, R. J., Bunker, B. B. (1996). 'Developing and Maintaining Trust in Work Relationships', in Roderick M. Kramer and Tom R. Tyler (eds), *Trust in Organizations*. Thousand Oaks CA: Sage, pp. 114–49.

Liebeskind, J. L., Oliver, A. L., Zucker, L., and Brewer, M. (1996). 'Social Networks, Learning and Flexibility: Sourcing Scientific Knowledge in the New Biotechnology Firms', *Organ Sci*, 7(4) 428–443.

—— —— (1998). 'From Handshake to Contract: Trust, Intellectual Property, and the Social Structure of Academic Research', in Cristel Lane and Reinhard Bachmann (eds), *Trust Within and Between Organizations*. New York: Oxford University Press, pp. 118–45.

Lodge, G. C. (1975). *The New American Ideology*. New York: Knopf.

Lorsch, J. W., and Allen, III. S. A. (1973). *Managing Diversity and Interdependence*. Division of Research, Graduate School of Business Administration, Harvard University, Boston, MA.

Luhmann, N. (1979). *Trust and Power*. Chichester, U.K.: Wiley.

Macaulay, S. (1963). 'Non-contractual relations in business', *Amer Soc Rev*, 28 55–70.

Macneil, I. R. (1980). *The New Social Contract*. New Haven CT: Yale University Press.

Marx, K. (1973). *Grundrisse: Foundations of Political Economy*. Harmondsworth: Penguin.

—— and Engels, F. (1959). 'Manifesto of the Communist Party', L. S. Feuer (ed.), *Marx and Engels Basic Writings on Politics and Philosophy*. Garden City: Doubleday.

Mashaw, J. L. (1983). *Bureaucratic Justice: Managing Social Security Disability Claims*. New Haven CT: Yale University Press.

Merton, R. K. (1973). *The Sociology of Science*. Chicago IL: University of Chicago Press.

Miller, G. J. (1992). *Managerial Dilemmas: The Political Economy of Hierarchy*. New York: Cambridge University Press.

Mintzberg, H. (1979). *The Structuring of Organizations*. Englewood Cliffs NJ: Prentice-Hall.

Nahapiet, J., Ghoshal, S. (1998). 'Social Capital, Intellectual Capital, and the Organizational Advantage', *Acad Management Rev*, 23(2) 242–266.

Nelson, R. R. (1988). 'Institutions Supporting Technical Change in the United States', in G. Dosi, C. Freeman, R. Nelson, G. Silverberg, and L. Soete (eds), *Technical Change and Economic Theory*. London: Pinter, pp. 312–329.

Nove, A. (1982). *The Economics of Feasible Socialism*. London: Allen and Unwin.

Nyland, C. (1998). 'Taylorism and the Mutual-Gains Strategy', *Indust Relations*, 37(4) 519–542.

OECD (1996). *Employment and Growth in the Knowledge-Based Economy*. Paris: Organization for Economic Co-operation and Development.

Organization Science (1998). Special issue on managing partnerships and strategic alliances, 9(3).

Ouchi, W. (1980). 'Markets, Bureaucracies and Clans', *Admin Sci Quart*, 25 (March) 125–141.

Paine, T. (1951) (1792). *The Rights of Man*. New York: E. P. Dutton.

Porter, M. E. (1985). *Competitive Advantage*. New York: Free Press.

Powell, W. (1990). 'Neither Markets nor Hierarchy: Network Forms of Organization', *Res in Organ Behavior*, 12: 295–336.

Prahalad, C. K., Hamel, G. (1990). 'The Core Competencies of the Corporation', *Harvard Bus Rev*, 86: 79–91.

Putnam, R. (1993). *Making Democracy Work: Civic Traditions in Modern Italy*. Princeton NJ: Princeton University Press.

Ramsay, H. (1977). 'Cycles of Control: Worker Participation in Sociological and Historical Perspective', *Sociology*, 11(3), 481–506.

Ring, P. S. (1996). 'Fragile and Resilient Trust and their Roles in Economic Exchange', *Bus Society*, 35(2) 148–175.

—— (1997). 'Transacting in the State of Union: A Case Study of Exchange Governed by Convergent Interests', *J Management Stud*, 34(1) 1–25.

—— and Van de Ven, A. H. (1992). 'Structuring Cooperative Relationships between Organizations', *Strategic Management J*, 13: 483–498.

Rosenberg, N. (1964). 'Neglected Dimensions in the Analysis of Economic Change', *Oxford Bull Econom Statist*, 26(1) 59–77.

Rothschild-Witt, J. (1979). 'The Collectivist Organization: An Alternative to Rational-Bureaucratic Models', *Amer Soc Rev*, 44 509–527.

Sabel, C. F. (1992). 'Studied Trust: Building New Forms of Co-operation in a Volatile Economy', in F. Pyke, and W. Sengenberger (eds), *Industrial Districts and Local Economic Regeneration*. Geneva: International Institute for Labour Studies.

—— and Zeitlin, J. (eds) (1997). *World of Possibilities: Flexibility and Mass Production in Western Industrialization*. Cambridge: Cambridge University Press.

Sako, M. (1992). *Prices, Quality and Trust: Interfirm Relations in Britain and Japan*. Cambridge: Cambridge University Press.

Salter, M. S. (1983). 'Tailor incentive compensation to strategy', *Harvard Bus Rev*, (March–April) 51(2) 94–102.

Satow, R. L. (1975). 'Value-rational authority and professional organizations: Weber's missing Type', *Admin Sci Quart*, 20 (Dec) 526–531.

Schindler, P. L., and Thomas, C. C. (1993). 'The Structure of Interpersonal Trust in the Workplace', *Psych Reports*, 73 563–573.

Schumpeter, J. (1976) (1942). *Capitalism, Socialism and Democracy*. New York: Harper.

Scott, W. R. (1992). *Organizations: Rational, Natural, and Open Systems*. Englewood Cliffs NJ: Prentice-Hall.

Seligman, A. B. (1997). *The Problem of Trust*. Princeton NJ: Princeton University Press.

Shapiro, S. P. (1987). 'The Social Control of Impersonal Trust', *Amer J Soc*, 93(3) 623–658.

Sparrow, M. K. (1994). *Imposing Duties: Government's Changing Approach to Compliance*. Westport CT: Praeger.

Spencer, M. E. (1970). 'Weber on Legitimate Norms and Authority', *British J Soc*, 21(2) 123–134.

Stiglitz, J. E. (1994). *Whither Socialism?* Cambridge MA: MIT Press.

Stinchcombe, A. L. (1985). 'Contracts as Hierarchical Documents', in Arthur L. Stinchcombe and Carol Heimer (eds), *Organization Theory and Project Management*. Bergen, Norway: Universitetsforslaget.

Tarrow, S. (1996). 'Making Social Science Work Across Space and Time: A Critical Reflection on Robert Putnam's *Making Democracy Work*', *Amer Political Sci Rev*, 90(2) 389–401.

Unger, R. M. (1975). *Knowledge and Politics*. New York: Free Press.

Uzzi, B. (1997). 'Social Structure and Competition in Interfirm Networks: The Paradox of Embeddedness', *Admin Sci Quart*, 42(1) 35–67.

Walton, R. E. (1985). 'Toward a Strategy for Eliciting Employee Commitment Based on Policies of Mutuality', in R. E. Walton, and P. R. Lawrence (eds), *HRM Trends and Challenges*. Boston MA: Harvard Business School.

Walzer, M. (1999). 'Rescuing Civil Society', *Dissent* 46(1) 62–67.

Weber, M. (1947). *The Theory of Social and Economic Organization*. New York: Free Press.

Wenger, E. (1998). *Communities of Practice*. New York: Oxford University Press.

Wicks, A. C., Berman, S. L., Jones, T. M. (1999). 'The Structure of Optimal Trust: Moral and Strategic Implications', *Acad Management Rev*, 24(1) 99–116.

Williamson, O. E. (1975). *Markets and Hierarchies*. New York: Free Press.

Williamson, O. E. (1981). 'The Economics of Organization: The Transaction Cost Approach', *Amer J Soc*, 87 548–577.

—— (1991). 'Economic Institutions: Spontaneous and Intentional Governance', *J Law Econom Organ*, 7 159–187.

—— (1993). 'Calculativeness, Trust, and Economic Organization', *J Law and Econom*, 36 453–502.

Zelizer, V. A. (1996). 'Payments and Social Ties', *Soc Forum*, 11(3) 481–496.

Zenger, T. R., and Hesterly, W. S. (1997). 'The Disaggregation of Corporations: Selective Intervention, High-Powered Incentives, and Molecular Units', *Organ Sci*, 8(3) 209–222.

Zucker, L. G. (1986). 'Production of Trust: Institutional Sources of Economic Structure. 1840–1920', *Res Organ Behavior*, 8 53–111.

10

Tightening the Iron Cage: Concertive Control in Self-Managing Teams

James R. Barker

In this paper, I provide an ethnographic account of how an organization's control system evolved in response to a managerial change from hierarchical, bureaucratic control to concertive control in the form of self-managing teams. The study investigates how the organization's members developed a system of value-based normative rules that controlled their actions more powerfully and completely than the former system. I describe the organization and its members and provide a detailed account of the dynamics that emerged as concertive control became manifest through the members' interactions. This account depicts how concertive control evolved from the value consensus of the company's team workers to a system of normative rules that became increasingly rationalized. Contrary to some proponents of such systems, concertive control did not free these workers from Weber's iron cage of rational control. Instead, the concertive system, as it became manifest in this case, appeared to draw the iron cage tighter and to constrain the organization's members more powerfully.

I don't have to sit there and look for the boss to be around; and if the boss is not around, I can sit there and talk to my neighbor or do what I want. Now the whole team is around me and the whole team is observing what I'm doing.

'Ronald,' a technical worker in a small manufacturing company, gave me this account one day while I was observing his work team. Ronald works in what contemporary writers call a postbureaucratic organization, which is not structured as a rule-based hierarchy. He works with a team of peers who are all equally responsible for managing their own work behaviors. But Ronald described an unexpected consequence of this team-based design. With his voice concealed by work noise. Ronald told me that he felt more closely watched now than when he worked under the company's old bureaucratic system. He said that while his old supervisor might tolerate someone coming in a few minutes late, for example, his team had adopted a 'no tolerance' policy on tardiness and that members monitored their own behaviors carefully.

Ronald's comments typify life under a new form of organizational control that has prospered in the last decade as a means of avoiding the pitfalls of bureaucracy. This form, called 'concertive control,' grows out of a substantial consensus about values, high-level coordination, and a degree of self-management by members or workers in an organization. This paper describes and analyzes the development of concertive control after Ronald's company. 'ISE Communications,' converted to self-managing (or self-directing) teams, a concertive structure that resulted in a form of control more powerful, less apparent, and more difficult to resist than that of the former bureaucracy. The irony of the change in this postbureaucratic organization is that, instead of loosening, the iron cage of rule-based, rational control, as Max Weber called it, actually became tighter.

The Problem of Control

Control has been a central concept in organizational theory since the time of Weber and remains perhaps the key issue that shapes and permeates our experiences of organizational life. Barnard (1968 : 17) best stated the importance of control when he wrote that a key defining element of any organization was the necessity of individuals to subordinate, to an extent, their own desires to the collective will of the organization. For individuals to achieve larger goals they must actually surrender some autonomy in organizational participation. Because of this basic tension, control is always problematic in any organization.

To work through this problem, an organization's members—managers and workers alike—must engage in ongoing formal and informal 'processes of negotiation in which various strategies are developed... [that] produce particular outcomes' for the organization (Coombs, Knights, and Willmott 1992 : 58). Herein lies the essence of control as it becomes manifest in organizational activity. For any organization to move toward its goals and purposes, its 'particular outcomes,' its members must interactively negotiate and implement some type of strategy that effectively controls members' activities in a manner functional for the organization.

Edwards' Three Strategies of Control

Edwards (1981) has identified three broad strategies that have evolved from the modern organization's struggle with controlling members' activities. First is 'simple control,' the direct, authoritarian, and personal control of work and workers by the company's owner or hired bosses, best seen in nineteenth-century factories and in small family-owned companies today. Second is 'technological control', in which control emerges from the physical technology of an organization, such as in the assembly line found in traditional manufacturing. And third and most familiar is bureaucratic control, in which control derives from the hierarchically based social relations of the organization and its concomitant sets of systemic rational-legal rules that reward compliance and punish noncompliance.

A pivotal aspect of Edwards' model is that the second and third strategies, technological and bureaucratic control, represent adaptations to the forms of control that preceded them, each intended to counter the disadvantages of the previous form. Technological control resulted not only from technological advances in factories but also from worker alienation and dissatisfaction with the despotism too often possible in simple control. But technological control proved subject to such factors as worker protests, slow-downs, and assembly-line sabotage. The stultifying effects of the assembly line, with workers as just cogs in the machine, still produced worker alienation from the company. The bureaucratic form of control, with its emphasis on methodical, rational-legal rules for direction, hierarchical monitoring, and rewards for compliance such as job security, already existed in the nineteenth century and was further developed to counter the problems inherent in technological control. The bureaucracy and bureaucratic control, which become manifest in a variety of forms (Riggs 1979; Perrow 1986), have matured into the primary strategy available to managers to control work effectively in the modern organization. But, as with its predecessors, this strategy of control, too, is problematic.

Bureaucratic Control and the Iron Cage

Weber articulated the bureaucracy as the dominant form of modern control, in both positive and negative senses. While the bureaucracy offers the fairest and most efficient method of control, its system of rational rules may become troublesome, as seen in the infamous 'red tape' that constrains and slows the bureaucracy and makes it unresponsive to environmental changes. Also, as Weber warned us, we, in our desire for organizational order and predictability, tend to focus too much on the rationality of the rules in and of themselves, overintellectualizing the moral and ethical values critical to our organizational lives and making decisions according to the rules, without regard to the people involved (Kalberg 1980 : 1158). We become so enmeshed in creating and following a legalistic, rule-based hierarchy that the bureaucracy becomes a subtle but powerful form of domination.

This notion of the inevitable, highly rational, but powerfully oppressive bureaucracy refers to what Weber (1958 : 180–1) called the 'iron cage'. Weber saw the bureaucracy and bureaucratic control as an irresistible force of high rationality that would commandeer and consume all other forms of control. For Weber (1978), we would, out of our desire for order, continually rationalize our bureaucratic relationships, making them less negotiated and more structured. These structures ultimately become immovable objects of control: "Once fully established, bureaucracy is among those social structures which are the hardest to destroy. Bureaucracy is *the* means of transforming social action into rationally organized action (Weber 1978 : 987). As organizational activity increasingly becomes saturated by bureaucratic rationalization processes, it is increasingly constrained by them. A rule requiring a customer service representative to have all refund decisions approved by someone two hierarchical levels above may impede the representative's ability to meet a customer's demands for a quick response. Thus a rule that apparently benefits an organization's effectiveness (getting managerial approval and oversight of refunds) also constrains its effectiveness (slows down response). In Weber's (1978 : 987–8) words, the individual organizational actor in a modern bureaucracy "cannot squirm out of the apparatus into which he has been harnessed."

Weber's image of how we become trapped in an iron cage of bureaucratic control suggests that control, as it becomes manifest as organizational activity through Edwards' three strategies, has become less apparent, or not as readily personal, as it has become more imbedded in the social relations of organizational members (Tompkins and Cheney 1985; Barker and Cheney 1994). Control in the bureaucratic organization becomes impersonal because its authority rests ultimately with the system, leaving organization members, in many cases, with what Weber (1958 : 182) called 'specialists without spirit, sensualists without heart.' Whereas the nineteenth-century mill owner overtly controlled workers, ordering, directing, and firing them at will, the bureaucracy's rules are more indirect: They control workers by shaping their knowledge about the 'right' ways to act and interact in the organization. A worker seeks supervisory approval for a decision because that is what the worker is supposed to do. The 'apparency' of control becomes hidden in the bureaucracy's seemingly natural rules and hierarchy. Thus, bureaucratic control leaves us in a paradoxical situation. The same rational activities that enable collective organizational interaction eventually come to constrain that activity in ways often difficult for us to perceive, much less comprehend, the consequences and ramifications. Our bureaucratic rules ultimately confine us as solidly as if we were in a cage bound by iron bars.

Concertive Control as a Fourth Strategy

Almost since the beginning of modern organizational study, influential theorists have argued that decentralized, participative, and more democratic systems of control offer the most viable alternatives to the bureaucracy's confining routines and rules (e.g. Follett 1941; Lewin 1948). This continual push toward participation and a flat organizational structure has become something of an obsession in managerial literature in the last decade or so (Eccles and Nohria 1992). Contemporary writers have unleashed a flood of literature announcing the 'coming demise of bureaucracy and hierarchy' (Kanter 1989 : 351) and detailing the dawn of a postbureaucratic age in which control emerges not from rational rules and hierarchy but from the concertive, value-based actions of the organization's members (Soeters 1986; Ogilvy 1990; Parker 1992). Characteristic of this movement are influential business consultants such as Tom Peters (1988) and Peter Drucker (1988) who have urged corporate executives to de-bureaucratize their firms and adopt more ideologically based designs drawn around unimpeded, agile authority structures that grow out of a company's consensual, normative ideology, not from its system of formal rules. By cutting out bureaucratic offices and rules, organizations can flatten hierarchies, cut costs, boost productivity, and increase the speed with which they respond to the changing business world.

Tompkins and Cheney (1985) argued that the numerous variations these authors have offered on the postbureaucratic organization represent a new type of control, 'concertive' control, built on Edwards' three traditional control strategies. This form represents a key shift in the locus of control from management to the workers themselves, who collaborate to develop the means of their own control. Workers achieve concertive control by reaching a negotiated consensus on how to shape their behavior according to a set of core values, such as the values found in a corporate vision statement. In a sense, concertive control reflects the adoption of a new substantive rationality, a new set of consensual values, by the organization and its members.

This negotiated consensus creates and recreates a value-based discourse that workers use to infer 'proper' behavioral premises: ideas, norms, or rules that enable them to act in ways functional for the organization. For example, a newly concertive company may have a vision statement that states, 'We are a principled organization that values teamwork.' This value may lead one of its members to create a discourse that calls out the premise that 'To be principled and value teamwork, we all must come to work on time.' The actors can then infer a method of acting (coming to work promptly at 7:00 A.M. not at 7:30), without the traditional supervisor's direction, that is functional for the organization. Thus concertive control becomes manifest as the team members act within the parameters of these value systems and the discourses they themselves create. These new collaboratively created, value-laden premises (manifest as ideas, norms, and rules) become the supervisory force that guides activity in the concertive control system. In concertive control, then, the necessary social rules that constitute meaning and sanction modes of social conduct become manifest through the collaborative interactions of the organization's members. Workers in a concertive organization create the meanings that, in turn, structure the system of their own control. Rule generation moves from the traditional supervisor-subordinate relationship to the actors' negotiated consensus about values.

A second and more important difference between the concertive control model and its bureaucratic predecessor lies in the locus of authority. In the concertive organization, the locus of authority, what actors see as the legitimate source of control to which they are willing to submit (Whitley 1977), transfers from the bureaucratic system and its rational–legal constitutive rules to the value consensus of the members and its socially created generative rules system. Under bureaucratic control, employees might ensure that they came to work on time because the employee handbook prescribed it and the supervisor had the legal right to demand it, but in the concertive system, employees might come to work on time because their peers now have the authority to demand the workers' willing compliance.

The key question is whether or not the concertive system offers a form of control that conceptually and practically transcends traditional bureaucratic control. I address this question by examining the process through which actors in a concertive organization collaborate to form the rules that structure their day-to-day work and how they give this process legitimate authority. I report on the processes of control that became manifest as a manufacturing organization changed and adapted to a concertive-based structure, in the form of a self-managing, or self-directed team design.

Self-Managing Teams: An Exemplar of Concertive Control

Currently, the most popular planned organizational change to a postbureaucratic structure is the transformation of a traditional, hierarchically based organization to a flat confederation of concertively controlled self-managing teams. Xerox, General Motors, and Coors Brewing have all initiated this kind of change over the last few years. Although self-managing teams have gained much of their popularity in recent years, they are not a new phenomenon. Research and writing on the subject originally dates from Trist's study of self-regulating English coal miners in the 1950s (Trist et al. 1963; Trist 1981) and includes the Scandinavian experience with semiautonomous teams (Bolweg 1976; Katz and Kahn 1978) and early US team experiences, most notably the Gaines Dog Food plant in Kansas (Walton 1982; Ketchum 1984). The contemporary version of the self-managing team concept draws on both the past experiences with teams in Europe and the US and the more recent influence of Japanese-inspired quality circles in Western organizations (Sundstrom, De Meuse, and Futrell 1990; Sewell and Wilkinson 1992).

Proponents of self-managing teams have described it as a radical change in the traditional managerial and authority structure of an organization (e.g. Orsburn et al. 1990; Wellins, Byham and Wilson 1991). In line with the impulse toward postbureaucratic, concertive-based organizations, they assert that traditional management structures entail inflexible hierarchical and bureaucratic constraints that stifle creativity and innovation. These rigid organizations are top-heavy with managers and unresponsive to changing, dynamic markets, ultimately reducing their competitive viability. From the proponents' viewpoint, US organizations must radically change their managerial structure by converting to worker-run teams and eliminating unneeded supervisors and other bureaucratic staff (traditional management structures). Proponents argue that self-managing teams make companies more productive and competitive by letting workers manage themselves in small, responsive, highly committed, and highly productive groups. Thus, the self-management perspective proposes a 'radical' shift from hierarchical supervision to hands-off, collaborative worker management.

This change from supervisory to participatory structures means that workers in a self-managing team will experience day-to-day work life in vastly different ways than workers in a traditional management system. Instead of being told what to do by a supervisor, self-managing workers must gather and synthesize information, act on it, and take collective responsibility for those actions. Self-managing team workers generally are organized into teams of 10 to 15 people who take on the responsibilities of their former supervisors. Top management often provides a value-based corporate vision that team members use to infer parameters and premises (norms and rules) that guide their day-to-day actions. Guided by the company's vision, the self-managing team members direct their own work and coordinate with other areas of the company.

Usually, a self-managing team is responsible for completing a specific, well-defined job function, whether in production or service industries. The team's members are cross-trained to perform any task the work requires and also have the authority and responsibility to make the essential decisions necessary to complete the function. Self-managing teams may build major appliances, process insurance claims, assemble component parts for computers, or handle food service for a large hospital. Along with performing their work functions, members of a self-managing team set their own work schedules, order the materials they need, and do the necessary coordination with other groups. Besides freeing itself from some of the shackles of bureaucracy and saving the cost of low-level managers, the self-managing company also gains increased employee motivation, productivity, and commitment. The employees, in turn, become committed to the organization and its success (Orsburn et al. 1990; Mumby and Stohl 1991; Wellins, Byham and Wilson 1991).

Most current research on self-managing teams concentrates on the functional or economic outcomes of the change to teams. Another body of practitioner-oriented writing recounts how self-managing teams increase organizational productivity, profitability, and employee satisfaction, as well as how corporations deal with problems encountered during the transition to teams (Dumaine 1990; Lewis 1990). Other research on self-managing teams tends toward organizational design issues that concern implementing the change (Andrasik and Heimberg 1982; Carnall 1982), attitudinal attributes of teamwork (Cordery, Mueller and Smith 1991), and leadership requirements within and outside the team (Manz and Sims 1987). As Sundstrom, De Meuse and Futrell (1990) and Hackman (1986) have pointed out, however, we still have very little empirical knowledge of how self-managing teams construct new and functional forms of control and how these forms compare with how we have conceptualized control in the past. ISE Communications offered me a useful case for examining this aspect of organizational control longitudinally.

Methods

ISE Communications

ISE Communications, a small manufacturing company located in a mountain-state metropolitan area, converted from a traditional manufacturing structure to self-managing teams in 1988. ISE manufactures voice and data transmission circuit boards for the telecommunications industry and employs about 150 people, with approximately 90 in manufacturing. ISE was originally a division of a large telecommunications firm, and the ISE management team bought it outright in 1984, although the large firm still remains ISE's largest customer. ISE has the traditional manufacturing, engineering, sales/marketing, human resources, and executive staffs found in most production companies. ISE pays its manufacturing employees by the hour, while the support staff members are on salary.

As expected of a manufacturing company in a large metropolitan area, ISE's production workers represent a cross-section of the local working-class community. Out of 90 manufacturing workers (the worker population when I ended my research in Fall 1992), the ratio of females to males fluctuates but tends to stay around two-thirds female to one-third male. Latino/as, African-Americans, and Asian-Americans are ISE's main ethnic groups, making up about 60 percent of the workforce. At any given time, ISE's manufacturing department employs around 15 percent temporary workers that the company trains in-house. In fact, only one job on the teams, an electronic technician, requires training not provided by ISE.

Manufacturing circuit boards involves requesting board parts (resistors, potentiometers, transistors, etc.) from the supply room, assembling these parts onto a circuit board, and soldering the parts to the boards. The workers must then test the boards for electronic problems, trouble-shoot any problems they find, and make any necessary repairs. This becomes a time-consuming and labor-intensive process. After a board passes the final tests, the workers must package it and process the necessary shipping paperwork. Building and testing boards requires repetitive tasks that easily become monotonous. Unfortunately, the errors that arise from monotony mean costly and lengthy retesting delays or repairs. The work requires close attention to detail and tightly coordinated effort.

Early in my research (Spring 1990), ISE was struggling to survive in a highly competitive and innovative marketplace that demanded flexibility, an emphasis on customer service, and increasing productivity. By the time I wrote this paper two and a half years later, ISE had increased both productivity and profitability. ISE's executives believed that the change to teams was a major reason for their company's success.

'Jack Tackett', the manufacturing vice president and one of ISE's founding members, developed and instigated the company's change to self-managing teams. After reading the works of Crosby, Peters, Drucker, and other consultants, studying manufacturing philosophies like 'Just In Time' (JIT)—a company-specific manufacturing method that emphasizes low inventories, first-line decision making, and fast, effective employee action—and taking the pulse of ISE's competition, Jack decided that his company's very survival depended on converting to self-management. As he told me:

I thought that if we did things the same way all the time, we were headed for disaster. We could not meet customer demands anymore. Hierarchy insulates people from the customer. The traditional organization cannot know the customer, they are in the dark about what goes on around them with the manager making all the decisions. You can't succeed with that anymore. The demands of the market are too dynamic for a company to be controlled by a handful of managers. The whole company needs to be focused on customer needs and I needed to marshal the resources of the whole organization, not just a few. . . . You have to look forward and say what will it take to survive. You can't look inwardly all the time. You can't look back and say, "Well, we survived this way." I say that we aren't going to survive if we always consider what we're doing now to be successful for the future.

In 1986, Jack proposed a plan for implementing self-managing teams at ISE to his management staff. Jack actually convinced many of them that the change to teams was absolutely necessary for ISE to survive—which, for some of them, meant giving up their management jobs, although Jack did arrange lateral moves for them within ISE—and recruited them to help him institute the change. Some thought that the change was a 'stupid idea.' But Jack was adamant that self-management was *the* way to revitalize the company:

I had it firmly set in my mind that this was the way we had to go and these guys [the reluctant supervisors] were going to come up to speed or I was gonna get rid of them. And this team process was the natural opportunity to give people the chance to either get on board on their own or to fall by the wayside.

And the change proceeded with surprisingly little managerial turnover.

After more than a year of planning and training in teamwork skills, which included drafting and distributing ISE's vision statement, Jack and his advisory group started one self-managing team on a trial run in early 1988. He planned slowly to convert the entire production department to teams over the course of a year.

After working through some difficulties, the new team soon began to work better than Jack or anyone else had expected, so Jack and his group decided to expedite the complete conversion. First, they increased the pace of employee training in teamwork, self-supervision, and JIT manufacturing. Then, over a weekend in August of that year, Jack had the manufacturing area completely remodeled and set up for three self-managing teams, originally called red, white, and blue teams. His group rearranged machines, worktables, and other equipment to form three distinct and self-sufficient work areas that gave each team all the necessary equipment needed to produce the types of circuit boards that the new teams would build. The work areas had separate sections for circuit board assembly, testing, repair and touch-up, trouble-shooting, and packaging/shipping, all the key tasks required in making a complete circuit board. On Monday, Jack divided the workers into three teams and assigned each team to manufacture or configure two or three particular types of boards (the teams did not make the same types of boards). Table 1 summarizes the differences between ISE's operations before and after the change.

Table 1. Structure of ISE before and after the Change to Teams

Before the change	After the change
1. Three levels of managerial hierarchy between the vice president and the manufacturing workers.	1. Managerial hierarchy extends directly from the manufacturing teams to the vice president.
2. Manufacturing assembly line organizes the plant. Workers manufacture boards according to their individual place on the line.	2. Team work areas organize the plant. Teams are responsible for complete fabrication, testing, and packaging of their assigned circuit boards.
3. Line and shift supervisors form the first managerial link.	3. Teams manage their own affairs, elect one person to coordinate information for them.
4. Workers have little input into work-related decisions. Managers make all decisions and give all directions.	4. Team members make their own decisions within guidelines set by management and the company vision statement. Teams have shared responsibility for their own productivity.
5. Management disciplines workers.	5. Team members discipline themselves.
6. Management interviews and hires all new workers.	6. Team members interview, hire and fire their own members.

Jack, the former managers, and the workers now began the difficult process of adjusting to their new work environment. The workers struggled with establishing concertive control, which meant they had to negotiate such supervisory issues as accepting responsibility, making decisions, and setting their own ground rules for doing good work, such as deciding who was going to perform which tasks, whether or not the team needed to work overtime or on weekends, and whether to hire or fire team members. For his part, Jack tried to build a supportive climate for the teams. He put three of the former supervisors into a nonsupervisory support group focused on helping the teams solve technical problems. He also provided new team-building and interpersonal-skill training programs. If a team came to him with a problem, Jack would only offer suggestions, requiring the team to make the decision. Then he would support the decisions that the teams made, right or wrong, as long as the teams learned from their mistakes.

I began my research at ISE during this initial phase of adjustment to self-management, as the new teams were creating the collaborative process that characterizes the dynamics of concertive control.

My interest in self-managing teams came from my own experience with them. Prior to returning to graduate school, I worked as the 'leader' of a self-managing team for a large trucking company, which gave me a well-informed perspective on ISE's experience. I first met Jack at a social event in January 1990, where, after finding out about our mutual interest in teams, he invited me to come study what was happening at ISE.

Data Collection

When I first arrived at ISE, Jack introduced me as a researcher from the university interested in writing about self-managing teams and told me to roam around the plant as I wanted. I initially set about meeting people and getting to know the workplace. I spent my first six months there talking with members of each team and various management and support personnel. I watched workers at different stages of production and asked questions about how and why they were doing various tasks. During this period, I cultivated key informants on each team and developed plans and guides for in-depth worker interviews.

During my initial learning phase, I established a schedule of weekly, half-day (four-hour) visits to ISE. I normally alternated between morning and afternoon visits, and I also included some early evening observations of the second shift. I decided on a weekly schedule, mainly because ISE was a 90-minute drive from my residence. Occasional schedule variations occurred, when key events were happening at ISE and I would visit more than once a week, and when I had academic constraints, which would limit my visits to once every two weeks or so for brief periods.

After my first six months, I began an extended process of gathering data, primarily from in-depth interviews, observations, and conversations with key informants, but also from such sources as company memos, flyers, newsletters, and in-house surveys. Then I would withdraw from the setting to analyze the data, write, and develop revised research questions. I would repeat this process by returning to the setting, collecting more data, and then analyzing, writing, and revising again. I also observed and recorded team and company meetings, collected examples of naturally occurring team interactions, and closely followed one team's experiences for four months. In addition, I interviewed nonmanufacturing workers and former ISE employees. When my data collection ended, I had accumulated 275 research hours and conducted 37 in-depth interviews that ranged from as short as 45 minutes to as long as two hours.

In conducting the interviews, I tried as much as possible, given the constraints of voluntary participation, to stratify the interviews roughly across teams, including full-time and temporary employees and crossing ethnic and gender lines. I also interviewed Jack, the team coaches, and a few other members of the management and support staffs. I asked open-ended questions about how the teams made decisions, solved problems, and did day-to-day work. Finally, I probed into their responses for key examples.

During all phases of my data collection, my observer role at ISE did not change. The team members knew that I was studying and writing about their work processes. They were very cooperative and generally accommodated my needs for observation space and interview time. While I would, on occasion, discuss my observations with Jack, I have never filled a formal consulting role, nor has Jack ever asked me to disclose what I considered to be sensitive information about my informants.

Data Analysis

I began my analysis by working from the basic question, 'How are the control practices in ISE's new team environment different from the control practices in place prior to the change to teams?' This basic question allowed particular themes about control to emerge from my data that I could compare, revise, and refine as I collected more data and grew more familiar with the case. The particular themes and data analyses I present here emerged from my application to the database of sensitizing concepts (Jorgensen, 1989) primarily drawn from Tompkins and Cheney's (1985), Giddens' (1984), and Weber's (1978) theories of value-based control and constitutive rules. For example, I would examine my data by asking such general questions as, 'How has a value-consensus occurred in the team's interactions?' or 'Have any teams developed new decision premises or rules?' As significant themes emerged from my data, I would ask about them in subsequent interviews, which allowed their inter-related patterns and subthemes to take shape.

From this analysis I developed an analytical description of the general character of concertive control as it became manifest during ISE's experience with teams, which I present below. To help ensure the validity of this analytical conceptualization and its attendant claims, I cross-checked my interview data with my field notes and observations, interviews with management or support staff, and relevant hard data (team performance results, consultant surveys, human resource data, previous team-training programs). Finally, I reviewed my analysis, claims, and conceptualizations with colleagues not familiar with or participating in the setting (Adler and Adler 1987).

The result of my analysis is a three-part narrative about the three phases of the evolution of concertive control at ISE. The first phase covers the period of consolidation following the turbulence of the change to teams (late-1988 to late-1990). In this phase, the teams began to develop and apply concertive consensus about values that allowed them to infer functional decision premises and interact effectively with each other. The second phase (late-1990 to late-1991) saw the teams develop strong norms from their value consensus and begin to enforce these norms on each other as a set of rules. The third phase (late-1991 to mid-1992) saw the stabilization and formalization of these new systems of rules. The rules became rationalized and codified and served as a strong controlling force of team actions.[1]

The Development of Concertive Control

Phase 1: Consolidation and Value Consensus

Phase 1 began with the chaos of Jack's abrupt changing of the manufacturing area to teams over that weekend in August 1988. While the workers knew that the change was coming, they still walked into a whole new experience on Monday morning. Bonnie, an original ISE employee, described the scene for me:

Well, it was mass confusion. Nobody knew where they were sitting, what team they were on. They had an idea of what was going on at that point and what the team aspect was all about. As far as details, no idea! So, basically, everybody was just kind of like WOW, this is kinda fun! Because everything was different, it was wonderful in a way, the atmosphere had changed. It was fun to see who you were going to be sitting with, what team you were going to be on, what you were going to be doing. For me it was like, what board am I going to be working on? 'Cause before, I had a certain board that I had worked on from the beginning [of her tenure at ISE] and I still wanted to be working on it.

Jack assigned workers to the three new teams by drawing names out of a hat. He also assigned a former manager to coach each of the teams for six to nine months until they got used to managing themselves. Jack directed these coaches, who had themselves been key players (and believers) in the transition to teams, not to direct the teams overly but to let them learn how to manage themselves. The coaches saw their role primarily as preventing disasters and helping the teams to keep the production flowing.

The challenge for the teams during this first phase was learning how to work together and supervise themselves functionally: They had to learn how to get a customer's order manufactured and out the door. To do this, they had to merge, or consolidate, a variety of differing perspectives on how to do good work. For example, the new team members knew the separate activities involved in circuit board production, but they did not know how to control their individual efforts so that they could complete the whole process themselves. They knew how their former supervisors valued good work, but they lacked a means of articulating this value for themselves. To meet this need, the teams began developing their own value consensus as to what constituted, both collectively and individually, good work for the teams and patterns of behavior that put this consensus into action. Jack had already provided the foundation of this consensus in the vision statement that he had written for his new teams.

When ISE began converting to self-managing teams, Jack, along with ISE's president, crafted a vision statement that articulated a set of core values and goals, which all employees were to use to guide their daily actions. ISE's seven-paragraph vision statement functioned in the consolidation phase as a socially integrating myth that merged basic human values and 'day-to-day [employee] behavior with long-run [organizational] meaning and purpose' (Peters and Waterman 1982 : 282). Within this context, ISE's vision statement gave Jack a formula for creating his new concertive organization that centered on all the new team members working together in concert under the guidance of shared values rather than the old ISE managerial hierarchy.

The vision's fourth paragraph detailed the essential values that the teams would draw from during the consolidation phase:

We will be an organization where each of us is a self-manager who will:
—initiate action, commit to, and act responsibly in achieving objectives
—be responsible for ISE's performance
—be responsible for the quality of individual and team output
—invite team members to contribute based on experience, knowledge and ability.

The values expressed here, such as personal initiative, responsibility, commitment to the team, quality of individual and team contributions, along with Jack's directive for all to be self-managers, provided the necessary and legitimated preconditions for the teams to draw their value consensus, essential for concertive control.

Early in my research I saw a framed copy of the vision statement near Jack's desk and asked him what he saw as its purpose. He replied, 'The vision provides the company the guiding light for driving day-to-day operations for each of the teams.' The goals and values in ISE's vision statement served as the nexus for consolidating the teams' material reality (how work gets done) with their ideational reality (their values) (Jermier et al. 1991 : 172). When ISE converted to self-management, Jack distributed copies of the vision statement to all team members, and framed copies appeared in each team's area and in central locations like the break room. This led the new team members to talk with each other separately and at team meetings about the vision, particularly its fourth paragraph, and how it related to their work. Out of this talk came the functional patterns that allowed the teams to work together.

When I first began my research (early 1990), I readily noticed the results of this process. The team members talked openly about initiating action, taking ownership for their team's success, taking responsibility for satisfying ISE's customers' needs, emphasizing team quality, and expecting member contributions. The teams had learned to direct their work through planned and ad-hoc team meetings run by a peer-elected coordinator who did just that—coordinated information, such as production schedules, parts supplies, and companywide memos. All the teams met formally for about 15 minutes at the start of the workday to plan the day and solve any known problems. When serious problems arose during the workday, such as an unknown parts shortage holding up production, the teams would meet briefly and decide how to deal with the problem.

During team meetings workers would spend some time talking in administrative terms about the work they had to do and in abstract terms about values expressed in the vision: responsibility, quality, member contribution, commitment to their team and the company. The most prevalent example of these discussions occurred when team members had to decide whether or not to work overtime to meet their production schedules. My illustration comes from my field notes of one of many such situations the blue-team members found themselves in while I was tracking their decision making during the fall of 1990.

Early Friday afternoon, Lee Ann, the coordinator, was anxiously awaiting word from the stockroom that a shipment of circuit potentiometers had arrived. The vendor, about 800 miles away, had promised the shipment would arrive that morning, and the blue team had to get a customer's board order out that evening. Jim, from the stockroom, came running down to the blue team's area about 12:30 to tell Lee Ann that the potentiometers had just arrived, and she called the other eleven members of the team together for a short meeting.

> She looked at the team, "We've got the 'pots' in but it's gonna take us two extra hours to get this done. What do you want to do?"
> Larry groaned, "Damn, I've got plans for five-thirty!"
> Suna spoke up, "My daughter's school play's tonight!"
> Johnny countered, "But we told Howard Bell [their customer] that we would have these boards out today. It's our responsibility."
> Tommy followed, "We're gonna have to stay. We have to do this right."

What followed was a process in which the team negotiated which values and needs (individual or team) would take precedence here and how the team would work out this problem. The team decided to work late; members valued their commitment to a quality product delivered on time to their customer more than their individual time. Lee Ann volunteered to coordinate for the late shipment and to tell Jack Tackett that they would be working overtime (they could do this without his approval). Another team member went to arrange for the building to stay open for them. Larry said that he could put off his plans for two hours. The team agreed to let Suna leave, but she promised to work late the next time they were in a bind.

This vignette depicts how the teams concertively reached a value consensus that, in turn, controlled their individual and collective work. They brought the abstract values of the vision statement into concrete terms. The team members agreed on the priority of their commitment to the team's goals and responsibility for customer needs, and they acted based on this value consensus. These points of agreement also set strong precedents for future action. The blue team's agreement to work overtime to meet customer needs was not a one-time quick fix; it became a pattern that team members would follow as similar situations arose. In a conversation some time after the above meeting, Diego described for me the continuing power of the blue team's value consensus about personal responsibility: 'I work my best at trying to help our team to get stuff out the door. If it requires overtime, coming in at five o'clock and spending your weekend here, that's what I do.'

Although there were slight differences, this value consensus and these decision premises emerged powerfully and with remarkable consistency across the new teams. Early in 1991, I was sitting with Wendy watching her work with the blue team. I asked her how she reacted to missing a customer requirement:

I feel bad, believe it or not. Last Friday we missed a shipment. I feel like / missed the shipment since I'm the last person that sees what goes to ship. But Friday we missed the shipment by two boards and it shouldn't have been missed. But it was and I felt bad because it's me, it's a reflection on me, too, for not getting the boards out the door.

Over time, the teams faced many situations that called for members to reach some sort of value consensus. Other values, not explicitly stated in the vision but influenced by its general thrust, began to appear in the team members' talk and actions. These values helped them unite, learn how to work together, and navigate the turbulence of the change and the possible failure of the company. Team members like Wendy talked about taking ownership of their work, being committed to the success of their team, and viewing ISE as a family and their teammates as family members. Debbie, another original team member, told me about this new feeling of ownership: 'Under the old system, who gave a hoot if the boards shipped today or not? We just did our jobs. Now, we have more buy-in by the team members. We feel more personal responsibility for the product.' Other values included the need for everyone to contribute fully. The team members called this 'saying your piece' at team meetings so that the team's decision would be better (and their consensus stronger). Another part of this value was the need for all team members to learn all the jobs required by the team so that they could fill in and cover for each other.

This was also a time when ISE was struggling desperately and almost went under. In mid-1990, layoffs reduced the teams from three to two. The power of their values helped the teams navigate this difficult period. One of my most vivid memories of this time comes from Liz, who became one of my primary key informants. In August 1990, when the workers did not know if ISE would survive the quarter, she told me how she thought of ISE as a family and how she 'spends more time with these people than my real family.' She told me that if ISE closed down, 'I'm gonna turn the lights out. I love this place and these people so much, I've got to be the last one out. I've gotta see the lights go out to believe it.'

The teams' value-based talk and action during the consolidation phase created, in Weber's terms, a new substantive rationality. The team members had committed themselves 'first and foremost to substantive goals, to an ethic' that overrode all other commitments (Rothschild and Whitt 1986 : 22). Substantive rationality, in this context, extends from what Weber called 'a unified configuration of values' (Kalberg 1980 : 1164) held by a collectivity of people, in this case ISE's team members. This value configuration, or consensus, is intellectually analyzable by the members; they use it to make sense of and guide their everyday interactions. In an organizational situation, a consensus about values informs and influences members' outlooks on and processes of work activity, such as decision making. In doing this, the members place a psychological premium on themselves to act in ethical ways in terms of their values (Weber 1978 : 36; Kalberg 1980 : 1165). These values, then, are morally binding on the team members because they represent the will of the teams and were arrived at through the democratic participation of the team members (Homans 1950 : 125–7; Rothschild and Whitt 1986 : 50). The old rationality and ethic of obeying the supervisor had given way to a new substantive rationality, the teams' value consensus, and a new form of ethical rational action, working in ways that supported the teams' values: Wendy's taking personal responsibility for her team's failure, Debbie's buying in to the team's success, Johnny's reminding the team of its customer commitment, and Diego's willingness to come in at 5 A.M. all illustrate this point.

These examples also point out another significant aspect of substantive rationality. The ethical rational action spawned by a value consensus will take on a methodical character (Kalberg 1980 : 1164): The teams will develop behavioral norms that put their values into action in consistent patterns applicable to a variety of situations, just as team members applied their norm of working overtime to meet customer demands to a variety of situations requiring extra work. Thus, the teams could turn their value consensus into social norms or rules. The teams had manifested the essential element of concertive control: Their value-based interactions became a social force that controlled their actions, as seen in Larry's willingness to forego his plans in order to work overtime for the team. Authority had transferred from ISE's old supervisory system to the team's value consensus. These norms of ethical action, based in consensual values, penetrate and subjugate other forms of action by the team members. As this occurs, these norms take on a 'heightened intensity' (Kalberg 1980 : 1167); they become powerful social rules among the team (Hackman and Walton 1986; Hackman 1992). This process played a pivotal role in the next phase of ISE's experience with teams.

There were four key points in the consolidation phase: (1) The teams received ISE's vision statement, which framed a value system for them; (2) the teams began to negotiate value consensus on how to act in accordance with the vision's values; (3) a new substantive rationality emerged among the teams that filled the void left by the former supervisors and the formal rationality associated with following their directives (the teams' values now had authority); and (4) the teams began to form normative rules that brought this rationality into social action.[2] The consolidation phase left ISE with a core group of long-time ISE team workers, committed to the company and to teamwork. The employees had developed a consensus about what values were important to them, what allowed them to do their work, and what gave them pride. And they would guard this consensus closely.

Phase 2: Emergence of Normative Rules

ISE did survive through 1990. In early 1991, the company began to prosper, and a large number of new workers had to be integrated into the teams. These workers were unfamiliar with the teams' value consensus and they posed an immediate challenge to the power relationships the older employees had formed. Further, when ISE began to hire new workers, they hired them on a temporary basis and let the teams decide who to hire on as full-time workers. ISE also added four new teams to the two remaining original teams, for a total of six—red, blue, a new white, and green, silver, and aqua. Jack had to place some of the older, experienced workers on these new teams to help them get organized, and the teams had to integrate their new teammates into their value-based social order. As the team's value consensus and particular work ethic began to penetrate and subjugate the new members' individual work ethics, this process took on a heightened intensity. The substantive rationality of the teams' values gave them authority, which they would exercise at will.

Members of the old teams responded to these changing conditions by discursively turning their value consensus into normative rules that the new workers could readily understand and to which they could subject themselves. By rationalizing their value-based work ethic, the new team members could understand the intent and purpose of their team's values and norms (e.g. why it was important to work overtime to meet a customer need), use the norms to make sense of their daily work experience, and develop methodical patterns of behavior in accordance with the team's values (Miller and O'Leary 1987; Hackman 1992). The longer-tenured team members expected the new workers to identify with (they called it 'buy into') the teams' values and act according to their norms. By doing this, ISE's teams were asserting concertive control over the new workers: The new members began to take part in controlling themselves. Slowly, the value-based norms that everyone on the team once 'knew' became objective, rationalized rules that the new members could easily understand and follow.

Around March–April 1991, I began to notice that the way the team members talked, both informally and at team meetings, had changed. They did not talk so much about the importance of their teamwork values as they did about the need to 'obey' the team's work norms. Team meetings began to have a confrontational tone, and the new workers' attitudes and performance became open topics for team discussion. When the longer-tenured team members saw someone not acting in accordance with their norms, such as not being willing to do whatever it took for the team to be successful, they said something about it. Liz, an original team member, told me of the old team workers' feelings: 'We've had occasions where we've had a person say, "I refuse to sit on the [assembly] line." And we had to remind him, "Hey, you are a part of the team and you go where you're needed and you do it".' Team meetings became a forum for discussing norms and creating new rules. Team members could bring up anybody's behavior for discussion. Again, Liz clarified their feelings: 'If you notice that somebody's not getting anything done, then we can bring it up at a meeting, you know, and ask them what the problem is, what's causing them not to be able to get their work done.'

The new team members began to feel the heat, and the ones who wanted to be full-time members began to obey the norms. The teams' value-based concertive control began to penetrate and inform the new workers' attitudes and actions. Stephi, who was a temporary employee at the time, told me how she personally tried to conform to the values and norms of her team:

When I first started I really didn't start off on the right foot, so I've been having to re-prove myself as far as a team player. My attitude gets in the way, I let it get in the way too many times and now I've been watching it and hoping they [her team] will see the change in me and I can prove to them that I will make a good ISE employee.

Stephi's words indicate that concertive control at ISE now revolved around human dignity. The team members rewarded their teammates who readily conformed to their team's norms by making them feel a part of the team and a participant in the team's success. In turn, they punished teammates who had bad attitudes, like Stephi, with guilt and peer pressure to conform (Hackman and Walton, 1986; Mumby and Stohl, 1991; Hackman, 1992). The power of the team's concertive work ethic had taken on its predicted heightened intensity.

A pivotal occurrence during this phase was the teams' value-based norms changing from a loose system that the workers 'knew' to a tighter system of objective rules. This transformation most often occurred when new members were not acting according to the team's work norms, such as coming to work on time. Danny told me how easily this change came about:

> Well we had some disciplinary thing, you know. We had a few certain people who didn't show up on time and made a habit of coming in late. So the team got together and kinda set some guidelines and we told them, you know, "If you come in late the third time and you don't wanna do anything to correct it, you're gone." That was a team decision that this was a guideline that we were gonna follow.

The teams experienced the need to make their normative work ethic easily understandable (and rewardable and punishable), and they responded by making objective guidelines.

The team members' talk turned toward the need to follow their rules, to work effectively in concert with each other. In mid-1991 I found Ronald, a technician and my key informant on the green team, angrily cleaning up a mistake made by a new technician who had not followed the rules: 'All this should have been caught three months ago, and I'm just now catching it. And upon looking into it, it was because the tech wasn't taking his responsibility for raising the flag or turning on the red light when he had a problem.' Later that day, I was sitting with the silver team when I saw Ryan confront a newer team member who was working on four boards at a time instead of one, which the team had discovered increased the chance for error. Ryan stood above the offender and pointed at him, 'Hey quit doing that. You're not allowed to do that. It's against the rules.'

By turning their norms into rational rules, the teams could integrate new members and still be functional, getting products out the door on time. The 'supervisor' was now not so much the teams' value consensus as it was their rules. You either obeyed the rules and the team welcomed you as a member, or you broke them and risked punishment. This element of concertive control worked well. As Danny, a temporary worker at this time told me, 'If you're a new person here, you're going to be watched.'

Even the coordinator's role and responsibilities became more objectified during this phase. Some teams agreed on five specific tasks for the coordinator to do, other teams had seven. The teams now elected coordinators for six-month periods rather than one month. The coordinator role began to take on the aura of a supervisor. People began to look to coordinators for leadership and direction. Lee Ann, a coordinator at this time, told me one day, 'Damn, I feel like a supervisor, I just don't get paid for it.'

The second pivotal occurrence during this phase involved how authority worked among the teams. After the consolidation phase, authority had moved from the former supervisory system to the new value consensus of the teams, but during the second phase, the old team members, all full-time employees, were the keepers of this new system. They identified strongly with it and expected new members to demonstrate their worthiness to participate with them in the concertive process. They began to use rewards and punishments to encourage compliance among the team members. Temporary workers either obeyed the rules and became integrated into this system, or they found the door. The teams' interactions left little room for resistance. This placed strong pressure on the temporary workers to conform to their team's rules. Tommy, a temporary worker then, explained the pressure:

Being temporary, you could come in any day and find out you don't have a job no more. So, that's kind of scary for a lot of people who have, you know, kids and a lot of bills to take care of. So they tend to hold it in, what they want to say, to the point where they can't do it anymore and they just blow up, which causes them to lose their job anyway.

Before the change to teams, the line supervisors would generally tolerate some degree of slackness among the workers and allow someone many chances to screw-up before taking drastic action. But now the team members exercised their new-found authority with much less patience. In mid-1991 I walked into the blue team's area one morning and found the temporary workers very agitated and the full-time workers nowhere around. I asked Katie what was happening. She said that the full-time workers had gone off to fire Joey. Joey was a temporary who worked hard but had a tendency to wander off across the shop and socialize. While he did not do this often, he had the knack of doing it when Martha, the coordinator, or another full-time worker happened to notice his absence. The previous day, Joey had been caught again. That morning, after the team meeting, the full-time workers said that they were going to go to the conference room to talk about Joey's problem. Right before I came to the team's area, they had called him back to the conference room. Katie looked back over her shoulder toward the conference room and sighed, 'He's a good worker, but they [the full-time workers] don't see that. They don't know him. Now they're back there, judge, jury, and executioners.'

While peer pressure may be essential to the effective work of any team (Walton and Hackman 1986 : 186; Larson and Lafasto 1989 : 96), the dynamics of ISE's teams during this phase go much deeper. The above episode was not a simple case of the full-timers beating up on the temporaries. What seemed to be peer pressure and power games on the surface was in fact a manifestation of concertive control. Authority here rests in the team's values, norms, and now rules. Team members rewarded themselves for compliance and punished themselves for noncompliance. They had invested their human dignity in the system of their own control (Parker and Slaughter 1988; Mumby and Stohl 1991). As participants in concertive control, the team members had begun a process of functionally constructing both their work activity and their own identities (Cheney 1991).

The second phase represents a natural progression of the value-based substantive rationality the teams had created in phase 1. The teams demystified their value consensus for new members by making it intellectually analyzable. The norms of phase 1 now became guidelines or rules, increasingly objectified and clarified for the team members, which allowed for effective interaction. The values forming the teams' substantive rationality provided the boundaries of action and interest within and among the teams (Kalberg 1980 : 1170), but the control of actions and interests in the teams is not stable; it has to be fixed at particular points in time. The emergence of rational rules during the second phase served this function. These rules made concertive control concrete, almost as tangible as their old supervisor's book of job descriptions. It was the locus of authority resting with the teams themselves, however, that gave the rules their power. It empowered the teams to enable certain activity and constrain others. The locus of authority made concertive control work for ISE's teams.

Four key points characterize the development of concertive control at ISE during the second phase: (1) The teams had to bring new members into the particular value-based social systems they had created during phase 1; (2) To meet this need, the teams began to form normative rules for doing good work on the teams, creating what Hackman and Walton (1986 : 83) called a team's 'core norms.' Longer-tenured team members expected the new members to identify and comply with these rules and their underlying values; (3) The rules naturally began to take on a more rationalized character; and (4) Concertive control functioned through the team members themselves sanctioning their own actions. While the influx of new members may have served as a catalyst for the emergence of normative rules on the teams, the rules came about through the natural progression of the team's value consensus into what Weber called a 'methodical way of life' on the organizational/team level (Kalberg 1980 : 1164). This was how the new members could learn their teams' value consensus and participate in their new form of control. Further, these particular tensions between full-time and temporary workers were not enduring. What did last was the impact of rationalizing the rules and the fact that authority rested with the peer pressure of the teams.

Phase 3: Stabilization and Formalization of the Rules

During this time (late-1991 to mid-1992), the company began to stabilize and turn a profit. A large number of temporary workers had been integrated into the full-time pool during phase 2, which resulted in the number of temporary workers falling from a high of almost 50 percent at times in phase 2 to as few as 10 percent during phase 3. But the stabilization phase also saw the teams' normative rules become more and more rationalized: Their value-based substantive rationality was giving way to rationalization (Cooper and Burrell 1988 : 93). What were simple norms in phase 1 (we all need to be at work on time) now became highly objective rules similar to ISE's old bureaucratic structure (if you are more than five minutes late, you're docked a day's pay). On the surface, day-to-day control still looked much different than when ISE had traditional supervisors, but, on a deeper level, this control seemed hauntingly familiar and much more powerful.

The most noticeable change occurred in the coordinator's role. From my first days at ISE, I had tracked a continual pressure to make the coordinator's duties clearer and more specified. Thus, the coordinators' work gradually had become more formalized. If the team members needed something from the human resources department, they would ask the coordinator to get it. If Jack needed information about a team's work, he would ask the coordinator for it. The coordinators began to take on more and more specific tasks: scheduling, tracking production errors, holding regular meetings with each other, and so forth. In early 1992, the role became formalized as a permanent position, now called facilitator. The teams nominated workers for the six positions, and a committee of workers and managers (including Jack) interviewed the nominees and selected the new facilitators. These six workers received a 10 percent boost in their hourly wage to signify their new importance. They also drew up a list of duties for the role, which really just formalized what the old coordinators had already been doing. Lee Ann, who became the blue team's facilitator saw this process, too, as she told me about a month after assuming the new role: 'It's more formalized acceptance that somebody is gonna be the one to answer the questions, and you might as well have someone answering the questions of the team and of management. And, I get paid for it, too.' The most interesting aspect of the change in the coordinator role for me was that the workers wanted it, not so much to reinvent hierarchy on the teams but because formalizing their work life seemed so natural to them.

Formalizing the aspects of their work appeared to give the teams a sense of stability that would insulate them from the turmoil of the past year, and so rules proliferated in all aspects of the teams' activity. As Brown (1978 : 368) suggested, the rules were taking on their own rationality and legitimacy. What was once an abstract value, such as 'a team member should be able to do all the work roles on the team', had now became a set of specific guidelines for how long new members had to train for a specific function (assembling, testing, repairing, etc.) and how long a team member would have to work in assembly before rotating to a new team job, such as repair.

During phase 3, I saw the teams' social rules become more and more rigid. The teams seemed to be trying to permanently fix their social rules. Two examples stand out for me. In mid-1992 I was talking with Liz, who had also become a facilitator, about how members directed each other's actions now, as opposed to three years before. Liz told me that her team had been talking about drafting a 'code of conduct' for team members that spelled out the behaviors needed to be a good team member. She began to get very excited about the possibilities of making these actions clear and concrete. She said, 'If we can just get this *written down* [emphasis hers]. If we can just get our code of conduct in writing, then everyone will know what to do. We won't have so many problems. If we can just get it written down.' I found the second telling example when I visited ISE again two weeks later. I had been following how the teams were dealing with attendance and how their rules for coming into work on time were becoming more specific. A team member who came in five minutes or more late would be charged with an 'occurrence' and considered to be absent for the whole day. If a worker accumulated four occurrences in a month, the team facilitator would place a written warning in that person's company file. A worker who came in less than five minutes late received a 'tardy', and seven tardies equaled one occurrence. While I knew that all the teams had some kind of attendance policy, what I found this day truly surprised me. When I walked into the red team's area, I saw a new chart on its wall. The chart listed each team member's name down the left-hand side and had across the top a series of columns representing days of the week. Beside each name were color-coded dots that indicated 'on time,' 'tardy,' or 'occurrence.' The team had posted this board in plain sight for all team members to see, and the team updated its board every day. I found a similar chart in use by the other teams.

Three thoughts went through my mind. The first was the powerful insight of Ronald's comment, which opened this paper: 'Now the whole team is around me and the whole team is observing what I'm doing.' The second was that this policy seemed uncannily similar to something I would have expected to find in the old supervisory system. The third was that the teams had now created, in effect, a nearly perfect form of control. Their attendance behavior (and in a way their human dignity) was on constant display for everyone else on the team to monitor: an essentially total system of control almost impossible to resist (Foucault 1976). The transformation from values to norms to rules had gained even more heightened intensity.

The fact that the teams were creating their own rational rule systems was not lost on all the team members, but they expressed the feeling that these rules were good for them and their work. As Lee Ann told me at this time:

We are making a lot of new rules, but most of them come from, "Well see, because so and so person did such and such, well we're not gonna allow that anymore" [concertive control at work]. But the majority of the rules that we are putting in are coming from what the old rules were [before the change to teams]. They had a purpose. They did stop people from making, like expensive mistakes.... With more people on the teams, we have to be more formal. We have seventeen people on my team. That large amount of people moving is what's causing the bureaucracy to come back in.

Lee Ann's use of 'bureaucracy' perplexed me. Had ISE's teams reinvented a bureaucratic system of control? Certainly the substantive rationality and its focus on value consensus that characterized phase 1 now had become blurred with a new formal rationality that focused on making rules, which appeared to fit with Weber's prediction that 'a *multiplicity* of rationalization processes ... variously conflict and coalesce with one another at all societal and civilizational levels' (Kalberg 1980 : 1147), including among ISE's teams. And certainly much of the pressure toward formalization came from the team's need to be productive and efficient in order for ISE to survive in its competitive market (Kalberg 1980 : 1163). But as I later reflected on Lee Ann's comment and my experience at ISE, the nature of this blurring of substantive and formal rationality became clearer.

The progression of the teams' value-based work ethic from norms to rational rules indicated that the workers had created micro-level disciplines that rationalized their work behaviors so to make them purposeful, functional, and controlled (Foucault 1980; Barker and Cheney 1994). Discipline, here, refers to a willingly accepted social force that rationalizes organizational work to ensure normalized and controlled individual and collective action. During phase 3, the teams developed formalized rule systems out of the normative ethics of their original value consensus. These disciplinary systems enabled the teams to work effectively, integrate new members easily, and meet their production demands. The team members willingly accepted these disciplines because they themselves had created them. And these disciplines appeared to work. During phase 3, ISE became profitable again. ISE's top management believed that the change to teams was one of the key reasons (along with other key changes in engineering and marketing) for the company's success. Jack credited the change to teams with cutting his factory costs 25 percent since 1988.

But the teams' formalization of their value system and norms did not mean that they had recreated a bureaucracy. Authority in ISE's concertive system rested with the teams and their interactions with each other. The character of ISE's concertive control was still much different than when it operated under bureaucratic control. As they integrated more temporary workers into the ranks of full-time members, the team members still held authority over each other. They still expected each other to follow the rules and, as evidenced by their attendance charts, still monitored each other's behavior carefully. The team members themselves still rewarded or punished each other's behavior. They did not give this function to the new facilitators: they kept it for themselves.

Close to the end of my data collection, Liz told me of an incident that had occurred a few days before, involving Sharon, a single mother who had some difficulty getting to work at 7 A.M. The team had been sensitive to her needs and had even given her a week off when one of her children was sick. The day before the incident, enough time had passed for Sharon to drop one of her many occurrences. She even announced this to the team by making a joke of it, 'I just dropped one occurrence, so that means I can have another.' The next morning one of her children was sick again and she was late. And the team remembered her 'joke' of the night before.

When Sharon showed up, the team reacted in the same way a shift supervisor in ISE's old system might have. The team confronted Sharon immediately and directly. They told her that they were very upset that she was late. They bluntly told her how much they had suffered from having to work short-handed. Stung by the criticism of her peers. Sharon began to cry. The team's tack shifted to healing the wounds they had caused. They told her that they had not meant to hurt her feelings but that they wanted her to understand how her actions had affected them. They asked her to be certain to contact them immediately when she had a problem. The episode closed with the team telling her, 'we really count on you to be here and we really need you here.' When I checked a month later, Sharon had not recorded another occurrence.

In phase 3, the team members still kept the authority to control each other's behaviors: concertive control still occurred within the teams. In many ways,the formalization of the team's normative rules made this process easier, as seen in the incident with Sharon. The teams had created an omnipresent 'tutelary eye of the norm,'[3] with the team members themselves as the eye, that continually observed their actions, ready either to reward or, more importantly, punish. Being under the constant eye of the norm appeared to me to have an effect on the workers. To a person, the older team workers told me that they felt much more stress in the team environment than they had under the old ISE system. The newer members also complained of the constant strain of self-management. This sense of heightened stress that ISE's workers expressed to me was similar to that found in other team-based organizations (e.g. Grenier 1988; Mumby and Stohl 1991). Parker and Slaughter (1988) even called the self-management concept management by stress.

My key informants also appeared more strained and burdened than in times past. I had watched Liz change from the totally committed team member in 1990, who saw her team as a family and wanted to be the last one to turn out the lights, to a distant, distracted facilitator in 1992, too harried and pressured to take any enjoyment in her team or to think of it as a family. Lee Ann, in a conversation with me in August 1992, expressed the same feelings:

After you've been here awhile, you're gonna get super-involved, then you're gonna get burned out. I see this with person after person. You get really involved, you take it home with you, you eat with it, you sleep with it. You work 12, 16-hour days and you just burn out. You may step out just a bit, let someone else get super-involved for awhile, then you'll pick it up again. But you won't have that enthusiasm anymore.

The tutelary eye of the norm demanded its observants become super-involved or risk its wrath, and critical to this phase, the eye also demanded that its observants demonstrate this involvement by following its rules, its rational routine. That was work life in the eye of the norm, in ISE's brand of concertive control.

In phase 3, the teams' activity appeared to stabilize around sets of formalized rules that provided a rational and effective routine for their day-to-day actions. As in the previous phases, this formalization did not change the locus of authority in the teams but rather strengthened it. The team members directed and monitored each other's actions. Concertive control still occurred within the teams themselves. Four key points characterize phase 3: (1) The normative rules of phase 2 became more and more objective, creating a new formal rationality among the teams; (2) The teams appeared to 'settle in' to the rational routine these formal rules brought to their work. The rules made it easier for them to deal objectively with difficult situations (such as Sharon's coming in late) by establishing a system of work regulation and worker self-control; (3) The team members felt stress from the concertive system, but they accepted this as a natural part of their work. They did not want to give up their feeling of being self-managers, however, no matter how intense the system of control became; and (4) The work life at ISE stabilized into a concertive system that revolved around sets of rational rules, as in the old bureaucracy, but in which the authority to command obedience rested with the team members themselves, in contrast to the old ISE. The team members had become their own masters *and* their own slaves.

Consequences of Concertive Control at ISE

Table 2 summarizes and juxtaposes the manifest and latent consequences emerging from the system of concertive control that evolved at ISE between 1988 and 1992. This table depicts how concertive control, in a process akin to Lewin's (1946) model of 'unfreezing-moving-refreezing', matured from a

Table 2. Manifest and Latent Consequences of ISE's Experience with Concertive Control

Manifest	Latent
1. Teams developed value consensus by drawing from ISE's vision statement.	1. Teams began to form a value-based substantive rationality, which led them to develop a mutually shared sense of ethical rational action at work.
2. Team members identified with their particular value consensus and developed emotional attachments to their shared values.	2. Authority transferred from ISE's old bureaucratic control system to the team's value system. The team members' human dignity became invested in submitting to this authority.
3. Teams formed behavioral norms from the values that enabled them to work effectively, thus put their values into action.	3. The teams became methodical about putting their values into action. Their values began a natural progression toward rationalization, which allowed the values and norms to be intellectually analyzable by all members.
4. Older team members expected new members to identify with the norms and values and act in accordance with these value-based norms.	4. Concertive control became nested in the team. Members themselves took on both superior and subordinate roles, monitoring and directing.
5. The teams' normative rules grew more rationalized. Team members enforced their rules with each other through peer pressure and behavioral sanctions.	5. ISE's concertive system became a powerful force of control. Since they had created it themselves, this control was seemingly natural and unapparent to the team members.
6. Teams further objectified and formalized the rules and shared these rules with each other. The work environment appeared to stabilize.	6. The teams had developed their own disciplines that merged their substantive values with a rule-based formal rationality. These disciplines enabled the teams to work efficiently and effectively. The teams controlled their work through a system of rational rules and the self-monitoring of their own individual and collective actions.

loosely held consensus about abstract values to a tightly bound system of rational rules and powerful self-control. ISE's experience with teams and the analysis I have reported here are consistent with other research reports of self-management systems at the level of the worker (e.g. Grenier 1988), which suggests that concertive control has a particular character: Concertive control, as it becomes manifest in organizational interaction, is more powerful and has a greater ability to control than the bureaucratic system it replaces.

Writers on concertive control have warned that this new system could become a stronger force than bureaucratic control. Tompkins and Cheney (1985 : 184) asserted that concertive control would increase the strength of control in its system, and Tannenbaum (1968) proposed that if management will give up some of its authority to the workers, it will, in turn, increase the effectiveness of control in the firm. Tannenbaum (1968 : 23) wrote that partici-pative (self-managing in this case) organizations could not be productive 'unless they have an effective system of control through which the potentially diverse interests and actions of members are integrated in concerted, that is, organized behavior. The relative success of participative approaches, therefore, hinges not on reducing control but on achieving a system of control that is more effective than that of other systems.' This 'more effective system of control', in terms of self-managing teams, comes from the authority and power teammates exercise on each other as peer managers.

Peer management increases the total amount of control in a concertive system through two important dynamics. The first is that concertive workers have created this system through their own shared value consensus, which they enforce on each other. But in doing so, as seen in ISE's experience, the teams necessarily create a system of value-based rational rules, such as their strict attendance policy. They have put themselves under their own eye of the norm, resulting in a powerful system of control.

The second reason for the increased power of concertive control is that the way it becomes manifest is less apparent than bureaucratic control. Team members are relatively unaware of how the system they created actually controls their actions (Tompkins and Cheney 1985). Concertive control is much more subtle than a supervisor telling a group of workers what to do. In a concertive system, as with ISE, the workers create a value-based system of control and then invest themselves in it through their strong identification with the system (Barker and Cheney 1994). Because of this identification, the team members are socially constructed by the system they have created (Mumby and Stohl 1991). When this happens, the team members readily accept that they are controlling their own actions. It seems natural, and they willingly submit to their own control system. ISE's team members felt that developing a very strict and objective attendance policy was a natural occurrence. Likewise, their challenging Sharon's personal dignity when she violated the policy was another natural occurrence. And ISE's teams work effectively without Jack's constant (i.e. more apparent) monitoring. Thus, ISE's team workers are both under the eye of the norm and *in* the eye of the norm, but from where they are, in the eye, all seems natural and as it should be. Their system of rational rules winds tighter and tighter about them as the power of their value consensus compels their willful obedience.

ISE's experience with concertive control, then, is consistent with two theoretical predictions about the future of organizational activity. The first, which extends from Weber (1978) to Foucault (1976, 1980), asserts that organizational life will become increasingly rationalized and controlled. The second, which emerges primarily from Tompkins and Cheney (1985), Tannenbaum (1968), and Edwards (1981), posits that organizational control will become less apparent and more powerful.

The development of concertive control at ISE also complements the traditional literature on work-group norms and team development (e.g. Sundstrom, De Meuse and Futrell 1990; Hackman 1992). ISE's experience with concertive control illuminates the linkages between the emergence of group norms and the broader organizational issues of authority, rationality, power, and control.

ISE's teams developed a concertive system of control that grew from value-laden premises to strong norms, to rational rules for good work in the teams. ISE's system became deeply embedded in the social relations of the members, which served to conceal the character of concertive control. Because of this, the concertive, value-based rules increased the overall force of control in the system, making it more powerful than bureaucratic control had been. Unlike the bureaucratic hierarchy, authority and the possibility of appeal first and finally resided in the peer pressure of the teams.

ISE's experience with concertive control still begs the question: Does the concertive system offer a form of control that conceptually and *practically* transcends traditional bureaucratic control? My analysis of ISE's experience with teams indicates that, on the one hand, a concertive system creates its own powerful set of rational rules, which resembles the traditional bureaucracy. But, on the other hand, the locus of authority has transferred from the hierarchical system to the teams' values, norms, and rules, which does not resemble the bureaucracy. Concertive control works by blurring substantive and formal rationality into a 'communal-rational' system (Barker and Tompkins 1993). Concertive workers create a communal value system that eventually controls their actions through rational rules.

More importantly, however, my analysis suggests that concertive control does not free workers from Weber's iron cage of rational rules, as the culturalist and practitioner-oriented writers on contemporary organizations often argue. Instead, an ironic paradox occurs: The iron cage becomes stronger. The powerful combination of peer pressure and rational rules in the concertive system creates a new iron cage whose bars are almost invisible to the workers it incarcerates. ISE's team workers, as Weber (1978 : 988) warned, have harnessed themselves into a rational apparatus out of which they truly cannot squirm. As ISE's experience demonstrates, uncommitted workers do not last in the concertive system. Concertive workers must invest a part of themselves in the team: they must identify strongly with their team's values and goals, its norms and rules. If they want to resist their team's control, they must be willing to risk their human dignity, being made to feel unworthy as a 'teammate.' Entrapment in the iron cage is the cost of concertive control.

Acknowledgement

I wish to thank Patricia A. Adler, Phillip K. Tompkins, George Cheney, Brenda J. Allen, Lars Thøgar Christensen, and Michael Pacanowsky for their advice and criticisms during the writing of this essay. In addition, John H. Puckett provided the necessary support and coordination that enabled me to complete the research project.

Notes

1. Although the line that divides the point at which an idea in a worker's mind becomes a behavioral norm and then a rule is very indistinct, the concepts of concertively generated and collaboratively held value consensus, norms, and rules are important heuristics for explaining the processual nature of concertive control. Simon (1976 : 223) distinguished between value-based and factual-based decision premises. No longer guided by the old factual premises of the traditional supervisor, ISE's workers found themselves in a process of creating value premises and turning them into factual premises. Adopting these heuristic concepts and expressing their relationship as a transition from value consensus to norms to rules enables me to discuss this elusive process analytically.
2. ISE's teams developed in ways consistent with traditional studies of small groups and teams, most notably Tuckman's (1965), Homans' (1950), and Lewin's (1946) models of group formation and Walton and Hackman's (1986) model of work-group value and norm development. While cognizant of the parallels ISE's teams have to these fundamental models, I have sought to situate the story of how the teams developed a new form of control within the broader framework of the social forces (rationality, authority, social rule generation, etc.) that shaped the teams' organizational context.
3. I am indebted to Professor Lars Thøgar Christensen of Odense University in Denmark for coining this phrase.

References

Adler, P. A., and Adler, P. (1987). *Membership Roles in Field Research*. Beverly Hills CA: Sage.

Andrasik, F., and Heimberg, J. S. (1982). 'Self-management procedures', In Lee W. Frederiksen (ed.), *Handbook of Organizational Behavior Management*. New York: Wiley, pp. 219–47.

Barker, J. R., and Cheney, G. (1994). 'The Concept and the Practices of Discipline in Contemporary Organizational Life', *Communication Monographs*, vol. 60.

Barker, J. R., and Tompkins, P. K. (1993). 'Organizations, Teams, Control, and Identi-fication', unpublished manuscript, Department of Communication, University of Colorado, Boulder.

Barnard, C. (1968). *The Function of the Executive* (originally published in 1938) Cam-bridge MA: Harvard University Press.

Bolweg, J. F. (1976). *Job Design and Industrial Democracy*. Leiden: Martinus Nijhoff.

Brown, R. H. (1978). 'Bureaucracy as Praxis: Toward a Political Phenomenology of formal organizations', *Administrative Science Quarterly*, 23: 365–382.

Carnall, C. A. (1982). 'Semi-autonomous Work Groups and the Social Structure of the Organization', *Journal of Management Studies*, 19: 277–294.

Cheney, G. (1991). *Rhetoric in an Organizational Society: Managing Multiple Identities.* Columbia SC: University of South Carolina Press.

Coombs, R., Knights, D., and Willmott, H. C. (1992). 'Culture, control, and competi-tion: Towards a Conceptual Framework for the Study of Information Technology in Organizations', *Organization Studies*, 13: 51–72.

Cooper, R., and Burrell, G. (1988). 'Modernism, Postmodernism, and Organizational Analysis: An Introduction', *Organization Studies*, 9: 91–112.

Cordery, J. L., Mueller, W. S. and Smith, L. M. (1991). 'Attitudinal and Behavioral Effects of Autonomous Group Working: A Longitudinal Field Study', *Academy of Manage-ment Journal*, 34: 464–476.

Drucker, P. E. (1988). 'The Coming of the New Organizations', *Harvard Business Review*, Jan.–Feb.: 45–53.

Dumaine, B. (1990). 'Who needs a boss?', *Fortune*, May: 52–60.

Eccles, R. G., and Nohria, N. (1992). *Beyond the Hype: Rediscovering the Essence of Management*. Cambridge MA: Harvard Business School Press.

Edwards, R. C. (1981). 'The Social Relations of Production at the Point of Production', in Mary Zey-Ferrell and Michael Aiken (eds), *Complex Organizations: Critical Perspec-tives*, Glenview IL: Scott, Foresman, pp. 156–182.

Follett, M. P. (1941). *Dynamic Administration: The Collected Papers of Mary Parker Follett*, Henry C. Metcalf and L. Urwick (eds) London: Pitman.

Foucault, M. (1976). *Discipline and Punish*. New York: Vintage.

—— (1980). *Power/Knowledge*. New York: Pantheon.

Giddens, A. (1984). *The Constitution of Society: Outline of the Theory of Structuration*. Berkeley: University of California Press.

Grenier, G. J. (1988). *In human Relations*. Philadelphia: Temple University Press.

Hackman, J. R. (1986). 'The Psychology of Self-Management in Organizations', in Michael S. Pallak and Robert O. Perloff (eds), *Psychology and Work: Productivity, Change, and Employment*. Washington, DC: American Psychological Association, pp. 89–136.

—— (1992). 'Group Influences on Individuals in Organizations', in Marvin D. Dunn-ette and Leaetta M. Hough (eds), *Handbook of Industrial and Organizational Psychology*, 2nd edn., 3: (199).–267. Palo Alto, CA: Consulting Psychologists Press.

Hackman, J. R., and Walton, R. E. (1986). 'Leading Groups in Organizations', in Paul S. Goodman and Associates (eds), *Designing Effective Work Groups*. San Francisco: Jossey-Bass, pp. 72–119.

Homans, G. C. (1950). *The Human Group*. New York: Harcourt, Brace & World.

Jermier, J. M., Slocum, J. W. Jr., Fry, L. W. and Gaines, J. (1991). 'Resistance Behind the Myth and Facade of an Official Culture', *Organization Science*, 2: 170–194.

Jorgensen, D. L. (1989). *Participant Observation: A Methodology for Human Studies*. Newbury Park CA: Sage.

Kalberg, S. (1980). 'Max Weber's Types of Rationality: Cornerstones for the Analysis of Rationalization Processes in History', *American Journal of Sociology*, 85: 1145–1179.

Kanter, R. M. (1989). *When Giants Learn to Dance*. New York: Simon & Schuster.

Katz, D., and Kahn, R. L. (1978). *The Social Psychology of Organizations*. New York: Wiley.

Ketchum, L. D. (1984). 'How redesigned plants really work', *National Productivity Review*, 3: 246–254.

Larson, C. E., and Lafasto, F. M. J. (1989). *Teamwork: What Must Go Right/What Can Go Wrong*. Newbury Park CA: Sage.

Lewin, K. (1946). 'Research on Minority Problems', *Technology Review*, 3: 48.

—— (1948). *Resolving Social Conflicts: Selected Papers on Group Dynamics*. New York: Harper & Row.

Lewis, B. (1990). 'Team-Directed Workforce from a Worker's View', *Target*, Winter: 23–29.

Manz, C. C., and Sims, H. P. (1987). 'Leading Workers to Lead Themselves: The External Leadership of Self-Managing Work Teams', *Administrative Science Quarterly*, 32: 106–128.

Miller, P., and O'Leary, T. (1987). 'Accounting and the Construction of the Governable Person', *Accounting, Organizations and Society*, 12: 235–265.

Mumby, D. K., and Stohl, C. (1991). 'Power and Discourse in Organizational Studies: Absence and the Dialectic of Control', *Discourse and Society*, 2: 313–332.

Ogilvy, J. (1990). 'This Postmodern Business', *Marketing and Research Today*, Feb.: 4–20.

Orsburn, J. D., Moran, L., Musselwhite, E. and Zenger, J. H. (1990). *Self-Directed Work Teams: The New American Challenge*. Homewood IL: Irwin.

Parker, M. (1992). 'Post-Modern Organizations or Postmodern Organizational Theory?', *Organization Studies*, 13: 1–17

Parker, M., and Slaughter, J. (1988). *Choosing Sides: Unions and the Team Concept*. Boston: South End Press.

Perrow, C. (1986). *Complex Organizations: A Critical Essay*. New York: Random House.

Peters, T. J. (1988). *Thriving on Chaos*. New York: Knopf.

Peters, T. J., and Waterman, R. Jr. (1982). *In Search of Excellence: Lessons from America's Best-Run Companies*. New York: Harper & Row.

Riggs, F. (1979). 'Introduction: Shifting Meanings of the Term "bureaucracy".' *International Science Journal*, 31: 563–584.

Rothschild, J., and Whitt, J. A. (1986). *The Cooperative Workplace*. Cambridge: Cambridge University Press.

Sewell, G., and Wilkinson, B. (1992). '"Someone to Watch Over Me": Surveillance, Discipline and the Just-in-time Labour Process', *Sociology*, 26: 271–289.

Simon, H. A. (1976). *Administrative Behavior: A Study of Decision-Making Processes in Administrative Organizations*, 3rd edn. New York: Free Press.

Soeters, J. L. (1986). 'Excellent Companies as Social Movements', *Journal of Management Studies*, 23: 299–312.

Sundstrom, E., De Meuse, K. P., and Futrell, D. (1990). 'Work Teams: Applications and Effectiveness', *American Psychologist*, 45: 120–133.

Tannenbaum, A. S. (1968). *Control in Organizations*. New York: McGraw-Hill.

Tompkins, P. K., and Cheney, G. (1985). 'Communication and Unobtrusive Control in Contemporary Organizations', in Robert D. McPhee and Phillip K. Tompkins (eds), *Organizational Communication: Traditional Themes and New Directions*. Newbury Park CA: Sage, pp. 179–210.

Trist, E. L. (1981). 'The Evolution of Socio-Technical Systems', *Occasional Paper* No. 2. Toronto: Quality of Working Life Centre.

Trist, E. L., Higgin, G., Murray, H. and Pollock, A. B. (1963). *Organizational Choice*. London: Tavistock.

Tuckman, B. W. (1965). 'Development Sequences in Small Groups', *Psychological Bulletin*, 63: 384–399.

Walton, R. E. (1982). 'The Topeka Work System: Optimistic Visions, Pessimistic Hypothesis, and Reality', in Robert Zager and Michael P. Roscow (eds), *The Innovative Organization*. New York: Pergamon, pp. 260–87.

Walton, R. E., and Hackman, J. R. (1986). 'Groups under Contrasting Management Strategies', in Paul S. Goodman and Associates (eds), *Designing Effective Work Groups*. San Francisco: Jossey-Bass, pp. 168–201.

Weber, M. (1958). *The Protestant Ethic and the Spirit of Capitalism*. New York: Scribner's.

—— (1978). *Economy and Society*. Guenther Roth and Klaus Wittich (eds). Berkeley: University of California Press.

Wellins, R. S., Byham, W. C., and Wilson, J. M. (1991). *Empowered Teams: Creating Self-Directed Work Groups that Improve Quality. Productivity, and Participation*. San Francisco: Jossey-Bass.

Whitley, R. (1977). 'Organizational Control and the Problem of Order', *Social Science Information*, 16: 169–189.

11

The Managing of the (Third) World

Bill Cooke

Introduction

This article is about the relationship between management and the Third World. Its significance, however, is for understandings of management in and of both First and Third Worlds. It builds from an agreement with Diana Wong-MingJi and Ali Mir (1997) that what is taken as 'management' in the First World, in the field of management and organization studies (MOS), its associated journals and texts, and the business and management schools that train its academics and practitioners, has ignored, with few significant exceptions, the Third World. But this is only a beginning; the purpose of this article is to identify the existence and implications of a largely separated set of First World managerial theories and practices, which takes and indeed helps constitute the Third World as its subject. This separated discipline was once known as 'development administration', and now more typically as 'development management' or 'development administration and management' (henceforth DAM, considered in comparison with the 'management' of business schools, MOS, etc.).

DAM, despite this separation, has connections to 'management'. It uses some of its techniques and language, and claims to be subset of public administration. Although these connections appear to be strengthening, DAM maintains its distinctive self-identity through its 'developing country' orientation. This in turn points to the two fundamentals of DAM that identify it as separate. First, 'management' has historically taken 'the organization' as its basic unit of analysis and action. This is often a tacit assumption or, if not, one that passes unremarked, as in the very conflation of MOS—'management *and* organization studies'. Ferguson's statement, however, that 'the development paradigm insists on taking *the country* as the basic unit of analysis' (1990 : 60), and, it can be added,

244

action, is also true for its subfield, DAM. Second, whereas management assumes that its primary subjects (organizations being managed) are situated within modernity (or, for some, beyond it, in postmodernity), DAM assumes that its primary subjects (countries being managed) have yet to achieve modernity, which is why they are deemed to need 'development'.

Formal definitions provide some insights into the distinctivenesses claimed by the DAM orthodoxy and in this article. Thus, Schaffer (1973 : 245) defines development administration as:

development programmes, policies and projects in those conditions in which there are unusually wide and new demands and in which there are peculiarly low capacities and severe obstacles to meeting them.

The specification of a particular set of conditions (i.e. wide and new demands, low capacities, severe obstacles) and the particular task of development is a tacit distinction from generic public administration. It is also another way of saying 'Third World countries requiring modernization'. Making this point explicit, Luke argues (1986 : 74) that 'the context of the struggle for development in the Third World gives the subject ... [its] peculiar status', going on to quote Swerdlow (1975 : 347) that development administration 'must be limited to the administration of those countries that are seeking development and are starting at low levels of economic productivity'.

How this separation/connection between DAM and 'management' manifests itself in practice is illustrated in a job advertisement in *The Economist* (8 April 2000 : 137). It sought a 'Chief, Office of Democracy and Governance' in Kenya to provide 'intellectual leadership in the design, implementation, management and evaluation of programs needed to support democratic local governance ... '. Required qualifications included:

1. Experience in providing leadership in the following areas: rule of law, elections and political processes, civil society and governance;
2. Ability to carry out analyses of Kenyan democratic development and formulate appropriate Mission's objectives, targets and strategies for achieving them;
3. Ability to design and manage the implementation of programs and projects through which the strategies are implemented;
4. Ability to evaluate the results of projects and their effect on the related objectives in the democracy and governance sector in Kenya ....

The job is open only to 'a US citizen or US resident alien'. For this post with USAID (US Agency for International Development) the selected individual 'will be required to obtain a US government secret security clearance'. While she or he will have to have 'excellent communication skills in English', 'fluency in Swahili' is only 'recommended'.

What is going on here, then, is a First World intervention in the political processes of another nation-state. The post-holder will not manage a modern (or beyond) organization, which is what 'management' has assumed managing is all about. Yet this is an advert for a manager, as the use of the managerialist terminology of leadership, objectives, strategy and strategies, programme and project, implementation and evaluation (not to mention 'manage') makes clear.

So, despite their differences, 'management' and 'DAM' are both versions of management in its most broad and generic sense (perhaps it is clearer to say that they are both versions of managerialism). They are both cases of 'a common sense and taken for granted reality of management' in which 'management is what managers do' (Grey 1999 : 569); that is, management as a conflation of a certain set of distinctive managerial activities ('what managers do') with an occupational category possessing a distinct managerial identity (i.e. 'managers'). This is more than a parallel between different sets of technocrats and technocracies; as the illustration shows, 'management' language and practices are used in DAM. Ironically, this helps conceal the fundamental differences that there nonetheless are. In turn, this article will show, this combination of similarity and difference hides the contemporary complicity of both DAM and 'management' (when used in DAM) in a neo-liberalizing global modernization project.

The goals of this project—diminution of the state, extension of the market, evident in the removal of the public sector from enterprise, the reduction in the size of the state in terms of expenditure, numbers employed and services delivered, the espousal of free trade, policies to introduce labour market flexibility, and so on—are well known (e.g. Fotopoulous 2001). But besides the globally familiar consequences of neo-liberalism (for example, privatization), this article also discusses others more specific to the Third World, most obviously the extension of direct user charges for essential services (health, education, potable water). These had initially been introduced in an earlier cycle of externally imposed reforms called Structural Adjustment Programmes (SAPs).

The Logic and Structure of the Article

This brings me, then, to the underpinning logic and structure of the article, which is as follows. It has three more main sections. In the next of these, 'DAM and "Management" Compared', I will explore the relationships between DAM and 'management'. These are assessed in terms of the institutional settings in which DAM and management are produced and, regarding DAM in particular, its claimed theoretical underpinning.

The section following this, 'DAM in Practice', moves on from DAM in theory to consider how it is put into practice by the largest and most influential development agency, the World Bank. In particular, it is shown how the use of 'management' ideas for development management ends in the Bank's Comprehensive Development Frameworks (CDFs) and Poverty Reduction Strategy Papers (PRSPs) is intended to facilitate the establishment of neo-liberal institutional frameworks in the Third World.

The last section is the conclusion. This begins, first, by anticipating possible criticisms of the choice of the World Bank as a case study of DAM in practice. It continues by exploring the implications of the preceding sections for understandings of the various versions of management discussed thus far—international management, the 'management' of MOS and DAM. It rounds off by exploring the implications of my analysis for critical management studies (CMS).

DAM and 'Management' Compared

Esman's account of DAM begins as follows:

While the field's pioneers confronted the dilemmas of the declining colonial era with its hesitant and post-World War II commitment to development, the subject was transformed by the precipitous expansion of US imperium into terra incognita in Asia, Latin America, and Africa. These encounters through technical assistance with the realities of Third World governments revealed that the conceptual equipment of Western, particularly American, public administration was inadequate to the task at hand. This challenge produced several nodes of activity among them . . . Indiana . . . Michigan State . . . Syracuse . . . Southern California . . . Harvard . . . Pittsburgh. (1991 : 1)

It was argued in Cooke (2001a) that this statement ignores the continuance of formal imperialism well past the end of the Second World War, underplays the extent of US imperialism pre- and post-1945 and fails to recognize the old imperial power of the UK's contribution to DAM. Relevant to this paper, it was pointed out that the common term 'technical assistance' (and elsewhere 'technical cooperation') helps DAM represent itself as technocratically neutral, with the words 'assistance' or 'cooperation' implying a non-existent parity of power between the technical helpers and helped. In specifying new 'nodes of activity' and inadequate public administration conceptual frameworks, Esman also points to an institutional separation. This, it is argued here, sustains the conceptual separation, which is at once claimed and concealed in Esman's alignment to an inadequate public administration.

247

DAM Institutions

Evidence of the institutional separation of 'management' and DAM is provided by contemporary calls for its diminution by senior staff in international development agencies. The vision for the United Nations Development Programme (UNDP) of its head, ex-World Bank Vice-President Malloch-Brown, is that it must become like the archetypal management consultancy: '[w]e need to become a kind of McKinsey for the developing world' (in Morgan 2000 : 5). The former Head of Social Development at the UK government's Department for International Development (DfID), Ros Eyben, argues that, 'as orthodox development loses its dominant position, so we can take advantage of recent postmodernist organizational theory which has been developed in business management faculties to explain the success of certain transnational corporations' (2000 : 10). Eyben does not subsequently discuss this theory (although it is returned to below). Institutionally, in naming 'business management faculties' as it source, she implies a distinction and a turn away from the 13 or so development departments in the UK, as well as those listed by Esman in the USA, where DAM or some aspect thereof is taught (CDSC 2000).

As the introduction noted, this institutional separation has been confirmed empirically, in relation to 16 leading management journals, by Wong-MingJi and Mir (1997). Their concern was the global spread of international management (IM), but their methodology means that their research is equally about 'management' generally. Wong-MingJi and Mir analysed every article in these journals (3,649 articles in total) according to the country of authors' institutional affiliation, and the nations represented in articles besides those where a given journal was published.[1] All the journals are published in the First World, and within them Third World countries were overwhelmingly underrepresented: 37.41 percent of articles originated from the USA, and 15.68 percent each from Canada and the UK, whereas the highest percentage from a Third World nation was 2.25 percent from India; 98 countries had no representation amongst contributors, and 89 countries were not represented as subjects. Those that did not feature among either contributors or subjects included Barbados, Bolivia, Botswana, Cuba, Ecuador, Guatemala, Jamaica, Kenya, Mozambique, Oman, Sri Lanka, Syria, Trinidad and Tobago, and Zimbabwe. The highest representation as subject in percentage terms was the 1.73 percent of articles that featured India, 1.51 percent the Third World per se, and 0.36 percent Nigeria.

There are, however, other First World journals that claim countries engaged in modernization as their subject. Of these, generic development journals include *World Development* ('a multidisciplinary monthly journal of development studies. It seeks to explore ways of improving standards of living and the human condition generally...'), *Development and Change* ('an interdisciplinary journal devoted to the critical analysis and discussion of current issues of development'), and *Journal of International Development* ('wishes to publicise any work which shows promise in confronting the problems of poverty and underdevelopment in low income countries'). All have published articles about DAM as part of their broader development remit (see, for example, Brinkerhoff 2000; Hirschmann 1999; Thomas 1996).

Some are more directly development management oriented, for example *Development in Practice* ('a multi-disciplinary journal of practice-based analysis and research concerning the social dimensions of development'), which has recently published a collection of its articles under the title *Management and Development* (Eades, 2000), and *Public Administration and Development (PAD)* ('reports and reviews the practice of public administration ... where this is directed to development in less industrialized and transitional economies. It gives special attention to the management of all phases of public policy formulation and implementation which have an interest and importance beyond a particular government and state. *PAD* also publishes articles on the experiences of development management in the NGO sector').[2]

At the same time, the institutional separation between management and DAM has never been absolute. What for some are separate identities are for others merged. Thus, from Tanzania, Malloch-Brown's aspiration for the UNDP might appear pointless, because McKinsey is the 'McKinsey for the Developing World'. Max's primer on Tanzanian local government notes the central role of 'McKinsey and Co. Inc, an international capitalist consultancy firm specialised in development management' in its ruinous decentralization in 1973 (1990 : 84). Some development institutes teach 'management' topics such as human resource management or management information systems, although often segregated from similar business/management school classes in the same university (CDSC 2000). *Organization* was not included in Wong-MingJi and Mir's analysis, but has, particularly in its early years, addressed the failure of development (Escobar 1995a), global organization (Gergen 1995), feminist international development (Ferguson 1996), and a sub-field of management (Organization Development, OD) read from the Third World (Holvino 1996). This article supports some parts of these earlier contributions, for example Ferguson's concerns for the hegemonic nature of the IMF/World Bank, and for the role of practitioners acting at their behest. However, it does so in meeting a remit hitherto unaddressed, in acknowledging the existence of DAM per se and in exploring the DAM/'management' nexus and results in different, and more current, findings. Elsewhere, public administration journals do from time to time publish articles on DAM (e.g. *Public Administration Review* of Brinkerhoff and Coston 1999). Elsewhere still, Blunt et al. (1992) and Kiggundu (1989) have applied management/organization theories in the

Third World, but still with organizations primarily understood as instrumentalities of the development process.

There is nonetheless much else in DAM journals and books that readers from a 'management' background would not recognize as management as they understand it. This is partly because of techniques and methods specific to the DAM domain that do not occur elsewhere, for example institutional development, the logical framework and participatory rural appraisal (PRA) (Cooke 1998; Chambers 1997). But mutual understanding is also constrained because DAM and 'management' work from different sets of paradigms. Accordingly, Cooke (1997) recognizes that a development practitioner adopting an MOS Burrell and Morgan multi-paradigm approach would nonetheless still be working within the development paradigm. The same applies to a 'management' practitioner working in DAM. The difficulties of cross-paradigmatic understanding, on the one hand, and the 'management' in common, on the other, sustain the obliviousness of management practitioners and theorists to the switch from modernity to modernization, from organization to nation-state, and even from 'management' to DAM, as the former is applied in the latter.

The Ideas of DAM

In addressing the paradigmatic situation of DAM, a transition is made from its institutions to its ideas. To continue in this vein, but at the sub-paradigmatic level of DAM's representations of itself, it should be noted that it is not disputed that there is continuity between development administration and development management. Hirschmann's historical survey notes that for its internal disputes 'the theory and practice of Development Administration (or Management as it came to be known) have continued, and with some vibrancy' (1999 : 288). From the USA, Brinkerhoff and Coston's (1999) assessment of development management also acknowledges this continuity, tracking its history back to the 1950s. In the DAM tradition, they identify development management as an applied discipline, and locate it within a parent field of public administration. But they also say that it has changed, particularly in its emphasis on the state as a vehicle of development. Thus:

The trend has been away from a technocratic, universalist, public-sector administrative model toward a context-specific, politically infused, multisectoral, multiorganizational model. From its initial focus on institution building for central level bureaucracies and capacity building for economic and project planning, development management has gradually expanded to encompass bureaucratic reorientation and restructuring, the integration of politics and culture into management improvement, participatory and performance-based service delivery and program management, community and NGO [non-governmental organization] capacity building, and policy reform and implementation. (Brinkerhoff and Coston 1999 : 348–9)

This inclusion of community and NGO capacity-building, which elsewhere Brinkerhoff (2000) suggests should also include the private sector, shifts DAM further still from public administration. More generally, the shift of emphasis away from state bureaucracy to a variety of organizational forms and processes might be taken as suggesting notice has been taken of Eyben's call for post-modern organization, along the lines perhaps of that proposed by Clegg (1990). This is far from the case, as the following section will show. DAM is still very much about the attempt to achieve modernity, albeit the 'neoliberal modernity' Fotopoulous (2001 : 33) identifies as succeeding its 'statist' version.

Although they are DAM insiders, Brinkerhoff and Coston's assessment is nuanced. It does, for example, recognize DAM is about First World interventions in the Third World, identifying '[d]evelopment management as a means to foreign assistance agendas . . . most often sponsored by international aid agencies, all of which have their own . . . agendas; typically development management professionals enter the scene upon the request from a donor agency for a predetermined task'. In describing 'development management as values' they recognize explicitly that DAM requires political interventions in the status quo, but for the best of reasons, because it 'takes a normative stance on empowerment and supporting groups, particularly the poor and the marginalized, to take an active role in determining and fulfilling their own needs' (1999 : 349; emphasis in original).

There are according to Brinkerhoff and Coston two additional 'facets' of development management. Both contain substantial components recognizable as 'management' but at the same time differentiations that point to country as the unit of analysis and action. 'Development management as toolkit . . . promotes the application of a range of management and analytical tools adapted from a variety of disciplines, including strategic management, public policy, public administration, psychology, anthropology and political science' (1999 : 350), whereas:

Development management as process operates at three levels—[first] in terms of the individual actors involved it builds on process consultation and organization development . . . starting with the client's priorities needs and values . . . [second] at the organizational level, whether . . . individual agency or multiple organizations . . . concerned with the organizational structures and processes through which plans are implemented . . . [third] at the sector level—public, civil society, and private . . . [it] addresses broader governance issues, such as participation, accountability, transparency, responsiveness and the role of the state . . . this brings in empowerment in its societal and political dimensions. (Brinkerhoff and Coston 1999 : 350)

The relationship between 'management' and DAM is also explored from the UK by Alan Thomas, for whom a development management training curriculum should cover (1996 : 108):

1a. Development studies.
1b. Conventional management theory in a development context.
2. New areas arising from viewing development management as the management of intervention aimed at 'progress' in a context of conflicts over goals and values.
3. Radical participative management methods aimed at enabling and empowering, arising from cases where development management may be viewed as the management of interventions on behalf of the relatively powerless.

In sum, besides the extension of remit from the state alone to incorporate civil society and the private sector, there are three other changes evident in the transition from development administration to development management. First, according to both Thomas and Brinkerhoff and Coston, development management incorporates more of 'management'. The relationship between Brinkerhoff and Coston's four 'facets' is, however, more accurately conceived as hierarchical than, as they have it, in 'tension' (Brinkerhoff and Coston 1999 : 349), with 'foreign [i.e. First World] assistance agendas' informed by particular 'values' determining what is permitted in the management-orientated 'process' and 'toolkit'. Second, there is an emphasis on the use of participatory 'management' approaches (e.g. process consultation), as well as those developed separately in DAM, and their associated language of empowerment. Third, both recognize that development in theory and practice is contested. This is evident in Brinkerhoff and Coston's 'development management as values' facet, and in Thomas's argument (1996 : 102) that development's goals for social change are 'strongly subject to value based conflicts, derived from different conceptions of "progress" and development, and differences of interests'.

In relation to this last point, Brinkerhoff and Coston and Thomas suggest DAM takes a particular side, that of the powerless and the poor. Brinkerhoff and Coston present a version of development management in which implicitly this is what actually happens, although their acknowledgement of 'tensions' suggests that this is not always the case. Thomas is even more cautious, and makes a distinction between the 'management *of* development', the generic management of 'deliberate efforts at progress', i.e. 'development interventions', and 'management *for* development', where development is seen 'as an orientation towards progressive social change' (2000 : 46). For Thomas, authentic development management is the progressive management *for* development, but he is ultimately uncertain about whether or how this progressive orientation is maintained in practice: 'the majority of cases will be ... ambiguous, with value based conflicts, contestations over the definition of development and power struggles. Development management will often remain an ideal rather than a description of what takes place' (2000 : 51).

Thomas claims, accurately, that this alignment of participation with a radical, pro-poor agenda takes development management beyond mainstream 'management' versions of empowerment. This might offer hope to some of those focused on 'management' but at the same time outside it in critical management studies, seeking 'more humane' forms of management that are 'less irrational and socially divisive' (Grey and Fournier 2000 : 23). DAM does offer techniques unknown in 'management' and critical management (CM) for working with and organizing the poor and the marginalized—notably associated with Chambers' (1997) PRA. Yet, at the same time, neither Thomas nor Brinkerhoff and Coston recognize the managerial orthodoxy's capacity to appropriate radical ideas (Burrell and Morgan 1979; Alvesson and Willmott 1996). Also not acknowledged in DAM are CM claims that participation and empowerment are used in the workplace as means of control (Cooke 1999), although similar analyses are now finding their way into critiques of participatory development (Cooke and Kothari 2001). In both cases, the argument is that participation and empowerment at the micro level (of, say, work teams or individual 'communities') can sustain, through co-optation and undermining resistance, macro-level inequalities and exploitation.

This appropriation and co-optation is what appears to be happening. The following section reveals how claims for pro-poor interventions, which it is claimed distinguishes DAM, mask interventions that have the opposite effect. It also shows how, at the level of practice, management's participatory processes, and those associated with organizational culture change more generally, have, via DAM, become implicated in management of change at the most macro levels possible, that is in the global, neo-liberal transformation of nation-states.

DAM in Practice

In 'management', the ideas of participation and empowerment are associated with the notion of collective psychological ownership by employees of the policies, processes and activities to which an organization is committed. This is particularly the case in relation to the management of organizational change (e.g. Schein 1987). Psychological ownership does not translate into literal ownership however, or control beyond the most micro levels of organizational processes; broader managerial goals are always taken as given and immutable, and, moreover, the desire and strategies for the achievement of such 'ownership' are always externally, i.e. managerially, impelled (Willmott 1993).

'Ownership' at the Country Level

The difference in DAM is that it is countries that are required to show 'ownership'. That is, there is a First World requirement that its interventions in the functioning of Third World nation-states are 'owned' by those states. As in 'management', the desire and strategies for ownership are managerially impelled—but in this case as a means to achieve DAM's 'foreign assistance agendas' facet (see also Cooke 2003).

This is demonstrated with greatest significance by the World Bank and its implementation of Comprehensive Development Frameworks (CDFs) and Poverty Reduction Strategy Papers (PRSPs) (shared with the IMF). The Bank is the largest development agency, with 8000 staff, and lending and guaranteeing around US$25 billion a year to 177 member countries. Headquartered in Washington DC, its executive board is dominated by representatives of First World nations. Its president, currently James Wolfensohn, is always chosen by the US government (Bretton Woods Project, 2001). The Bank is not merely a financial institution however; its lending is often tied to specific projects that it directly or indirectly manages. As the following section will also show, it increasingly sees itself (with the IMF) as the architect of global financial and political systems and processes and the global coordinator of First World development interventions in the Third World. Important in relation to the distinctiveness of contemporary development management, all this is done in the name of the World's poor. Bank web pages are tagged 'A World Free of Poverty', and its stated purpose is to help 'developing countries fight poverty and establish economic growth that is stable, sustainable, and equitable' (World Bank 2001a).

The Bank's claim to worldwide authority in this realm is evident, for example, in its Global Development Gateway, aimed at becoming 'the premier web entry point on poverty and sustainable development' (cited in Bretton Woods Project 2001). It is also evident in the term 'comprehensive' in Comprehensive Development Framework, one aspect of which signifies the Bank's intention that there should be a single, overarching development strategy (in Brinkerhoff and Coston's terms, 'foreign assistance agenda') for a given Third World country, to which individual First World nation development agencies (e.g. USAID, DfID) contribute. Within CDFs, poverty alleviation is a key goal, and addressed through country PRSPs, which are a joint Bank/IMF initiative. In the implementation of CDFs and PRSPs, there has also been a heavy incorporation of 'management' ideas and practices, as this section will go on to show. CDFs and PRSPs therefore show how DAM, embodying all Brinkerhoff and Coston's four facets (in the hierarchy I have suggested) and an apparent pro-poor management *for* development on Thomas's lines (and containing his three components) is practised by the most powerful development agency in the world (see George and Sabelli 1994).

The other aspect of CDF comprehensiveness, where comprehensive means thorough, and the centrality of ownership therein is stated by the Bank thus:

The CDF suggests a long term holistic approach to development that recognizes the importance of macroeconomic fundamentals but gives equal weight to the institutional, structural, structural underpinnings of a robust market economy. It emphasizes strong partnership among governments, donors, civil society, the private sector and other development actors. Perhaps most importantly, the country is in the driver's seat, both 'owning' and directing the developing agenda with the Bank and the country's other partners. (World Bank 2001b)

According to the latest figures available at the time of writing, 46 countries are involved in the CDF/PRSP processes (CDF Secretariat 2001). The relationship between PRSPs and CDFs is not clear. At the time of writing, the official line is that the PRSP is 'an operational vehicle which can be a specific output of a CDF or of processes based on CDF principles. Its intent is to integrate countries' strategies for poverty reduction into coherent, growth oriented macroeconomic frameworks and to translate these strategies into time bound action plans' (World Bank 2000:32). Again, ownership is required. The IMF states that '[c]ountry-ownership of a poverty reduction strategy is paramount. Broad based participation of civil society in the adoption and monitoring of poverty reduction strategy tailored to country circumstances will enhance its sustained implementation' (IDA/IMF 1999:6). At the time of writing, there is much more publicly available information (to a writer based in Britain) about the content of PRSPs compared with CDFs.

Country CDFs are to be drawn up according to a matrix, reproduced here as Table 1, which is to be accompanied by annexes. This reduces a nation's political, social and economic processes, its internal relationships between and within state, market and civil society and its external relationships with global organizations and processes to a single table, which in turn provides the basis for its management. As Paul Cammack (2002) points out, a CDF requires a detailed—indeed comprehensive—specification of government policy to the Bank's satisfaction if Bank/IMF support (which includes some relief of existing debts) is to be given. Cammack quotes Wolfensohn (1999:24) that 'the matrix will be a summary management tool', behind each of its headings being annexes, which 'set forth where the country stands in terms of achievement, and where they want to go', followed by 'a strategy for implementation with a timeline'. This is to be followed with 'a more detailed listing of projects achieved, projects underway, and projects planned, together with a listing of those institutions providing assistance, and a detailed description of the projects planned and undertaken with their results'.

Bill Cooke

Table 1. The Comprehensive Development Framework Matrix

MATRIX	Structural/ Institutional	Social/Human	Physical/ Rural/Urban	Macroeco- nomic/Finan- cial
Government				
Private Sector				
NGO/CSOs				
Bilateral Partners				
UN Partners				
RDBs				
World Bank				
IMF				
EU				
NGO/CSOs:	Non-governmental organizations/civil soviety organizations			
RDBs:	Regional Development Banks			
IMF:	International Monetary Fund			
EU:	European Union			

Source: Excerpted from World Bank (2001b)

What Wolfensohn proposes is very close to a standard description of a strategic or business plan. However, as the matrix headings make clear, what is being managed is not a work organization but a nation-state, which is required to prioritize and taxonomize its activities according to the Bank's matrix to the Bank's satisfaction. In achieving ownership of CDFs, the Bank also clearly sees a need to buttress hard systems change embodied in the matrix with change in so-called softer systems, mimicking, for example, Saithe's (1985) approach to organizational culture change. Hence, '[f]undamentally the CDF approach calls for a change in internal culture and mindset and it is evident from the pilot countries that this is beginning to happen' (World Bank 2001c).

The Culturalist Management of Nations

The Bank itself produces examples of how this culture change is to be achieved globally in Table 2, reproduced verbatim (World Bank 2000 : 37). The headings of each column—leadership behaviour, organizational environment, learning approach—and the 'culturalist' (in the sense described by Kunda 1992) language in the boxes are evidently from 'management'; but the application is to

Table 2. Promising Changes in the Bank's Way of Working. Examples from Bank's way of working with pilot countries that facilitated incorporation of CDF principles (one country per region shown)

	Leadership Behaviour (roles, skills, attitudes)	Organizational Environment (structure, processes, culture)	Learning Approach (learning, context, content, process)
Bolivia	*Empowering teams incl. ACS [ ]staff and infusing passion* inspiring a higher level of effort and forged more committed internal and external relationships.	*Decentralization of decision making* facilitated receptiveness to emerging opportunities.	*Using a results- and decision-oriented learning approach* promoted a results- and decision-oriented work culture together with the government.
Ghana	*Giving priority to national experience and capacity* encouraged government to take stronger leadership role.	*Building a culture of mutual respect and trust* gave the government the opportunity to present their long-term country strategy directly to the Board	*Building upon lessons* learned in Bolivia and applying an action-learning approach sped the process of joint learning.
Morocco	*Adapting our CAS* [Country Assistance Strategy] *practices* to the dynamics in the country and to the timing of the national process for developing country strategy improved the relationship between government and Bank.	*Developing cross-sectoral working practices* promoted movement towards a more holistic approach.	*Facilitation of country team retreat by process expert* enhanced team process skills and effectiveness.
Romania	*Being more innovative and working within the broader context* together with the government is helping to create a network for change inside the country and to open up dialogue between the government and the private sector and other members of civil society.	*Leveraging the matrix structure* facilitated intersectoral teams, both within the Bank and within the government.	*Leveraging external change process expertise into a joint learning experience* supported vigorous national dialogue, including with civil society.

Table 2. Promising Changes in the Bank's Way of Working. Examples from Bank's way of working with pilot countries that facilitated incorporation of CDF principles (one country per region shown)—continued

	Leadership Behaviour (roles, skills, attitudes)	Organizational Environment (structure, processes, culture)	Learning Approach (learning, context, content, process)
Vietnam	*Performing a networking role* and ceding leadership to others facilitated synergies among development partners.	*Modelling more open and transparent work culture and processes* encouraged government to take a more open and inclusive approach with civil society and private sector.	*Sharing of knowledge and joint learning* supported the institutionalizing of bi-annual mini-CG-meetings, bringing together nternal and external stakeholders.

Source: World Bank (2000: 37), published with permission of the World Bank

countries. The names in the first column, again, represent nation-states not the regional offices of a transnational organization.

Claims are also made for action learning, recognizing 'that people learn better by using a "hands-on" approach than the traditional classroom setting', which for the Bank helps focus on the 'need to deliver real country products in real time'. The US Society for Organizational Learning was commissioned by the Bank to evaluate its action-learning programme in the CDF pilot phase, and concluded that 'the approach catalyzed innovative institutional change, enhanced leadership competencies consistent with the CDF requirements, and led to enthusiastic support for the new way of doing business'.[3] According to the World Bank Country Director for Bolivia, action learning 'was essential in producing effective stakeholders discussions. I have never seen this in the Bank before—where you go through the process of discussion, have so many perspectives at once, but you have action at the end. And there was not just a unilateral decision, but everyone was involved' (all quotes from World Bank 2001c).

There is an unspoken consequent implication that what happened before, when decisions were unilateral, lacked legitimacy. Certainly, a substantial proportion of the debt that PRSPs are a stipulated prerequisite to relieving does include that accrued through questionable First World loans. Many of these were made without due diligence on the part of the lenders in the First World private banking sector to Third World private enterprise, and were subsequently forced on Third World governments as state liabilities (as Chossudovsky 1997, says, they were nationalized). Other loans were made to dictatorial regimes, for example Thieu of South Vietnam, Smith of Zimbabwe,

Mobutu of D.R. Congo, the South African apartheid state, and the Brazilian military dictatorship (Chossudovsky 1997; Ransom 1999; Hanlon 1999).

Problems with the pre-1999 action-learning CDF/PRSP strategy of Structural Adjustment Programmes (known as austerity programmes) were also attributed by the Bank to a lack of ownership. Others saw the civil unrest that ensued in many countries as resulting from the social harshness of reform that the SAPs required, for example the removal of subsidies for essential goods and services, privatizing and downsizing, and introduction of user fees, which had a disproportionately damaging effect on the poor, on women, on children, on people with disabilities and on the elderly (Cornia et al. 1987; Bernstein 1990; Elson 1991).

Accountability and remedy for harmful past Bank/IMF practice are not issues being addressed in the Bank's apparently participative, mindset-changing, ownership-engendering learning processes. This is not surprising, given the control that it exerts over them. No contradiction is recognized in calling for participation and PRSP ownership, on the one hand, and the initial prescription of 'Factors Governments May Wish to Consider in Drawing Up their Participatory Process', on the other (IDA/IMF 1999 : 12). This in turn has developed into hundreds of pages of analysis and recommendations on the conduct of PRSP participation, which can be downloaded from the World Bank PRSP website, including a 69-page report by Brinkerhoff and Goldsmith (2001) entitled *Macroeconomic Policy, PRSPs and Participation*.

Throughout, though, there has been no Bank departure from the understanding that '[m]ajor multi-lateral institutions—including the bank and the fund—would need to be available to support the process, as would other donors' (IDA/IMF 1999 : 13). This 'support' is extensive. Bank/IMF 'teams will need to cooperate closely' with one another, 'and seek to present the authorities with a coherent overall view, focusing on their traditional areas of expertise':

[For IMF staff] this would include prudent macroeconomic policies; structural reforms in related areas such as exchange rate, and tax policy; and issues related to fiscal management, budget execution, fiscal transparency and tax and customs administration. The Bank staff will take the lead in advising the authorities in the design of poverty reduction strategies . . . the design of sectoral strategies, reforms that ensure more efficient and responsive institutions, and the provision of social safety nets; and in helping the authorities to cost the priority poverty reducing expenditure through Public Expenditure Reviews and the like and in other structural reforms such as privatization and regulatory reform. Many areas will need to be shared between the two staffs, such as the establishment of an environment conducive to private sector growth, trade liberalization, and financial sector development. (IDA/IMF 1999 : 13–14)

The implication is that sovereign governments' ownership is therefore supposed to derive from their responsibility for everything else; though what else remains is not specified. A detailed World Development Movement

(WDM) review (Marshall and Woodroffe 2001) of 16 country PRSPs or Interim PRSPs (I-PRSPs) demonstrates an absence of ownership and participation in both process and content. Globally, trades unions have been excluded from participation. More generally, negotiations over PRSPs have been conducted in private between Bank and government officials, with evidence that the latter have tried to second-guess what the Bank wants in order to gain debt relief. In Cambodia, PSRP documentation was not available in the Khmer language by the time the final draft was put before cabinet. 'Foreign technical consultants of major donor institutions [are] setting the parameters of Cambodia's poverty reduction strategy' (Marshall and Woodroffe 2001 : 36). Ghanaian women's organizations argued that the requirement that civil society speak 'with a single voice . . . would mean subordinating women's gender interests to men's'. In Tanzania, there are 157 policies attached to the I-PRSP, which 'pressure the Government of Tanzania [GOT] to carry out political, economic and social reforms designated by the IMF and World Bank and acceded to by the GOT. Such excessive conditionality amounts to micromanagement of the GOT by its creditors' (Global Challenge Initiative 2000, in Marshall and Woodroffe 2001 : 39). Having met these conditionalities, debt relief will not be absolute however. Thus Tanzania will still be required to pay the equivalent of US$3 million a week to service its debt (Denny and Elliott 2000).

The WDM review identifies the compilation of a PRSP as an intensively political process and provides examples of the manipulation of consultation processes by governments and oppositions and the exclusion of civil society organizations (CSOs). It does not, however, quite go so far as to raise the broader questions of the legitimacy and accountability of CSOs and their right to participate. However, according to the Bank itself, those who are elected but outside government have little involvement. For both CDFs and PRSPs, 'parliaments are mostly absent from the debate' (CDF Secretariat 2001 : 4). That there is therefore a divergence between espoused and actual practice when it comes to participation and empowerment is only part of the case. CDFs and PRSPs have been produced and adopted, so what the Bank proudly claims for action learning, team-building, changing leadership behaviours and so on seems to have had some effect. That effect may have been the co-optation and ideological conversion of technocratic/political elites achievable through participative culture change processes (Cooke 1999, 2001b) or to engineer their knowing yet unwilling capitulation to the realities of Bank/IMF power. Bond (2000) suggests the former in the case of South Africa and the World Bank generally; Marshall and Woodroffe (2001) provide evidence of the latter. Either way, the result is a highly homogeneous set of PRSP outputs that belie the claims made for participation. Marshall and Woodroffe state that 'the consistency of policies put forward is remarkable given the different histories, characteristics and drafting processes of the . . . countries surveyed' (2001 : 14).

Consistent Neo-liberal Outcomes

Marshall and Woodroffe's tabulation of components of individual nations' PRSP/I-PRSPs demonstrates conclusively that each one amounts to an extensive neo-liberal reform package, the assumption being that economic growth leads to poverty reduction, although the logic behind this trickle-down approach is never explained or justified. All 16 countries proposed macroeconomic policy based on 'economic growth . . . , macro-economic stability . . . prudent monetary/fiscal/ budgetary policies', and private sector development. Central are liberalization and privatization. The former includes the removal of price controls (on e.g. gas, cotton, petroleum, transport, electricity, water, telecommunications, seeds), the removal of trade barriers and tariffs, and the promotion of foreign trade and direct investment. Core privatization policies 'across all countries' include privatization of telecommunications, ports, energy, railways, posts, and public enterprises, and making the private sector the engine of growth (Marshall and Woodroffe 2001 : 14). PRSP social policy is built on the idea of cost recovery, that is, that users of services such as education, health and clean water should pay for that service at the point of delivery and that the private sector should deliver such services (how Brinkerhoff and Coston's enabling 'the poor and the marginalized . . . to take an active role in determining and fulfilling their own needs' is realized). This is the face of pre-existing detailed evidence that user fees exclude the poor from the receipt of such essential services.

At the same time, there are common absences from PRSPs and I-PRSPs of policies that would directly help the poor. In the few places where land reform is considered, it is in terms of clarifying ownership not of redistribution. Labour laws, in terms of a minimum wage and safety and employment legislation, are barely mentioned, except in relation to the states' roles in deregulation. No strategies mention children's rights, and other vulnerable groups receive little attention (again, Marshall and Woodroffe 2001 : 22). Nor is income redistribution mentioned, despite the Bank's own earlier acknowledgment that 'the greater the improvement in income inequality over time, the greater the impact of growth on poverty reduction' (World Bank 1996 : 46), which is also reiterated on the current Bank PRSP website. Marshall and Woodroffe go on to comment in detail on the likely negative consequences for the poor not just of user fees but of the other detail of PRSP policies. They are able to do so because, in contrast to claims for 'innovative' organizational (or institutional?) learning on the part of the Bank, PRSP policies so closely resemble those of SAPs. If there is any difference it is that PRSPs extended privatization further—into public sector essential services— than was the case with SAPs; and that national economies are deliberately further exposed to global markets than had previously been the case.

Moving to Comprehensive Development Frameworks (CDFs), given there is little CDF content currently in the public domain, the focus can be on only the mechanics of and plans for the CDF process. Cammack (2002) addresses the 'hard' dimension of the CDF matrix alone but, despite this methodological difference and a classical Marxist philosophical and political position not shared by the WDM, his analysis of CDFs parallels that of the WDM on PRSPs: namely that the rhetoric of ownership and the managerialist practices of conditional participation conceal and facilitate a neo-liberal agenda.

The CDF is absolutely rigid in the set of fundamental macroeconomic disciplines it imposes. It prescribes on top of these a range of economic and social policies without parallel in their scope and in the depth and intensity of intervention they represent in the affairs of supposedly sovereign states. Presented as a vehicle for incorporating social and structural policies into an agenda previously dominated by macroeconomic policy alone, it is in fact a means of *shaping* social and structural policies so that they reinforce and extend macroeconomic discipline, and *subordinating* them to imperatives of capitalist accumulation. (2002 : 50)

Cammack goes on to summarize Bank/IMF plans for the extension of the CDF/PRSP framework to middle-income countries, concluding that it has be 'trialed with the most heavily indebted countries, prior to being extended to the remaining clients of the Bank and the Fund as a generalized means of intervention in economic and social policy and political governance'. For Cammack, the Bank, via the CDF/PRSP initiative and matrix, is becoming the 'mother of all governments' (all quotes 2002 : 50). In so doing, it appears to be using the mother of all managements.

Discussion and Conclusion

The preceding sections have set out the nature of the similarity and simultaneous difference between DAM and 'management'—institutionally, conceptually and in practice. They have demonstrated how this paradoxical mix results in a version of managerialism that absorbs and applies the ideas of organizational change management but seeks to change not organizations but Third World nation-states, and does so to establish a particular, neo-liberal political economic order. This statement is sweeping, yet I believe it is accurate. Nonetheless, I accept some nuance and detail are lost in producing this big picture; and there may be criticisms that ostensibly arise as a consequence. Two of these can be anticipated before the implications of my analysis are explored for the various versions of management that have appeared in this article.

Anticipating Criticism

First, if the World Bank is taken as a case study of DAM, there is the possibility of the usual question of generalizing from cases. The Bank is not the only institution through which DAM is operationalized, and other development agencies might have agendas that allow for a DAM that is different in process and output. There are, however, no such agencies of remotely comparable significance; moreover, the Bank's policy of sub- and sub-sub-contracting its work directly and via other donors means that apparently independent agencies are drawn within the Bank's sphere of influence. This is as true of academic institutions where DAM is taught, which rely on development agency payment of student fees and commissioned research and consultancy income, as it is of other NGOs. Also, the World Bank has been selected not as a representative case study but precisely because it is the World Bank, with power that derives from that status.

This leads to a second potential criticism, that to accept the World Bank as a centre of global power is to reinforce that power. It might be argued that the World Bank's political position is not as unprecarious or unchallenged as the previous section implies. There is also difference and debate within the Bank— it is not a homogeneous organization (see Kanbur 2001; Wade 2001, on the debate on income redistribution). Bank agendas are challenged and negotiated by First World governments and civil society organizations. Some Third World states, which are not homogenous, reified entities either (so perhaps ruling élites is more accurate), have also historically subverted Bank agendas, for social as well as individual gain (see Storey 2000). By the World Bank's own account, things are not going absolutely smoothly in the implementation of CDFs/PRSPs; for example, new national governments have not automatically accepted their predecessors' CDF/PRSP commitments. (The Bank response is to include opposition parties in the participatory process, making the unitarist assumption that consensus is possible and natural; CDF Secretariat 2001). Kothari's (2001) Foucauldian analysis of the dynamics of power in participatory development points to a need to understand its micro circulations and manifestations as well as its national and institutional operation, and again to recognize the opportunities for subversion therein.

It has to be accepted, in the face of all this, that the terrain is contested; but it is still terrain of the Bank's choosing. In the end, the outcomes of the CDF/PRSP processes are much as the Bank would want; or, if we acknowledge how debate within the Bank plays out, as the victorious anti-redistribution neo-liberals in the Bank would want (again, see Kanbur 2001; Wade 2001). Participatory processes may open up some space for resistance and for reshaping Bank strategy; yet at the same time the imbalance of power relations means that this occurs only within First World boundaries, which proscribe genuinely empowering options. One such would be unconditional debt relief: as we have seen, nations are still paying back huge proportions of GNP to First World creditors, which the Bank is using to leverage 'management' practices that substitute for government and politics to result in neo-liberal policy change.

International Management, DAM and 'Management'

This article has tried to demonstrate how this leveraging has been aided by the unspoken differentiation of DAM from 'management', where the former tries to engineer the neo-liberal modernization of nation-states while simultaneously using and cloaking itself in 'management' language and practices. This is not good new for the various versions of management that this article has covered, namely international management, DAM and 'management'. It also has implications for the state of critical management studies.

Briefly, for international management, Wong-MingJi and Mir's finding that it has ignored the Third World is even more problematic for its disciplinary claims to authority, given the extent to which 'management' does pervade the Third World within DAM. For DAM, its explicit and actioned desire to intervene on the side of the poor and the oppressed clearly has not precluded its sustaining, through co-optation or choice, supposedly 'pro-poor' interventions that have the opposite effect. Moreover, a commitment to participation and empowerment has not stopped, but facilitated, this. Saving DAM might begin, therefore, by stipulating which of the contested versions of development (which hitherto have only been acknowledged) it will and will not engage with. Second, the potential for manipulation and co-optation in 'participation' and 'empowerment' noted within CMS should be acknowledged, and might form the basis for a move towards a critical development management.

Critical Management and Development

In that it has sought to further reveal management as a political rather than a technocratic instrument, this article might be located within CMS; and Alvesson and Willmott's discussion of CMS offers DAM the possibility of more than critique in at least two cases. First, in relation to a specific aspect of DAM practice, they set out a version of action learning—critical action learning—that goes beyond the version appropriated by the World Bank. Critical action learning deliberately sets out to enable learners to confront social and political phenomena (in this context, it might be hoped, international financial institutions and their favoured ideologies) posing as 'givens'.

More profound, perhaps, is their proposition of a version of management grounded in Critical Theory, which, among many, many things, explores the opportunities for a genuinely emancipatory management, not 'a gift to be bestowed' through managerialist empowerment but rather 'an existentially painful process of confronting and overcoming socially and psychologically unnecessary restrictions'. But none of this is unproblematic.

Not least, the idea of a Critical DAM assumes that the idea of development in itself is worth preserving. As CMS is to management, so a range of critics— sometimes collectivized as 'post-development' thinkers but heterogeneous and conflicting in outlook—identify the development paradigm as intellectually and practically problematic, if not bankrupt (see, for example, Escobar 1995b, and others in Crush 1995; Rahnema and Bawtree 1997; and Williams 2000). The development paradigm and/or the development discourse (distinctions between the two not being clearly drawn) are seen as an interweaving body of knowledge and practice that enable the management (in the most general sense) of the Third World. Paradigm or discourse, the idea of development provides a false logic to and legitimation of processes such as, *inter alia*, the infliction of debt and of structural adjustment. Ironically, these analyses draw on much the same social theory that one finds in CMS, for example Foucault in the case of Ferguson (1990), whose critique, like that of CMS, is of the idea of a technocratic neutrality. In his analysis of the activities of international development agencies in Lesotho, Ferguson describes their operation as a technocratic 'anti-politics machine'. He notes that, 'by uncompromisingly reducing poverty to a technical problem, and by promising technical solutions to the sufferings of the powerless, and oppressed people, the hegemonic problematic of "development" is the principal means through which the question of poverty is de-politicized' (1990 : 256).

As the argument of this article leads one to expect, despite the commonalities of theory and analysis, these considerations of management, on the one hand, and development, on the other, have barely touched. One exception is Banerjee (2000), who has used postdevelopment and postcolonialist theorizing to reveal the exploitative nature of a stakeholderism and to critique the postmodernist tendency within CMS. Agreeing with Radhakrishnan (1996), Banerjee points to the Eurocentrism of postmodernism in the assumptions it makes about the global universality of its ontology and epistemology and its exclusionary consequences for those in struggle with the forces of self-proclaimed modernization in the Third World.

The other seriously critical and reflexive attempt to consider the relation between CMS and some aspects of development is in Parker (2002). Parker is possibly within the bounds of CMS as some would define it, in that he seeks to challenge the hegemony of managerialism. Yet, as he recognizes, this boundary is ill defined, moving and contested; and he also is concerned to critique CMS itself, and so can be situated outside it. Either way, what Parker sees is non-engagement: part of his critique is of CMS's failure to connect, in its theorizing or its practices, with anti-corporate writing and protest, and, *inter alia*, its opposition to the World Bank, the IMF, the WTO and so on. Parker also recognizes explicitly that these bodies have contributed to the impoverishment of the Third World and institutionalized a neocolonial dependency relationship. Certainly this article supports Parker's view of an emerging global managerial class, spreading with missionary zeal the message that 'the market is now king and management its representative on earth' (2002 : 184). But it also suggests that CMS's non-engagement is all the more problematic given the extent to which the Word Bank et al. are using management, which is what CMS exists to critique.

Banerjee and Parker aside, then, that parts of the world are deemed to yet require modernization, that modernization interventions per se are theorized and take place, are largely ignored by CMS. This is not to accept the categorization of 'requiring modernization (or pre-modern)/modern/post-modern'. Instead it is to recognize that it has an existence (explicit or tacit) in the work of development agencies, in the separations and linkages between DAM and 'management', and in the construction of the latter and its critique in CMS. This article has shown that the failure to address this categorization, combined with a largely exclusive focus on organization as unit of analysis, means that the role of 'management' (as appropriated by DAM, exemplified above by action learning) and of management in the broader sense of the introduction (i.e. encompassing both 'management and DAM') as an instrument of attempted national, neo-liberal modernization is lost. Once this is acknowledged, management's engagement with international public institutions and, through them, Third World nations might usefully be reassessed as more than public sector mimesis of the private and a symptom of market extension. This article demonstrates that it is also complicit in a global project to create the institutional circumstances that enable that extension. In so doing, it creates more opportunities for itself, as the management practices of the World Bank demonstrate.

Missing from any analysis of management thus far, then, is recognition of its specific role as a global, institutional (more than organizational), modernizing change agent. The change could ultimately be seen to be in the cause of Hardt and Negri's (2000) de-nationed Empire, or de-nationed capital (Cammack 2002), or US business interests (Govan 2000). This article suggests a need to extend analyses of management to consider its role in interventions in the international (or, some would have it, global) political economy. Until this happens, both critique and, from CMS quarters, proposals for emancipation can be only partial, primarily focusing as they do on the micro, organizational and sub-organizational level of analysis. Again, this concurs with Parker; but where I diverge is on organization. Parker is *against management* (the title of his book) but *for organization* (the title of its final chapter, 2002 : 182). Here, organization, or at least its prioritization, is also problematic. It is perhaps stating the too obvious, but nonetheless, for all the supposed difference between MOS paradigms, and now discourses, the debates on (in)commensurability and the role of CMS, one transcendent, common factor is taken for granted. To go back to the start of this article, organization is privileged as the most important category of social activity and arrangement, and those arrangements and activities are idealized accordingly. That they might be better understood as, for example, institutions, nation-states or societies is ignored. So, as a result, is the managing of the Third World.

Notes

1. The 16 journals and the years of their first issue are: *Academy of Management Journal* (1958); *Academy of Management Review* (1976); *Administrative Science Quarterly* (1956); *California Management Review* (1958); *International Studies of Management and Organization* (1971); *Journal of International Business Studies* (1969); *Journal of Business Studies* (1980); *Journal of General Management* (1974); *Journal of Management* (1965); *Journal of Management Studies* (1961); *Long Range Planning* (1968); *Management International Review* (1961); *Management Science* (1954); *Organization Studies* (1980); *Sloan Management Review* (1960); *Strategic Management Journal* (1980) (Wong-MingJi and Mir 1997 : 344–5).

2. All statements are from the journals' aims, 2001 volumes.

3. The use of the word 'institution' by management specialists who might normally have chosen 'organization' is often, as here, an indicator of the switch between 'management' and DAM taking place. Institutions (some of which might also be organizations, although not all are) are distinctive because they have a particular, often managerially unacknowledged and possibly contested, societal role (Cooke 1998).

References

Alvesson, M. and Willmott, H. (1996). *Making Sense of Management*. London: Sage.

Banerjee, S. B. (2000). 'Whose Land Is It Anyway? National Interest, Indigenous Stakeholders and Colonial Discourses', *Organization and Environment*, 13(1): 3–38.

Bernstein, H. (1990). 'Agricultural "Modernisation" and the Era of Structural Adjustment: Observations on SubSaharan Africa', *Journal of Peasant Studies*, 18(1): 3–35.

Blunt, P., Jones, M. and Richards, D. (1992). *Managing Organizations in Africa*. Berlin: De Gruyter.

Bond, P. (2000). *Elite Transition: From Apartheid to Neoliberalism in South Africa*. Scottsville: University of Natal Press.

Bill Cooke

Bretton Woods Project (2001). *Background to the issues*, http://www. brettonwoodsproject.org/about/background.htm, accessed 2 October 2001.

Brinkerhoff, D. (2000). 'Democratic Governance and Sectoral Policy Reform: Tracing Linkages and Exploring Synergies', *World Development* 28(4): 601–16.

Brinkerhoff, D. and Coston, J. (1999). 'International Development Management in a Globalized World', *Public Administration Review*, 59(4): 346–61.

Brinkerhoff, D. and Goldsmith, A. (2001). *Macroeconomic Policy, PRSPs and Participation, Action Learning Program on Participatory Processes for Poverty Reduction Strategies*, Washington DC: World Bank; http://www.worldbank.org/participation/web/webfiles/macrosynthesis.htm, accessed 20 November 2001.

Burrell, G. and Morgan, G. (1979). *Sociological Paradigms and Organizational Analysis*. London: Heinemann.

Cammack, P. (2002). 'The Mother of All Governments: The World Bank's Matrix for Global Governance', in R. Wilkinson and S. Hughes (eds), *Global Governance: Critical Perspectives*. London: Routledge, pp. 36–53.

CDF Secretariat (2001). *Comprehensive Development Framework: Meeting the Promise? Early Experience and Emerging Issues*. Washington DC: World Bank, 17 September.

CDSC (2000). *Development Studies in Britain. A Select Course Guide 1999/2000*. Manchester: Conference of Directors of Special Courses.

Chambers, R. (1997). *Whose Reality Counts? Putting the First Last*. London: IT Publications.

Chossudovsky, M. (1997). *The Globalization of Poverty.* Penang: Third World Network.

Clegg, S. (1990). *Modern Organizations*. London: Sage.

Cooke, B. (1997). 'The Deceptive Illusion of Multi-Paradigm Development Practice', *Public Administration and Development*, 17(5): 479–86.

—— (1998). 'The Theory of Institutional and Organization Development', IDPM Discussion Paper 52, IDPM: University of Manchester.

—— (1999). 'Writing the Left out of Management Theory: The Historiography of the Management of Change', *Organization*, 6(1): 81–105.

—— (2001a). 'From Colonial Administration to Development Management', paper presented at US Academy of Management, Washington DC, August.

—— (2001b). 'The Social Psychological Limits of Participation', in B. Cooke and U. Kothari (eds), *Participation: The New Tyranny?* London: Zed Books.

—— (2003). 'A New Continuity with Colonial Administration: Participation in Development Management', *Third World Quarterly*, 24(1).

Cooke, B. and Kothari, U. (2001). 'The Case for Participation as Tyranny', in B. Cooke and U. Kothari (eds), *Participation: The New Tyranny?* London: Zed Books.

Cornia, G. A., Jolly, R. and Stewart, F. (eds) (1987). *Adjustment with a Human Face Volume 1: Protecting the Vulnerable and Promoting Growth*. Oxford: Oxford University Press.

Crush, J. (ed.) (1995). *Power of Development*. London: Routledge.

Denny, C. and Elliott, L. (2000). 'Hand to Mouth in the Clinics the West Forgot', *The Guardian*, 18 April, p. 29.

Eades, Deborah, (ed.) (2000). *Development and Management*. Oxford: Oxfam.

Elson, D. (1991). 'From Survival Strategies to Transformational Strategies: Women's Needs and Structural Adjustment', in L. Beneria and S. Feldman (eds), *Economic Crises, Household Strategies and Women's Work*. Boulder, CO: Westview Press.

Escobar, A. (1995a). ' "Living" in Cyberia', *Organization*, 2(3/4): 533–7.

—— (1995b). 'Imagining a Post-Development Era', in Crush, J. (ed.), *Power of Development*. London: Routledge.

Esman, M. (1991). *Managerial Dimensions of Development, Perspectives and Strategies*. West Hartford, CT: Kumarian.

Eyben, R. (2000). 'Development and Anthropology: A View from Inside the Agency', *Critique of Anthropology*, 20(1): 7–14.

Ferguson, A. (1996). 'Bridge Identity Politics: An Integrative Feminist Ethics of International Development', *Organization*, 3(4): 571–87.

Ferguson, J. (1990). *The Anti-Politics Machine: 'Development' Depoliticization and Bureaucratic State Power in Lesotho*. Cambridge: Cambridge University Press.

Fotopoulos, T. (2001). 'The Myth of Postmodernity', *Democracy and Nature*, 7(1): 27–76.

George, S. and Sabelli, F. (1994) *Faith and Credit: The World Bank's Secular Empire*. London: Penguin.

Gergen, K. (1995). 'Global Organization: From Imperialism to Ethical Vision', *Organization*, 2(2/4): 519–32.

Govan, P. (2000). *The Global Gamble: Washington's Faustian Bid for World Dominance*. London: Verso.

Grey, C. (1999). ' "We Are All Managers Now"; We Always Were: On the Development and Demise of Management', *Journal of Management Studies*, 36(5): 561–85.

Grey, C. and Fournier, V. (2000). 'At the Critical Moment: Conditions and Prospects for Critical Management Studies', *Human Relations*, 53(1): 7–32.

Hanlon, J. (1999). 'Take the Hit', *New Internationalist*, 212, May: 1–4.

Hardt, M. and Negri, A. (2000). *Empire*. Cambridge MA: Harvard University Press.

Hirschmann, D. (1999). 'Development Management versus Third World Bureaucracies: A Brief History of Conflicting Interests', *Development and Change*, 30: 287–305.

Holvino, E. (1996). 'Reading Organization Development from the Margins: The Outsider Within', *Organization*, 3(4): 520–33.

IDA/IMF (International Development Association/International Monetary Fund) (1999). 'Poverty Reduction Strategy Papers: Operational Issues', mimeo, 10 December.

Kanbur, R. (2001). 'Economic Policy, Distribution and Poverty: The Nature of Disagreements', *World Development*, 29(6): 1083–94.

Kiggundu, M. (1989). *Managing Organizations in Developing Countries: An Operational and Strategic Approach*. Hartford CT: Kumarian.

Kothari, U. (2001). 'Power, Knowledge and Social Control in Participatory Development', in B. Cooke and U. Kothari (eds), *Participation: The New Tyranny?* London: Zed Books.

Kunda, G. (1992). *Engineering Culture. Control and Commitment in a High-Tech Corporation*. Philadelphia PA: Temple University Press.

Luke, D. (1986). 'Trends in Development Administration: The Continuing Challenge to the Efficacy of the Post-Colonial State in the Third World', *Public Administration and Development*, 6(1): 73–85.

Marshall, A. with Woodroffe, J. (2001). *Policies to Roll Back the State and Privatise? Poverty Reduction Strategy Papers Investigated*. London: World Development Movement.

Max, J. (1990). *The Development of Local Government in Tanzania*. Dar es Salaam: Educational Publishers and Distributors.

Morgan, O. (2000). 'New Role for the UN: McKinsey for the Developing Nations', *The Observer*, 27 February, Business Section, p. 5.

Parker, M. (2002). *Against Management*. Cambridge: Polity.

Radhakrishnan, R. (1996). *Diasporic Mediations*. Minneapolis, MN: University of Minnesota Press.

Rahnema, M. and Bawtree, V. (1997). *The Post-Development Reader*. London: Zed Books.

Ransom, D. (1999). 'The Dictatorship of Debt', *New Internationalist*, 212, May: 1–4.

Saithe, V. (1985). 'How to Decipher and Change Corporate Culture', in R. H. Kilmann, M. J. Saxton and R. G. Serpa (eds), *Gaining Control of Corporate Culture*. San Francisco: Jossey Bass.

Schaffer, B. (1973). *The Administrative Factor*. London: Frank Cass.

Schein, E. H. (1987). *Process Consultation Volume 2: Lessons for Consultants and Managers*. Reading MA: Addison Wesley.

Storey, A. (2000). 'The World Bank, Neoliberalism and Power: Discourse Analysis and Implications for Campaigners', *Development in Practice*, 3/4, August: 361–70.

Swerdlow, I. (1975). *The Public Administration of Economic Development*. New York: Praeger.

Thomas, A. (1996). 'What Is Development Management', *Journal of International Development* 8(1): 95–110.

—— (2000). 'What Makes Good Development Management', in T. Wallace (ed.), *Development and Management*. Oxford: Oxfam GB.

Wade, R. H. (2001). 'Making the World Development Report 2000: Attacking Poverty', *World Development*, 29(8): 1435–41.

Williams, G. (2000). 'Studying Development and Explaining Policies', Keynote Address to the Finnish Society for Development Studies, 4 February.

Willmott, H. (1993). 'Strength Is Ignorance; Slavery Is Freedom: Managing Culture in Modern Organizations', *Journal of Management Studies*, 30(4): 515–52.

Wong-MingJi, D. and Mir, A. (1997). 'How International Is International Management?', in P. Prasad, A. Mills, M. Elmes and A. Prasad (eds) *Managing the Organizational Melting Pot: Dilemmas of Workplace Diversity*. Thousand Oaks, CA: Sage, pp. 340–66.

Wolfensohn, J. (1999). 'A Proposal for a Comprehensive Development Framework', Memo to the Board, Management and Staff of the World Bank Group. Washington DC, World Bank, 21 January.

World Bank (1996). *Poverty Reduction and World Bank: Progress and Challenges in the 1990s*. Washington DC: World Bank.

—— (2000). *Comprehensive Development Framework Country Experience March 1999—July 2000*. Washington DC: World Bank.

—— (2001a). *About Us: What We Do*, http://www.worldbank.org/about/whatwedo, accessed 2 October 2001.

—— (2001b). *Background and Overview of the Comprehensive Development Framework*, http://www.worldbank.org/cdf/overview.htm, accessed 2 October 2001.

—— (2001c). *Facing up to New Challenges in the Way We Work. Applying the Principles of the CDF*, http://www.worldbank.org/cdf/story4.htm, accessed 2 October 2001.

12

The Making of the Corporate Acolyte: Some Thoughts on Charismatic Leadership and the Reality of Organizational Commitment

Heather Hopfl

He enters the room, assured and confident. A wry smile plays on his lips. He casts an indulgent eye over his audience. They in turn stop their chatter and take their measure of the man. This after-dinner speech has been well publicized. Most of those present are there because they fear the consequences of being absent, but they have not articulated this thought. The man is middle-aged. He is not handsome but, at the same time, he is not unattractive. His clothes are expensive and conservative: they make a statement. The man stands before them, examines his manicured nails and then, with the same perceptive eye, scrutinizes the menage of middle management gathered to hear him. The audience shift warily in their seats. Mentally, they come to attention. The man draws up a bar stool. He sits at right-angles to the rows of seats. He folds his arms. He is about to begin.

The scene which is about to unfold is not unfamiliar to those who attend management training courses with large organizations. What is about to take place is the reading of the corporate gospel, the 'Hear, O Israel', the *sursum corda*. What we are about to hear is how much the company loves, cherishes and needs these poor unworthy servants; how, if they will only give their heart, soul and mind to the company, they can take their place with the chosen ones, the elect. The language is thick with quasi-religious imagery, eclectic and all-embracing. It speaks to the Humanist, to the Christian, to the Jew, to the

Muslim. It is all-purpose, higher order, well practised. It is unashamedly sentimental. It offers fear and comfort in equal measure. No reasonable person could object to these platitudes. If the company be for us, who can be against us?

So, hearts are lifted, the symbolic response is made—a metaphorical *et cum spiritu tuo*—and there is rapturous applause. The man stands, arms uplifted, in the gesture of the priest. The offering is made. He is transfigured. He is the multiplicity of their hopes and aspirations held in the oneness of his being. Blessed are the meek for they shall inherit the earth.

In recent years, I have seen this performance enacted on numerous occasions. The management prophet descends from Mount Sinai, either as a missionary from the Board Room or a bought-in corporate evangelist. His message is simple. It is the Gospel of the Sunday School and it says, 'God Lives. He Loves You. If you want to enjoy his favours, he must be obeyed.' Like the missionaries of the Christian church, he seeks conversion, a common credo, allegiance to a declared mission statement. He comes like an angel of light. And so he is, for he is Lucifer come to offer Faust his contract.

Missions and Meanings

I make no apology for the introduction to this article, I have tried to convey the flavour of this particular style of charismatic leadership. 'The language of charisma and the expectations for it are around us everywhere and every day' (Butterfield 1988 : 71). More often than not, it requires a high degree of style and skill. House expresses this very well when he asserts that charismatic leaders are able to induce 'similarity of followers' beliefs to those of the leader, unquestioning acceptance of the leader,... affection,... obedience,... identification with and emulation of the leader, emotional involvement of the follower in the mission, heightened goals of the follower...' (House 1977 : 191).

Indeed, this is observably the case with the specific range of influence of the performance. However, beyond this there is a difficulty. One of the major problems associated with the theory of leadership is the guiding assumption that whilst there may be a plurality of interpretations available to leaders, subordinates and others, it is the prerogative of leaders to manage the meaning of events (Smith and Peterson 1988 : 126) and, therefore, by implication to frame the experiences of others. Indeed, it has been argued that the primary function of managers is to create and manage culture (Schein 1985 : 2). What this means in practice requires careful examination.

273

There is a wealth of literature on the subject of leadership in general (Bennis and Nanus 1985; Burns 1978; Kipnis 1976; Schein 1985; Smith and Peterson 1988) and on theories of leadership in particular (Blake and Mouton 1964; Fiedler 1967, 1972, 1978; House 1971, 1984, 1987, 1988; Stogdill 1948, 1974; Vroom and Yetton 1973; Yukl 1981; and others). There is a long tradition of research and interest in charismatic leadership from Weber to Waterman (Weber 1947; Waterman 1987) with a recent revival of interest in the relationship between charismatic leadership and organizational culture (Avolio and Bass 1988; Boal and Bryson 1988; Broussine and Guerrier, 1985; House 1987; Pfeffer 1981; Pondy 1978). Schein has put forward some conceptual mechanisms for understanding the relationship between a leader's influence and the organizational culture (Schein 1985). Pondy (*op. cit.*) is specific that the capacity of leaders to make sense of organizational activities and make them meaningful through language to a large number of people gives leaders considerable leverage. This article is not concerned with the elusive nature of charisma or the exercise of power but, rather, with their combined implications. Consequently, what is at issue here is what is meant by 'the management of meaning' (Smith and Peterson *op. cit.*) by the organization for its individual members. Graham (1988 : 73) points out that the emphasis on attempts to understand leader behaviour at the expense of follower behaviour rests on a 'romantic simplification' of reality which she argues threatens to impoverish rather than enrich our understanding of organizations. This article looks at those people, usually in middle management, who are rewarded according to their role performance and who are called to serve and reinforce the corporate culture, its acolytes. Therefore, it is necessary to give some attention to the nature of this relationship, to consider how it is manifested and demonstrated in commitment or apparent commitment to the organization.

The subject of organizational commitment has received a considerable amount of attention in the social science and management literature of recent years. The main focus of much of this research has been on the ways in which commitment can be used in relation to theories of motivation and job satisfaction as an indicator or predictor of operational variables such as labour turnover (Mowday et al. 1982). Reichers (1985) has suggested abandoning the term in favour of identifying a set of 'commitment foci', Barling et al. (1990) argue that job satisfaction, organizational climate and job involvement are significant predictors of company commitment. Oliver (1990) offers empirical evidence to suggest that 'primary commitment targets are not . . . organizations *per se*, but rather the goals and values which they embody'. There have been empirical studies which attempt to identify the determinants of organizational commitment and its consequences (Griffin and Bateman 1986). Allen and Meyer (1990) concern themselves with the measurement of 'affective, continuance and normative commitment to the organization' in order to argue that future research may be able 'to identify commitment profiles that differentiate employees who are likely to remain with the organization and contribute positively to its effectiveness from those who are likely to remain but contribute little'. The difficulty with much of this research is that it treats the notion of commitment uncritically, that is, as unproblematic. The term commitment tends to be used to describe very different constructs, experiences, degrees of involvement and motivations. Moreover, despite the obvious affective dimensions of commitment, there is little or no attention to its emotional aspects as Hosking and Fineman (1990) point out in a more general comment on the widespread neglect of emotional processes in organizational research.

In broad terms, the literature on commitment, developing from Etzioni's early work on compliance, has considered calculative involvement with organizations and moral or attitudinal approaches (Amernic and Aranya 1983; Ferris and Aranya 1983). In contrast, this article adopts a social constructionist perspective (Berger and Luckmann 1971) and so takes its standpoint from 'a radical doubt in the taken-for-granted' world (Gergen 1985). It is addressed to the distinction between behaviour and experience and to the ways in which the individual gives meaning to the multiplicity of forms of experience that occur within one individual conscious life (Merleau-Ponty 1962 : 423). Experience is always 'in the making', extending in new permutations of experience (Georgoudi and Rosnow 1984). New experience is accommodated by the interpretive schema (Abercrombie 1960) of the individual and has direction in the plurality of successive states of the self (Bergson 1913 : 142). The process by which this is achieved involves the assimilation of the newly encountered experience by its comparison with some previously learned schema, a shaping of difference into recognizable form, a reduction of ambiguity: a process which Jaynes has termed 'conciliation' (Jaynes 1976 : 65). It is a drawing together of multiple possible states into an individual, personal unity (Shotter 1984 : 45). This is the habitual mode of consciousness. The processing of multiple states and options reflects the fluidity of the subjective experience to permit new perceptions, disjunct states, ambiguities, and insights to offer novel interpretations, new constructions. The individual is able to assign meaning to experience within a unique matrix of personal meanings. What is at issue here is the extent to which the perception of meaning held by leader and led is a shared one. Anyone who has witnessed the type of 'Come to Jesus' (Waterman 1987 : 299) crusades described at the beginning of this article will be aware of the wide discrepancy between the apparent allegiance of the conference room or auditorium and the bar-room dissension which often follows. It is here that disjunct meaning structures are most apparent and where the reduction of ambiguity or 'conciliation' is attempted. In practice, the interpretive schema is able to select the particular combination of perceptual structures which direct the interpretation of the world. In this sense, the interpretative schema is unique, dynamic and continuous, in equilibrium between past and present as new perceptual options are added.

Multiple Meanings

We inhabit a world made up of multiple realities. This is a common everyday experience. There are any number of 'finite provinces of meaning' each with its own cognitive style and attitudinal consistency (Schutz 1973 : 227–31). These finite provinces of meaning appear as enclaves within paramount reality (Berger and Luckmann, 1971) characterized by specific meanings and modes of experience. This has important implications for the development of theories of charismatic leadership.

Boal and Bryson (1988) attempt a phenomenological and structural approach to charismatic leadership. They identify what they describe as 'visionary charismatic leaders', those gifted with extraordinary qualities, and what they term 'crisis produced leaders' who are found in extraordinary circumstances which produce charismatic effects. According to Boal and Bryson (1988), what these two leadership styles have in common is the ability to create 'a phenomenologically valid' world for their followers. In this context, validity rests on the creation of a different world view or interpretive schema that is emotionally and behaviourally real for the followers of such leaders. This valuable contribution to leadership theory offers a way of understanding how leaders can control and manipulate the ways in which their followers make sense of their world, that is, can offer prospective coherence in return for commitment to a common understanding of the present. Clearly, charismatic leaders can produce powerful correspondence between behaviour and experience. However, the significance that can be attached to such correspondence and the extent to which it can be sustained in temporal terms is problematical. Boal and Bryson (1988) suggest that it is possible to consider such congruence in terms of internal and external validity, a consistency between inner states, behaviour and behavioural consequences. However, this presents a rather sanitary solution. Disjunct, conflicting, and contradictory states can happily co-exist within their own 'finite province of meaning'. Arguably, prolonged correspondence between the leader and the led is symptomatic of a pathological relationship, of delusion. In other words, complicity in the construction of meaning as guided by the corporate visionary may require a psychological maladjustment. Personal coherence as rooted in the existential self may be threatened by the powerful definition of reality offered by the organization and the discontinuity of meaning between self and situation which this creates.

That both negative and positive dimensions exist in the relationship between leaders and the led is to be expected. The co-existence of commitment, absence of commitment, performance activities, fantasies and an entire repertoire of behaviour mediating between the organization and the individual is the desirable state of affairs. The individual is a 'stance-taking entity' occupying a position between identification with the organization and opposition to it. Goffman (1968) asserts that total commitment requires a kind of selflessness and that it is in the contrary pull that the self emerges. Commitment to an organization is likely to be characterized by a plurality of states which may vary in strength and duration.

Cooper (1983) holds that, at an ontological level, the self knows itself only through the Other, that the nature of Otherness embodies the idea of reversibility. This reversibility involves a dialectic between disjunction and conjunction; alienation and integration. On this basis, movement toward and away from organizational commitment, toward acceptance of the synthesis presented, rejection of that synthesis, towards involvement, towards alienation, towards mere performance, towards selfhood, towards surrender of self can be viewed as a dialectical relationship which defines reality(ies) producing an accretion of meaning within the self such that movement is always 'towards' even when it is 'away from'. What is at issue here is the nature of control. It is important to make a distinction between those experiences which are under control of the self and those which are not. Work imposes a distinction between experiences which the individual can control and those which require 'management' to meet the demands of another.

The point is that whether or not an experience is regarded as part of the self, as defined by Rogers (1951), is determined by whether or not it is perceived to be within the control of the self (Rogers 1951 : section 16). Experiences which are not under the control of the self are experienced as being apart from the self. When employees are exhorted to greater commitment to the organization, they are effectively required to pledge more of themselves to the company than they would normally be required to commit to a marriage. The organization imposes its own specific and internally consistent cognitive styles and attitudinal constellations. There is a specific tension of consciousness which binds the individual to the life-world of work. To increase organizational commitment involves creating a greater tension and, by implication, places a strain on the other life-worlds in which there is partial inclusion.

Yet partial inclusion in multiple life-worlds does not necessary mean that each imposes partial demands (Luckmann 1970). There are conflicts of obligation and as the demands of the organization increase, the amount of time required to service and maintain oneself for work—resting, sleeping, eating, washing and household chores—means that increasing amounts of time become centred on the world of work (de Grazia 1962 : 246). The enclaves of time left may thus appear so insignificant that it is easier to marginalize them in order to avoid the threat of acknowledging them.

The Bribe of Bread

In Shaw's play, *Major Barbara*, Andrew Undershaft, the arms manufacturer, rebukes his Salvation Army daughter, Major Barbara, for achieving the conversion of souls with a Bible in one hand a loaf of bread in the other. Corporate conversion involves a similar offer. Some theorists (Amernic and Aranya 1983; Griffin and Bateman 1986) distinguish between those who comply with the organization in order to obtain specific, extrinsic rewards, that is, have a calculative orientation and those who identify with the organization through a moral involvement. Both of these definitions implicitly acknowledge an inextricable relationship between corporate commitment (or its semblance in performance) and the satisfaction of personal needs. A calculative involvement is essentially related to the future and so involves an instrumental view of the present. The apparently purposive nature of organizations reinforces this directional activity. Yet, planning and decision-making are a kind of 'make believe' (Cooper and Fox 1990 : 597) which arises from the indeterminate nature of the world. Means and ends become inseparable polythetic intents. Organizations may confer power, status, wealth; may meet needs for affiliation and belonging; may bolster self-esteem—yet, at a fundamental level, the issue of control, of order and ordering, it not resolved. The play of power is intrinsic to this process of order and giving orders. The relationship is characterized by a latency which holds within it the 'indestructible reversing of a command', 'a sting' (Cooper 1983 : 214). Cooper cites Canetti (1962) as saying, 'What spurs men on to achievement is the deep urge to be rid of the commands once laid on them'.

Hence, the rewards a company can offer, while they undoubtedly attach meaning to behaviour and experience, are in themselves insufficient to sustain individual coherence, particularly when considered in temporal terms. Here the necessary ambivalence of performance, the immediate and the prospective, bound in the moment of participation, acknowledges the discontinuity which is, in the day-to-day, concealed by acceptance. At a recent management development course for middle management where the theme was 'Your Future with the Company' two of the three senior managers who were due to speak on the first day were, in effect, fired the day before the course. Apart from the problem it gave the course organizers, the contradictory messages it sent to the participants produced some remarkable effects. Many managers present found it difficult to sustain a coherent view of the company's attitude to them or theirs to the company. The fact that the men who had been dismissed were both popular and not seen to be ineffective in their work caused confusion and cynicism. The participants could not sustain their definitions of reality in the face of two conflicting versions of their corporate destinies.

Under such circumstances, commitment requires a considerable leap of faith; the suspension of disbelief. Converts are received *ex haeresi*. The promise is liberation through submission. The reality is rather different. Long-term prisoners will often initiate a break with their families and refuse letters or visits because they cannot sustain two separate realities (Hopkins 1982). Similarly, candidates for the corporate priesthood must renounce or, at least, subordinate those life-worlds which are incompatible with their vocation. Moments of doubt or questioning are seen as 'back-sliding'. The novice masters/mistresses must offer and sustain a vision. This is one of the most important functions of charismatic leadership: the manufacture and maintenance of meaning. Skilful leadership is able to 'achieve a social order in which certain kinds of changes are seen to make sense' (Hosking and Morley 1988 : 91). This requires exceptional powers of invention and make-believe in order to permit the organization, in its actors, to create and recreate each successive moment, to achieve a presentation and re-presentation of appearance—a brilliant *Vorstellung*.

The meaning which is offered as part of the corporate definition of reality, located as it is in an instrumental approach to the present, is both conflictual and powerfully seductive. The problem is that it cannot be exposed or seen for what it is until some dislocation of expectation occurs, as in the example given above. In part, this is because instrumentality frustrates any immediate meaning by 'making sense of' behaviour and experience via the promise of future rewards and coherence. Absence of meaning in the present induces a range of ego-defensive strategies. The individual may take 'flight from immediacy' by retreating into a world of daydreaming or fantasy or else take 'flight into immediacy' by engaging in a level of activity which is so frenetic that it precludes the possibility of confronting immediate experience: a compulsive busyness. In this way, the individual is protected from the realization that a sacrifice is being made or that one finite province of meaning has assumed the role of mediator of paramount reality. The difficulty here is the strength and coherence of the apparent meaning of attachment to a corporate philosophy and the range of inducements which reinforce it. However, such commitment leads to a level of engagement with the world where the need for reflexive action is minimized. The individual adopts a strategy to avoid confrontation with the realization that control has been surrendered to an apparently consummate objectivity. While the persona is left to engage at the interface between being and the world, at play, in performance in the corporate drama, the self (as in Rogers 1951) is left paralysed by multiple realities and conflicting options over which it can exercise only limited control. It is only when the power of the corporate definition of reality is diminished—by distance, or drink, or disaster—that the underlying anxieties, perplexities and conflicts become apparent.

The Mirage of Meaning

The necessary conciliation between the world of the corporate culture and the other multiple life-worlds which the individual inhabits is achieved by an act of self-deception. In order to minimize the impact on self-perception, contradictions are ignored or denied. There is a gap between meaning as objectively perceived and subjectively experienced. However, this becomes apparent only when issues of control, personal unity, and personal meaning are thrown into focus and confronted. It is only in breaches of the taken-for-granted by disjunct experience that the difference between individual capabilities and objective demands exposes disorientation, detachment, internal conflict and anxiety. These are the manifest symptoms of the discrepancy in subjective experience. While the organization is able to sustain the illusion of being the mediator of meaning, its rewards have considerable power. It is, perhaps, not surprising that the so-called 'mid-life crisis' is often described as a period of self-realization and disillusionment.

It is necessary to relate this back to charismatic leadership. One standpoint is that charisma is to do with the ability to exert influence over other people through the force of one's personality (Broussine and Guerrier 1985). Charismatic leaders at senior levels in organizations appear to have the power to offer a corporate vision and to define the prevailing meaning with the organization to which its members must give at least apparent consensual commitment. Of course, leaders themselves are subject to the same psychological contracts and self-deceptions as their followers. This opens a range of interesting issues to do with the relationship between power and consensus, but it is beyond the scope of this article to deal with it here (Bacharach and Lawler 1980; Kets de Vries 1990; Kipnis et al. 1981; Mangham 1985; Pfeffer 1981; Podsakoff and Schriesheim 1985). This article has been concerned with the implications for individuals in organizations of the power of the organization, personified in its leaders, to define and maintain meaning. It has been argued that the power of corporate culture is such that it appears to be impossible for those who wish to enter to have less than a total commitment. The occupation acquires the status of a vocation. A necessary conciliation takes place between conflicting life-worlds: anxieties and dissatisfactions within the life-world of work are only revealed by role-slips and disjunctions. The relationship between identification with an organization, the contrary rejection of the organization, and the shifting of involvement and commitment in mediating between these two positions is an important starting point for understanding organizational commitment. More attention needs to be given to those aspects of organization which normally appear self-evident and so are taken for granted. There is a need for a greater understanding of the rich and complex nature of the experience of work. An appreciation of the dynamic tensions in organizations and their oscillation between their purposive nature and ambivalence in their actors, provides an opportunity for seeing organizations 'in emergence' rather than as categories and appearances.

References

Abercrombie, M. L. J. (1960). *The Anatomy of Judgement*. Harmondsworth: Penguin.

Allen N. J. and Meyer, J. P. (1990). 'The measurement and antecedents of affective, continuance, and normative commitment to the organization'. *Journal of Occupational Psychology*, 63, 1–18.

Amernic, J. H. and Aranya, N. (1983). 'Organizational commitment: Testing two theories'. *Relations Industrielles*, 38, 319–41.

Avolio, B. and Bass, B. M. (1988). 'Charisma and beyond: Research findings on transformational and transactional leadership'. In Hunt, J. G. et al. (eds.), *Emerging Leadership Vistas*. Boston: Lexington, pp. 29–49.

Bacharach, S. B. and Lawler, E. J. (1980). *Power and Politics in Organizations*. San Francisco: Jossey-Bass.

Barling, J., Wade, B. and Fullagar, C. (1990). 'Predicting employee commitment to company and union: Divergent models'. *Journal of Occupational Psychology*, 63, 49–61.

Bennis, W. G. and Nanus, B. (1985). *Leaders: the Strategies for Taking Charge*. New York: Harper & Row.

Berger, P. and Luckmann, T. (1971). *The Social Construction of Reality*. Harmondsworth: Penguin.

Bergson, H. (1913). 'An introduction to metaphysics, (duration and intuition)', in Stuart, J. C. C. (ed.) (1964), *Problems of Space and Time*. New York: Macmillan.

Blake, R. R. and Mouton, J. S. (1964). *The Managerial Grid*. Houston: Gulf.

Boal, K. B. and Bryson, J. M. (1988). 'Charismatic leadership: a phenomenological and structural approach' in Hunt, J. G. et al., pp. 11–28.

Broussine, M. and Guerrier, Y. (1985). *Surviving as a Middle Manager*. London: Croom Helm.

Burns, J. M. (1978). *Leadership*. New York: Harper & Row.

Butterfield, D. A. (1988). *Welcome Back Charisma*. In Hunt, J. G. et al., pp. 67–72.

Canetti, E. (1962). *Crowds and Power*. London: Gollancz. Cited in Cooper (1983).

Cooper, R. (1983). 'The Other: A model of human structuring'. In Morgan, G. (ed.), *Beyond Method, Strategies for Social Research*. Beverly Hills: Sage, pp. 202–18.

Cooper, R. and Fox, S. (1990). 'The "texture" of organizing', *Journal of Management Studies*, 27, 6, 575–82.

de Grazia, S. (1962). *Of Time, Work and Leisure*. New York: Twentieth Century Fund.

Ferris, K. R. and Aranya, N. (1983). 'A comparison of two organizational commitment scales'. *Personnel Psychology*, 36, 87–9.

Fiedler, F. E. (1967). *A Contingency Theory of Leadership Effectiveness*. New York: McGraw-Hill.

—— (1972). 'Personality, motivational systems, and behaviour of high and low LPC persons'. *Human Relations*, 25, 391–412.

—— (1978). 'The contingency model and the dynamics of the leadership process', in Berkowitz, L. (ed.), *Advances in Experimental Social Psychology*, 11. New York: Academic Press, pp. 59–112.

Georgoudi, M. and Rosnow, R. (1984). 'Towards a contextualist understanding of social psychology', *Personality and Social Psychology Bulletin*, 11, 1, 5–22.

Gergen, K. J. (1985). 'The social constructionist movement in modern psychology'. *American Psychologist*, 40, 3, 266–75.

Goffman, E. (1968). *Asylums*. Harmondsworth: Penguin.

Graham, J. W. (1988). 'Transformational leadership: fostering follower autonomy, not automatic followership', in Hunt, J. G. et al., 73–9.

Griffin, R. W. and Bateman, T. S. (1986). 'Job satisfaction and organizational commitment', in Cooper, C. L. and Robertson, I. (eds), *International Review of Industrial and Organizational Psychology*. New York: Wiley, pp. 157–88.

Hopkins, H. J. (1982). *The Subjective Experience of Time*. Unpublished PhD thesis, University of Lancaster.

Hosking, D. M. and Fineman, S. (1990). 'Organising processes', *Journal of Management Studies*, 27, 6, 583–604.

Hosking, D. M. and Morley, I. (1988). 'The skills of leadership', in Hunt, J. G. et al. (eds.), 189–207.

House, R. J. (1971). 'A path-goal theory of leader effectiveness', *Administrative Science Quarterly*, 16, 321–38.

—— (1977). 'A 1976 theory of charismatic leadership', in Hunt, J. G. and Larson, L. L. (eds.), *Leadership: The Cutting Edge*. Carbondale Ill.: Southern Illinois University Press, pp. 189–207.

—— (1984). 'Power in organizations: a social psychological perspective', Unpublished paper, Faculty of Management, University of Toronto.

—— (1987). 'The "All things in moderation" leader', *Academy of Management Review*, 12, 164–9.

—— (1988). 'Power and personality in complex organizations', in Staw, B. M. (ed.), *Research in Organizational Behavior*, Vol. 10. Greenwich CT: JAI Press, 305–57.

Hunt, J. G., Baliga, B. R., Dachler, H. P. and Schriesheim, C. A. (eds.), (1988). *Emerging Leadership Vistas*. Boston : Lexington.

Jaynes, J. (1976). *The Origin of Consciousness in the Breakdown of the Bicameral Mind*. Boston: Houghton-Mifflin.

Kets de Vries, M. (1990). 'The organizational fool: Balancing a leader's hubris', *Human Relations*, 43, 8, 751–70.

Kipnis, D. (1976). *The Powerholders*. Chicago: University of Chicago Press.

Kipnis, D., Schmidt, K., Price, K. and Stitt, C. (1981). 'Why do I like thee: Is it your performance or my orders?' *Journal of Applied Psychology*, 66, 324–8.

Luckmann, T. (1970). 'The small life-worlds of modern man'. *Social Research*, 37, 580–96.

Mangham, I. L. (1985). *Power and Performance in Organizations*. Oxford: Blackwell.

Merleau-Ponty, M. (1962). *Phenomenology of Perception*. London: Routledge & Kegan Paul.

Mowday, R. T., Porter, L. W. and Steers, R. M. (1982). *Employee–Organization Linkages: The Psychology of Commitment, Absenteeism, and Turnover*. New York: Academic Press.

Oliver, N. (1990). 'Rewards, investments, alternatives and organizational commitment: Empirical evidence and theoretical development', *Journal of Occupational Psychology*, 63, 19–31.

Pfeffer, J. (1981). 'Management as symbolic action: The creation and maintenance of organizational paradigms', in Cummings, L. L. and Staw, B. M. (eds.), *Research in Organizational Behavior*, 3, Greenwich CT: JAI Press.

Podsakoff, P. M. and Schriesheim, C. A. (1985). 'Field studies of French and Raven's bases of power: Critique, reanalysis and suggestions for future research', *Psychological Bulletin*, 97, 387–411.

Pondy, L. R. (1978). 'Leadership is a language game', in McCall, M. W. Jr and Lombardo, M. M. (eds), *Leadership: Where Else Can We Go?* Durham NC: Duke University Press, cited in Smith and Peterson.

Reichers, A. E. (1985). 'A review and reconceptualization of organizational commitment', *Academy of Management Journal*, 10, 465–76.

Rogers, C. (1951). *A Theory of Personality and Behavior in Client-Centred Therapy*. Boston: Houghton-Mifflin.

Schein, E. H. (1980). *Organizational Psychology*. Englewood Cliffs, NJ: Prentice-Hall.

—— (1985). *Organizational Culture and Leadership: A Dynamic View*. San Francisco: Jossey-Bass.

Schutz, A. (1973). 'Multiple realities', in Douglas, M. (ed.), *Rules and Meanings*. Harmondsworth: Penguin, pp. 227–31.

Shotter, J. (1984). *Social Accountability and Selfhood*. Oxford: Blackwell.

Smith, P. B. and Peterson, M. F. (1988). *Leadership, Organizations and Culture*. London: Sage.

Stogdill, R. M. (1948). 'Personal factors associated with leadership: A survey of the literature', *Journal of Psychology*, 25, 35–71.

Stogdill, R. M. (1974). *Handbook of Leadership*. New York: Free Press.

Vroom, V. H. and Yetton, P. W. (1973). *Leadership and Decision Making*. Pittsburgh: University of Pittsburgh Press.

Waterman, R. H. (1987). *The Renewal Factor*. London: Bantam.

Weber, M. (1947). *The Theory of Economic and Social Organization* (first published 1921). New York: Free Press.

Yukl, G. (1981). *Leadership in Organizations*. Englewood Cliffs NJ: Prentice-Hall.

13 Sexuality at Work

Rosemary Pringle

Sex is like paperclips in the office: commonplace, useful, underestimated, ubiquitous. Hardly appreciated until it goes wrong, it is the cement in every working relationship. It has little to do with sweating bosses cuddling their secretaries behind closed doors—though lots of that goes on. It is more adult, more complicated, more of a weapon.

Brenda Jones, NT, December 1972

... women are constantly and inescapably constructed *as women*... Men are sustained at the centre of the stage precisely because they can be 'people' and do not have to represent their masculinity to themselves. They... can never be displaced from the centre until they can be forced to recognise themselves as men and to take responsibility for this.

Black and Coward, 1981: 85

If the boss–secretary relation is organized around sexuality and family imagery this seems to place it outside the modern bureaucratic structures that are a feature of all large organizations. The relationship is often conceptualized either as archaic or as marginal to the workings of bureaucracy 'proper'. It is argued here that, on the contrary, the boss—secretary relationship is the most visible aspect of a pattern of domination based on desire and sexuality. Far from being an exception, it vividly illustrates the workings of modern bureaucracies. Gender and sexuality are central not only in the boss–secretary relation but in *all* workplace power relations.

Two bodies of theory are important to the development of this argument. A variety of feminist analyses, particularly of sexual harassment, indicate the ubiquity of *coercive* sexual encounters in the workplace; and theorists such as Marcuse and Foucault have indicated, in their different ways, the connections between sexual *pleasure* and the operations of power. By contrast, most organization theory continues to treat sexuality and gender as marginal or incidental to the workplace. In doing so, however, it expresses a widely held view that while gender was central to 'traditional' social relations it has become outmoded in 'modern' society which is more concerned with 'personhood'. Since degendering is implicit in the modernist emphasis on rationality and in the development of liberal democratic institutions, it is important to start by considering the ways in which gender is suppressed in the main texts.

For Weber bureaucracy is progressive in that it breaks down the old patriarchal structures and removes the arbitrary power held by fathers and masters in traditional society. He distinguishes between traditionalism, which is patriarchal, and the rational–legal order of the modern world which promises the end of tyranny and despotism and the development of liberal democracy. All attempts to theorise bureaucracy have been carried out in the shadow of Weber's classical account. He still sets the terms of the dominant frameworks for studies of power and organizations. Although the limits of his theory have been clearly shown in more than half a century of organization studies, Weber's version retains a powerful ideological hold. People's views of how organizations actually do work and how they 'ought' to work are still filtered through Weber and the theory becomes, in some sense, a self-fulfilling prophecy.

Weber has been given a favourable reading by liberal feminists because he does appear to provide a basis for understanding the breakdown of patriarchal relations. Equal Employment Opportunity and Affirmative Action plans, for example, emphasise the importance of excluding 'private' considerations and insist on the impersonal application of rules. Secretaries, it is thought, should ignore or reject the sexual and familial images and focus on skills and career ladders. The implication here is that secretarial work should be 'rationalized', made to fit the bureaucratic pattern. In her broadly liberal feminist analysis, *Men and Women of the Corporation*, Rosabeth Moss Kanter denies that gender or sexuality have much explanatory potential. She observes that 'what look like sex differences may really be power differences' and that 'power wipes out sex' (1977 : 201–12). In this framework the problem for secretaries is that they lack power; they are caught up in an old-fashioned patriarchal relationship that is out of kilter with 'modern' business practices. The question then becomes how can individual secretaries remove themselves from these back-waters and place themselves on the management ladder? Kanter's very lucid analysis of the power structure is designed to help individuals articulate their positions and thereby improve their own manoeuvring for power.

It is not surprising that Weber should have had such influence for he is one of the great spokespersons of 'modernity'. Thinkers of his stature are not easily 'overturned'. Even theorists who take a critical stance, or who self-consciously define themselves as 'postmodern', find themselves returning to at least some of the 'modernist' assumptions. Kanter herself was explicitly rejecting the Weberian emphasis on the rationality and goal-directedness of bureaucracies, yet by playing down gender and sexuality she eventually returned to that which she had criticized. Whatever modifications or even radical revisions are made to the theory it retains a core of 'truth' which makes it difficult to move outside it. This 'core' needs to be deconstructed if gender and sexuality are to be made central to the analysis of the workplace. While 'modernist' analyses and bureaucratic structures offer certain gains for women they are not, in fact, gender-neutral and may in fact represent a subtler and hence more stable version of male domination than the earlier models. Feminist and 'post-modern' critiques are therefore very important in informing political and workplace strategies.

According to Weber the overriding concerns of bureaucratic organizations are efficiency and consistency in the application of rules. Authority established by rules stands in contrast to the 'regulation of relationships through individual privilege and bestowals of favour' which characterises patrimonialism. Traditional forms of domination are based on the household unit and are patriarchal in the direct sense that the father, as head of the family, possesses authority. In larger forms of traditional organisation authority is patrimonial, that is, it takes the form of personal allegiance to the master. In bureaucracy, by contrast, loyalty is to an office not to a particular person. Impersonality and the separation of the public and private spheres distinguish bureaucracy from traditionalism. As theorised by Weber, bureaucracy 'has a "rational" character: rules, means, ends, and matter-of-factness dominate its bearing... The march of bureaucracy has destroyed structures of domination which had no rational character, in the special sense of the term' (Gerth & Mills 1958 : 244).

According to Weber's 'ideal type', bureaucracies are based on impersonality, functional specialisation, a hierarchy of authority and the impartial application of rules. There are well-defined duties for each specialized position and recruitment takes place on criteria of demonstrated knowledge and competence. Authority is held in the context of strict rules and regulations and graded hierarchically with the supervision of lower offices by higher ones. Authority established by rules stands in contrast to the 'regulation of relationships through individual privileges and bestowals of favour' which characterized traditional structures. Above all there is a separation of the public world of rationality and efficiency from the private sphere of emotional and personal life.

The boss–secretary relationship runs against every one of these criteria. By having direct access to the powerful, secretaries are outside the hierarchy of authority. Far from being specialised, they can be called upon to do just about anything, and their work may overlap with that of their bosses. The relationship is based on personal rapport, involves a degree of intimacy, day-to-day familiarity and shared secrets unusual for any but lovers or close friends, and is capable of generating intense feelings of loyalty, dependency and personal commitment. How are we to explain this least 'bureaucratic' of relationships? Is it merely an exception or does its existence suggest problems with the way bureaucracy itself has been theorised?

Organization theorists argue that Weber's 'ideal type' was never intended to have any empirical existence and that other kinds of relationship can coexist within bureaucracies. The boss–secretary relationship may thus be explained as a kind of pre-bureaucratic relic. Kanter portrays it as 'the most striking instance of the retention of patrimony within the bureaucracy' (1977 : 73). It is patrimonial in that 'bosses make demands at their own discretion and arbitrarily; choose secretaries on grounds that enhance their own personal status rather than meeting organisational efficiency tests; expect personal services with limits negotiated privately; exact loyalty and make the secretary a part of their private retinue, moving when they move . . . ': This begs the question of why bureaucracy would retain a relationship that appears to be 'irrational' and 'inefficient'. Theorists of bureaucracy have long recognised that the personal intrudes into the workplace all the time; even that it is necessary to have an informal arrangement alongside the formal structure to motivate people and to make things actually work. It is acknowledged that, far from being a limitation on bureaucracy, informal relations and unofficial practices actually contribute to efficient operations (Blau & Myer 1958 : 25). The 'human relations' theorists of the 1920s and 30s showed that people want more from their work than just pay and that the existence of cohesive bonds between co-workers is a prerequisite for high morale and optimum performance (Rose 1975, Part 3).

In these accounts the existence of 'the personal' in the workplace is seen as consistent with bureaucratic organization and even as supportive of it. While the human-relations theorists added an informal dimension, they did not challenge the theorising of the formal bureaucratic structures. In some ways they reinforced the idea of managerial rationality: while *workers* might be controlled by sentiment and emotion, *managers* were supposed to be rational, logical and able to control their emotions. The division between reason and emotion was tightened in a way that marked off managers from the rest. Where the secretary might have been seen as a source of order in the office, she too came to be positioned as the bearer of sexuality and emotion, while the boss was represented as cool and rational. The successful manager was the 'man' who could control his emotions, and women were perceived as 'temperamentally unfit' for management because they were too emotional (Kanter 1975 : 46–7). In making these assumptions explicit, Kanter opened up the potential for making sexuality and gender central to the analysis. Instead she veered away. She concentrated her critique on the 'rational bias' itself rather than on the ways in which the 'discourse' on rationality has operated to maintain male domination and exclude women. While rejecting much of Weber she was committed to the degendering strategies of liberal feminism and sought to explain differences between men and women in terms other than sex or gender. While drawing attention to the existence of separate organizational classes and internal labour markets, she overlooked the appearance of *new* forms of power and control based around the construction of sexuality.

Kanter, and other critics of Weber, argue that instead of thinking of one 'ideal type' of organization as characteristically modern it is useful to consider a range of different types. Part of the problem is the attribution of goals or purposes to the organization. This avoids the issue of the specific and possibly conflicting interests of the individuals or groups who are the actors in organizational settings. Silverman (1970) suggests that the 'structures' of organizations are a good deal less solid and permanent than is often suggested; that they should be seen as the transient outcomes of the actions and interactions of individuals and groups pursuing their own ends with whatever resources are available to them. This shifts the analysis away from the relation between formal and informal structures and opens up new ways of understanding power relations in organizations.

It remains important to analyze the discourse of 'bureaucratic rationality' as it affects men and women. This involves not so much a rejection of Weber as a rereading designed to bring out the underlying assumptions. It can be argued that while the rational–legal or bureaucratic form presents itself as gender-neutral, it actually constitutes a new kind of patriarchal structure. The apparent neutrality of rules and goals disguises the class and gender interests served by them. Weber's account of 'rationality' can be interpreted as a commentary on the construction of a particular kind of masculinity based on the exclusion of the personal, the sexual and the feminine from any definition of 'rationality'. The values of instrumental rationality are strongly associated with the masculine individual, while the feminine is associated with that 'other' world of chaos and disorder. This does not mean that men are in fact 'rational' or that women are 'emotional' but rather that they learn to recognise themselves in these conceptions.

Erotic Bureaucracies

It may be argued that 'rationality' requires as a condition of its existence the simultaneous creation of a realm of the Other, be it personal, emotional, sexual or 'irrational'. Masculine rationality attempts to drive out the feminine but does not exist without it. 'Work' and 'sex' are implicitly treated as the domains of the 'conscious' and the 'unconscious'. But far from being separate spheres the two are thoroughly intertwined. Despite the illusion of ordered rationality, workplaces do not actually manage to exclude the personal or sexual. Rather than seeing the presence of sexuality and familial relations in the workplace as an aspect of traditional, patriarchal authority, it makes more sense to treat them as part of modern organizational forms. I am concerned here not with 'actual' families but with the family symbolism that structures work as well as personal relationships. The media, advertising and popular culture are saturated in such imagery, which provides a dominant set of social meanings in contemporary capitalist society.

The gist of structuralist and post-structuralist work is that there is no unitary human consciousness and that 'identity' itself is a precarious achievement, constantly undermined by the repressed wishes which constitute the unconscious. It is the claim of psychoanalysis that conscious intentions are only a tiny part of our being and that the unconscious and its investments have to be investigated. A theory of the subject thus requires a theory of the unconscious. 'Subjectivity is formed as individuals become aware of their alienation from themselves, in the pre-oedipal imaginary realm which always remains with them; and then as through the oedipal process, individuals become aware of the structures of human sexuality which they acquire through the acquisition of language' (Weeks 1985 : 171). The 'I' comes about only through the 'discourse of the other', that is to say, through practices of signification. We are all subject to the laws of language and our task in childhood is to insert ourselves into that order so that we may secure a place from which to speak. Since the symbolic order is patriarchal, girls and boys, it is argued, enter it differently. In particular, they have to become aware of the presence or absence of the phallus, the signifier, in our culture, of sexual difference and of power.

Different schools of psychoanalysis have different ways of conceptualising gender identity. The object relations school, as represented by Nancy Chodorow (1978) stresses the identification with real people in the formation of different types of self, masculine and feminine, the one autonomous and the other relational. The structuralists, represented by Juliet Mitchell (1975) place less emphasis on the ego but also stress the formation of a core gender identity. In this approach women are constructed as 'non-men', making a 'negative entry into culture'. Recent post-structuralist readings of Lacan have a more fluid conception of sexual difference and gendered subjectivity. Jacqueline Rose, for example, argues that 'if psychoanalysis can give an account of how women experience the path to femininity, it also insists, through the concept of the unconscious, that femininity is neither simply rational–legal nor bureaucratic form presents itself as gender-unified but diverse, fragmented and contradictory.

If we accept that a series of discourses on sexuality underpin bureaucratic control it is possible to see secretaries not as marginal but as paradigmatic of how that power operates. Thus, the boss–secretary relation need not be seen as an anomalous piece of traditionalism or of an incursion of the private sphere, but rather a site of strategies of power in which sexuality is an important though by no means the only dimension. Far from being marginal to the workplace, sexuality is everywhere. It is alluded to in dress and self-presentation, in jokes and gossip, looks and flirtations, secret affairs and dalliances, in fantasy, and in the range of coercive behaviours that we now call sexual harassment. Rather than being exceptional in its sexualization, the boss–secretary relation is an important nodal point for the organization of sexuality and pleasure. This is no less true when the boss happens to be a woman.

Sex at work is very much on display. It is undoubtedly true that for both men and women sexual fantasies and interactions are a way of killing time, of giving a sense of adventure, of livening up an otherwise boring day. As Michael Korda put it, 'the amount of sexual energy circulating in any office is awe-inspiring, and given the slightest sanction and opportunity it bursts out' (1972 : 108). Marcuse was one of the first to recognize the pervasiveness of sexuality in the workplace and to try to theorize it. He recognized that it was not just an instance of incomplete repression but was encouraged as a means of gratification in otherwise boring jobs. If open-plan offices are about surveillance they are also, he suggests, about controlled sex.

Marcuse introduced the concept of 'repressive desublimation' to explain how people were being integrated into a system which in its sweeping rationality, which propels efficiency and growth, is itself irrational (1968 : 12). He pointed to the ways in which,

without ceasing to be an instrument of labour, the body is allowed to exhibit its sexual features in the everyday work world and in work relations . . . The sexy office and sales girls, the handsome, virile junior executive and floor worker are highly marketable commodities, and the possession of suitable mistresses . . . facilitates the career of even the less exalted ranks in the business community . . . Sex is integrated into work and public relations and is thus made susceptible to (controlled) satisfaction . . . But no matter how controlled . . . it is also gratifying to the managed individuals . . . Pleasure, thus adjusted, generates submission. (1968 : 70–1)

In Foucault's account, sexuality in the workplace is not simply repressed or sublimated or subjected to controlled expression. It is actively produced in a multiplicity of discourses and interactions. Modern Western societies have accumulated a vast network of discourses on sex and pleasure. We expect to find pleasure in self-improvement in both our work and non-work activities. Purposive activity operates not through the denial of pleasure but its promise: we will become desirable.

Foucault is concerned with the processes by which individuals come to think of themselves as 'sexual subjects'. Sex has become not merely another object of knowledge but the basis of 'identity'. The greater the valorization of the individual as the ideal subject, the greater the demand for techniques of individual training and retraining. The emphasis on individual choice is consonant with the maximizing of disciplinary controls. 'Controls' operate not to repress but to prolong, intensify and refine the possibilities of pleasure: 'Pleasure and power do not cancel or turn back against one another; they seek out, overlap, reinforce one another. They are linked together by complex mechanisms and devices of excitation and incitement' (Foucault, 1980:48). This may not be as far from Weber as it at first seems. Where Weber treated sex as 'irrational', Foucault looks at the ways in which sex came under the control of 'sexuality' operating through techniques of power. For Foucault power relations are always rational in the sense that they are 'imbued, through and through, with calculation' (1980:95) and they follow a series of aims and objectives. Both see rationalization as characteristic of modern life; but whereas Weber (and Marcuse) see it as a global historical process, and one based on a distinction between public and private, Foucault is concerned with specific rationalities that cut across the public/private division. For Weber and Marcuse the dominance of instrumental reason was a general process to which the whole society was assumed to be uniformly and inexorably subject. Where they are pessimistic about the future Foucault finds some grounds for optimism in the fact that resistance is ever present. While this may mean that resistance is merely an inherent part of the exercise of power it must also create the possibility of displacing that power. People are never just victims but free subjects faced with choices and real alternatives.

The dual possibilities of 'resistance' make it appealing for considering the situation of secretaries. Secretaries have been represented as sellouts, as victims, stooges of management, or alternatively as the potential bearers of a proletarian consciousness based on their deskilling and reduction in status. Rather than simply placing them on one side or the other, Foucault's analysis suggests a more fluid and confused situation:

Instead there is a plurality of resistances, each of them a special case: resistances that are possible, necessary, improbable; others that are spontaneous, savage, solitary, concerted, rampant, or violent; still others that are quick to compromise, interested, or sacrificial...the points, knots, or focuses of resistance are spread over time and space at varying densities, at times mobilizing groups or individuals in a definitive way, inflaming certain points of the body, certain moments in life, certain types of behaviour...(1980:96)

Far from being victims secretaries necessarily engage in resistance. This does not mean that they constitute a revolutionary group but neither are they totally inscribed within existing power relations.

The difficulty with both Marcuse and Foucault is that they are gender-blind. While they establish the centrality of sexuality in the workplace they pay very little attention to gender. Marcuse presumes that men and women are equally and similarly oppressed, ignoring the ways that women are required to market sexual attractiveness to men. Foucault acknowledges gender struggles but does not afford them any priority or permanence. Central to his work is the idea that there is no constant human subject or any rational course to history. If there is no human subject then for Foucault there is no gendered subject. Feminist struggles are, like any others, merely immediate responses to local and specific situations. Foucault's account of power is counterposed to any binary opposition between rulers and ruled. Though he underplays the significance of gender he does provide the basis for developing a more dynamic and fluid conception of power relations between men and women. 'Male power' is not simply and unilaterally imposed on women—gender relations are a process involving strategies and counter-strategies of power.

Harassing Sex?

Where organization theorists have maintained a division between sex and work, women are left in little doubt that the two go together. Women are constantly aware of sexual power structures and the need to put up barriers against men. Though they might enjoy male company and male jokes they are careful to limit their participation and to make it clear to men 'how far they can go'. Many secretaries have chosen their current jobs on the basis of minimizing any further experiences of sexual harassment. One head office, nicknamed the 'twenty five year club' because of the length of time most of the managers had been there, was regarded as something of refuge. If there was no sexual excitement on the sixteenth floor, at least there was no danger.

The term 'sexual harassment' came into the language around 1976 and was quickly taken up as a dimension of gender inequality at work. Mackinnon argued that 'intimate violation of women by men is sufficiently pervasive . . . as to be nearly invisible. Contained by internalized and structural forms of power, it has been nearly inaudible . . . Tacitly, it has been both acceptable and taboo; acceptable for men to do, taboo for women to confront, even to themselves' (1979 : 1). In the 1980s it became possible in Australia to bring sexual harassment cases under anti-discrimination legislation.

Sexual harassment has often been dismissed either as trivial and isolated or as referring to universal 'natural' behaviours. Secretaries who discussed it in the interviews tended to feel that they are responsible for controlling men's behaviour, that women should be able to deal with unwanted advances and preferably avoid getting into the situation in the first place. Yet a number of them had experienced sexual harassment and had even left jobs because of it. Feminists have insisted that sexual harassment is not only an individual problem but part of an organized expression of male power. Sexual harassment functions particularly to keep women out of non-traditional occupations and to reinforce their secondary status in the workplace.

The most claustrophobic example of control through sexuality (no one had yet labelled it 'harassment') concerns a legal practice which was, for a country town, quite large. The atmosphere was one of compulsory jocularity: solicitors and secretaries gaily exchanged insults and sexual banter with each other all day, and there was a great deal of friendly fondling and patting of bottoms. They also intermarried and had a shared social life of parties and barbeques. Ex-secretaries with their babies were regular visitors, and often came back to work on a part-time or temporary basis. Beneath the enforced egalitarianism and informality there was a rigidly enforced sexual division of labour. The partners could not imagine taking on a woman lawyer or the possibility that any of the 'girls' might have the capacity to do law—even though one of them boasted that he had got through the Leaving Certificate with five Bs and depended heavily on his more literate secretary to conduct his correspondence. The women were clear that their role was to service men and were willing to put up with what was constant sexual innuendo. The overall feel of the place was not dissimilar to a brothel. While the secretaries made continuous use of mockery and parody, it seemed only to reaffirm them in 'traditional' boss–secretary relationships.

Gutek and Dunwoody (1987) cite a lot of evidence that even non-harassing sexual behaviour has negative consequences for women. The office affair, particularly if it is with a supervisor, can have detrimental effects on a woman's credibility as well as her career. Many women report that they are not flattered by sexual overtures at work and experience even complimentary remarks as insulting. They would prefer to avoid all sexual interactions at work. Men, on the other hand, report virtually no work-related consequences of sexual behaviour and, if anything, are flattered by sexual overtures from women. While it is generally assumed that men are more sexually active than women, the cluster of characteristics usually associated with the male personality do not include a sexual component. Men can behave in a blatantly sexual way without it being identified. Playboys and harassers go largely unnoticed because 'organisational man', goal-oriented, rational, competitive, is not perceived in explicitly sexual terms. It is ironic that women are perceived as using sex to their advantage. They are much less likely to initiate sexual encounters and more likely to be hurt by sex at work.

Hearn and Parkin have pointed to the ways in which male managers use sexuality, harassment, joking and abuse as routine means of maintaining authority. This may be embedded in the taken-for-granted culture of the organization (1987 : 93). They also suggest that harassment can be interpreted as men's attempt to create some human contact as part of, or in reaction to, alienated working conditions. It may then be seen as 'a form of labour in which women become commodities for men, as a "reserve of sexual labour"' (1987 : 85).

Rosemary Pringle

The sexual division of labour is mediated by gender constructions that in numerous aspects bear on sexuality. Rich's notion of 'compulsory heterosexuality' (1983) can be applied here, for the sexual 'normality' of daily life in the office is relentlessly heterosexual. The norm is reproduced in concrete social practices ranging from managerial policies through to everyday informal conversations (Hearn and Parkin 1987 : 94–5). It involves the domination of men's heterosexuality over women's heterosexuality and the subordination of all other forms of sexuality. It was striking how few homosexuals, either bosses or secretaries, we turned up via our workplace visits, though we attempted to give cues that it was 'safe' to talk about the subject. Those who identified as homosexual were nearly all volunteers who had been contacted via 'non-work' channels. Few of them were 'out' at work in any more than a limited way. Those who were tended to be in 'creative' areas where it was acceptable, or they were treated by the rest of the office as the tame pervert. The only secretary who was completely open about her lesbianism was a woman who had been married and had children and could thus claim to have paid her dues to 'normality'. She said, 'I think I'm good PR for lesbians . . . because I'm so bloody ordinary. You know, I've been married, I've had children, I own a house, I own a car. I'm Ms Middleclass Suburbia!' Another secretary told me that she deliberately chose temporary work so that she could move on before having to face the chit-chat over morning tea about private life.

In naming and theorizing sexual harassment feminists have drawn attention to the centrality of sexuality in workplace organization. However, they have largely restricted sexuality to its coercive or unpleasurable dimensions. Radical feminists have emphasized sexual aggression and violence as the basis of men's power. If women experience pleasure it is treated as 'coerced caring' (Mackinnon 1979 : 54–5). In these accounts either virtually all heterosexual activity may be labelled as sexual harassment or a line has to be drawn between what is harassment and what is 'acceptable'. The identification of some activities as 'sexual harassment' may legitimate and obscure other forms of male power. But men control women not only through rape or through forcing them to do what they do not want to do, but through definitions of pleasure and selfhood. Control through pleasure may be more effective in that it is much less likely to provoke resistance than control through coercion.

At this point the argument becomes complicated for it is not clear where 'male power' begins and ends, whether women are in all cases 'victims' or whether they too can exercise sexual power. It is by no means certain that women are yanked screaming into 'compulsory heterosexuality'. Most actively seek it out and find pleasure in it. It is hard to know what a 'free' choice would be. Rich seems to assume some underlying bond with the mother that would be free to develop, flowing into 'lesbian continuum'. But women may choose heterosexuality precisely to get away from the constraints of the mother–

daughter relationship and because it does give them access to masculine power. If mothers were not held uniquely responsible for childcare the intensity and ambivalence of the mother–daughter bond may actually lessen. It is less likely that we would experience pressure to 'choose' between heterosexuality and homosexuality or that 'lesbian continuum' would be set up in contrast to 'compulsory heterosexuality'. We may see a construction of sexuality that did not favour men over women, heterosexuality over homosexuality, intercourse over other sexual acts.

While it has opened up discussion of sexuality and power in the workplace, sexual harassment is not an adequate way of conceptualising the issues. It is not sufficient merely to assert that secretaries are workers (as much feminist literature has done) and that sexuality and femininity have no place at work. There is an important additional step of deconstructing the boss–secretary relationship and analysing the place of gender and sexuality in workplace organization. Opposition to sexual harassment is only one component of a sexual politics in the workplace. It needs to be supplemented with analyses of the ways in which sexual pleasure might be used to disrupt male rationality and to empower women. Merely to attempt to drive sexuality from the workplace leaves the ideology of separate spheres effectively unchallenged.

Strategic Dilemmas

Foucauldian analyses situate 'bureaucratic rationality' in a larger context of discursive strategies in which sexuality and pleasure become central to the operations of power. In doing so they challenge the liberal and modernising assumptions behind organization theory as it has developed since Weber. However, they have little to say specifically about gender and tend to deny any fundamental antagonisms between men and women. Feminist analyses, on the other hand, emphasize the existence of gendered sexuality in the workplace. Whether sexual interactions in the workplace are coercive or voluntary, pleasurable or unpleasurable, they are seen as disadvantageous to women. Feminists thus appear to throw in their lot with neo-Weberian approaches in which sex is seen as an unwelcome invader which should be pushed out of the workplace. Feminist and Foucauldian approaches sit uneasily together and at many points contradict each other. They have different priorities and different understandings of power. Yet both offer important insights about the situation of secretaries and, by implication, all women in the workplace. While it would be premature, and perhaps undesirable, to try and integrate the two frameworks, it is necessary to keep them in some kind of tension.

What I have alluded to as 'modernism' covers a range of approaches that either deny the centrality of class, gender or sexuality or displace them. It includes technocratic, liberal or 'progressive' tendencies within capitalism as well as Marxist, feminist and other radical strands which are committed to the completion of the 'modernist' project through the transformation of the capitalist system. Most political conflict takes place within these parameters and it may seem surprising to have bracketed together movements and ideologies that are usually counterposed. When it comes to bosses and secretaries, they share some blind spots.

New technology is often represented as marking the end of the special relation between boss and secretary. Management consultants, employers, journalists and particularly computer retailers argue that in the new paperless office secretaries will either be redundant or transformed into all-round communications workers with sophisticated computer skills. Automation will break down 'traditional' relationships, removing the 'drudgery', and offering secretaries new opportunities. Marxist accounts are less sanguine but they too predict the end of the 'traditional' secretary. They concede that a small proportion of the workforce is becoming 'hyperskilled' but consider the vast majority are headed for proletarianisation or unemployment. The 'sexy secretary' with her 'bourgeois' pretensions is here overtaken by the *proletarian* figure experiencing similar conditions to those of factory workers. Her gender is subordinated to her changing class position. She loses control of her own work processes and becomes subject to time and motion studies. As the work becomes deskilled and routinized, health problems emerge that were once more typical of the factory than the office. In this account, secretaries disappear into the broader category of office workers, part of a new working class.

Feminists have taken up and extended both the liberal and marxist analyses. Liberal feminists are optimistic about the possibilities for secretaries to move into the management hierarchy and point out that far from being unemployed, secretaries are in short supply (Porat and Will 1983). Marxist feminists find themselves in a dilemma. Capitalist relations are seen to break down the old 'feudal' elements of the boss–secretary relationship while increasing exploitation. In their accounts 'secretary' disappears into that amorphous category of 'woman office worker'. What is most specific to her definition in other discourses, her sexuality and femininity, is deliberately ignored. It is easier to deal with the tangibles of health hazards, wage rates and unemployment.

Though the above approaches differ in significant ways all represent the boss–secretary relation as an archaic remnant of 'traditional' society that will be swept away by the extension of the bureaucratic model to all aspects of workplace organization. They view sex in the workplace as at best frivolous and time-wasting and potentially at least a form of harassment. 'Modernization' involves the application of a single, rational and objective standard to everyone. Sex discrimination legislation, equal employment opportunity and affirmative action programs may be seen as a logical extension and application of 'modernist' principles. Feminists of all kinds have supported such programs. Whatever their limits, their presence signals a whole new climate. 'Modernism' has become the official, though not necessarily the dominant discourse.

Most Australian states have had sex discrimination legislation since the late 1970s. New South Wales and some other states have also had equal employment opportunity (EEO) programs since 1980. These applied to government departments and public corporations, requiring them to draw up a management plan of action to overcome 'systemic' discrimination. Some private companies voluntarily set up similar programs. The Hawke Labor government passed a national Sex Discrimination Act in 1984. It had intended to include affirmative action with this legislation but this policy was sufficiently controversial for the government to decide to delay. Instead it set up a 'pilot' program involving some 25 companies and tertiary institutions. Each was to conduct research into patterns of discrimination in their workplace and come up with proposals for ending it. Most of the interviews were conducted during the period of this scheme (1985–87) and a number of companies visited were participating in the pilot. National affirmative action legislation finally became operational in March 1987 and applies to all companies with a staff or more than 100 (Ronalds, 1987). The legislation avoids any notion of 'positive discrimination', or the imposition of 'quotas' of women or minority groups. Instead it involves setting broad targets and establishing guidelines. Unlike the United States, the penalties for non-compliance are fairly nominal and implementation depends largely on the willingness of organisations to cooperate. Being 'named in parliament' is assumed to function as a deterrent.

Liberals hope that such programs will remove the last vestiges of inequality and discrimination and open up the career hierarchy to ability regardless of gender. For socialist and radical feminists they are but one starting point, and not necessarily the most important one, for addressing the structural inequalities at the heart of 'capitalist patriarchy'. They point out that the benefits are so far restricted to business and professional women who are already competing, albeit at some disadvantage, with men. These programs do not as yet direct much attention to the secretarial and clerical, sales and service jobs in which most women work. In the face of such criticisms, the attitude of organizations to secretaries has become something of a litmus test of their sincerity with regard to affirmative action. Some companies have begun to explore ways in which career opportunities might be opened up to secretaries and in a few cases set up senior secretaries' groups. Publicly at least they are obliged to treat secretaries with greater respect than they have done in the past. It remains to be seen whether these moves are any more than token.

By the time affirmative action legislation was passed and machinery set up to implement it nationally, many feminists had become disillusioned with it. At the 1987 socialist feminist conference in Sydney, women argued that it is token, that it sidetracks feminists from other demands and threatens to bury feminist politics under a mound of paperwork. Affirmative action operates in the public sphere and is not easily adapted to working on the public–private relation. Domestic problems, particularly lack of adequate childcare, have been largely excluded from liberal discourse even though they probably provide the greatest stumbling block to secretaries who wish to take up extra training or move into management. It remains to be seen whether the framework can be used as as a basis from which to push for further change. While some feminists (e.g. Eisenstein 1986) argue that it can be used to challenge the 'embeddedness' of male power, others have become more cynical. They claim that by trivial-ising gender differences and treating sexuality as the 'other' to be driven from the workplace, affirmative action actually preserves a form of patriarchal domination in the gender-neutral guise of 'bureaucratic rationality' (Game 1984). It allows women to make it as 'honorary men'. Critiques of affirmative action merge here with broader critiques of the phallocentricity of Western thought (e.g. Lloyd 1984) and the ways in which rationality and objectivity embody masculine values under the guise of gender-neutrality.

For many feminists secretaries are part of a disappearing act, either on the way to becoming part of management or in the process of being proletarian-ized. They have rejected the 'office wife' and 'sexy secretary' definitions, insisting that sexuality *should* have no place at work and analysing the particular vulnerability of secretaries to 'sexual harassment'. Only rarely have they considered why the discourses are there or the kinds of resistances that are open to secretaries within them. Perhaps because of a certain embarrassment about what secretaries represent, they have preferred to avoid sexuality and instead to talk briskly about the recognition of skills. Secretaries, along with nurses, were seen as suitable candidates for 'comparable worth' cases involving comparisons with appropriate groups of male workers. The fact that secretaries may not *like* being compared with groups like male truck drivers is left unanalysed. Many secretaries who work in companies and industries where the Federated Clerks' Union have 'closed-shop' agreements, are proud to have reached the point where membership of the union is no longer mandatory. 'Clause 31' exemptions are given on the basis of their closeness to management and the confidential nature of their work. To the Federated Clerks' Union, the rule-of-thumb definition of a secretary is, then, any clerical worker who can claim a 'clause 31' exemption.

Feminists have been wary of the 'servility' of secretaries, their femininity, their tendency to align themselves with management, their loyalty to their bosses and reluctance to insist on decent working conditions—their willing-ness, for example, to work long hours for no overtime. At best secretaries appear in feminist debates as 'victims', whether of technology, bosses, sexual harassment or of their own lack of assertiveness. This has created something of a gulf between feminists in general and those activist secretaries who have struggled for change. If feminists as a whole have embraced 'degendering' strategies it has not been so easy for secretaries to do so.

Secretaries cannot simply withdraw from the stereotypes and insert themselves into a 'degendering' approach, nor do they necessarily want to. While most share the feminist concerns for equal pay and equality of opportunity, they perceive feminists as either wanting to be 'like men' or hating men. Feminists are seen as both strident and joyless, obsessed with 'finding a rapist behind every filing cabinet'. In seeking to remove sexuality and femininity from the workplace they threaten to remove not only dangers but also pleasures. Secretaries do not necessarily want to take on 'masculine' work profiles and career goals, develop new skills, or perpetually be off on training courses in order to become part of management.

What the secretaries express is dissatisfaction and scepticism about an approach that attempts to set up one path for all workers. Though their militancy is limited they want a range of options based on recognition of skills, better pay, and working conditions that give them (rather than the employers) flexibility and security. Though they often prefer the predictability of bureaucracies over the more idiosyncratic decision-making of small organizations, they do not want sexuality or gender difference to be driven from the workplace. While feminists cannot be held entirely responsible for their unflattering media representations, all of this suggests the importance of reviewing our assumptions and priorities. Arguments about the relationship between 'equality' and 'difference' have been central to feminist theory for more than a decade but have had surprisingly little impact on practical politics or workplace struggles. Despite the emphasis placed on sexuality, the sexual investments that secretaries and other groups of women have in the existing system have not been understood or acknowledged.

Sexuality cannot be 'banished' from the workplace. Attempts to treat it as an 'intruder' are basic to the negative representation of women/sexuality/secretaries. It is by insisting on its presence, making it visible, asserting women's rights to be subjects rather than objects of sexual discourses, that bureaucracy can be challenged. This does not mean organizing orgies in the office, encouraging sexual harassment or sitting on the boss's knee! All of these things things would imply that women's pleasure is first and foremost in pleasing men. It is actually quite difficult to imagine a secretary sitting on the boss's knee in a way that was purely for her own pleasure and not pandering to his desire.

Making sexuality visible will involve an exploration of what it means to be sexual *subjects* rather than objects. Our culture has such a fear of female sexuality that its autonomous expression is viewed as horrendous: Salome demanding the head of John the Baptist. Given such images it is hard even to begin to imagine what subjectivity can mean for women. But there is a growing body of feminist work on female sexuality that is relevant. While some feminists have concentrated on the coercive aspects of sexuality: rape, incest, domestic violence, paedophilia, sexual harassment and so on, others have claimed that the priority given to danger and coercion has led to a marginalisation of female pleasure (Vance 1984). Lynne Segal (1987) and Gayle Rubin (1984) argue instead for a libertarian position. Segal simply wants a return to the early 1970s concern with sexual pleasure, claiming that sexuality has been overemphasised and that men's sexual domination is based on their social and economic power and not the reverse. Rubin, drawing on Foucault, points to the tendency in our culture to treat sex with suspicion, to sanction certain kinds of sexual activity and to create a hierarchy of sexual values. She wants to challenge this by siding with the 'outlawed' sexual minorities, destroying the notion of a single universal ideal sexuality by developing a pluralistic sexual ethics. The difficulty with both these writers is that they risk falling into an essentialism that takes any sexual desire as somehow authentic. They avoid any critical examination of the material basis of consent and historical shifts in sexual power.

On another tack, difference theorists celebrate the multiplicity of identities and pleasures based on the female body which they contrast with the one-dimensional, instrumental and abstract culture of the male. This enables them to develop a rhetoric of pleasure which completely bypasses current realities. Silverman (1984) argues that female sexuality has been constructed by the interaction of (male) discourse with the female body. She uses the Story of O to show the ways in which discourse quite literally maps meaning onto bodies. Women will not challenge the symbolic order from 'outside', she argues, but by altering their relation to discourse.

Given the difficulties involved in establishing women's subjectivity, it is important to be accepting of female sexuality as it is currently constituted. Rather than assuming, for example, that secretaries are always the pathetic victims of sexual harassment, it might be possible to consider the power and pleasure they currently get in their interactions with people and raise the question of how they can get what they want on their own terms. As Barbara Creed (1984) pointed out in her analysis of Mills and Boon novels, even here, in what is regarded as romantic trash, there are opportunities for subversion. While hardly feminist, these novels do cater for women's sexual pleasure and to some extent acknowledge their active sexuality, for example by presenting the male body as the object of their gaze. The acknowledgement of such pleasure may do something to bridge the negative representations that feminists and secretaries currently have of each other.

Establishing female subjectivity is only part of what is involved in making sexuality visible in the workplace. Just as important is exposing the masculinity that lurks behind gender-neutrality and forcing men to be responsible for their own sexual behavior. If the current stereotype of men is 'the perfect picture of asexuality' (Gutek and Dunwoody 1987 : 261), then it is masculinity, not femininity, that needs to be made visible, and it is men's 'refusal to recognise the effects of masculinity which constitutes the problem for women' (Black and Coward 1981 : 85).

In this context the insights of post-structuralism and / or postmodernism are of interest. While they do not replace modernism they do provide a critical stance and the possibility of deconstructing existing frameworks and thus opening up some blockages. Men's experience of themselves as unitary and autonomous is achieved through the repression of the 'feminine'. Given that 'identity' is at best a precarious achievement it may be that masculine identity is particularly vulnerable. While women have long been aware of the 'fragility' of the male ego, the implications for the larger structure of 'male' rationality are only just beginning to be explored. For women, the lesser likelihood of perceiving themselves as centre-stage, and their more decentred notions of self, may emerge as strengths rather than weaknesses. Should women struggle for autonomous identities or celebrate their fragmentation? The political consequences are complex.

While 'postmodernism' has as yet had little to say about the workplace it has been critical of the universalising tendencies of modern culture, the failure to acknowledge or celebrate difference and plurality. It is concerned with the politics of play and pleasure and its main strategies are exaggeration and parody. It delights in being 'over the top'. Oscar Wilde's version of *Salome* may be interpreted in this way, as parodying the puritanism and negative attitudes towards female sexuality of Jewish men. Among contemporary feminist theorists, Irigaray is most closely associated with mimicry and ridicule. In a similar way the 'Olympia' montage created by a community artist working with a group of Sydney secretaries in 1985 attempts to subvert existing definitions of secretaries. Instead of rejecting or moralizing about these images she recreates them in loving detail and plays with them. Here the naked reclining figure of Olympia the prostitute is brought together with every imaginable image of secretary, as sex object, femme fatale, temptress, worker, wife, mother holding the boss in the palm of her hand and so on. The whole thing is lit up with flashing lights; it is flamboyant, garish, loud, and above all celebratory. It is constructed to create the possibility of multiple interpretations and indeed everyone who looks at it sees something different. Whether it subverts or reproduces the discourses it parodies is an open question. The author cannot guarantee meaning or ensure that her audience will not take the parody seriously!

In their office humour and sometimes in public expression secretaries use parody of themselves and their bosses to powerful effect. Much pleasure is derived from imitating, exaggerating and ridiculing the existing stereotypes. These interventions are necessarily localized, sporadic, spontaneous and may amount to little more than a letting off of steam. To dispense with other political strategies in favour of parody would be a regressive move. Yet it is not unduly romanticising to suggest that parody has a place in the critical assessment of what 'modernism' has to offer and in the creation of a larger-scale politics of change.

....

References

Black, M. and Coward, R. (1981). 'Linguistic, Social and Sexual Relations', *Screen Education*, 39, Summer.

Blau, P. N. and Meyer, M. M. (1971). *Bureaucracy in Modern Society*. New York: Random House.

Chodorow, N. (1978). *The Reproduction of Mothering*. Berkeley: University of California Press.

Creed, B. (1984). 'The Women's Romance as Sexual Fantasy: "Mills & Boon"', in Women and Labour Publications Collective, *All Her Labours: Embroidering the Framework*. Sydney: Hale & Iremonger.

Foucault, M. (1980). *The History of Sexuality, vol. 1*. New York: Vintage.

Game, A. (1984). 'Affirmative Action: Liberal Rationality or Challenge to Patriarchy?', *Legal Services Bulletin*, 9, 253–57.

Gerth, H. H. and Mills, C. W. (eds) (1958). *From Max Weber: Essays in Sociology*. New York: Galaxy.

Gutek, B. A. and Dunwoody, V. (1987). 'Understanding Sex inthe Workplace', in A. H. Stromberg et al. (eds), *Women and Work (An Annual Review, vol. 2)*. Newbury Park: Sage.

Hearn, J. and Parkin, W. (1984). '"Sex" and "Work": Methodological and other difficulties in then study of sexuality in work organizations'. Paper at British Sociological Conference, University of Bradford.

Kanter, R. M. (1975). 'Women and the Structure of Organizations: Explorations in Theory and Behavior', in M. Millman and R. Kanter (eds), *Another Voice*. New York: Anchor.

—— (1977). *Men and Women of the Corporation*. New York: Basic Books.

Korda, M. (1972). *Male Chauvinism! How It Works*. New York: Random House.

Lloyd, G. (1984). *The Man of Reason*. London: Methuen.

MacKinnon, C. A. (1979). *Sexual Harassment of Working Women*. New Haven: Yale University Press.

Marcuse, H. (1968). *One Dimensional Man*. London: Sphere Books.

Mitchell, J. (1975). *Psychoanalysis and Feminism*. Harmondsworth: Penguin.

Porat, F. and Will, M. (1983). *The Dynamic Secretary*. New Jersey: Prentice-Hall.

Rich, A. (1983). 'Compulsory Heterosexuality and Lesbian Existence', in Snitow et al. (eds), *Powers of Desire*.

Ronalds, C. (1987). *Affirmative Action and Sex Discrimination*. Sydney: Pluto.

Rose, M. (1975). *Industrial Behaviour: Theoretical Development since Taylor*. London: Allen Lane.

Rubin, E. (1984). 'Thinking Sex: Notes for a Radical Theory of the Politics of Sexuality', in Vance (ed.), *Pleasure and Danger*.

Segal, L. (1987). *Is the Future Female?* London: Virago.

Silverman, D. (1970). *The Theory of Organisations*. London: Heinemann.

Silverman, K. (1984). 'Histoire d'O: The Construction of a Female Subject', in Vance (ed.), *Pleasure and Danger*.

Snitow, A. et al. (eds) (1983). *Powers of Desire: The Politics of Sexuality*. New York: Monthly Review Press.

Vance, C. (ed.) (1984). *Pleasure and Danger: Exploring Female Sexuality*. Boston: Routledge & Kegan Paul.

Weeks, J. (1985). *Sexuality and its Discontents*. London: Routledge & Kegan Paul.

14

Performance Appraisal and the Emergence of Management

Barbara Townley

Introduction

A number of articles have questioned approaches taken to the study of management (Carroll and Gillen 1987; Reed 1984; Stewart 1989; Whitley 1984, 1989; Willmott 1984, 1987). They echo Reed's (1984 : 279) argument that there is a need for 'a substantial reconsideration of the conceptual equipment through which management on a theoretical, methodological and empirical level is to be understood'. Studies of management are criticized for treating it as a technical, politically neutral activity, decontextualized and depoliticized (Willmott 1987). Stewart (1989) notes that management is all too often depicted as a static entity, a universally similar activity, prone to the development of lists. Such criticisms contain the kernel of remedial activity: for example, that the study of management should consider the political dimensions of its activity and emphasize the dynamic nature of its subject. However, this is to engage the studies in their own terms and, as such, it is questionable if this constitutes a fundamental rethink of the nature of management and its study.

A more serious criticism is that the study of management has suffered from reification, the action of taking conventional categories and treating them as if they were natural entities. By beginning an analysis with 'management' functions within an organization, management is already presaged in the analysis. Ontologically privileged, it exists as a theoretical antecedent, a structured, pre-given aspect of organizations. This gives rise to definitions, as for example, that of Penrose (1980) used by Whitley (1989 : 211), of management as 'the construction, maintenance and improvement of an administrative system which co-ordinated and transformed human and material resources into productive services'. Such definitions conceal an element of tautology. As Willmott (1984 : 354) notes, 'integral to this image of the manager is the implication that in the absence of direction and control, little or nothing would be produced, the potential of subordinates would be unfulfilled and the lack of objective information on current progress would exclude the possibility of reviewing their activities'. Management is defined in terms of itself—the functional prerequisite of that which it is hoped to study. Activities are defined in terms of their origin, labelled managerial because they emanate from management, either deriving from the person designated as such, or from an imputed function.

To advance the substantial reconsideration which Reed (1984) recommends, it is necessary to deconstruct management and, in doing so, substantiate or justify the designation of particular roles or functions as being managerial. Definitions of management, unfortunately, suffer from conceptual obscurity. Stewart (1984 : 323) maintains that the nature of management is 'elusive', whilst Astley (1984 : 267) holds that there is a 'clear lack of awareness over what constitutes the field's (management science) core of knowledge'. Rarely is management precisely defined. Managerial work, managerial jobs and managerial behavior are used interchangeably (Stewart 1989). Hales (1986 : 110) notes a failure to identify what is distinctive about managerial work, with the literature confining itself to 'what it is like, not what it is'. Given the lack of explicit definitions, management has to be imputed or deduced from studies of it. Based on the assumption that managerial work is done by those in managerial jobs, there has been the attempt to decipher what management 'is' from what managers 'do' (Stewart 1984). The value of such approaches is necessarily limited, as Whitley (1984 : 210) comments: 'most studies fail to justify their selection of individuals being studied as "managers" which rather vitiates any claims to draw general conclusions about the distinguishing features of "managerial" work'.

The demand for conceptual clarity is not motivated by a desire for more eloquent definitions. Conceptual clarity is important because it forces the recognition that 'management' has the status of a conceptual object, an abstraction. The concepts 'manager' and 'management', as Rosen (1984) reminds us, are 'social artifacts reflecting social relations'. Management is a 'given' within a conceptual framework; it has a summarizing function within an abstracted systematic statement. Management, however, has become such a norm of institutionalized knowledge that its status as a conceptual object, an abstraction, has become obscured. In recognizing management as a concept, it behoves us to examine it as a theoretical construct rather than assume its existence as a natural entity.

As Machin and Lowe (1983) note, management is something of an omnipresent process, with most individuals in an organization at some point carrying out 'managerial' activities. However a distinction drawn by Willmott (1984 : 350) is useful in dissociating the omniscient from the particularistic in the uses of the term. Recognizing that it is possible to be engaged in management without being a manager, he draws the distinction between 'management' as reflexive social action, intrinsic to human agency and management as being 'institutionally empowered to determine and/or regulate certain aspects of the actions of others'. It is this latter definition which will inform our consideration of management here.

As a definition it has three important implications. It emphasizes the social context of management—management operates *through* people, rather than being a disembodied practice. This identifies management as a relational activity—management manages in relation to something or someone. Its identity is derived from its relation to the 'other'. It is not an absolute and self-contained entity, intrinsic to a person or action. Although managerial work has been recognized as 'collective and interdependent' (Whitley 1989) involving a reliance on other people (Stewart 1984), this is understood as the interdependence or interplay of discrete actors (Roberts 1984). Management as a relational concept, however, involves the interdependence of meaning and activity. It is the rejection of an essentialist view of management and managerial practices. It also emphasizes the practice of management, its active construction as an activity or process.

The relational and the constitutive dimensions suggest a research strategy which decentres management. Defining management in these terms indicates that it is the relationship between elements which can aid an understanding of social phenomena, more so than an examination of properties in isolation may do (Whitley 1984). Rather than start with management as a pre-given entity, the central organizing focus through which it is to be understood, management should be denied its privileged status. Before outlining what such an approach would involve, the third dimension of management must be addressed.

Willmott's definition stresses the political dimension of management: the essence of managing is power. Within what may be termed orthodox approaches to management power remains implicit. Management is synonymous with organizational functioning, a necessary set of tasks and roles for the efficient achievement of organizational objectives. It is a systematic characteristic of organizations functioning in a model of means—end rationality (Lowe and Puxty 1989; Richbell 1983). Power is usually addressed as an analogue of authority, considered in analyses of leadership styles, decision-making, influence and networks, informing studies as to 'who has power?' or 'power to do what?'. Radical critiques of this approach are directed at its failure to confront adequately the issue of power, and its neglect of political economy and broader capitalist relations of production (Chua et al. 1989; Knights and Willmott 1986; Machin and Lowe 1983). They criticize the failure of the orthodox approach to acknowledge that portraying management as the selection and achievement of goals and the direction and coordination of organizational activity necessarily entails the operation of power and control (Otley 1983). For the radical critique, the concept of control is central to an understanding of management.

Both radical and orthodox perspectives, however, operate with an economic model of power. Not only is power deduced from, and in the service of, the economy; more importantly, the metaphor for understanding its operation is that of the commodity. Power is something externally 'held' or possessed, embodied in a person, an institution or a structure, to be used for individual, organizational or class purposes. As a commodity it is portrayed in zero-sum or negative terms, commonly presented as 'power over': the traditional representation of A's getting B to do something they would, or should, not otherwise do. Although the dimensions of power have been critiqued (Lukes 1974), initiating debates as to its nature and whether it resides in its potential or its exercise (Benton 1981; Hindness 1982, Isaac 1982), the underlying concept in both orthodox and radical approaches to management remains that of power as a commodity or possession.

This conception prompts the questions, 'who holds power?' or 'where does it reside?' It assumes a central organizing focus or source, the study of which involves examining how it percolates from organizational apex to base, informing a descending analysis of power. It involves a search for determinants, sought in the conscious intention or decision of voluntaristic subjects, or determining or constraining institutional sources of power. Explanations are thus caught in a dualism between agency and structure, a dualism which has been identified as being at the heart of the recent impasse in theorizing about management (Knights and Willmott 1985; Reed 1984; Willmott 1987).

The work of Foucault provides an alternative conceptualization of power. It also addresses the relational and the constitutive dimensions identified earlier as being important in an understanding of management. Foucault is critical of the economic model of power—power is not to be sought in a central point, something to be acquired or seized, 'a system of domination exerted by one group over another' (Foucault 1981 : 92). Rather, Foucault conceives of power as a property of relations. It is referred to as a relay or an interdependency. It is exercised rather than held, conceived of as a strategy, not as a property or possession. He writes 'power is neither given, nor exchanged, or recovered but rather exercised and only exists in action' (Gordon 1980 : 114). Foucault stresses the analytics of power relations, the specific mechanisms and technologies through which power circulates. Power is embedded in practice, and does not have a necessary centre. This relational concept of power is also, for Foucault, positive and creative.

This constitutive nature of power finds particular expression in the intimate connection between power and knowledge (Foucault 1977, 1981; Gordon 1980). Through the construct power/knowledge, Foucault draws attention to the fundamental role knowledge plays in rendering aspects of existence 'thinkable' and, as a result, able to be acted upon. Bodies of knowledge have direct implications for the way in which the conduct of individuals or groups may be directed. The process of making something known or visible, in other words, also makes it potentially governable. To 'know' something is to create a new power relation. In explaining the process of rendering a domain calculable and amenable to intervention, Foucault provides a valuable entree to the study of management.

The constitutive interdependence of power and knowledge has several implications. Knowledge is not detached and independent, a source of illumination. It is implicated in, and integral to, the system of administration and governance which becomes established. This is in direct contrast to orthodox considerations of management which separate the planning or directive roles ('management') from an essentially secondary information control function ('administration'). The latter is an aid to management designed to enhance rational decision-making, or even viewed as 'routine' (Whitley 1989). From a Foucauldian perspective, information systems are an integral and active component of an organization's system of management. They are directly implicated in the forms of organizational segmentation, hierarchy and control which emerge. Concepts of manager and management are actively constructed in particular ways and are inseparable from the practical means of administration which are implicated in their emergence and functioning.

This deconstruction of management redirects analysis. The focus becomes the regulatory mechanisms which make a domain or arena open to regulation. This approach highlights systems by which power is exercised through its intersection with knowledge, for example, methods of observation, techniques of registration—mechanisms for the supervision and administration of individuals and groups. 'The apparently humble and mundane mechanisms which appear to make it possible to govern . . . the indirect means of action and intervention' (Miller and Rose 1990 : 8). The focus becomes, in Miller and Rose's (1990) term, 'governmentality'—the processes of inventing, promoting and installing mechanisms of rule. Such an approach places a particular premium on language—the vocabularies of programmes through which power operates and the legitimacy of government is established.

Since concepts of power inform concepts of management, reconceptualizing power has implications for the way management is studied. Power as a relational activity stresses the practice of management—not 'what managers do', or 'who manages', but the 'how' of management. Following recommendations of organization theory (Morgan 1980) that it is more beneficial to privilege organizing rather than organization, the focus becomes the activity of managing rather than management as an extant object. As Dreyfus and Rabinow (1986 : 185) indicate 'if power is not a thing or the control of a set of institutions . . . then the task for the analyst is to identify how it operates . . . to isolate, identify and analyse the web of unequal relationships set up'. The aim is to identify how non-egalitarian, asymmetrical relationships become established and perpetuated and sedimented within organizations. In other words the position argued here is not that management gives rise to ways of managing or managerial practices, rather practices or methods of regulation give rise to management.

The questions arising from a Foucauldian approach to management are: if power is exercised what sort of exercise does it involve? In what does it consist? What is its mechanism? The method of tracing knowledge production and its power effects advances based upon a number of principles: a study of techniques rather than institutions; practices rather than intentions; webs of power rather than classes or groups; knowledge rather than ideology; and perhaps most importantly, an ascending analysis of power (Silverman 1985). The latter involves the study of power 'at its extremities, in its ultimate destinations' (Gordon 1980). Starting from its 'infinitesimal mechanisms', its aim is to delineate how these have been 'transformed, displaced, extended . . . by ever more general mechanisms' (Gordon 1980 : 114). It studies the way power is exercised, concretely and in detail—a relatively neglected area in studies of management.

This approach reinforces the recommendations which have been put forward for the empirical study of management: that such an approach be sensitive to the 'empirical diversity and social ambiguity' of managerial practices; analyse the mechanisms by which it becomes 'structured to take on a coherent and reasonably stable institutional state' (Reed 1984 : 279); and that it remains closely linked to the organizational context rather than abstracting managerial activities from the institutional arrangements in which they are carried out (Whitley 1989; Willmott 1987).

Method

It is useful to apply this method to an empirical case to explore how a Foucauldian approach is capable of providing an additional dimension to the study of management. The example used here is an analysis of performance appraisal systems recently introduced into UK universities (Townley 1990). Not traditionally associated with sites of management (Berry 1983; Gherardi and Strati 1990), the choice of universities allows for a broadening of the understanding of management in a context where this may not be readily discernable. It also provides the opportunity to view how what has been termed a relatively unrationalized social domain (Meyer 1983) is brought under the jurisdiction of a rational organizational structure.

Appraisal is usually identified as a managerial activity: the provision of data designed to ensure that resources are used efficiently in accomplishing organizational objectives. Associated with organizational reform and improvement, appraisal is recommended to enhance managerial and organizational performance and employee motivation (Randell 1989). In providing information on individual job performance it contributes to decision-making and resource allocation. Some accounts have questioned this view of appraisal for conveniently ignoring the political realities of the firm (Pym 1973; Barlow 1989), suggesting that appraisal functions as a mechanism for the control of employees. Indeed appraisals may differ, reflecting, as Pym (1973) indicates, the culture of the organization in which they operate, their functions mirrored in the particular details of a scheme: the choice of appraiser; links with promotion or discipline; appeal mechanisms; confidentiality of documents, etc. Both interpretations, however, reflect an approach to the study of management highlighted earlier—activities are defined in terms of their origin and imputed from an assumed intention or function; appraisal is a managerial activity to be judged in terms of its contribution to organizational effectiveness or managerial control.

The approach adopted here is to decentre 'management' as an organizing focus, dissociating power from structure or function. Rather, through an analysis of appraisal documentation as 'texts', Foucault's ascending analysis of power will be used to illustrate how management as a directional activity becomes articulated through minute organizational procedures. Limiting the approach to written texts may draw the criticism that management in operation is neglected. Texts, however, are important. They provide guides for action and present information which prompts the need for decisions and solutions. As Miller and Rose (1990 : 6) note, 'it is out of linguistic elements that rationalities of government are elaborated and seek to specify appropriate bases for the organization and mobilisation of social life'. Following, therefore, is a textual examination of appraisal systems based on appraisal documents, including forms and notes of guidance for appraiser and appraisee, which were collected from 30 universities. Proceeding from a detailed examination of the language of appraisal, how information is obtained and what is done with it thereafter, it illustrates how power relations are engendered. It is an exercise in the analysis of what Gowler and Legge (1983 : 198) refer to as the rhetoric of bureaucratic control: 'highly expressive language that constructs and legitimizes managerial prerogatives in terms of a rational, goal directed image of organizational effectiveness'.

The Appraisal Process

Appraisals vary in the extent to which they articulate a role for the appraiser, and the extent to which an explicitly managerial role becomes written into existence. The premiss of appraisal is that the appraiser is 'present', the embodied persona essential to 'validate' the information which emerges during the appraisal process. The role which is articulated for this person varies greatly and is to some extent dependent on the process by which individuals are obliged to provide information about themselves and their jobs. For example, variation can be seen in terms of the structuring of the appraisal interaction: thus, 'the appraiser submits points for discussion arising from the appraisee's self appraisal'; 'the appraiser's role is to make the appraisee aware of the structure of the review meeting'; 'the appraiser should begin by giving a member of staff his/her observations on the appraisee's performance'. In each, the role of appraiser becomes structured in terms of initiating and controlling discussion especially through setting the agenda. This may be contrasted with:

the paper work involved requires the member of staff to give a good deal of thought to the job and its priorities and how they spend their time, it is only later in the process that the [appraiser] enters the situation in an active way. Both [appraiser] and employee become involved in actively seeking the right basis for constructive action as a joint professional task.

An explicitly managerial role is found in the articulation of the appraiser's role once the appraisal discussion has been conducted: 'the appraiser records comments on the appraisee's activity and development, including an assessment of performance'. Others are more directive as, for example, where the appraiser is required to 'make notes on job performance, the capability and potential of employees, including strengths of work, areas needing improvement and suggestions for further development'. This is to be contrasted with schemes which do not require the appraiser's comments, with the latter's role limited to responding, as required, to the appraisee's self assessment during the appraisal discussion.

The significance of written documentation is important. Again the role here varies. Some schemes explicitly require the appraiser's comments to be an *agreed* record of the appraisal discussion and an *agreed* statement of objectives. Others are less specific on this—'the appraiser makes written and hopefully agreed summary comments reviewing overall performance'. The more managerial stipulate that:

following the meeting the appraiser will complete the appraisal record and forward it to the member of staff stating a summary of objectives and activities in the last year, comments on achievements, problems and constraints, a summary of objectives for the following year, comments on expected standards, methods of achievement, timescales and specific action points including training and development.

The tasks of appraiser as monitor may be firmly established thus: 'the aim is to judge (and record) the quality of performance and to identify ways to improve it which can be checked at a subsequent appraisal'. In some cases the appraiser's role becomes an explicitly judgemental one:

some members of staff will chiefly need to be told that their work is excellent and that it is appreciated. Some will need to be encouraged to identify and then pursue new activities or areas of work of interest to them. Others may need to be encouraged to a greater effort...a few may need to be told that parts of their work are not up to the necessary standard.

The appraisal procedures vary in the extent to which they specifically articulate the nature of the appraiser's authority and the extent of a judgemental role. Most systems deny the element of judgement, depersonalizing the process by appealing to notions of a seemingly externally verifiable objectivity. Thus: 'the comments by the head of department will be of a judgemental nature, it is vital that comments are as objective and fair as possible'; or 'appraisal is to contribute to common aims. That purpose would be frustrated by an inept exercise of procedure in which it appeared that a head was exercising self-indulgent authority. Authority will have to be exercised and sometimes severely but it must be exercised clearly in the common good.' This is in contrast to 'the term appraisal usually implies a judgement by a superior of a subordinate, that is a process which is unilateral and top down. A shift to "staff review" recognises that this approach will be unacceptable within a university environment.' Making judgements 'on a colleague's personal worth' is under this perspective explicitly rejected.

One area at issue is control over the labour process and the degree of individual control over work. Appraisal has important implications for this, varying in the extent to which control over work is seen as being something to be discussed in consultation with colleagues or directed by the emergent hierarchy. Thus, for example, a more collegially based system states 'one objective is to help the employee set personal goals at an acceptable and realistic level and discuss the means by which they can be realised'. For others, 'management' emerges by becoming inextricably linked to control over the labour process: 'appraisal provides the opportunity for individuals to discuss what performance is expected of him/her and receive feedback'. Appraisal, structured within a formally hierarchical relationship, assumes the directly experienced elements of managerial control found in the judgement of work and deriving from this the 'legitimacy' to influence its subsequent direction. 'Targets' become externally established as, 'the head of department should use his/her expectations of what is required of a member of staff as criteria for measurement and in the interview should invite staff members' comments on criteria chosen'. Targets may become centrally established as, for example, the notes for guidance for appraisers in one appraisal system which makes reference to three to four research papers being set as an example of a target set per year. Sometimes there are constraints on the ability of appraisers to impose targets by ensuring explicit reference on the appraisal form to problems or difficulties in achieving them.

In other circumstances control over the labour process, although not directly or explicitly articulated as a 'managerial' activity may be circumscribed by the format in which work is discussed, for example, 'it is important that target setting be relevant to goals which are valued and focus on the specific and the measurable, the realistic and the attainable, they should be actions which it will be possible to review in a years time'. Sometimes this is quite specific:

Please find ways of stating objectives which make them: quantifiable (wherever possible make them objective and thus measurable), capable of being tested (define the constraints within which they are to be achieved, within a definite timescale), precise (clear, well defined and written in as few words as possible).

Work then becomes articulated in terms of target setting—thus 'statements made at previous appraisals will be considered in order to review how far agreed goals and targets have been achieved'. What emerges is another component of the rhetoric of bureaucratic control identified by Gowler and Legge (1983 : 198) as that of a 'rational, goal directed image of organizational effectiveness'. What is being privileged is the 'quantitative, results-orientated, explicitly rational . . . and independently verifiable' (Earl 1983 : 115). Credence is given to what Morgan (1988 : 480) calls the over-arching metaphor of the numerical view of reality. Some appraisals explicitly reject this, however, 'the difficulties of trying to quantify output in any useful way and of trying to judge progress within specialized areas would present almost insuperable problems'.

Analysis of the emergence of management cannot, however, rely solely on an analysis of process. Content is also important. This can be seen in particular in the appraisals of heads of departments, where the appraisal of the managerial role is predominant. Many appraisals reflect the view that 'the outcome of appraisal carries as much purport for appraisers and reviewers about the quality of leadership and management as it does for employees about individual performance'. Although appraised in performance as academics, administrative and 'managerial qualities' are also scrutinized. In one university the hierarchical appraisal of the Head or Chair Role is on whether there is 'efficient and effective use of departmental resources; the extent to which they [heads] maximize the opportunities and performance of staff of the department, ensuring optimal quality in teaching, research and consultancy'. In some cases this is supplemented by assessment against departmental and faculty indicators. What emerges is the definition of the head in an explicitly managerial way in terms of directing the actions of others, with the subsequent appraisal of him or her in this capacity subsequently reinforcing this.

Throughout is the implicit assumption of 'objective' information external to appraiser and appraisee, accessible through the appraisal process, the truth of which is more likely to be discerned by the appraiser. This 'externalization' of knowledge as existing 'out there' becomes inextricably linked to control and is particularly observable in issues which relate to the source of the information to be used in appraisal. In some appraisals information is restricted to that provided by the appraisee, in others however the source of information can be quite wide ranging, including 'information known directly to the appraiser, and information solicited by the appraiser from other relevant members of the department' or 'other staff both within and outside the department'. Or, as in one case, 'in order to appraise the chair...and conduct a broader appraisal of managerial effectiveness the Vice Chancellor (VC) should be able to take informal soundings from professors and other senior staff within departments on a confidential basis as is required'. In this case the VC is also able to take informal soundings outside the university in relation to research performance.

Student evaluations are obviously an important source of information and again are variously handled indicating differing concepts of individual autonomy and the managerial role. In some cases evaluation lies within the discretion of the appraisee: 'the *curriculum vitae* should make reference to the methods of obtaining feedback and attempts at improvement'. In others the methods to be used are stipulated. For example, 'teaching is to include a questionnaire which is subject to approval by the staffing committee'. Again the role of the appraiser varies: 'questionnaires may not be issued to students without prior discussion between the appraiser and appraisee, completed questionnaires being part of the appraisal process and will be confidential to the appraiser and appraisee'. Alternatively, the review of teaching is seen as a departmental or university responsibility, the results of which are then to be communicated to the appraisee—'student opinion about the quality of the lectures will be sought and made known to the lecturer'.

This examination of the 'extremities of power', the techniques of notation, in the textual variation amongst appraisal documents illustrates how nonegalitarian, asymmetrical relationships may become structured and established in a variety of different areas and have implications for control over work, individual autonomy and the way relationships with others are handled. Continuing this ascending analysis of power it is important to trace further power effects of knowledge systems.

Control of Information and the Emergence of a Managerial Strata

Access to and control of information is crucial to an appraisal scheme. However, this introduces one of the inherent paradoxes of appraisal—that the information required to ensure effective work organization will not be forthcoming if it is thought this will jeapordize the individual. If this indicates restricted access to documents at the local level there are other, counter pressures, which promote the need for a wider circulation. Once the initial decision has been taken to introduce appraisals, others follow as, for example, if and how it is to be monitored. Incremental decision-making reinforces these dynamics. As one observer commented: 'heads of department and deans argued that if access [to appraisal documents] was restricted, why was the university spending money on appraisal, the university wants to get a return from appraisal'. Not only does the knowledge created in appraisal require the legitimation of the appraiser, in many cases the documented process which results must be verified by a higher level. Appraisal records must be viewed to ensure a 'consistency of review'. The 'need' to monitor appraisal prompts additional documentation in terms of the procedures used to ensure appraisal has been completed, and examine how they have been conducted. This then leads to questions as to how detailed the monitoring process is required to be and the degree of visibility of lower organizational levels to higher tiers.

Access to documentation prompts its own intervention. Rarely is information viewed 'for its own sake'; it has to be viewed 'with a purpose'. Monitoring is not just the recording of processes, but provides the basis of intervention and with it, the creation of a managerial role. In conventional discussions of appraisal the assumption is made that documentation merely records summaries, agreed or otherwise, and that this encapsulates an independent and separate reality. On the contrary, summaries constitute independent texts. Removed from the context from which they were drawn, written comments lose an important facet of their meaning and, given the inherent creativity of language, become open to differing interpretations as they are reviewed by those further up the hierarchy. Information from a particular form allows information to be re-presented in an arena where decisions are to be made.

The meaning summaries acquire as a subset of the context in which they are written is lost as new interpretations are imposed on them. Intervention may therefore be prompted in individual cases as differing interpretations are placed on 'the case' from those more immediate to its recording.

In addition to manufacturing a distinct managerial role, appraisal also has implications for structures within the organization. As Hacking (1986 : 27) notes 'a new body of knowledge brings into being a new class of people or institutions that can exercise a new kind of power'. Thus, as one appraisal committee minutes noted, 'complete consistency will never be achieved but steps must be taken to ensure that basic principles are understood. *Some new machinery will need to be created*' (emphasis added). New committees are thus established to oversee the procedure and the emergence of another managerial layer derives almost axiomatically from the appraisal process. Once a committee is established, the need for it to be seen to do something in order to justify its existence may serve to further centralize decision-making in the organization. Given the 'garbage can' model of decision-making (Cohen et al. 1972), this process may develop along very *ad hoc* lines, but develop nonetheless.

One form of intervention is that which can occur under the rubric of an 'aid to participants'. In one appraisal committee which was observed in which a number of completed appraisal documents were sent for review following a pilot scheme, it was suggested, half in jest at the time, that one of the appraisal records might be circulated to subsequent appraisees as an example of the style of report which the appraisal committee wished to see. The particular record in question happened to be of an academic who had had a particularly successful publication record that year, having just had a number of books and articles published. The jocular tone of the suggestion that the form might provide an example was accompanied by a number of comic responses about 'production rates', and 'giving the troops some idea of what was required'. The tone of the meeting then turned more serious, concluding that the suggestion 'wasn't a bad idea'; a 'model' should be found; appraisees would appreciate it; and appraisers would have a clearer idea of what to look for. Thus a specific style of appraisal becomes favoured and a 'norm' becomes established against which to judge other appraisees and appraisers.

The appraisal procedure epitomises a process whereby procedures of notation are then removed to centres where calculations or judgements are made. What emerges, however, is how a functioning network arises from a loose assemblage of activities, not as something centrally planned or directed. The essence is adhocracy as problems and solutions evolve into structures and coping mechanisms, rather than a ubiquitous and omniscient management establishing structures to set objectives.

The Information Panopticon

In many respects appraisal functions as the paper equivalent of the panopticon—an 'information panopticon' (Zuboff 1988). Originally designed to inform prison construction, the panopticon is an architectural model. It involves the construction of a central observation tower around which are housed the 'inmates' of the prison and from which they are open to observation. The central tower was to house 'the administrative functions of management, the policing functions of surveillance, the economic functions of controlling and checking, the religious functions of encouraging obedience and work; from here all orders would come, all activities would be recorded, all offences perceived and judged' (Foucault 1977 : 174). In combining hierarchy, unilateral observation and a normalizing judgement, the panopticon has been defined as the principle of disciplinary organization. It offers this possibility through combining knowledge production and power effects.

Appraisal operates as a form of panopticon with its anonymous and continuous surveillance as seen in the articulation of a monitoring role. For example, 'academic deans may not need to see all appraisal forms below head of department. They will ask to see a sample range of completed forms so that they can monitor how the scheme is being operated in practice'. Often monitoring and hierarchical access to records is introduced under the guise of fairness, for example, 'it is important for the integrity of the system that employees receive equality of treatment'; 'the pro-VC responsible for staffing matters will examine a random sample of proforma from time to time for the purpose of monitoring the scheme and ensuring common standards of judgement are being applied across the university and follow up action is being pursued'. Monitoring functions conflict with the confidentiality of the scheme, a dilemma which may not always be recognized, however, for example:

the university officers are to monitor the scheme and have the same access to appraisal documentation as other personal data concerning members of staff while at the same time creating an atmosphere of trust between appraiser and appraisee.

As a system of surveillance, appraisal, although discontinuous in action, is rendered permanent in its effects. Its functioning principle is that the individual never knows whether he or she is under surveillance or not. It represents the exercise of control at a distance both spatially and temporally, 'allowing the absence of face to face contact without the absence of control' (Robson and Cooper 1989 : 103). This effect is magnified in those systems where the source of information to be used in appraisal, and the access to final documentation, is unrestricted. Although operating through visibility, as a technology of power its effects remain largely invisible. It is the exercise of control, a method by which the powerful are helped to observe the less powerful but rarely, it must be noted, *vice versa*.

It is a feature of appraisal which is recognized by those who have to operate it. As one head of department commented:

it would spoil relationships if there was a formal review. If things are formalised they spoil relationships. It would introduce the feeling that every relationship has to be watched. That you have to creep about. It would introduce a bogus element into the relationship which you don't have now.... We operate as a team. This would be destroyed with the idea of spies around.

The panopticon effect is not just on those at the base of the hierarchy, but functions through a network of relations from base to top. Not only does monitoring serve to keep an independent check on what is happening, it also functions as an appraisal of appraisers: 'supervisers perpetually supervised' (Foucault 1977 : 177). As one system reports: 'The head will keep all documents in the attempt to ensure a uniformity of approach within departments and units, the staff development officer will be in touch with the head of department regularly to ensure as much uniformity as is possible throughout the university'. For others access to documents as a form of monitoring is explicit as a means of enabling 'the VC to review the professors to see how they manage their staff'. It has the function of reporting up the internal hierarchy. As indicated, its operation over time may serve to reinforce organizational hierarchy and centralization, as objectives are channelled down the organization and their subsequent implementation is monitored. As one consultant explained of one appraisal: 'the VC saw the initial benefit in terms of information seeking, the task-setting element would be tightened up in the years ahead'. It also ensures that the 'centre' may strengthen its control over the organization: 'Failure to conduct appraisals should be rapidly pursued by personnel . . . a continued unwillingness to undertake appraisals in the manner agreed should bring firm action from the pro vice chancellor'.

The value of the panopticon for Bentham, whose design it was, was that it represented a power relation operating in a mechanistic way, independent of the person who operates it. In practical terms there is the advantage of the exercise of power with the least cost, as the system is operational with limited manpower. Continuous and autonomous surveillance becomes the technology of power, as Bentham's recommendations for it reveal:

it makes it possible to perfect the exercise of power. It does this in several ways: because it can reduce the number of those who exercise it, while increasing the numbers on whom it is exercised . . . its strength is that it never intervenes . . . it constitutes a mechanism whose effects follow from one another . . . it is a great new instrument of government; . . . its great excellence consists in the strength it is capable of giving to any institution it may be thought proper to apply it to . . . .(quoted in Foucault 1977 : 206).

The metaphor which emerges is that of visibility—making 'possible for a single gaze to see everything constantly' (Foucault 1977 : 173). The emphasis is placed on observation, supervision, invigilation, 'each actor is alone, perfectly individualised and constantly visible' (Foucault 1977 : 200). It is not insignificant that of all the appraisal systems analysed none saw the unit to be examined as being the department, all identified the individual as the unit of production. The particular pattern of visibility which is chosen effects change in an organization. Some of the patterns illustrated here result in the gradual dissolution of collegial systems of organization and their replacement by more explicitly managerial forms. The position of 'supervisor' as monitor and evaluator becomes established. Equally the supervisor's work is subject to evaluation and control. Themes of hierarchy and accountability emerge to the extent that an explicit and active managerial hierarchy becomes the organizing principle. The effect therefore, if not intent, of such a procedure is to resemble the panopticon.

The mechanism by which this takes place, however, is not at the instigation of a particular omniscient group or strata within the organization. It is not the exercise of some people with 'power' operating on those without. There is no 'centre' of power in the sense of a controlling or directing force, although one may be nominally identified. The 'point of origin' of these changes is dispersed. For Foucault it is the effect of 'a multiplicity of often minor processes of different origins and scattered locations, which overlap, repeat or imitate one another, support one another'. Techniques which are invented for one purpose spill over into other aspects of a governmental role. Although actions are informed by a series of aims and objectives, with individuals and groups jockeying for advantage, this does not indicate that the broader consequences of these actions are co-ordinated. Introduced with the functional aim of improving individual and organizational performance through the provision of information, appraisal sets in train specific power dynamics, the effects of which over time are by and large unpredictable. As Foucault (1982 : 787) phrases it 'people know what they do, they know why they do it, but what they don't know is what they do does'.

The effect *may* be to change the character of the organization, and the individual experiences of work sufficiently, the disciplinary effect of which may even be counter to the wishes of those who operate it. This may or may not happen. It is not an 'unproblematic unfolding'. As Miller and Rose (1990 : 10) remark, 'whilst "governmentality" is eternally optimistic, "government" is a congenitally failing operation . . . the will to govern needs to be understood less in terms of its success than in terms of the difficulties of operationalising it'.

These developments are not axiomatic or inexorable. There is always resistance to programming or rendering a sphere or an arena programmable, depending on the perceptions of those involved, and the extent to which resistance is articulated. Technologies are used by people for different means and result in unplanned outcomes or unexpected consequences. They may be modified according to those involved in its operation, or there may be collective patterns of resistance. As Hindess (1982) notes, power is not the playing out of a script. The privileging of a particular system of managing, conflicting with long established patterns of relationships between colleagues or personal definitions of what 'the job' entails, may prompt resistance. The emergence of a managerial role gives formal power but may detract from the authority and effectiveness likely to be required to introduce change, and thus be eschewed. Equally the productive role of power with appraisal acting as an aid to subjective well-being may lead to support for certain types of appraisal processes (Knights 1990; Knights and Willmott 1985).

Conclusion

The purpose of this article has been to contribute to debate on the study of management. Its premise has been to decentre 'management' as an organizing focus, arguing that a more productive approach to its study is generated by an investigation of the technologies or practices which give effect to managing. Practices have been examined for their power effects, without presupposing intention or imputing interests. In denying the link between power and interests, management is not reduced to the actions of a manager, or a coherent and calculating organizational force which holds power. Adopting Foucault's ascending analysis of power—the study of power at its extremities—the lived experience of those within organizations is considered whilst at the same time enabling the constitutive effects of such practices to be considered.

Appraisal illustrates a technology active in the constitution of managing. It is an example of the operation of power/knowledge, rendering aspects of existence thinkable, calculable, and thus manageable. Through an examination of the various stages in an appraisal process it is possible to see how texts help to articulate asymmetrical power relations and enhance the capillary functioning of power. Appraisal illustrates how knowledge of the individual and the work performed articulates the managerial role as a directional activity. The routinized provision of information operates so as to affect organizational segmentation and create new bases for administrative expertise, with patterns of organizational visibility articulating specific forms of management structure.

Minute organizational procedures contribute to the transformation in the mode of government of organizations. In some cases there is a tendency for it to function over time by sedimenting a more hierarchical, centralized and disciplinary model of the organization.

A Foucauldian—ascending—analysis illustrates how activities initially become articulated as managerial, which, over time, acquire institutional consequences and actively create a managerial structure. It emphasizes that management, in both its role and structure, is not 'given' but evolves out of structured practices, constructed through processes which, over time, modify and reinforce institutional arrangements. This deconstruction of management and an examination of processes within organizations at their most basic levels helps to illustrate the processes of organizational transformation with greater clarity.

Acknowledgement

I should like to thank the anonymous reviewers and Richard Marsden for their helpful comments on earlier drafts of this article.

References

Astley, G. (1984). 'Subjectivity, sophistry and symbolism in management science', *Journal of Management Studies*, 21, 3, 259–71.

Barlow, G. (1989). 'Deficiencies and the perpetuation of power: latent functions in managerial appraisal', *Journal of Management Studies*, 26, 449–517.

Benton, T. (1981). 'Objective interests and the sociology of power', *Sociology*, 15, 161–84.

Berry, A. (1983). 'Open social systems and management control', in Machin, J. and Lowe, T. (eds), *New Perspectives in Management Control*. New York: St Martins Press.

Carroll, S. and Gillen, D. (1987). 'Are the classical management functions useful in describing managerial work?', *Academy of Management Review*, 12, 38–51.

Chua, W., Lowe, T. and Puxty, T. (eds.) (1989). *Critical Perspectives in Management Control*. Basingstoke: Macmillan.

Cohen, M., March, J. and Olsen, J. (1972). 'A garbage can model of organizational choice', *Administrative Science Quarterly*, 17, 1–25.

Dreyfus, H. and Rabinow, P. (1986). *Michel Foucault, Beyond Structuralism and Hermeneutics*. Brighton: Harvester Press.

Earl, M. (1983). 'Accounting and management', in Earl, M. (ed.), *Perspectives on Management: a Multidisciplinary Analysis*. Oxford: Oxford University Press.

Barbara Townley

Foucault, M. (1977). *Discipline and Punish: the Birth of the Prison*. London: Allen Lane.

Foucault, M. (1981). *The History of Sexuality, Volume One, an Introduction*. London: Penguin.

Foucault, M. (1982). 'The subject and power', *Critical Inquiry*, 8, 777–95.

Gherardi, S. and Strati, A. (1990). 'The "texture" of organizing in an Italian University Department', *Journal of Management Studies*, 27, 6, 605–18.

Gordon, C. (1980). *Power/Knowledge: Selected Interviews and Other Writings by Michel Foucault*. New York: Pantheon Books.

Gowler, D. and Legge, K. (1983). 'The meaning of management and the management of meaning: a view from social anthropology', in Earl, M. (ed.), *Perspectives on Management: a Multidisciplinary Analysis*. Oxford: Oxford University Press.

Hacking, I. (1986). 'The archaeology of Foucault', in Couzens Hoy, D. (ed.), *Foucault: A Critical Reader*. Oxford: Blackwell.

Hales, C. (1986). 'What do managers do? a critical review of the evidence', *Journal of Management Studies*, 23, 88–115.

Hindess, B. (1982). 'Power, interests and the outcomes of struggles', *Sociology*, 16, 498–511.

Isaac, J. (1982). 'On Benton's "Objective interests and the sociology of power": a critique', *Sociology*, 16, 440–4.

Knights, D. (1990). 'Subjectivity, power and the labour process', in Knights, D. and Willmott, H. (eds.), *Labour Process Theory*. London: Macmillan.

Knights, D. and Willmott, H. (1985). 'Power and identity in theory and practice'. *Sociological Review*, 33, 22–46.

Knights, D. and Willmott, H. (eds) (1986). *Managing the Labour Process*. Aldershot: Gower.

Lowe, T. and Puxty, T. (1989). 'The problem of a paradigm: a critique of the prevailing orthodoxy in management control', in Chua, W., Lowe, T. and Puxty, T. (eds), *Critical Perspectives in Management Control*. Basingstoke: Macmillan.

Lukes, S. (1974). *Power: a Radical View*. London: Macmillan.

Machin, J. (1983). 'Management control systems: whence and whither?', in Machin, J. and Lowe, T. (eds), *New Perspectives in Management Control*. New York: St. Martins Press.

Machin, J. and Lowe, T. (1983). 'Introduction', in Machin, J. and Lowe, T. (eds), *New Perspectives in Management Control*. New York: St. Martins Press.

Machin, J. and Lowe, T. (eds.) (1983) *New Perspectives in Management Control*. New York: St Martins Press.

Meyer, J. (1983). 'On the celebration of rationality: some comments on Boland and Pondy', *Accounting, Organizations and Society*, 8, 235–40.

Miller, P. and Rose, N. (1990). 'Governing economic life', *Economy and Society*, 19, 1–31.

Morgan, G. (1980). 'Paradigms, metaphors, and puzzle solving in organization theory'. *Administrative Science Quarterly*, 3, 605–22.

Morgan, G. (1988). 'Accounting as reality construction: towards a new epistemology for accounting practice', *Accounting, Organizations and Society*, 13, 477–85.

Otley, D. (1983). 'Concepts of control: the contribution of cybernetics and systems theory to management control', in Machin, J. and Lowe, T. (eds.) *New Perspectives in Management Control*. New York: St. Martins Press.

Pym, D. (1973). 'The politics and ritual of appraisals', *Occupational Psychology*, 47, 221–24.

Randell, G. (1989). 'Employee appraisal', in Sisson, K. (ed.), *Personnel Management in Britain*. Oxford: Blackwell.

Reed, M. (1984). 'Management as a social practice', *Journal of Management Studies*, 21, 273–85.

Richbell, S. (1983). 'Management control and worker participation in management', in Machin, J. and Lowe, T. (eds.), *New Perspectives in Management Control*. New York: St Martins Press.

Roberts, J. (1984). 'The moral character of management practice', *Journal of Management Studies*, 21, 3, 287–302.

Robson, K. and Cooper, D. (1989). 'Power and management control', in Chua, W., Lowe, T. and Puxty, T. (eds.), *Critical Perspectives in Management Control*. London: Macmillan.

Rosen, M. (1984). 'Myth and reproduction: the contextualization of management theory, method and practice', *Journal of Management Studies*, 21, 3, 303–21.

Silverman, D. (1985). *Qualitative Methodology and Sociology*. Aldershot: Gower.

Stewart, R. (1984). 'The nature of management? a problem for management education', *Journal of Management Studies*, 21, 3, 323–30.

Stewart, R. (1989). 'Studies of managerial jobs and behaviour: the ways forward', *Journal of Management Studies*, 26, 1–10.

Townley, B. (1990/91). 'The politics of appraisal: lessons of the introduction of appraisal into UK universities', *Human Resource Management Journal*, 1, 2, 27–44.

Whitley, R. (1984a). 'The fragmented state of management studies: reasons and critiques', *Journal of Management Studies*, 21, 3, 331–48.

Whitley, R. (1984b). 'The scientific status of management research as a practically-oriented social science', *Journal of Management Studies*, 21, 4, 369–90.

Whitley, R. (1989). 'On the nature of managerial tasks and skills: their distinguishing characteristics and organization', *Journal of Management Studies*, 26, 209–24.

Willmott, H. (1984). 'Images and ideals of managerial work: a critical examination of conceptual and empirical accounts', *Journal of Management Studies*, 21, 349–68.

Willmott, H. (1987). 'Studying managerial work: a critique and a proposal', *Journal of Management Studies*, 24, 249–70.

Zuboff, S. (1988). *In the Age of the Smart Machine: the Future of Work and Power*. London: Heinemann; New York: Basic Books.

15

Studying Managerial Work: A Critique and a Proposal[1]

Hugh Willmott

Introduction

A striking point about empirical studies of managerial work in capitalist enterprise is their disregard for its institutional formation and significance.[2] In general, the institutional conditioning and consequences of managerial work is either bracketed, taken for granted, or treated as an independent variable.[3] The purpose of this article is to highlight the hiatus between 'behavioural' and 'institutional' accounts of managerial work and to suggest a means of overcoming this dualism between 'action' and 'system' (Giddens 1976; 1979; 1984). More specifically, the paper focuses upon the neglect of institutional analysis in behavioural studies of management practice.

Studies of managerial work are found wanting in four inter-related respects. First, as already noted, they abstract the activities of individual managers from the institutional arrangements in and through which they act. In doing so, such studies generally disregard how the work of the manager is accomplished by enacting, and thereby reconstituting, institutionally produced rules and resources. Second, and relatedly, their focus is upon differences of individual behaviour or group allegiance, and not upon managerial work as expressive of the (developing) institutional arrangements that are at once a condition as well as a consequence of managers' actions. Third, these studies uncritically trade upon a distinction between the technical/formal and the political/formal elements of managerial work. Technical/formal elements are assumed to be legitimate or politically neutral because they are officially sanctioned. What is 'political' is thereby restricted to 'informal' departures or deviations from an officially sanctioned order, and even then such departures are generally understood to be of only local, organizational significance.

The final limitation of these studies concerns the lack of revealed awareness about the problematical relationship between the observer (researcher) and the observed (manager). They do not appreciate the value-relevant (Weber, 1949) and cognitive interest-dependent (Habermas, 1972) nature of accounts of managerial work.[4] This failure to reflect upon, and stimulate an appreciation of, the intrinsically open and problematical nature of the relationship between observer and observed allows existing studies to *appear* to provide a mirror image of the reality of managerial work. This is especially the case when they do little more than reflect commonsense accounts of what managers do, and when so few alternative accounts, informed by a critical perspective, have been undertaken.[5] In this respect, it is relevant to acknowledge that the proposed framework does not escape dependence upon particular values and interests.[6] Specifically, it is guided by a concern to highlight the unavoidably social or relational—and, therefore, moral and political–character of managerial action, as well as by an interest in revealing how this action may both preserve and conceal what is problematical within organizations and society.

The article falls into three main sections. In the first section, alternative conceptualizations of management are briefly outlined before critically reviewing three major empirical studies of managerial work by Dalton, (1959) Kotter (1982), and Mintzberg (1973). The second section extends the critical examination of these studies by considering alternative frames of reference for making sense of capitalist work organization. Finally, in the third section, Giddens' theory of structuration is advanced as providing an alternative methodological framework for the study of managerial work. Its relevance is then illustrated by reference to empirical materials presented by Nichols and Beynon (1977) in *Living with Capitalism*.

....

Accounting for Managerial Work

In his textbook treatment of management, Child (1977) distinguishes between three different conceptualizations, or images of management. The first image of management is of the 'economic resource' that performs technical, administrative functions. A second, related image is that of the 'professional corps' which is identifiable less by its function than by its expertise and credentials. Under-developed in comparison, Child suggests, is an image of the 'political aspect' of management (ibid. 113). When examined from this aspect, management is conceptualized as 'a system of power and authority within which different personal and group strategies are pursued' (ibid.).

[handwritten at top left: Threads, like in a rope]

Hugh Willmott

[handwritten margin marks: i, ii, iii]

Within the 'political' literature on management, Child identifies three strands: studies that locate managers in the class structure (e.g. Nichols 1969; Stanworth and Giddens, 1974), studies that attend to managers' orientations within and between different organizational and cultural settings (e.g. Sofer 1970; Turner 1971) and, finally, studies that focus upon the social and political processes embodied in managerial work (e.g. Dalton 1959; Mintzberg 1973). However, although these strands are exposed in Child's overview, the rifts between them are not. 'Institutional' writers have studied managers' positions in the 'system of power and authority' independently of the examination of managers' personal and group strategies. And, on the other hand, 'behavioural' writers have researched managers' strategies without understanding these to be a medium and outcome of a wider 'system of power and authority'. The contention that research has been premised upon a dualistic separation of institutional and behavioural dimensions will now be explored and illustrated by reviewing briefly three major contributions to the study of managerial work.[7]

Mintzberg

In *The Nature of Managerial Work* (1973), Mintzberg presents an analysis of the work of five chief executives. To interpret his findings, he builds upon role theory to advance a contingency view of managerial work in which variations between managerial role sets are attributed to the deterministic influence of four nested sets of variables: 'environmental', 'job', 'person' and 'situational'. Or, as he puts it, 'the work any manager does at a certain point in time can be described as a function of the four "nested" sets of variables'. Mintzberg's approach represents the reality of managerial work as a set of discrete, 'observable' activities. *[handwritten margin: separate, discontinuous]* The mix of these activities is then associated with the occupancy of a formal office or position which is seen to be shaped and modified by the four nested sets of variables. By conceptualizing the content of managerial work in terms of discrete activities, and by drawing upon contingency theory to account for variations in managerial work, Mintzberg effectively disregards the *social* or *relational* nature of managerial work. Not that he fails to note the significance of 'environmental' and 'situational' variables. But this recognition that managerial work is shaped by institutional 'variables' does not lead him to develop a relational understanding of its reality.

Instead, Mintzberg seems to be saying this: when we make sense of managerial work, we must not make the mistake of explaining it solely in terms of the personality characteristics ('person' variable) of the individual manager. In addition, we must recognize the impact of institutional and interpersonal forces: the 'environmental', 'job' and 'situational' variables. In this way, Mintzberg appears to take account of the social nature of managerial work.

But he does so without appreciating the relational and *contested* production of this reality. Yes, he does conceptualize managerial work as the outcome of an interaction between 'social' variables. However, in his structured observational method, where work content is equated with commonsense description, and also in his theory, which involves the unproblematic identification of roles and variables, all appreciation of the social formulation and maintenance of the 'content' of managerial work is excluded.[8] And so, despite an espoused concern to examine managerial work in terms of the institutional roles performed by managers, Mintzberg's methodology and conceptual framework effectively deny him the possibility of studying the historical and political processes that underpin, channel and provide rationales for the work that managers do.

Dalton

In turning to consider Dalton's *Men Who Manage* (1959), it might be anticipated that a more penetrating account of the 'political aspect(s)' of managerial work would be found. Certainly, the method of participant observation enabled Dalton to get beneath the surface of the formal and/or officially sanctioned features of managerial work. In doing so, he exposes much of the underlife of organizations (cf. Goffman 1959) in which 'informal' arrangements replace, impede and are 'mixed' with formal, official procedures.

However, on closer inspection, it is apparent that Dalton's appreciation of the social and political processes of managerial work is quite limited. There is much reporting of the shifting individual and clique-based strategems developed by managers to 'loosen controls on themselves and tighten them on others' (Dalton 1959 : 19). But the focus of Dalton's research is almost exclusively upon the psychological struggles of the individual manager who is seen to strive to reconcile (unreconcilable) 'rational, emotional, social and ethical claims' in the context of large, impersonal corporations (ibid. : 258). In elaborating and illustrating the existence of tensions between roles and their players, Dalton's analysis conceptualizes these tensions primarily as the result of personal sentiments rather than, say, the contradictory, oppressive structure of social relations. There is minimal detailed description or theoretical penetration either of role tensions or of the structural source of the rules and resources drawn upon by managers in the pursuit of their 'personal' values and interests.

Kotter

The final study to be considered is Kotter's *The General Managers* (1982). Like Mintzberg, Kotter focuses his attention upon the work of a number of senior managers. In doing so, he concurs with Dalton in the view that 'real progress' in the study of managerial work depends upon the use of unstructured observation methods (ibid. : 153). These, Kotter indicates, are essential if the researcher is to get 'inside' descriptions of activities undertaken or roles played in order to reveal how managers construct and maintain their *relationships* with others.

Kotter's study begins to disclose how 'effective' managers skilfully use their access to institutional resources to build political alliances and influence people. He reveals, for example, how managers contrive to glean information and support from supervisors without appearing to be over-demanding or inadequate; how they seek to motivate and supervise subordinates, and how they elicit co-operation from corporate and external groups despite resistance, etc. (cf. Blau 1965). As Kotter observes, the managers in his study:

> tried to make others feel legitimately obliged to them by doing favours or by stressing their formal relationships. They acted in ways to encourage others to identify with them. They carefully nurtured their professional reputations in the eyes of others. They even manoeuvred to make others feel that they were particularly dependent on the general managers for resources, or career advancement or support. (Kotter 1982 : 69–70).

It might be said that Kotter's observations are merely statements of the obvious. Don't we already know that managers, like everyone else, skilfully construct and employ symbols and other 'stage props' to secure the sense and solidity of their position and prerogative? Perhaps we do, but most studies of managerial work serve to dim rather than heighten our awareness of this, as Kotter (1979; 1982) forcefully points out. His major contribution, then, has been to highlight the building and maintaining of networks of 'relationships' in a *sine qua non* of general managerial work. In doing so, he reveals that the power that is exercised and replenished through the successful management of inter-personal networks should not be regarded as peripheral to managerial activity nor be treated as a deviation from formally or officially defined roles.

In these aspects, Kotter's study goes further than most of its predecessors in acknowledging and stressing the central importance of social relationships and power in the routine accomplishment of managerial work (cf. Sayles 1979). However, Kotter's interest in relationships and power extends only to the identification of their significance and potential for achieving a more effective use of the individual manager's talents. The 'position-power' of managers is perceived to be unproblematical. According to Kotter, 'politicking' by managers is necessary only because of the complexity of large organizations that makes it difficult to obtain reliable current information about diverse operations. No mention whatever is made of the structures of social and economic relations that support the legitimacy of the rules and the accessibility of the resources drawn upon by managers in defining, refining and defending the content of their work. A unitarist or perhaps pragmatically pluralist view of the organization is thus taken for granted (Kelly 1982) as the pursuit of existing priorities by more effective managers is assumed to be in the interests of everyone.

To summarize this section, it has been argued that prominent and influential studies of managerial work have been guided by frameworks of interpretation that have disregarded or trivialized its institutional reality and significance. By separating work from its social context, these 'behavioural' studies have largely disregarded the 'political aspect' of managerial work; or they have identified it exclusively with the skills and strategies devised and applied by individual managers to perform their formally defined roles and/or to advance their career interests. Overlooked or obscured are the institutional grounds of managerial work as an expression of politico-economic relations of power. This critical assessment of the capacity of such studies to illuminate the political aspect of management will now be expanded. To do this the 'unitary' and 'pragmatically pluralist' assumptions common to these studies will be compared and contrasted with an alternative, 'radical' view of the structure of power relations in organizations and society.

Towards an Alternative Account of Managerial Work

In the previous section, the political aspect of management was equated with the view of management as a 'system of power and authority within which different personal and group strategies are pursued' (Child 1977 : 113). The particular virtue (and vice) of this formulation is its capacity to include (and its failure to differentiate between) the structural principles of the system and the associated structuring of individual's strategic conduct. To characterize the variety of ways in which 'system' and 'strategic conduct' can be conceptualized, it is relevant to refer briefly to Fox's (1973; 1974) distinction between unitary, pluralist and radical frames of reference. By drawing selectively and critically upon Fox's analysis, differences in the formulation of the relationship between observer (researcher) and observed (managers) can be highlighted.

Unitary, Pluralist and Radical Views of Management

From a unitary standpoint, the structure of social relations within organizations is seen to embody rational efforts to develop the most efficient and effective means of achieving common interests and objectives. When studied in this light, managerial work is regarded primarily as an expression of the technical division of labor required to realize organizational goals. In other words, the work of managers is accounted for as a functional element of organization whose responsibility is for the rational design of all aspects of organization so that the shared objectives of its members can be secured. This view of the structure of social relations is most clearly evident in classical and human relations accounts of the role of management. However, as noted earlier, strong traces of this perspective can also be found in recent studies of managerial work (e.g. Mintzberg 1973).

Pluralist s.p. From a pluralist standpoint, the unitary perspective is unconvincing because, in large modern organizations, the complexity of the technical division of labour is such that individuals are conditioned by specialized training and motivated by self-interest to form coalitions for the pursuit of sectional object-ives. Conflicts between a plurality of power-holders within organizations is thus seen to be endemic, and managerial work is understood to involve a continu-ous effort to gain consent and/or contain conflicts of interest in ways which, in the long run, allow at least minimal fulfilment of all members' sectional objectives. This perspective has been advanced by theorists who have regarded the classic, unitary view of management as an unobtainable ideal. Desirable as this ideal might be, to confuse it with reality or to strive to make reality conform to it, is perceived as self-defeating. Again, evidence of elements of this pragmatic pluralist framework is present within studies of managerial work reviewed earlier (e.g. Kotter 1982).

Radical s.p. Finally, the radical standpoint challenges assumptions made in both pluralist and unitary accounts of the structure of social relations in organizations (and society). The basic charge levelled against them concerns their failure to recog-nize the politico-economic nature of the technical division of labour. From a radical perspective, the horizontal and vertical differentiation of tasks between individuals and groups cannot adequately be explained by references to func-tional imperatives. Instead, it is understood to reflect and sustain the structure of power relations within society. Managers are seen to play specialist, technical roles in the division of labour. But these roles are perceived to be primarily conditioned by the political economy of labor processes in capitalist society.

Capitalist Work Organization

Central to Fox's conceptualization of the radical frame of reference is a distinction between spontaneous and manipulated forms of 'consensus'.[9] Whereas spontaneous forms of consensus are understood to arise when all involved are 'moved by a common cause', a manipulated consensus describes the position when one group has the physical or institutional power to exploit others' dependence in the pursuit of its own sectional interest. As Fox (1974 : 284) puts it:

People do not come together freely and spontaneously to set up work organizations, the *propertyless many are forced by their need for a livelihood to seek access to resources, owned or controlled by the few* (emphasis added).

Fox highlights the structural dependence of the many upon the few. He also emphasises that the latter's influence in shaping expectations and aspirations tends to create a situation in which socially arbitrary conventions and principles are in effect naturalized. However, conspicuous by its absence from his analysis is any sustained appreciation of the existence and significance of structural contradictions and forms of resistance within social systems. Certainly, he remarks upon the asymmetrical distribution of power and the conflicting objectives represented in the existence of low discretion roles. But little or nothing is said of the structural cleavages of interest—the contradictory forms of unity—that can be said to be inherent within capitalist relations of production. Indeed, it would seem that, in Fox's allegedly radical frame of reference, the powerful have the unassailable power to suppress or over-rule such contradictions by using their power to 'determine the power of the many' (ibid. : 284).

In contrast, the position taken here is that relations of production are premised upon and structured around a basic contradiction between the 'principles' of socialized production and private appropriation (Giddens 1979 : 136–7). Following Marx, Hindess and Hirst (1977) have outlined the central structural dynamic of those relations although, as they observe in a later publication, it is 'capitals', not capitalists, which exist in capitalism in its socialized form (Cutler et al. 1977 : 312).

Capitalists buy means of production and items of personal consumption from each other. They buy labour power from labourers in exchange for wages. With these wages the labourers buy items of personal consumption from capitalists and must then sell their labour power for a further period in order to be able to buy further means of personal consumption. Appropriation of surplus labour here depends on a difference between the value of labour power and the value that may be created by the means of the labour power. Surplus labour takes the form of surplus value. . . . Thus capitalist relations of production define a mode of appropriation of surplus labour in the form of surplus value, and a social distribution of the means of production so that these are the property of non-labourers (capitalists), while the labour power takes the form of a commodity which members of the class of labourers are forced to sell to the class of non-labourers. (Hindess and Hirst 1977 : 10).

This contradiction between private appropriation (possession) and socialized production (non-possession) underpins and succours (but does not determine) a class division of labour. This is reflected in tensions within structures and

331

strategies of control as capital depends on labour for the cycle of production and valorization to be sustained (Cutler et al. 1977; Storey 1985a). As the servants of socialized capital, managers are formally required to organize the resources at their command to ensure the extraction of surplus value. In performing this function, management is required to forestall or check resistance to control that arises out of the contradiction between socialized production and private appropriation (Storey 1983). As Winkler (1974) and Zeitlin (1974) have found, *top* managers, at least, tend to espouse values and priorities that are very similar to those of shareholders (and creditors). More generally, the (albeit ambiguous) class position and institutional role of managers at all levels inclines them towards ideas and actions that are not markedly opposed to the reproduction of a social order in which they enjoy a position of comparative advantage (Goldthorpe 1982).

However, formal requirements and concrete practices do not necessarily coincide. Managers are not omniscient. Even when intending to safeguard shareholders' interest, conflicting interpretation and judgement inevitably enter which, with hindsight, can be questioned. To put this another way, the interests of capital like those of labour, are not given. They have to be organized. Moreover, they are organized by managers who themselves do not occupy an unambiguous position within the structure of capitalist relations of production. The variable measure of autonomy enjoyed by managers can be used to organize and defend their own (specialist and hierarchically positioned) values and interests. Moreover, despite being employed to preserve the interests of capital, most managers share with workers an oppressive requirement to sell their labour power to provide for the items of personal consumption.

For these reasons it should not be assumed that managerial action is unmediated by 'opposition and resistance, opportunism and sheer irrationality and incompetence' (Storey 1983 : 7). What managers actually do cannot be convincingly analysed without allowing for the influence of 'sectional conflicts, professional strategies, internal bargaining, occupational closure and so forth' (Reed 1984; Salaman 1982). However, in taking this into account, it is equally important not to be distracted or become preoccupied with conflicts within management (e.g. Dalton 1959; Pettigrew 1985). Otherwise, as Tinker (1984 : 70) has cautioned, 'the "moderators" and "intervening factors" take on greater significance than that which is being moderated—structural conflict itself'.

To classify managers simply as 'part of the capitalist class' and 'members of the bourgeoisie', as for example Carchedi (1975 : 48) does, is to overlook how their social location and work situation is constructed in the context of competition and struggle within classes as well as between classes. Crucially, the reproduction of class relations of production founded upon the contradiction between socialized production and private appropriation does not exist independently of non-economic forces (Coward and Ellis 1977;

Pecheux 1982). Indeed, political and ideological elements may not only condition but also contain, conceal and thereby postpone indefinitely the resolution of this contradiction. In a similar vein, Burawoy (1985) has noted how the process of ideological and political struggle between classes can mollify the opposition of interests. The 'crucial issue', he argues is that:

the interests that organize the daily life of workers are not given irrevocably; they cannot be imputed... To assume, without further specification, that the interests of capital and labour are opposed leads to serious misunderstandings of capitalist control. (pp. 28–9).

'Serious misunderstandings' arise where it is assumed that the interests of workers/managers can be 'read off' from the primary economic contradiction of capitalist relations of production. In concrete social practices, political and ideological elements, whose plausibility and legitimacy is conditioned by the distinctive features of the capitalist mode of production, can obscure or minimize the class nature of the structure of production relations. In the factory or at the office, workers do not directly confront 'the class of possessors'. Rather, they encounter managers who, like themselves, exchange their labour for wages,[10] and who may appear merely to be engaged in the universal, technical task of coordinating a complex labour process. From this perspective, the social function of management, which involves preserving a (profitable) difference between the price paid for labour power and the value it creates, may be invisible to workers and managers alike. The extraction of surplus value is obscured from view as wages appear to cover all the hours at work, not just the hours necesary for the reproduction of labour power; and the individual or collective wage bill appears to be determined, in a quasi-fatalistic manner, by the impersonal mechanism of the market, without awareness of how the allowance for unpaid labour is already incorporated into the structural operation of this mechanism.[11]

Moreover, even those who recognize the class structure of capitalist relations of production may pledge or resign themselves to getting what they, individually or collectively, can out of 'the system'. For, as Storey (1985b : 282) has stressed, 'labour is not simply in the position of being subject to capital, it also has a crucial stake in it... many workers see their fortunes enmeshed in the prevailing order. People deeply critical of this order also act to make it work'. 'Cooperation' may thus be as much the product of informed calculation as it is an expression of ignorance, manipulation or false-consciousness. Reflecting such ideas, the notions of a 'fair' wage is regularly formulated in relation to differentials and comparabilities rather in terms of the difference between necessary and surplus labour time. Nonetheless, from the perspective advanced here, such ideas, which serve to reproduce exploitative and oppressive relations of production are regarded as an expression of these class relations. For, as Giddens (1982 : 40) has observed:

it is quite possible to conceive of circumstances in which individuals are not only not cognisant of being in a common class situation, but where they may actively deny the existence of classes—*and where their attitudes and ideas can nevertheless be explained in terms of class relationships.* (emphasis added)

In sum, managerial work cannot adequately be studied and accounted for simply by identifying its economic function. Nor can it satisfactorily be explained purely in terms of its checking of resistance from below. Nor, finally, can it be understood only in terms of the autonomous, if ambiguous, values and interests of managers. Instead, the argument of this article is that managerial work is theorized better as reflecting and sustaining a fundamentally contested structure of social relations in which an institutionalized organization of the interests of capital is tempered and compromised: first by systematic contradictions; second, and relatedly, by individual and collective resistance from below; and, third, by managers themselves who, at the very least, interpret and act out their 'functional roles' in the light of their own (minimally) autonomous cultural and ideological values. This understanding will now be explored and illustrated by drawing upon Giddens's theory of structuration and Nichols and Beynon's *Living with Capitalism*.

[margin note: moderated/ mitigated]

....

The Theory of Structuration and the Study of Managerial Work

It has been argued that if the study of managerial work is to take account of its institutional contexts as well as the strategic conduct of individual managers, then managerial work must be analysed as an expression of the strategic conduct of individuals and as a product of the institutional order. Giddens (1976; 1979; 1984) has recently developed a conceptual framework that provides a means of doing precisely this: to overcome the dualism in social and organizational theory between 'action' and 'system' (Ranson et al. 1979; Willmott 1979). His theory of structuration will first be outlined before illustrating how it provides an alternative framework for the study of managerial work.

The Duality of Structure in Interaction

Central to the theory of structuration is the idea of structure as a duality. Instead of employing the concept of structure to describe a context in which social practices are situated or played out, it is conceived as the medium of strategic conduct. Structure is thus understood to reside within social practices and not to exist as an external context of constraint upon them (cf. Bhaskar 1978). The particular value of the theory of structuration is that it does not reduce 'action' to a function of 'the system'; nor does it neglect or take for granted the structural conditions and consequences of 'action'. Instead, by conceptualizing structure as a duality—that is, as a medium as well as an outcome of (managerial) action—it is possible to better grasp the inter-relatedness of the 'institutional' and the 'strategic' dimensions of social practice.

In the process of acting, agents are conceived by Giddens as mobilizing interpretative schemes, norms and other facilities which, collectively, are described as the modalities of structuration (see Figure 1). Analytically, the modalities provide the linkage between the process of interaction and the structural components of social systems. Modalities are understood to be drawn upon by actors in the production of interaction. And, at the same time, they are the media of the reproduction of the structural components of systems of interaction. By placing an epoché upon the institutional dimension, the modalities appear in the form of the communication of meaning, the use of power and the application of norms. Conversely, when bracketing the strategic dimension, the modalities appear as the structural properties of social systems—as expressions of signification, domination and legitimation.

Interaction	Communication	Power	Sanctions
(Modality)	Interpretative Schemes	Facilities	Norms
Structure	Signification	Domination	Legitimation

Fig. 1. *The duality of structure in interaction* (Giddens 1979 : 82)

To elaborate, from the standpoint of strategic conduct, the three analytically separable modalities are examined in relation to individuals' efforts to achieve their purpose and/or pursue their interests. From this perspective, the modalities appear as rules and resources strategically drawn upon by agents in the accomplishment of interaction. From an insitutional standpoint, in contrast, these rules and resources are studied as features of systems of social interaction. To repeat, the analytical significance of the modalities is that they provide 'the coupling elements' whereby the analysis of the 'dimension of interaction—centred upon the communication of meaning, the operation of relations of power and the application of normative sanctions—is linked to the analysis of the structural components of social systems—where the analytical focus is upon signification, domination and legitimation. In this way, whether the analytical focus is upon actors' strategic conduct or the structural components of social systems, Giddens's conceptual framework incorporates the recognition that

The communication of meaning in interaction does not take place separately from the operation of relations of power, or outside the context of normative sanctions...no social practice expresses, or can be exploited in terms of, a single rule or type of resources. Rather, practices are situated within intersecting sets of rules and resources. (Giddens 1979: ibid. : 81–2)

When the institutional dimension of social practices is methodologically bracketed, actors are seen to draw upon the structural properties of social systems so as to 'bring off' everyday social interaction. Conversely, when the dimension of strategic conduct is bracketed, it is not the involvement of these properties in the accomplishment of social practices that is of interest, but, rather, their particular composition within a given social system. As Giddens (ibid. : 80) puts it:

To examine the constitution of social systems as *strategic conduct* is to study the mode in which actors draw upon structural elements—rules and resources—in their social relations. 'Structure' here appears as actors' mobilization of discursive and practical consciousness in social encounters. *Institutional* analysis, on the other hand, places an epoché upon strategic conduct, treating rules and resources as chronically reproduced features of social systems.

To this, Giddens adds:

It is quite essential to see that this is only a methodological bracketing: *these are not two sides of a dualism, they express a duality, the duality of structure.* (ibid. emphasis added)

Giddens's theory of structuration offers a conceptual framework for connecting the 'strategic' and 'institutional' aspects of managerial work. By employing this theory, the social practices that constitute managerial work can be studied as the skilled accomplishment of agents *and* as an expression of the structural properties of systems of interaction. Thus, on the one hand, they are seen to be accomplished by managers who strategically develop and enforce rules and deploy resources. From this 'strategic' standpoint, it is evident that they are actively engaged in accomplishing and restructuring regularized relations of interdependence both amongst themselves and with other groups. On the other hand, such conduct is understood to be possible only because of the institutional rules and resources that are (presently) at their disposal. The value of this framework will now be illustrated by drawing upon empirical material presented by Nichols and Beynon in *Living with Capitalism*. This study is of particular relevance because of its authors' explicit concern to connect action and structure. For, as Nichols and Beynon lucidly observe in the preface

So much of what passes for 'theory' (even Marxist theory) fails to connect with the lives that people lead, whereas most descriptive social surveys too often fail to grasp the structure of social relations and the sense which people make of them.[12]

Living with Capitalism

The specific focus of *Living with Capitalism* is the relations of production within a modern factory named Chem Co. Included in this is an examination of 'the labour of superintendence' (i.e. managerial work) in the context of the management strategy for the organization and control of the labour process. The following extract is illustrative of the practice of the 'new industrial relations' at Chem Co. in which managerial work involves the artful application of social psychological theories and skills. In common with most qualitative research, it is based upon one informant's account of a set of events. Clearly, it would be of interest, for other purposes, to explore other accounts of the same events. However, for the present purposes of illustrating Giddens's framework, it is not necessary to be detained by considerations of the 'accuracy' or 'impartiality' of this particular account.

In the following extract from *Living with Capitalism*, Colin Brown, a comparatively young and inexperienced manager describes how he uses a case of poor time-keeping to manage his relationship with a shop steward. Brown reflects:

Every man is born to do something and my function in life is to manage. I think this is a problem that most managers have failed to get to grips with. Now take an example. As far as I can see, any man who takes on the job of shop steward wants his ego boosting. But you've got to boost his ego in the proper manner. Now, if I get a bit of trouble—now take an example, perhaps of a serious case of a man who has been perpetually late. Now, I'm the manager, and it's my function to manage. It's my function to discipline this particular man. But I have to deal with the steward. So, what do I do? I take the shop steward aside and tell him that in half an hour's time this man Smith is going to walk into this room. That I'm going to stamp and bang the table and tell him that I'm going to put him out on the road.

Then I'll say to the shop steward, 'and what *you* can do will be to intervene at this time. Make a case for the man. And we'll agree to let the man off with a caution'.

Now the man comes in and I bang the table and the steward says 'Come on, Mr. Brown. Couldn't you give him one more chance?' I relent. The shop steward gets out of the meeting and says to him 'I've got you off this bloody time but don't expect me to do it again'. You see the shop steward gets his ego boosted. He gets what he wants and I get what I want. That's what good management is about (Nichols and Beynon 1977 : 122).

Applying Giddens's framework, Colin Brown can be seen to draw upon a number of *interpretative schemes* to *communicate* the reality of his managerial work. He begins by employing the notion that everyone is born to do something, and that his predetermined mission, for which he is naturally fitted, is to manage. This scheme includes the understanding that in any organization there will be a separation between managers and managed. It is this inevitable fact,

Brown suggests, that most managers have 'failed to get to grips with'. Brown's belief in the division between managers and managed within the natural order of things is also reflected in his view that shop stewards aspire to quasi-managerial positions because they have a need to get their ego boosted. This, Brown observes, presents the manager with a challenge, to boost the steward's ego in a way that is 'proper' for the effective execution of the management function. The notion of 'proper' reflects a second interpretative scheme. Namely, that good management is about the calculated contribution and negotiation of situations in ways that produce the maximum benefit for the minimum cost.

These interpretative schemes allow Brown to make sense of and to organize his work. They underpin and are supported by his skilful use of facilities as he manages his interaction with the steward and Smith, the poor time-keeper. His use of facilities—rules and resources—enables him to 'take the steward aside', to rehearse his performance and generally stage-manage the disciplinary scene. Brown makes strategic use of his facilities, (e.g. his power to put Smith 'out on the road') by creatively identifying a low-cost opportunity to reinforce the relationship of domination over the steward. More specifically, Brown stage-manages the situation so that, in the process of getting his ego boosted, the steward becomes both incorporated into the management process and indebted to Brown for enabling him to play out his (managerially defined) role as shop steward.

Norms are drawn upon by the various parties to the interaction. On this occasion at least, the steward seemingly accepts the right of the manager to discipline Smith. Conversely, the manager 'recognizes', and indeed exploits, the right of the steward to make out a case for his union member. The positive sanction of the ego boost is used by Brown to ensure that the steward follows his script to the letter, and with gratitude. As long as it works—and this depends appreciably upon the schemes of interpretation and facilities at the command of the steward—the asymmetrical relationship of power between the manager and the steward is hegemonically concealed in the very process of its reproduction.

It should be clear from the discussion of this example that the distinction between the three modalities is purely analytical. In practice, interaction involves a simultaneous and interdependent employment of interpretative schemes, facilities and norms. But, so far, we have considered only how Brown draws strategically upon the modalities to manage his relationship with the steward.[13] The particular value of Giddens's notion of the duality of structure, however, is that is apprehends how the strategic use of modalities involves a mobilization of structural properties.

For example, in the interaction between Brown and the steward, their communication can be seen to depend upon the sign or *signification* systems employed by both parties to discern or 'read' the reality of the situation and, in particular, the ontology of self and the other. Brown 'reads' the situation as an interaction between a self who has 'just got to manage' and another, the steward, who 'wants his ego boosting'. The interaction is accomplished as Brown identifies self and other within this system of signification. Of course, Brown's understanding may not have been fully shared by the steward. But, for practical purposes, the steward's possible disbelief is suspended as he complies with Brown's script and acts out his role (albeit that this may have been played at a distance).

Similarly, Brown's exercise of power over the steward depends upon his command over resources. More specifically, Brown draws upon and reproduces a system of *domination* which gives him authority over others as well as the power to allocate material resources, such as Smith's job. It is this system that shapes and naturalizes the disciplinary function of the manager. Brown can perform this function only because he acts as the agent of the owners of the material resources and has the power to command others legally invested in him (in the employment contract and in company law).

The interaction between Brown and the steward also illustrates how a system of *legitimation* supports the normative regulation of interaction. What empowers Brown to act is the symbolic value of the role he performs. It is the taken for granted legitimacy of his social position that enables him to take the steward aside. The normative regulation of such interaction is secured through the idea that 'good management' is achieved when the interests of seemingly opposing factions (e.g. capital/labour; Brown/Smith) are seen to be concretely coordinated, thereby preserving the basic structure of capitalist relations of production. In uncritically acting out the role of advocate for Smith, the steward colludes with Brown in legitimating the form of his power-play. It is, of course, possible that the steward saw straight through Brown's 'spoofing' and played his role at a distance—perhaps because he preferred a quiet life, perceived himself to be powerless or wanted to lull Brown into a false sense of power or even because he wanted the (ego-boosting) satisfaction of outsmarting Brown at his own game. However, whatever the steward's intent, the effect of his behaviour is to confirm, for the moment, the 'objective' reality and legitimacy of the normative order.[14]

This analysis of the interaction between Brown and the steward, as reported by Brown, can be further developed by drawing upon the concept of *contradiction*, discussed earlier, which is also central to Giddens's theory of structuration.

In Giddens's terminology, contradiction refers to disjunctions or oppositions between the structural principles of social systems. Its major analytical contribution lies in their capacity to illuminate the dynamics of social life. The existence of mutually incompatible or contravening principles of system organization helps to explain why stability and continuity in social systems is impermanent and problematic and, relatedly, why conflicts of interest arise and are worked out but rarely resolved. In the example of Brown's managerial work, Brown requires 'his' men's labour to be reliable: to get to work when it is useful or valuable to him. Moreover, in contrast to other, less visible, breaches of discipline, (e.g. skiving), poor time-keeping poses a direct challenge to management's authority to police the labour process. On the other side, Smith, the man whom he is to discipline, has an interest in minimizing the time that he is subjected to managerial and organizational discipline.[15]

This conflict between the manager and the worker is expressive of the primary contradiction of capitalist society discussed earlier; that is, the contradiction between the principle of the *private* appropriation of wealth which presumes, yet is conditional upon and negated by, the principle of *socialized* production. Brown, acting on behalf of the owners of the means of production, requires Smith, as a unit of labour cost, to arrive at work on time so that goods can be produced that will realize a surplus. Needless to say, as an individual, Smith is unimportant and dispensable; Brown repeatedly refers to Smith as 'the man'. As Brown threatens, this man can be 'put out on the road' and replaced by a more 'responsible' worker. What is crucial is the issue at stake, the issue of managerial discipline. For if Smith is seen to 'get away' with poor time-keeping, the danger for Brown is that others will follow Smith's example. Thus, Brown's interview with Smith also indicates his own vulnerability in respect of labour on whom he, as an agent of capital, depends. More specifically, it can be seen how the class nature of the division between manager and managed acts as an obstruction to productive activity. Ironically, Smith's labour is necessarily idle during the period of the interview. Moreover, Brown is obliged to discipline Smith by making threats that can only deepen the divide between them, an effect that is in direct conflict with the conciliatory design of Brown's 'spoof'. In short, the contradictions of capitalist relations of production both facilitate the occasion and constrain the effectiveness of Brown's disciplining of labour.[16]

Conclusion

The purpose of this article has been, first, to develop a critique of prominent and influential empirical studies of managerial work and, secondly, to outline and illustrate an alternative approach based upon Giddens's theory of structuration. Through an examination of the research of Dalton, Kotter and Mintzberg a number of major limitations were identified and explored. In general, these studies were found to abstract the behaviour of managers from the institutional settings and media of managerial work. Drawing upon Giddens's theory of structuration, the proposal is to advance the study of managerial work by appreciating how, within capitalist relations of production, the work of managers is both a medium and outcome of the structural properties of a social system founded upon the contradiction between socialized production and private appropriation. As Storey (1983; 1985a) has argued, such an approach appreciates how inter-subjective reality requires perpetual reconstruction and, at the same time, recognizes that managerial work, as a labour process, is accompanied within a totality of social relations containing contradictory forms of unity. The claim of this article has been that Giddens's concept of structure as a duality is consistent with such an approach, and that it provides a valuable alternative conceptual framework for advancing critical empirical research into managerial work.

Notes

1. In making revisions to this article I have been stimulated and guided by comments and suggestions from Stewart Clegg, David Knights, John Storey, Paul Thompson and Richard Whitley as well as from two referees. I would like to thank them for their assistance, while taking responsibility for any remaining inadequacies of the paper.
2. The paper is restricted to an examination of managerial work within capitalist enterprises. It does not aspire to contribute to the comparative analysis of management within the public sector or within non-capitalist economies.
3. For example, empirical studies of managerial work rarely relate the behaviour of managers to the so-called 'managerial revolution' in which power is alleged to pass from the owners to managerial elites within large corporations (e.g. Berle and Means 1932; Burnham 1941; Galbraith 1967). Nor, equally, do these studies connect with the writings of critics of the managerial revolution thesis (e.g. Baran and Sweezy 1968; Herman 1982; Scott 1979).
4. The lack of reflexivity in these studies does not, of course, invalidate their utility. Clearly, in terms of their own (generally implicit) purposes, they have been found to be of (limited) value.
5. Here it is relevant to note the existence of 'critical' studies that are broadly comparable with Giddens's framework. Clegg (1975) and Silverman and Jones (1976) both provide theoretically sophisticated analyses of managerial work. In Clegg's case, however, his proposed framework (which is similar to that of Giddens, see Clegg 1979) is somewhat detached from the brief analysis of his empirical materials. Silverman and Jones (1976) provide a much more detailed analysis of their materials, but present only a sketchy outline of the theoretical framework that informs their study. Two papers by Golding (1979; 1980) also make an important

contribution to the critical study of managerial work by revealing how symbols play a central role in the depoliticizing and legitimation of managerial power. Roberts and Scapens (1985) present a lucid account of the potential of Giddens' framework for analysing managers' use of accounting information. However, this paper is disappointing in its failure to provide any systematic analysis of empirical data.

6. Nor is it invulnerable to criticism. See, for example, Archer 1981; Dallmayr 1982; Gane 1983; Layder 1981; Thompson 1984; Willmott 1986.

7. It is clearly impractical to review all recent studies of managerial work within this paper. Had space permitted, more attention could have been paid to other relevant studies (e.g. Pettigrew 1973; Sayles 1979; 1972). For more comprehensive reviews of the literature on managerial work, see Campbell et al. 1970; Glover 1977; Glover and Martin 1986; Mintzberg 1973; Willmott 1984.

8. Mintzberg recognizes that managers do have some discretion in shaping their commitments. But he does not explore the issue of how roles are negotiated or how collectively managers are involved in enacting/managing the 'external' and organizational contexts which, in Mintzberg's model, are reduced to 'environmental' and 'job' variables. Instead, he regards the exercise of discretion as a defining characteristic of successful management. To quote: 'all managers appear to be puppets. Some decide who will pull the strings and how, and they then take advantage of each move that they are forced to take. Others, unable to exploit this high-tension environment, are swallowed up by this most demanding of jobs' (Mintzberg 1973 : 51).

9. It is significant that Fox employs the term consensus rather than, say, compliance. Certainly, he acknowledges that those in control 'do not enjoy a monopoly of ideological communication' (1974 : 92). He also recognizes that occupants of low discretion roles tend to regard them 'as expressive of management's intent to use them as instruments towards ends they do not share' (ibid. : 93). But these sources of resistance and disaffection are, in Fox's assessment, marginal because 'the few can use their power to determine the power of the many not only directly but also indirectly through the many agencies of socialization, communication and attitudeformation' (ibid. : 284). Fox's formulation of the radical frame of reference thus conveys a strong impression that only incompetence or misjudgement on the part of the owners and controllers of resources is likely to destabilize the working consensus (cf. Wrong 1961). This impression is reinforced by his contention that 'society is already in the shape which serves their essential interests' (ibid.: 278); and, further, that 'all the social institutions, mechanisms and principles which it is crucially important for them to have accepted and legitimized are accepted and legitimized already' (ibid. : 277).

10. However, in contrast to workers, a greater proportion of managers' labour is employed 'unproductively' to ensure that surplus value is appropriated and realized. The cost of this unproductive labour is, of course, met from the surplus value produced by workers and (to a lesser extent) managers when performing a co-ordinating role. This burden upon labour is also routinely obscured, for reasons discussed below.

11. In this respect, the obscuring of class exploitation is made easier to the extent that employed labour may be buffered from the harsher effects of continuing rationalization of productive processes by the establishment of a strong competitive or monopolistic advantage in product markets and/or the profitable investment of income in capital markets, etc. In this light, the strategic control of labour processes and the concrete organization of workers' interests must be examined not only in relation to workers' capacity to resist the displacing devaluing, deskilling and intensifying of their labour, but also in relation to the capacity of corporate managers to pursue and exploit alternative avenues for achieving a favourable return on capital (Knights and Willmott, 1986; Knights, Willmott and Collinson 1985; Littler and Salaman 1982).

12. Although Nichols and Beynon set out with the intention of connecting social action and social structure, they are only partially successful. Certainly, they highlight the fundamental, systemic contradictions and conflicts of interest that are characteristic of capitalist relations of production. They also acknowledge that 'to talk of capital is to talk of a social relationship' and that 'if social class means anything at all it is to be found in the real lives of real people' (Nichols and Beynon 1977 : 76). However, very little is presented that reports and analyses actual interaction between classes and members (e.g. managers and managed) at Chem Co. Nor, indeed, is it clear how Nichols and Beynon theorize managerial work. For, on the one hand, they assert that it 'can increasingly be seen as labour (ibid. XV), while, on the other hand, managers appear not to act in any way as labour. That is, they are portrayed and theorized as pliant and passive agents of capital who are 'driven by the impersonal force of capital' (ibid.) and, again, whose actions are subject to the dictates of an impersonal force—capital' (ibid. : 42). While labourers are seen to engage in various forms of resistance—albeit marginal, individualistic and often futile—managers are presented as mere functionaries. Moreover, when managers are perceived to deviate from their functional roles, this is explained in psychologistic terms. For example, the deviations of Edwards Blunsen are related to his personal ambition, those of George Smith are associated with his personal values and those of John Baird are analysed in terms of his youthful innocence. No doubt an appreciation of these personality traits and biographical details is important for understanding each man's distinctive approach to his work. But if the intention is to study the work of these managers as an expression of class relations, then it is necessary to develop a *dialectical* analysis of the connection between individual character and social structure. The basic shortcoming of Nichols and Beynon's account of managerial work is that it embodies a dualism between individual and relational action. Instead of studying 'the labour of superintendence' as they call it, as a relational activity, the actions of individual managers are theorized as a deterministic product of the social structure of capitalism. Despite their stated intention to reveal the interdependence of action and structure, Nichols and Beynon consistently treat the latter as a container and/or determinant of the former. Or, as they themselves summarize 'we have attempted . . . to see the way class relations bear on the individual and to locate individuals always with class relations' (ibid. : 203–4, emphasis added). What is lacking theoretically is a

conceptual framework capable of penetrating and overcoming the analytical dualism between action and structure. Empirically, what is absent is observational data on the actual conduct of class relations/managerial work and Chem Co. For a more developed critique of Giddens's theory of structuration as well as Nichols and Beynon's *Living with Capitalism*, see Knights and Willmott, 1985.

13. To be more precise, it is an example of managerial work as accounted for by Brown and mediated by Nichols and Beynon.

14. With reference to these structural properties, it is worth repeating the point that the distinction between systems of signification, domination and legitimation is an analytical one. As Giddens (1979 : 106–7) stresses, 'if signification is fundamentally structured in and through language, language at the same time expresses aspects of domination, and the codes that are involved in signification have normative force. Authorization and allocation are only mobilized in conjunction with signifying and normative elements and, finally, legitimation necessarily involves signfication as well as playing a major part in co-ordinating forms of domination'.

15. Of course, for most employees, for most of the time, the comparative loss of discretion or control over their labour power is not challenged through a collective struggle between management and labour. This is because managerial and organizational discipline is widely regarded as more or less legitimate insofar as the contract is perceived to be entered into more or less freely. However, the fact that organized resistance is exceptional certainly does not imply that contradictions do not exist. Nor, relatedly, does it suggest that there are no endemic conflicts of interest.

16. Potentially, union organization provides the means of countering, or at least curtailing, managers' powers to exploit the weak position of atomized workers. Strong union organization can protect the position of labour by making it less dispensable or substitutable, and thereby exploiting the fundamental dependence of capital upon it. Simply because collective resistance presents the greatest potential challenge to management control, it is this source of power that Brown and the more progressive managers at Chem Co. strove to undermine by stealth. The policy of incorporating trade unionism into management is well illustrated in the stage-managed meeting between Brown, Smith and the steward. Instead of seeking to exclude the trade union representative, Brown invites him to play an 'active' part in the disciplinary proceedings. Through a petty conspiracy between Brown and the steward, Smith is given the impression that his steward has successfully defended his interests, and the illusion of sound union representation is maintained. At the same time, instead of taking the hard line by carrying out his threat to put Smith 'out on the road', Brown engineers a low-cost demonstration of the fair and enlightened nature of Chem Co. as an employer. At the very worst, from Brown's point of view, he will be obliged to suffer Smith's poor time-keeping for a few more days before 'putting him on the road', with the steward's consent. Balanced against this minimal cost, his 'spoofing', if undetected, plays a mundane but nonetheless essential role in managing the fundamental contradiction between private appropriation and socialized production.

References

Archer, M. (1981). 'Morphogenesis versus structuration', *British Journal of Sociology*, 31, 2, 346–61.

Baran, P. and Sweezy, P. M. (1968). *Monopoly Capital*. Harmondsworth: Penguin.

Berle, A. A. and Means, G. C. (1932). *The Modern Corporation and Private Property*. New York: Macmillan.

Bhaskar, R. (1978). 'On the possibility of social scientific knowledge and the limits of naturalism', *Journal for the Theory of Social Behaviour*, 8, 1, 225–52.

Blau, P. (1965). *The Dynamics of Bureaucracy*. University of Chicago Press.

Burnham, J. (1941). *The Managerial Revolution*. Harmondsworth: Penguin.

Burawoy, M. (1985). *The Politics of Production*. London: Verso.

Campbell, J. P., Dunnette, M. D., Lawler, E. E. and Weick, K. E. (1970). *Managerial Behaviour, Performance and Effectiveness*. New York: McGraw-Hill

Carchedi, G. (1975). 'On the economic identification of the new middle class', *Economy and Society*, 4, 1–86.

Child, J. (1977). 'Management', in Parker, S. R., Brown, R. K., Child, J. and Smith, M. A. *The Sociology of Industry*, 3rd edn. London: Allen and Unwin.

Clegg, S. (1975). *Power, Rule and Domination*. London: Routledge and Kegan Paul.

Clegg, S. (1979). *The Theory of Power and Organisation*. London: Routledge and Kegan Paul.

Coward, R. and Ellis, J. (1977). *Language and Materialism*. London: Routledge and Kegan Paul.

Cutler, A. J., Hindess, B., Hirst, P. Q. and Hussain, A. (1977). *Marx's Capital and Capitalism Today*. Vol. 1. London: Routledge and Kegan Paul.

Dallmayr, F. (1982). 'The theory of structuration: a critique', in Giddens A. (ed.), *Profiles and Critiques in Social Theory*. London: Macmillan.

Dalton, M. (1959). *Men Who Manage*. New York: Wiley.

Fox, A. (1973). 'Industrial relations: a social critique of pluralist ideology', in Child, J. (ed.), *Man and Organization*. London: Allen and Unwin.

Fox, A. (1974). *Beyond Contract*. London: Faber.

Galbraith, J. K. (1967). *The New Industrial State*. London: Hamish Hamilton.

Gane, M. (1983). 'Anthony Giddens and the crisis in social theory', *Economy and Society*. 12, 368–98.

Giddens, A. (1976). *New Rules of Sociological Method*. London: Hutchinson.

—— (1979). *Central Problems in Social Theory*. London: Macmillan.

—— (1982). 'Power, the dialectic of control and class structuration', in Giddens, A. and Mackenzie, G. (eds.), *Social Class and the Division of Labour*. Cambridge University Press.

—— (1984). *The Constitution of Society*. Cambridge: Polity Press.

Glover, I. (1977). 'Managerial work: a review of the evidence', *Social Science Research Council Report*.

Glover, I. and Martin, G. (1986). '*Managerial Work—An empirical and cultural contradiction in terms?* Mimeo, Dundee College of Technology.

Hugh Willmott

Goffman, E. (1959). *Asylums*, Harmondsworth: Penguin.

Golding, D. (1979). 'Symbolism, sovereignty and domination in an industrial hierarchical organization', *Sociological Review*, **27**, 1, 169–77.

Golding, D. (1980). 'Establishing blissful clarity in organizational life: managers'. *Sociological Review*, **28**, 4, 763–82.

Goldthorpe, J. (1982). 'On the service class, its formation and future', in Giddens, A. and Mackenzie, G. (eds), *Social Class and the Division of Labour*. Cambridge University Press.

Habermas, J. (1972). *Knowledge and Human Interests*. London: Heinemann.

Herman, E. S. (1982). *Corporate Control, Corporate Power*. Cambridge University Press.

Hindess, B. and Hirst, P. (1977). *Mode of Production and Social Formation*. London: Macmillan.

Kelly, J. E. (1982). *Scientific Management, Job Redesign and Work Performance*. New York: Academic Press.

Knights, D. and Willmott, H. C. (1985). 'Power and identity in theory and practice'. *Sociological Review*, 33, 1, 22–46.

Knights, D., and Willmott, H. C. (eds) (1986). *Managing the Labour Process*. Aldershot: Gower.

Knights, D., Willmott, H. C., and Collinson, D. (eds) (1985). *Job Redesign*. Aldershot: Gower.

Kotter, J. P. (1979). *Power in Management*. New York: Amacon.

Kotter, J. P. (1982). *The General Managers*. New York: McGraw-Hill.

Layder, D. (1981). *Structure, Interaction and Social Theory*. London: Routledge and Kegan Paul.

Littler, R. C. and Salaman, G. (1982). 'Bravermania and beyond: recent theories of the labour process', *Sociology*, 16, 2, 251–69.

Mintzberg, H. (1973). *The Nature of Managerial Work*. New York: Harper and Row.

Nichols, T. (1969). *Ownership, Control and Ideology*. London: Allen and Unwin.

Nichols, T. and Beynon, H. (1977). *Living with Capitalism*. London: Routledge and Kegan Paul.

Pecheux, M. (1982). *Language, Semantics and Ideology*. London: Macmillan.

Pettigrew, A. (1973). *The Politics of Organizational Decision-Making*. London: Tavistock.

Pettigrew, A. (1975). *The Awakening Giant*. Oxford: Basil Blackwell.

Ranson, S., Hinings, B. and Greenwood, R. (1980). 'The structuring of organizational structures', *Administrative Science Quarterly*, 25, 1–17.

Reed, M. I. (1984). 'Management as a social practice', *Journal of Management Studies*, 21, 3, 273–85.

Roberts, J. and Scapens, R. (1985). 'Accounting systems and systems of accountability— understanding accounting practices in their organisational contexts'. *Accounting, Organisations and Society*, 10, 4, 443–56.

Salaman, G. (1982). 'Managing the frontier of control', in Giddens, A. and Mackenzie, G. (eds), *Social Class and the Division of Labour; Essays in Honour of Ilya Neustadt*. Cambridge University Press.

Sayles, L. R. (1979). *Leadership*. New York: McGraw-Hill.

Scott, J. (1979). *Corporations, Classes and Capitalism*. London: Hutchinson.

Silverman, D. and Jones, J. (1976). *Organizational Work*. London: Collier-Macmillan.

Sofer, C. (1970). *Men in Mid-Career: A Study of British Managers and Technical Specialists*. Cambridge University Press.

Stanworth, P. and Giddens, A. (1974). *Elites and Power in British Society*. Cambridge University Press.

Storey, J. (1983). *Managerial Prerogative and the Question of Control*. London: Routledge and Kegan Paul.

Storey, J. (1985a). 'The means of management control', *Sociology*, 9, 2, 193–211.

Storey, J. (1985b). 'Management control as a bridging concept', *Journal of Management Studies*, 22, 3, 269–91.

Thompson, J. B. (1984). *Studies in the Theory of Ideology*. Cambridge: Polity.

Tinker, A. M. (1984). 'Theories of the state and the state of accounting: economic reductionism and political voluntarism in accounting theory', *Journal of Accounting and Public Policy*, 3, 55–74.

Turner, B. A. (1971). *Exploring the Industrial Subculture*. London: Macmillan.

Weber, M. (1949). *The Methodology of the Social Sciences*. New York: Free Press.

Willmott, H. C. (1979). 'The structuring of organizational structure: a note', *Administrative Science Quarterly*, 26, 470–4.

Willmott, H. C. (1984). 'Images and ideals of managerial work', *Journal of Management Studies*, 21, 3, 349–68.

Willmott, H. C. (1986). 'Unconscious sources of motivation in the theory of the subject; an exploration and critique of Giddens' dualistic models of action and personality', *Journal for the Theory of Social Behaviour*, 16, 1, 105–22.

Winkler, J. T. (1974). 'The ghost at the bargaining table: directors and industrial relations', *British Journal of Industrial Relations*, 12, 191–212.

Wrong, D. (1961). 'The over-socialised conception of man in modern sociology', *American Sociological Review*, 26, 2, 183–98.

Zeitlin, M. (1974). 'Corporate ownership and control: the large corporations and the capitalist class', *American Journal of Sociology*, 79, 1073–119.

The development of CMS has been accompanied—and in part enabled—by a range of overviews, commentaries and critiques of CMS itself. Sotirin & Tyrell (1998) conclude their review by referring to CMS as an 'oxymoron', and the same term is used as the starting point for Zald's (2002) exploration, which itself is the opening contribution to a special issue of the journal *Organization* devoted to debating CMS. The paradox to which these writers are referring is the coupling of 'critical' and 'management'.

The idea of CMS as oxymoronic arises primarily because of its institutional location in business schools, discussed in the introduction to this volume. To the extent that business schools have defined both management and management studies in managerial terms, then this does indeed minimize the possibility of critical understandings. However, a central part of CMS is to dispute such managerial definitions. Were it to be successful in that dispute then the oxymoron would disappear. That is not, however, to deny that there are many tensions, ambiguities and perhaps even paradoxes entailed by CMS, and these have been assiduously debated from a range of positions.

Martin Parker's (2002) book *Against Management* is both informed by, but also contains a critical discussion of, CMS. It is the discussion which we reproduce here. Parker notes—with regret—that much of the debate about CMS has been conducted as a scholastic dispute between, approximately, critical realists and neo-marxists on the one hand and post-structuralists and postmodernists on the other (see also section two of this volume). Parker, drawing in part upon Fournier & Grey (2000), seems more sympathetic to a pluralistic understanding of CMS which can encompass all of these kinds of positions. However, even if such a state of affairs came to pass, he remains concerned about the paradoxes and limitations created by CMS's primary location in university business schools. Given this location, he sees CMS as being able to achieve only a compromised enrolment into the well-worn path of managerial humanism or, alternatively, to preach critique so successfully that business schools disappear, and CMS with them!

Parker alludes to the hostility between different traditions of critical thought and the debates which have taken place between adherents of each. This has had a particular impact upon CMS. For a start, in a rather parochial way, CMS as a 'movement' can to some extent be thought of as having developed out of a thriving Labour Process Analysis (LPA) movement from the 1970s onwards. Initially mainly concerned with Marxist sociology and political economy there was a gradual growth of interest in post-structuralism and issues of subjectivity. CMS took over this set of interests (and others besides) so that debates which previously had been conducted within the umbrella of LPA have increasingly been articulated as debates between LPA and CMS. It is within this context that **Paul Thompson's** (2004) vitriolic attack on CMS, reproduced here, is to be understood. For Thompson, CMS is necessarily post-structuralist and post-modern and, therefore, in his view irredeemably relativist. If Thompson's assessment is accepted, it poses problems for both the theoretical adequacy and the practical purchase of CMS. On the latter point it means that CMS, at best, is an exercise in scholasticism and academic career-building which is an effective critique not of management but only (and if that) of management *studies*. Thompson prefers a form of critical realism which, in principle, accepts the inherent incompleteness of knowledge and certainly rejects the positivism of the mainstream but which identifies trends, and locates empirical knowledge within structural mechanisms and the material reality of divergent interests. Like Parker, but with considerably less sympathy, Thompson draws upon Fournier & Grey (2000) for many of his definitions of CMS but he regards their claim that these definitions are pluralistic, and so capable of including critical realism, as 'tokenistic'.

Whether or not Thompson is right in the latter accusation (see Grey, 2005), what is unquestionably true is that the attempt to hold together a diverse set of positions under the CMS label is difficult to achieve. For it is not just that Thompson and those with similar views (e.g. many contributors to Ackroyd & Fleetwood 2000; Fleetwood and Ackroyd 2004; Tinker 2002) object to CMS; so too do some of those who hold the post-structuralist and/or postmodern views that he says characterize CMS.

The paper by **Ed Wray-Bliss** (2002) is a case in point. It provides a critique of CMS research and more particularly that of the 'Manchester School' of Labour

Process Theory (which, in essence, is the research that for Thompson defines CMS *in toto*). This research is largely post-structuralist in character, yet Wray-Bliss regards it as reproducing a problematic realism which is de-personalized, ethically deficient and reliant upon the depersonalised authority of academics at the expense of silenced and marginalized research subjects. Indeed, this is not just a resurrection of realism, argues Wray-Bliss, but in fact a 'marriage' of post-structuralism and positivism.

In this regard, the assessment of CMS has moved beyond a debate in which opposing camps quarrel directly with each other to a situation where each attacks CMS for its failure to espouse an adequate version of criticality. This indirect terrain of conflict perhaps demonstrates the success of CMS in establishing itself. But it also points to the difficulties of coming to grips with CMS if it can be simultaneously regarded as entirely and disgracefully rejecting realism and also as disgracefully embodying realism.

The optimistic reading of this situation is that the range of ways in which CMS can be interpreted, positively and negatively, is a necessary feature of attempts to sustain it as pluralistic undertaking: vigorous debate is a sign of intellectual health. The pessimistic view is that CMS is failing to reach beyond its inner sanctum. One measure of this is the absence of any engaged response from the mainstream. This silence can be interpreted in a variety of ways. It might suggest that CMS is seen as insufficiently significant to merit a response. Or perhaps the mainstream is simply incapable of mounting an effective defence. But in any case, the ultimate assessment of CMS will be the extent to which it succeeds in making a critical—reflective and emancipatory—difference to understanding, studying, teaching and practicing management.

References

Ackroyd, S. and Fleetwood, S. (eds) (2000). *Realist Perspectives on Management and Organisations*. London: Routledge.

Fleetwood, S. and Ackroyd, S. (eds) (2004). *Critical Realist Applications in Organisation and Management Studies*. London: Routledge.

Fournier, V. and Grey, C. (2000). 'At the Critical Moment: Conditions and Prospects for Critical Management Studies', *Human Relations*, 53, 1: 7–32.

Grey C. (2005). 'Critical Management Studies: Towards a More Mature Politics', in Howcroft, D. and Trauth, E. (eds) *Handbook of Critical Information Systems Research*. London: Edward Elgar in press.

Sotirin, P. and Tyrell, S. (1998). 'Wondering About Critical Management Studies', *Management Communication Quarterly*, 12, 2: 303–336.

Assessing Critical Management Studies

Tinker T. (2002). 'Disciplinary Spin', *Organization* 9, 3: 419–427.

Zald M. (2002). 'Spinning Disciplines: Critical Management Studies in the Context of the Transformation of Management Education', *Organization* 9, 3: 365–385

16

Writing Critical Management Studies

Martin Parker

CMS is still a new baby in academic terms. Newer even than business ethics. At the time of writing it is probably approaching its tenth birthday, a birthday which might be commonly dated with the publication of Alvesson's and Willmott's *Critical Management Studies* in 1992. Since then, the title has become a term—even a 'brand' (P. Thompson 2001)—and it is now possible to identify yourself as someone who does CMS, as opposed to managerial studies of business, the latter including most of business ethics. In making such an identity claim, and hence claim to be a member of the CMS community too, the author will be saying something about his or her political sympathies—broad left, pro-feminist, anti-imperialist, environmentally concerned and so on—as well as usually expressing a certain distrust for conventional positivist formulations of knowledge within the social sciences.

This combination of political and epistemological radicalism is now a recognizable identity on the margins of academic studies of business and management, just as it has become a central one in some other social sciences, cultural studies for example. Though not nearly as institutionalized as business ethics—there are no chairs in critical management, and no research institutes—the process is beginning. In the English-speaking world the intricate apparatus of academic legitimacy is slowly being constructed. In the UK, there has since 1999 been a bi-annual CMS conference, and at least two seminar series have been funded by the Economic and Social Research Council. 'Critical' panels have been held at more orthodox conferences, 'critical' texts and readers have been published, academic superstars are emerging and certain departments are identified as having a critical mass of critical researchers. In the US, the most high-profile development was the establishment, in 1998, of a CMS workshop (CMSW) for 'critters' which is attached to the huge annual Academy of Management Conference. There have also been some suggestions that a special interest group of the Academy might now be established that would further legitimize and disseminate critical work. Crossing these national boundaries, there is also a well-established email discussion list and an increasing number of paper and internet journals which are self-consciously identified as places where critical papers can find a home.

Though it is very difficult to summarize the work which gathers, or is gathered, under the CMS label, Sotirin and Tyrell (1998), in their review of various critical texts, suggest the following very general forms of theoretical agreement. A general critique of instrumental reason, often manifested as a suspicion of modernism; some attention to historical-empirical specificities; the assumption that language is constitutive not representational; a degree of reflexivity about method and authorial position; and a commitment to intervene in relations of oppression. In terms of actual writings they note a tendency to use guru literature as a foil; some intention to transform management education curricula and pedagogy; an emphasis on non-US knowledges and concern with the negative effects of globalization; a concern to use metaphorical and utopian languages; as well as the promotion of alternative theories and methodologies. Yet, as is obvious, this is still a very vague and wide area. At one extreme, we have empirical studies of power and oppression which contrast what gurus say with what actually happens, at the other, theoretically sophisticated attempts to dethrone the demons of modernism, positivism and managerialism. In between, a variety of attempts to introduce new themes—gender, the body, the environment, ethnicity—and new methods—ethnographic, deconstructive, discursive, rhetorical, narrative, psychodynamic, feminist, and so on.

So what else ties these disparate mobilizations and literatures together? The most explicit programme can be found on the CMSW website, with a mission statement that is intended to be implicitly endorsed through membership. Given what I have already argued about mission statements in Chapter 3, this one could be seen as an example of the subversion of a managerial form, or the formalization of subversion. The text itself has three main strands. Firstly, it asserts that managerialist bottom-line versions of organization pay little or no attention to 'justice, community, human development, ecological balance' and so on. The development of critical interpretations of the hegemonic system of business and management is intended to right this balance by providing an alternative to the orthodoxy. Second, the statement explicitly claims to be non-sectarian in theoretical terms—to include critical theory, feminism, Marxism, postmodernism, critical realism and so on. No exclusions are made on the basis of adherence to one particular school of thought or another. Third, the CMSW group will work within the Academy *of* Management to ensure that it does not become an Academy *for* Management. This is not an attempt to dethrone existing academic institutions, but an entryist strategy of revising them from within. Whilst there are clearly problems with using this 'mission statement' as definitive, it does signal some of the central boundary problems for CMS. First, that this is a political project aimed at some form of substantive social change. The ghost being exorcized here is presumably a managerialist version of academic labour as handmaiden of capital, one that regards its duty as collecting facts about organizations in order that managers might meet their avowed goals more effectively. Second, the document seems to recognize that different theoretical traditions might formulate 'the critical' in rather contradictory ways. Marxists who wish to insist on the primacy of class will be one of the problems for feminists. Post-modernists who wish to insist that everything is just another story are likely to be accused of political quietism by materialist radicals, and so on. Finally, these grand aims are to be achieved from within academic institutions and networks. Supporters of CMSW are encouraged to educate, agitate and organize with other groups of people too, but their central location is, and will continue to be, the university, and even more specifically, the B-School.

A second seminal piece for defining CMS, though somewhat reluctantly, is Valerie Fournier and Chris Grey's review article 'At the Critical Moment' (2000). This time reflecting UK concerns more than US ones, Fournier and Grey argue that, internal disputes notwithstanding, CMS can usefully be characterized in three ways. Firstly, that it has a 'non-performative' intent, which is to say that it is not concerned with providing tools that are intended to assist managerial efficiency through re-engineering minimum inputs for maximum outputs. Second, that it 'denaturalizes' that which is usually taken for granted. If the imperatives which are often assumed to be immutable in mainstream research (efficiency, profit, the right to manage and so on) can be shown to be social constructions embedded in specific historical moments, then they potentially become amenable to some kind of progressive change. Third, CMS is philosophically and methodologically reflexive, which is to say that it attempts to problematize (to a lesser or greater extent) its own claims to know things about the world. As with the CMSW mission, these characterizations are more concerned to say what CMS is *not*, rather than what it *is* and, in so doing, articulate the output of the B-School as a key problem and Big Other. Consequently both texts describe the mainstream in ways that many orthodox B-School academics might not recognize very easily. It is performative, assumes that there is no radical alternative to the present state of affairs and is unreflective about its truth claims. As P. Thompson (2001: 12) puts it, 'CMS needs the bogeyman'. This demonization of what surrounds CMS invokes a boundary but leaves the content of what lies inside relatively open. This is a strangely paradoxical exercise, as Fournier and Grey acknowledge. In order to define the critical, they need to exclude work that they believe is uncritical, but these exclusions are intended to be generous enough to include work with a diverse variety of epistemological and political commitments. Rather like the construction of a political party, diversity can be encouraged, but only up to a certain point.

So, as a result of these exclusions, much of the work that I have covered in this book so far might be deemed to be outside CMS as it has been defined here. The nostalgic and turbo-managerial critiques of bureaucracy; consensual formulations of organizational citizenship, culture or community; and mildly reformist versions of ethics and corporate social responsibility all fail on one or more of Fournier and Grey's three tests. In fact, since much conventional work in management is concerned with 'humanizing' work organizations in order to achieve better productivity, it might be argued that any work that directly or indirectly contributes to the perpetuation of existing managerial capitalist relationships, even if it ameliorates them to some degree, is outside CMS. But, and here is the paradox, this very same work might be critical if viewed in another light. So the radical Weberian critique of bureaucratic rationalization, or du Gay's defence of the bureaucratic ethos within democratic administration (2000), attempts to insist on industrial citizenship rights within organizations, as well as communitarian critiques of the dominance of market relationships, together with ethically led regulation of the social and environmental responsibilities of managers and organizations, could all lie within CMS too. It seems to depend on interpretation, and not some absolute dividing line between the critical and the co-opted.

Lurking behind this seems to be a Kantian sense of an evaluation of the good intentions of particular authors. This would be a judgement as to whether they treat people as means to achieve a more efficient form of managerial capitalism or treat people as ends in themselves. Does their work intend to contribute to the maintenance of managerial capitalism? If yes, then it is outside CMS. Does the work intend to contribute to emancipation, to remaking the world in less instrumental ways? If yes, then it is on the inside. But the problem with Kantian formulations is that we do not have access to the contents of people's heads. We can only judge intentions through action, so deciding whether a particular person is 'really' critical can only depend on our assessment of what we read, hear and see. An academic may, as Fournier and Grey acknowledge briefly and P. Thompson (2001) suggests strongly, be jumping on the critical bandwagon because it helps their career, because they must publish or perish and so on. They might, as I suggested of business ethics, be being 'strategically' critical. But how could we tell? On what grounds might we decide whether an academic was a person of good character or not? This might well be the subject of whispered chats at conferences, but is hardly a serious and consistent basis on which to adjudicate the differences between 'one of us' and 'one of them'.

Perhaps a different way into the question might attempt to evaluate the distinctions between the two positions in terms of consequences—the utilitarian ends of action rather than their wellsprings. What if, for example, the work is intended to assist in the development of better health and safety legislation? It may be explicitly performative, entirely reliant on taken-for-granted categories and unreflexive about the use of accident statistics. Does that mean that attempts by academics to show that existing health and safety legislation is inadequate are uncritical, and that they should fall outside the CMS project? Or, to take another example, Ricardo Semler's *Maverick* (1994) describes his organization, Semco, in Brazil as an anti-hierarchical, democratic manufacturing company with a self-governing and self-managing workforce. It (if Semler is to be believed) has no organization chart; has flexible working hours; encourages people to wear what they like and decorate their workspaces as they see fit; encourages union membership and upward appraisal and so on. In many ways this is a new-model capitalist organization, and one that has been widely lauded by business gurus. Yet it also seems to be doing something, in very practical terms, about the complaints voiced by CMS academics. So does Semco represent something that CMS is opposed to? And what about Tom Peters? He, and a great deal of the business guru literature, what Gibson Burrell has called 'Heathrow Airport Organization Theory', announces itself as critical of the established order (du Gay 2000). It too is concerned to denaturalize and radicalize, but somehow CMS must announce that these are not real revolutions—merely the death of an old king and the crowning of a new one.

In terms of ends, we are then into the knotty problem of what ends we deem to be desirable. More money for less work, or the end of work and money altogether? Less hierarchically managed organizations and more teamworking, or the end of hierarchy altogether? Ethical capitalism, or the end of capitalism? Critical academics, or anyone else for that matter, will find it hard to judge the greatest happiness of the greatest number by comparing the possible future merits of reformist and revolutionary utopias. Unless human happiness can really be added up on the scales of justice. As Fournier and Grey acknowledge, these are not easy matters to adjudicate upon. Should CMS academics attempt to work towards humanizing work organizations, and run the danger of being co-opted, or refuse to engage with managerial practice at all, and run the danger of being ignored? In practice, much of what has been labelled as CMS has tended towards the latter rather than the former, tending to stress theoretical purity as a proxy for moral purity, and disengagement from the B-School hegemony as a virtue in itself. More on this later, but next I want to consider some of the components of critical thought on organizations more generally in order to ask some questions about the particular nuances and histories of B-School CMS at the turn of the millennium.

Disciplining CMS

As I hinted before, this description of CMS as a collectively unified vanguard movement, as the B-School's nemesis in waiting, is very wide of the mark. It suggests a coherence to something that is better described as a series of connected debates. Indeed, it might be said that (as it used to be claimed of postmodernism) it is easy to find someone who is against some aspect of it, and very hard to find someone who is unconditionally for it. There is, in practice, very little agreement about the nature and boundaries of what counts as critical work on organizations and this is partly because of the diverse variety of lineages that this work can make reference to. I will classify these histories in two ways, different disciplines and different theories, and deal with the latter in the next section.

A fairly obvious point to make about CMS is that it is primarily located in the 'organizational behaviour' parts of B-Schools. To be more precise, its debts are primarily, even if rather vaguely, to those parts of sociology and social psychology that constitute much of the canon in this area. To be sure, there is a substantial body of work in critical accounting, a little in marketing, and a few pieces of work on strategy, operations, information systems and so on. However, in many of these latter areas, it is possible to argue that the trajectory of the work has been aimed at 'sociologizing' the taken-for-granted by showing, for example, that the construction of accounting is not a neutral technical matter, but a social practice that represents power for its own interests and ignores other stakeholders—the environment, social costs and so on. Yet by far the largest body of work emerges from organization studies and human resource management. It is here, perhaps in the domains that are most committed to human beings (rather than numbers, or machines), from which CMS has primarily grown. In the UK there are, as Fournier and Grey (2000) and M. Parker (2000b) have argued, some rather more prosaic reasons too. The lack of career opportunities for sociologists and other social scientists during the 1980s, combined with a massive expansion in business and management teaching, resulted in many students with postgraduate training in sociology and related disciplines being forced to find work outside sociology departments. Many of the ideas which now shape CMS can be traced back to the consequent importation of Marxism, critical theory, post-structuralism and so on into the B-school from the 1980s onwards.

But, despite this migration, there is a kind of forgetting built into much of CMS as it tends to stress its novelty and contemporary relevance. After all, a great deal of work in organizational sociology from Weber onwards and organizational psychology from Maslow onwards was implicitly or explicitly critical of rationalization, the division of labor, alienation and the various psycho-pathologies which supposedly followed from certain forms of management and labour. To take the former, in the second chapter of this book I noted that the anti-bureaucratic critique has a long history, and I mentioned that it gained particular importance in US sociology after the Second World War when a number of writers were deeply concerned to evaluate both the efficiency and the morality of an organization form which was by then associated with corporate power and fascist versions of efficiency. So Mills, Gouldner, Blau, Selznick, Adorno, Merton and so on wrote much on the inefficiencies of bureaucratic structures, on the bureaucratic personality, and on the increasing domination of a managerial power elite and mode of thought which was intimately connected to the military-industrial complex. In quite parallel ways, humanistic psychologists such as Maslow, Argyris, Likert and McGregor bemoaned the shortcomings of autocratic management styles, the lack of meaning in contemporary workplaces and the extent to which the managerial strategies of the time were turning employees into resentful dependent children. Yet, for CMS, much of this work is either forgotten, or regarded as the uncritical predecessor of the enlightenment that begins with Alvesson and Willmott in 1992. This also seems to mean that in contemporary sociology, what little that is left of the sociology of organizations hence has little connection to CMS. Sociologists have turned to culture and social policy, or have continued researching various 'classic' forms of inequality, but they seem relatively uninterested in organizing and organizations as such. So the two areas, both broadly denaturalizing, reflexive and non-performative, proceed on relatively independent tracks. It seems that one of the perils of boundary work is that it excludes potential friends as well as obvious enemies.

In this regard, it is worth noting other literatures which are critical of the corporate managerial complex, but are also largely excluded. Within what might be called international political economy, there is an established body of thought on the role of business lobbies in structuring state and multilateral decision-making (Sklair 1995). I'll cover some of this material in chapter 8, in terms of anti-corporate protest, but just briefly mention the watering-down of climate change legislation as an example. As Newell and Paterson (1998) argue, an unholy alliance of pro-capitalist state and energy lobbies representing fossil fuels and transportation companies has been systematically defending its interests through public relations, research grants, positions on key decision-making bodies and so on. George W. Bush's decision in early 2001 to break with the Kyoto protocols and massively invest in further exploiting non-renewable energy resources was a testament to the power of this group of interests. Yet, once again, the B-School focus of CMS has meant that these macro-political issues are rarely considered. Of course, it might be said that this is largely because CMS is concerned with organizational issues, and this is a fair defence. All disciplines have their boundaries by definition. Yet, as I argued with reference to business ethics in the previous chapter, these boundaries can easily result in exclusions that are positively unhelpful when viewed from outside.

Similar points can be made in terms of literatures on feminist collective organization, the ecological critique of growth and the postcolonial literatures on structures of racism. For CMS, managerialism is often enough identified as patriarchal, environmentally disastrous and deeply complicit with an imperial order. However, with a very few exceptions, these connections are undeveloped and tend to be largely rhetorical. This is not to accuse CMS practitioners of sin by deliberate commission or omission, but to note that this is what academic labels and disciplines do. They divide up territories and allow for particular forms of legitimate enquiry to be practised, but in so doing this labour of division leaves certain matters in the shadows, or as properly the work of someone else. CMS spends most of its energy attacking B-School versions of the organization, the employee, human resource management, culture and so on. It is therefore perhaps hardly surprising that it should have little energy left to lengthen its history or widen its focus. If it did this, then CMS would no longer be engaged in its very important institutional battle with myopic market managerialism. But perhaps the most contested exclusion is related to the debate between two forms of European social theory, both deeply related but now the subject of some heated and intense disagreement—Marxism and post-structuralism.

Theorizing CMS

This moves me from disciplinary division to theoretical division. Of course, the two are related but, in the case of CMS, there is a sense in which theory has become the battleground for defining the heart of the critical project. Various forms of Marxist analysis have pretty much defined oppositional approaches to capitalism for much of the last century. Whether we refer to Marx's own writings, Marxist-Leninist practice, the Frankfurt School of critical theory, or post-Braverman labour process analysis, it is difficult to imagine a robustly critical analysis of organization and management making sense without some form of residual commitment to Marxism. Yet that is exactly the point at issue here, with the central concern being to define exactly what kind of Marxism, neo-Marxism or post-Marxism CMS should be based upon. In a way that echoes the intense sectarianism of the left more generally—critical academics have been busily worrying about epistemology while Seattle was burning.

I don't want to spend too much time on the detail of this debate, but it is necessary to draw a general picture. The cleavage here is between a variety of labour process academics who are mostly indebted to Braverman's analysis of managerialism in his 1974 *Labor and Monopoly Capital*. This book was widely seen as invigorating Marxist analyses of work and organizations and directly led to the founding of the UK Labour Process Conferences in 1983. However, since the early 1990s, CMS has grown away from these origins and become more concerned to theorize subjectivities rather than structures. This has led to some heated disagreements. First, for labour process theorists, CMS academics (who are mostly characterized as adherents to Foucauldian forms of post-structuralism or postmodernism) are accused of a distraction from the critical project by sponsoring a largely irrelevant form of social or organizational theory that both denies the specificity of the employment relationship and appears to have little relation to Marxism proper. Second, it is suggested that their post-structuralist epistemology makes them unable to distinguish key dualisms—manager/managed, oppression/emancipation and so on—which are essential to any analysis of ideology in work organizations. Finally, that the above two points lead to a general inability to articulate a political position more generally because CMS has, through its sustained intellectual hypochondria, disqualified all the grounds for judgement. Perhaps the previous chapter would be a good example of this particular disease. CMS academics respond by agreeing that their approach is a development and revision of labour process Marxism but that this is entirely consistent with historical and dialectical thinking. Marxism is not a fixed corpus of ideas, and new intellectual currents should not be excluded. Second, they acknowledge that academics, or anyone else, can't do intellectual work without dualisms but that all critical authors must continually attempt to be aware of their contingent nature and the extent to which they perform identity work for the people who deploy them. Third, that this does not mean the end of politics—merely the end of the kind of representational politics that was characteristic of modernism and its replacement with a more modest, reflexive and local practice. There is, in other words, no secure place outside discourse to accuse other people of suffering from false consciousness whilst your own ideology goes unquestioned.

The labour process position seems to be premised on the assumption that the CMS position is inherently relativist because subjectivist. In other words, it ends up as a stance that cannot contribute to emancipation because (amongst other things) it questions the objective reality of power inequalities. On the other hand, CMS researchers argue that the opposing position adopts (or constructs) a fictional 'high moral ground' and is masculinist, humanist, defensive and dualist. It therefore has difficulty in contributing to emancipatory struggles because it relies on elitist and conservative assumptions about the relationship between researcher and researched and refuses to debate the nature of emancipation itself. Whatever the rights and wrongs of this debate, the clear implication has been that many critical researchers do not identify

CMS as their home, but as a fashionable form of relativism that is incapable of being politically critical. As one of them said during a debate at a labour process conference, 'I feel like my language has been stolen from me.' Labour process analysis, with its materialist or realist commitments, predates CMS by decades yet is having its critical credentials appropriated. A politically ambivalent form of idealism and scepticism is colonizing the very words that have provided such powerful ammunition in the past. But for CMS academics, such a response adds up to a remarkable degree of defensiveness. CMS should include Marxism, as the CMSW mission and Fournier and Grey make clear, but is not solely constituted by it. Marxism is not irrelevant, but (for CMS) needs supplementing by new theories and methodologies in order to undertake a more ambitious critical programme.

This is a sad state of affairs. The remarkable mobilizations that seem to have had the potential to develop an internal critique of the B-School, of managerialism and the political economy of the corporation seem to be running into the sands of academic debate. As Jaros has put it 'we seem to spend more time debating each other about political economy than we do the right wing forces that are carrying the day' (2001: 38). Instead of inciting a storm of informed dissent, we have a flurry of academic papers and replies in learned journals. But let me be clear about my complaint here, because I am as complicit in this as anybody else. My pastiche of the issues at stake is unsubtle, it uses the wrong words and names the wrong names. In any case, many of the academics involved in these debates spend most of their time doing other things— engaging in theoretically informed empirical analyses of management and organizations, writing about power and inequality at work, teaching students about these and other ideas, perhaps even being involved in other political activity outside the academy altogether, and so on. This debate about the inside and outside of CMS is a side-show and not the main event. Nonetheless, it seems to me symptomatic of what happens to ideas when academics get hold of them. Critical? Critical of capitalism, or managerialism, or corporate domination? Critical of patriarchy, or imperialism, or heterosexism? What can be included and what must be excluded? Further, are we to be critical of positivism, of the hegemony of the scientific method? Or should we be suspicious of any claims to truth, whether realist or interpretivist? And if our critique becomes accepted, perhaps the cornerstone of a new hegemony, should we switch positions and become critical of that too? No doubt this is why Hancock (1999) ironically suggests a new acronym which provides a place for these questions—CCMS, critical of critical management studies. Perhaps the most characteristic way for an academic to answer a question is with 'it depends what you mean by . . .'. That is, after all, our job. To think hard about words and things. Sadly, though, at least at the time of writing, CMS (and CCMS) does not seem to be achieving much else. But then perhaps I was expecting too much from academics.

References

Alvesson, M., and Willmott, H. (1996). *Making Sense of Management: A Critical Introduction*. London: Sage.

Braverman, H. (1974). *Labor and Monopoly Capital*. New York: Monthly Review Press.

du Gay, P. (2000). *In Praise of Bureaucracy*. London: Sage.

Fournier, V., and Grey, C. (2000). 'At the Critical Moment: Conditions and Prospects for Critical management Studies', *Human Relations*, 53/1: 7–32.

Hancock, P. (1999). 'The Management of Everyday Life: The Idea'. Paper presented at the First International Critical Management Studies Conference, Manchester.

Jaros, S. (2001). 'Labor Process Theory', *International Studies of Management and Organizations*, 30/4: 25–39.

Newell, P., and Paterson, M. (1998). 'A Climate for Business', *Review of International Political Economy*, 5/4: 679–703.

Parker, M. (2000). 'The Sociology of Organizations and the Organization of Sociology: Some Reflections on the Making of a Division of Labour', *Sociological Review*, 48/1: 124–46.

Semler, R. (1994). *Maverick*. London: Arrow.

Sklair, L. (1995). *Sociology of the Global System*. Hemel Hempstead: Prentice-Hall.

Sotirin, P., and Tyrell, M. (1998). 'Wondering about Critical Management Studies', *Management Communication Quarterly*, 12/2: 303–36.

Thompson, P. (2001). 'Progress, Practice, and Profits: How Critical is Critical Management Studies?' Paper presented to the 19th Labour Process Conference, Royal Holloway College, March.

17 Brands, Boundaries and Bandwagons:
A critical reflection on critical management studies

Paul Thompson

> No postmodernist would believe they have the right answers, only that there are subjects whose knowledge and identity have been constituted as privileged in a particular setting.
>
> (Palmer and Hardy 2000 : 281)

Perhaps we can interpret the above as indicating that postmodernists know how to be in the right place at the right time. Certainly, critical management studies has been a major growth area, now with its own conference in the UK and a lively US-based discussion list. While any new forums for radical exploration of management and organisation are welcome, appearances can be deceptive. The diversity of people attending conferences and even contributing to discussions is not entirely indicative of the nature of the beast. For critical management studies is also Critical Management Studies, and for its adherents a brand of sorts.[1]

This can be seen in the detailed and useful account of the origins and characteristics of CMS by Fournier and Grey (2000). The authors make reference to a plurality of intellectual traditions that include varieties of 'neo-Marxism', psychoanalysis and environmentalism, but that proves ultimately tokenistic. For all their qualifying statements, they state that 'the boundaries are drawn around issues related to performativity, denaturalisation and reflexivity' (2000 : 17).[2] There is, thus, no significant difference between claims on behalf of CMS and those made for post-structuralism and postmodernism in general. The reference to 'issues' around the three boundaries is somewhat disingenuous. Though occasionally reference is made to enemies beyond the gate, the debates are overwhelmingly within it—cms becomes CMS the brand.

Given that, what this chapter seeks to do is use Fournier and Grey's framework as a starting point for investigating the CMS phenomenon, whilst attending to some of the variations within and beyond its boundaries. Anyway, let us return to their three boundaries. Reflexivity can be seen as part of the unwillingness to take received wisdoms and practices for granted that constitutes much of the appeal of CMS. As Hardy et al. (2002) note, some post-structuralists have gone beyond examining ways in which knowledge is situated within research communities and how research processes shape outcomes, to (over-)emphasising authorial identity and 'confessional melodramas'. But the issue of reflexivity is passed over fairly quickly by Fournier and Grey without trying to give it an explicit or distinctive twist. For this we should be grateful. For even the most enthusiastic adherent of CMS would find it difficult to claim that reflexivity is a specific trait of CMS. Rather it is a shared inheritance of critical approaches to social science in general, including interpretive (such as symbolic interactionist) and critical realist perspectives. For example, reflexivity has been one of the five 'domain assumptions of a critical approach to the study of organisations' in Thompson and McHugh's *Work Organizations* (3rd edn., 2002) for over a decade.[3]

However, the other boundary criteria—non-performativity and de-naturalisation—more explicitly reveal the post-structuralist, postmodern character of the CMS brand. What reflects is a major shift in radical analyses, from ontological to epistemological scepticism.[4] As Epstein (1997 : 137) notes, this draws on the general postmodernist attitude of 'radical scepticism towards the truth, or toward claims that there is an objective reality that is to some extent knowable'. The outcome of this shift and the means through which the shift is achieved have deeply negative consequences.

The triumph of epistemological relativism

In Fournier and Grey's words, denaturalisation is about 'deconstructing the reality of organisational life' and 'effacing the process of construction behind the mask of science' (2000 : 18). Critiques of the 'naturalistic fallacy' associated with positivism have been prominent in the social sciences and sociology of knowledge since at least the work of Mannheim.[5] As with reflexivity, a type of de-naturalization is, therefore, part of the shared history of critical social science. A soft postmodern epistemology attracts many to this type of approach to the social sciences—that is a recognition of the socially mediated perceptions of reality and socially constituted character of knowledge, and therefore the difficulty of making truth claims or resolving them. But Founrier and Grey give de-naturalisation a specific imprint that reflects a harder relativist kernel, a strong version, that is the meta-theoretical core of postmodernism and the version of CMS postulated by them. Such a version 'takes the form of an extreme social constructionism, a view that identities, relations and political positions are constructed entirely through interpretation, that there is no identifiable social reality against which interpretations can be judged' (Epstein 1997 : 137). The hard epistemology moves beyond a contingent explanation for being unable to access the real (because it is too fragmented) to an all-purpose one ('truth' is merely the will to power). If it is impossible to adjudicate between 'truth claims', then all we can do is show the construction of a perspective and how it is translated for action (Czarniawska 1999).

Socially constructing science

Czarniawska is typical of CMS writers in making a critique of scientific orthodoxy—a rejection of what is called the 'logico-scientific mode of knowing'—the prime means to accomplish the shift from ontological to epistemological scepticism. This deserves, therefore, some detailed consideration. In support of her claim that organization theory can be treated as a literary genre because there is no difference between fiction and any other form of writing, science can be considered as mere 'conversation', whose logic of enquiry is rhetorical (1999 : 10). Much of the force of this argument comes from a reading of the philosopher of science, Thomas Kuhn (1962, 1970). Indeed Czarniawska (1999 : 18) argues that, 'the insight that scientific knowledge is grounded in metaphorical thinking has been more or less commonly accepted (thanks to writers such as Kuhn 1964/66, McCloskey 1986, Morgan 1986)'.[6]

It seems from this statement that Czarniawska has read Morgan's *Images of Organisation* a lot more closely than she has Thomas Kuhn. So, it's worth recapping Kuhn's argument. He challenged the accepted, positivist view that science was based on the linear, patient, disinterested collection of facts, leading to hypotheses that were then tested or 'falsified' until the truth was discovered. Examining the development of physics and related disciplines, he showed that intellectual development took place within a dominant paradigm, excluding that which challenged its way of thinking. Only occasionally would these periods of puzzle-solving within 'normal science' be disrupted by irresistible forces of change based on the inability of the old paradigm to explain a large number of anomalies, and the existence of an alternative, incommensurable paradigm that would displace the old one. In that struggle, protagonists are not merely comparing findings to the real world, but making judgements about what is acceptable in their own professional domain. Science, then, is not wholly rational, and is shaped by ideologies and power.

Czarniawska is far from alone in her misuse of Kuhn. Post-structuralism in general, and CMS in particular, draw on a woefully partisan and partial reading.[7] Short references to his work seldom mention that it was subject to heavy criticism from within the scientific community, and that Kuhn accepted much of it, drawing back from radical interpretations of paradigm wars (see Caldwell, 1982 : 70–8, for a summary). Even more importantly, we should keep in mind that for all the talk of social influences on science, Kuhn did not deny that the outcomes of science were real physical laws, or claim that science is mere discourse. He argued that observation and experiment drastically restrict the range of admissible belief, that progress takes place in the state of knowledge, and that the distinction between the scientific and non-scientific is real. Within his model of 'normal science', there is full recognition that empirical investigation creates 'anomalies'—empirical results that contradict theoretical expectations—and which alter the course of action. As Armstrong (2001 : 161) notes, 'Social construction, on the Kuhnian model, is interwoven with impacts against the real, not an alternative to them.' In short, what we can say from Kuhn is that scientific judgements involve both the comparison of paradigms with varying modes of reality and with each other.

Safe in their social constructionist readings, relativists appear to be entirely ignorant of the complexities of such debates. They are also seemingly unconcerned with long-running debate on the left about the nature of science. Re-reading Donald McKenzie's excellent twenty-year old article, 'Science and social relations', is to be reminded that the dangers of what Hilary and Steven Rose called 'hyper-reflexivity' have been around a long time, but then were more likely to have their roots in a crude and determinist Marxism that 'reduces science to a mere image of the society in which it develops; destroys the boundary between truth and falsity, science and ideology' (McKenzie 1981 : 48).

Given that nobody would leave the house, let alone get on an aeroplane or submit themselves to surgery if science had not discovered truths bounded by the laws of probability, constructionists and deconstructionists are either lying to the world or to themselves. Czarniawska addresses this with a typical pragmatic evasion: 'It is practical to *believe* in the world of causes "out there"; it works most of the time. This does not equal saying that there are ways of describing this world "as it is"' (1999 : 10, emphasis in original). But actually it does. Unless processes of scientific discovery had revealed that particular bit of the world as it is, we would not know what works. 'Belief' is antecedent to that fact.

Post-structuralists need their partisan readings of Kuhn because he is a scientist and thus adds legitimacy. Their wilful ignorance and willingness to believe their own rhetoric can, however, be the undoing of epistemological postmodernism. This is nicely illustrated through the Sokal controversy. For the uninitiated, Sokal (1997; Sokal and Bricmont, 1997), a professor of physics, submitted a paper to the leading postmodern US journal *Social Text* purporting to deconstruct accounts of quantum gravity. It was a hoax—containing 'deliciously daft assertions' that crossed 'the boundaries of lunacy' (Sardar 2000 : 7), plus numerous citations of postmodern masters—but was nevertheless accepted and lavishly praised (until, of course, the hoax was revealed in the press and subsequent book).[8]

Beyond the stereotypes

Whether with respect to science, or theoretical knowledge in general, it is perfectly possible to recognize the various forms of social influence on the processes of *discovery*, without accepting the harder relativist baggage concerning *outcomes*. There are three serious bodies of work that critical workplace scholars would find particularly congenial: accounts of the institutional influences upon scientific work, with particular reference to the operation of scientific fields as reputational communities (see Whitley 2000); the 'strong programme' of the sociology of knowledge originally associated with the Science Studies Unit at Edinburgh University (Barnes, 1974); and the treatment of the work of scientists as a labour process (promoted by the *Radical Science* journal; see McKenzie 1981).

A failure to draw on any of these streams of the sociology of knowledge is indicative of the way in which CMS ignores any middle-ground positions. Instead, post-structuralists promote a stereotypical opposition between (bad) positivism and (good) social constructionism. As Ackroyd and Fleetwood (2000 : 3–4) note:

Here we arrive at the commonly held position that there are two basic perspectives on offer: either the world is objectively and unproblematically available and capable of being known by the systematic application of the empirical techniques common to positivism, or it is not knowable objectively at all; and in the place of claims to objectivity, we find that what is known is merely the product of discourses.

The language of 'truth claims', 'correspondence theory' and 'essentialism' functions as an intellectual halt sign: signalling that what is in fact merely difficult is in substance impossible. The study of work and organizations, like other social science domains, needed to recover a sense of feasible social science based on a recognition that while we cannot ever wholly know the real, reality can nevertheless bite back. With this in mind, 'reality claim' is more accurate than the pejoratively loaded 'truth claim'. There is an alternative, middle ground between positivism and relativism. As a philosophy of science, *critical realism* accepts that social structures and the meanings actors attribute to their situation have to be recognized in the way we construct explanations (Bhaskar, 1989; Collier, 1994), However, while our knowledge is inherently constrained and shaped by the social process of its production, entities such as labour markets and gender relations exist independently of our perceptions and investigations of them (see Tsoukas 2000, for a specific application to management and organization).

As Ackroyd and Fleetwood (2000) argue, the ontological question, 'what exists?' is often confused with the epistemological one, 'how can we know what exists?' Hence, as our knowledge is bound up with our conceptions, the misleading conclusion is drawn that all that exists is our concepts or discourse. The difficulties of establishing absolute certainty should not be used to assert that we can make *no* reality claims. In his defence of postmodern epistemology, Newton asks, 'How can we be sure that we have found "the real"?' (1996 : 22). The short answer is that we cannot be totally sure, but that is a far cry from not knowing anything: realists, 'want to hold that better and worse forms of knowledge exist and that there are reliable procedures for producing knowledge of things and events' (Ackroyd and Fleetwood 2000 : 15).

What we know is inherently incomplete, but we require a capacity to generate generalisable knowledge and to identify trends, if not laws. Critical realists eschew the positivist search for laws, preferring to identify tendencies associated with the operation of structural mechanisms in open system conditions (see Fleetwood 2001). This is not to say that critical realism has solved all epistemological problems and provides a fully formed toolbox for researchers. As with all such frameworks, realists can hide absences and unsolved questions behind formally elegant language. But it is not necessary to fully embrace critical realism in order to accept that while there cannot be an exact correspondence between reality and our representations of it, good research aims to grasp the real with as much accuracy and complexity as is feasible in given conditions. For example, we know that the vast majority of studies of empowerment demonstrate, through a variety of quantitative and qualitative methodologies, a massive gap between managerial claims of delegated decision-making and workplace outcomes. Not only can we attempt to distinguish between particular representations and the socially real, it is fundamental to a healthy social science that we seek to do so. In other words, good empirical work helps us to distinguish between rhetorics of the powerful and the realities of power.

What is the point of all this with respect to critical management studies? Simply this—extreme epistemic suspicion or hyper-reflexivity has been disastrous for the field of study. It has encouraged dumbed down empirical work based on ignorance of or hostility towards the full range of social science methodologies, particularly of a quantitative nature. In addition, we have been either plagued with endless and often obscure meta-theorizing, or drawn away from challenging the ontological claims associated with managerialist orthodoxies. When it is fashionable for social science to problematize everything, the focus is always on what we don't know rather than what we do. While there is a role for deconstruction, when it becomes the sole purpose of analysis, the outcomes are ultimately arid and self-defeating. CMS is predisposed to problematize everything and resolve nothing.

....

Strategies for (non-) explanation—power without responsibility

The argument in this chapter now turns towards the strategies employed in CMS in order to theorize about 'what exists'. It is based on the simple premise that theorising without accessing the real is impossible. If this is the case, what we get from post-structuralists is the worst of both worlds—non-transparent forms of explanation, the power to persuade without the responsibility to account for explanation.

Three overlapping directions can be identified:

1   Retreat Wholly into the Text

If 'truth claims' are based wholly on the power to persuade, then text itself becomes the only source of legitimacy. Or as Armstrong puts it, 'If all we can know of text is text itself, questions of validity dissolve into rhetorical pragmatics' (2001 : 157). The most obvious manifestation of this is quoting your mates, or referring only to those who support your argument. If we go back to Czarniawska's (1999) book, we find that her arguments are justified and legitimated time and again by reference to small number of co-thinkers such as Rorty, Macintyre, Lyotard and Latour. The economist McCloskey is quoted twelve times in the book in support of her relativist claims about the non-scientific nature of economics and other disciplines, yet no other work of economics appears in the index. It is as if this particular claim encompasses the whole discipline, despite, for example, a strong critical realist presence (e.g. Lawson 1998). Postmodernists are big on hearing alternative voices until any of those voices say anything that disputes their line of thinking. These approaches are given further underpinning by notions of paradigm incommensurability.

Such highly selective readings are not merely examples of 'bad practice'. It is the likely outcome of treating the literature as the sole or main source of authoritative reinforcement/consensus: 'Thus the doctrine of the discursively constituted self encourages the authors to infer the penetration of a discourse from the mere fact of its presence' (Armstrong 2001 : 156).

There is a further dimension to this. Having dismissed any notion of the real and any sense in which research is based on a process of discovery, all references are equal. They need not indicate the status of a work or what empirical evidence it does or does not rest upon. To return to the Czarniawska example, she refers to Kuhn, McCloskey and Morgan as her sources for the view that there is near consensus on the rhetorical nature of science, yet the first is misread (on the basis of a single reference); the second appears to be the only economist in the world who believes that her discipline consists of nothing more than metaphors and stories; and the third writes about the usefulness of metaphors, but *Images of Organisation* does not explicitly discuss the nature of scientific knowledge at all.

2 Indirect Reference to the 'Real'

CMS texts, while denying the possibility of making truth claims, litter their discussions of contemporary organizational life with references to 'new realities', though often with quotation marks to indicate ironic distance. Logically, an approach that rejects narrative and totalizing pictures should be hostile to or uninterested in an alternative conception of society, but there is considerable evidence of what Armstrong calls 'the persistence of unreconstructed truth claims within avowedly anti-realist texts' (2001 : 7). Even those who have most resolutely avoided any engagement with the empirical cannot resist reference to 'the changing conditions of modern life', to justify their calls for conceptual shifts in the body of organization theory, or in this case the theory of the organizational body (Dale and Burrell 2000 : 25).

The main example I want to use is Shenhav's study of the 'engineering foundations of the managerial revolution'. He assures us that he does not wish to 'evaluate the ontological status of the propositions and claims presented in the engineering texts' (1999 : 135) that he draws on in his fascinating account of the emergence of management systems in the USA. Yet almost every page is replete with description of events that asserts particular interpretation, sometimes of a strong character. For example, we are told that 'The engineering rhetoric is a form of colonizing the mind—the minds of employers and workers as well as of politicians, social scientists and policy-makers. This book explores how this "colonizing of the mind" was realised' (1999 : 201). Except that it doesn't. Too often it presents the discourses of *American Machinist* and other journals as if words were deeds. Reality claims are made, but epistemological responsibility evaded.

Finally, in a classic example of having your cake and eating it, Fournier and Grey advance an analysis of the intellectual, political and socio-economic conditions under which the critical and management came together. It is replete with confident claims about agency and context,[9] yet they preface the analysis with the following: 'we should make it clear that we do not see these conditions as having "caused" or determined the emergence of critical management studies' (2000 : 10). On what grounds, then, should the reader accept what they say?

3   The Discursive Production of Reality

These two tendencies—to retreat into the text and use it as a source of uncontested authority, and the finding of ways to indirectly refer to the real—come together in a third strategy of creating facts from discourse. As Armstrong observes, qualitative research by post-structuralists in the management field does make substantial reality claims:

Talk and action are reported as support for the writer's interpretation of them.... Whilst presenting a surface of empirical engagement, the style actually incorporates a general-purpose interpretative filter through which all possible realities can be assimilated to its theoretical core. (Armstrong 2001 : 162)

He then proceeds to illustrate this primarily through the work of du Gay.

Armstrong's observations parallel a similar exercise carried out by Thompson and Findlay (1999). Their paper seeks to identify strong claims from weak evidence made in CMS studies by, among others, Rose, Grey and McCabe and Knights. For example, it demonstrates that even where qualitative material is collected in case studies, it is often simply attributed to respondents' concerns with identity, concerns which are seen as distinct and discontinuous with traditional terrains of work and management. Ironically, this truly is an example of a way of doing research that is theoretically determined as well as theory-laden.

In conclusion to this section, we would argue that if reality claims are inevitable, we need to have transparent, shared ways of discussing and resolving them—however partial and limited they may be. The enhanced epistemological freedom for the postmodern theorist from anything other than self-referential accountability is secured at the expense of organizational theory in general. Before we get to the third Fournier and Grey boundary, it is worth noting and discussing a fork in the CMS road.

....

An epistemological escape hatch: multi-paradigm perspectives

Some proponents of CMS/post-structuralism have become unhappy with the consequences of relativism. Unwilling to accept or ignorant that critical realism offers an alternative to positivism and social constructionism, they have to seek other ways out of the relativist *cul-de-sac*, which allow some means of making judgements and making a difference.

The chief escape hatch from pure reliance on deconstruction is development of 'multi-paradigm thinking', under the banner of diversity, dialogue and democracy, so the chapter focuses on a critique of multi-paradigm analysis. Originally promoted by Hassard (1991), who interprets empirical data on the fire service in the UK through the paradigmatic 'eyes' of each of Burrell and Morgan's original quartet, the argument is that the approach reflects the diverse and multi-faceted nature of reality which no single approach can grasp (Schultz and Hatch 1996).

This has been developed in a number of more recent contributions. For example, Kamoche argues that unless human resource management is ana-lysed from within each paradigm, we may be 'ignoring the insights that other perspectives have been shown to yield' (1991 : 13). A 'multi-perspective' ap-proach is also utilised by Daymon (1999), drawing on Martin's (1992) well-known integration, differentiation and fragmentation framework for analysing culture. She asserts that a single analytical lens is insufficient to explain the complex realities of life in new organizational forms such as television stations.

Hassard's argument is superficially attractive. Who, after all, could be against dialogue, or resist the call for greater 'democracy' in organization theory? (1991 : 296). In addition, there is no doubt that such exercises are fruitful individual exercises in collective and individual learning. But, as Parker and McHugh (1991) observed of Hassard's effort, the ability to hop between languages is not the same as demonstrating its analytical usefulness. The practice of multiple paradigm analysis tends to be closure by any other name, for each speaks from behind its own walls. Indeed, Hassard (1988) treats meta-theories as distinct language games in which we can be trained. The normal purpose of dialogue is to resolve issues or move beyond disagreements. This is difficult for postmodernists, given their denial of any grounds against which to make judgements.

It may be true, as Kamoche says, that paradigms generate different insights, but what if those insights are based on competing claims, for instance about the relative weight of hard and soft HRM in contemporary workplace practice? Alternatively, what if the competing insights refer to an entity that is accepted as both entirely discursive and extra-discursive? Similarly, in her previously discussed analysis of competing perspectives on culture in a TV station, Daymon says that an integration lens is useful, because 'commonly held beliefs are found about the need to make profits in order to survive' (1999 : 131). But this is not just a belief, it is a real consequence of competitive markets. Other perspectives on culture cannot negate that reality. The relativist twist that everything is of equal value merely adds to the problem and is open to the same objections that were raised by Reed of Morgan's use of metaphors: that we end up taking products down from the shelf as uncritical consumers, rather than promoting rigorous debate and research.

It may well be the case that a single analytical lens is insufficient to explain the complex realities of life in new organizational forms such as television stations. But what if competing claims are being made? For example, integration perspectives are often not just about how things are managed, but are discourses used by management to explain the world in unitary terms. This frequently clashes with how employees (in differentiated or fragmented terms) see and experience the *same* events. Daymon tries to get round this by distinguishing between paradigms and perspectives; the latter being empirically derived without any consistent association with particular methods or epistemologies. The distinction is useful, but the argument, that 'the three separate portrayals of CTV are simultaneously accurate' (1999 : 131), is open to the same objections.

Whatever virtues it may have, this mode of analysis reproduces the weaknesses of relativism by other means. There is no solution to the core problem of loss of explanatory power. In addition it draws attention away from a more worthwhile approach—multi-level analysis. It is perfectly legitimate to have a more structural or a more micro emphasis on management or some other aspect of organizational life. Moreover, it is possible to creatively combine micro and macro. The key is not to analytically close off the possibilities of 'seeing' the other dimension, and that observations made about action and structure at different levels—workgroup, organisational, societal—are compatible with one another (Ackroyd 2000).

To go further, it is even possible to argue that such dimensions are sometimes most effectively addressed by different perspectives. Kellner (1999 : 194) says that, 'McDonaldization is a many-sided phenomenon and the more perspectives that we can bring to its analysis the better grasp of the phenomenon one will have.' This 'more the better' outlook may be overdoing it, but Kellner does persuasively argue that postmodern concepts can be successfully deployed to explain a later development of McDonaldization, when a modernist emphasis on mass production was complemented by a set of practices around consumption and management of global identities. Kellner's analysis partly avoids this trap because he utilises different perspectives to explain different things—in his case production and consumption relations—and in different time periods.

Performance

Critical work on management must have 'non-performative intent'. Fournier and Grey (2000 : 17) define performativity in a number of ways: part process—'inscribing knowledge within means–ends calculation'—and part potential outcome—'the aim is to contribute to the effectiveness of managerial practice'. On this basis they go on to make a distinction between legitimately invoking notions of power, inequality and control; and the illegitimate invocation of efficiency, effectiveness and profitability. So, for example, they criticize harnessing diversity in the name of effectiveness.

It is difficult to find practical or political grounds to sustain such an interpretation. Once again, critical researchers have long questioned the construction of performance categories. The work of Nichols (1986) or Williams et al. (1989) are examples of critical scholarship that challenge (and not merely deconstruct) the terms of existing concepts and practices focused on different aspects of performance. But they do not reject making judgements on the basis of performance or outcome (Rosenau 1992: glossary). After all, what is seen as illegitimately performative—efficiency, effectiveness and profitability—is the terrain through which the capitalist labour process is reproduced and contested. Earlier in their paper, Fournier and Grey themselves (2000 : 11) talk of management incompetence and the lack of effectiveness, or is this just discourse? It is certainly difficult to identify the grounds on which they would evaluate the relevant practices.

And why is this terrain illegitimate in itself? In any feasible economic relations some organisations or practices will be more effective and efficient than others, though how this is measured and what action follows from it will always be open to dispute. Productivity matters to employees as well as managers. It is reasonable to argue that HRM or equal opportunity can be positive for efficiency, as long as this is not the only criterion on which progressive practices are advocated. A refusal to engage at this level makes the genuine attempts by CMS to debate grounds for ethical choice or emancipation ultimately hollow. It is also apparent that CMS applies performativity criteria to anyone but academics.

Inscribing knowledge within mean–ends calculation sounds pretty much like what we do with our research choices and publishing 'strategies'. It is difficult to see why academic performativity (producing yet another journal article that next to nobody reads) is morally superior or practically more beneficial than, let's say, attempts to improve work design.

CMS is locked into this *cul-de-sac* of non-performativity, not simply because of its location within a business context, but because of the postmodern rejection of the idea of progress or reason in general. Suspicion of performativity can quickly slip into rejection of *any* practice. While the individual politics of postmodernists varies, if there are no grounds for privileging or de-privileging any discourse, the politics in general tends to despair or disengagement. A stance of pure criticism, refusing to assert any values (other than its own relativism), postmodernism cannot provide a basis for a radical alternative, given that 'left politics requires a conception of a better society and an assertion of a better set of values than those that now prevail' (Epstein 1997 : 143).[10]

It is worth noting that aversion to performativity is not characteristic of all in the CMS camp. To illustrate this it is worth quoting Palmer and Hardy's dismissal of 'hard postmodernism' in full:

Such an approach, or anything close to it, presents difficulties in organisation and management theory because, according to this view 'postmodern organisation' is a contradiction in terms. Not surprisingly the field has proven resistant to such intrusions. Consequently many postmodern writers on organisations have limited their role to one of critique. Rather than abandon modernity and reason altogether, they often advocate a soft or optimistic version of postmodernism, which recognises the ontological existence of the social world, however precarious and fluid, and focuses on the location of alternative interpretations, marginalized voices and different readings. (Palmer and Hardy 2000 : 265)

In seeking to apply the insights of postmodernism to practice, they place themselves in the soft camp, yet their formulation combines both a softer relativism and a desire to shape practice. As we shall see in the next section, both directions are present, in varying degrees and combinations, among CMS writers more generally.

....

Performativity escape hatches: ethical and managerial enlightenment

With reference to practice, the search for an escape hatch has been more tortuous, but in the absence of any social science criteria to make judgements, the focus has been on normative grounds, notably ethics (Parker 1998). This has been debated and critiqued elsewhere, the essential point being made that whatever the merits of a critical ethics, if there is no body of meaningful evidence in organization theory, 'starting with ethics means finishing with nothing to argue about but our own value preferences' (see Thompson et al., 2000 : 1156). Fournier and Grey also search for ways 'to sever the logical link between epistemological and moral or political relativism' (2000 : 21). But after rehearsing the arguments between hard and soft relativism, they proclaim the debate to have been 'challenging', but reach no conclusions and pass on to the next issue.[11]

There is another, more direct, escape hatch. As Fournier and Grey (2000 : 25–6) admit, there is now a small, but flourishing industry of books and consultancy that seeks to use the insights of postmodernism to enlighten management. Palmer and Hardy go explicitly down this line arguing that such insights can help managers encourage multiple stories, diagnose problems, and live with ongoing tensions between the new and old, external and internal, etc. This can promote more successful innovation, learning, change (2000 : 283–4). Differences from the humanistic wing of management, or progressive sounding pop management writers, are difficult to spot. Generally, such approaches at least have the virtues of honesty and the modest possibilities for organizational reform. However, the orientation towards management as an agent or alternative consultancy sits rather uneasily with a claim to be within the domain of critical management studies. Or does it?

....

How not to be critical of management

Ultimately the question is—what is CMS critical of? It is certainly not management itself. When Paul Adler (2000 : 3) argued on the American CMS list that 'our critique should be primarily but not exclusively in the name of working people', responses were largely hostile. Such divisions between management and labour were 'dualistic' and had to be 'problematized'.

One critic worried about taking such an oppositional stance towards 'our MBA students and consulting clients'. Treating them as 'other' would be 'subtly and unintentionally hostile towards them' (Chumer 2000 : 7). Palmer and Hardy (2000 : 276) reinforce the more general point: 'Postmodern approaches draw our attention to the irrelevance of cutting up the world into distinctions that may no longer be meaningful. One arena where this may be particularly important is the distinction between non-managers and manager.'

While decades of activity on the left has inoculated me against making claims in the name of labour or anyone else, critical workplace researchers cannot ignore the interests of labour and management (albeit fractured in each case). But, for CMS, in the name of fragmented identities and refutation of dualisms, the material reality of divergent interests is set aside, or consigned to the compartment labelled 'out of date and no longer relevant'.

Shorn of such an orientation, the only object left is management theory. In other words, it is the *studies*, not the management, that CMS emphasizes. Shut off from performance in the wider world, this kind of CMS can only be concerned with performance in the academic equivalent—in other words with the effectiveness of critique of the mainstream on the one hand, and in the sphere of management education on the other.

This is not a single response. As Fournier and Grey show, there is a continuing divide between purists and pragmatists. The former, whether in the guise of meta-theorists or paradigm warriors, see engagement with management as dilution of the message. The alternative of 'permanent critique' is, however, in itself problematic. For this purpose to be meaningful, it must have orthodoxy to constitute itself against. Yet in many British management schools and some segments of organisation theory, CMS has *become* the orthodoxy.[12] What will it then have to critique? If 'critique has to follow the practices that constitute its target' (Fournier and Grey 2000 : 19), CMS needs the bogeyman.

For some within, or attracted to CMS, it is not enough to leave purely 'textual markers' (Perriton 2000 : 229). Perriton, echoing previous themes from Anthony (1998), goes on to argue that CMS must attend to the diverse performances of management pedagogy and to suggesting alternative management identities. Practical engagement equals management education, or educating management: 'The work of critical educators in this context will be a form of guerrilla warfare on the reproduction of the current managerialist identity of "manager".' While any form of critical practice is welcome, the statement merely draws attention to the limitations of detaching identities from interests.

Having said all that, it is not easy to take a moral high ground. We all have careers to make, reputations to enhance and interests to pursue. Those of us in business schools need to make meaningful to ourselves, to managers and would-be managers what we are teaching. But it still seems legitimate to ask of CMS—is this all there is? Palmer and Hardy refer to postmodern practices 'rattling the cage' (2000 : 284), but what cage are we talking about? It certainly doesn't appear to be Weber's iron cage of labour. Their preference for playing devil's advocate, embracing the new or ephemeral, seeing all sides of stories and continually critiquing assumptions is an underwhelming response to the range of intellectual and policy issues facing us. But it is a response that suits the occupational interests of academics, particularly at a time of increased regulation and measurement.

In this sense, the final argument of Fournier and Grey (2000 : 27) that the best we can do is ensure that the cacophony of critical voices 'is heard by students of management, "undistorted" by the performative intent (hence the importance of management education for CMS)' is both naive about manage-ment and silent about academic performativity. Meanwhile, they are worried that, 'the spectacle of "critical" is being appropriated in ways which are so extensive as to make its meaning indistinguishable from that which was formerly the target of critique' (2000 : 27). Well, what a surprise—welcome to the bandwagon effect. In the mid-1980s labour process theory went through the same process. It came out the other side with less adherents and influence, but still with something to say and, in recent years, a determination to connect with public policy and wider constituencies. The choice for CMS is this—does it want to be a (postmodern) brand or a genuine, additional forum for a variety of critical workplace researchers? I have no problem with Fournier and Grey debating or defining the boundaries of a diverse critical community in order to shake some of the bandwagon jumpers off the wagon train. But I do draw the line at locking the enterprise into a brand identity in the name of a broad critical community that far outstrips the sectarian imprint they seek to give it.

Notes

1. I am not assuming that the brand is identical in every context. As in all matters, institutional specificity leaves its mark and, for example, the US-based CMS network appears to be less influenced by postmodernism.
2. How Fournier and Grey arrive at these criteria is not obvious. They say that CMS is 'constituted through a process of inscription within a network of other inscriptions that serve to create obligatory points of passage in terms of work referenced and vocabulary or concepts used for analysis' (2000 : 16). What this seems to mean is that you are part of the brand if you quote the right people and use the designated language.
3. For a detailed discussion of issues around reflexivity, see Alvesson and Sköldberg (2000). Interestingly, it has also been argued that contemporary cultures are so knowing that reflexivity has become the norm, and therefore emptied of any radical content (Zizek 1999).
4. In his review of postcolonial writings and the work of Spivak in particular, Eagleton makes a similar point, that it is 'rather more audacious about epistemology...than about social reconstruction' (1999 : 5).
5. I'm grateful to Graham Sewell for enlightening me on this and a number of other points in the chapter.
6. Metaphor itself is not necessarily connected to social constructionism. Lewis (1999) makes a strong case that the use of metaphor performs a useful cognitive role in scientific theorising in that it is part of the linguistic context through which models are suggested and described.
7. Fournier and Grey have a standard one line dismissal of 'the supposed objectivism of natural science' by reference to Kuhn (2000 : 13).

8. Sardar is in the broadly postmodern camp, and his excellent pamphlet is recommended reading for those sceptical of just how wrong-headed most social constructionist writing on science actually is.

9. This appears to consist of a kind of elective affinity between the raised but inherently problematic profile of management in the workplace and broader polity, and the increased numbers, better location and enhanced legitimacy of those in a position to critique it from within academia.

10. Disengagement from social change is also reinforced by the tendency of CMS writers to emphasise what Palmer and Hardy refer to as 'constrained actors' (2000 : 272). Such constraints derive from concepts of power and identity in which, though resistance if possible, it is ultimately ineffective. As this has been critiqued elsewhere (Thompson and Ackroyd 1995; Ackroyd and Thompson 1999), I shall say no more here.

11. For similar inconclusive agonizing that eventually settles for 'existential angst', see Newton (1996).

12. This is obviously not the case everywhere, particularly in the USA. But there can be little doubt that, even there, the numerical weight and intellectual confidence of the so-called positivist-functionalist orthodoxy in organization theory has been severely dented.

References

Ackroyd, S. (2000). 'Connecting organisations and societies: a realist analysis of structures?', in S. Ackroyd and S. Fleetwood (eds), *Realist Perspectives on Management and Organisations*. London: Routledge.

Ackroyd, S. and Fleetwood, S. (2000). 'Realism in contemporary organisation theory and management studies', in S. Ackroyd and S. Fleetwood (eds), *Realist Perspectives on Management and Organisations*. London: Routledge.

Ackroyd, S. and Thompson, P. (1999). *Organizational Misbehaviour*, London: Sage.

Adler, P. (2000). 'Critical in the name of who or what?', Critical Management Studies Workshop Essay. Available at http://www.owner-c-m-workshop@jiscmail.ac.uk (and see comments by Chumer, Kreisher, Willmott and Kaghan).

Alvesson, M. and Sköldberg, K. (2000). *Reflexive Methodology: New Vistas for Qualitative Research*. London: Sage.

Anthony, P. (1998). 'Management education: ethics versus morality', in M. Parker (ed.), *Ethics and Organization*. London: Sage.

Armstrong, P. (2001). 'Styles of illusion', *The Sociological Review*, 49 (2): 155–73.

Barnes, B. (1974). *Scientific Knowledge and Sociological Theory*. London: Routledge and Kegan Paul.

Bhaskar, R. (1989). *Reclaiming Reality*. London: Verso.

Caldwell, B. (1982). *Beyond Positivism: Economic Methodology in the Twentieth Century*. London: Routledge.

Chumer, M. (2000). Comment on Adler, P., 'Critical in the name of who or what?', Critical Management Studies Workshop Essay. Available online at: http://www.owner-c-m-workshop@jiscmail.ac.uk.

Coleman, G. (1991). *Investigating Organisations: A Feminist Approach*. Bristol: SAUS Publications.

Collier, A. (1994). *Critical Realism*. London: Verso.

Czarniawska, B. (1999). *Writing Management: Organization Theory as a Literary Genre*. Oxford: Oxford University Press.

Dale, K. and Burrell, G. (2000). 'What shape are we in? Organization theory and the organized body', in J. Hassard, R. Holliday and H. Willmott (eds), *Body and Organization*. London: Sage.

Daymon, C. (1999). 'Tensions in television: quality, profits, and career aspirations', paper for the 17th Annual Labour Process Conference, Royal Holloway.

Eagleton, T. (1999). 'In the gaudy supermarket', *London Review of Books*, 21 (10): 13.

Epstein, B. (1997). 'Postmodernism and the left', *New Politics*, 6 (2): 130–45.

Fleetwood, S. (2001). 'Causal laws, functional relations and tendencies', *Review of Political Economy*, 13 (2): 201–22.

Fournier, V. and Grey, C. (2000). 'At the critical moment: conditions and prospects for critical management studies', *Human Relations*, 53 (1): 7–32.

Hardy, C., Harley, B. and Alvesson, M. (2002). 'Reflexivity in discourse analysis: how far have we come?', paper for EGOS Conference, Barcelona, July.

Hassard, J. (1988). 'Overcoming hermeneutics in organization theory: an alternative to paradigm incommensurability', *Human Relations*, 41 (3): 247–59.

—— (1991) 'Multiple paradigms and organizational analysis: a case study', *Organization Studies*, 12 (2): 275–99.

Kamoche, K. (1991). 'Human resource management: a multiparadigmatic analysis', *Personnel Review*, 20 (4): 3–14.

Kellner, D. (1999). 'Theorising/resisting McDonaldization: a multiperspectivist approach', in B. Smart (ed.), *Resisting McDonaldization*. London: Sage.

Kuhn, T. (1962, 2nd edn. 1970). *The Structure of Scientific Revolutions*. Chicago: University of Chicago Press.

Lawson, T. (1998). *Economics and Reality*. London: Routledge.

Lewis, P. (1999). 'Metaphor and critical realism', in S. Fleetwood (ed.), *Critical Realism in Economics*. London: Routledge.

McKenzie, D. (1981). 'Notes on the science and social relations debate', *Capital and Class*, 14: 47–60.

Martin, J. (1992). *Cultures in Organisations: Three Perspectives*. New York: Oxford University Press.

Newton, T. (1996). 'Postmodernism and action', *Organization*, 3 (1): 7–29.

Nichols, T. (1986). *The British Worker Question*. London: Routledge and Kegan Paul.

Palmer, I. and Hardy, C. (2000). *Thinking About Management*. London: Sage.

Parker, M. (1998). 'Capitalism, subjectivity and ethics: debating labour process analysis', *Organization Studies*, 20 (1): 25–45.

Parker, M. and McHugh, G. (1991). 'Five texts in search of an author: a response to John Hassard's "Multiple Paradigms and Organizational Analysis: A Case Study"', *Organization Studies*, 12 (3): 451–6.

Perriton, L. (2000). 'Verandah discourses: critical management education in organizations', *British Journal of Management*, 11: 227–37.

Rosenau, P. M. (1992). *Postmodernism and the Social Sciences: Insights, Inroads and Intrusions*. Princeton: Princeton University Press.

Sardar, Z. (2000). *Thomas Kuhn and the Science Wars*. Cambridge: Icon Books.

Schultz, M. and Hatch, M.-J. (1996). 'Living with multiple paradigms: the case of paradigm interplay in organizational culture studies', *Academy of Management Review*, 21: 529–57.

Shenhav, Y. (1999). *Manufacturing Rationality: The Engineering Foundations of the Managerial Revolution*. Oxford: Oxford University Press.

Sokal, A. (1997). 'A plea for reason, evidence and logic', *New Politics*, 6 (2): 126–9.

Sokal, A. and Bricmont, J. (1997). *Intellectual Impostures*. London: Profile Books.

Thompson, P. and Ackroyd, S. (1995). 'All quiet on the workplace front? A critique of recent trends in British industrial sociology', *Sociology*, 29 (4): 1–19.

Thompson, P. and Findlay, P. (1999). 'Changing the people: social engineering in the contemporary workplace', in A. Sayer and L. Ray (eds), *Culture and Economy After the Cultural Turn*. London: Sage.

Thompson, P. and McHugh, D. (2002). *Work Organisations*, 3rd edn., London: Palgrave.

Thompson, P., Smith, C. and Ackroyd, S. (2000). 'If ethics is the answer, you've been asking the wrong questions: a reply to Martin Parker', *Organization Studies*, 21 (6): 1149–58.

Tsoukas, H. (2000). 'What is management? An outline of a metatheory', in S. Ackroyd and S. Fleetwood (eds), *Realist Perspectives on Management and Organisations*. London: Routledge.

Whitley, R. (2000). *The Intellectual and Social Organization of the Sciences*. Oxford: Oxford University Press.

Williams, K. *et al.* (1989). 'Do labour costs really matter?', *Work, Employment and Society*, 3 (3): 281–305.

Zizek, S. (1999). 'You may! The post-modern superego', *London Review of Books*, 21 (6).

18 Abstract Ethics, Embodied Ethics: The Strange Marriage of Foucault and Positivism in Labour Process Theory

Edward Wray-Bliss

'When we write about the experiences of a group to which we do not belong, we should think about the ethics of our action, considering whether or not our work will be used to reinforce and perpetuate domination.' (bell hooks 1989 : 43)

This paper is an exploration and critique of the ethics and effects of our actions as academics and researchers engaged in critical management studies.[1] I draw upon Foucauldian ethical commitments and the example of the 'Manchester School's' labour process theory (LPT) to illustrate and contextualize my discussion.[2] In using the Manchester school's LPT as an example, it is not my intention for this work to be read as either singling out particular authors for specific criticism, or as a contribution to the 'divide' between 'Foucauldian' and 'Marxist' LPT/organizational studies. Rather, I would ideally like you the reader to use the examples and arguments in this paper to reflect upon the ethics and politics of your/our own research practices and processes and their unintentional subordinating effects in whatever 'school' of 'critical' management studies you engage with.

To encourage this, I organize the paper into three parts. In the second and third parts, I explore the resonances between the Manchester school's LPT and Foucauldian ethical commitments. In particular, I suggest that the school's writings may be understood as *theoretically or abstractly* resonating with Foucauldian ethical themes (second part), but that the authors do not seek to *embody* these themes or feelings in their research practices and processes (third part). This lack of embodiment may, I argue, be seen to have problematic effects for the researched, effects which are detrimental to our ability to confidently proclaim LPT (and by implication other 'critical' organization/management studies research) *as* 'critical' or 'political' academic work.[3] Before this, I use the first part of the article to draw out my understanding of Foucauldian ethics. Specifically, I draw out four ethical *themes* or *feelings*, which are threaded throughout the paper to structure my discussion. These are:

- understanding 'ethics' as intimately connected with 'politics';
- a critique of notions of sovereign subjectivity;
- a broadening of what we understand as political action or agency to include processes hitherto marginalized as 'merely personal';
- a commitment to permanently problemize, not authorize or normalize, our understandings, behaviours and representations.

Finally, perhaps a note is needed on the nature of my discussion of Foucauldian ethics in the first part. Like a growing number of other critics and academics, I experience many academic discussions of 'theory' as unnecessarily complex and inaccessible. Like others, I understand such writings to function as a form of exclusionary practice, with the effects of reproducing a problematic 'expert' elitist academic authority and culture (Seidman 1992; Stanley and Wise 1983). Based upon this understanding, I have tried to introduce or draw out Foucauldian ethical themes or feelings through what I hope will be an accessible medium—a medium that facilitates and enables the reader's active engagement with the issues rather than submission to the presumed authority of the Foucauldian 'expert' theorist. Specifically, I draw out 'Foucauldian' ethical themes through a discussion of sex(ual ethics), and in particular the themes of monogamy and non-monogamy grounded in a male character's justification of his decision not to have sex, taken from Phillipe Djian's novel *Betty Blue* (Djian 1988). If you are not put off finishing the paper by this unconventional style, you will also notice metaphors of sex, monogamy/ non-monogamy, marriage, divorce and separation threaded throughout the paper—starting with the title of the first part, below.

....

Fucking around with Foucault's Ethics

The title heading to this part of the article indicates or alludes to two aspects of my discussion. First, it alludes to my way of relating to theory and theorists (see also Wray-Bliss 1998; Wray-Bliss and Parker 1998). Specifically, I am not concerned to reproduce or claim either an 'expert' knowledge or 'truth' about Foucauldian ethics, or to claim that Foucault himself would have agreed with my interpretation of his work. I understand such conventional ways of dealing with theory and theorists to reproduce problematic authority relations, relations that I explicitly critique in this paper (see third part headed 'A Marriage of Convenience and the Divorce of Researcher from Researched'). Rather, I play around ('f**k around') with the ethical themes, feelings, or commitments that Foucault, his colleagues and critics have inspired in me.

Second, I illustrate and draw out what I understand to be Foucauldian ethical themes through discussing a male character's choice not to 'fuck around', as he phrases it in Phillipe Djian's novel *Betty Blue* (Djian 1988). I explore the complex interrelationships and social/political effects that such a nominally 'personal' or 'ethical' choice may reproduce or transgress. I do this to open up the broader theme of this paper, which is to explore the ethical/political effects and implications of our nominally 'personal' presence as researchers and writers for those we research and represent.

'... listen to me,' I went on. 'I was never much for fucking around, I never got much out of it. I know everybody else does it; but it's no fun if you do it like everybody else. To tell you the truth, it bores me. It does you good to live according to your ideas, to not betray yourself, not cop out at the last minute just because some girl has a nice ass, or because someone offers you a huge check, or because the path of least resistance runs by your front door. It's good for the soul.' I turned around to tell her the Big Secret: 'Over Dispersal I choose Concentration. I have one life—the only thing I'm interested in is making it shine.' (Djian 1988)[4]

A starting point of a Foucauldian ethical critique may be understood as a concern to de-naturalize or '*problemize*' (Foucault 1984c : 389) authoritative or prescriptive representations of self (Foucault 1984a : 352), relations with others (Foucault 1984d : 44), and society (Foucault 1981). Such authoritative or prescriptive representations are understood as a form of limitation of other possibilities, other ways of being.[5]

How might this 'Foucauldian' concern to problemize authoritative prescriptions/descriptions of self, relations and society be used to explore the above issue of monogamy/non-monogamy? First, we could highlight the *normalization* of monogamy by (western) religious, governmental and medical authorities.[6] We might, for instance, explore the ways that particular religious and political leaders and authorities routinely privilege monogamy (particularly when institutionalized as marriage [Rose 1996]) *over* non-monogamy. Drawing on this critique to re-read the extract from *Betty Blue*, we might interpret the speaker's concern to 'make his life shine' through resisting the temptation of sex, as the glow of self-righteousness, reflecting an official image of religious or moral dogma.

Second, we could highlight how casting monogamy as the natural, moral and god-fearing choice has functioned and does continue to function to *oppress* people. We might, for instance, explore understandings of monogamy as the institutionalization of women as the private property of individual men (codified, for example, in marriage vows 'to have and to hold'), and links between such 'property' relationships and domestic and sexual violence against women—evidenced, for instance, in the only recent criminalization of rape in marriage (1991/1992). We could link religious and governmental normalization of monogamy to the continual pathologization and oppression of those who identify (or are identified) as gay, lesbian, or bisexual. Thus, we might highlight the ways that gays, lesbians and bisexuals are still routinely represented and understood as promiscuous (if not paedophilic), and thus as not only 'immoral', but now also 'dangerous' or 'unsafe' (Watney 1996). Finally, we could explore the ways that the privileging of monogamy intersects with and legitimizes a colonial racialized discourse where black people, and particularly black African men, are pathologized by being represented as 'irresponsibly' promiscuous and not accepting the need to use condoms, and thus problemized (by a seemingly progressive discourse of AIDS awareness) as responsible for the predicted 'epidemic' of AIDS on the African continent.

The above critiques of the oppressive other(ing) side of dominant discourses of monogamy highlight how that which we might conventionally understand as an apparently personal, individual, everyday, or ethical decision (to be monogamous or not to be—to have sex with this person or not) can be *re-presented as* and *re-connected with* politics (Foucault 1984b).[7] Our 'personal', 'private', or 'ethical' relations and identifications are also inescapably wrapped up in and reproduce wider power relations which continue to pathologize other behaviours and people.[8] By drawing upon Foucault, we may therefore *broaden* what we understand as political oppression to include also spheres such as sexuality (Foucault 1992) frequently excluded from mainstream/malestream political discourse (Hearn and Parkin 1987).

By broadening what may be understood as political oppression, Foucault's work also opens up our appreciation of resistance to these 'new' forms of oppression as political agency (Simons 1995). For example, some gay, bisexual, queer, lesbian and/or feminist individuals and groups have explicitly explored non-monogamy as personal–political practice (e.g. Campaign for Homosexual Equality 1972; Gay Liberation Front 1971). In Foucauldian terms, these groups may be represented as understanding monogamy to be a personally and socially oppressive *limit experience* (McNay 1994; Simons 1995) containing policing and property relationship to self and others. And, further, a limit experience which needs to be *transgressed* so that other ways of relating to self and others may be created (Best 1995; Foucault 1977).[9]

It is important to highlight that gay, lesbian, bisexual, feminist and other groups and individuals that critique 'compulsory monogamy' call for the *practical/embodied* transgression of limit(ing) experiences of monogamy. Non-monogamy is, therefore, not only explored as an abstract or intellectualized personal/sexual politics. Such intellectualized politics may also enable the theoretical critique of oppression while the practical effects of such relations are still inscribed in our relationships and deeper sense of self. Like these groups, Foucauldian ethics asks us to pay attention to the politics of (our) bodies (Foucault 1988), to *embody* our ethics/politics,[10] based upon the understanding that the forces of normalization are not imposed *on us* as an alien power from above but rather are daily reproduced *by us* in our everyday embodied reproduction of 'normal life' (Foucault 1980:94, 98, 1984b; see also Best 1995; McNay 1994).

As I have used a Foucauldian ethic to discuss some of the oppressive effects of normalized monogamy, and highlighted some of the groups explicitly resisting these effects through practical, emotional and conscious transgression, the reader might assume that the discourse of non-monogamy is being privileged by my reading of Foucault as *the* politically progressive sexual relationship choice. We might even begin to understand non-monogamy as the new 'truth' of proper, non-oppressive, sexual relations, with likely effects such as pathologizing those, such as the speaker in the passage from *Betty Blue*, who practise monogamy as sexually repressed and/or necessarily oppressing others. Thus, we might begin to understand non-monogamous selves as 'liberated' or 'true' selves whereas monogamous 'others' are presented as not knowing, and needing educating about, the true nature of their oppressive/oppressing sexuality.

Though this reproduction of truths and expert knowledges can be an effect of a Foucauldian problemization of normalized understandings and behaviours, Foucault's work does not have to reproduce such effects (see also the third part headed 'A Marriage of Convenience and the Divorce of the Researcher from the Researched'). Indeed, Foucault's critiques are notorious for problemizing orthodoxies or truth claims about society and self (Foucault 1980:131, 1991, 1992), and problemizing these truths/knowledges whether they are presented as progressive or not (see, for example, Foucauldian critiques of Marxism [Foucault, 1984c; Poster, 1984]; prison reform [Foucault 1991]; and 'liberal' attitudes to sexuality [Foucault 1992]).[11] The problemizing gaze of Foucauldian ethics is, in this sense at least, 'promiscuous'. There is no comfortable, secure, politically progressive, or enlightened haven outside of relations of power or within relations of power. Rather, we are exhorted to continually reconsider or *permanently critique* (Simons 1995) the potentially problematic effects of the new (power) relations we have entered into and are thereby reaffirming and re-enacting.

To further problemize the issue of non-monogamy, we may highlight, as the speaker in *Betty Blue* does, the possibility that having sex with a person might represent the 'path of least resistance', a 'cop-out', or in some sense a 'betrayal' of self. Further, we could highlight the links between non-monogamy and historically masculine and contemporary 'post-industrial'/consumer society discourses of objectifying and commodifying sexual partners and securing sense of self through our conspicuous (sexual) consumption (e.g. Kundera 1984).

Thus, though the character in *Betty Blue* personally rejects 'fucking around', this is presented as a common, if not expected, practice in his circles ('I know everybody else does it'). Further, this practice is implicitly linked to the objectification of sexual partners as sexual objects, thus in his speech women are reduced to 'girls' possessing a 'nice ass'. Finally, the commodification and objectification of women are linked with a discourse of consumption in the equation of woman ('girl') and money ('check'/cheque) ('It does you good to live according to your ideas, to not betray yourself, not cop out at the last minute *just because some girl has a nice ass, or because someone offers you a huge check*'). Next, we could render visible how sexual exploitation and abuse can be rationalized away or obscured by apparently 'progressive' discourses of non-monogamy, with the effect of, for instance, legitimizing new property relations whereby young women or men may be passed around as possessions. Finally, we might highlight how an exhortation to transgress the limiting moral conventions of monogamy may itself become a restrictive new orthodoxy of non-monogamy, enshrining new relations of obedience and repression. In this context, we could understand the whole of the above speech/extract from *Betty Blue* as expressing the speaker's felt need to justify and legitimize his monog-amy in a context where he felt pressure to be non-monogamous. As Stanley and Wise have argued (1983 : 74), such new pressures or relations of obedience that apparently cut across the grain of restrictive conventional moral codes may be experienced as even more pernicious and censoring through being represented as *the* radical or political choice.

The above critiques (the limits) of non-monogamy seem to turn us back, almost full circle, to monogamy, but this time monogamy understood as a *transgression* of the limits, restrictions and oppression of compulsory non-monogamy ('it's no fun if you do it like everybody else. To tell you the truth, it bores me. It does you good to live according to your ideas'). And yet, as I have argued above, the discourse of monogamy *is also* and *is still* a potentially restrictive and normalizing discourse. What the Foucauldian permanent pro-blemization of our subjectivities and practices does, therefore, is to problemize a discourse, any discourse, as inherently anything. Thus, for instance, as I have argued, the discourse of monogamy may be understood *both* as an embodi-ment and reproduction of masculine and capitalist patterns of ownership *and* as an attempt to resist masculine and contemporary consumerist relationships of conspicuous (sexual) commodification and consumption. Understanding and using Foucauldian ethics in this way encourages us to pay attention to what is *created* through our actions, relations and assumptions, and not to rely upon their essentialized rightness or treat a moral/political code as a non-problem-atic or authoritative truth (Foucault 1983a, 1983b, 1984a).[12] This act of creation may be represented as embodied in the *Betty Blue* character's concern to make his life 'shine', where this 'shine' is understood as a process of self-transformation or aesthetic self-creation, honing and polishing the self so that it reflects back the image one wants to create, rather than the dull, singular and official image prescribed by authorities.[13]

Through this discussion of monogamy / non-monogamy, I have tried to draw out a 'feeling' for some of the themes of a Foucauldian ethics. In particular, I have drawn out: (i) an *intimate connection between* what we might understand as, on the one hand, the personal, *ethical*, everyday and, on the other, *political* issues and effects; such that our personal *embodied behaviours* are understood to reproduce or rebel against wider relations that bind your / our 'private' selves with the lives of others. This understanding has the effects of: (ii) showing the modernist conceptualization of the *independent atomized individual to be a myth*,[14] we are interdependent not independent beings, our actions have consequences for ourselves and others; and (iii) *broadening* what we may understand and relate to as of political concern to include areas conventionally marginalized as 'only' ethical, personal, or inconsequential. Further, (iv) I have highlighted the Foucauldian exhortation to *permanently problemize* the ways that we authorize or normalize our practices and identifications so that we may be more aware of how these may function to pathologize, or contribute to the oppression of, others (or in the words of Skunk Anansie [1996]: 'yes it's fucking political, everything's political').

The exhortation to permanently problemize provides us with no easy escape from power relations and removes from us the comforting but ill-founded ability to authorize our practices or identifications as beyond critique. For some critics of Foucault, this has been understood to mean that Foucault was a 'prophet of entrapment who induces despair by indicating that there is no way out of our subjection' (Simons 1995 : 3).[15] If, these critics argue, there is nothing outside of power relations, nothing without the potential to oppress or silence others, then everything is equally bad and we have no reason to act, no way of justifying or legitimizing our agency (Thompson and Ackroyd 1995). Clearly, it is possible to read Foucault this way. However, it is not necessary to do so. In contrast, it is possible to see the other side of the permanent problemization of closure, as the privileging of openness. Thus, for instance, a Foucauldian ethics may be understood as focusing our ethical/political attention upon: revolt, transgression and resistance (Simons 1995), and the importance of (metaphors of) self-stylization and aesthetics, embodied in the focus upon the *creation* of relations to self and others rather than privileging static authoritative truths of self. In Foucault's words, we need to open up a 'critique and creation of ourselves in our autonomy' (1984d : 44), or in the words of the male character in *Betty Blue*: 'I have one life—the only thing I'm interested in is making it shine'. Further, if everything is highlighted as potentially oppressive/restrictive by a Foucauldian ethics, this is not necessarily a cause for a loss of political agency, but, on the contrary, this may be understood as a call for heightened political vigilance, reflection and activism:

My point is not that everything is bad, but that everything is dangerous, which is not exactly the same as bad. If everything is dangerous, then we always have something to do. (Foucault 1984a : 343)

In the next two parts, I draw upon this Foucauldian ethical commitment to 'permanently problemize' to explore our 'critical' management research practices and understandings. In particular (using Foucault's phrasing in the above quote), I explore in the next part of the article what the Foucauldian-inspired Manchester school's LPT has 'done' and how this resonates with a Foucauldian ethics. In the third part, I explore what is 'dangerous' with this 'Foucauldian' LPT and what the 'something to do' might be for us as 'critical' management researchers reflecting upon these dangers.

....

The Marriage of Foucault and LPT?

In this part of the article, I suggest resonances between the Manchester school's LPT and the four Foucauldian ethical themes or feelings drawn out and illustrated in the previous discussion.[16] To recap, these are a commitment to:

- see ethics as politics;
- critique sovereign subjectivity;
- broaden politics;
- permanently problemize.

Ethics as Politics

The first theme or feeling that I have suggested can be understood to constitute a Foucauldian ethic is the intimate connection between what we may have hitherto represented as the separate realms of the private, everyday, personal, or 'ethical' (e.g. sexual relationships), and the wider public realm of the 'political' (e.g. discourses of patriarchy, homophobia, sexism and racism).

Here, I suggest that we can understand the Manchester school's critique of orthodox labour process theory and development of a Foucauldian-inspired LPT as similarly drawing upon Foucauldian ethical concerns to re-connect what has been conventionally marginalized as the 'personal', individual, or apolitical issue of workers' subjectivities and identities, with wider politics of capitalist labour process.

First, Manchester school authors have argued against orthodox LPT's *separation* of the personal/everyday from the political in the form of LPT's marginalization or exclusion of the issue of workers' subjectivity as ahistorical and astructural bourgeois social science (Knights and Willmott 1989). Far from being a 'fatal distraction' (Thompson 1993) from the proper 'political' concerns of LPT, the authors argue that the neglect of workers' subjectivity, in favour of a concentration upon the 'objective' dimension of class, means that LPT is unable to adequately account for the continual reproduction of relations of domination and subordination enshrined in the capitalist labour process.

Second, building upon this critique of orthodox LPT, the school's authors argue that it is only by concentrating upon, rather than marginalizing, workers' subjectivity that we can appreciate how power relations are actually sustained within, what Willmott calls, 'the micro-politics of interaction' (1994 : 105). The 'micro-politics of interaction' in the labour process (the process by which capitalist relations are daily reproduced) is a product and outcome of workers' attempts to develop and sustain a stable sense of personal identity. In seeking a stable sense of identity in conditions that continually threaten its erosion, workers invest 'their subjectivity in familiar sets of practices'; this has the effect of 'inhibit[ing] the potential for disruption by representing it as a threat to (workers') identity/sense of reality' (Knights and Willmott 1989 : 554). The 'personal' issue of a worker's subjectivity and identity, including even their sense of their own masculinity/femininity (Collinson 1994; Knights and Collinson 1987; Knights and Willmott 1989), is *intimately* and *unavoidably* bound up in the reproduction and contestation of existing relations of power.

By focusing upon the ways that workers' 'existential struggles with self identity are promoted by, and serve to sustain, the contradictory organization and control of the capitalist labour process' (Willmott 1993 : 701), the authors' writings may be understood to resonate with or reproduce what I have argued is a Foucauldian ethical concern to *critique the separation*, and *explore the intimate connection between*, the 'personal', everyday, ethical, micro-practices of self, and wider 'political' relations of oppression and domination.

A Critique of Sovereign Subjectivity

The second Foucauldian ethical theme is problemization of our understanding of our selves as separate from and independent of others. I highlighted two effects of this critique of independent/sovereign subjectivity in my earlier discussion of non/monogamy. First, I highlighted how nominally 'individual' choices and behaviours are inextricably bound up in and reproduce effects for/upon others. Second, I highlighted how Foucauldian ethics problemizes the authorization of any particular understanding of self as the 'truth' of our essential selves. In this section, I suggest that we may similarly understand the Manchester school's Foucauldian-inspired LPT to similarly draw upon and resonate with this ethical theme.

First, the school's key criticism of Burawoy's (1979) reconstruction of LPT is levelled at his understanding of workers as possessed of some inner creative essence blocked by capitalist production regimes (Knights and Willmott 1989; Willmott 1993). This construction of workers' essential subjectivity is understood to be a dangerous product of humanist/enlightenment thinking that serves the problematic effect of separating off workers' 'subjectivity' from the social context within which it is/they are enacted and constructed. Burawoy is therefore presented as having performed the valuable role of refocusing attention upon workers' subjectivity and its effects upon the politics of production, but then inhibiting analysis and reflection upon this by imposing an a priori definition of what this subjectivity *is*. Rather than reproducing this humanist 'truth' of workers' subjectivities, Manchester school authors draw upon Foucault's writings to understand subjectivity as an ' "openness" to the possibilities of our relationship to nature and social life' (Knights and Willmott 1989 : 552). Drawing upon this Foucauldian privileging of openness, the authors thereby represent workers' constructions of their subjectivities/identities as attempts at closure, attempts to control and silence the existential angst which accompanies the ever-present alternative 'field of possibilities' for expressing one's relationship to self and others (Knights and Willmott 1989 : 553). Therefore, far from being reducible to objective class interests, workers' constructions of subjectivity, even the notion of subjectivity itself, needs to be examined and reflected upon in local social/political contexts (see, for example, Collinson 1994; Knights and Collinson 1987; O'Doherty and Willmott 1998).

Second, the Manchester school's writings further resonate with the Foucauldian critique of sovereign subjectivity by reflecting upon the social/political *effects* of the particular constructions or understandings of their subjectivity that workers employ. For instance, Knights and Collinson (1987) argued that the (male) shopfloor workers they studied constructed and relied upon a gendered (masculine) sense of their own identity, which privileged 'masculine' themes such as a sense of independence, straight talking and honesty. Further, the authors argued that there were several problematic effects of the workers' construction of a gendered subjectivity. First, the workers were rendered complicit, even 'collaborators' (1987 : 471), in their own oppression—the construction of a gendered subjectivity was 'a subjectivity position that could not acknowledge the reality of labour's actual *dependence* on the company since this would deny the very autonomy which was the foundation of shopfloor dignity' (Knights and Collinson, 1987 : 472, authors' original emphasis). Second, the authors argue that male workers' elevation of the importance of (a particular) sense of masculinity discredits and devalues that which they construct as 'feminine', with likely divisive outcomes and oppressive effects for women both in, and outside of, the workplace.

By so drawing upon Foucault to examine and critique subjectivity, the Manchester school opens up understandings of subjectivity as *fluid, as socially and self-constructed, and as inescapably interrelational and political* in opposition to the historical essentialization and/or problemization of subjectivity in LPT. In these ways, the school's LPT writings may therefore be seen to resonate with what I have suggested is a Foucauldian ethical critique of sovereign subjectivity.

Broadening Politics

The third Foucauldian ethical theme is the *broadening of what we may understand as political agency* to include behaviours and identifications (e.g. resisting compulsory monogamy) conventionally marginalized as 'only' ethical or personal.

Here, I suggest that we may understand the Manchester school's Foucauldian-inspired LPT as similarly drawing upon/reproducing this Foucauldian ethical concern to broaden what we may understand and relate to as political action or agency—specifically, to include micro, personal and local practices as potential, and necessary, sources of political agency and an effective challenge to oppressive relations.

First, having made connections between workers' understandings of 'sovereign' subjectivity and relations of self-subordination to oppressive relations within the capitalist labour process (see under 'Ethics as Politics' and 'A Critique of Sovereign Subjectivity' above), the authors highlight the historically marginalized arena of workers' identity constructions as a crucial location for workers' resistance to oppression. Willmott (1994) draws out this point explicitly when he writes that, to effectively challenge modern power relations, people need to engage in a political process of 'de-subjection' that acts to 'dissolve the sense of sovereignty upon which, through the media of anxiety, guilt and shame, the powers of domination, exploitation and subjection routinely feed' (Willmott 1994 : 123).

Through such a focus upon practices of the self, the school's authors may be understood as engaged in a process of enriching and extending 'politics' in LPT by introducing a historically problematized focus upon a politics of identity/identifications into the traditional labour politics focus of LPT.

Second, the authors have researched the issue of workers' identity in actual/specific organizational contexts (Collinson 1994; Knights and Collinson 1987; Knights and McCabe 1998a, 1999b, 2000), rather than merely read off an assumed oppositional class identity from workers' objective position of subordination in the capitalist labour process. By so doing, these writings concentrate our attention upon local, everyday, micro-organizational practices as an important site for workers' engagement in, and our investigation of, political agency. As Knights (1997 : 6) writes:

It is not 'experts' at a distance representing problems on a grand narrative scale that are needed, but workers actively participating in producing context-related and localized responses to a set of political, ecological and social conditions with which they are confronted.

This endorsement to locate analysis and critique of this oppression within local/micro-organizational practices and an identity politics of 'de-subjection' may be seen to resonate with a Foucauldian ethical concern to broaden what we understand by 'politics' so as to also include historically marginalized areas of identity, the 'personal' and local/micro practices.

Permanently Problemize

The fourth, and last, Foucauldian ethical theme is the concern or broad commitment to *problemize (any/all) truth or authority claims.* This is based upon the understanding that such claims are unavoidably founded upon and reproduce the silencing and pathologization of other positions and people. This ethical concern could perhaps be summarized as a general antipathy towards, and attempt to subvert, closure and privilege openness. Here, I suggest that the Manchester school's LPT writings may be similarly understood as concerned with this ethic of permanent problemization.

First, the school's authors theorize and promote the subversion of closure in their articles (Willmott 1998). For example, we are encouraged to 'cherish impermanence' (Willmott 1994), and understand subjectivity as simply an 'openness' to the possibilities of our relationships with each other and life (Knights and Willmott 1989). As I have argued earlier, such openness is to be embodied in problemizing ideas of sovereign subjectivity and embracing (political) practices of 'de-subjection' (Willmott 1994).

Second, the authors seem to problemize what some would construct as some of the central defining foci of LPT (Martinez Lucio and Stewart 1997; Rowlinson and Hassard 1994; Thompson 1993; Thompson and Ackroyd 1995). For example, through their introduction of subjectivity understood as a struggle with the existential openness of life, the authors challenge LPT's traditional privileging of 'class' struggle specifically located within the workplace over other forms of oppression and resistance (Thompson 1993).

The Manchester school's empirical writings further risk the censure of colleagues, if not the possible accusation of embodying an anti-working class sentiment, by their problemization of the ways that working class men resist the effects of the labour process. In particular, the school's authors represent (male) workers as constructing themselves and their behaviours in ways that: (i) are macho and sexist (Knights and Collinson 1987); (ii) result in inhibiting 'real' resistance (Knights and Collinson 1987 : 465); and (iii) unwittingly result in the workers becoming 'collaborators' (Knights and Collinson 1987 : 471) in their own oppression. They further argue that these effects occur outside of the comprehension of the workers themselves who maintain the 'illusion' (Knights and Collinson 1987 : 472, 474) that they are resisting management (see also Collinson 1994; Knights and McCabe 1998a, 1999b).

Such problemizations of LPT orthodoxies and established ways of knowing are a central, perhaps the central, contribution of the Manchester school's post-structuralist informed writing. It is a contribution readily acknowledged and celebrated by the authors (see, for example, Willmott 1993 : 701). It is also a contribution that has been made explicitly and extensively enough for some to consider the writings as too far removed from LPT's core values to be properly understood *as* LPT (Martinez Lucio and Stewart 1997; Thompson 1993). Such a critique would suggest perhaps that the school's writings should not be seen as a form of Foucauldian 'permanent problemization', transgressing both the limits of workplace oppression *and* the normalizing boundaries and effects of nominally 'critical' literatures that claim a new and problematic authority for their critiques, but should more properly be understood as merely another branch of 'uncritical' management theory or bourgeois sociology. However, as Parker (1999) observes, the school's authors clearly represent their post-structuralist theory and problemizations of LPT orthodoxies to be within the spirit of furthering an effective critique of oppressive and subordinating relations (see also Knights and Vurdubakis 1994). As such, they position themselves broadly within the critical spirit (though perhaps not always the letter) of a Marxist informed critique of the capitalist labour process (Willmott 1993).

These writings may be seen to be reproducing what I have argued is a Foucauldian ethical concern to *permanently problemize subordinating forms of closure*, irrespective of whether they are conventionally represented as oppressive (e.g. the capitalist labour process) *or* progressive (e.g. the orthodoxies of LPT).

....

A Marriage of Convenience and the Divorce of Researcher from Researched

Above, I have drawn out resonances between what I have suggested as themes or feelings of a Foucauldian ethics and the Manchester school of labour process writings. I have been concerned, specifically, to argue that there *is* an apparent marriage (to use a metaphor that continues the monogamy/non-monogamy theme) between the concerns of this school and Foucauldian ethics. I now question, however, whether this may be understood as more of an *abstract engagement* with Foucauldian ethics than an attempt to *explore and embody* these ethics, particularly in the context of the researcher's relationship with the researched. The marriage between Foucauldian ethical concerns and the Manchester school appears, I suggest, to be intellectual rather than embodied, in the head rather than the heart. In other words, it is a *marriage of convenience* and a marriage that ends in a positivist *divorce* of researcher from researched.[17] This divorce risks ending in an unequal settlement whereby the professional academic accrues cultural capital and resources and the researched are left poorer as a result of their engagement with the 'political' academic.[18]

I make these arguments by drawing upon the same four Foucauldian ethical themes or feelings drawn out in the first part of this article and threaded through the second part above. In this part, these themes translate as:

- a *disconnection* between ethics and politics;
- the *reproduction* of the sovereign and independent researcher;
- *neglected opportunities* for exploring politics;
- the author's problemization of others and *authorization of self*.

Disconnection of Ethics and Politics

Earlier in this article, I suggested that we could understand the Manchester school's focus upon workers' subjectivity in the politics of production as resonating with a Foucauldian ethical commitment to explore the intimate connections between the (marginalized) 'personal', individual, or ethical and the (privileged) 'political'. Here, I argue that, although the school's authors challenge the neglect of the 'personal' issue of workers' identity in theory; they then reproduce this neglect by producing *depersonalized*, 'realist' (Van Maanen 1988), academic representations of the workplace. They compound this neglect by failing to reflect and act upon the problematic subordinating/silencing effects of producing such depersonalized 'authoritative' representations.

Van Maanen writes that, of all the ways of writing up empirical research, realist tales 'push most firmly for the authenticity of the cultural representations conveyed in the text' (1988 : 45). Principally, realist tales do this by *depersonalizing* the representations they produce, by removing the person of the researcher from the account produced, removing the knower from the known:

Ironically, by taking the 'I' (the observer) out of the ethnographic report, the narrators' authority is apparently enhanced, and audience worries over personal subjectivity become moot. (Van Maanen 1988 : 46)

Where the 'I' does figure in such realist tales, it is in:

... brief, perfunctory, but mandatory appearance in a method footnote tucked away from the text. The only other glimpse of the ostrich-like writer is a brief walk-on cameo role in which he puts into place the analytic framework. The voice assumed throughout the tale is that of a third-party scribe reporting directly on the life of the observed. (Van Maanen 1988 : 64)

I argue here that the Manchester school's empirical LPT writings may be understood as reproducing this problematic realist form of representation.[19]

First, the authors' discussions of methodology in their empirical papers reproduce realist conventions by being brief, formal and serving to further authorize the particular representations they produce. Knights and McCabe's (1998a) recent article is illustrative of these points (see also Knights and McCabe 1998b, 1999a, 2000; Knights and Murray 1994). A one-and-a-half page discussion of 'Theory and Methodology' employs several typical realist devices to push for the 'authenticity of the cultural representation conveyed in the text'. Methodology is discussed as a series of unproblematic formal techniques (formal interview, documentary investigation, observational research, triangulation), suggesting the authors are skilled researchers trained and experienced in the use of a variety of analytical techniques. The discussion stresses the time and depth of the research undertaken (six months, 25 staff interviewed, 10-hour-long weekly team meetings, five meetings of 10 team leaders), suggesting the authors possess a unique 'experiential authority' (Van Maanen 1988 : 46) to correctly interpret the culture. Finally, the discussion of 'Theory and Methodology' is clearly sectioned off from the rest of the paper, suggesting that the following representation is unproblematic, incontestable and authentic: matters of methodology (or how the authors came to 'know' what is 'known') have, it seems, already been dispensed with.

Second, the Manchester school's writings reproduce the realist myth of being 'third party scribes reporting directly on the life of the observed' by removing and obscuring their presence in the material they present. Thus, empirical material is typically presented without reference to the context of its production, the conversations that preceded or followed a particular quote, or the possibility of alternative interpretations other than that presented by the authors. Perhaps in anticipation of criticisms of such uncontextualized/unproblematized quotes being used as evidence of what those studied 'really think', Manchester school writings periodically include one or more sentences disclaiming the authority of their representations. For example, Knights and Collinson (1987 : 458) put their faith in a 'consensus theory of truth' and the 'plausibility to the reader' of their analysis; Knights and McCabe (1998a : 175, 1998b : 777) acknowledge that all representations are social constructions; Knights and McCabe (2000 : 151–5) say in an endnote that 'this record of our methods is not intended as a claim to authoritative representations devoid of any human concern for the lives of those employees'; and Knights and Murray (1994 : 130–1) state that 'we are not of the (positivist) school that believes it possible to eradicate values from research'. However, like the authors' brief, formal discussions of methodology, such sentences are spatially, and I would suggest emotionally, separated from the depersonalized, third-person and apparently objective and authoritative representations of the workplace produced in the rest of their papers and/or book. For example, such recognition (or disclaimers) of the socially constructed, and problematical, nature of representations of reality do not lead the authors to question their own interpretations, or seriously explore other possible readings, or make explicit their ethical/political reasons for constructing their representations as they do, much less produce 'multivocal texts where an event is given meaning first in one way, then another' (Van Maanen 1988 : 52; see also Wray-Bliss 2001). Rather, they implicitly claim a kind of 'interpretive omnipotence' (Van Maanen 1988 : 51) over the particular workplace studied, and present carefully selected uncontextualized quotes and descriptions as unproblematic evidence supporting their depersonalized authoritative analysis of workplace relations and even their analysis (and problemization) of other peoples' identities.

This depersonalized authority reproduces a skewed power relationship vis-a-vis the researched. The LPT theorist's social/professional standing becomes less vulnerable the more they authorize their research and the more they apparently remove themselves from that which they write. The researched, however, do not have access to this strategy. For:

> . . . to be vulnerable is an everyday hazard for 'the researched', for little research is done on those people powerful enough to force the non-publication or recantation of results they don't like. The researched are vulnerable in the sense that their lives, feelings, understandings, become grist to the research mill and may appear, in goodness knows what mangled form, at the end of the research process. And whatever mangled form it is, its form is unlikely to be subject to control by them. (Stanley and Wise 1983 : 180)

The problematic vulnerability that may result from the depersonalized authority of the academic text may be illustrated with the example of Knights and Collinson's (1987) 'Disciplining the Shopfloor'. In this paper, the authors use the typical conventions of realist writing (uncontextualized extracts as quotes, depersonalized reporting style, minimal 'formal' discussion of methodology) to problemize/pathologize the resistance *and* identities of the shopfloor workers they research and to authorize their own selective interpretations. For instance, despite the shopfloor workers spending much more 'time in the field' than the authors, and considerably more time constructing and living with their own identities than the authors did deconstructing them, Knights and Collinson present as being able to know that the workers' valued sense of identity and dignity is 'illusionary' (Knights and Collinson 1987 : 474), that their resistance is not 'real' resistance (Knights and Collinson 1987 : 465) and that the men should properly be understood as 'politically docile' (Knights and Collinson 1987 : 474) and 'collaborators' in their own subordination (Knights and Collinson 1987 : 471—for similar problematic dynamics reproduced in the Manchester school writings see Collinson 1994; Knights and McCabe 1998a; O'Doherty and Willmott 1998 : 18 discussion of Sosteric 1996).

Knights and Collinson's pathologization of the researched highlights two aspects of the depersonalized authority of the realist tale. First, as Stanley and Wise (1983) argue above, the removal of the 'personal' presence of the researchers can have subordinating political effects for those we research (see also bell hooks 1989). Thus, not only could Knights and Collinson's problemization of workers' resistance and identities be experienced as patronizing and dismissive, but it also carries the warranting force of 'realist' academic authority. Second, without extensive reflection upon, and discussion of how the authors came to know what they know, of the context of quotes and observations, and of the researched's own responses to how they were being represented, Knights and Collinson's pathologizing 'realist' representation does not *in itself* contain sufficient material for us to accept their subordinating representation of these shopfloor workers. The fact that we *do* accept this representation (and that journals normalize such realist empirical articles) highlights a final problematic quality of the depersonalized realist tale. A realist tale is not accepted wholly, or even primarily, because of its internal content, rather:

... a good deal of what is by and large the unproblematic quality of fieldwork authority rests on the background expectancies of an audience of believers. (Van Maanen 1988 : 46)

Thus, we, the wider audience of 'critical' academics and 'political' LPT writers, are a crucial complicit link in creating and sustaining the subordinating authority of the depersonalized realist tale.

From the above, I argue that the Manchester school's 'Foucauldian' LPT does not seek to embody the Foucauldian ethical commitment to link the 'personal' (presence of the authors in all aspects of the research process) with the 'political' (LPT representations they produce). Rather, and in common with most LPT writings, the authors unreflexively reproduce a depersonalized 'realist' academic authority. As Willmott (1998 : 87) reminds us, post-structuralist ethical critiques, like Foucault's, highlight how authority 'is founded upon forms of arbitrary, forceful exclusion or repression'. I have drawn upon such an understanding of Foucauldian ethical themes or feelings here to highlight the subordinating 'exclusion' or 'repression' of the researched that is a consequence of the mystification of the personal and its replacement with the depersonalized authoritative in the school's writings.

Sovereign and Independent Researcher

Previously, I argued that the Manchester school's authors are explicitly concerned to utilize a Foucauldian framework to problemize humanist notions of independent, essential, sovereign subjectivity (see Knights and Willmott 1989; Knights and Collinson 1987; Knights 1997; Willmott 1993, 1994). This task of problemization/deconstruction is founded upon the authors' understanding that relating to ourself/selves as independent from others (and their/our shared processes of continual social co-construction) renders us vulnerable to reproducing social practices that reaffirm our valued sense of self at the cost of our subordination to their routine oppressive effects and knowledges. Thus:

> ... resistance to the development of more rational, harmonious social institutions does not arise simply from vested interests in preserving the status quo but also, and no less fundamentally, from a modern, humanist belief in the existence and continuity of self-identity, the confirmation of which is frequently dependent upon sustaining prevailing power relations. (Willmott 1994 : 93)

The author's critique of such understandings of sovereign, independent subjectivity is levelled not just at workers 'out there', but also at mainstream and critical (especially LPT) academics who utilize and reproduce such constructions in their writings (see under 'A Critique of Sovereign Subjectivity' above). With regard to these writings, the authors are 'uncomfortable with a methodological strategy that involves a separation of "objective" and "subjective" moments of social reproduction' (Willmott 1993 : 691; also Knights 1992). In the place of problematic, 'humanist', dualistic constructions of (independent, essentialized) sovereign 'self' and (independent, essentialized) sovereign 'other', what is needed is a process of practical 'de-subjection' or 'de-differentiation' of self and other, subject and object, I and they:

> ... the theory and practice of de-subjection can enable us to recognize and overcome the habitual desire to define and secure the sense of self as sovereign entity. (Willmott 1994 : 125–6)

While the school's critique of independent sovereign subjectivity and advocation of practices of 'de-subjection' clearly resonates with Foucault's writings and ethics, an (ethical/political) problem with the work is that the authors apply this critique only 'to problems of dualistic *theorizing* in organization studies' (Knights 1997 : 2 (*my emphasis*); also O'Doherty and Willmott 1998). They do not use this Foucauldian ethical commitment to reflect upon their own dualistic and problematic research and scholarly *practices*, but routinely separate themselves from those they study through reproducing the depersonalized conventions of a realist representation. In their empirical accounts, the research object/subject (the worker) is rendered visible/vulnerable in the text while the researcher remains separate and aloof. The researcher and researched are constructed as independent, rather than interdependent, with the researcher revealing and commenting upon, rather than co-constructing and contributing to, the lives of the researched.[20] Such a (modernist/positivist) dualist construction of research relations reproduces problematic subordinating and silencing effects for the researched, and specifically the subordination to the depersonalized ('sovereign'?) authority of the researcher/LPT expert—bell hooks' words could have been written with just such a relationship in mind:

> Even if perceived 'authorities' writing about a group to which they do not belong and/or over which they wield power, are progressive, caring, and right-on in every way, as long as their authority is constituted by either the absence of the voices of the individuals whose experiences they seek to address, or the dismissal of those voices as unimportant, the subject–object dichotomy is maintained and domination is reinforced. (bell hooks 1989 : 43)

Interestingly, Knights and McCabe (1998b) seem to anticipate such a critique in one of their articles. The authors argue that publicly funded academic research should 'be for the benefit of the population' and that a crucial way to explore this is to 'give voice to those who are often the targets of power' (Knights and McCabe 1998b : 777). Unfortunately, however, they then do not explore any of the ways academic research has been, and could be, constructed so as to facilitate 'giving' (?) voice to the historically silenced. Rather, they end up privileging one voice, their own, throughout their traditionally narrated text and even legitimize their (depersonalized) authority further by defining (their) research as '*the* voice of dissent and enquiry that challenges and questions taken-for-granted assumptions which those who relish power would sooner not have asked or exposed' (Knights and McCabe 1998b : 778 (*emphasis added*)). Similarly, Knights (1995) discussing the politics of research and the politics of IT highlights the contribution that research can make by 'giving voice to dissent from the official line' (Knights 1995 : 233). He argued that senior managers' silencing of dissent in the case study organization was clearly problematic and was in need of 'disruption' (Knights 1995 : 247). His article 'recommends' (Knights 1995 : 248) case study research of the kind that he has produced as 'facilitat(ing) the processes of such disruptions' (Knights 1995:248) through, for instance, having 'the practical implications . . . to disrupt the masculinity of practitioners in their aggressive and compulsive search for "correct answers" ' (Knights 1995 : 239). However, as in Knights and McCabe (1998b) above, recognition of such potential of research to 'give' voice or 'practically disrupt' local instances of silencing or subordination are un(der)explored in the text. Such potentialities for research remain a theoretical rather than embodied possibility.

If Manchester school authors are to be consistent in their commitment to critique the dualisms of (sovereign) self–(problematized) other, then the expert/depersonalized *researcher/observer* and misguided/self-subordinating *researched* dualism too needs to be 'practically de-differentiated' (Willmott 1994 : 113). The 'independent sovereign' (even if well intentioned) researcher roaming imperially over the workplaces and identities of others needs to be practically 'de-subjected'.

Without wanting to constrain or limit, and without the space here to really explore, the multiple and diverse ways through which this project/process might be enacted, such practices of de-differentiation/de-subjection of the researcher–researched dualism might include exploring ways of trying to construct and conduct research 'with' rather than 'on' others (Reason 1994). Thus, we could engage with and learn from traditions of participatory research and participatory action research (Griffin and Pheonix 1994; Henwood and Pigeon 1995; Reason and Bradbury 2001), particularly as explored, reflected upon and debated within the personal–political traditions of (some) feminist literatures, where crucial issues of inclusion/exclusion, speaking for/speaking with, appropriation and emancipation are cogently and practically explored (Abbot and Wallace 1992; Aitken 1996; Opie 1992; Lincoln 1995). Further, we could seriously reflect upon what it means to understand our representations as our *relationship with others* (Jodelet 1991), such that it becomes incumbent upon us to consider our writings as our shared ethical/political agency within the politics of production (see Collins and Wray-Bliss 2000a; Wray-Bliss 1998). Thus, we would write because of—and only because of—our understanding of the ethical/political effects of our writing (to start with ethics—Parker 1999), and not to hide behind a discredited elitist/positivist assumption that we are writing to represent 'truth' or that we produce our particular/partial representations because of some kind of epistemological necessity. To paraphrase Willmott, the appeal and value of such disciplines, traditions and literatures that attempt to blur the problematic separation between researcher and researched would reside 'in their capacity to debunk and dissolve *practically* the dualistic illusion of individual sovereignty that is deconstructed intellectually by [the Manchester school's] poststructuralist forms of analysis' (Willmott 1994 : 90, author's original emphasis, my brackets/contents).

That the Manchester school's authors (and other LPT writers) do not explore such practices in their research relations raises questions about the authors' commitment to a Foucauldian ethical critique of sovereign, independent subjectivity. But, more importantly, the subordinating effects that the authors argue are a consequence of a 'sovereign' subject's relationship to prevailing oppressive power relations are likely reproduced and reinforced within research subjects' relationships with the nominally 'political' but in practice independent and expert labour process theorist.

Neglected Politics

I have argued in the last two sections that the Manchester school authors leave untheorized and unexplored their own reproduction of subordinating, and (according to my reading of Foucault) ethically/politically problematic, effects and relations in the research process. In this section, I extend this critique by arguing that, in addition to reproducing these 'negative' effects, the authors fail to reflect upon and explore the 'positive' political possibilities of their presence as researchers situated within the micro-politics of production.

A significant contribution of the school's Foucauldian-inspired writings has been to (re)introduce an appreciation of the political nature of nominally 'personal' or individual acts and understandings (see under 'Broadening Politics' above). In particular, the authors have highlighted workers' identity as a crucial fulcrum through which oppression may be reproduced and as an essential site through which effective resistance to such oppression must be mounted (Willmott 1994; Knights and McCabe 1999a; Knights and Willmott 1989). Despite this theoretical recognition of the importance of transgressing the gap between 'personal' and 'political', the authors neglect to explicitly consider the political implications and possibilities of their own personal presence in the workplaces they study as a political issue or resource.

To illustrate, I draw upon the process of 'consciousness raising' historically privileged by feminists as an important personal–political process. Though sometimes maligned now as an outdated (according to 'new' women, spice girls, post-feminists) and/or arrogant, expert, practice, consciousness raising may be considered an explicit attempt to link 'political' understandings with 'personal' practices and identifications. As such, a variation of consciousness raising might be one process that the Manchester school could explore as a means of embodying their Foucauldian commitments to link the personal/ethical with political practices and knowledges.[21] In fact, given the school's authors' apparent ability to make authoritative (see under 'Disconnection of Ethics and Politics' above) pronouncements over what forms of resistance are or are not effective, will or will not fail (e.g. Knights and Collinson 1987; Collinson 1994; Knights and McCabe 1998a), and their ability to divine when another person's identity constructions are tying them into unwittingly reproducing self-subordination, then sharing these insights with those they judge/analyse would seem an obvious process for the Manchester school to explore. This may then both help the workers not to fall into the traps the researcher can apparently uniquely 'see', and/or the schools to have their ideas explored or exposed in practice. This might be one way to enable the school's authors to avoid being what Knights problemizes as ' "experts" at a distance representing problems on a grand scale' and to explore what it means for an academic to 'actively participate(e) in producing context-related and localized responses to a set of political, ecological and social conditions with which they are confronted' (1997 : 6). However, despite this call by Knights for 'context-related and local-ized responses', exploring the researcher's presence as a political resource or process is presumably too local for the school's authors to consider in their labour process research—or so the glaring omission of *any* explicit exploration of the political possibilities of their presence in their writings would suggest. Instead of serious reflection upon or evidence of any attempt to 'actively participate in producing context-related and localized responses' to the politics of production, Manchester school authors have instead responded by: (i) signal-ling a 'hope' that 'on reading this alternative insight into the impact of BPR at work, both managers and staff may be persuaded to reflect on the practices they adopt' (Knights and McCabe 1998a : 188)—this hope is mentioned without any discussion in the text of how or whether the research *was* made available to staff and managers, or discussion of any effects of the researched's readings and reflections upon the text (see also Knights 1995; Knights and McCabe 2000);[22] and (ii) by privileging other experts as the *only* ones capable of making sense/use of their work. As Knights and Collinson say of their research:

Its only potential then must lie with the audience of academic accountants who, in recognising the enormous disciplinary power of accounting knowledge, may give more attention to the moral and political consequences of their practice. (1987 : 474)

I am aware that outside of these problematic, limited, published responses, colleagues who have not sought to explicitly address issues of the ethics and effects of their research in their writings and public academic practices some-times privately confess feelings of disquiet or anxiety about the lack of rele-vance of their work for the lived politics of production. However, I would argue that such private expressions of guilt are not an acceptable or adequate response to these concerns. Given that other academics and researchers (e.g. Aitken 1996; Aitken and Burman 1999; Henwood and Pigeon 1995; Lincoln 1995; Marks 1993; Opie 1992; Reason 1994; Seidman 1992; Stanley and Wise 1983) have done and do continue to explicitly explore and publish ways of reconstructing the research process as more participative and political, the marginalization of these issues to private guilt, or the 'real ale bar' as one author advocated (Jackson 1995), suggests that once more malestream/main-stream 'critical' academia is silencing or individualizing voices, challenges and concerns that it finds uncomfortable.

Problemize Others, Authorize Self

Under the heading 'Permanently Problemize' above, I argued that the Manchester school may be understood to be engaged in a Foucauldian ethical process of problemizing normalized conventions and assumptions in LPT. However, throughout this final part of the article, I have argued that the authors direct this problemizing gaze at others rather than at themselves. Thus, I have suggested that the Manchester school: (i) draws upon conventions of the realist tale to authorize its own depersonalized representations; (ii) problemizes others' 'sovereign independent' subjectivity, but then enshrines this in its own relations with the researched; and (iii) problemizes workers' forms of resistance but does so at a distance without exploring the possibilities of participating/researching with others, and so exempts its own understandings of 'effective' resistance from any similar critique. These effects combine to make the school's authors ever more invulnerable and seemingly authoritative the more the researched are rendered vulnerable and problemized.

A possible rationale or defence that could be made of this inequity is that the authorization of the critical academic's voice is an unfortunate necessity if our critique is to be effectively heard and taken note of by our wider community. I explore this position as my conclusions to this work.

Rationalizing the authority of the researcher as a necessary political device or resource *might* be a tenable defence if labour process theorists were able to persuasively show that their voice *is* heard and that they *do* have positive effects in changing oppressive political practices in the workplace. However, in the context of recent critiques of LPT's 'lack' of impact (Martinez Lucio and Stewart 1997; Rowlinson and Hassard 1994), and in the complete absence of research that I am aware of that explores the effects of our writings and research upon the politics of production, this argument risks appearing more like a self-interested legitimation. The glaring lack of study of the effects of our 'critical'/'political' research, writings and resources seems to suggest four possible implications.

The first is that we *don't actually care* about the effects of our work for others. If this is the case, then (like Parker 1999 : 41) 'my engagement with (and sympathy for) the papers stops here, because I can see no other very convincing reason for practising critical organization studies'.

Second, we don't conduct research into the effects of LPT because *we are confident* of its progressive political effects upon the politics of production. I have argued in this paper that this confidence is premature at best and seriously misplaced or delusional at worst.

Third, we don't explore the effects of our research because we have an uncomfortable and unsilenceable suspicion that we *don't have* appreciable positive effects. While I empathize with the sentiments, I have argued through-out that this private 'guilt' response is not sufficient, but rather should be mobilized as a resource to explore ways of conducting research with others into the practical resolution or mitigation of subordinating and oppressive relations. Some of the references contained within this paper might provide one preliminary starting point for this process.

Finally, we don't explore the effects of our research because we (say that we) *do not want to have* effects, perhaps seeing such a desire as an arrogant masculine drive for mastery, out of place in the 'modest' and 'diverse' postmodern academy (Knights 1997). This justification or legitimation for not exploring the effects of our research seems the most significant to me, for several reasons, and I make some comments on these to end this paper.

The charge of heroic masculinity is significant because it is a charge that has already been used to criticize (or marginalize) another organizational studies author's attempts to raise questions about the ethics and effects of our aca-demic practices. For instance, Jackson (1995 : 571) labelled Parker's (1995) attempt to stimulate reflections upon our practices as the 'chest thumpings' of the 'angry young man of organization theory'.[23]

Further, Foucault's writings and ethics have also been criticized for failing to differentiate enough from an individualistic discourse of heroic masculinity and self-mastery (McNay 1994; Simons 1995)—a discourse that I deliberately and visibly reproduced, rather than hid or mystified, in my discussion of the ethics of the male characters 'resistance' of female sexual advances in the first part of this article. For instance, referring to the initial quote from the male character in *Betty Blue*: clearly the ability to effectively 'resist' sexual advances and/or expectations is differentiated around an axis of gender. The male character refuses sexual advances purely by the force of his speech and, further, can use this encounter as an opportunity to 'impart' his own 'wisdom' or philosophy to/upon the other, female, character. In stark contrast, we as a society still have organized campaigns to limit male sexual violence against women and to make men understand that when a woman says 'no' it means *no*.

Relatedly, what some critics have understood as the heroic individualism of Foucault's ethics may also be seen as gendered (McNay 1994). Arguably, it is easier for a man to conceptualize and create his life as an individual 'work of art', and to transgress boundaries of normalized acceptable behaviour, because: (i) generally men have more latitude in society and are subject less to the control of others than women; and (ii) women are still primarily constructed as 'carers', as principally social rather than individual, and as primarily responsible for, and tied to, the lives and welfare of others. To resist and transgress in overt, explicit ways might therefore be understood as more risky and dangerous for women, in that it will likely subject them more readily and harshly to the official disciplinary powers of medical, social and legal authorities. Foucault's ethics of explicit transgression might therefore be constructed as potentially liberating for men (including those in the, male-dominated, LPT profession and the male workers whom they principally study), but is in need of considerable reworking if the ethic is to speak to or be useful for the majority of women.

Finally, throughout this last part of the paper I have proffered one reading, one tale of LPT. Through this process, I might have been experienced as reproducing a (masculine) form of closure: closing off other possible interpretations of the LPT writings that I cite in my masculine drive and desire to make my own narrative appear superior and authoritative. In other words, I might be *legitimately* accused of reproducing relations of silencing and subordination vis-a-vis the writings I represent—relations that contradict the paper's, and my own, explicit ethical/political positions and commitments. As I am critiquing others' texts, I am aware I may be experienced in part as problemizing other people('s labour). And, worse still, potentially elevating myself and my voice further through this process of problemizing others, a process that I have highlighted as ethically problematic. In a number of ways I have tried to mitigate this effect (for instance, I have presented these and similar arguments at conferences in the presence of the main authors I cite; the main authors I critique have each received a copy of this paper well in advance of its publication; I have edited the paper in the light of referees', reviewers' and others' comments; I have tried to convey an argument I feel passionate about while still representing generously the papers I critique; and I have tried to write this paper in a spirit of what *we* need to start exploring as critical organization researchers rather than pretend that I am somehow exempt from my own critique). Despite these attempts to mitigate some of my authorial power, I cannot, nor should I seek to, wish away my responsibility as researcher to the 'researched' of this paper. However, neither do I feel that we should forget the significant or qualitative differences between the 'researched' of this paper (i.e. senior academics with the opportunity, resources and record of having their voice authorized in national and international publications) and the 'researched' of the majority of ('Foucauldian' or other) LPT papers, namely working class employees of organizations who historically and continually suffer from having their voices subordinated to those of academic, managerial and other authorities. In short if, as I have argued, I owe a responsibility to 'the researched' of this paper—people who undeniably have far greater access than I to having their versions and voices authorized and heard—then this is also a marker of how under-explored and under-acknowledged our responsibility is to our 'normal' community of researched people, those who are so much more likely to be 'represented' by us without 'representation' by them.

Throughout this paper, I have highlighted why I am not confident that 'Foucauldian' (or indeed other) LPT has yet sufficiently explored these issues.

I am convinced, however, that these are *crucially important concerns*, concerns which must figure centrally in any attempt to construct research as simultaneously more (consciously) political, more participative, and less exclusionary and subordinating. Like Aitken and Burman (1999), Henwood and Pigeon (1995), Lincoln (1995), Opie (1982), Marks (1993), Seidman (1992), Spivak (1985), Stanley and Wise (1983) and other writers outside of our management studies community who debate and attempt to work with and through these issues while holding onto an idea of a different way of *doing* research or *being* academic, we too as an academic community and discipline need to have these debates in (*our*) publica*tions*. If we do not then we risk privatizing and marginalizing politics or assuming, without public debate, that exploring alternative ways of understanding and conducting research is necessarily oppressive and silencing. Such a nihilistic 'everything is bad' conclusion is one that I understand the Manchester school of LPT writers to have been arguing against in relation to Foucault's work for the last decade.

To end, I encourage us to discuss, debate, reflect, learn, and undoubtedly make mistakes and silence some while we privilege the voices and concerns of others, while exploring less depersonalized and authoritative, and more participative and political research relations and practices. My concern at present is that it might be more comfortable for us as 'critical' academics not to try and work with and through these concerns and our ethical/political commitments, but to instead apply easy labels (e.g. modernist, heroic, masculine, etc.) as a way of marginalizing the felt need to explore such an unfamiliar, uncertain, and personally and professionally challenging process. Such labels, I would argue, are being cynically misused if they serve as a ready-made excuse, legitimizing our collective failure to explore other traditions and as justification of our *espousal* rather than *embodiment* of our 'critical' ethical/political commitments.

Acknowledgement

I would like to thank Gill Aitken, Gary Brown, Peter Case, Helen Collins, Scott Lawley, Beverley Leeds, Martin Parker, Hugh Willmott, Frank Worthington and those at the 1999 CMS ethics stream for their comments and help. Also, thank you to the anonymous reviewers for your encouraging comments, thought-provoking questions and useful revisions.

Notes

1. Thank you to one of the reviewers for drawing my attention to the different ways that 'critical' may be used within 'critical management studies' (Alvesson and Willmott 1992; Fournier and Grey 2000). When I use the term in this paper, I am

assuming some commitment by the 'critical' academic to explore the emancipatory potential of (their) academic work, however loosely or differentially defined (see also Fournier and Grey 2000 : 19).

2. I use the term 'Manchester School' to signify a loose community of labour process writers who use Foucauldian frameworks to reintroduce and explore subjectivity in LPT. Not wanting to gloss over the dissimilarities and differences between members of this comprehensive 'school' (as one of the reviewers rightly asked me not to do), I concentrate principally upon the texts authored and co-authored by those who might be characterized as its 'head masters': principally David Knights and also Hugh Willmott (see O'Doherty and Willmott 1998; Parker 1999 for discussions of differences between these authors' texts). I still use the collective term of the 'Manchester school' throughout, however, rather than, for instance, Willmott's (1993) use of the more individualizing phrase 'Knights et al.' and 'Knights and his co-authors' because the feeling that I wish to convey in this text is not one of singling out specific authors for individual criticism (even though I appreciate that this text may be read by some as doing this). Rather, I hope that the examples I use encourage us to reflect further upon our own texts and practices, as I feel that the criticisms that I make apply across much 'Foucauldian', as well as 'Marxist', other, and my own, LPT research.

3. I feel it is important to note that a similar critique of the ethics and effects of academic research relations that I make here through a Foucauldian framework could equally have been made by drawing upon other ethical/political traditions. In particular, I have drawn heavily upon, and been inspired by, feminist writings and concerns to re-connect the personal, political and academic (see, for example, Aitken 1996; bell hooks 1989; Henwood and Pigeon 1995; Lincoln 1995; Marks 1993; Opie 1992; Stanley and Wise 1983). These literatures and concerns could have been used to explore and critique LPT's disembodied focus upon 'gender' (Collins and Wray-Bliss 2000b). Further, I am inspired/informed by Marxist ethics and commitments (Wray-Bliss and Parker 1998). And might have used Marxist ethical themes to critique the alienating effects of more self-consciously 'Marxist' LPT. Similarly, the critiques that I make of our 'critical' management research in the third part of this article resonate with critiques made within queer theory and post-colonial writings (for example, Morton 1996; Spivak 1985; Ware 1992; Williams and Chrisman 1993; Young 1990), and therefore might have been more explicitly organized around these labels and resources (Wray-Bliss in press). Rather than organize the paper around these other traditions, however, I choose to explicitly use a Foucauldian ethical label and framework in this paper purely for strategic reasons. I hope that by so using a Foucauldian ethics the critique I make and issues I raise might be more likely heard, and less easily marginalized, by those who draw upon Foucault in their own writings. However, I also hope that those critical management writers who do not use Foucault in their work will still engage with and reflect upon the critique I make here. Finally, I recognize that there is a danger that, by drawing upon insights and arguments also raised in these other traditions, but organizing this work around Foucauldian themes, I might be understood to be contributing again to the appropriation and marginalization of feminism, queer theory and post-colonial writings within mainstream/malestream academia. With-

out denying this danger, my hope is that this work inspires the readers to commit to read and engage with these literatures' critiques and explorations of the issues I begin to raise here.

4. The problematic heroic masculine/self-mastering nature of this quote is explicitly acknowledged and considered in relation to similar critiques of Foucauldian ethics in the section headed 'Problemize Others, Authorize Self' in the third part of this paper—see also McNay 1994 for a critique of the under-explored, unacknowledged masculinity in Foucault's ethics.

5. Foucault may be understood as directing some of his strongest criticism at social relationships where institutions and authorities extended and reproduced power effects by codifying, defining and controlling knowledge that people draw upon to understand their hitherto private lives or personal practices and decisions (Best 1995 : 123). Thus, for instance, Foucault criticized the church and psychiatry for extending the power of religious authorities and medical professionals into the 'private' realm of a person's sexuality (Foucault 1992). By codifying and disseminating 'authoritative' knowledges about sexuality, these institutions normalized (literally constructed as 'normal') some sexuality (e.g. heterosexual) and problemized other sexualities (e.g. homosexuality) as a sin, pathology, crime, or moral failing, and other people (e.g. gays, lesbians and bisexuals) as criminals, perverts, or mentally/physically ill.

6. While Foucault wrote extensively on issues of sexuality and ethics, I am not claiming to represent in this part of the article what Foucault's views were, or divine what they would have been, about non/monogamy. Rather, I am trying to conjure up a 'feeling' for what I understand, or how I suggest we may use, a Foucauldian-inspired ethical critique. I merely use the example of non/monogamy as an ethical issue many or most of us have made (do make) choices about as a 'way in' to explore and engage with often (unnecessarily) complex/abstract discussions of Foucault and ethics.

7. 'I would more or less agree with the idea that in fact what interests me is much more morals than politics or, in any case, politics as an ethics' (Foucault 1984b : 375).

8. Though I have argued that Foucault's writings concentrate out attention on the intimate connection between identity/identifications, the ethical, personal and the political realms, other writers have argued that Foucault's aesthetic ethics risks reproducing individualistic apolitical relationships. McNay (1994 : 160), for instance, argues that the absence of an 'explicit commitment to a set of normative goals' means that Foucault apparently privileged 'the act of aesthetic self-creation per se, regardless of normative content, that seems to constitute the only basis for an ethics of the self'. Foucault himself in certain passages also apparently argued for the divorce of ethics and politics: 'For centuries we have been convinced that between our ethics, our personal ethics, our everyday life, and the great political and social and economic structures, there were analytical relations, and we couldn't change anything, for instance, in our sex life or our family life, without ruining our economy, our democracy, and so on. I think we have to get rid of this idea of an analytical or necessary link between ethics and other social or economic or political structures' (Foucault 1984a : 350).

9. The ideas of transgression, refusal and revolt against limits were centrally import-ant points for Foucault's writings and ethics: 'Perhaps one day it [the idea of transgression] will seem as decisive for our culture, as much a part of its soil, as the experience of contradiction was at an earlier time for dialectical thought' (Foucault 1977 : 33 in Best 1995 : 120). 'It is through revolt that subjectivity (not that of great men but of whomever) introduces itself into history and gives it the breath of life. A delinquent puts his life into the balance against absurd punishments; a madman can no longer accept his confinement and the forfeiture of his rights; a people refuses the regime which oppresses it' (Foucault 1981 in Bernauer and Matron 1994 : 153).

10. The importance to Foucault of embodying our ethical/political or 'critical' aca-demic commitments is clear in the following passage: 'The key to the personal poetic attitude of a philosopher is not to be sought in his ideas, as if it could be deduced from them, but rather in his philosophy as life, in his philosophical life, his ethos. Among the French philosophers who participated in the Resistance during the war, one was Cavailles, a historian of mathematics who was interested in the development of internal structures. None of the philosophers of *engagement*— Sartre, Simone de Beauvoir, Merleau-Ponty—none of them did a thing' (Foucault 1984b : 374, author's original emphasis).

11. Foucault's writings, like those of other poststructuralists, have (in)famously pro-blemized a modernist privileging of, or faith in, 'truth'. Truth, wrote Foucault, 'is a thing of this world: it is produced only by virtue of multiple forms of constraint. And it induces regular effects of power' (Foucault 1980 : 131).

12. A focus upon what is created through our actions and relationships to others and self, and a refusal of notions of essential or static truths of self, is a central strand of Foucault's 'aesthetic' ethics: 'What strikes me is the fact that in our society, art has become something which is related only to objects and not to individuals, or to life. That art is something which is specialised or which is done by experts who are artists. But couldn't everyone's life become a work of art? Why should the lamp or the house be an art object, but not our life?' (Foucault 1984a : 350). 'For me intellectual work is related to what you could call aestheticism, meaning trans-forming yourself . . . you see that's why I really work like a dog and have worked like a dog all my life. I am not interested in the academic status of what I am doing because my problem is my own transformation . . . Why should a painter work if he is not transformed by his own painting?' (Foucault 1983b : 14).

   By privileging metaphors of 'art' and 'aesthetics', however, Foucault has also been criticized for writing an ethics of 'dandyism', or as appearing as a modern apologist for an ancient Greek (elitist and male) ethics of pleasure and virility. Such criticisms are worth holding in mind when using and interpreting Foucault (see, for example, Wray-Bliss 1998). McNay (1994) is perhaps one of the best examples of how we can interpret and use Foucault's writings, yet remain wary and critical of such effects.

13. There are strong similarities between this interpretation of Foucault's ethics and interpretations of Marxist ethics (see, for example, Brenkert 1983; Wray-Bliss and Parker 1998).

14. McNay writes: 'Foucault's whole oeuvre is orientated to breaking down the domination of a fully self-reflexive, unified and rational subject at the centre of thought in order to clear a space for radically other ways of being' (McNay 1994 : 4).

15. Critics' fear that Foucault's permanent problemization necessarily leads to a kind of 'political paralysis' applies not only to Foucault's work but also to the key concepts of other 'post' writers. As Derrida comments on the sentiment and practice of deconstruction: 'deconstruction . . . should seek a new investigation of responsibility, an investigation which questions the codes inherited from ethics and politics. This means that, too political for some, it will seem paralyzing to those who only recognize politics by the most familiar road signs. Deconstruction is neither a methodological reform that should reassure the organization in place nor a flourish of irresponsible and irresponsible making destruction, whose most certain effects would be to leave everything as it is and to consolidate the most immobile forces within the university' (Derrida 1982, quoted in Culler 1989 : 156). The similarities between 'deconstruction' and 'permanent problemization' suggest that it is very possible to draw jointly upon both Foucault and Derrida's writings to construct a passionate and reflexive ethics, despite some authors' representation of chasms between the two authors' works (see, for example, Norris 1987 : 217). Thank you to the anonymous reviewer who highlighted these similarities of concern between Foucault's and Derrida's works.

16. Readers who are not familiar with the British labour process debates generally, and the contribution of the 'Manchester school' in particular, can find useful, and quite different, summaries in Willmott (1993) and Thompson and Findlay (1996).

17. I use the term 'positivism' here in a broad sense to signify the relations of strict separation between those who do the knowing and that which is known (Reason 1994; Stanley and Wise 1983). I understand this separation to be a condition of possibility of more traditional or narrow understandings of positivism as, for instance, a methodology that is defined by 'the provision of laws and predictions' (Fournier and Grey 2000 : 13). (Social) scientific research that produces such laws and predictions would seem to be (normally) based upon an understanding that the phenomena studied exist 'out there' independent from the one doing the predicting. The underlying, broader understanding of positivism as defined by relations of strict separation is the one I call upon when representing LPT texts that clearly separate the 'knowing' researcher from the 'known' researched as positivist.

18. In critiquing, in this part of the article, the Manchester school's reproduction of what I argue are subordinating and oppressive relations between researcher and researched, relations which cut across the school's Foucauldian commitments, it is not my intention to deny the school's theoretical 'Foucauldian' contribution to LPT (see the second part of this article). To borrow Foucault's (1984a) phrasing, I do not understand it to be necessary to say that 'everything is bad' about the Manchester school because some of its practices are 'dangerous'. Such either/or, good/bad, all-for/all-against dichotomies are, though popular in British LPT at the moment, probably less than helpful (see also Parker 1999). I *celebrate* the school's introduction of Foucauldian ethics/theory into LPT, and ask the authors to *take*

this further by seeking to embody these ethical commitments in their research practices and relations.

19. It is not just the 'Manchester school' authors who reproduce this realist form of representation, or indeed the other problematic relationships that I critique in this part of the article. Rather, such forms of representation and research practices might almost be understood as the normalized convention of empirical LPT writing, irrespective of whether such writings are informed with Marxist and/or Foucauldian theory. If readers do know of published LPT works that challenge these conventions and would like to collaboratively explore such possibilities, or have had difficulty publishing such writings, I would love to hear from you.

20. Interestingly, Knights (1992) levels a similar critique of the objectifying and positivistic practices of treating the research subject 'whether this be an individual, a group, or a class of activities (such as an organization) as if it were no different from an *object* in the natural sciences' (Knights 1992 : 514). He goes on to critique: 'representational approaches to knowledge production [that] rest on a privileging of the consciousness of the researcher who is deemed capable of discovering the 'truth' about the world of management and organizations through a series of representations' (Knights 1992 : 515). And argues that these forms of research reproduce a problematic 'dualism between the subject or agent (e.g. researcher) and the object or subject matter of knowledge' (Knights 1992 : 515). Again, my critique in this section, and indeed the whole paper, is not with the theoretical or 'abstract' arguments Knights makes here, but rather in the apparent lack of 'embodiment' of these in the empirical work that he and other LPT writers produce.

21. Rather than use this paper to attempt an in-depth exploration of 'consciousness raising', participatory or emancipatory action research, or other possible processes through which we might seek to embody our 'critical'/political commitments in our academic work, I aim for it to be an 'incitement' to the 'critical' management studies community to explore these processes for your/ourselves.

22. Endnote (3) of Knights and McCabe's (2000) paper on teamworking again illustrates the expression of 'hope' that somehow critical academic research might have some effects somewhere: 'our accounts may strengthen the resilience of our respondents and perhaps students to refuse the subjugating aspects of teamworking' (p. 1515). Similarly, Knights's (1995) endnote (9) describes his research as 'a political act in support of subordinates and a theoretical challenge to the norms of hierarchy'. Again, rather than merely voicing a hope or stating that one's research is *by definition* political, if this is a felt ethical legitimization for 'critical' academic research then I argue it warrants rather more serious and central consideration in our research practices *and* texts.

23. As one reviewer of this paper highlighted, Jackson also invokes here the accusation (?) of youth to marginalize Parker's concerns. Thus, we might be forgiven for reading into Jackson's comments the patronizing 'everyone wants to change the world at your age' put down, which can serve as legitimization for a speaker's own lack of political engagement.

....

References

Abbott, P. and Wallace, C. (1992). *An Introduction to Sociology: Feminist Perspectives.* London: Routledge.

Aitken, G. (1996). 'Exploring "Race" and Gender in Referrals to, and Engagement in, Clinical Psychology Services', unpublished ClinPsyD thesis, University of Manchester.

Aitken, G. and Burman, E. (1999). 'Crossing and Keeping Professional and Racialised Boundaries: Implications for Feminist Practice', *Psychology of Women Quarterly,* 23(2).

Alvesson, M. and Willmott, H. (eds) (1992). *Critical Management Studies.* London: Sage.

bell hooks (1989). *Talking Back: Thinking Feminist, Thinking Black.* London: Sheba Feminist Publishers.

Bernauer, J. and Matron, M. (1994). 'The Ethics of Michael Foucault', in G. Gutting (ed.), *The Cambridge Companion to Foucault.* Cambridge: Cambridge University Press, pp. 115–40.

Best, S. (1995). *The Politics of Historical Vision.* New York: The Guilford Press.

Brenkert, G. (1983). *Marx's Ethics of Freedom.* London: Routledge & Kegan Paul.

Burawoy, M. (1979). *Manufacturing Consent: Changes in the Labour Process under Capitalism.* Chicago: University of Chicago Press.

Campaign for Homosexual Equality (CHE) (1972). *Introducing CHE.* Manchester: Campaign for Homosexual Equality.

Collins, H. and Wray-Bliss, E. (2000a). 'Equal Opportunities Policies: The Authority of Discrimination', paper presented at 15th Annual ERU Conference, 'Work Futures', Cardiff Business School.

Collins, H. and Wray-Bliss, E. (2000b). 'Women's Consciousness, Man's World: (Un)-learning Patriarchy and LPT', paper presented at 18th Annual International Labour Process Conference, University of Strathclyde, Scotland.

Collinson, D. (1994). 'Strategies of Resistance: Power, Knowledge and Subjectivity in the Workplace', in J. Jermier, D. Knights and W. Nord (eds), *Resistance and Power in Organizations: Agency, Subjectivity and the Labour Process.* London: Routledge, pp. 25–68.

Culler, J. (1989). *On Deconstruction.* London: Routledge.

Derrida, J. (1982). 'The Conflict of Faculties', in M. Riffaterre (ed.), *Languages of Knowledge and of Inquiry.* New York: Columbia University Press.

Djian, P. (1988). *Betty Blue: The Story of a Passion.* New York: Grove/Atlantic Inc.

Foucault, M. (1977). *Language, Counter-memory, Practice.* Ithaca, NY: Cornell University Press.

Foucault, M. (1980). *Power/Knowledge: Selected Interviews and Other Writings, 1972–1977,* ed. C. Gordon. New York: Pantheon.

Foucault, M. (1981). 'Is it Useless to Revolt?', trans. J. Bernauer. *Philosophy and Social Criticism* 8(1): 5–9.

Foucault, M. (1983a). 'Structuralism and Post-structuralism: An Interview with Michel Foucault', *Telos,* 55: 195–211.

Foucault, M. (1983b). 'The Minimalist Self', in L. Kritzman (ed.) *Michel Foucault: Politics, Philosophy, Culture*. London: Routledge, pp. 13–16.

Foucault, M. (1984a). 'On the Genealogy of Ethics: An Overview of Work in Progress', in P. Rabinow (ed.), *The Foucault Reader*. Harmondsworth: Penguin, pp. 340–72.

Foucault, M. (1984b). 'Politics and Ethics: An Interview', in P. Rabinow (ed.), *The Foucault Reader*. Harmondsworth: Penguin, pp. 373–80.

Foucault, M. (1984c). 'Polemics, Politics and Problemizations', in P. Rabinow (ed.), *The Foucault Reader*. Harmondsworth: Penguin, pp. 381–90.

Foucault, M. (1984d). 'What is Enlightenment?', in P. Rabinow (ed.), *The Foucault Reader*. Harmondsworth: Penguin, pp. 32–50.

Foucault, M. (1988). 'The Ethic of Care for the Self as a Practice of Freedom', in J. Bernauer and D. Rasmussen (eds), *The Final Foucault*. Cambridge MA: MIT Press.

Foucault, M. (1991). *Discipline and Punishment: The Birth of the Prison*. London: Penguin.

Foucault, M. (1992). *The Use of Pleasure: The History of Sexuality Vol. 2*. London: Penguin.

Fournier, V. and Grey, C. (2000). 'At the Critical Moment: Conditions and Prospects for Critical Management Studies', *Human Relations*, 53(1): 7–32.

Gay Liberation Front (GLF) (1971). *Manifesto*. London: GLF.

Griffin, C. and Phoenix, A. (1994). 'The Relationship between Qualitative and Quantitative Research: Lessons from Feminist Psychology', *Journal of Community and Applied Social Psychology*, 4: 287–98.

Hearn, J. and Parkin, W. (1987). *'Sex' at 'Work': The Power and Paradox of Organization and Sexuality*. London: Harvester Wheatsheaf.

Henwood, K. and Pigeon, N. (1995). 'Remaking the Link: Qualitative Research and Feminist Standpoint Theory', *Feminism & Psychology*, 5: 7–30.

Jackson, N. (1995). 'To Write, or not to Right?' *Organization Studies*, 16(4): 571–3.

Jodelet, D. (1991). *Madness and Social Representations*. (Translated by T. Pownall; edited by G. Duveen). London: Harvester Wheatsheaf.

Knights, D. (1992). 'Changing Spaces: The Disruptive Impact of a New Epistemological Location for the Study of Management', *Academy of Management Review*, 17(3): 514–36.

Knights, D. (1995). 'Refocusing the Case Study, the Politics of Research and Researching Politics in IT Management', *Technology Studies*, 2(2): 230–54.

Knights, D. (1997). 'Organization Theory in the Age of Deconstruction: Dualism, Gender and Postmodernism Revisited', *Organization Studies*, 18(1): 1–19.

Knights, D. and Collinson, D. (1987). 'Disciplining the Shopfloor: A Comparison of the Disciplinary Effects of Managerial Psychology and Financial Accounting', *Accounting, Organisation and Society*, 12(5): 457–77.

Knights, D. and McCabe, D. (1998a). 'What Happens when the Phone goes Wild? Staff, Stress and Spaces for Escape in a BPR Telephone Banking Work Regime', *Journal of Management Studies*, 35(2): 163–94.

Knights, D. and McCabe, D. (1998b). 'When "Life is but a Dream": Obliterating Politics through Business Process Reengineering?', *Human Relations*, 51(6): 761–98.

Knights, D. and McCabe, D. (1999a). 'Are there no Limits to Authority? TQM and Organizational Power', *Organization Studies*, 20(2): 197–224.

Knights, D. and McCabe, D. (1999b). 'How Would You Measure Something Like That? Quality in a Retail Bank', *Journal of Management Studies*, 34(3): 371–88.

Knights, D. and McCabe, D. (2000). 'Bewitched, Bothered and Bewildered: The Meaning and Experience of Teamworking for Employees in an Automobile Company', *Human Relations*, 53(11): 1481–517.

Knights, D. and Murray, F. (1994). *Managers Divided*. Chicester: John Wiley & Sons.

Knights, D. and Vurdubakis, T. (1994). 'Foucault, Power, Resistance and All That', in J. Jermier, D. Knights and W. Nord (eds), *Resistance and Power in Organizations: Agency, Subjectivity and the Labour Process*. London: Routledge, pp. 167–98.

Knights, D. and Willmott, H. (1989). 'Power and Subjectivity at Work: From Degradation to Subjugation in Social Relations', *Sociology*, 23(4): 535–58.

Kundera, M. (1984). *The Unbearable Lightness of Being*. London: Faber & Faber.

Lincoln, Y. (1995). 'Emerging Qualitative Criteria', *Qualitative Inquiry*, 1: 275–89.

McNay, L. (1994). *Foucault: A Critical Introduction*. Cambridge: Polity.

Marks, D. (1993). 'Case Conference Analysis and Action Research', in E. Burman and I. Parker (eds), *Discursive Analytic Research: Repertoires and Readings of Texts in Action*. London: Routledge, pp. 135–54.

Martinez Lucio, M. and Stewart, P. (1997). 'The Paradox of Contemporary Labour Process Theory: The Rediscovery of Labour and Disappearance of Collectivism', *Capital & Class*, 62: 49–77.

Morton, D. (ed.) (1996). *The Material Queer: A LesBiGay Cultural Studies Reader*. Oxford: Westview Press.

Norris, C. (1987). *Derrida*. London: Fontana.

O'Doherty, D. and Willmott, H. (1998). 'Recent Contributions to the Development of Labour Process Analysis'. Paper presented at the Labour Process Conference (April), Manchester.

Opie, A. (1992). 'Qualitative Research, Appropriation of the "Other" and Empowerment', *Feminist Review*, 40: 52–69.

Parker, M. (1995). 'Critique in the Name of What? Postmodernism and Critical Approaches to Organization', *Organization Studies*, 16(4): 553–64.

Parker, M. (1999). 'Capitalism, Subjectivity and Ethics: Debating Labour Process Analysis', *Organization Studies*, 20(1): 25–45.

Poster, M. (1984). *Foucault, Marxism and History: Mode of Production versus Mode of Information*. Cambridge: Polity.

Reason, P., ed. (1994). *Participation in Human Inquiry*. London: Sage.

Reason, P. and Bradbury, H., eds (2001). *Handbook of Action Research*. London: Sage.

Rose, S. (1996). 'Against Marriage' in S. Rose, C. Stevens et al. (eds), *Bisexual Horizons*. London: Lawrence & Wishart, pp. 119–21.

Rowlinson, M. and Hassard, J. (1994). 'Economics, Politics and Labour Process Theory', *Capital and Class*, 53: 65–97.

Seidman, S. (1992). 'Postmodern Social Theory as Narrative with a Moral Intent', in S. Seidman and D. Wagner (eds), *Postmodernism and Social Theory*. Oxford: Basil Blackwell, pp. 47–81.

Simons, J. (1995). *Foucault and the Political*. London: Routledge.

Skunk Anansie (1996). 'Yes it's Fucking Political', from the album *Stoosh*. Chrysalis Music.

Smith, C. and Thompson, P. (1992). 'When Harry Met Sally. . . and Hugh and David and Andy: Reflections on Ten Years of the Labour Process Conference'. Paper presented to 10th International Labour Process Conference, Aston University.

Sosteric, M. (1996). 'Subjectivity and the Labour Process: A Case Study in the Restaurant Industry', *Work Employment and Society*, 10(2): 297–318.

Spivak, G. C. (1985). 'Can the Subaltern Speak? Speculations on Widow Sacrifice', *Wedge*, 7(8): 120–30.

Stanley, L. and Wise, S. (1983). *Breaking Out: Feminist Consciousness and Feminist Research*. London: Routledge.

Thompson, P. (1993). 'Postmodernism: Fatal Distraction', in J. Hassard and M. Parker (eds), *Postmodernism and Organizations*. London: Sage.

Thompson, P. and Ackroyd, S. (1995). 'All Quiet on the Workplace Front? A Critique of Recent Trends in British Industrial Sociology', *Sociology*, 29(4): 615–33.

Thompson, P. and Findlay, P. (1996). 'The Mystery of the Missing Subject', paper presented at 14th International Labour Process Conference (25–7 March), Aston University.

Van Maanen, J. (1988). *Tales of the Field: On Writing Ethnography*. Chicago: University of Chicago Press.

Ware, V. (1992). *Beyond the Pale: White Women, Racism and History*. London: Verso.

Watney, S. (1996). 'Powers of Observation: AIDS and the Writing of History', in D. Morton (ed.), *The Material Queer*. Oxford: Westview Press.

Williams, P. and Chrisman, L. (eds) (1993). *Colonial Discourse and Post-colonial Theory: A Reader*. London: Harvester Wheatsheaf.

Willmott, H. (1993). 'Breaking the Paradigm Mentality', *Organisation Studies*, 14(5): 681–719.

Willmott, H. (1994). 'Bringing Agency (Back) into Organizational Analysis: Responding to the Crisis of (Post)modernity', in M. Parker and J. Hassard (eds), *Towards a New Theory of Organizations*. London: Routledge, pp. 87–130.

—— (1998). 'Towards a New Ethics? The Contribution of Poststructuralism and Posthumanism', in M. Parker (ed.), *Ethics and Organizations*. London: Sage, pp. 76–121.

Wray-Bliss, E. (1998). 'The Ethics and Politics of Representing Workers: An Ethnography of Telephone Banking Clerks', PhD thesis, School of Management, UMIST.

—— (2001). 'Representing Customer Service: Telephones and Texts', in A. Sturdy, I. Grugulis and H. Willmott (eds), *Customer Service: Empowerment and Entrapment*. Basingstoke: Palgrave.

—— (in press). 'Interpretation-Appropriation: (Making) An Example of Labour Process Theory', to appear in *Organizational Research Methods*, feature topic 'Interpretive Genres of Organizational Research Methods', 5(1): 80–103.

Wray-Bliss, E. and Parker, M. (1998). 'Marxism, Capitalism and Ethics', in M. Parker, *Ethics and Organizations*. London: Sage, pp. 30–52.

Young, R. (1990). *White Mythologies: Writing History and the West*. London: Routledge.

Index

Index

Index

Index

Index

Index

Index

Index

Index